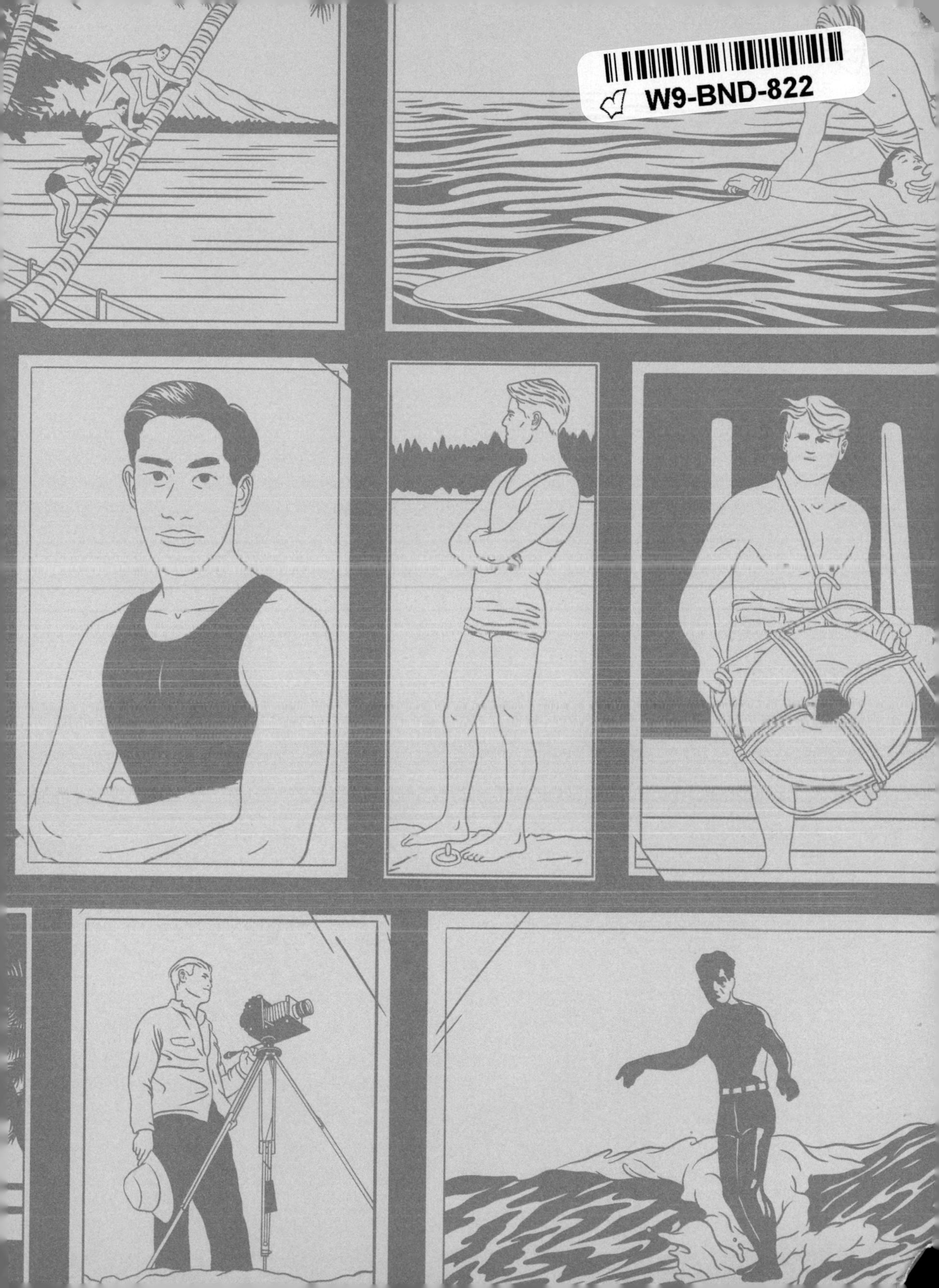

FOR KRISTEN

IN WAVES

AJ DUNGO

NOBROW
LONDON | NEW YORK

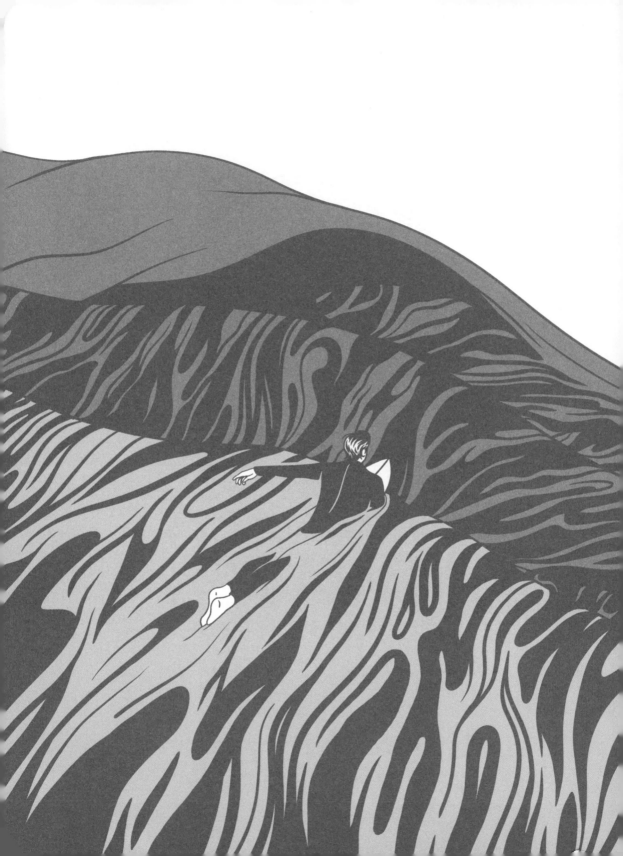

I MUST ADMIT, I AM NOT THE MOST QUALIFIED SOURCE
TO TEACH YOU ABOUT THE SUBJECT OF SURFING.

I'M JUST AN OVERZEALOUS TOURIST.

I CAN'T CLAIM SURFING AS MY OWN BUT
ITS CHARACTERS DO RESONATE WITH ME.

WE SHARE AN OBSESSION FOR RIDING WAVES, A DEEP
REVERENCE FOR THE OCEAN, AND A BROKEN HEART.

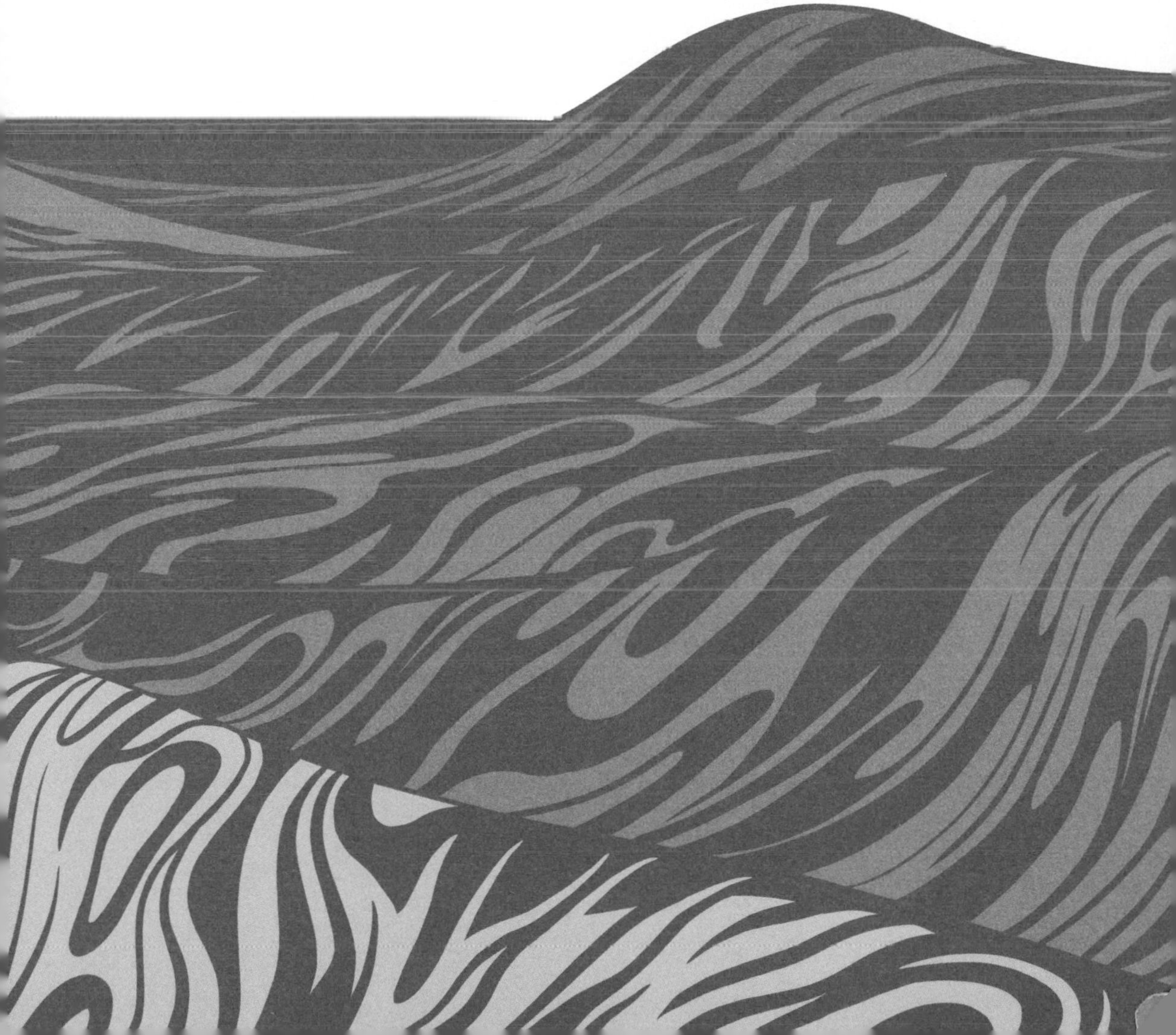

I. ORIGINS

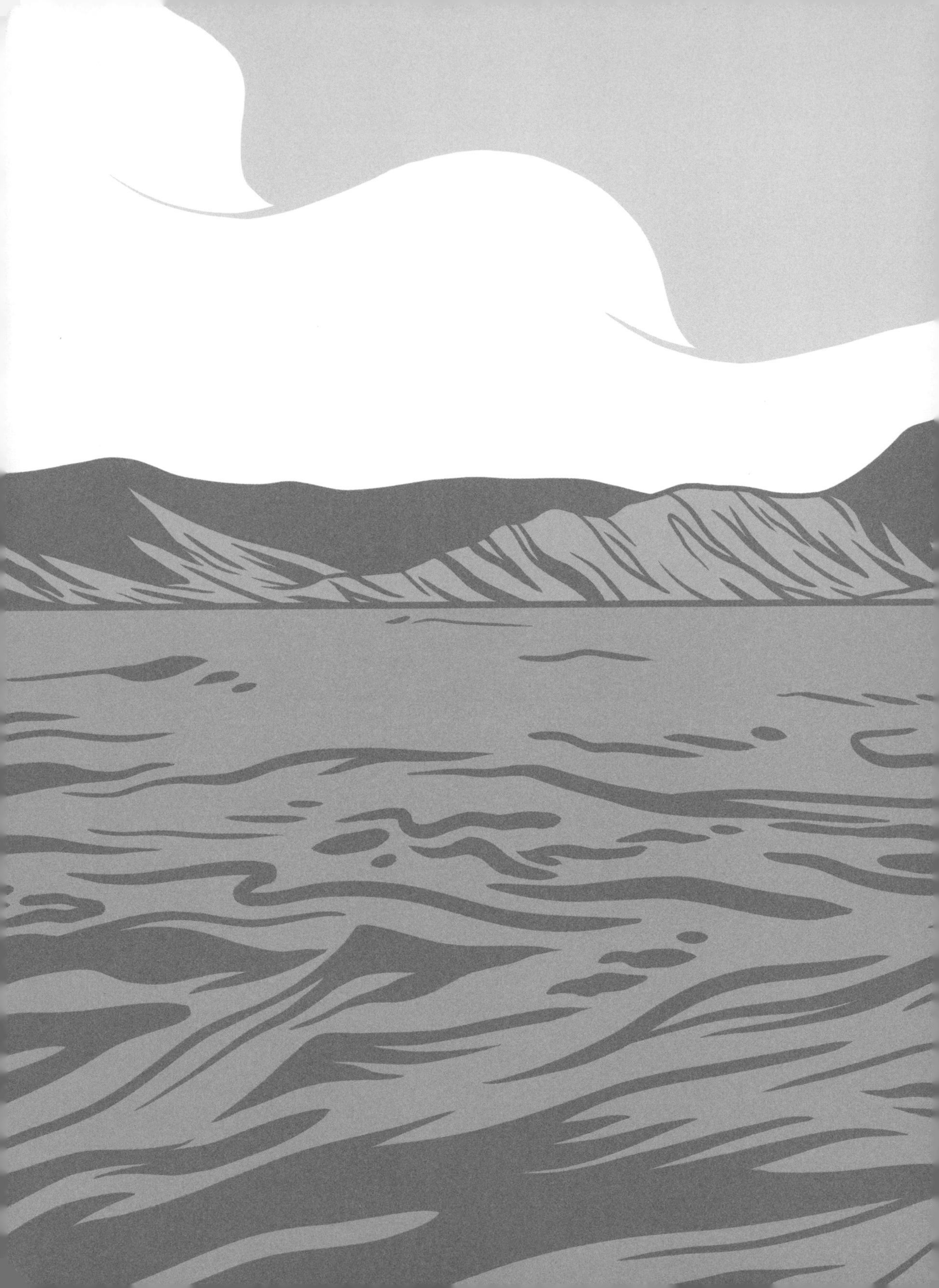

Spring
1800

The Hawaiian Islands

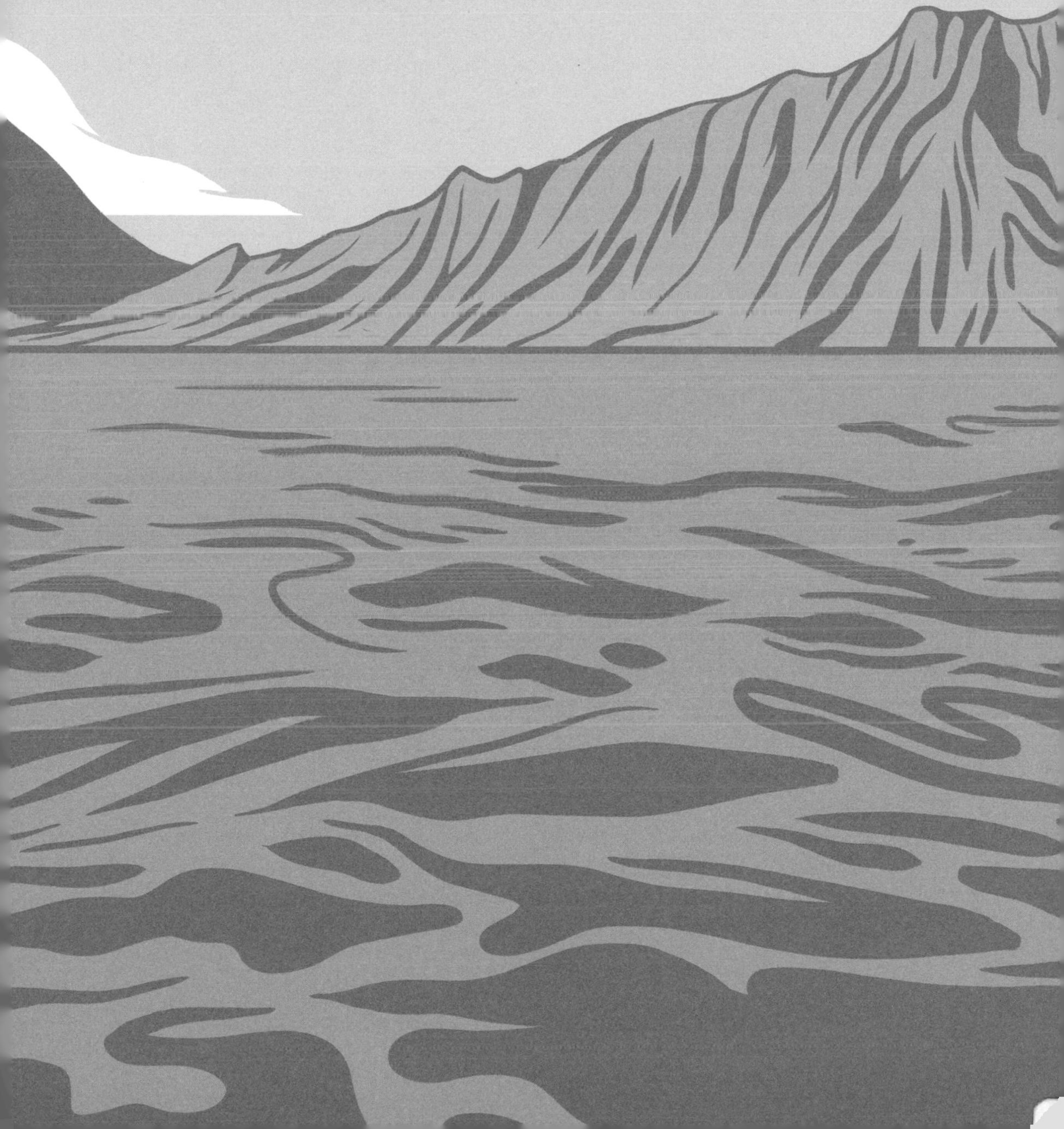

SURFERS HAVE ALWAYS FOUND SOLACE IN THE WATER.

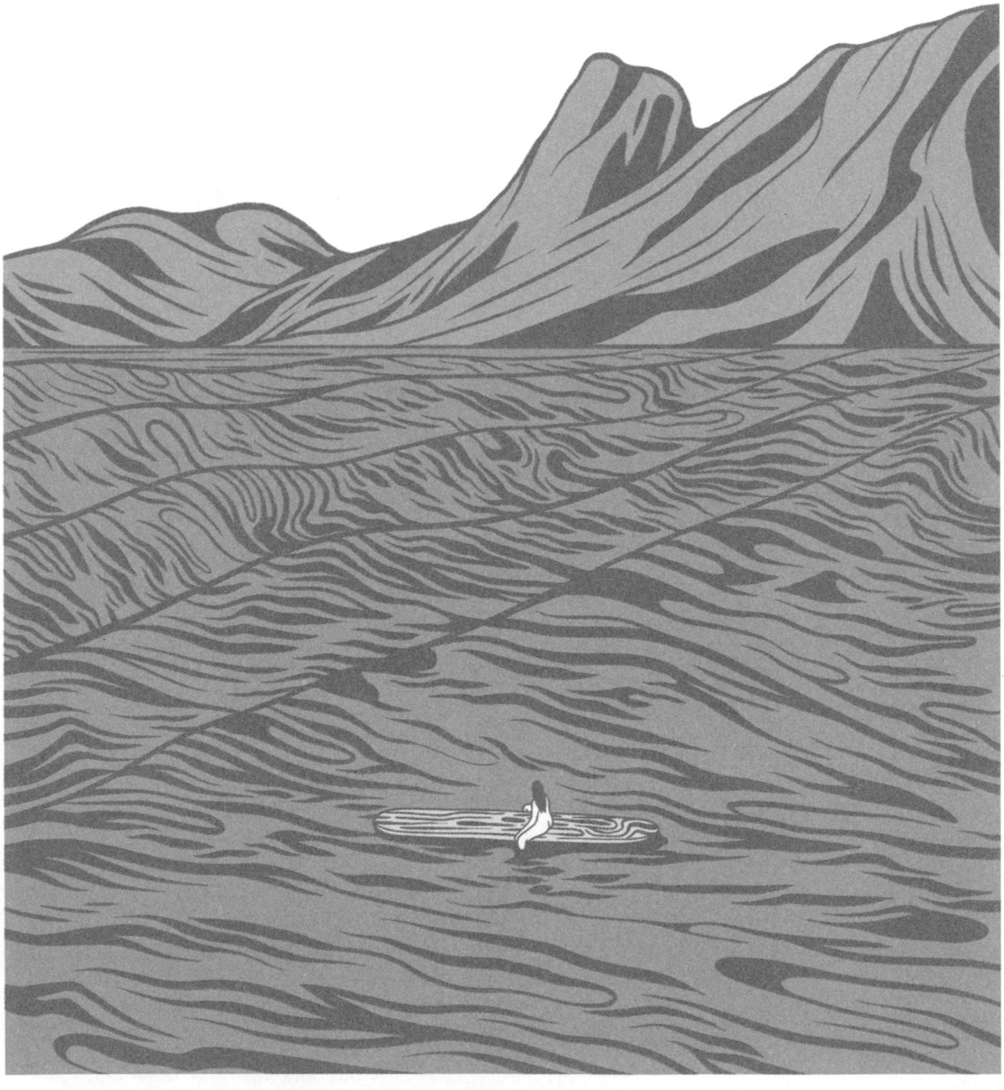

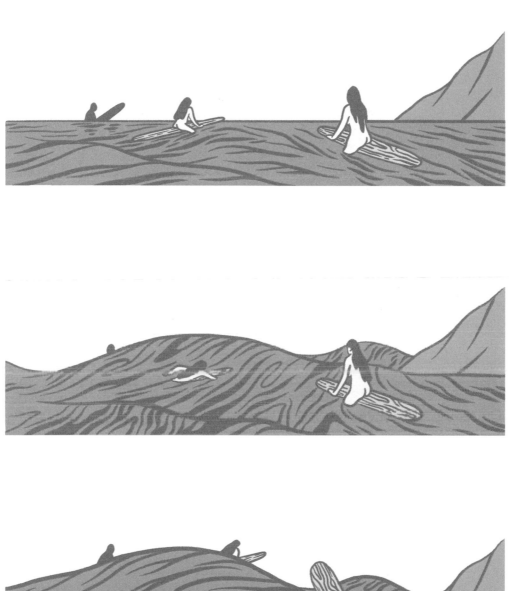

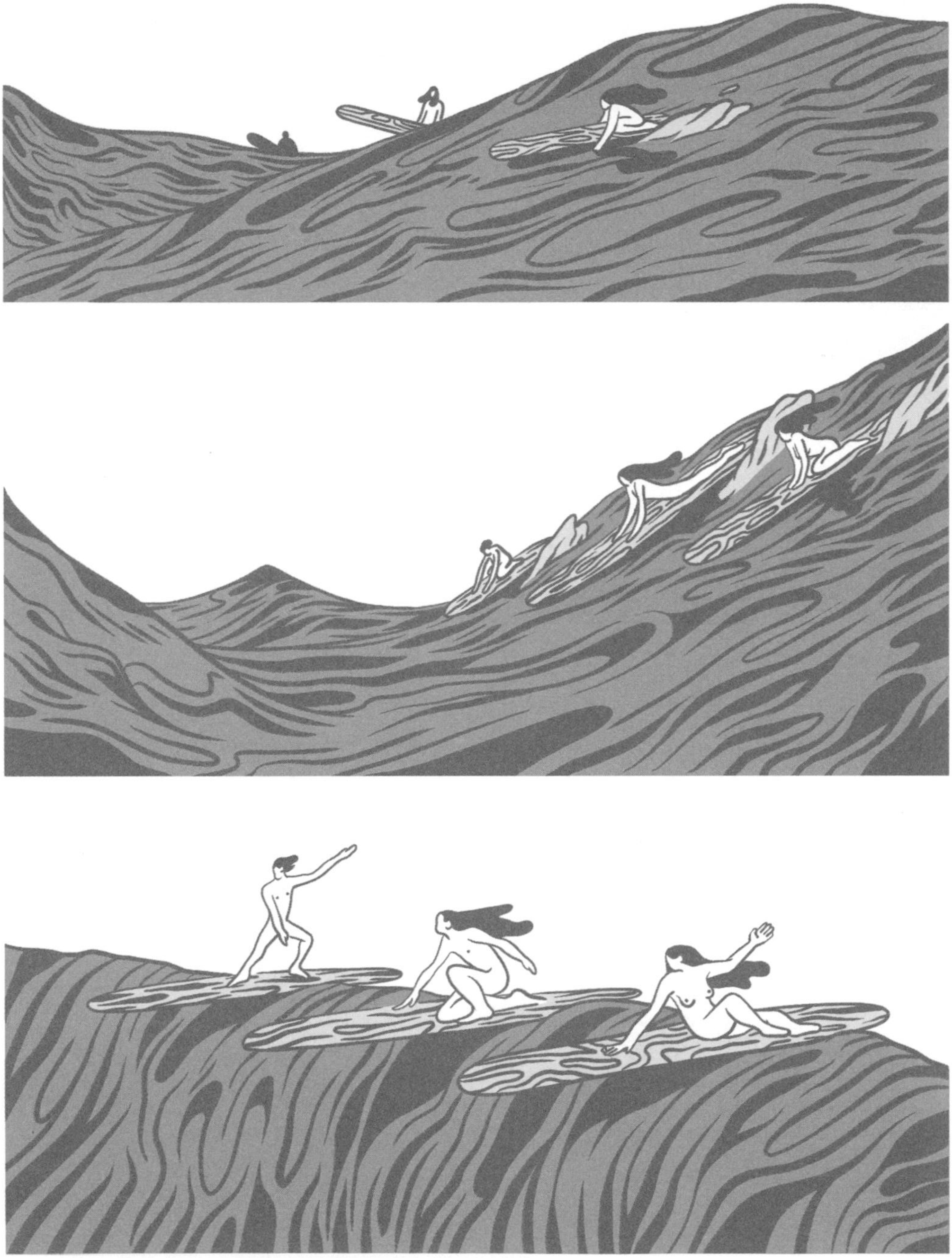

FOR EARLY POLYNESIANS, SURFING WAS A UNIVERSAL INDULGENCE.

A SPIRITUAL EXPERIENCE THAT BROUGHT THE ISLANDERS TOGETHER,

IT WAS WOVEN INTO THE FABRIC OF EVERY HAWAIIAN'S DAILY LIFE.

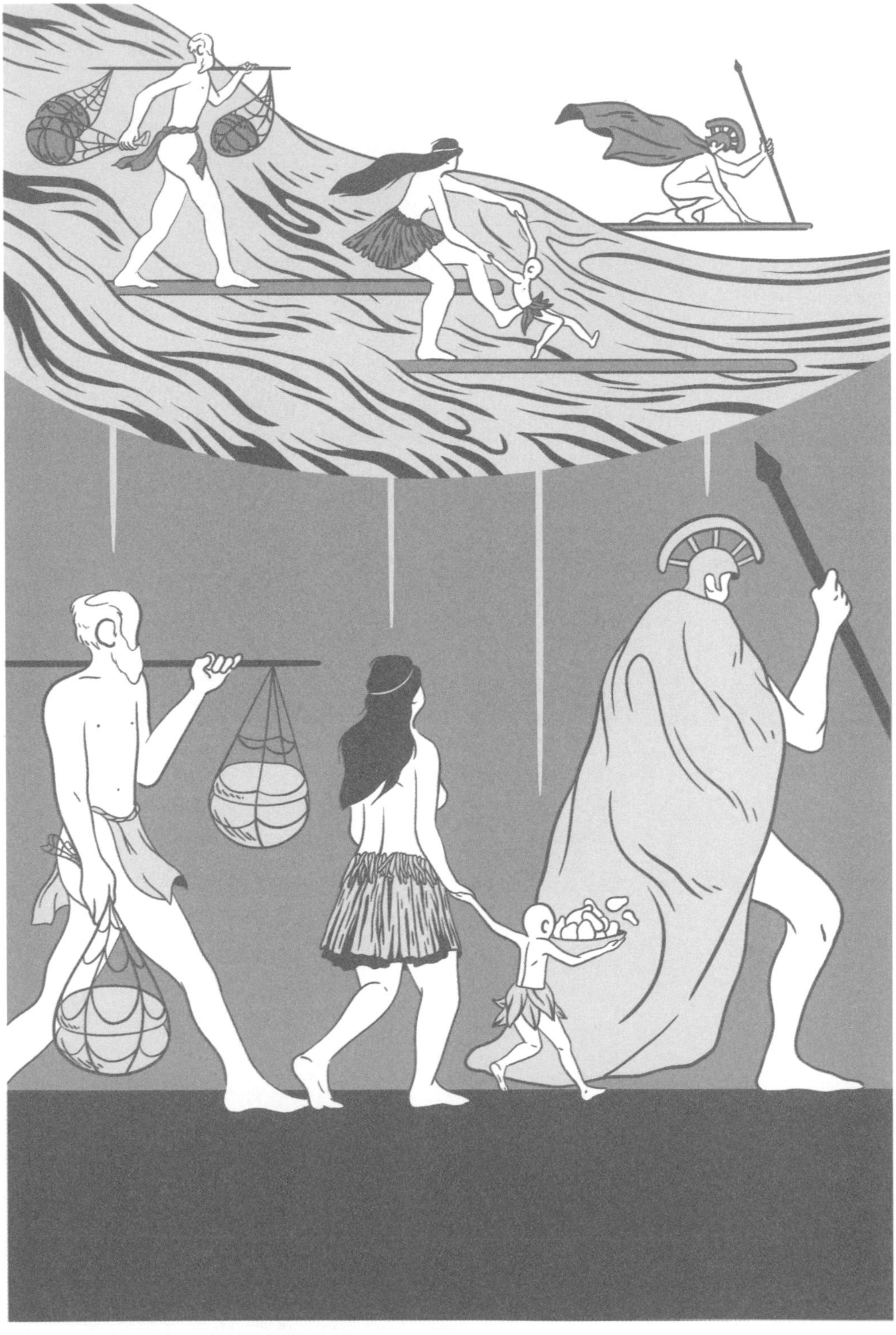

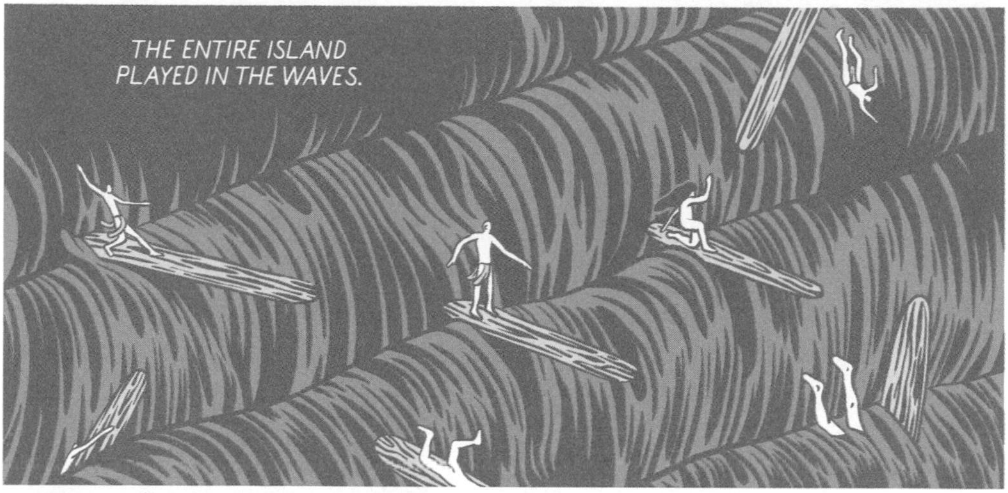
THE ENTIRE ISLAND PLAYED IN THE WAVES.

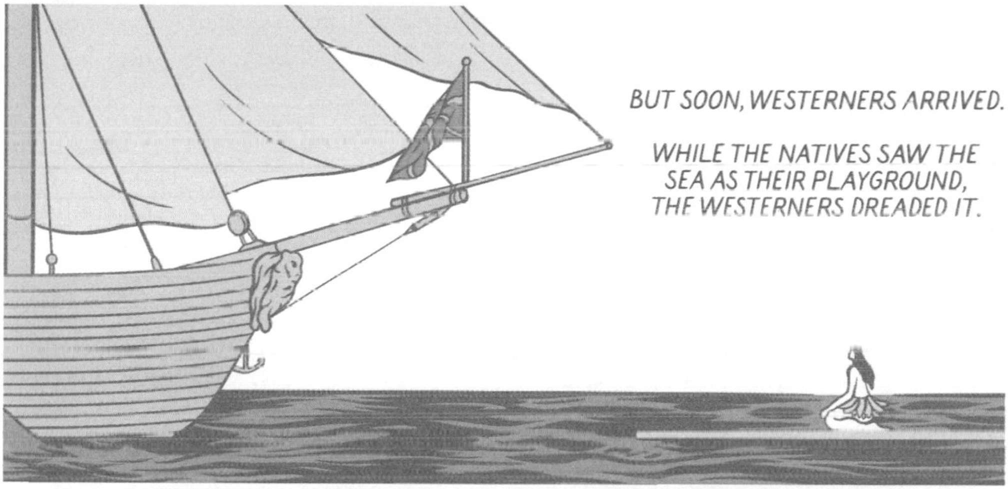
BUT SOON, WESTERNERS ARRIVED.
WHILE THE NATIVES SAW THE SEA AS THEIR PLAYGROUND, THE WESTERNERS DREADED IT.

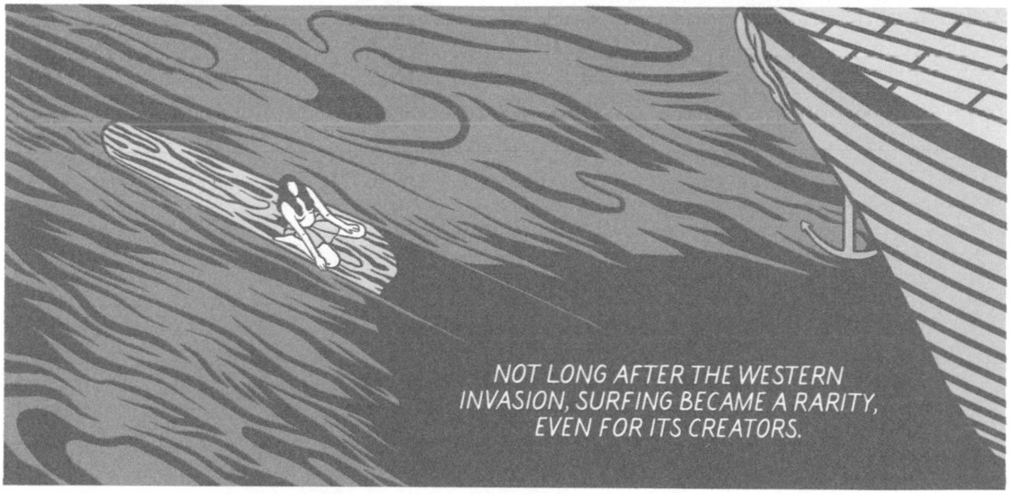
NOT LONG AFTER THE WESTERN INVASION, SURFING BECAME A RARITY, EVEN FOR ITS CREATORS.

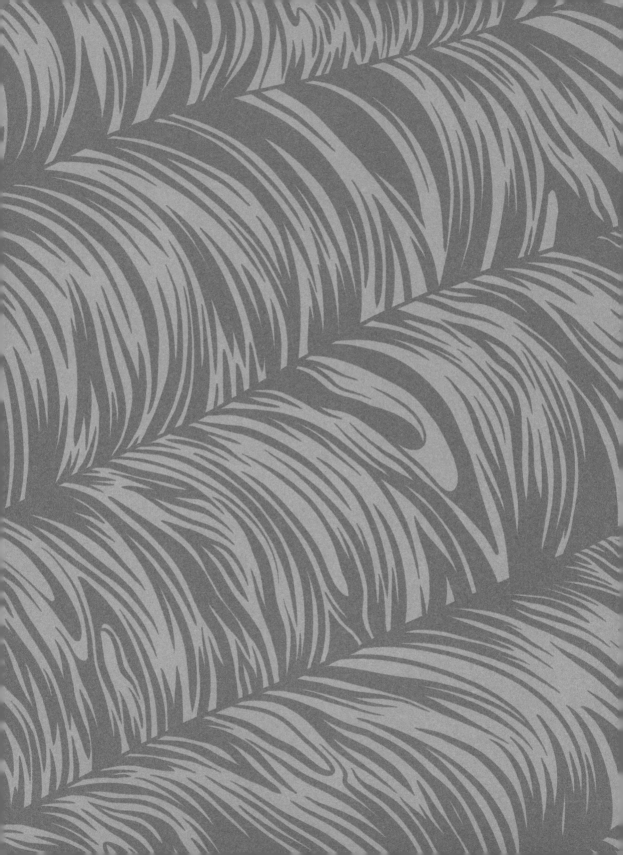

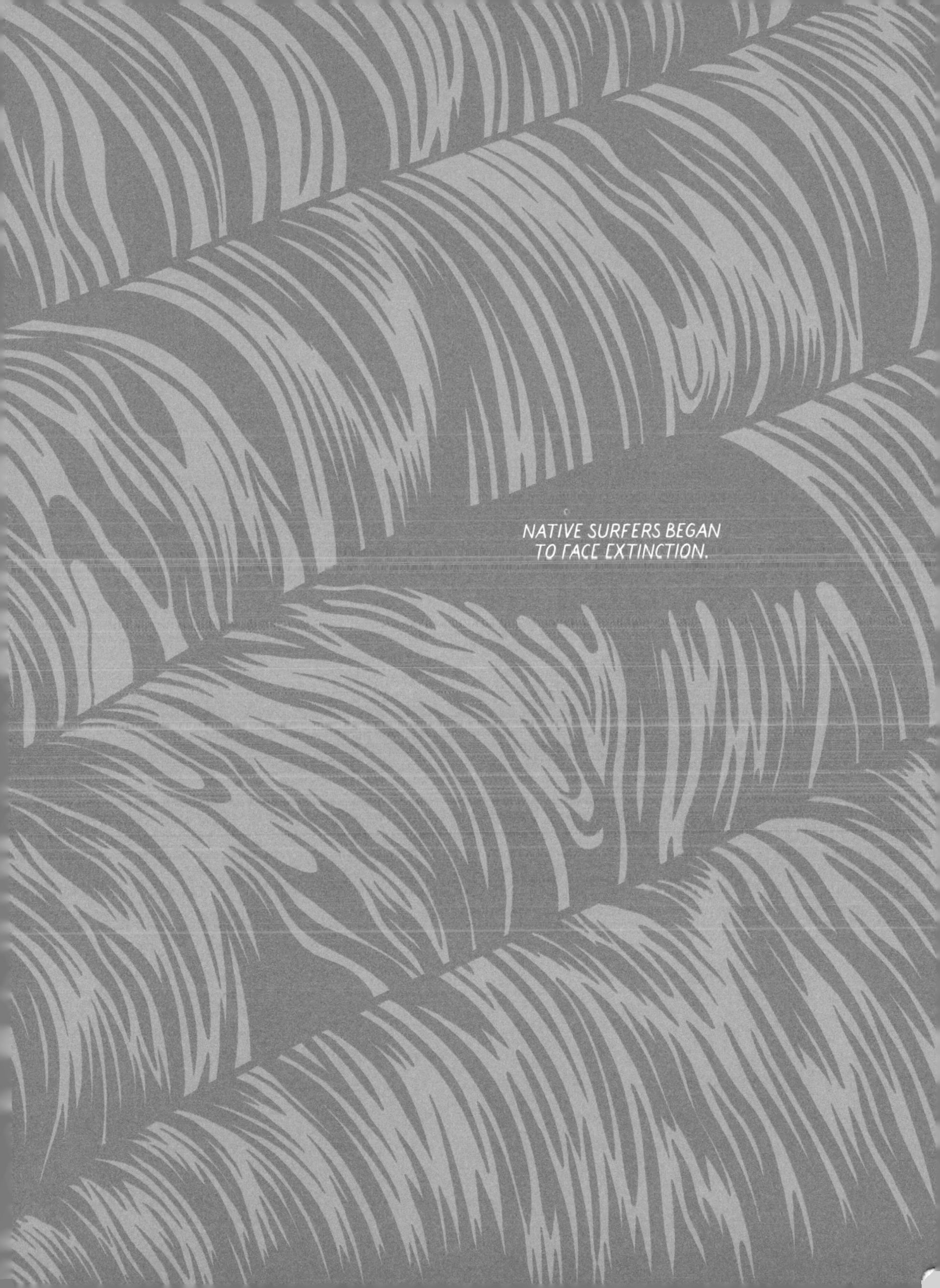
NATIVE SURFERS BEGAN TO FACE EXTINCTION.

WITH THE WESTERN
MISSIONARIES,

ALSO CAME INDUSTRY
AND DISEASE,

AND IT DECIMATED
TRANQUIL ISLAND LIFE.

IN RESPONSE, THE REMAINING NATIVES SOUGHT ASYLUM IN THE PLACE THE FOREIGNERS FEARED MOST.

SURFING BECAME A WAY TO ESCAPE THEIR TROUBLES,

TO PROTEST THEIR COLONIZATION,

TO HOLD ONTO THEIR DISAPPEARING CULTURE.

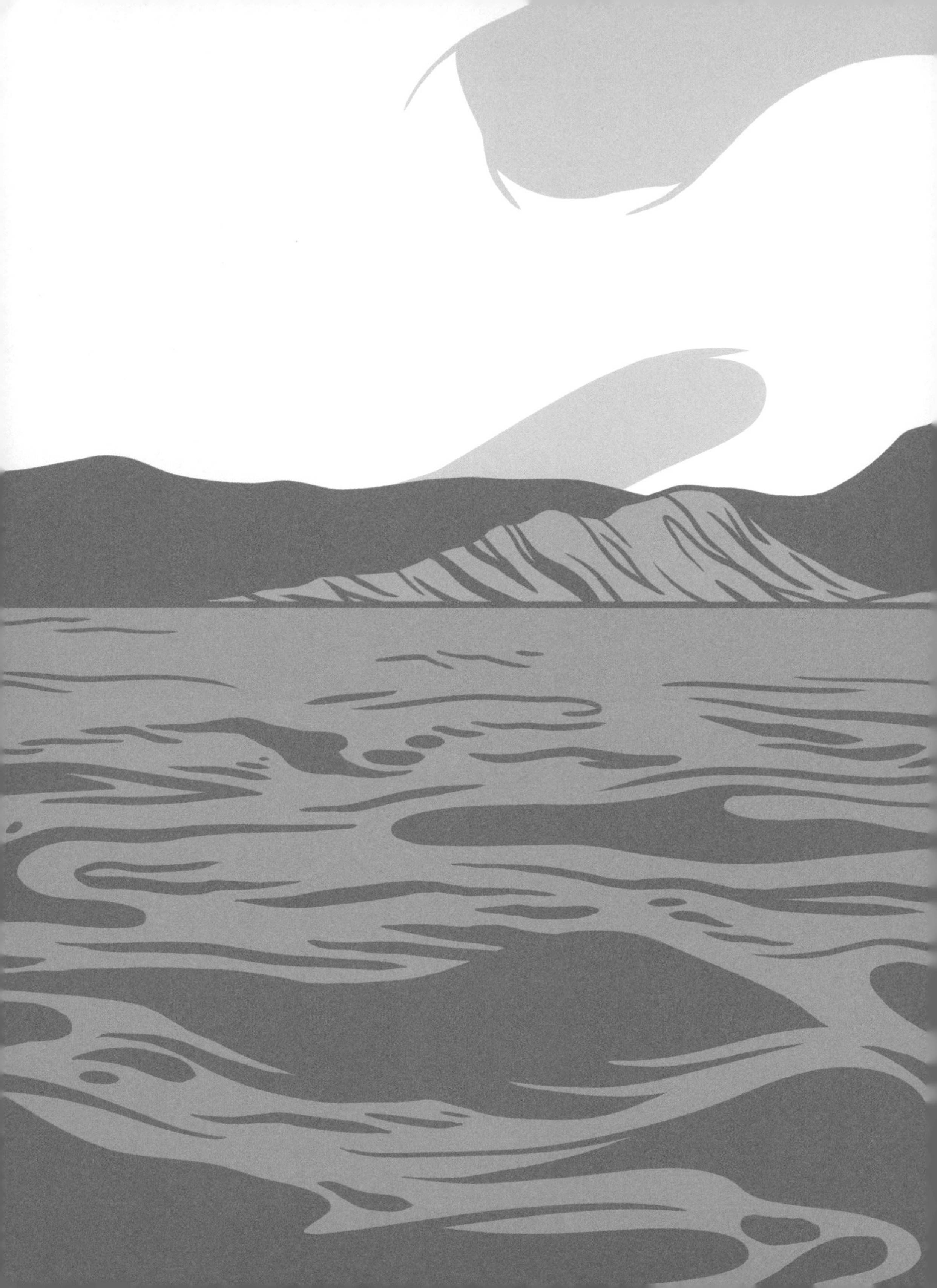

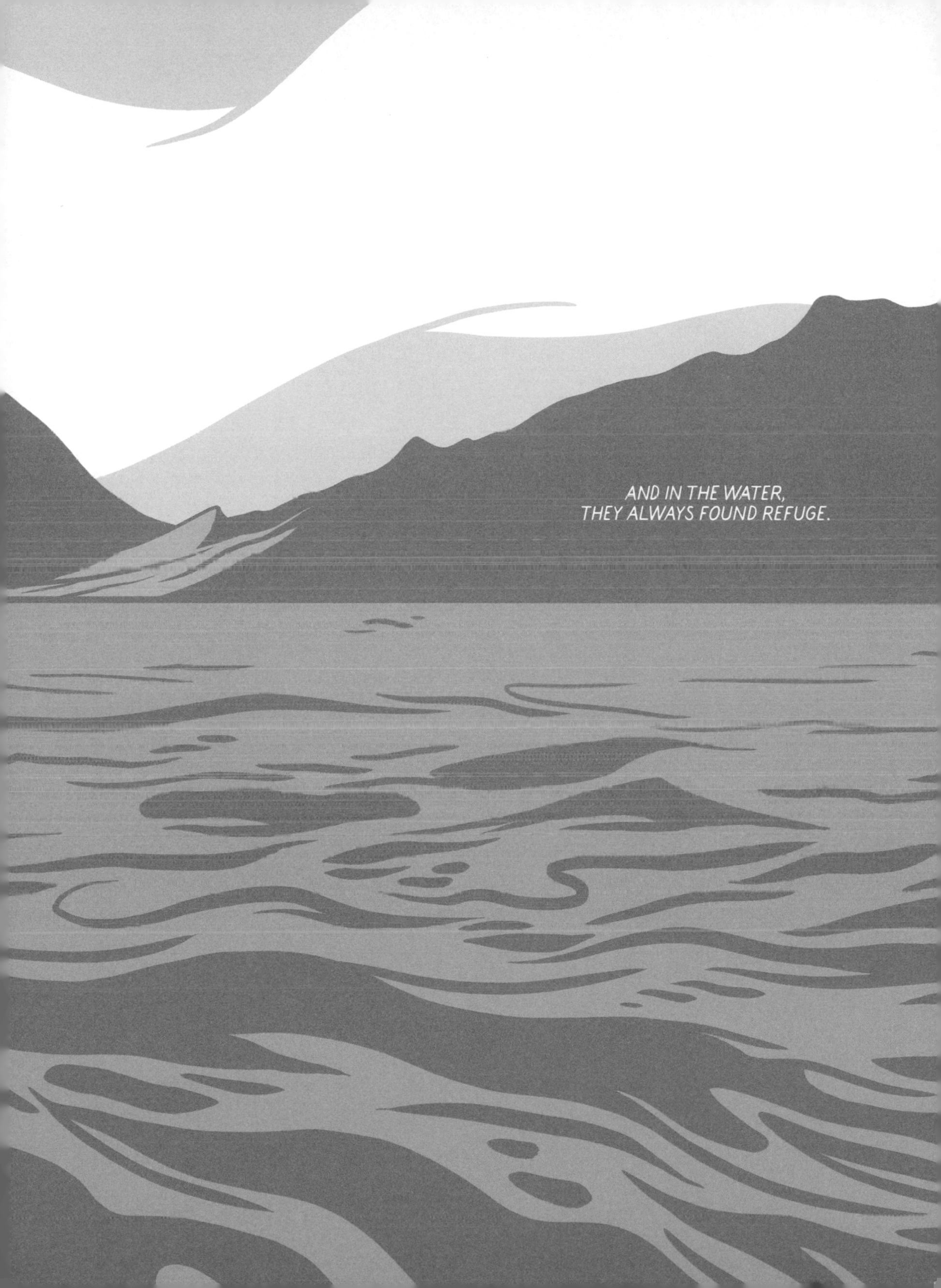
AND IN THE WATER,
THEY ALWAYS FOUND REFUGE.

II. LAST SUMMER

Summer 2015

Bolsa Chica, California

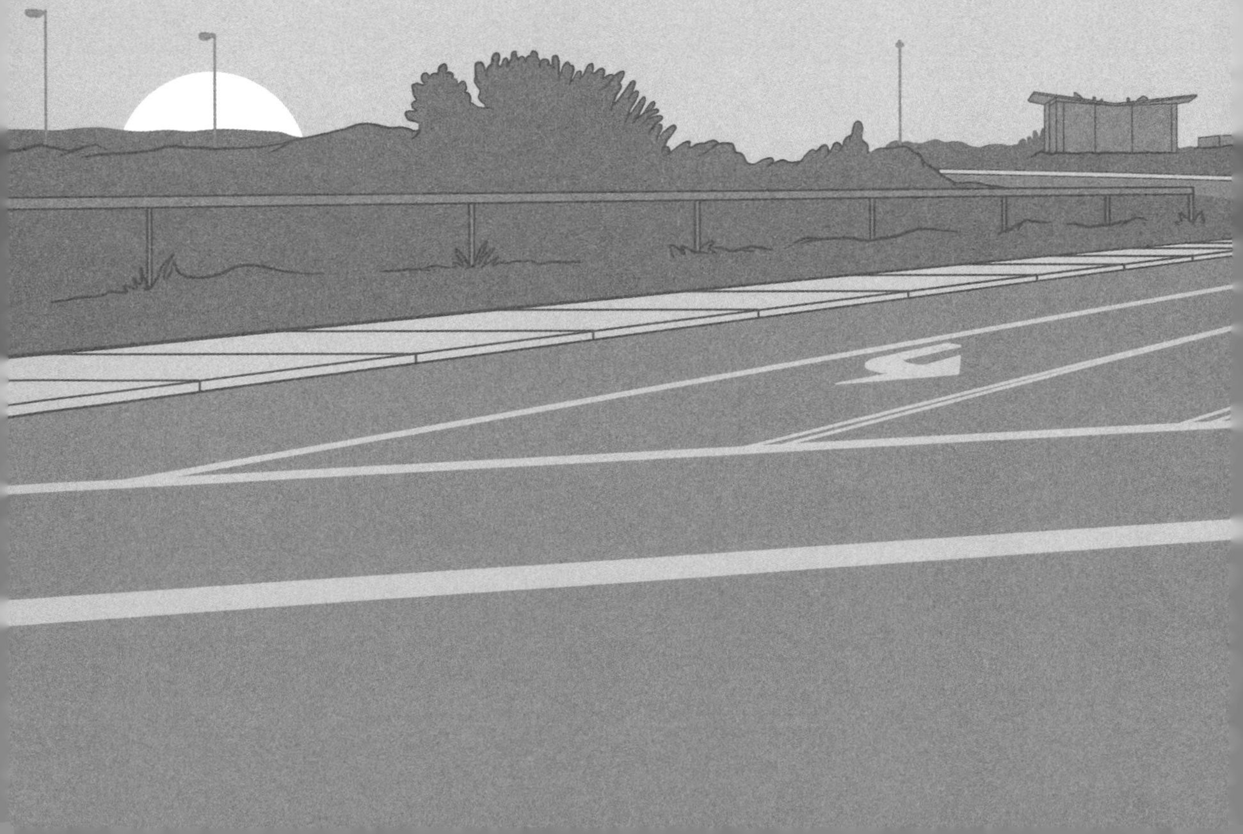

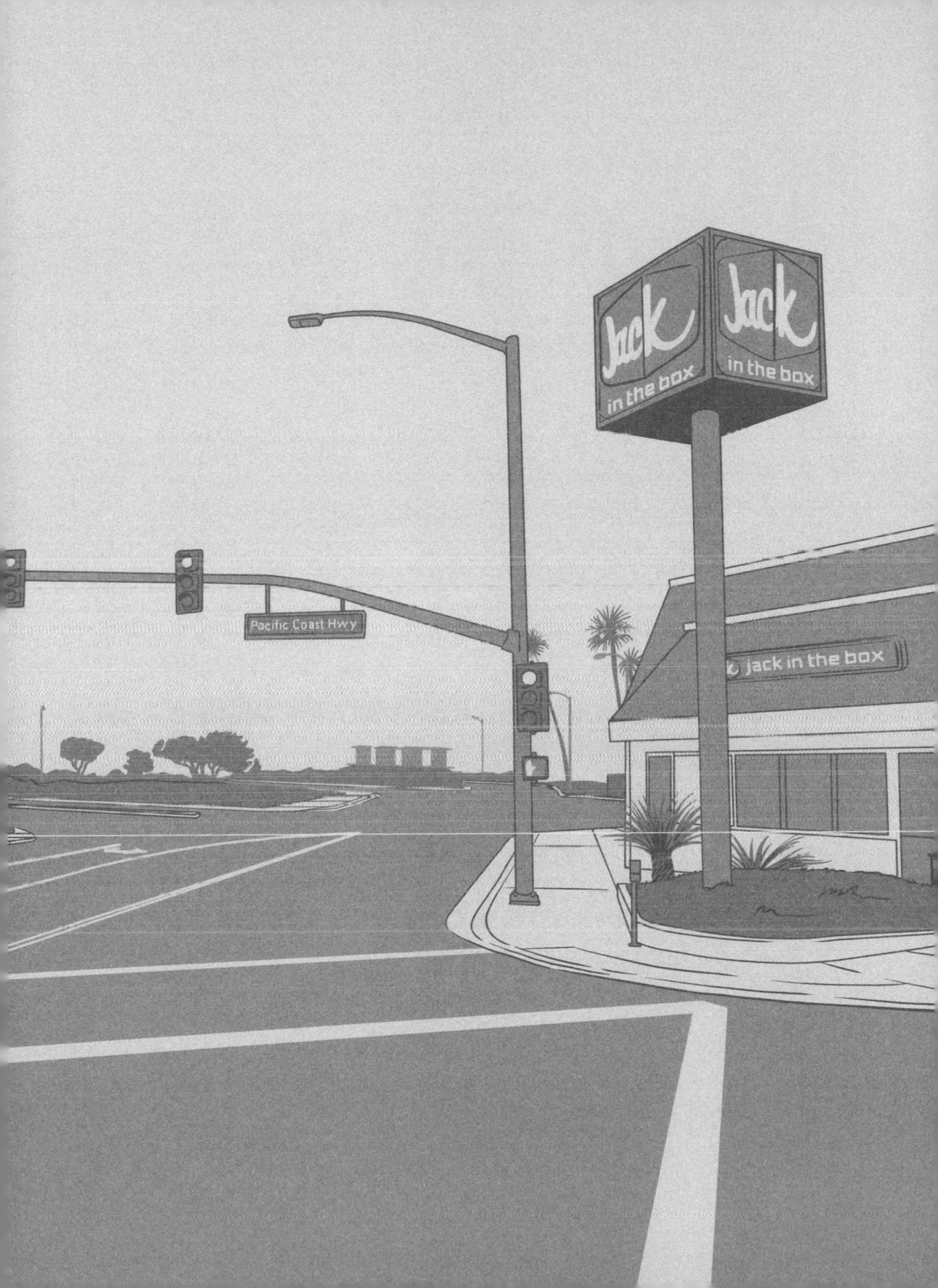
Jack
in the box
Jack
in the box
Pacific Coast Hwy
jack in the box

JULY 31ST WAS
KRISTEN'S BIRTHDAY.

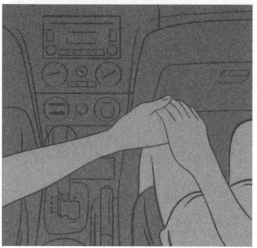

SHE HADN'T BEEN IN THE
WATER SINCE SHE GOT SICK.

THERE WAS A SURPRISE
PARTY PLANNED AND
HER FAMILY WERE WAITING
FOR US TO ARRIVE.

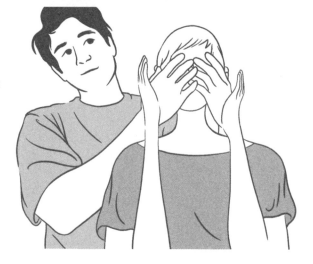

I DON'T THINK I HAD SEEN HER AS OVERJOYED AS SHE WAS IN THAT MOMENT.

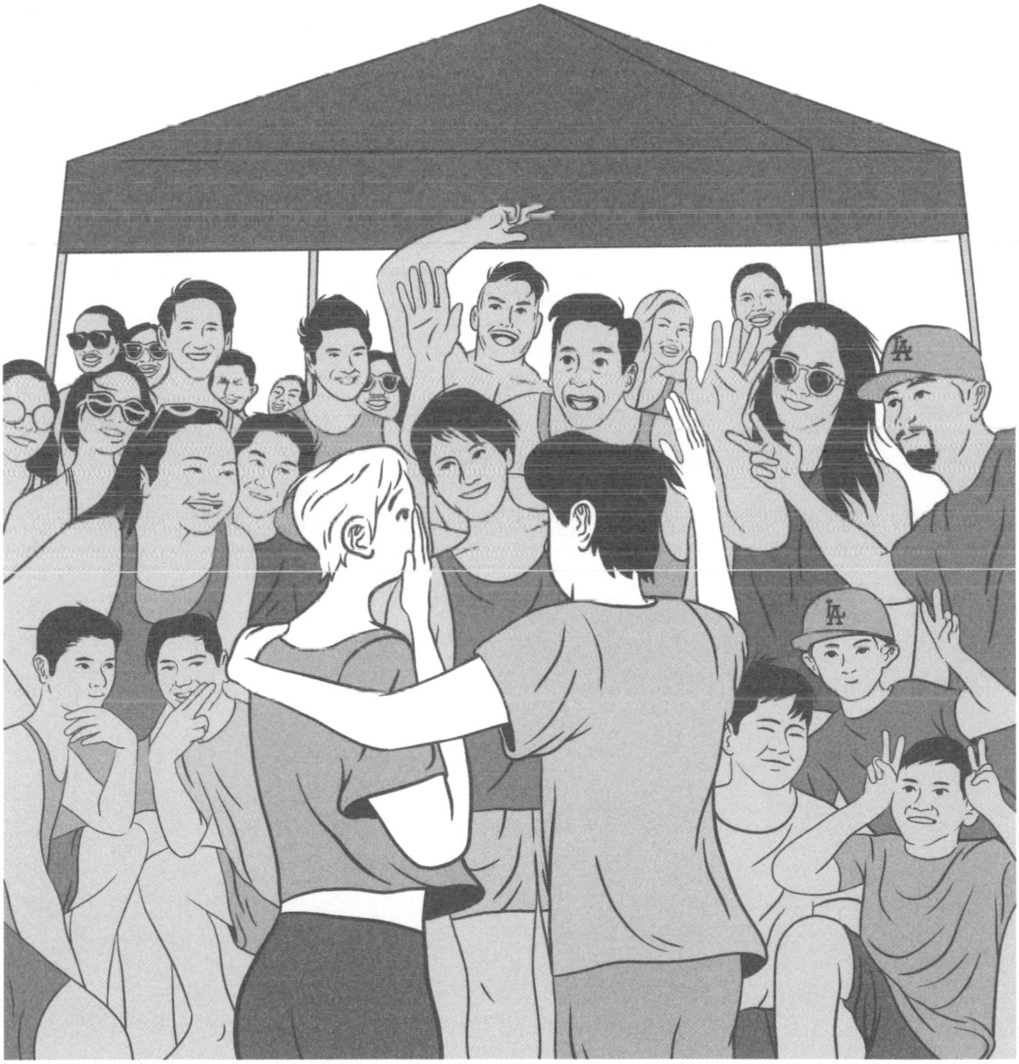

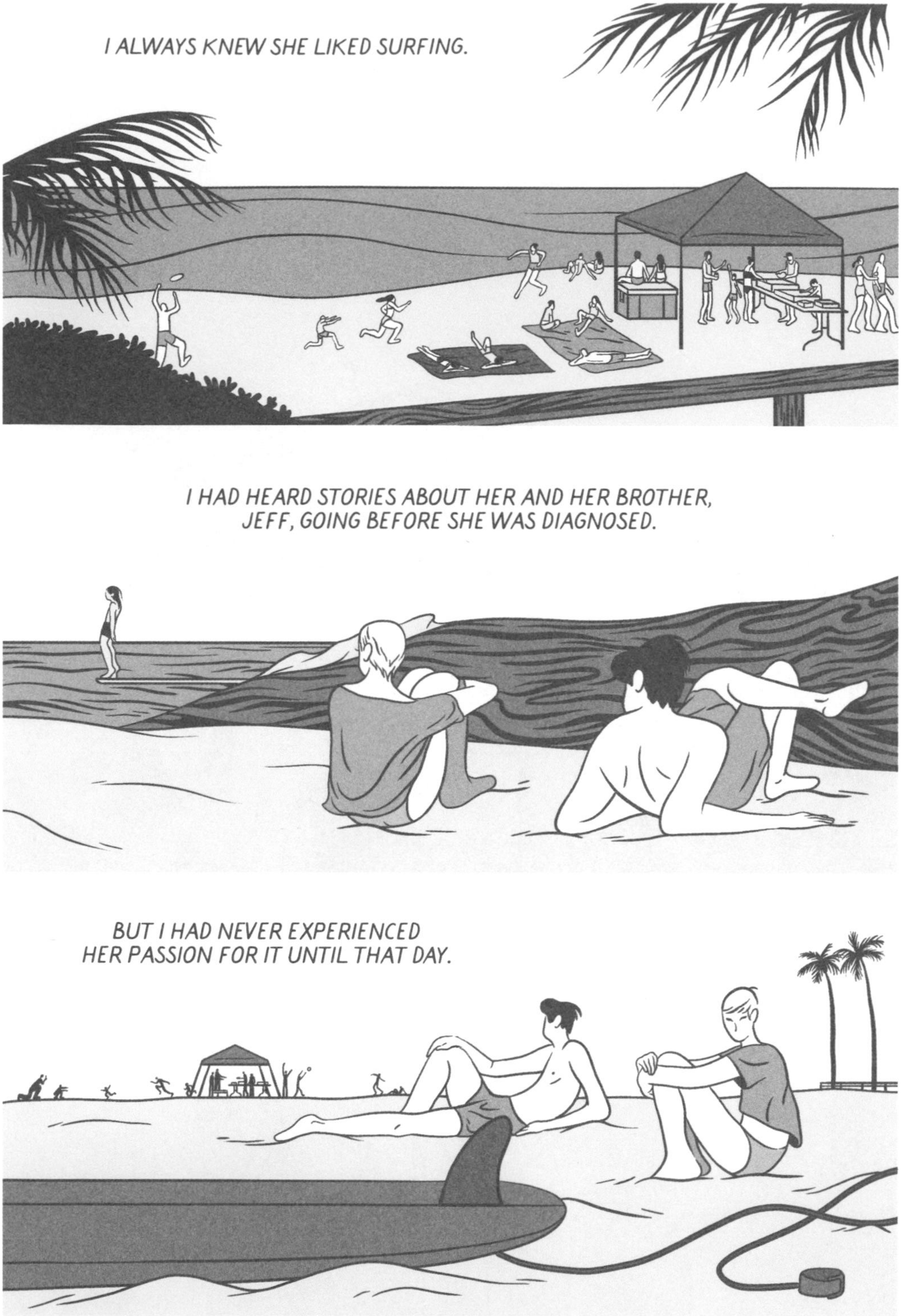
I ALWAYS KNEW SHE LIKED SURFING.
I HAD HEARD STORIES ABOUT HER AND HER BROTHER, JEFF, GOING BEFORE SHE WAS DIAGNOSED.
BUT I HAD NEVER EXPERIENCED HER PASSION FOR IT UNTIL THAT DAY.

WATCHING HER WADE INTO THE WATER,
SPARKED SOMETHING IN ME.

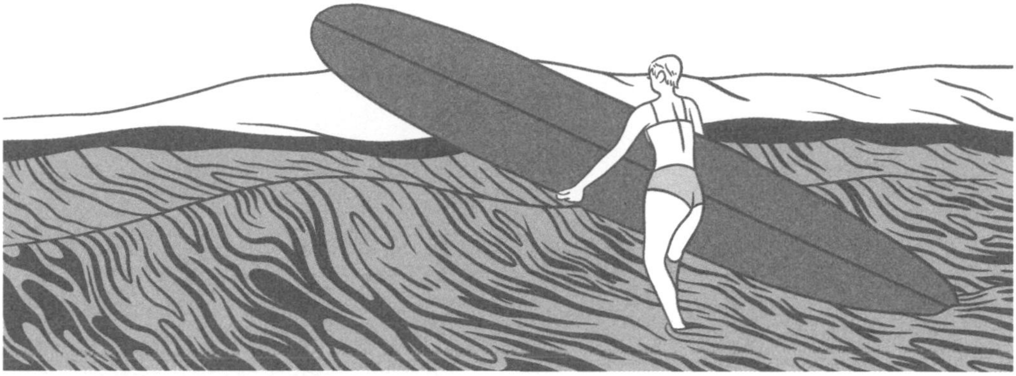

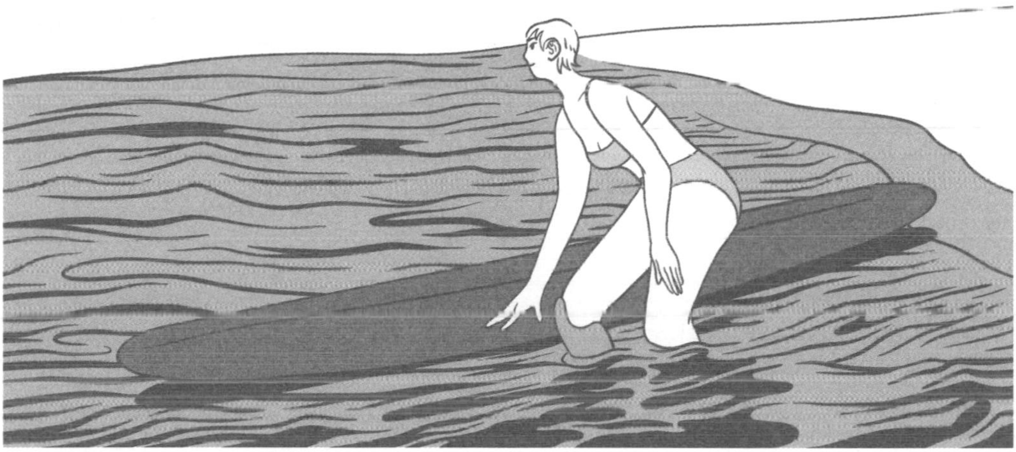

SHE SPARKED SOMETHING
IN HER FAMILY TOO.

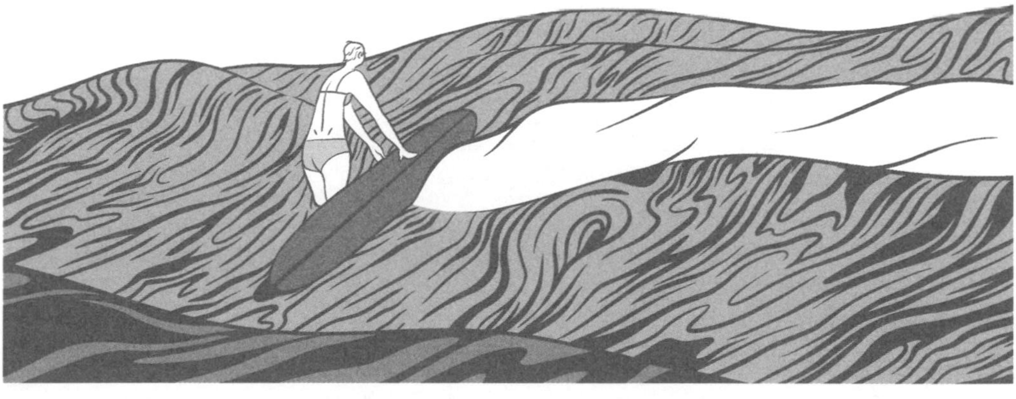

AS SHE WALKED TOWARD THE LINEUP;
JEFF, HER COUSINS, AND I, FOLLOWED.

WE HELPED HER GET PASSED
THE BREAK AND WAITED WITH HER.

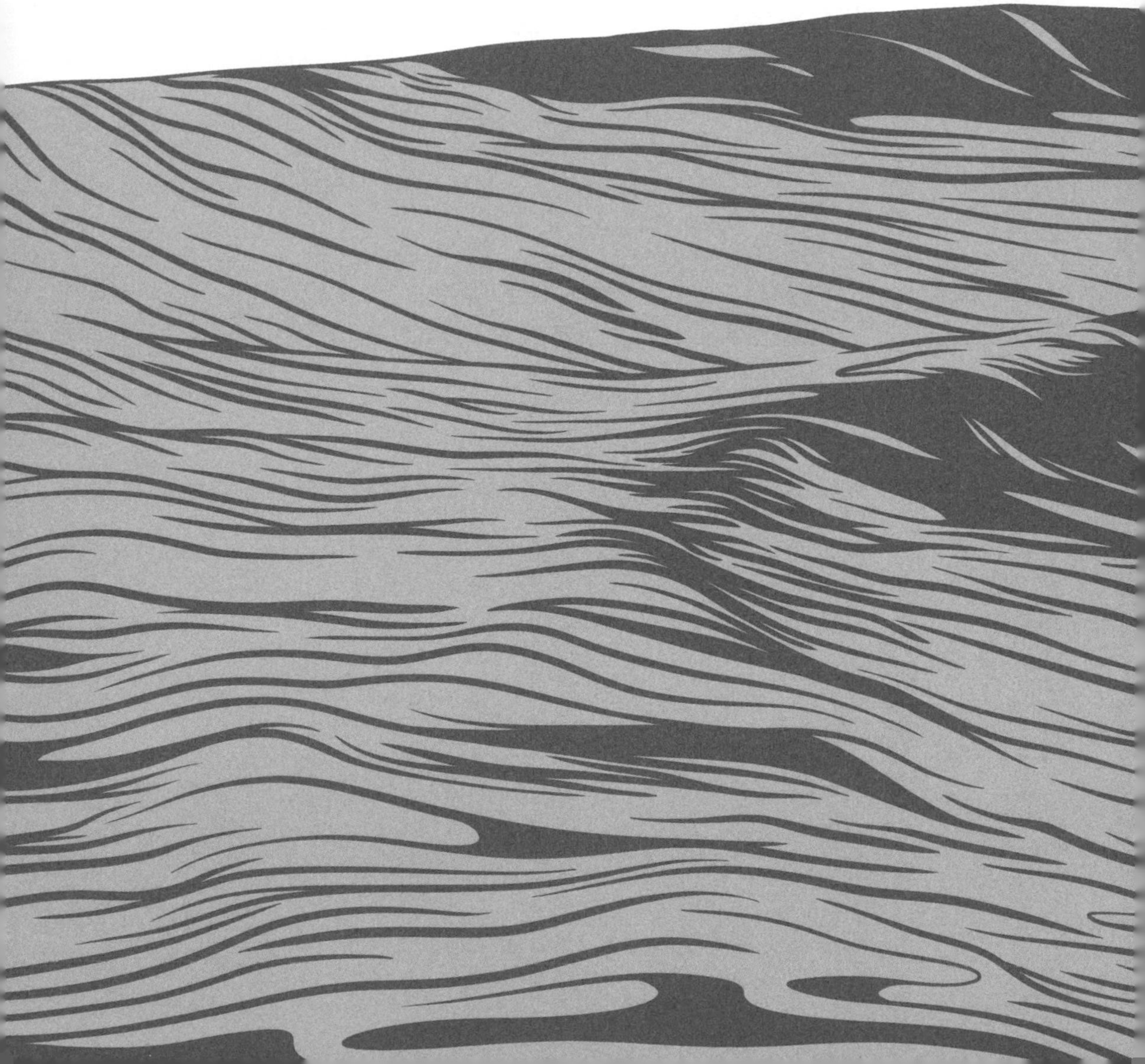

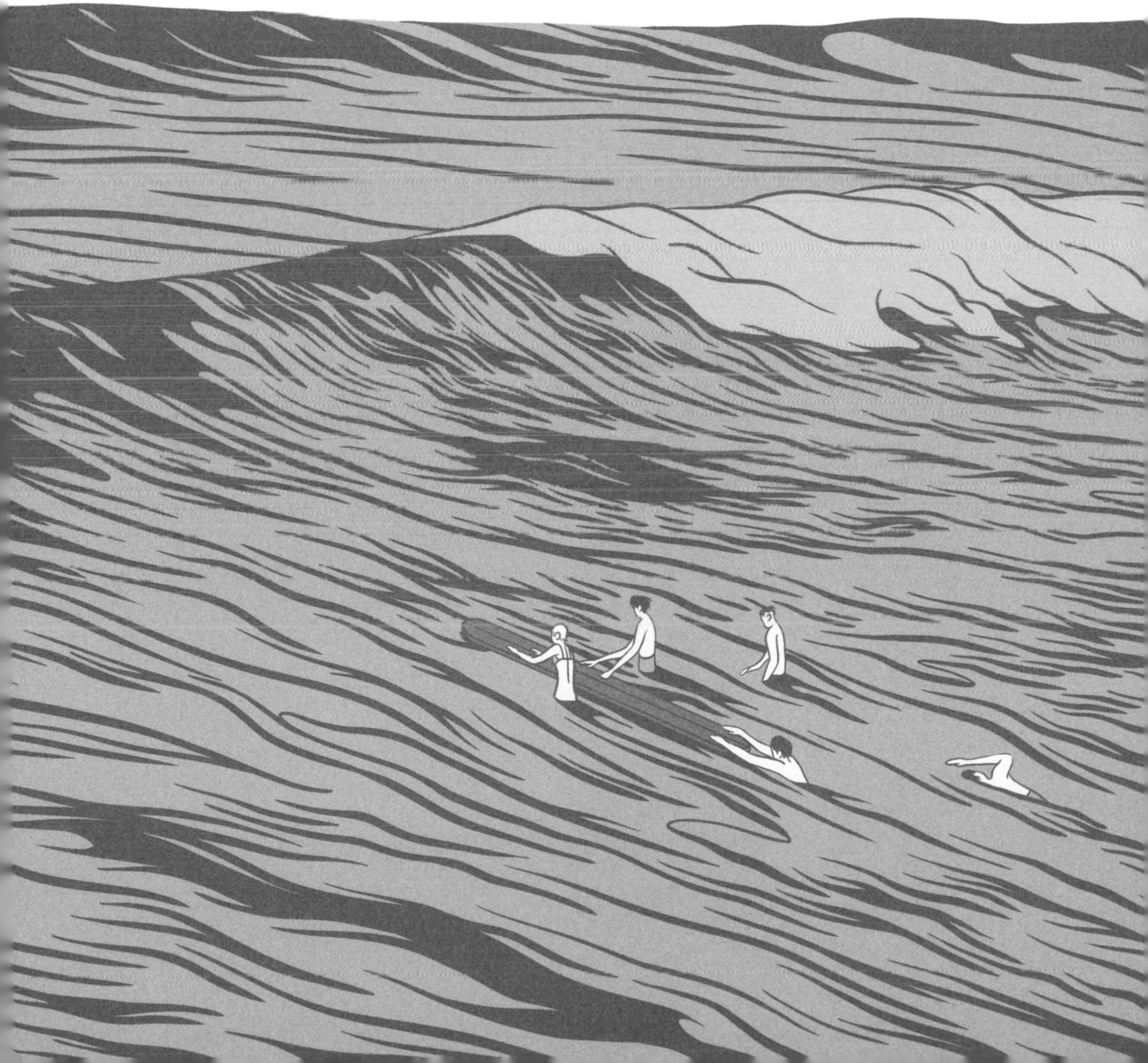

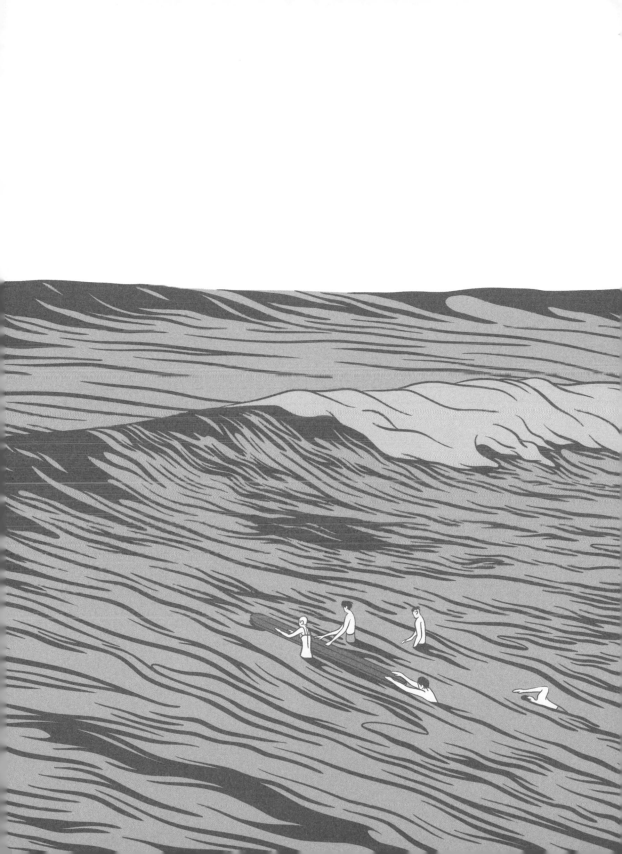

ONE WAVE STARTED TO TAKE SHAPE.

WE NUDGED HER INTO IT
AND SHE TOOK IT FROM THERE.

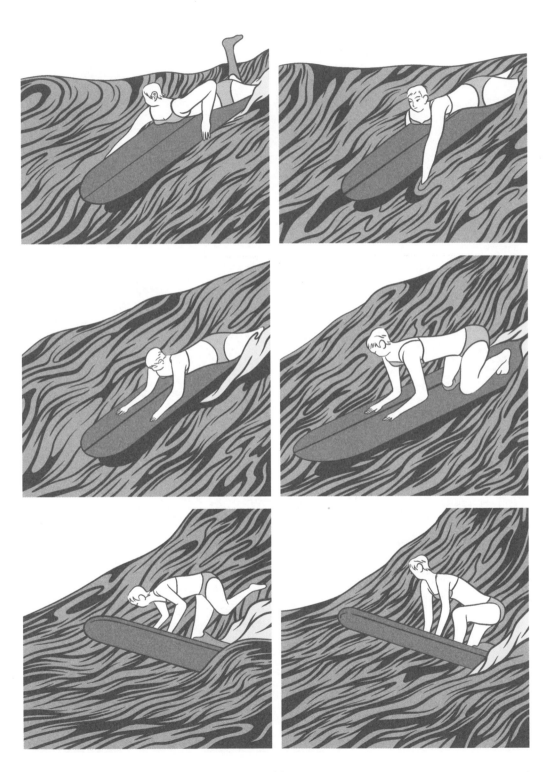

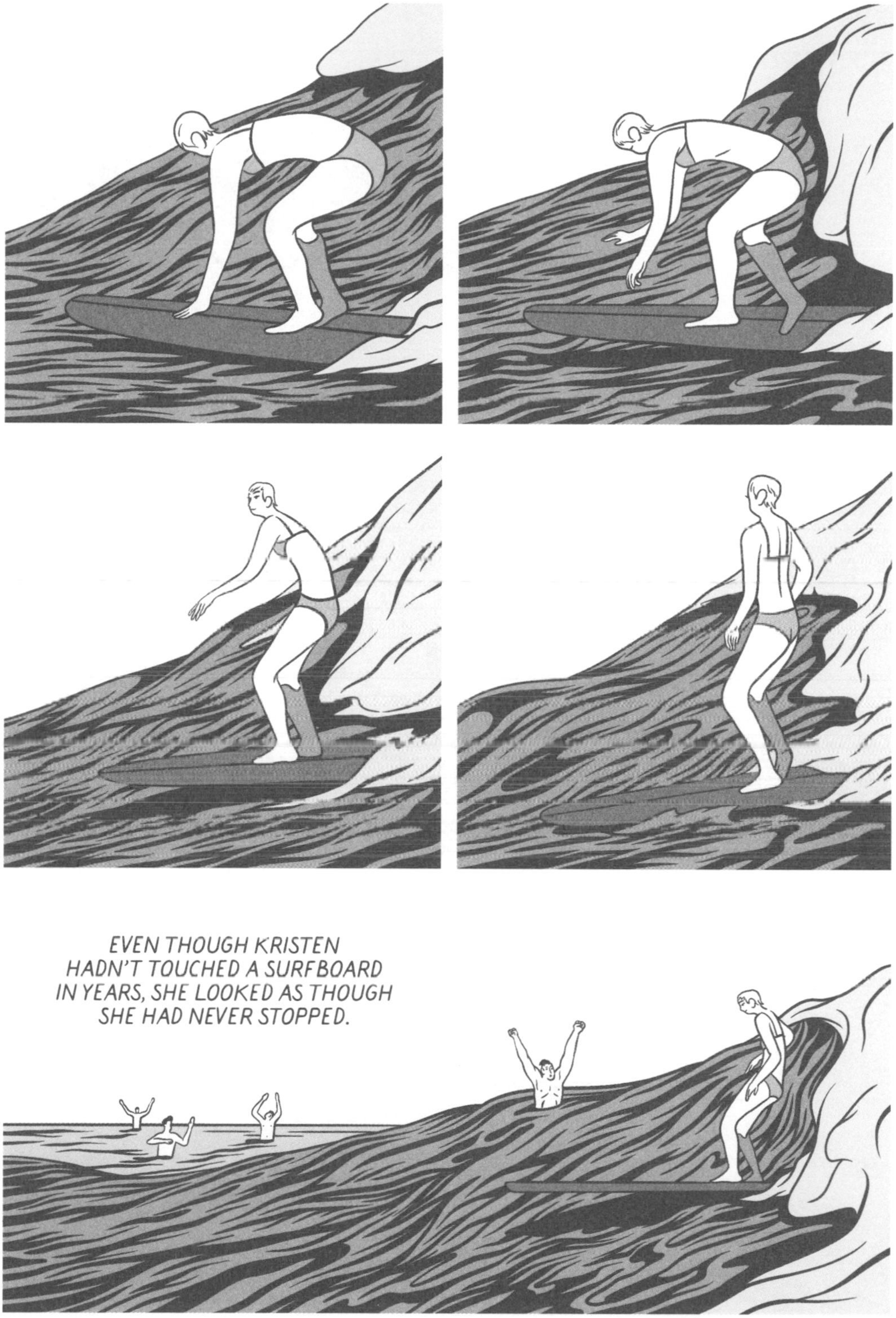
EVEN THOUGH KRISTEN HADN'T TOUCHED A SURFBOARD IN YEARS, SHE LOOKED AS THOUGH SHE HAD NEVER STOPPED.

WE WENT EVERY DAY AFTER THAT.

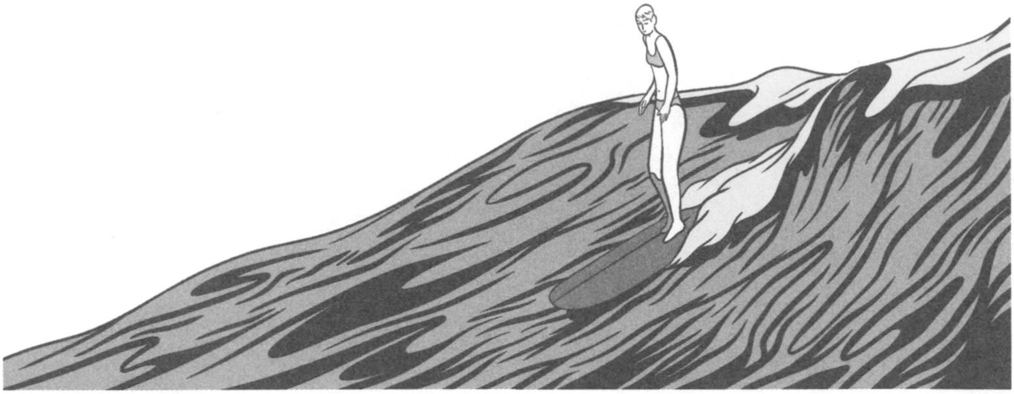

KRISTEN INSPIRED US ALL TO PICK UP A SURFBOARD.

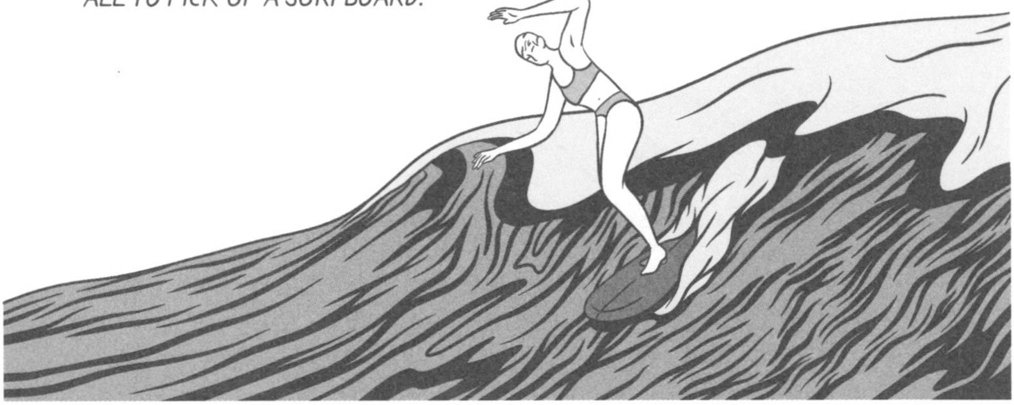

IT'S ALL WE TALKED ABOUT. ALL WE THOUGHT ABOUT.

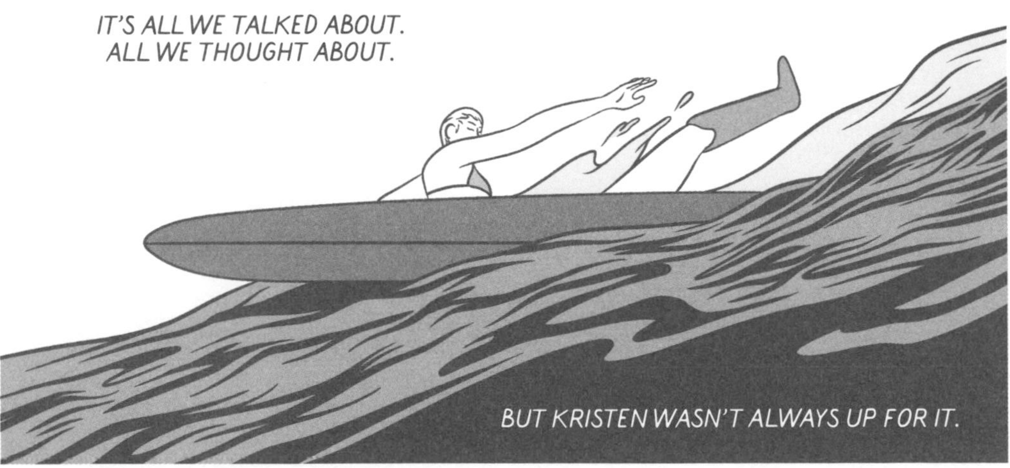
BUT KRISTEN WASN'T ALWAYS UP FOR IT.

HER BODY HAD ITS LIMITS.

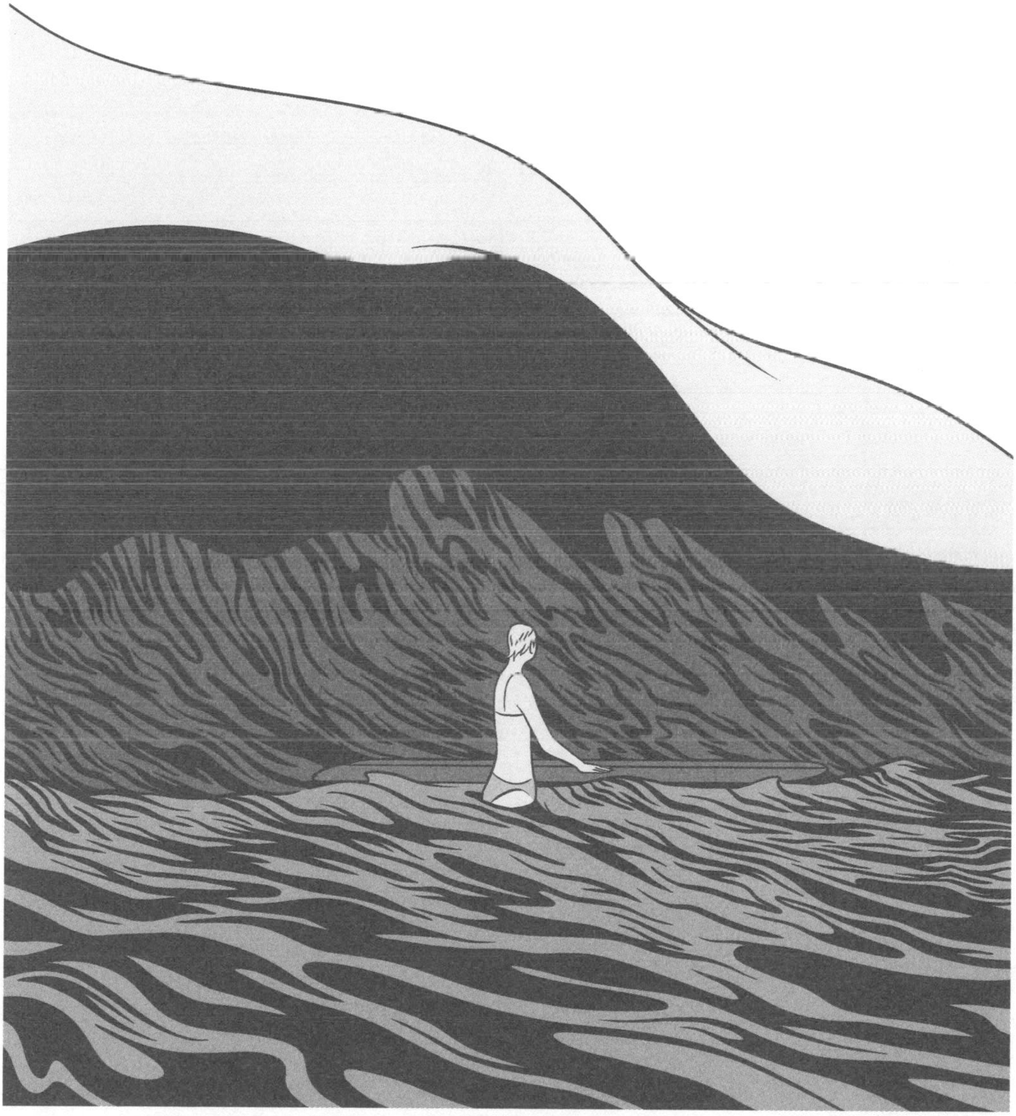

III. THE KISS

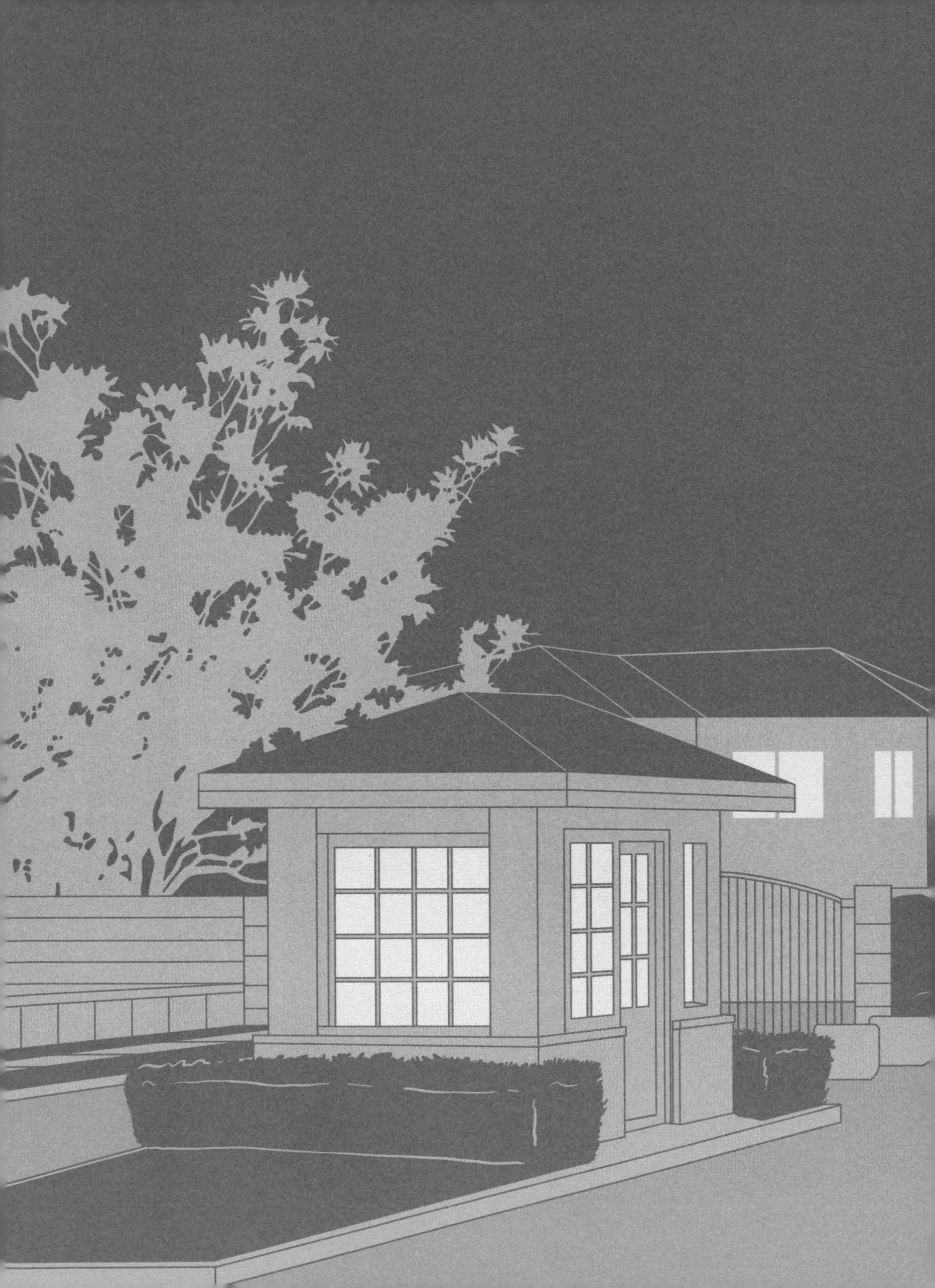

Winter
2008

Lakewood, California

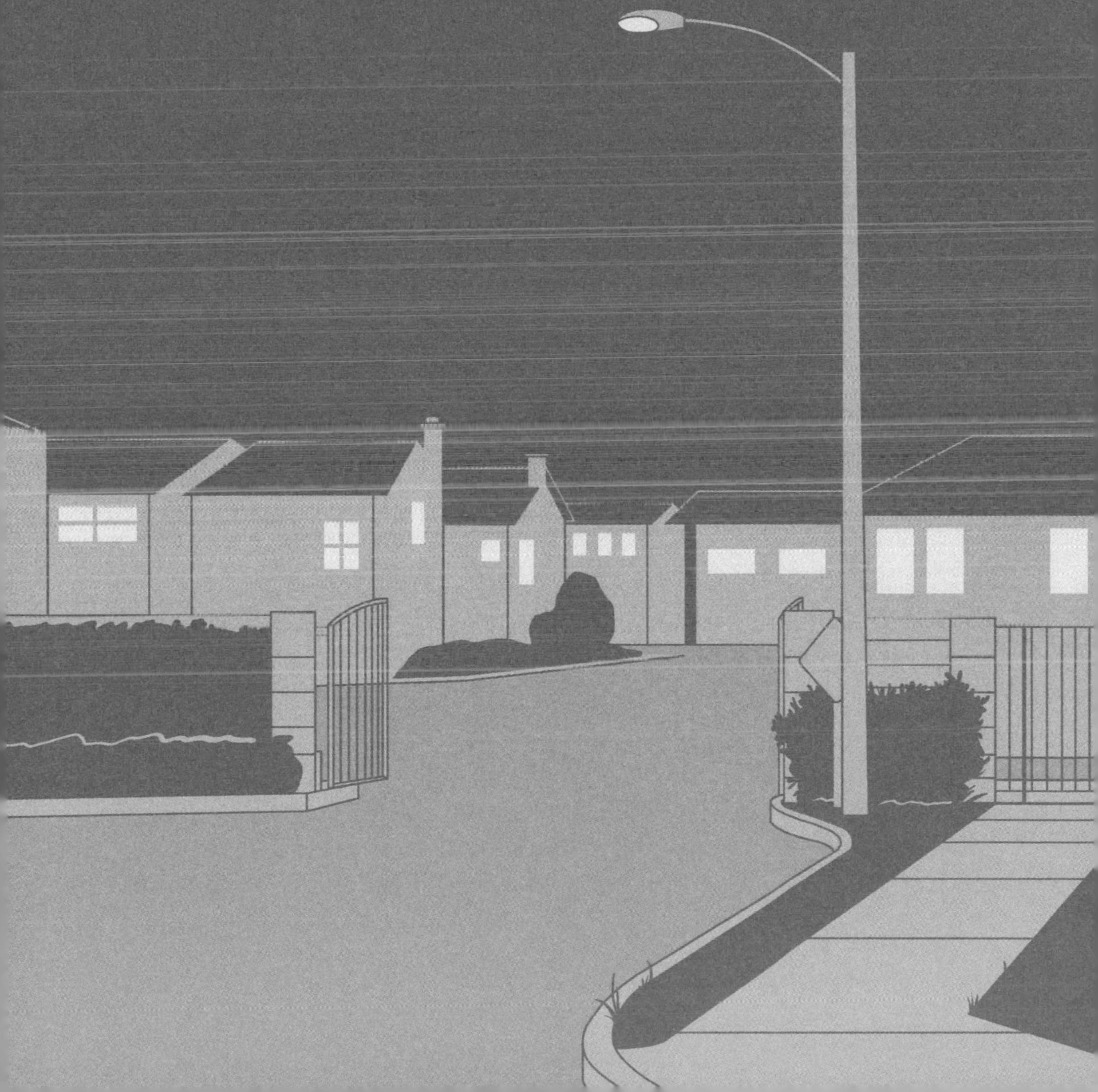

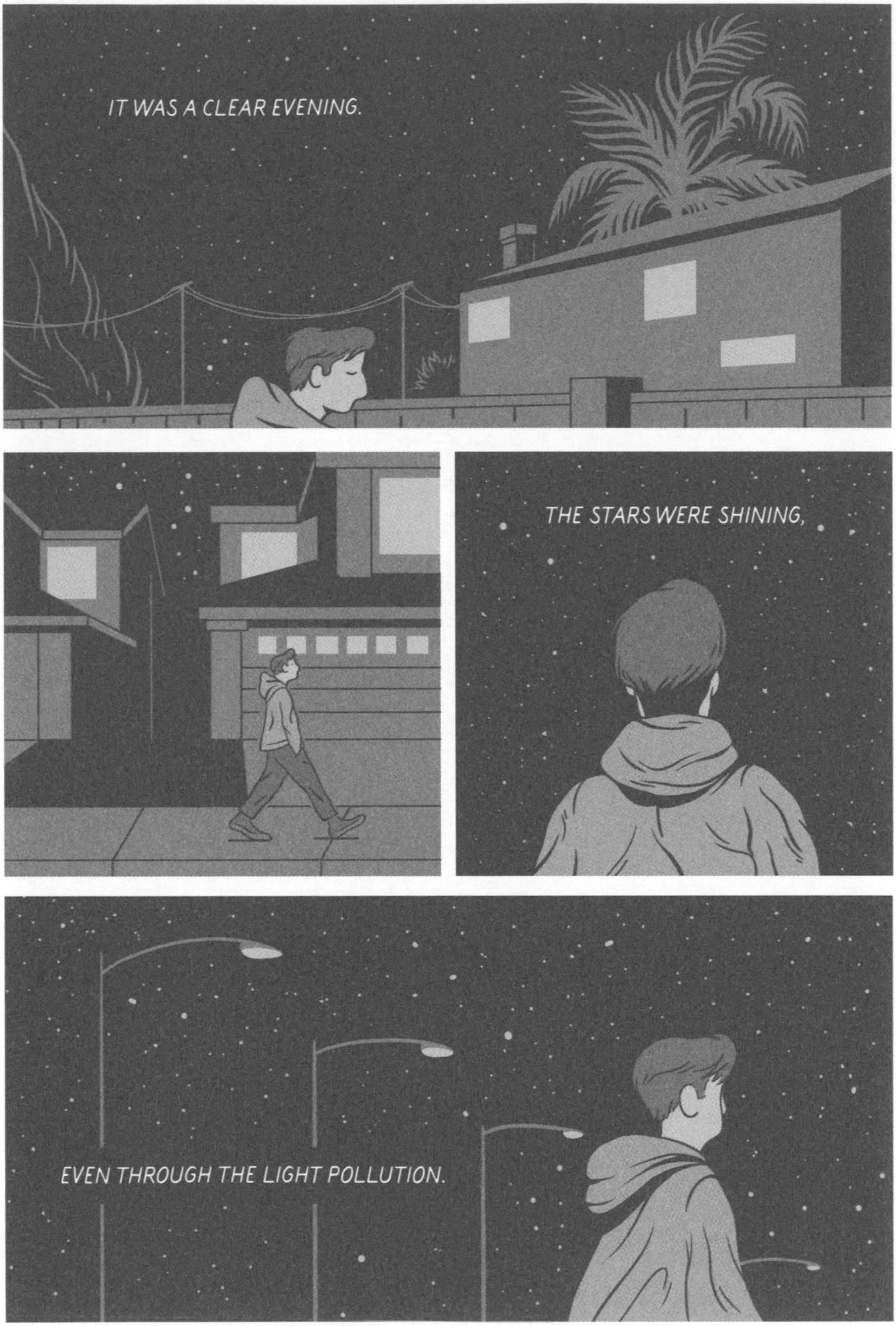
IT WAS A CLEAR EVENING.
THE STARS WERE SHINING,
EVEN THROUGH THE LIGHT POLLUTION.

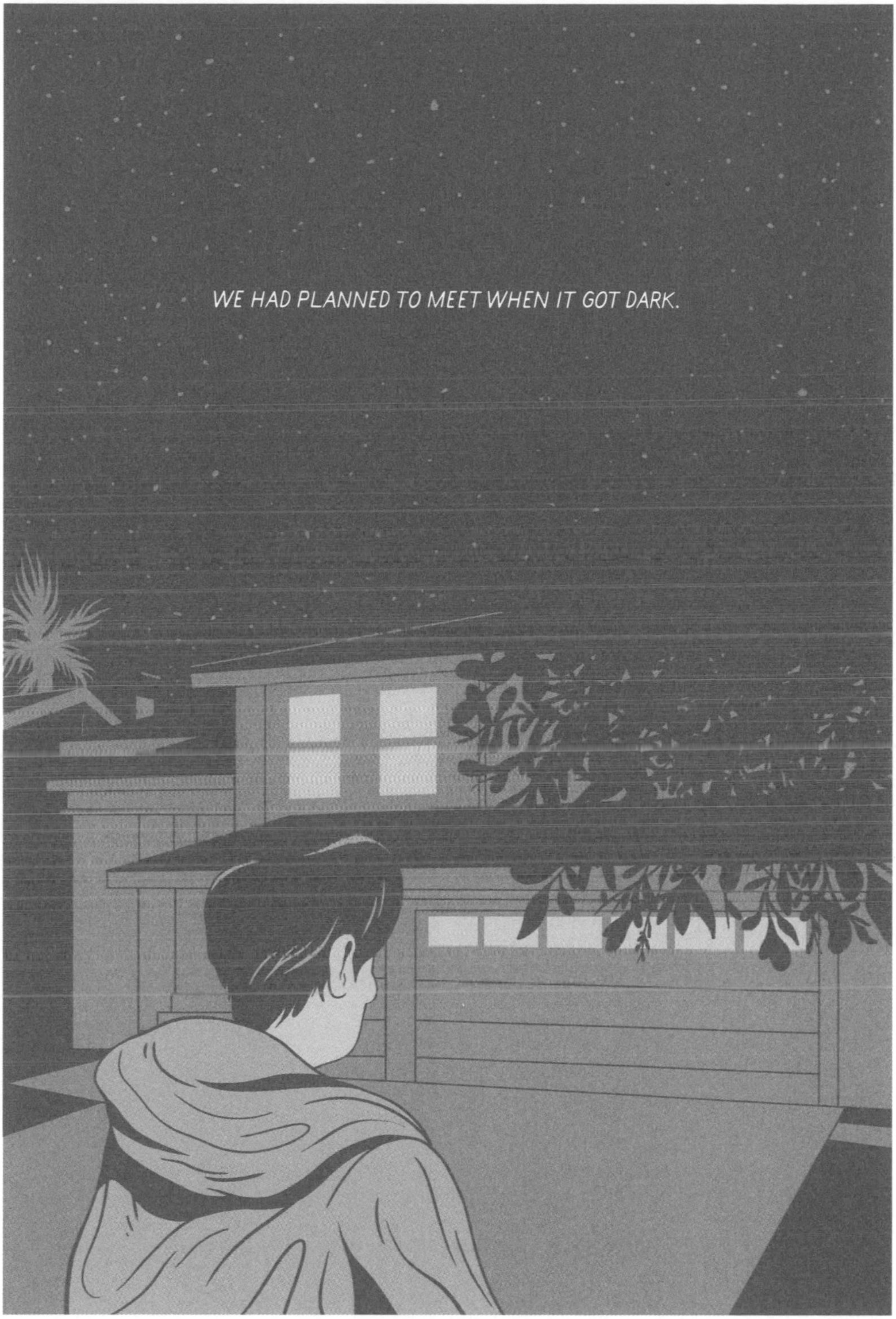
WE HAD PLANNED TO MEET WHEN IT GOT DARK.

SHE WAS HOME ALONE,

*BUT TOO NERVOUS
TO LET ME IN THE HOUSE.*

*HER PARENTS WOULD
BE BACK SOON.*

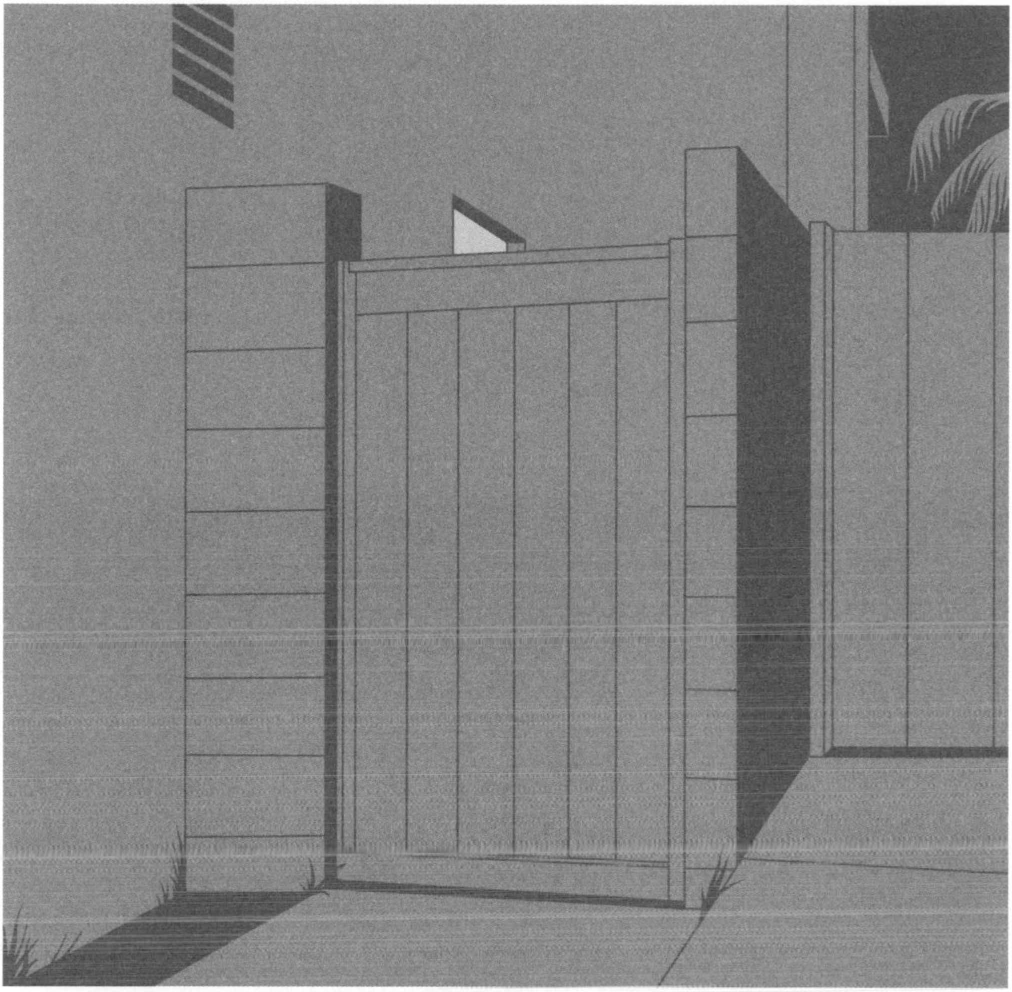

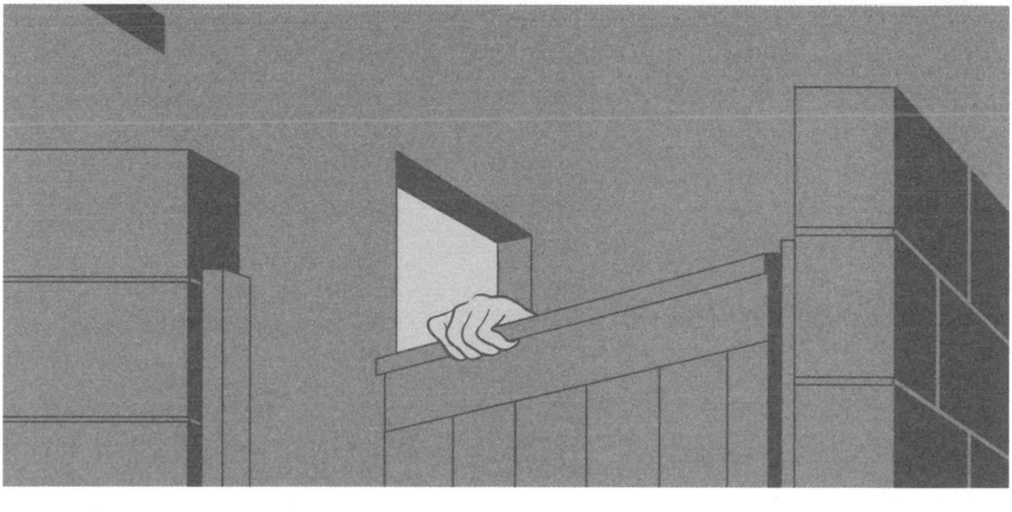

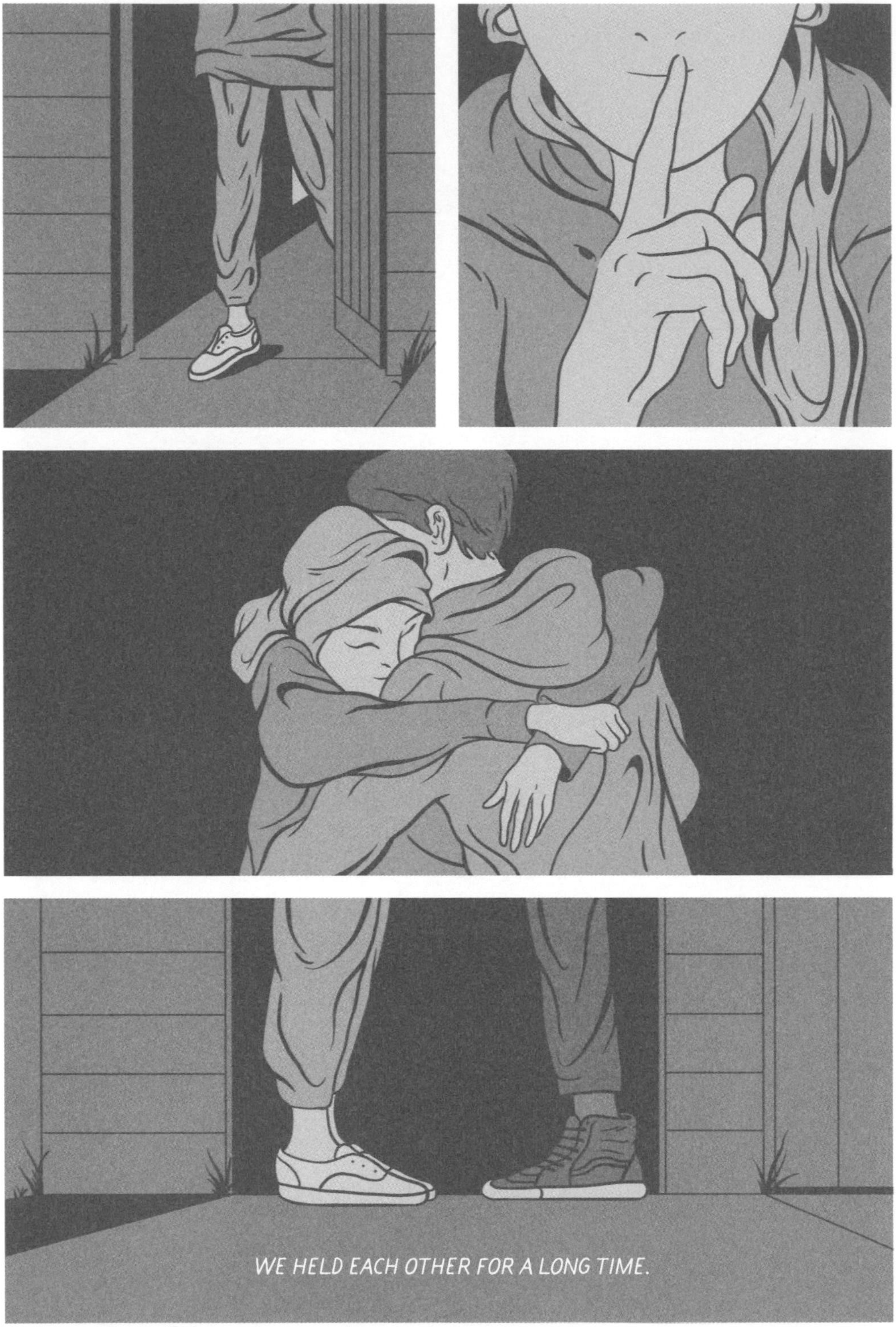
WE HELD EACH OTHER FOR A LONG TIME.

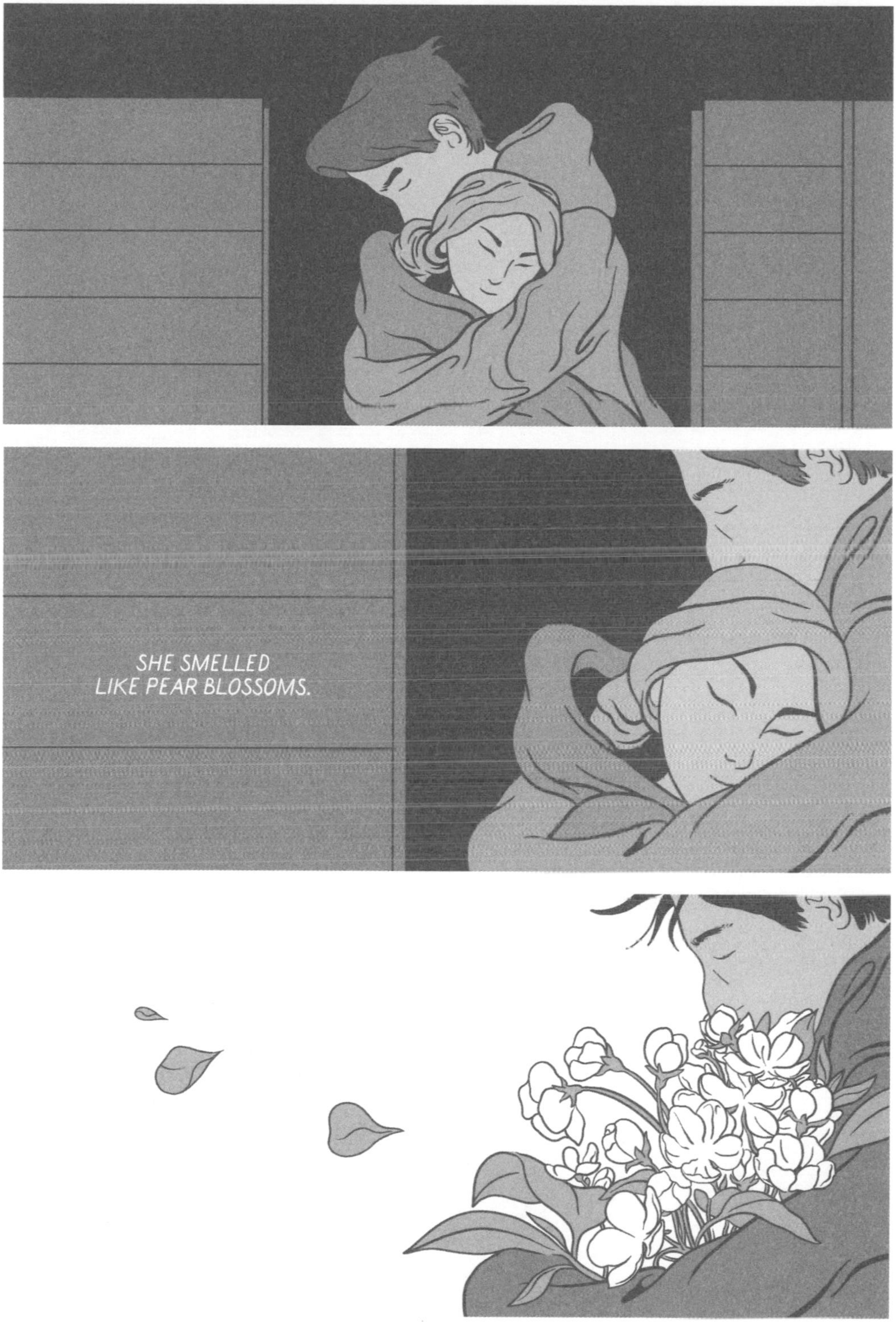
SHE SMELLED
LIKE PEAR BLOSSOMS.

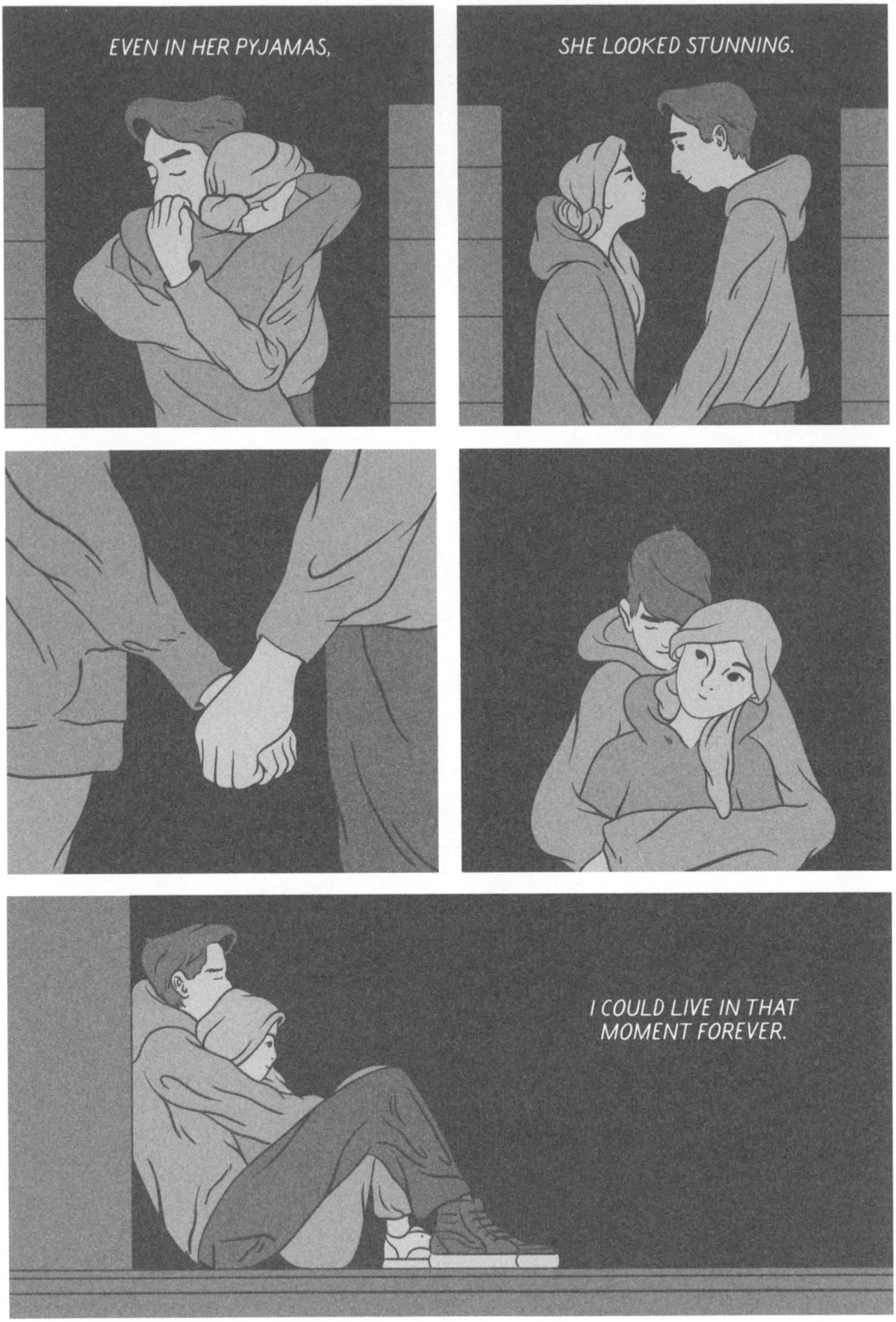
EVEN IN HER PYJAMAS,
SHE LOOKED STUNNING.
I COULD LIVE IN THAT MOMENT FOREVER.

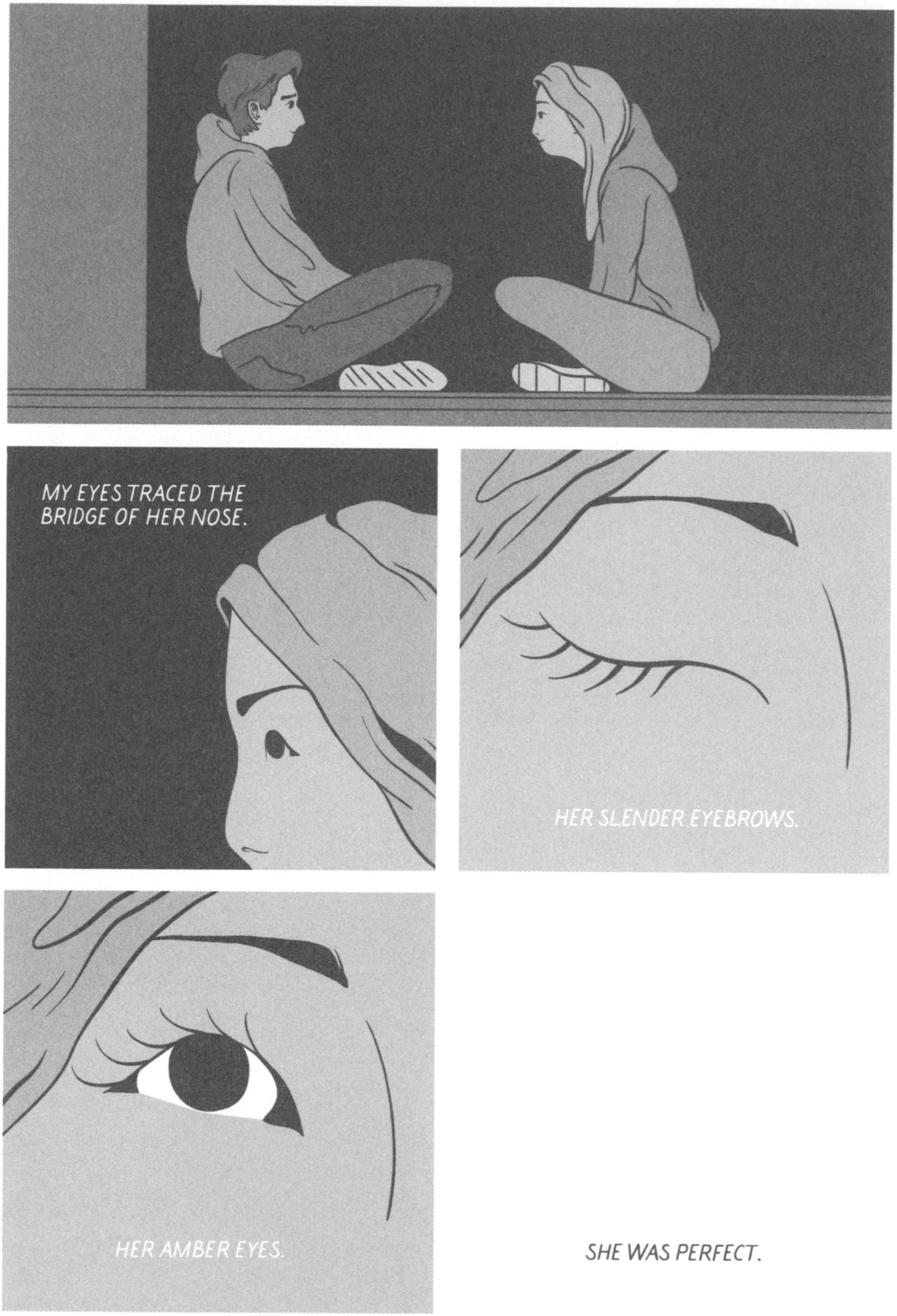
MY EYES TRACED THE BRIDGE OF HER NOSE.
HER SLENDER EYEBROWS.
HER AMBER EYES.
SHE WAS PERFECT.

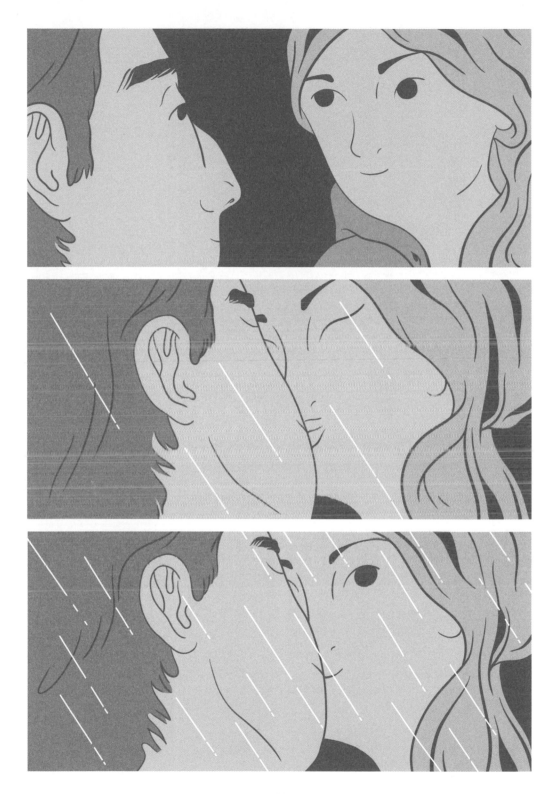

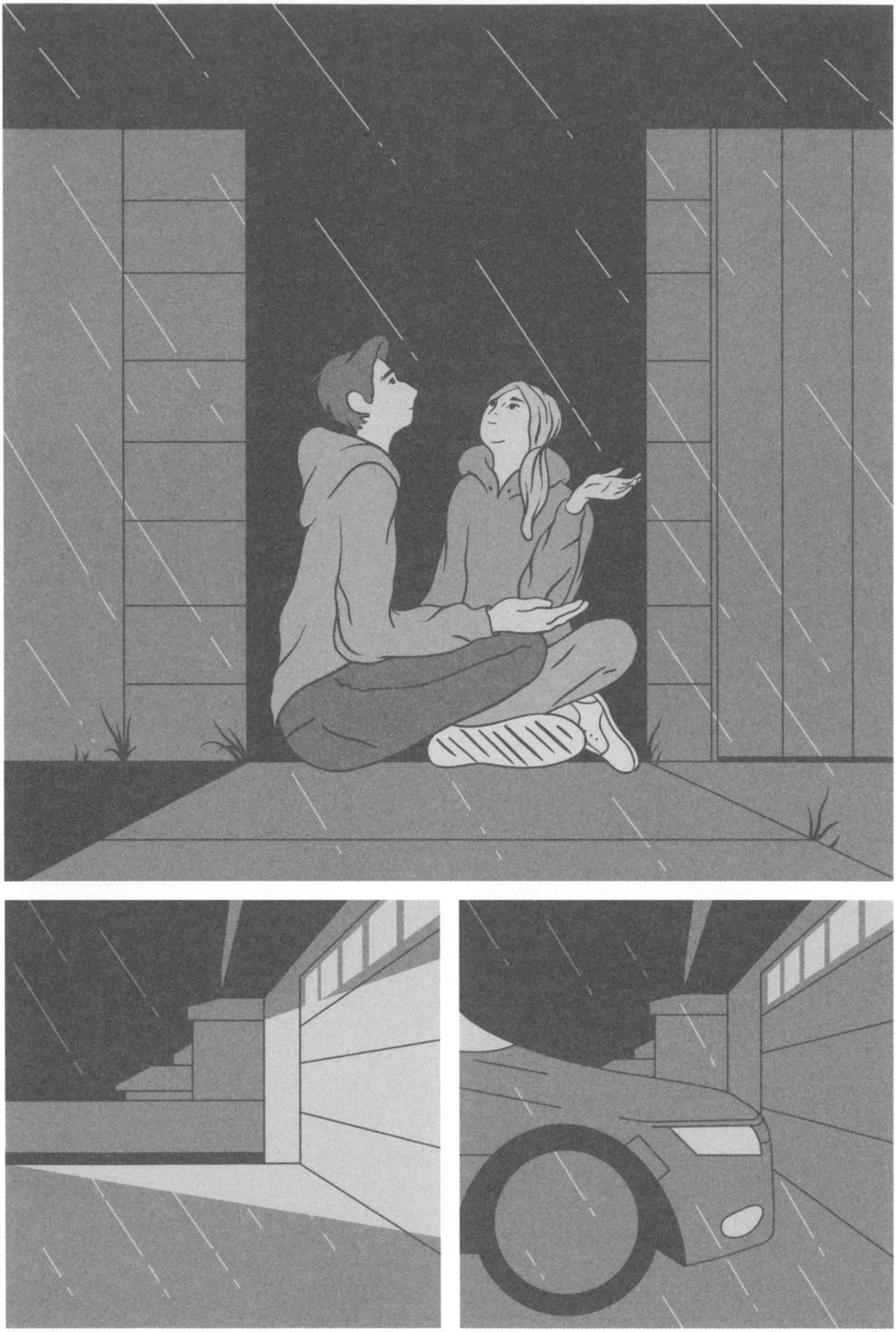

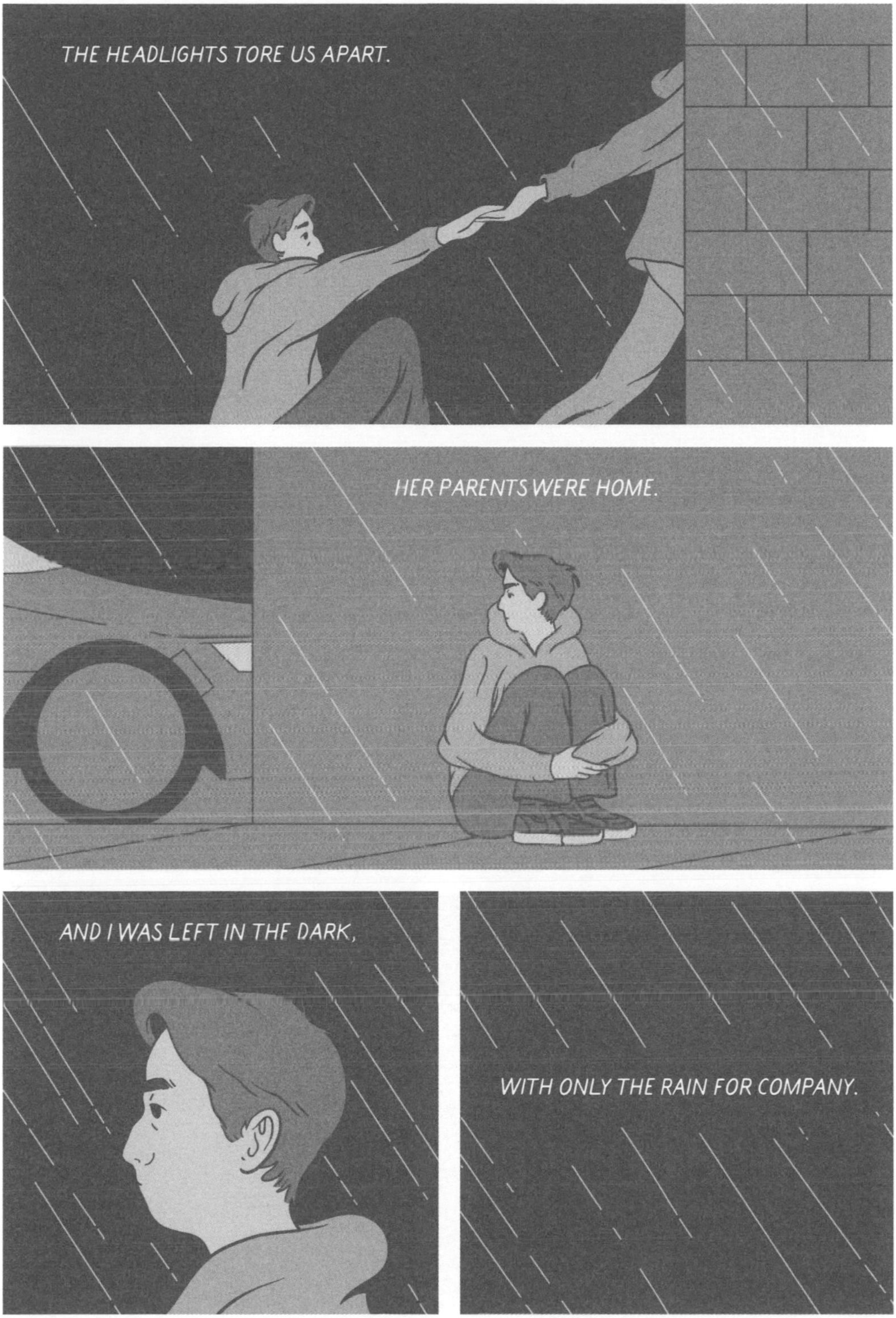
THE HEADLIGHTS TORE US APART.
HER PARENTS WERE HOME.
AND I WAS LEFT IN THE DARK,
WITH ONLY THE RAIN FOR COMPANY.

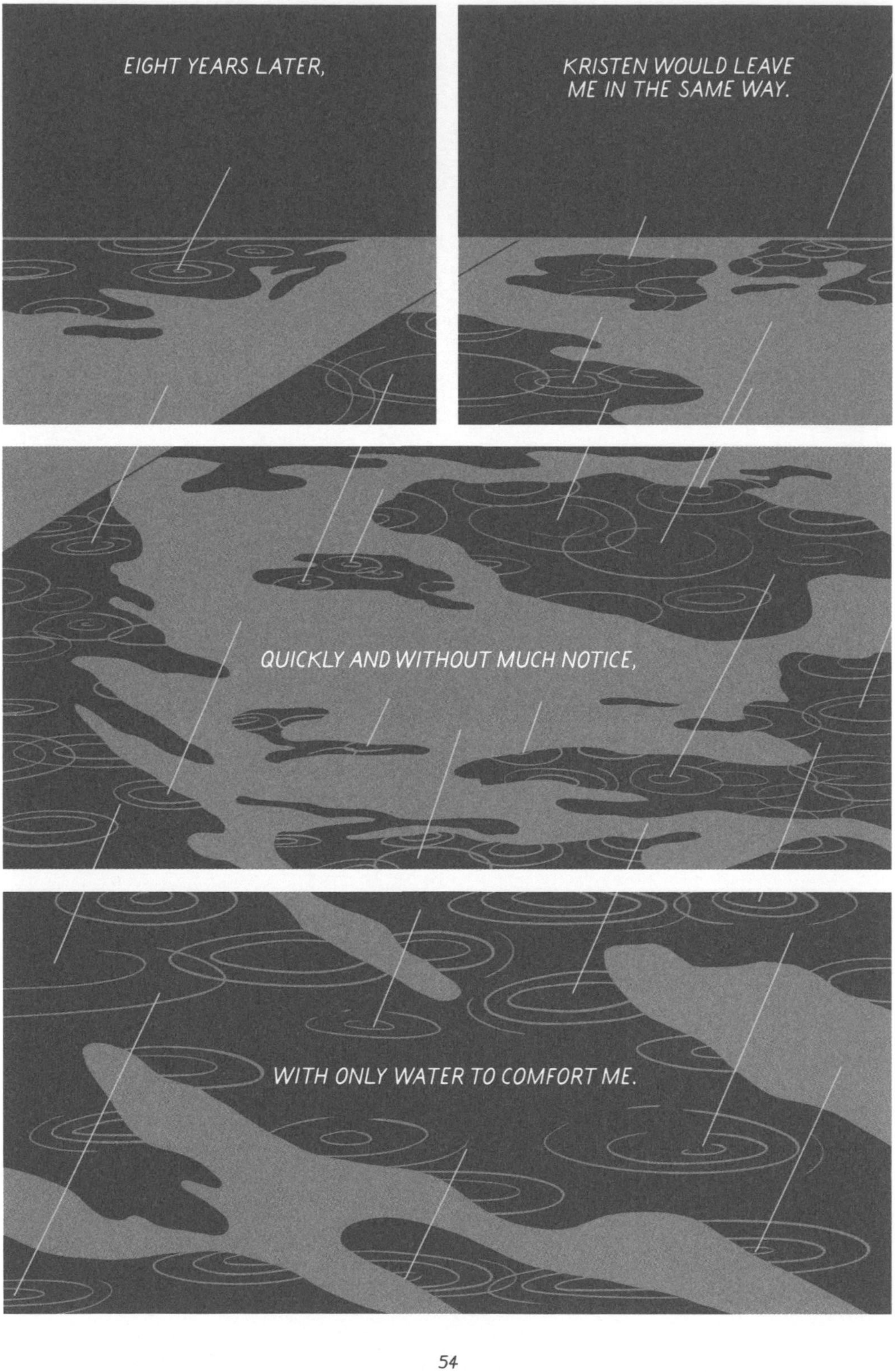
EIGHT YEARS LATER,
KRISTEN WOULD LEAVE ME IN THE SAME WAY.
QUICKLY AND WITHOUT MUCH NOTICE,
WITH ONLY WATER TO COMFORT ME.

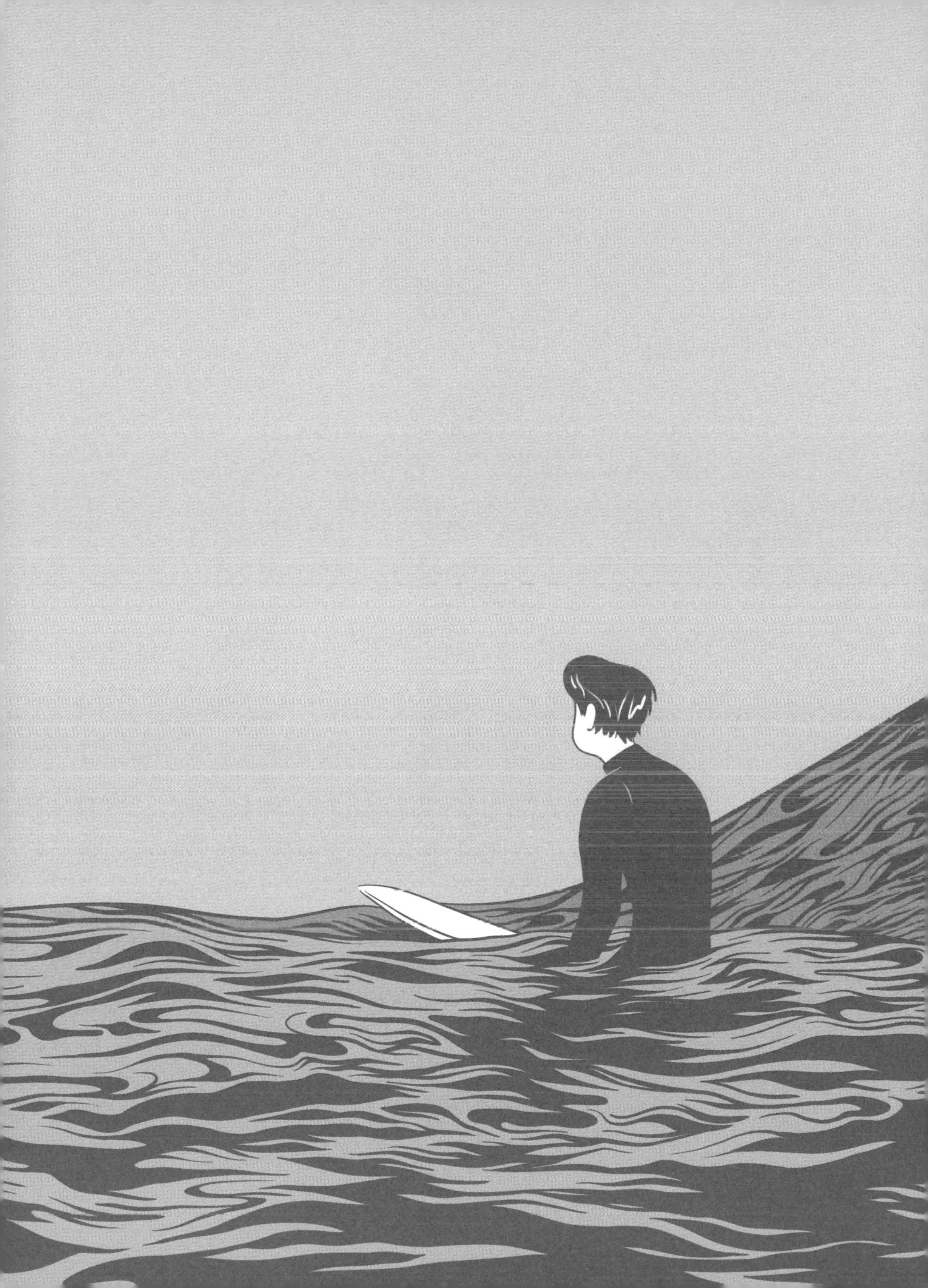

IV. BEACH BOYS

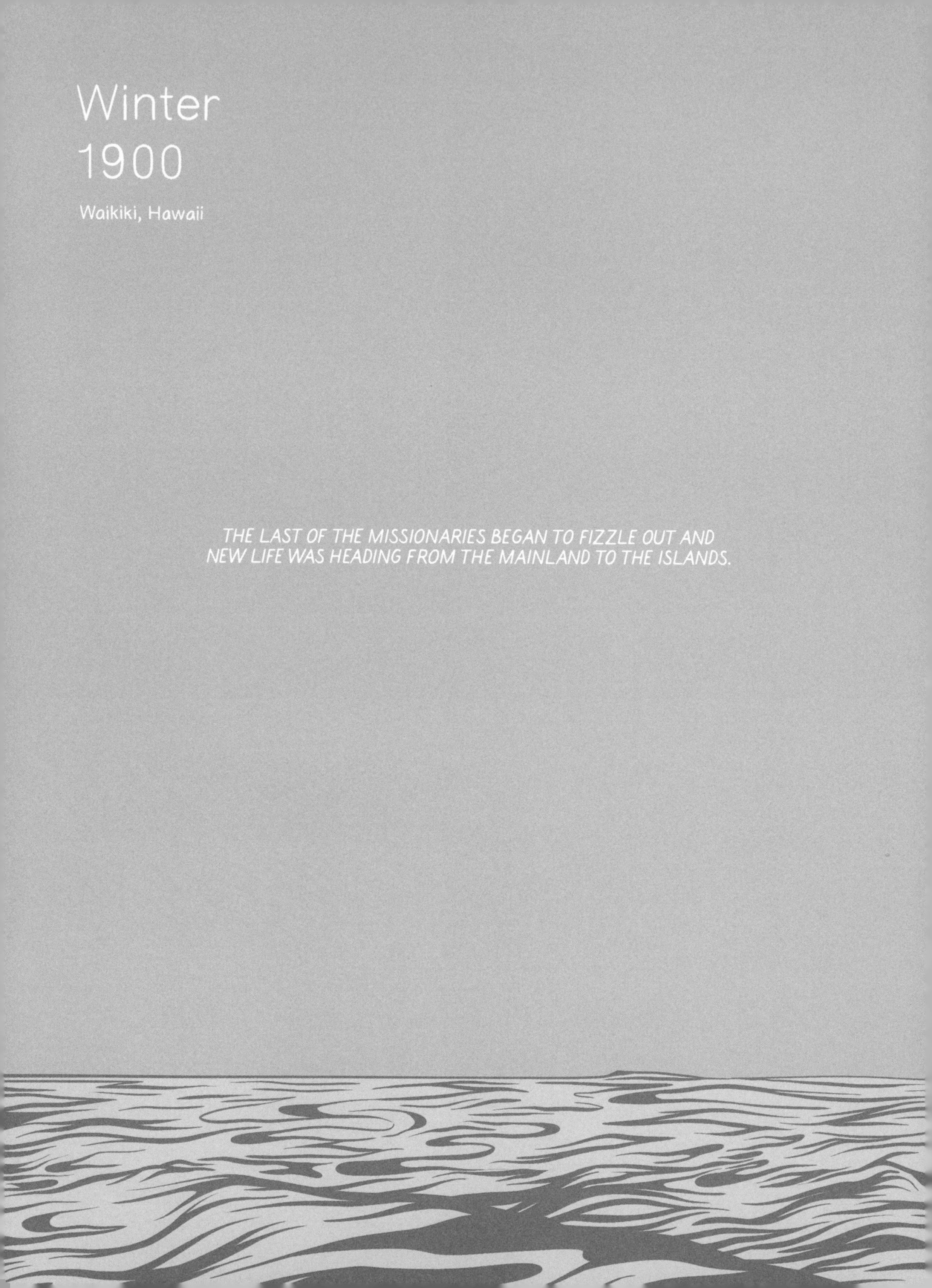
Winter
1900
Waikiki, Hawaii
THE LAST OF THE MISSIONARIES BEGAN TO FIZZLE OUT AND NEW LIFE WAS HEADING FROM THE MAINLAND TO THE ISLANDS.

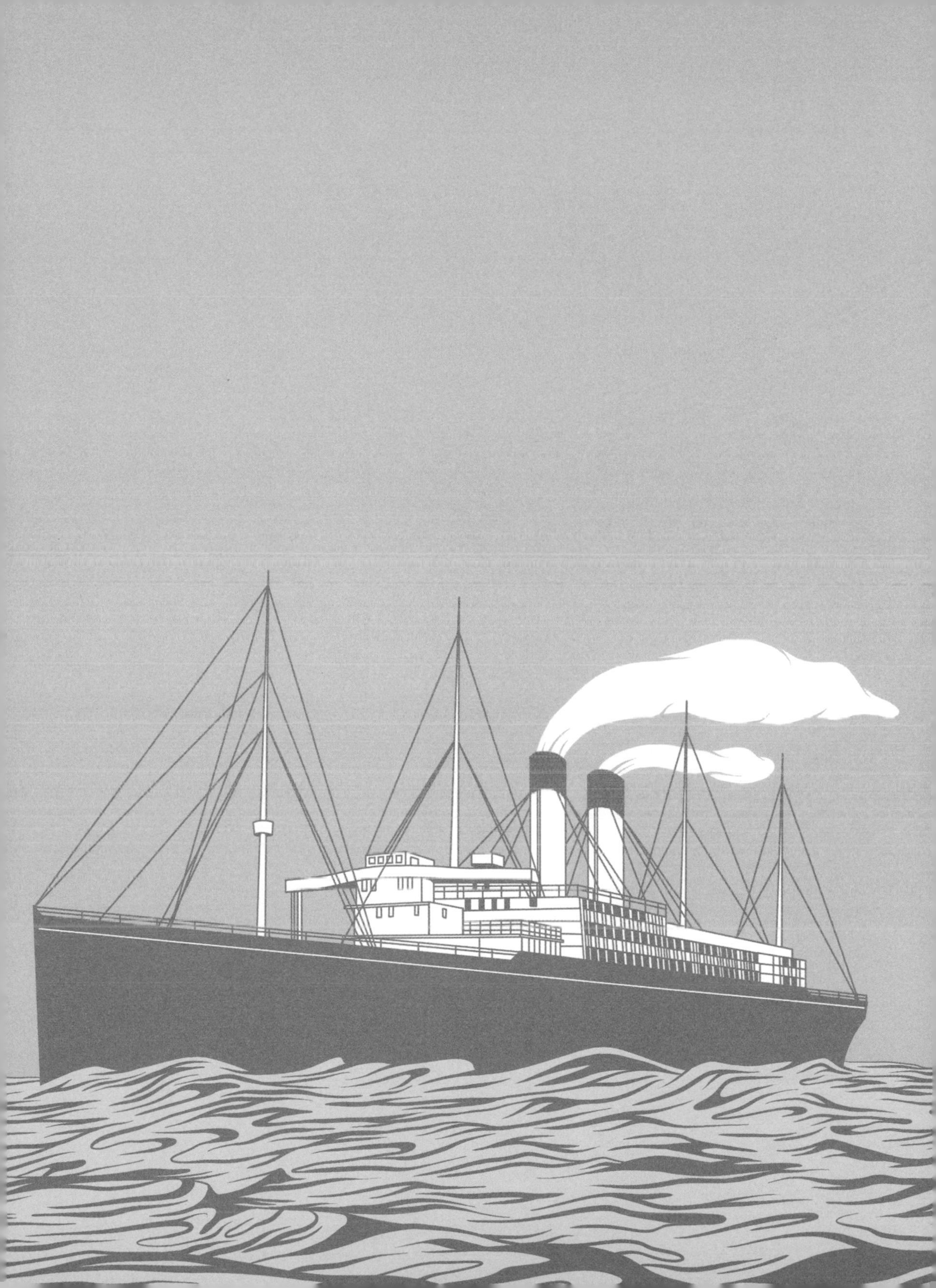

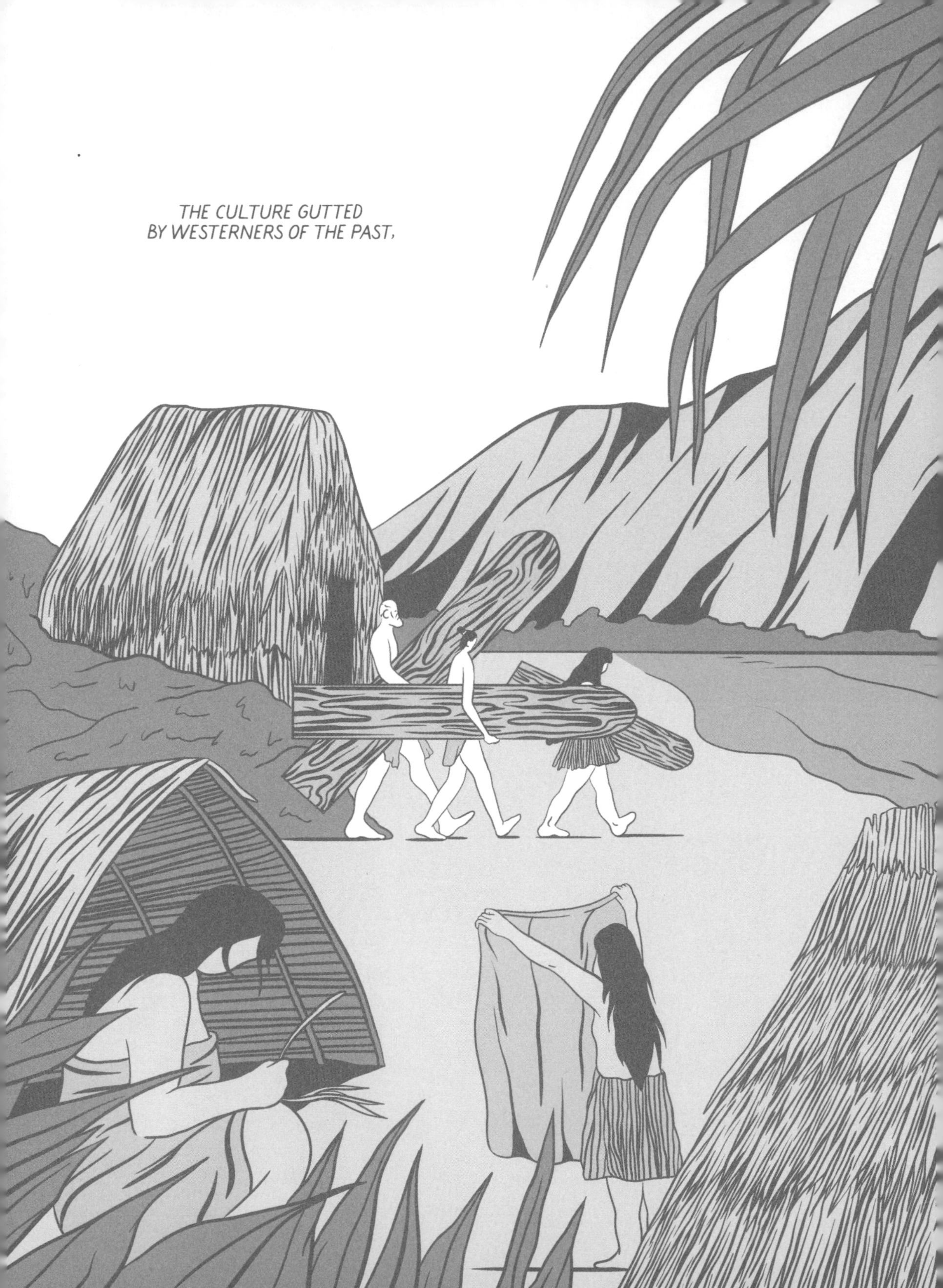
THE CULTURE GUTTED
BY WESTERNERS OF THE PAST,

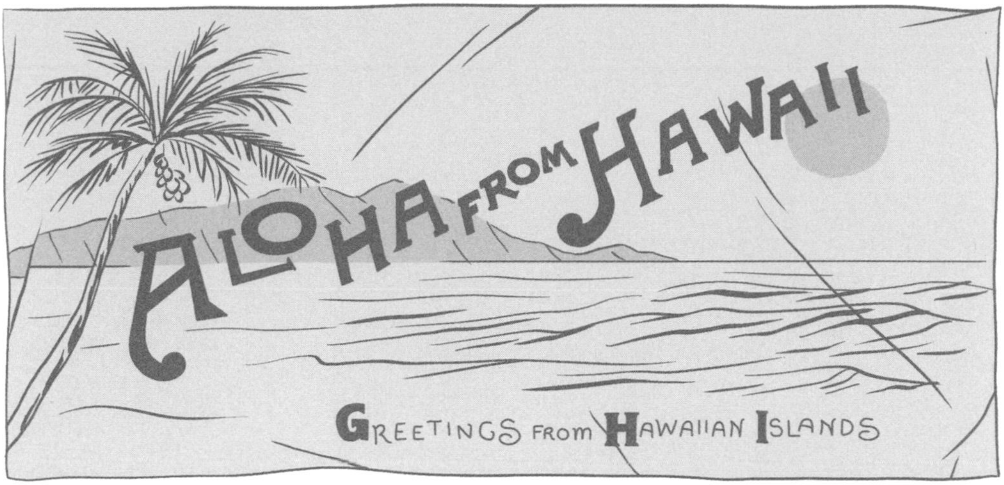
ALOHA FROM HAWAII
GREETINGS FROM HAWAIIAN ISLANDS

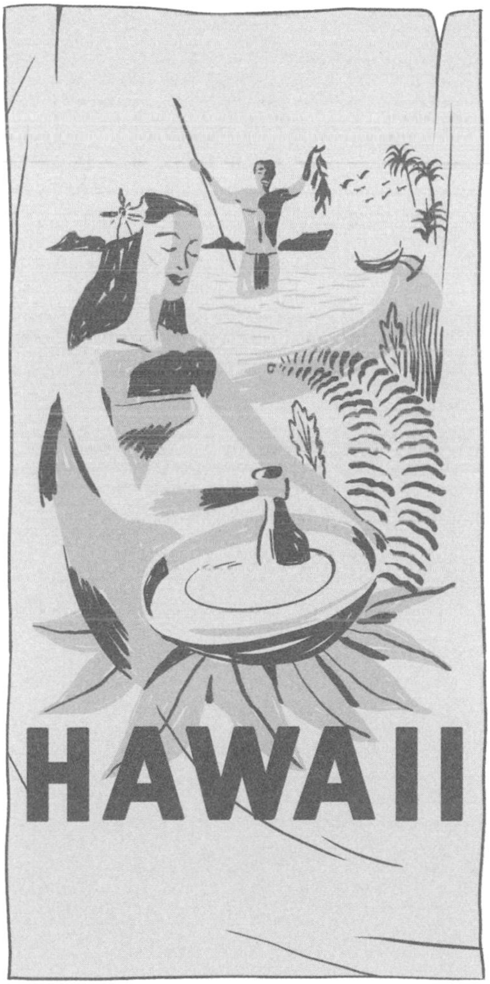
HAWAII

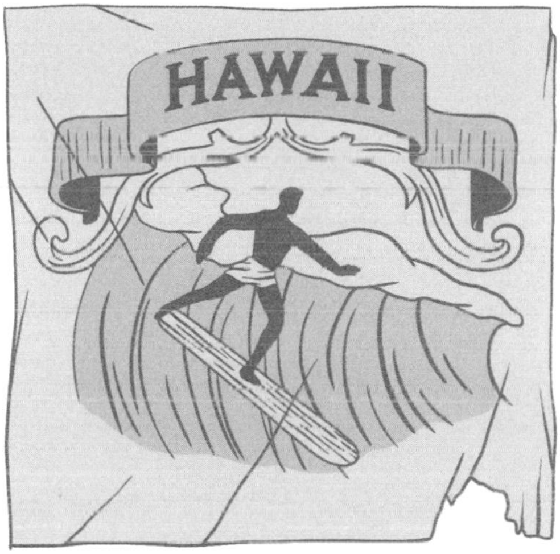
HAWAII

WAS THEN REBRANDED TO WEALTHY MAINLANDERS AS AN EXOTIC NOVELTY.

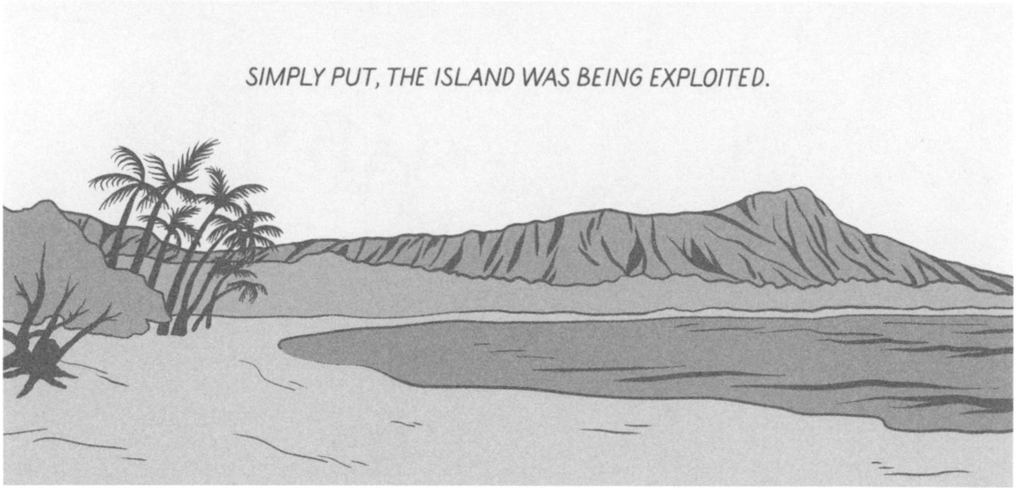
SIMPLY PUT, THE ISLAND WAS BEING EXPLOITED.

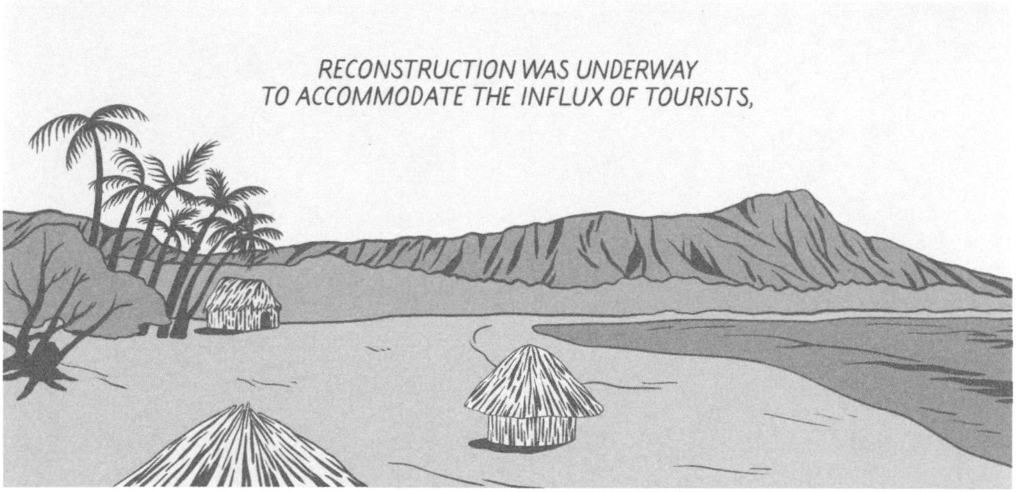
RECONSTRUCTION WAS UNDERWAY
TO ACCOMMODATE THE INFLUX OF TOURISTS,

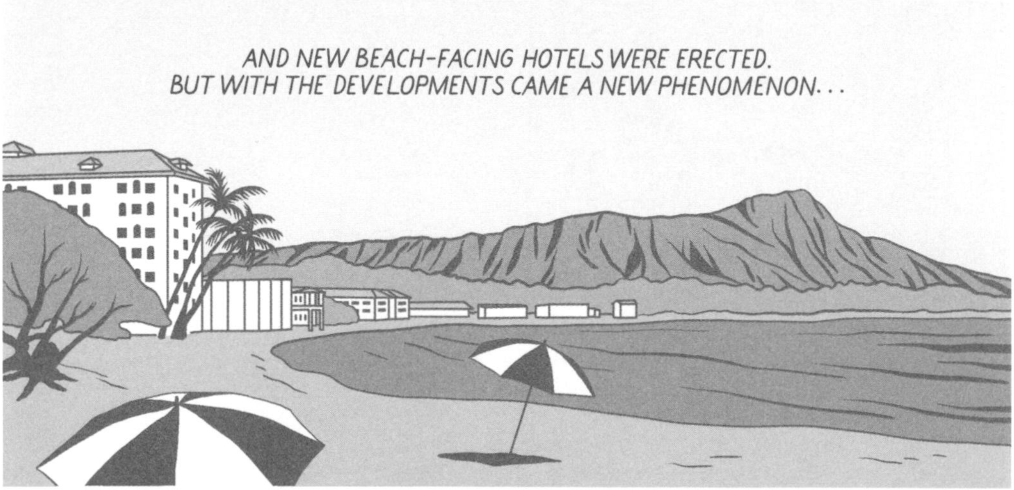
AND NEW BEACH-FACING HOTELS WERE ERECTED.
BUT WITH THE DEVELOPMENTS CAME A NEW PHENOMENON...

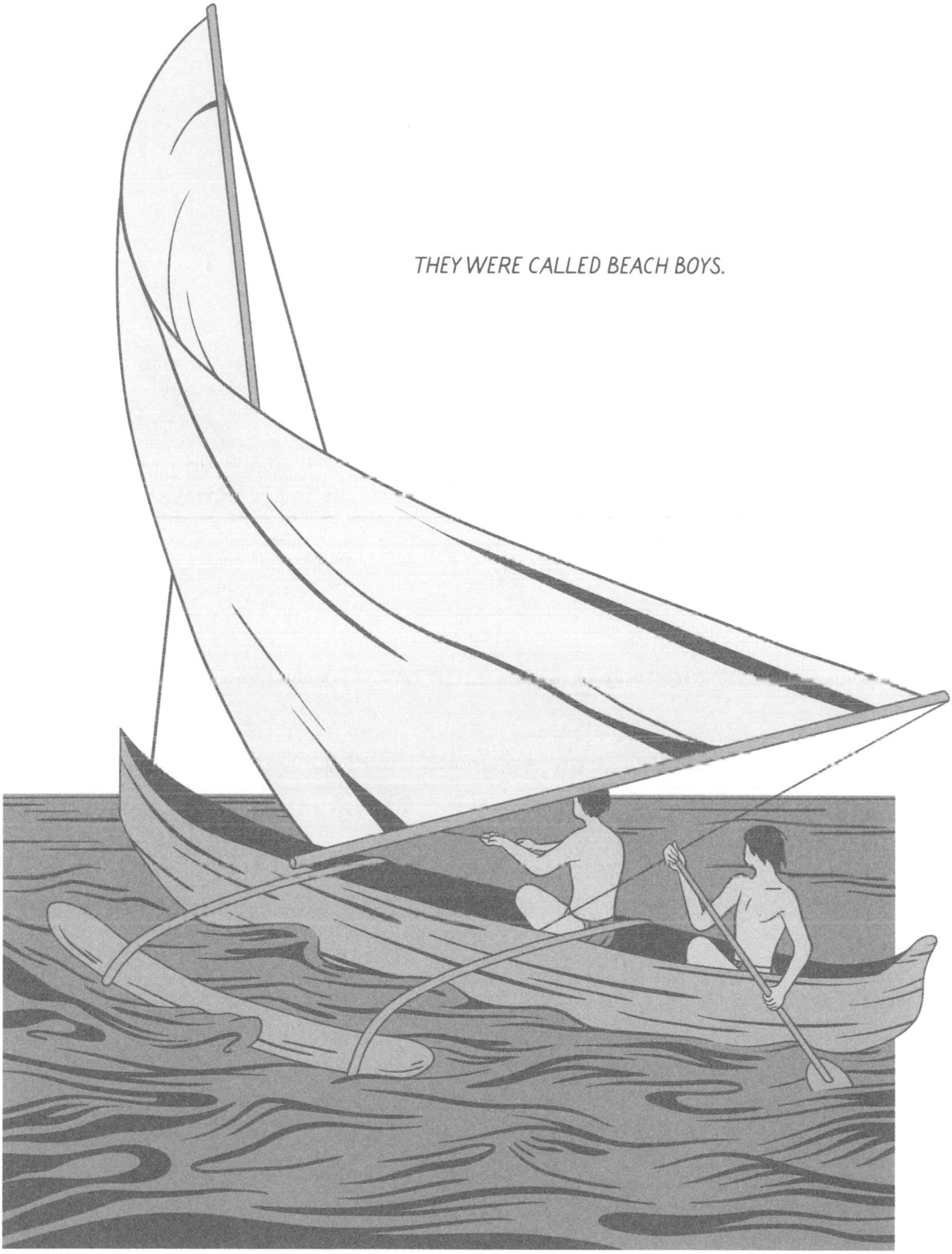
THEY WERE CALLED BEACH BOYS.

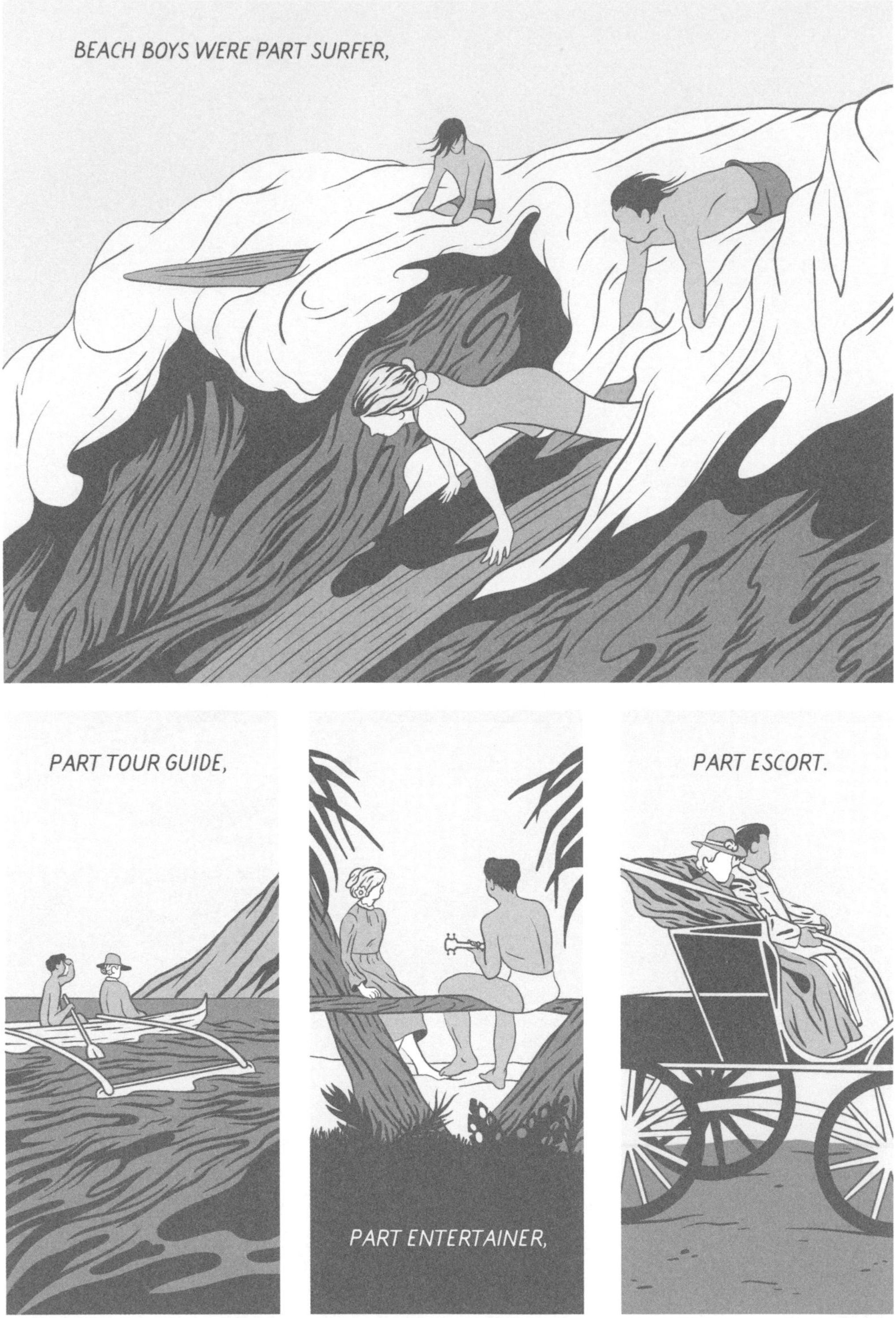
BEACH BOYS WERE PART SURFER,
PART TOUR GUIDE,
PART ENTERTAINER,
PART ESCORT.

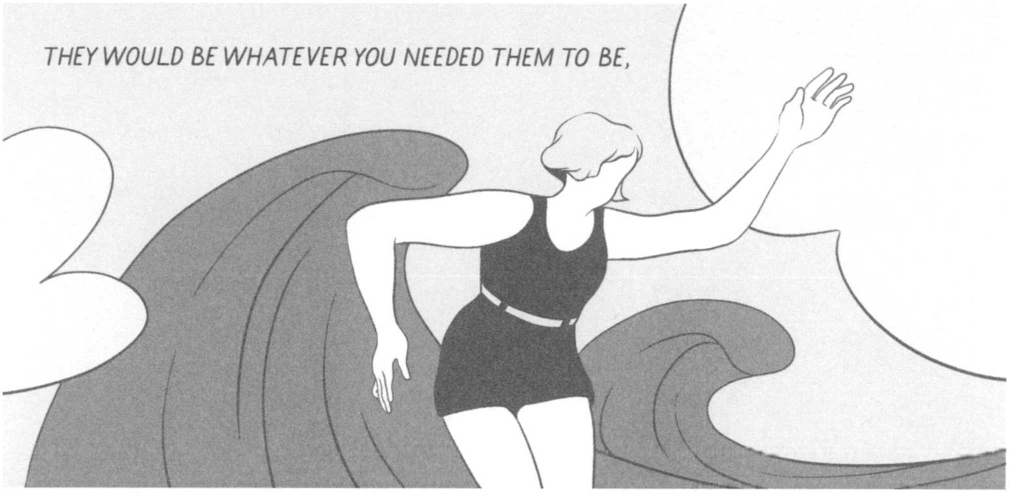
THEY WOULD BE WHATEVER YOU NEEDED THEM TO BE,
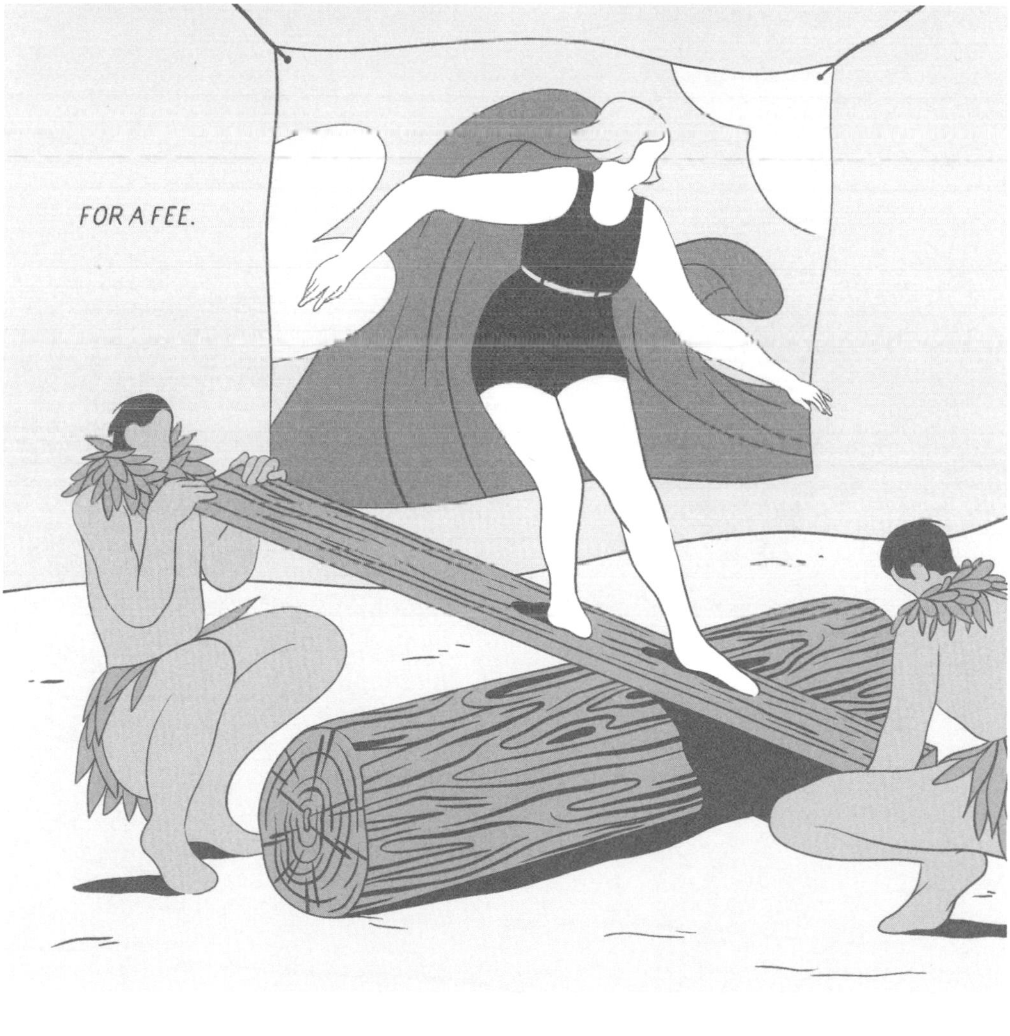
FOR A FEE.

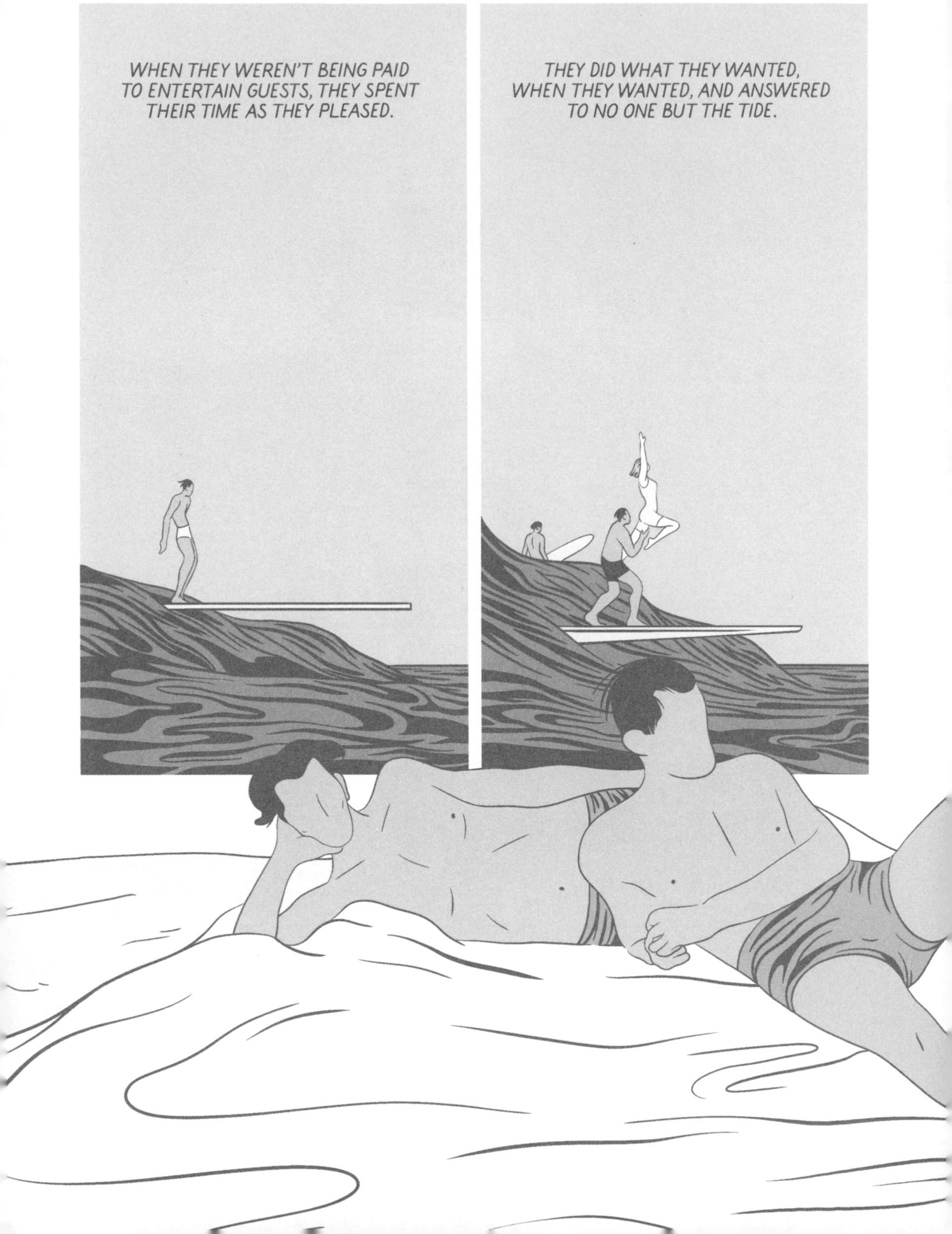
WHEN THEY WEREN'T BEING PAID TO ENTERTAIN GUESTS, THEY SPENT THEIR TIME AS THEY PLEASED.
THEY DID WHAT THEY WANTED, WHEN THEY WANTED, AND ANSWERED TO NO ONE BUT THE TIDE.

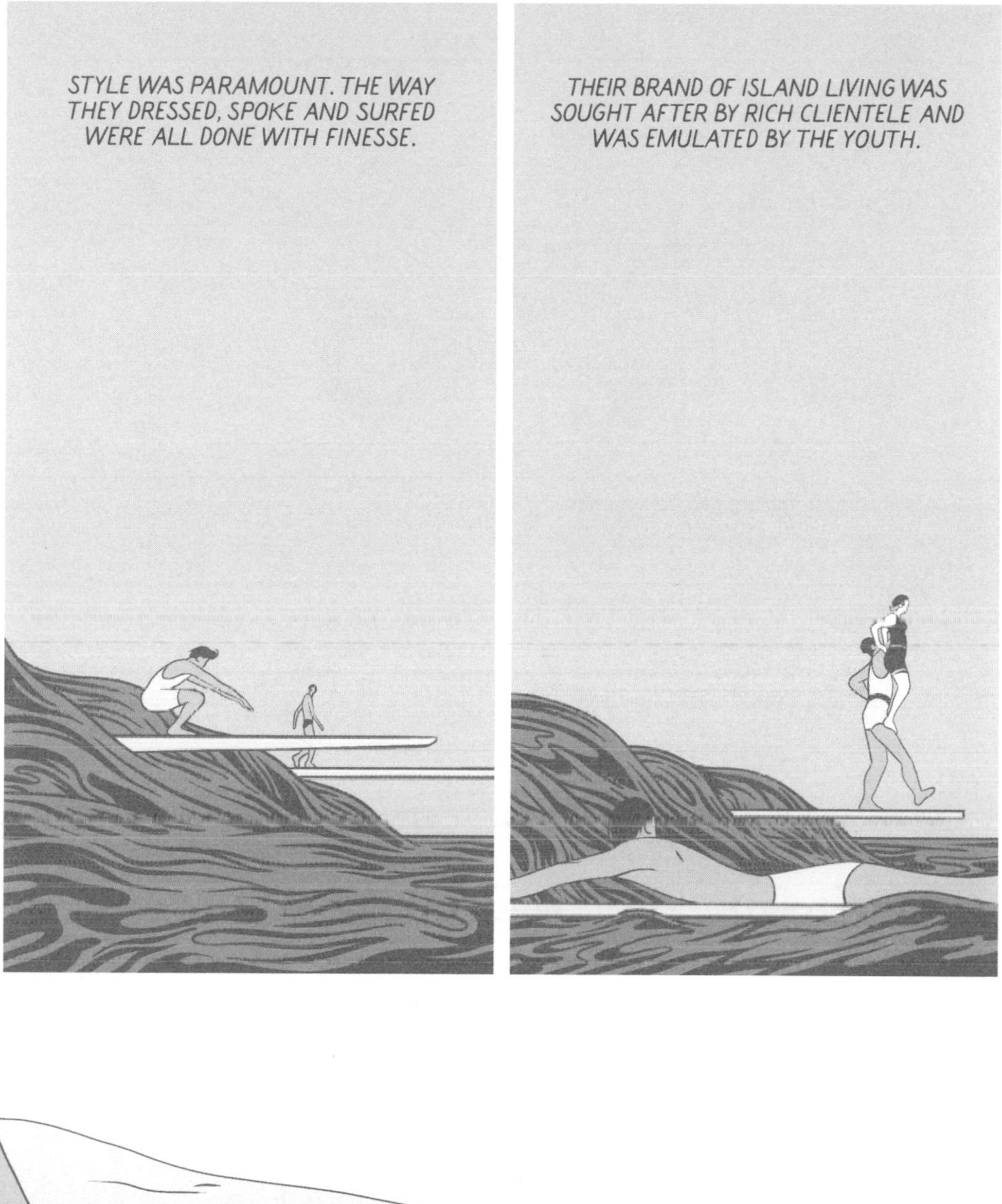
STYLE WAS PARAMOUNT. THE WAY THEY DRESSED, SPOKE AND SURFED WERE ALL DONE WITH FINESSE.
THEIR BRAND OF ISLAND LIVING WAS SOUGHT AFTER BY RICH CLIENTELE AND WAS EMULATED BY THE YOUTH.

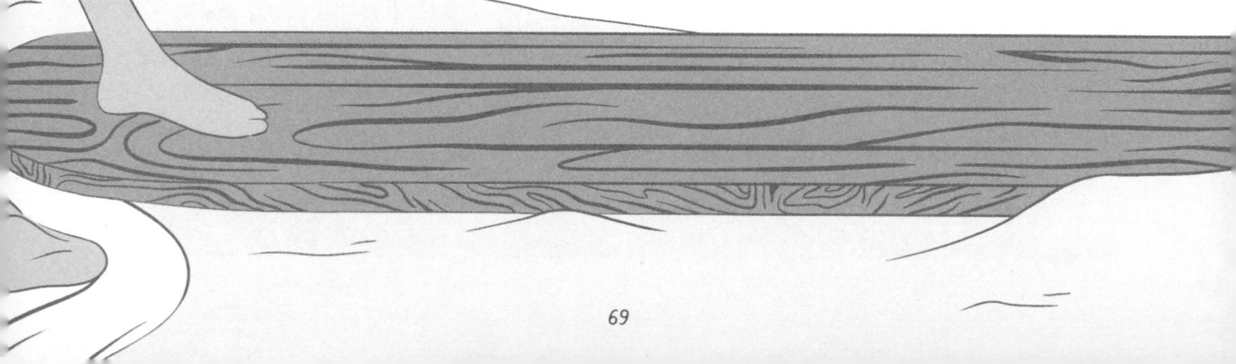

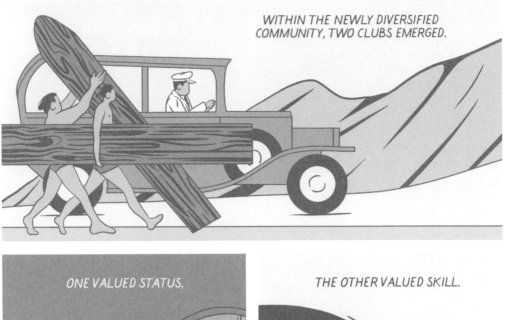

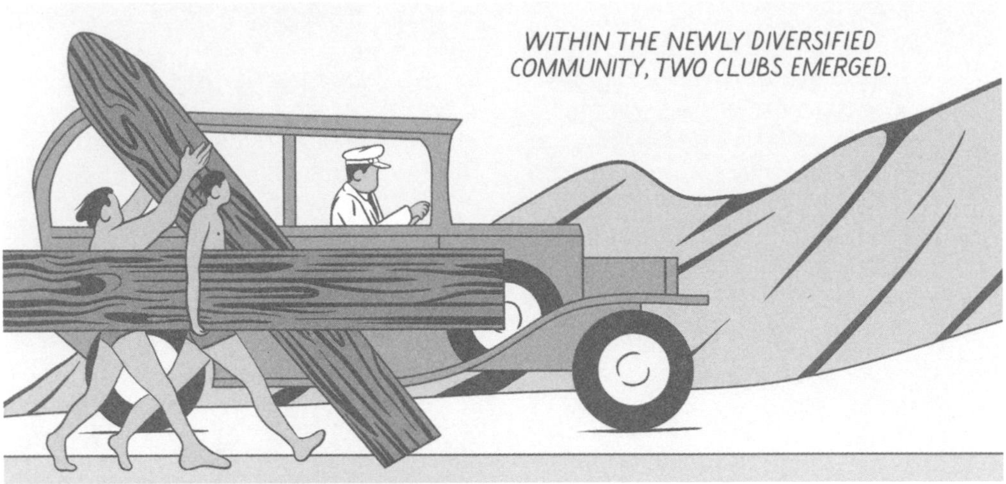
WITHIN THE NEWLY DIVERSIFIED COMMUNITY, TWO CLUBS EMERGED.

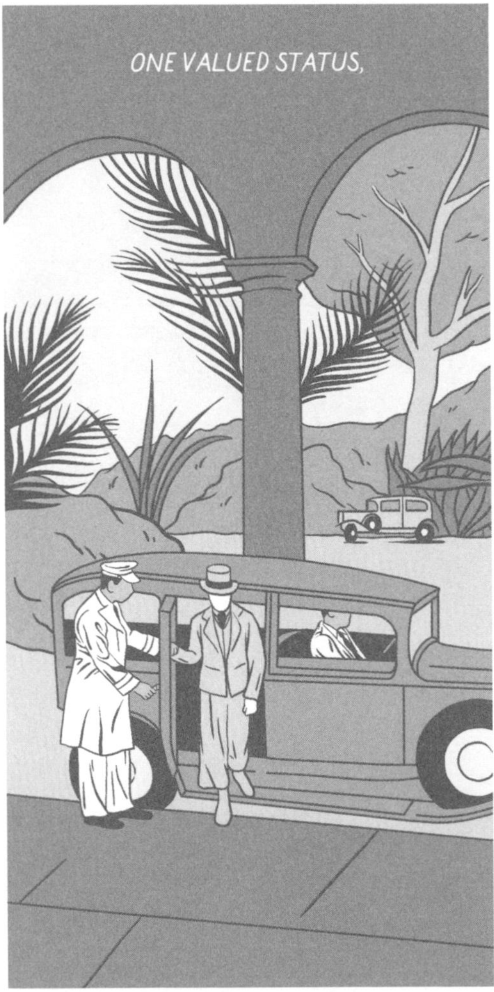
ONE VALUED STATUS,

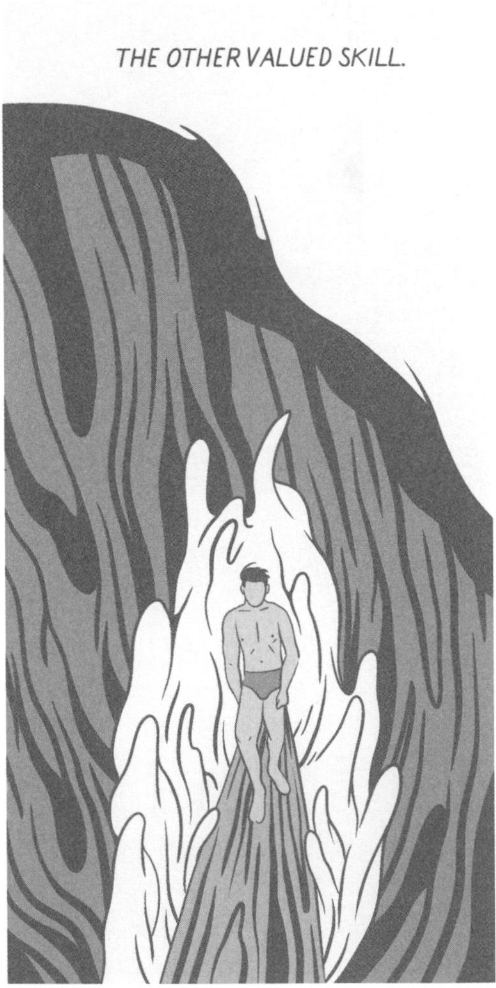
THE OTHER VALUED SKILL.

ONE PROVIDED STRUCTURE,

THE OTHER PROVIDED SHADE.

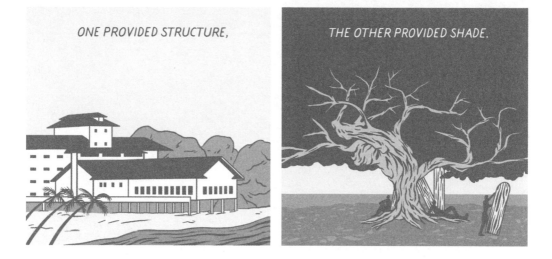

OVER TIME, THE SHADE OF THE TREES WAS
REPLACED BY THE SHADOW OF STRUCTURE.

WHAT REMAINED, HOWEVER,
WAS THE ULTIMATE BEACH BOY.

V. BRO

Summer 2017

Bolsa Chica, California

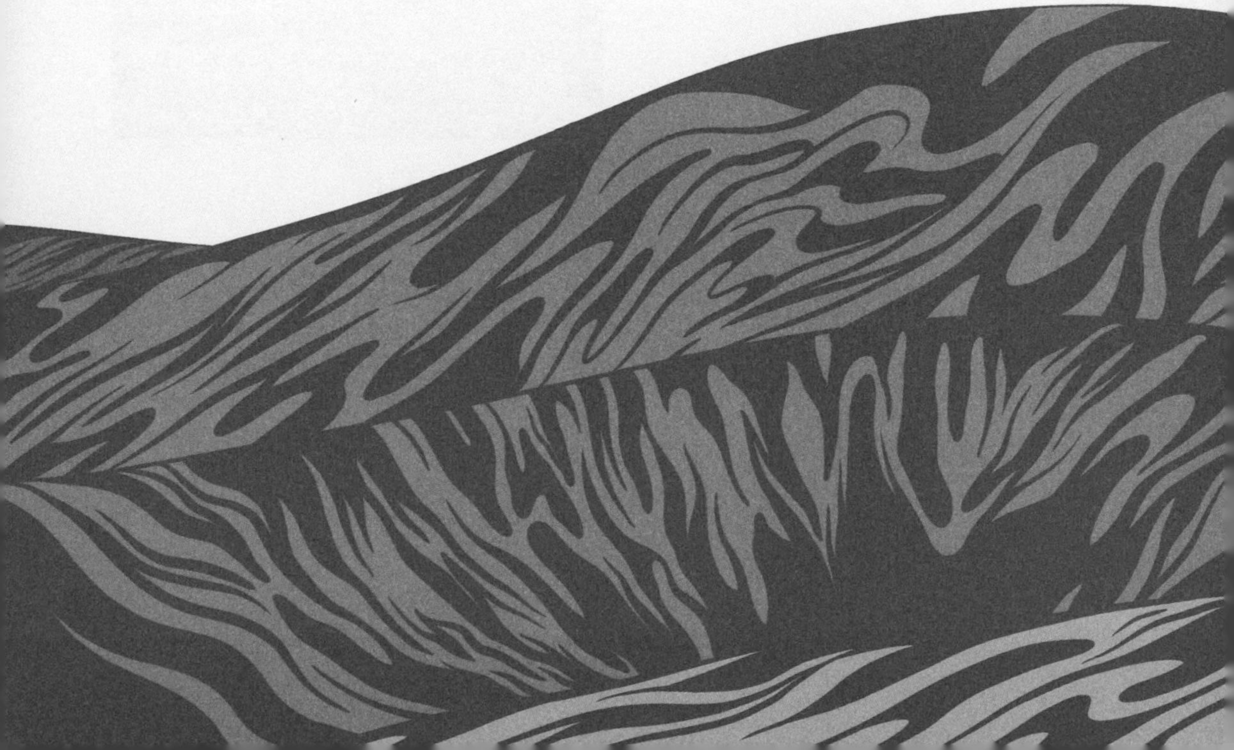

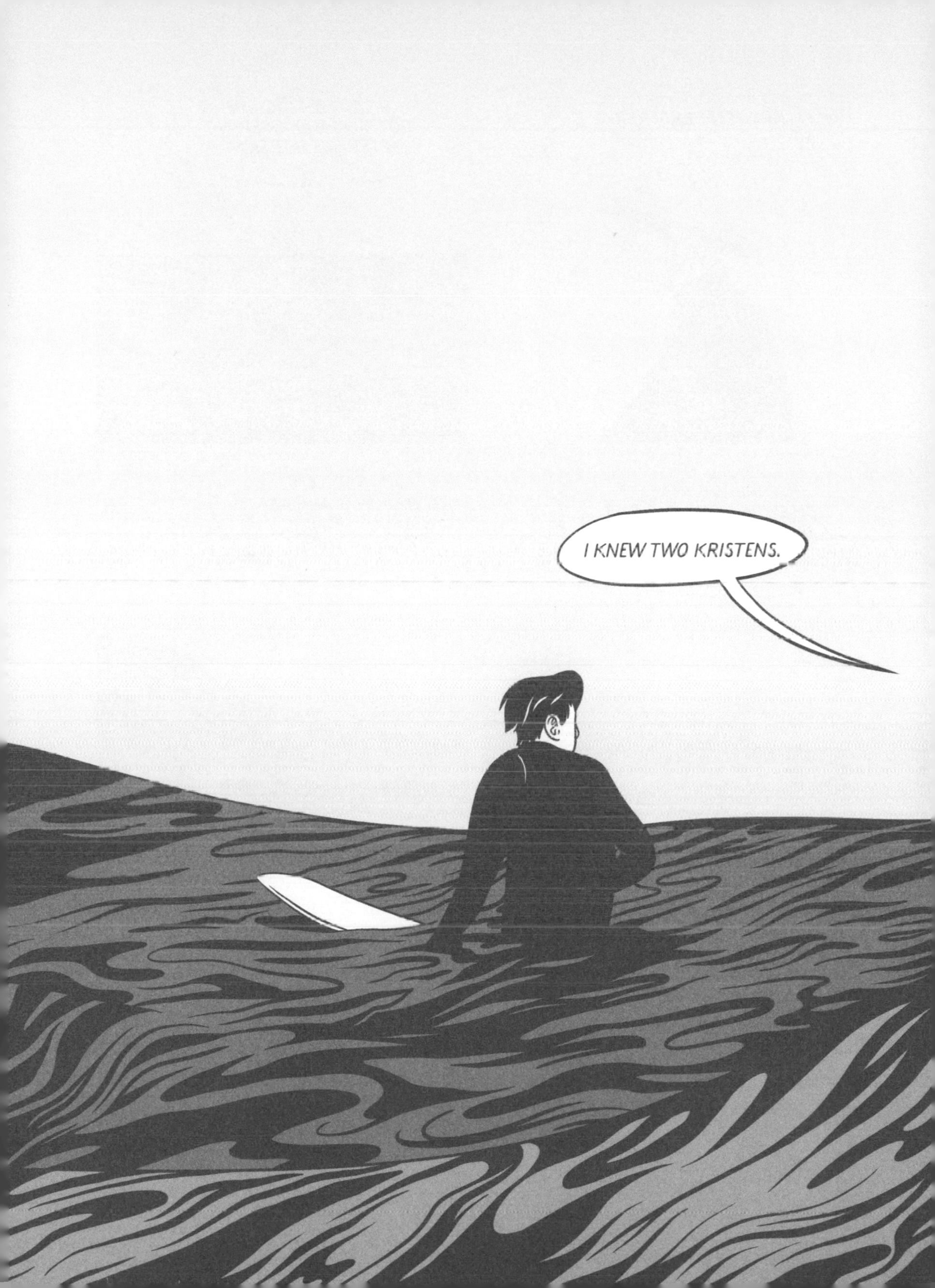
I KNEW TWO KRISTENS.

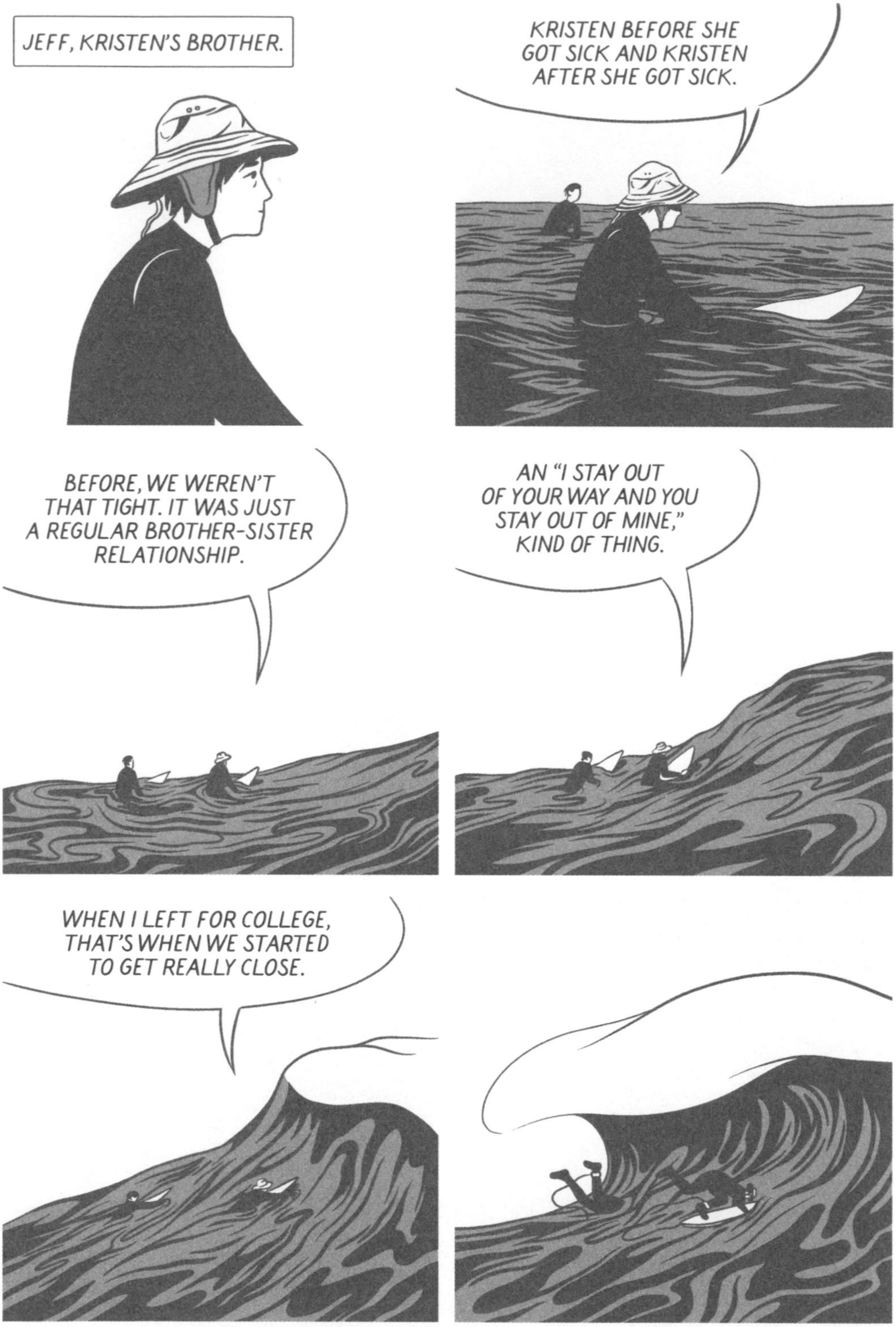
JEFF, KRISTEN'S BROTHER.
KRISTEN BEFORE SHE GOT SICK AND KRISTEN AFTER SHE GOT SICK.
BEFORE, WE WEREN'T THAT TIGHT. IT WAS JUST A REGULAR BROTHER-SISTER RELATIONSHIP.
AN "I STAY OUT OF YOUR WAY AND YOU STAY OUT OF MINE," KIND OF THING.
WHEN I LEFT FOR COLLEGE, THAT'S WHEN WE STARTED TO GET REALLY CLOSE.

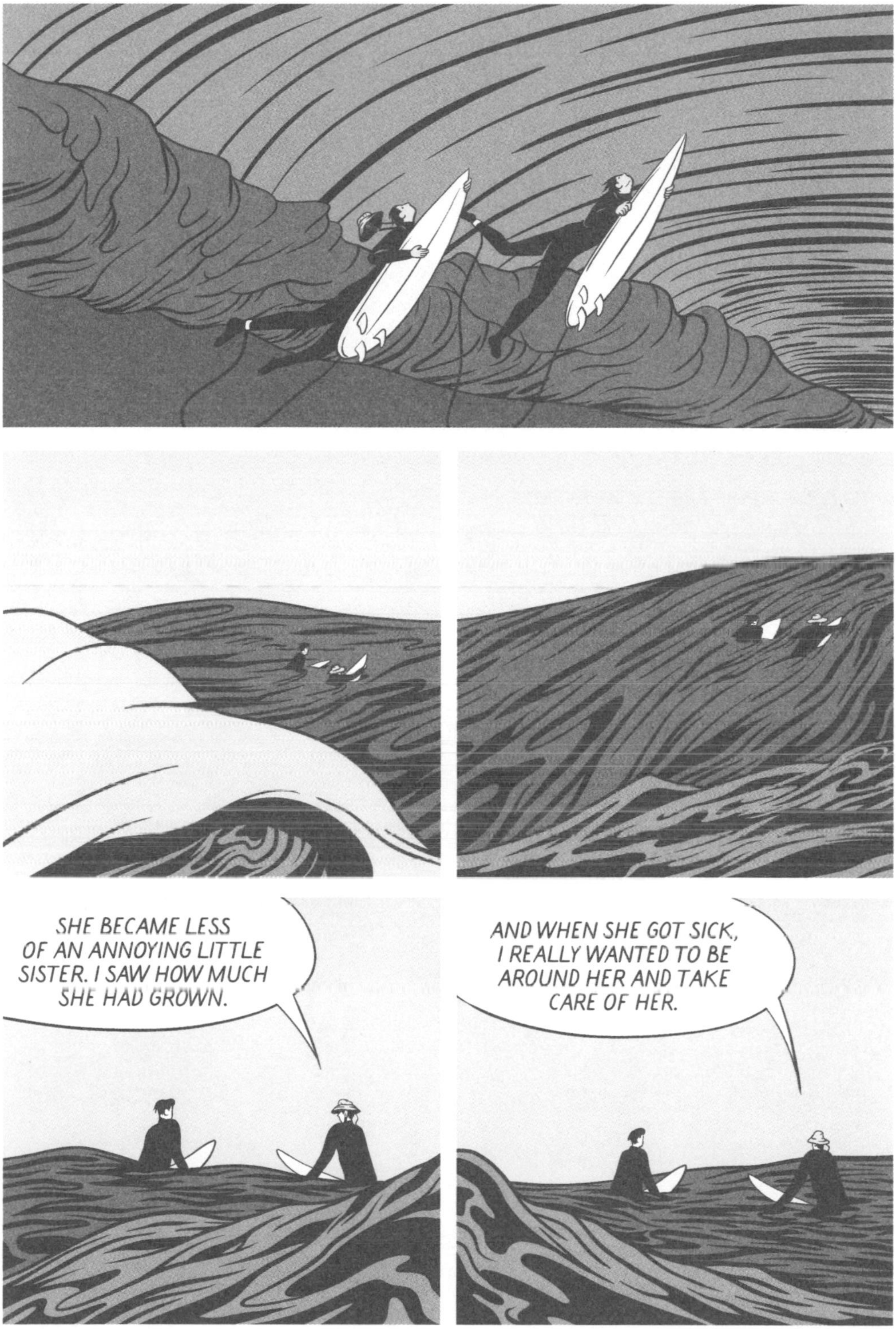
SHE BECAME LESS OF AN ANNOYING LITTLE SISTER. I SAW HOW MUCH SHE HAD GROWN.
AND WHEN SHE GOT SICK, I REALLY WANTED TO BE AROUND HER AND TAKE CARE OF HER.

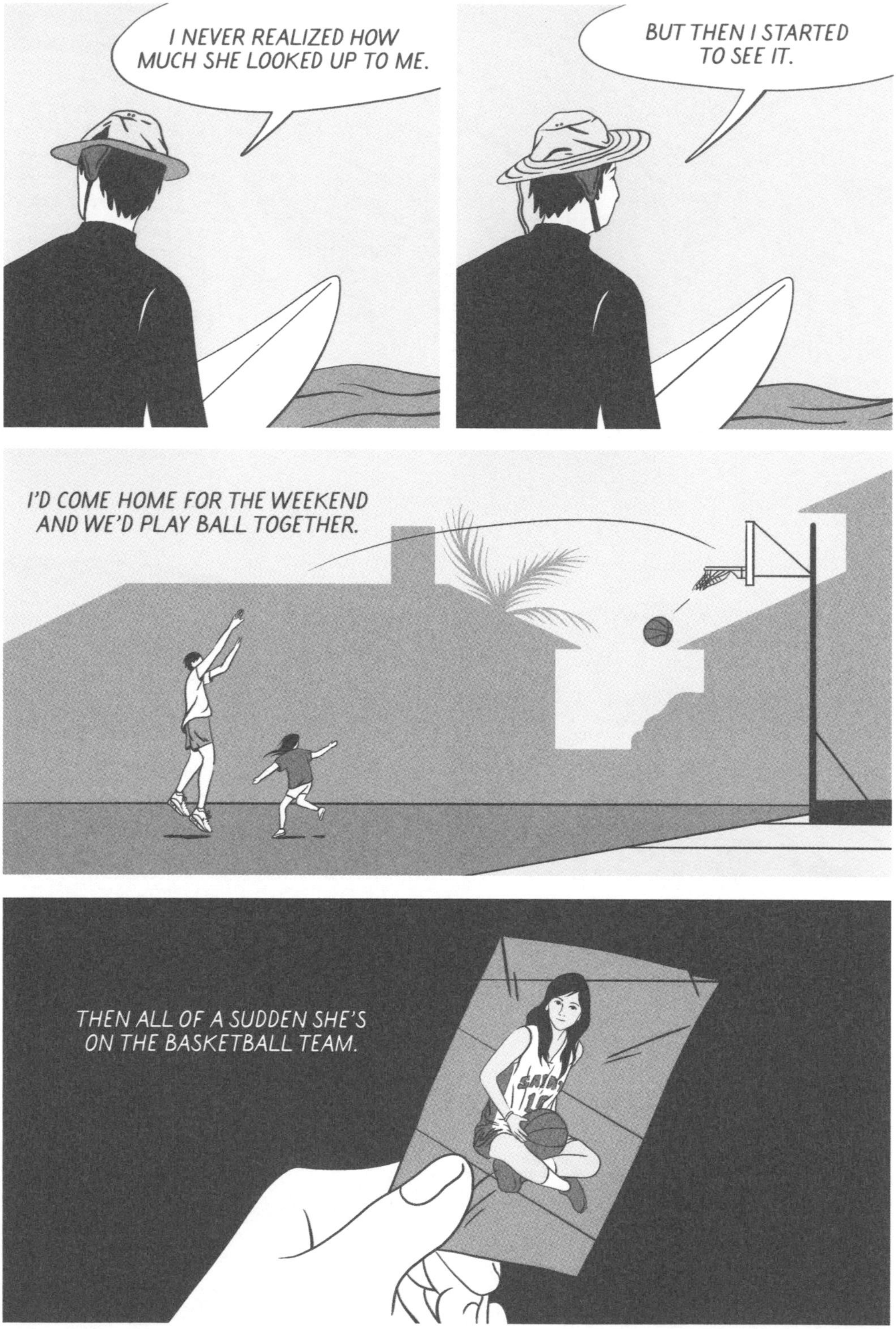
I NEVER REALIZED HOW MUCH SHE LOOKED UP TO ME.
BUT THEN I STARTED TO SEE IT.
I'D COME HOME FOR THE WEEKEND AND WE'D PLAY BALL TOGETHER.
THEN ALL OF A SUDDEN SHE'S ON THE BASKETBALL TEAM.

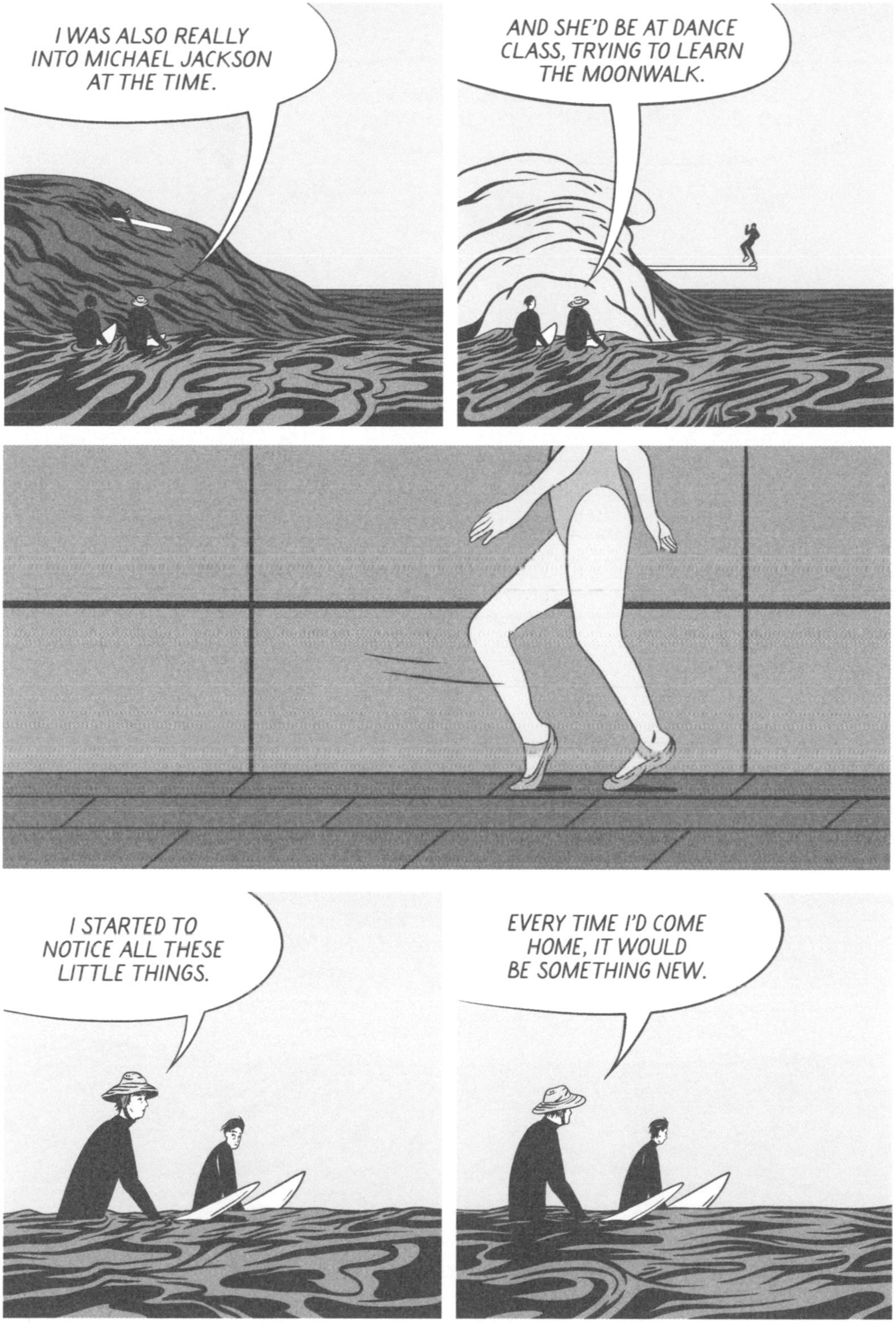
I WAS ALSO REALLY INTO MICHAEL JACKSON AT THE TIME.
AND SHE'D BE AT DANCE CLASS, TRYING TO LEARN THE MOONWALK.
I STARTED TO NOTICE ALL THESE LITTLE THINGS.
EVERY TIME I'D COME HOME, IT WOULD BE SOMETHING NEW.

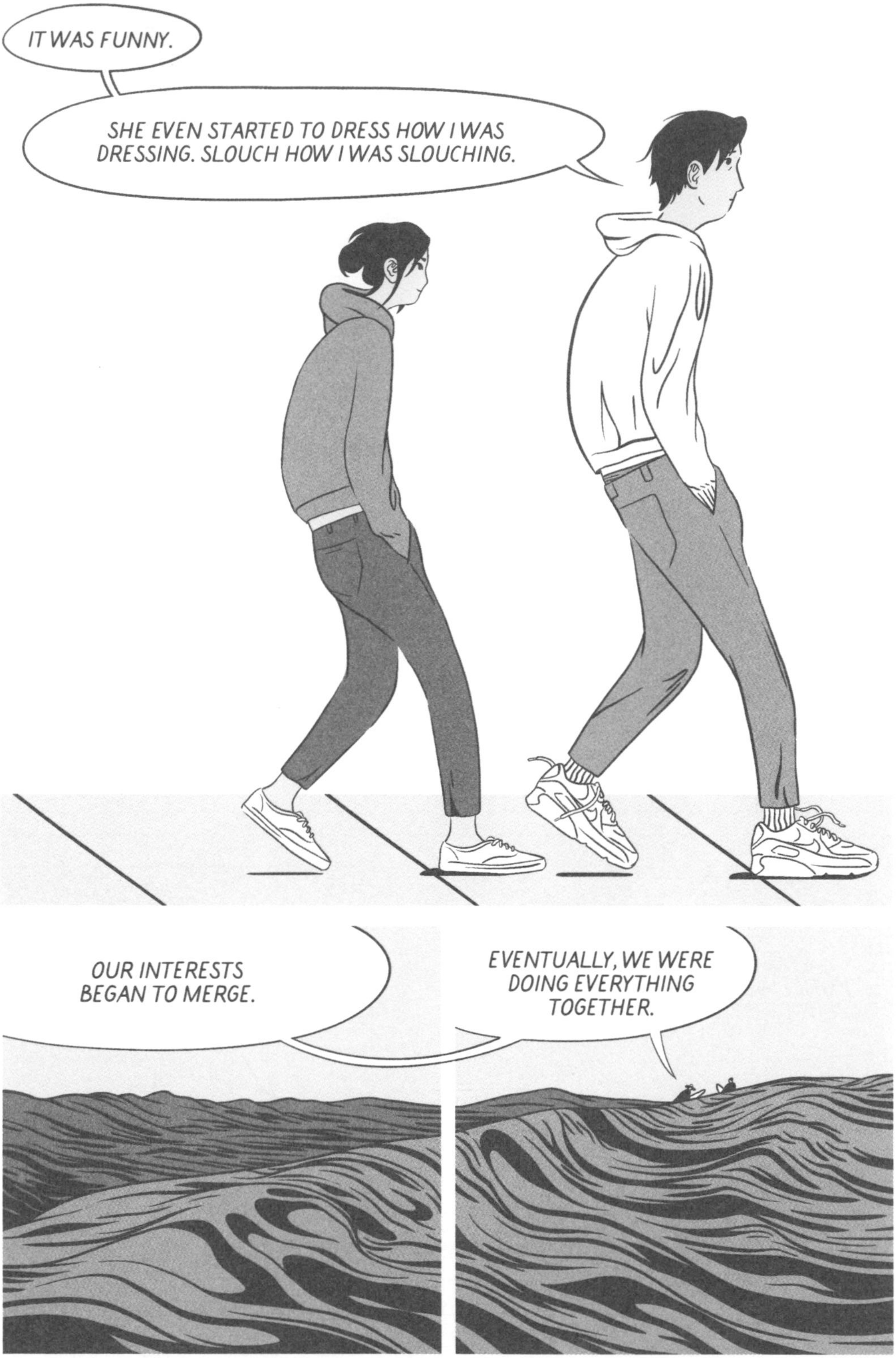
IT WAS FUNNY.
SHE EVEN STARTED TO DRESS HOW I WAS DRESSING. SLOUCH HOW I WAS SLOUCHING.
OUR INTERESTS BEGAN TO MERGE.
EVENTUALLY, WE WERE DOING EVERYTHING TOGETHER.

FOR SOME REASON SHE REALLY LIKED THE ZELDA GAME, "OCARINA OF TIME."

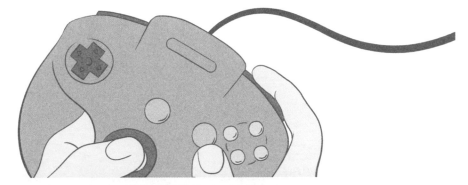

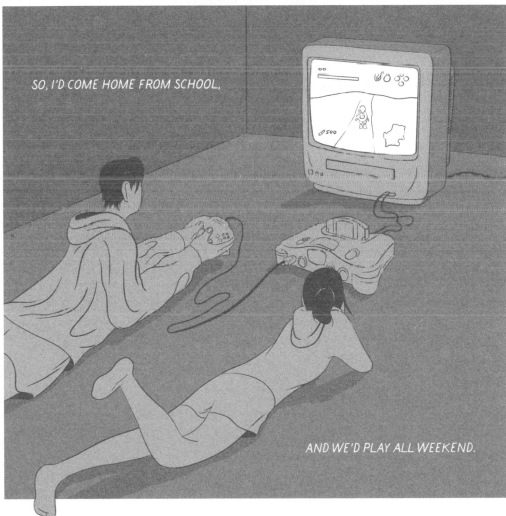

SO, I'D COME HOME FROM SCHOOL,

AND WE'D PLAY ALL WEEKEND.

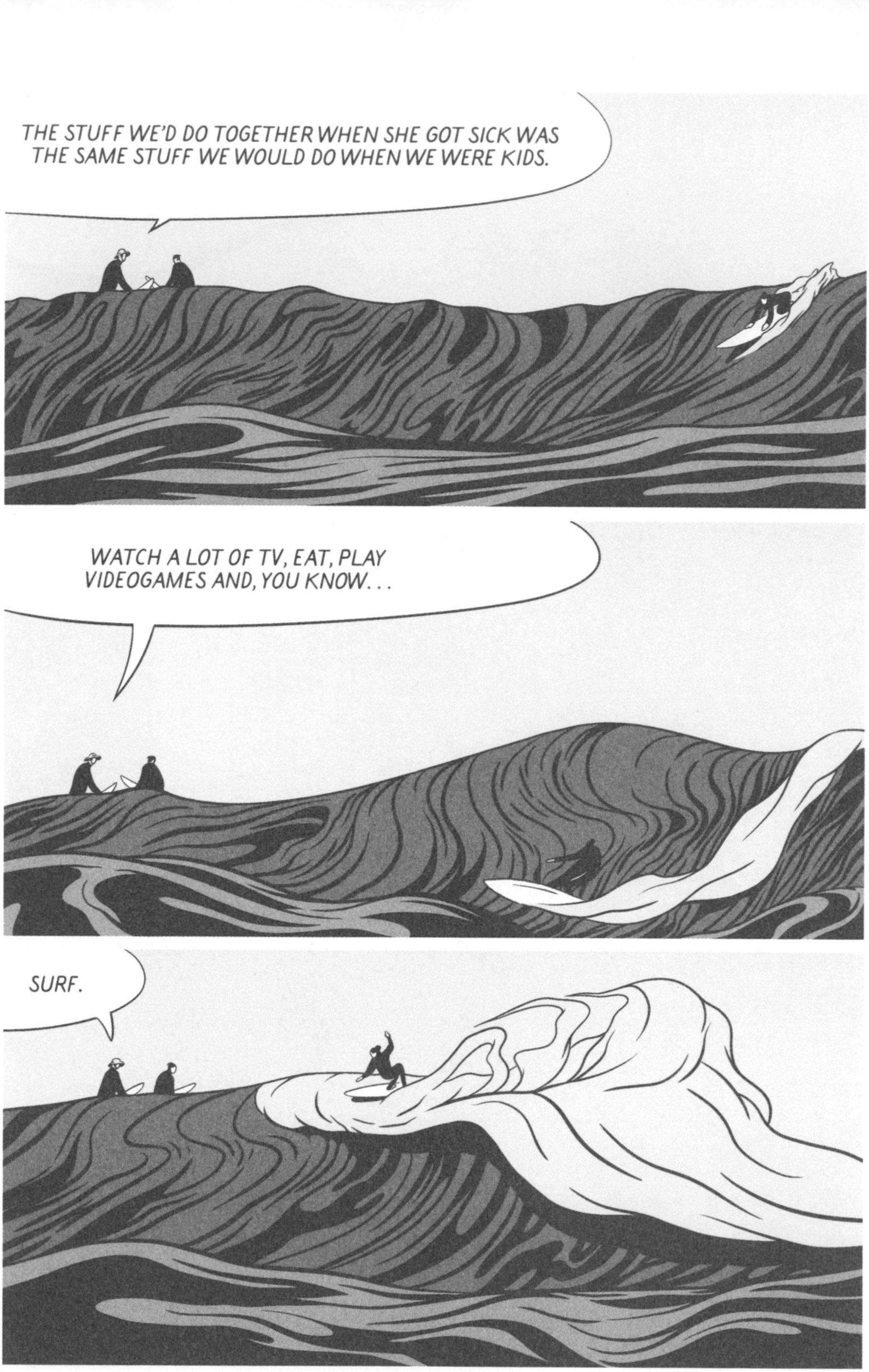
THE STUFF WE'D DO TOGETHER WHEN SHE GOT SICK WAS THE SAME STUFF WE WOULD DO WHEN WE WERE KIDS.
WATCH A LOT OF TV, EAT, PLAY VIDEOGAMES AND, YOU KNOW. . .
SURF.

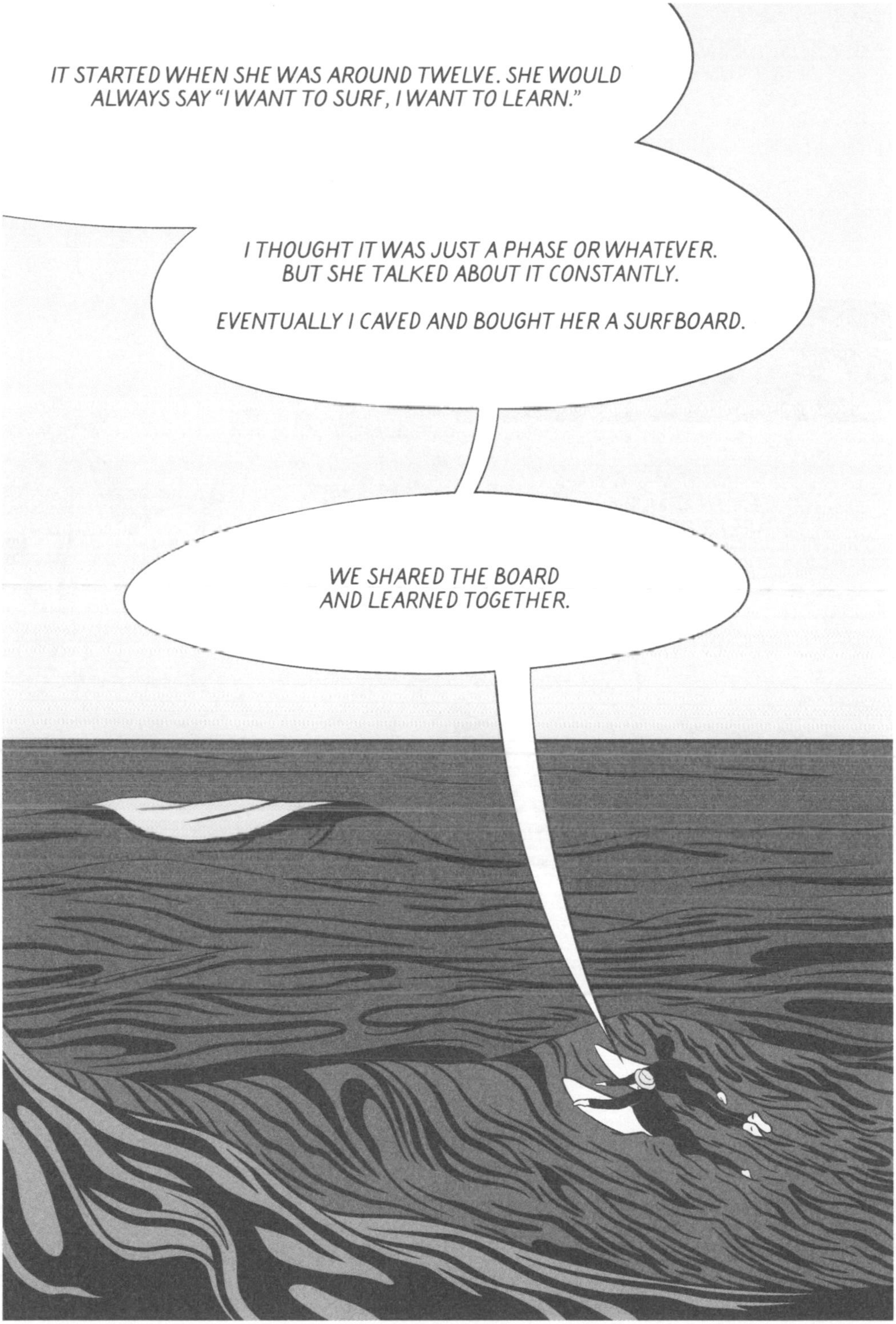
IT STARTED WHEN SHE WAS AROUND TWELVE. SHE WOULD ALWAYS SAY "I WANT TO SURF, I WANT TO LEARN."
I THOUGHT IT WAS JUST A PHASE OR WHATEVER. BUT SHE TALKED ABOUT IT CONSTANTLY.
EVENTUALLY I CAVED AND BOUGHT HER A SURFBOARD.
WE SHARED THE BOARD AND LEARNED TOGETHER.

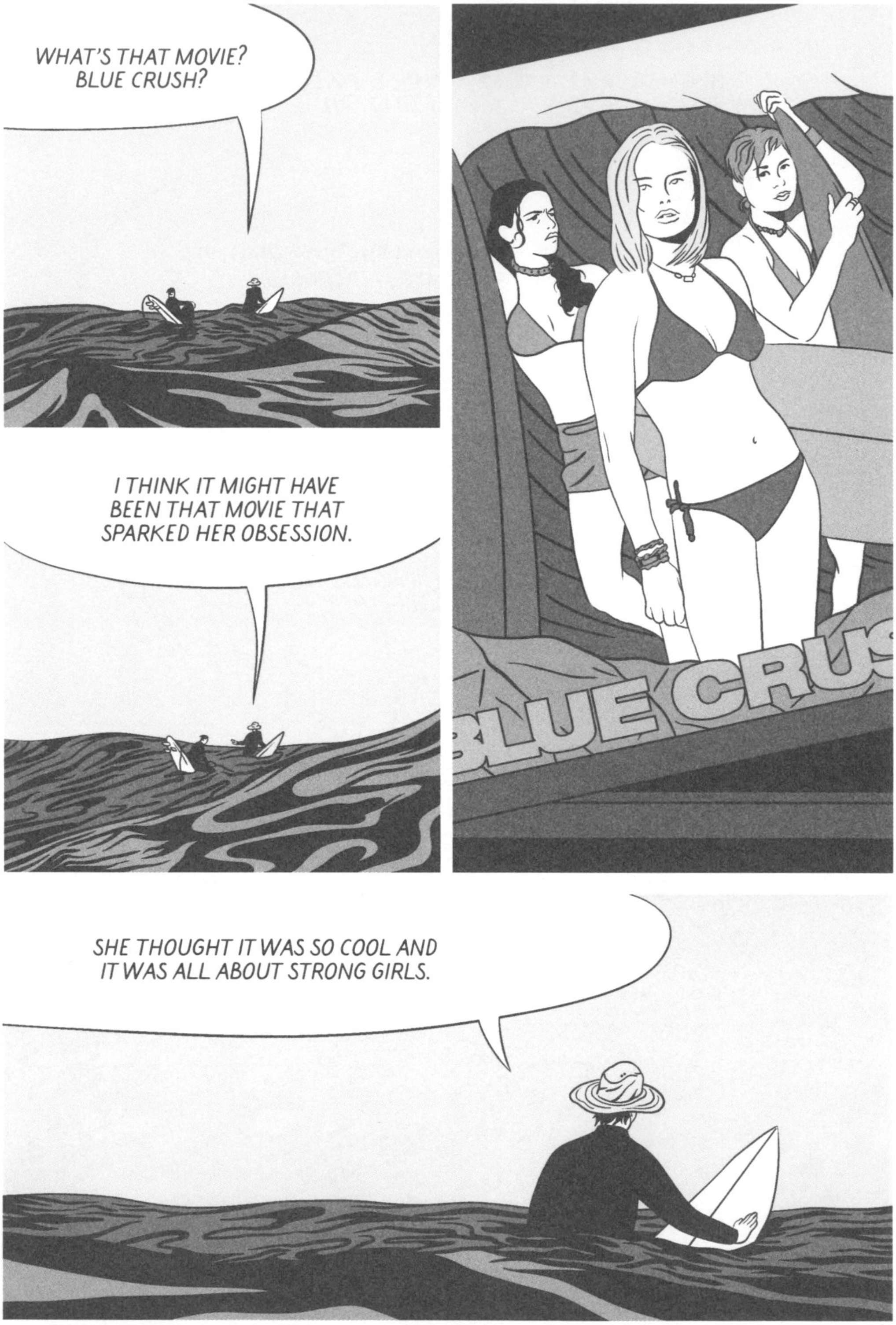
WHAT'S THAT MOVIE? BLUE CRUSH?
I THINK IT MIGHT HAVE BEEN THAT MOVIE THAT SPARKED HER OBSESSION.
BLUE CRUS
SHE THOUGHT IT WAS SO COOL AND IT WAS ALL ABOUT STRONG GIRLS.

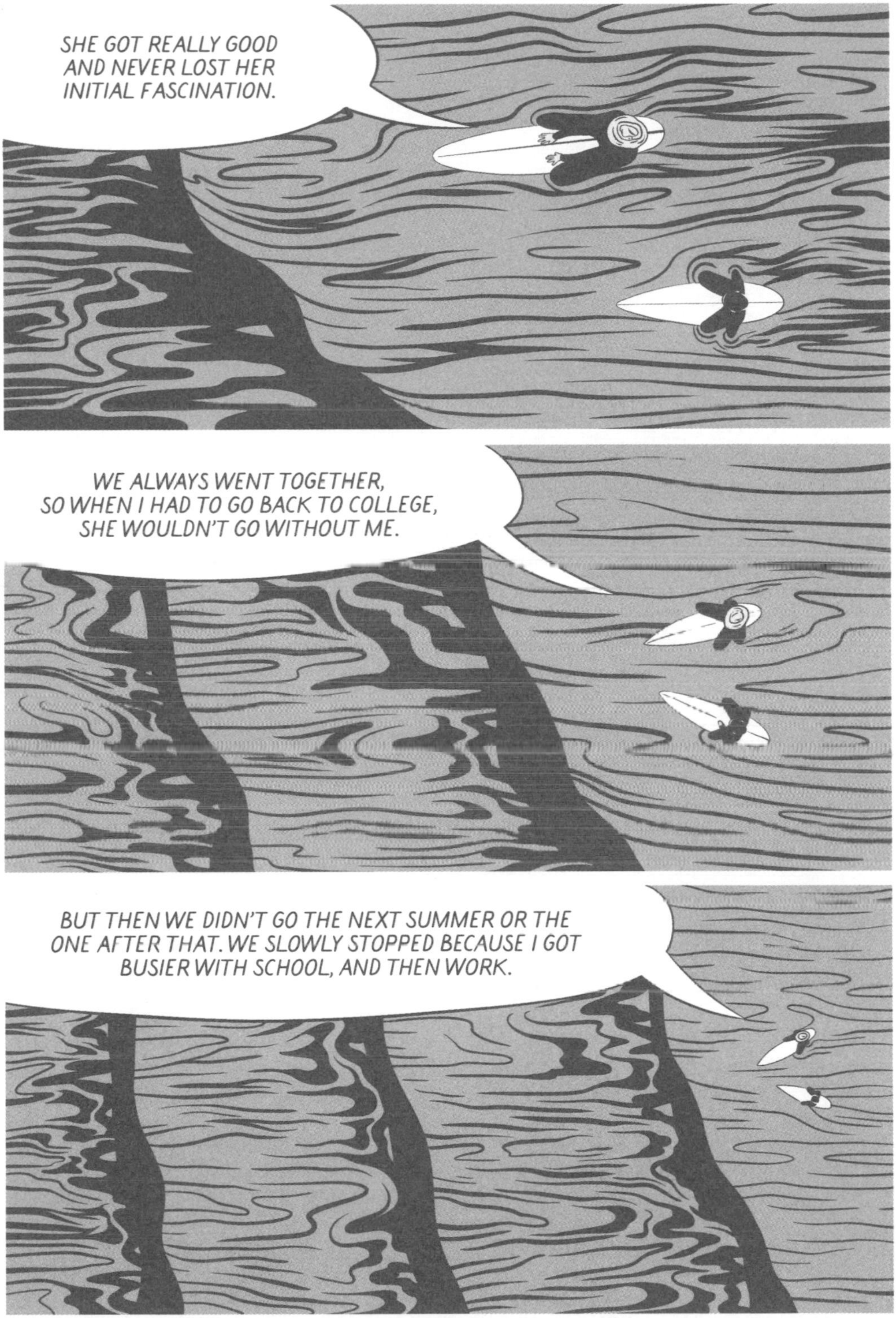
SHE GOT REALLY GOOD AND NEVER LOST HER INITIAL FASCINATION.
WE ALWAYS WENT TOGETHER, SO WHEN I HAD TO GO BACK TO COLLEGE, SHE WOULDN'T GO WITHOUT ME.
BUT THEN WE DIDN'T GO THE NEXT SUMMER OR THE ONE AFTER THAT. WE SLOWLY STOPPED BECAUSE I GOT BUSIER WITH SCHOOL, AND THEN WORK.

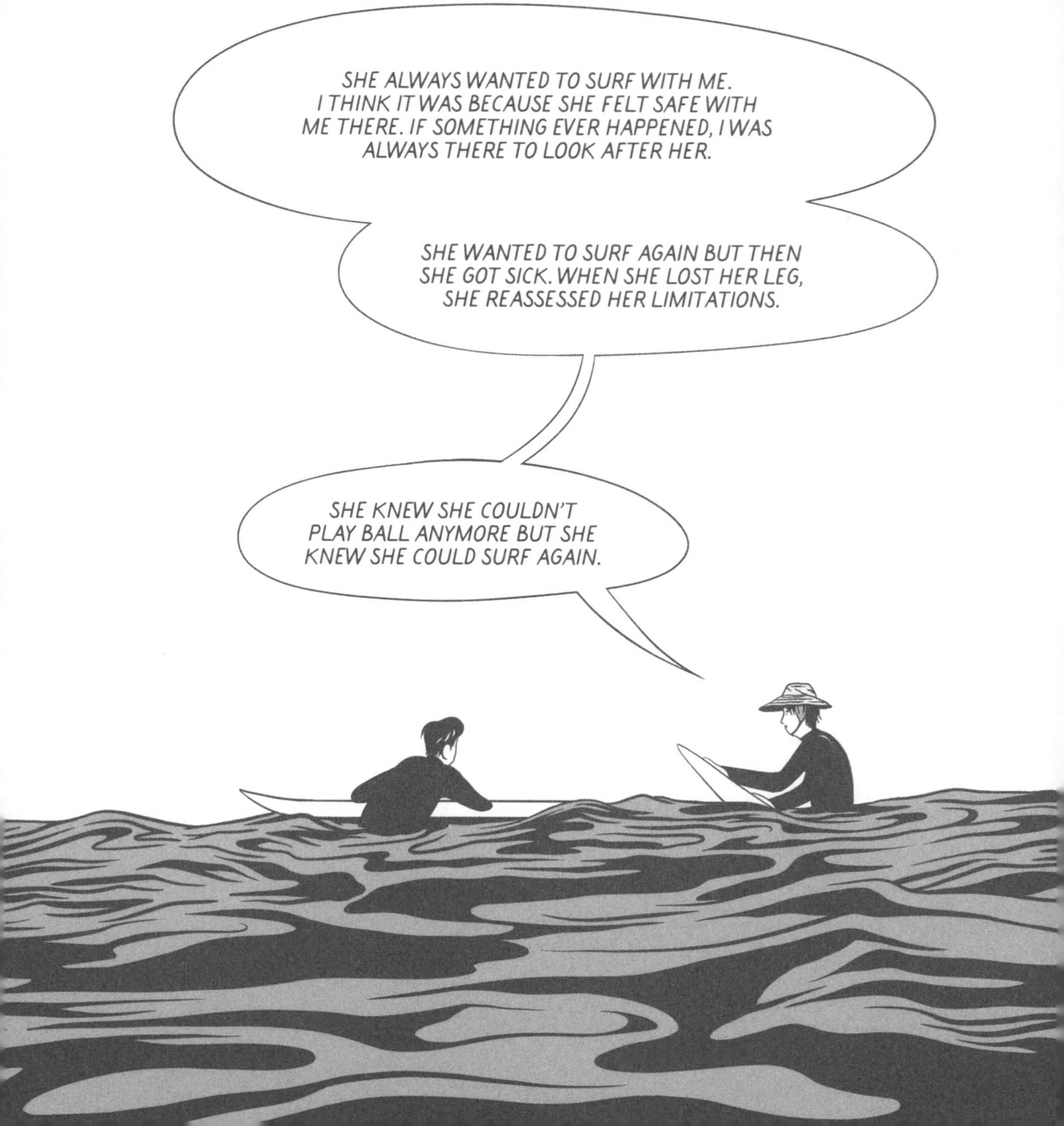
SHE ALWAYS WANTED TO SURF WITH ME. I THINK IT WAS BECAUSE SHE FELT SAFE WITH ME THERE. IF SOMETHING EVER HAPPENED, I WAS ALWAYS THERE TO LOOK AFTER HER.
SHE WANTED TO SURF AGAIN BUT THEN SHE GOT SICK. WHEN SHE LOST HER LEG, SHE REASSESSED HER LIMITATIONS.
SHE KNEW SHE COULDN'T PLAY BALL ANYMORE BUT SHE KNEW SHE COULD SURF AGAIN.

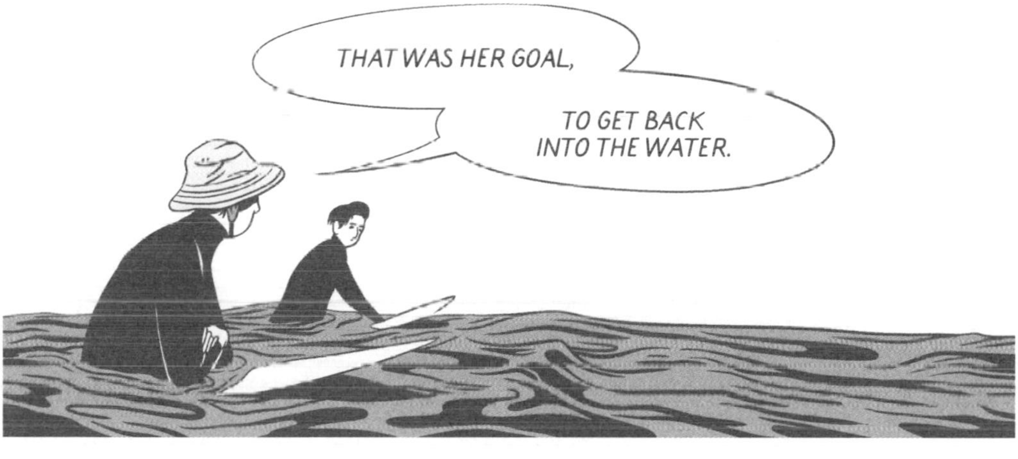
THAT WAS HER GOAL,
TO GET BACK INTO THE WATER.

VI. THE AMBASSADOR

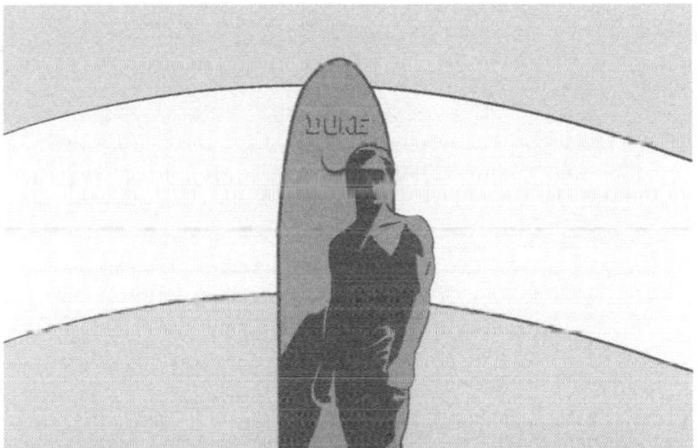
DUKE

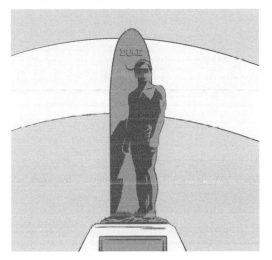

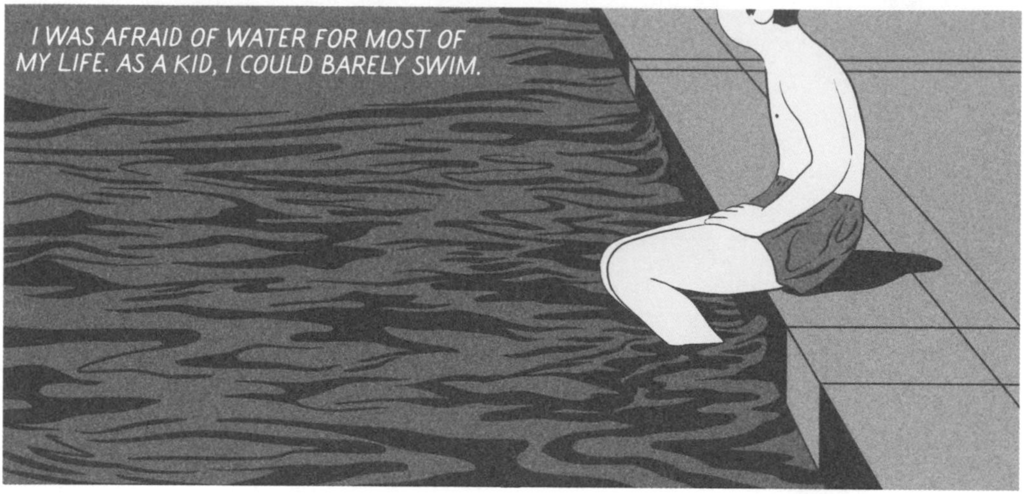
I WAS AFRAID OF WATER FOR MOST OF MY LIFE. AS A KID, I COULD BARELY SWIM.

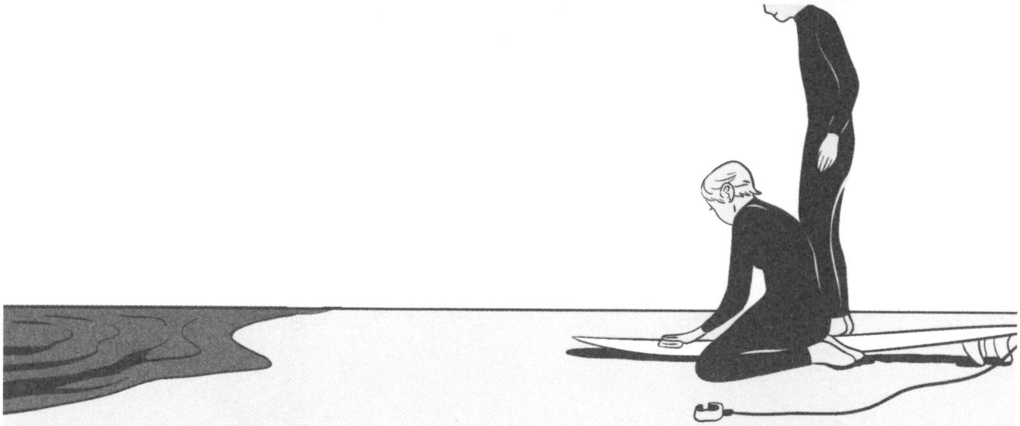

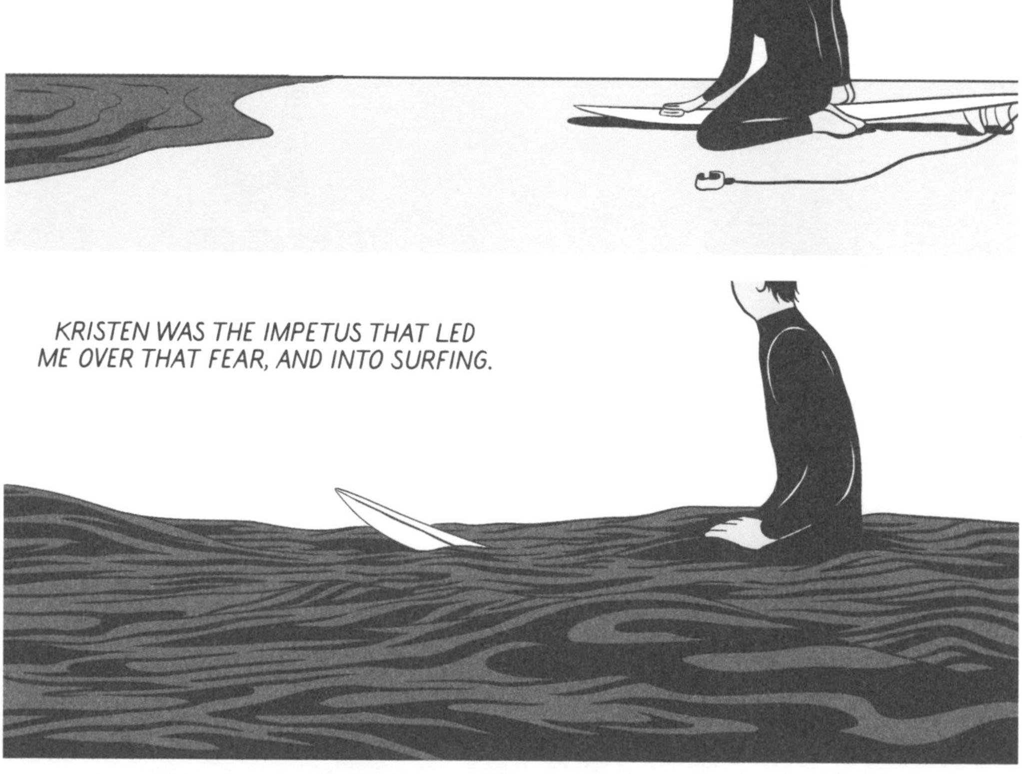
KRISTEN WAS THE IMPETUS THAT LED ME OVER THAT FEAR, AND INTO SURFING.

BUT I GOT INTO IT LATER THAN MOST.

MOST SURFERS KNOW THAT DUKE IS THE GREATEST WATERMAN OF ALL TIME.

MY ONLY CONNECTION TO DUKE WAS AN AGING BRONZE STATUE IN FRONT OF A LOCAL SURF SHOP,

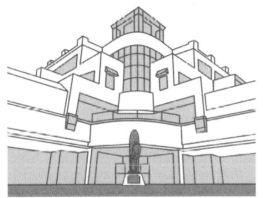

AND A HAWAIIAN SEAFOOD RESTAURANT AT THE START OF THE HUNTINGTON BEACH PIER.

I NEVER KNEW THAT THIS TOURISTY BRUNCH SPOT WAS NAMED AFTER HAWAII'S CROWN JEWEL.

DUKE KAHANAMOKU WAS
CALLED BY MANY NAMES
THROUGHOUT HIS LIFE.

NEWSPAPER HEADLINES
FREQUENTLY GAVE
HIM NICKNAMES.

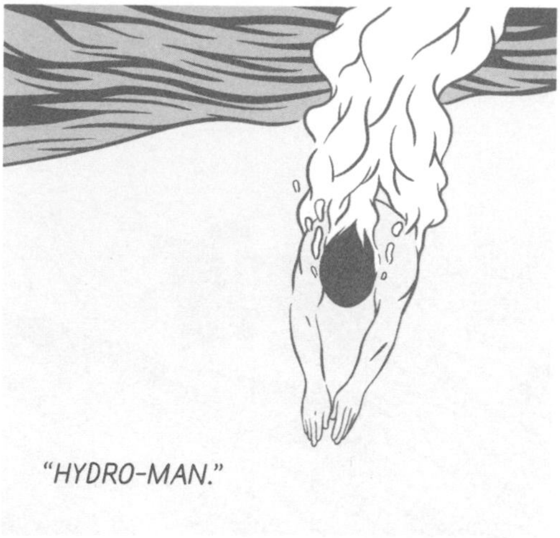
"HYDRO-MAN."

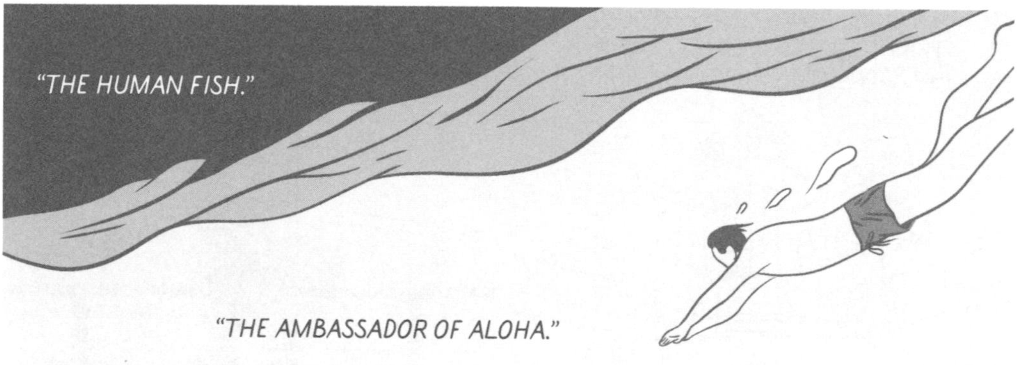
"THE HUMAN FISH."
"THE AMBASSADOR OF ALOHA."

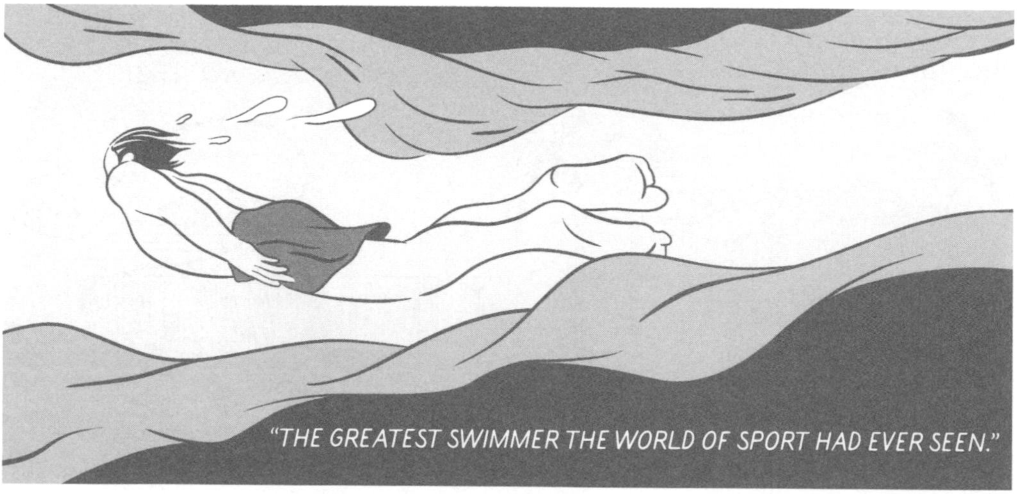
"THE GREATEST SWIMMER THE WORLD OF SPORT HAD EVER SEEN."

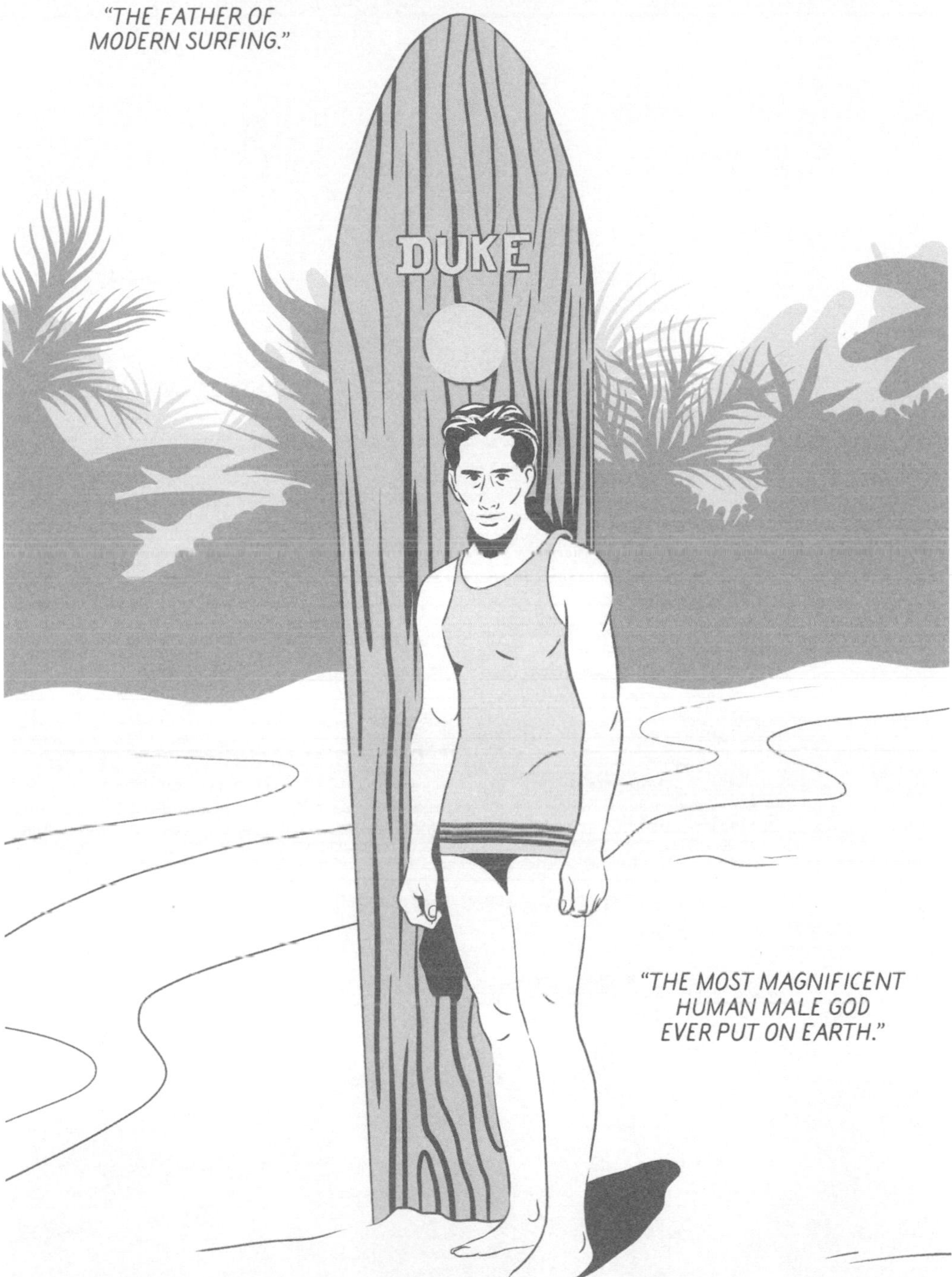
"THE FATHER OF MODERN SURFING."
DUKE
"THE MOST MAGNIFICENT HUMAN MALE GOD EVER PUT ON EARTH."

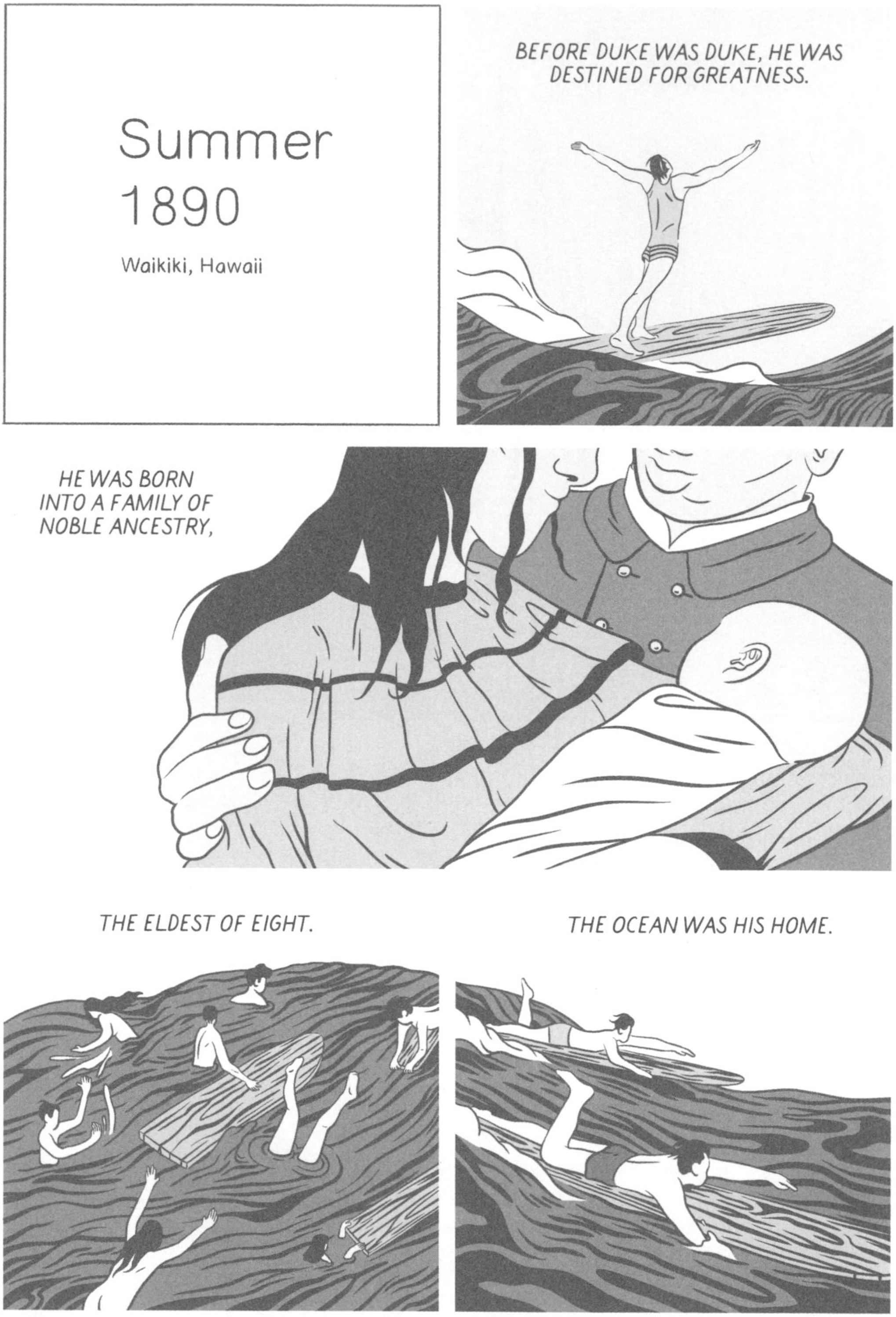
Summer
1890
Waikiki, Hawaii
BEFORE DUKE WAS DUKE, HE WAS DESTINED FOR GREATNESS.
HE WAS BORN INTO A FAMILY OF NOBLE ANCESTRY,
THE ELDEST OF EIGHT.
THE OCEAN WAS HIS HOME.

HE SPENT HIS DAYS AT WAIKIKI BEACH HONING HIS CRAFT.

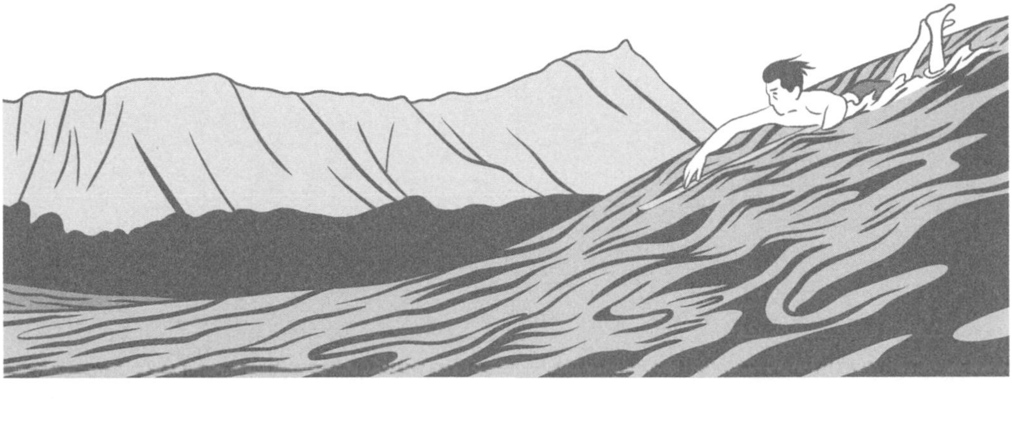

IT DIDN'T TAKE LONG FOR HIM TO DANCE ON THE WAVES.

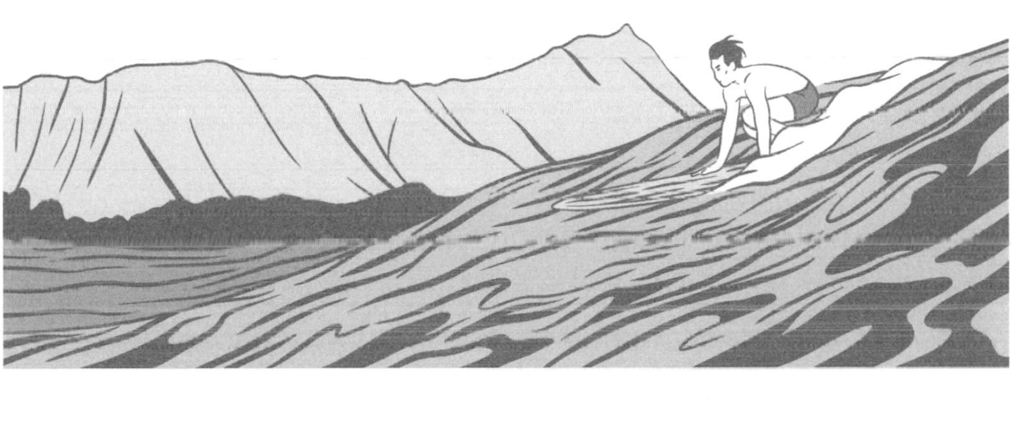

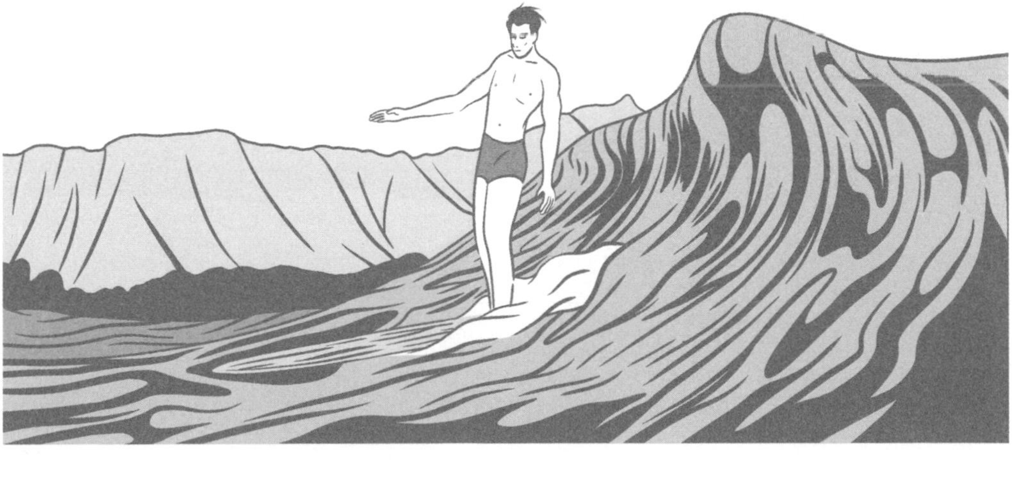

Summer 1900

Waikiki, Hawaii

DUKE'S LIFE REVOLVED AROUND THE WATER.

FOR MONEY, HE WOULD DIVE FOR PASSENGERS AS STEAMSHIPS ROLLED INTO THE HARBOR.

HE WOULD COLLECT THE COINS THROWN INTO THE OCEAN AND STORE THEM IN HIS MOUTH.

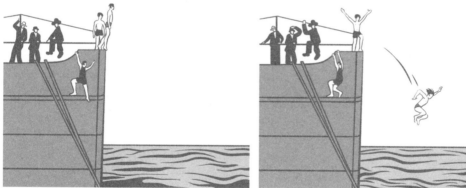

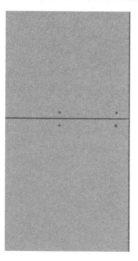

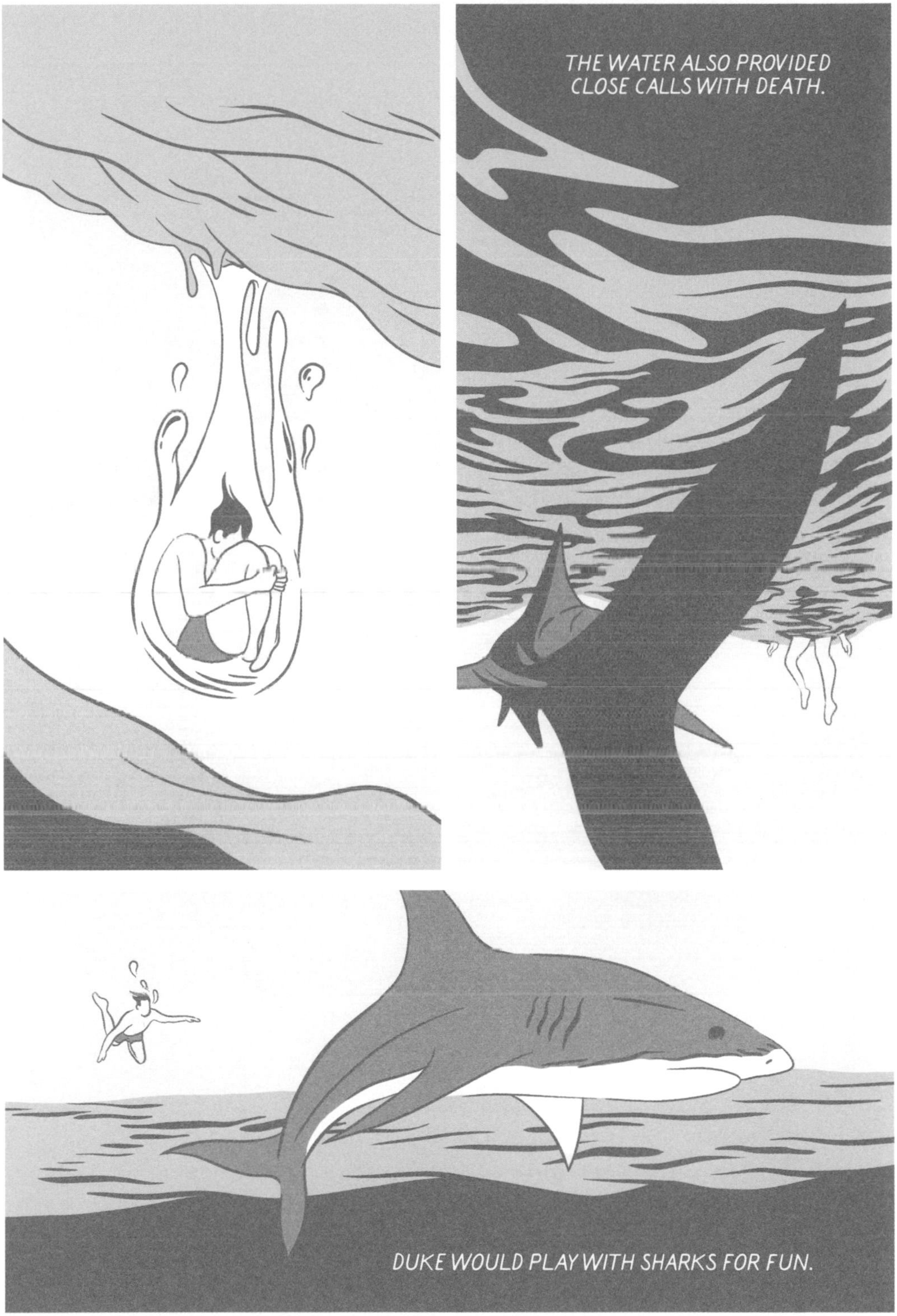
THE WATER ALSO PROVIDED CLOSE CALLS WITH DEATH.
DUKE WOULD PLAY WITH SHARKS FOR FUN.

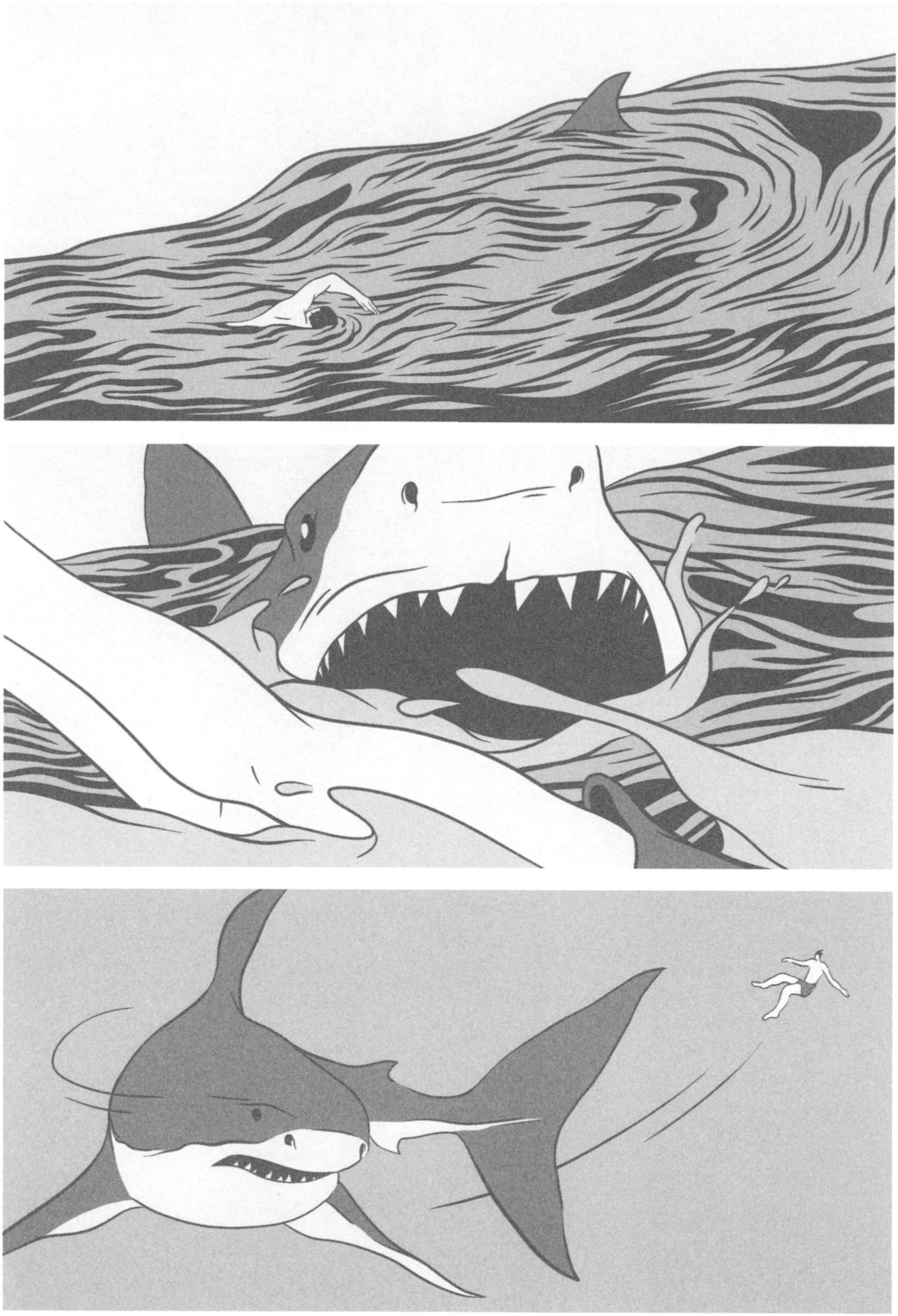

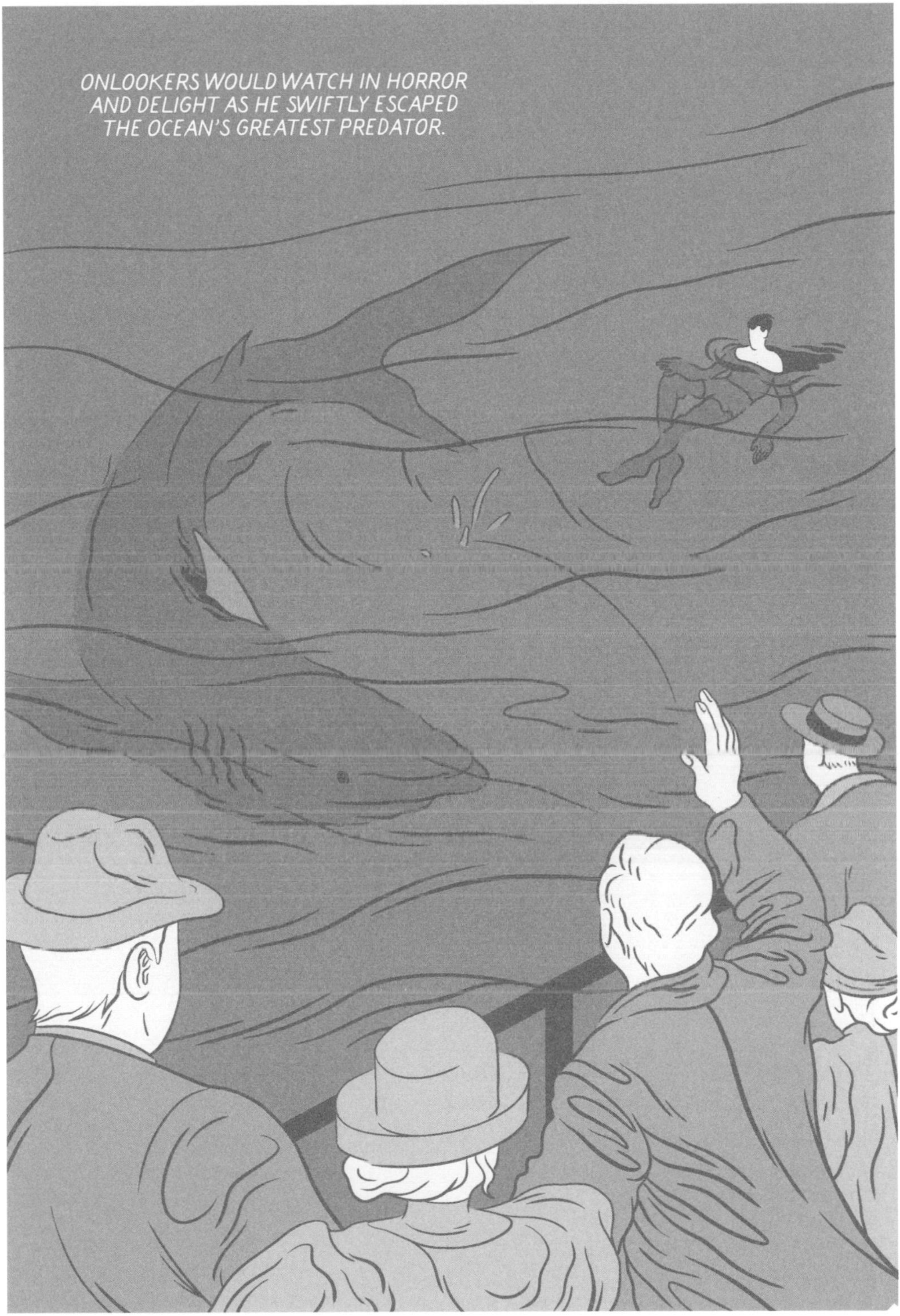
ONLOOKERS WOULD WATCH IN HORROR AND DELIGHT AS HE SWIFTLY ESCAPED THE OCEAN'S GREATEST PREDATOR.

Summer
1911

Waikiki, Hawaii

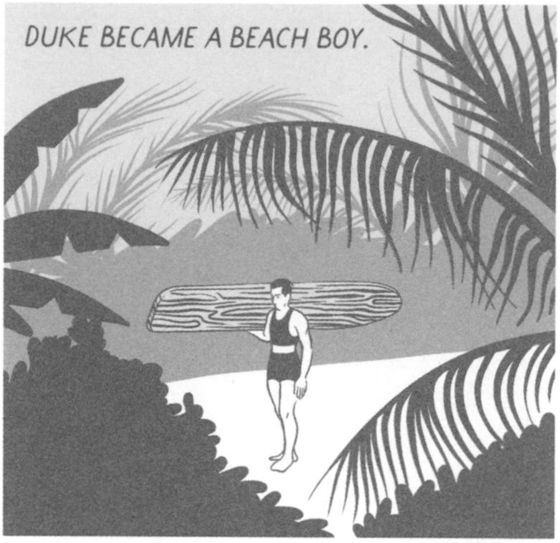
DUKE BECAME A BEACH BOY.

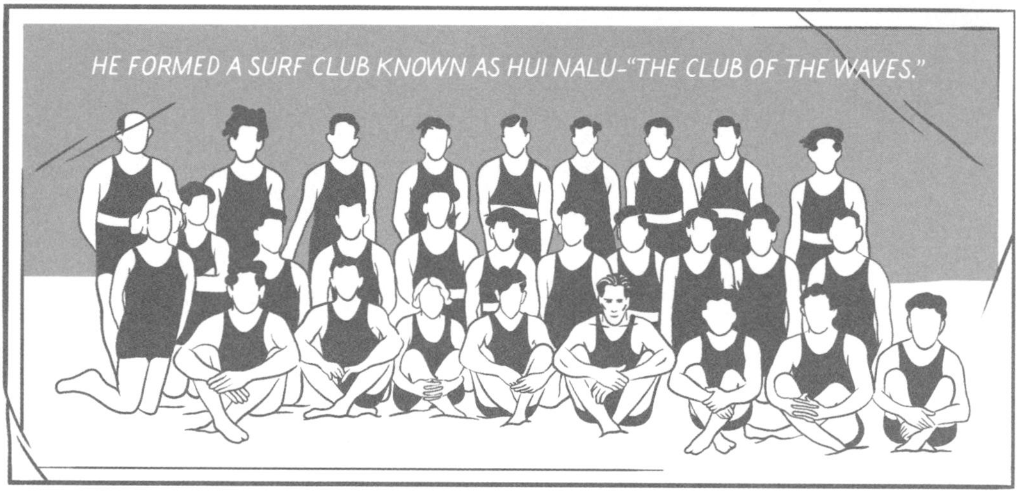
HE FORMED A SURF CLUB KNOWN AS HUI NALU-"THE CLUB OF THE WAVES."

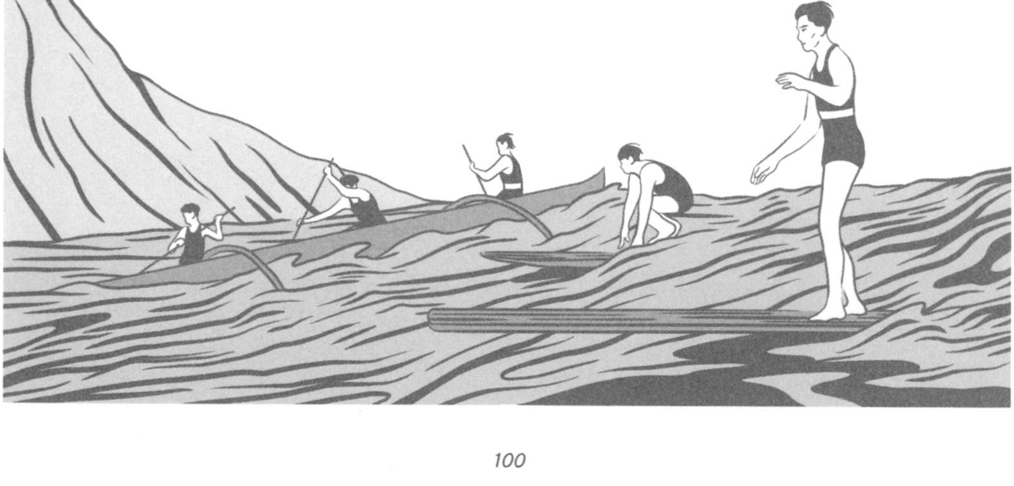

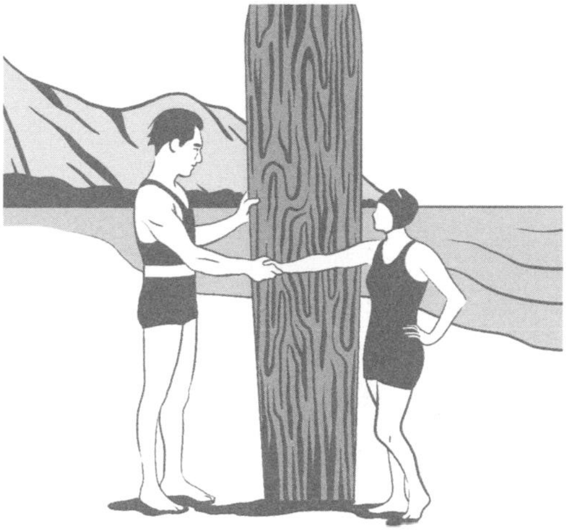

HE WOULD SHOW TOURISTS
THE ISLAND AND INTRODUCE THEM
TO HIS WORLD WITHIN THE WATER.

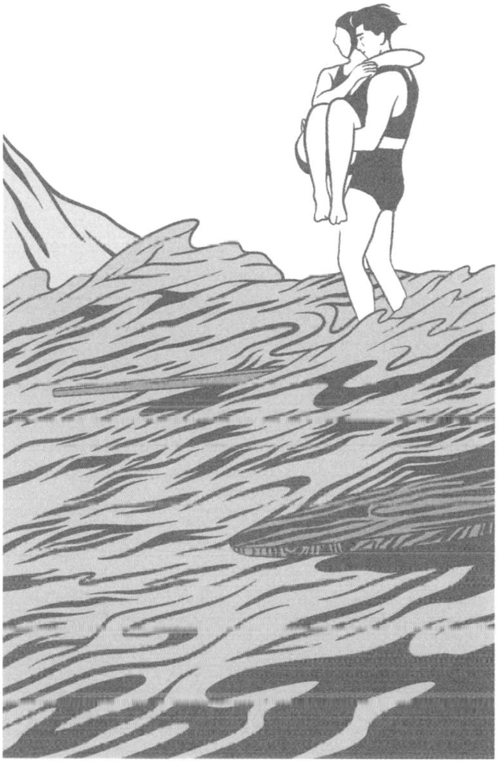

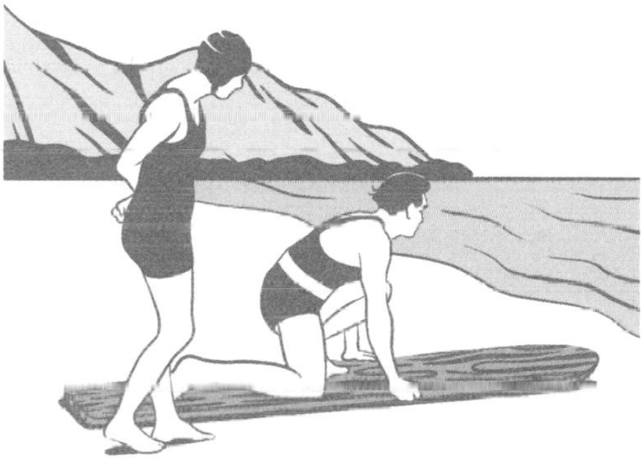

DUKE AND HIS CREW ARE WIDELY CONSIDERED RESPONSIBLE
FOR THE REBIRTH OF SURFING IN HAWAII AT THIS TIME.

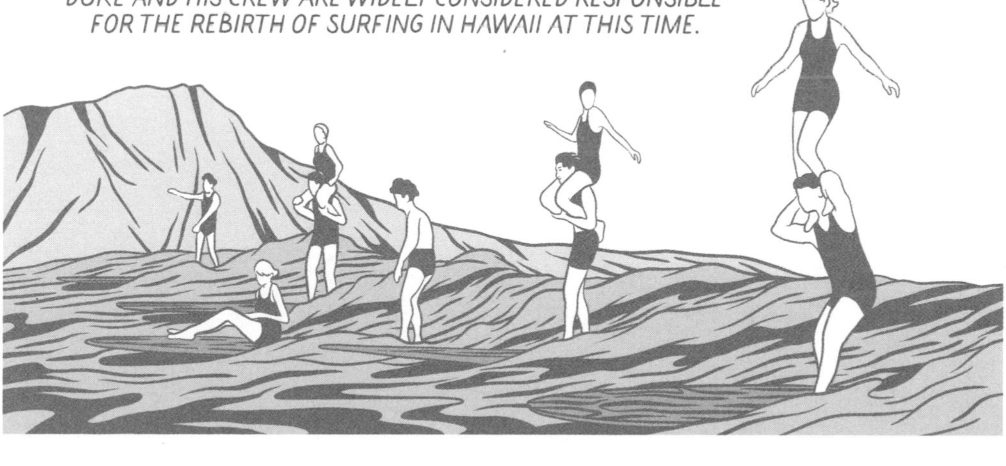

Summer
1912

Stockholm, Sweden

*DUKE'S TIME IN THE WATER SERVED HIM WELL
AND LED HIM TO THE COMPETITIVE ARENA.*

*AT HAWAII'S FIRST AMATEUR ATHLETIC UNION
SWIM MEET, DUKE BROKE BOTH THE 100-YARD
FREESTYLE RECORD AND THEN LESS THAN
AN HOUR LATER, BROKE THE 50-YARD RECORD.*

*HE QUICKLY BECAME AMERICA'S FAVORITE
FOR THE UPCOMING OLYMPICS.*

AT THE 1912 OLYMPICS IN STOCKHOLM, THE EYES OF THE WORLD WERE ON DUKE.

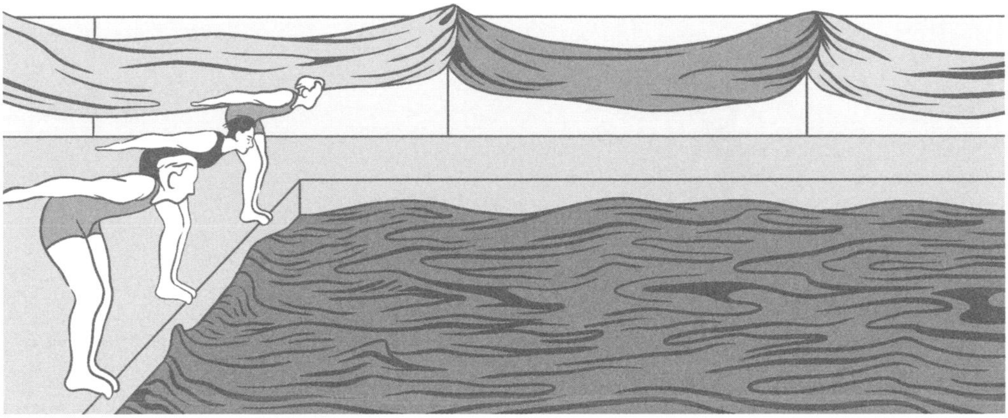

HE SET A WORLD RECORD DURING HIS 100 METER FREESTYLE AND EARNED A GOLD MEDAL FOR THE USA.

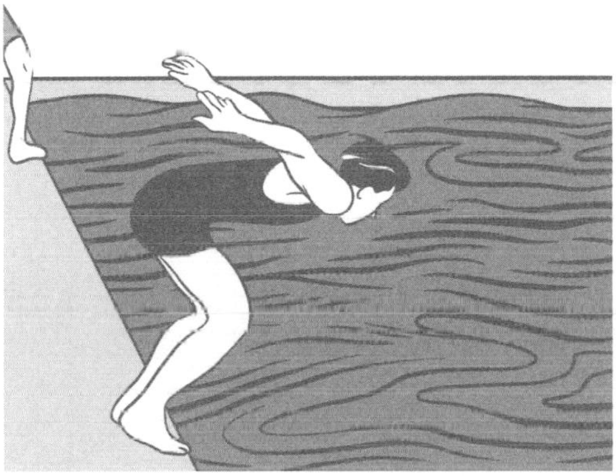

AT ONE POINT DURING HIS RACE,

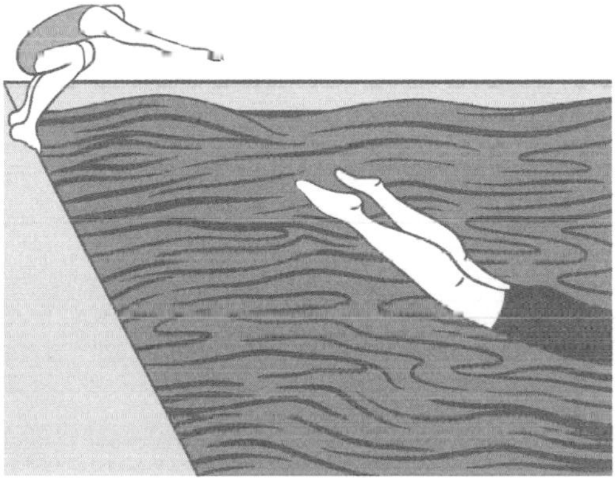

DUKE WAS SO FAR AHEAD OF HIS COMPETITION,

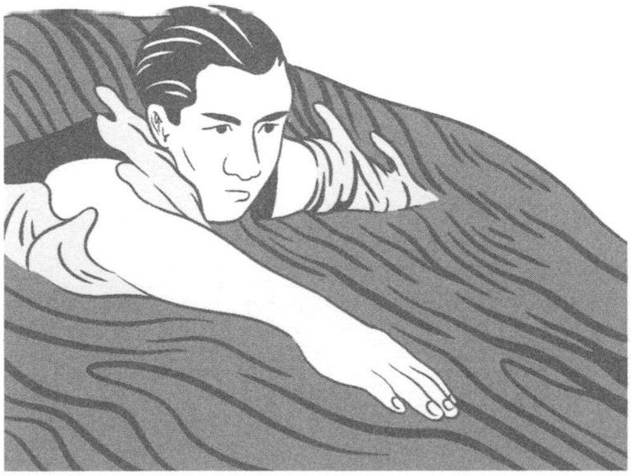

THAT HE PAUSED, MID-STROKE, TO GLANCE BACK AT THEM IN HIS WAKE.

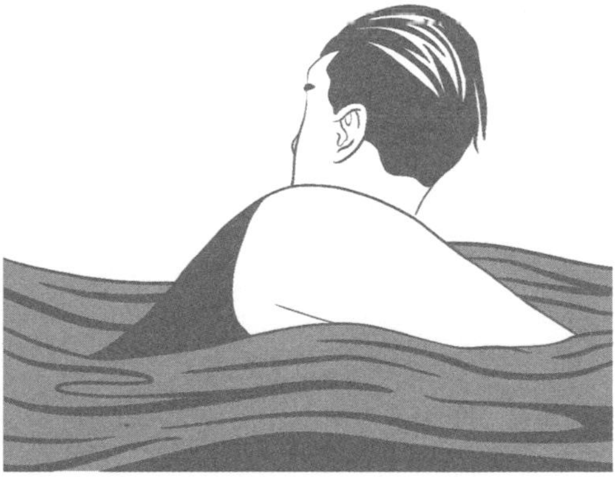

HOMEWARD BOUND AFTER THE OLYMPICS, DUKE TOOK THE OPPORTUNITY TO INTRODUCE SURFING TO THE WORLD.

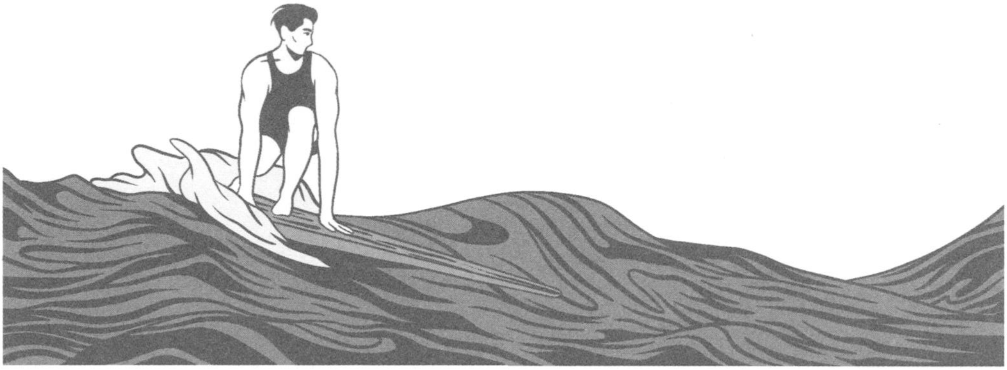

HE USED HIS STARDOM TO BRING SURFING TO THE PUBLIC FOR THE FIRST TIME AND HELD EXHIBITIONS IN WESTERN EUROPE, AND ALL OVER AMERICA.

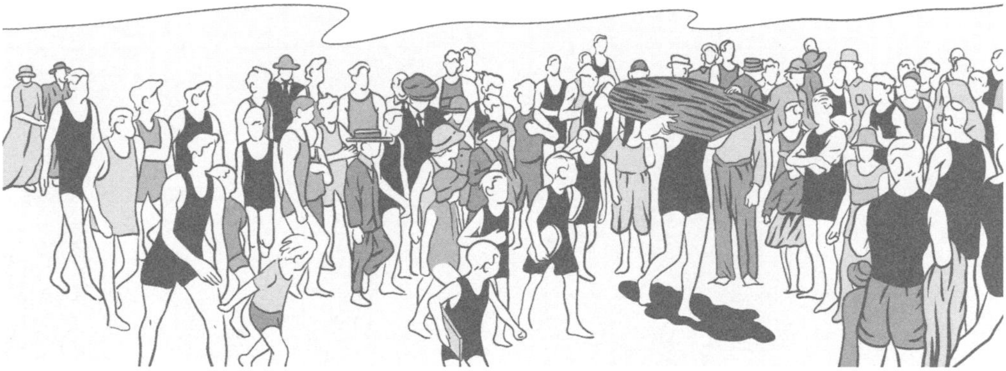

THESE TOURS WOULD LEAVE A LASTING IMPRESSION ON THE NEXT GENERATION OF SURFERS ACROSS THE GLOBE.

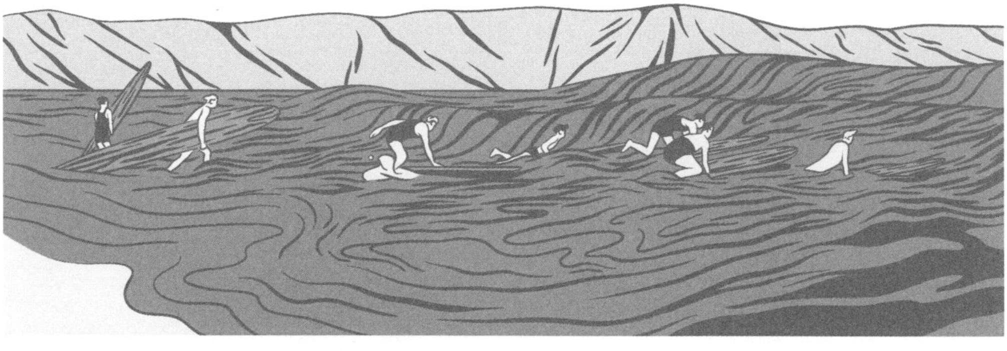

WHEN DUKE RETURNED HOME, HE WAS THE UNDISPUTED HERO OF HAWAII.

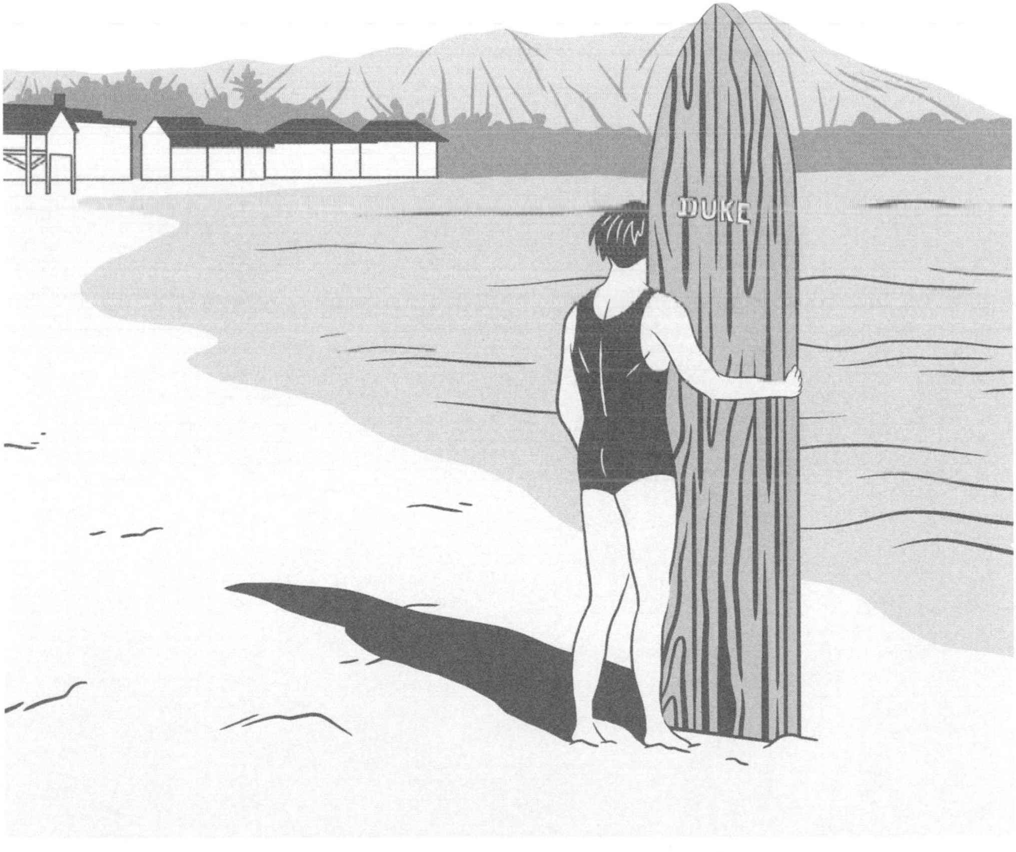
DUKE

VII. SUNSET SESSION

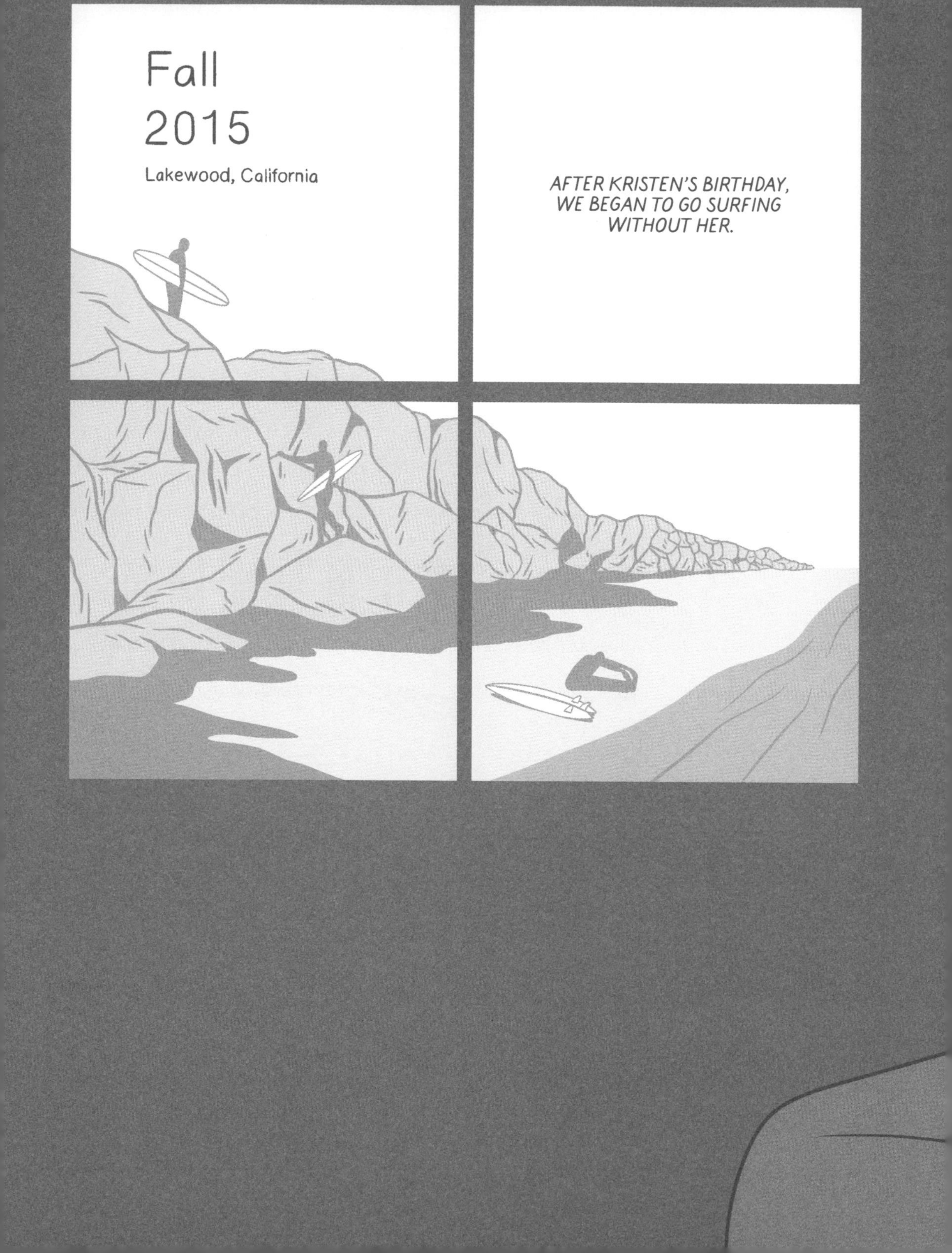
Fall
2015
Lakewood, California
AFTER KRISTEN'S BIRTHDAY, WE BEGAN TO GO SURFING WITHOUT HER.

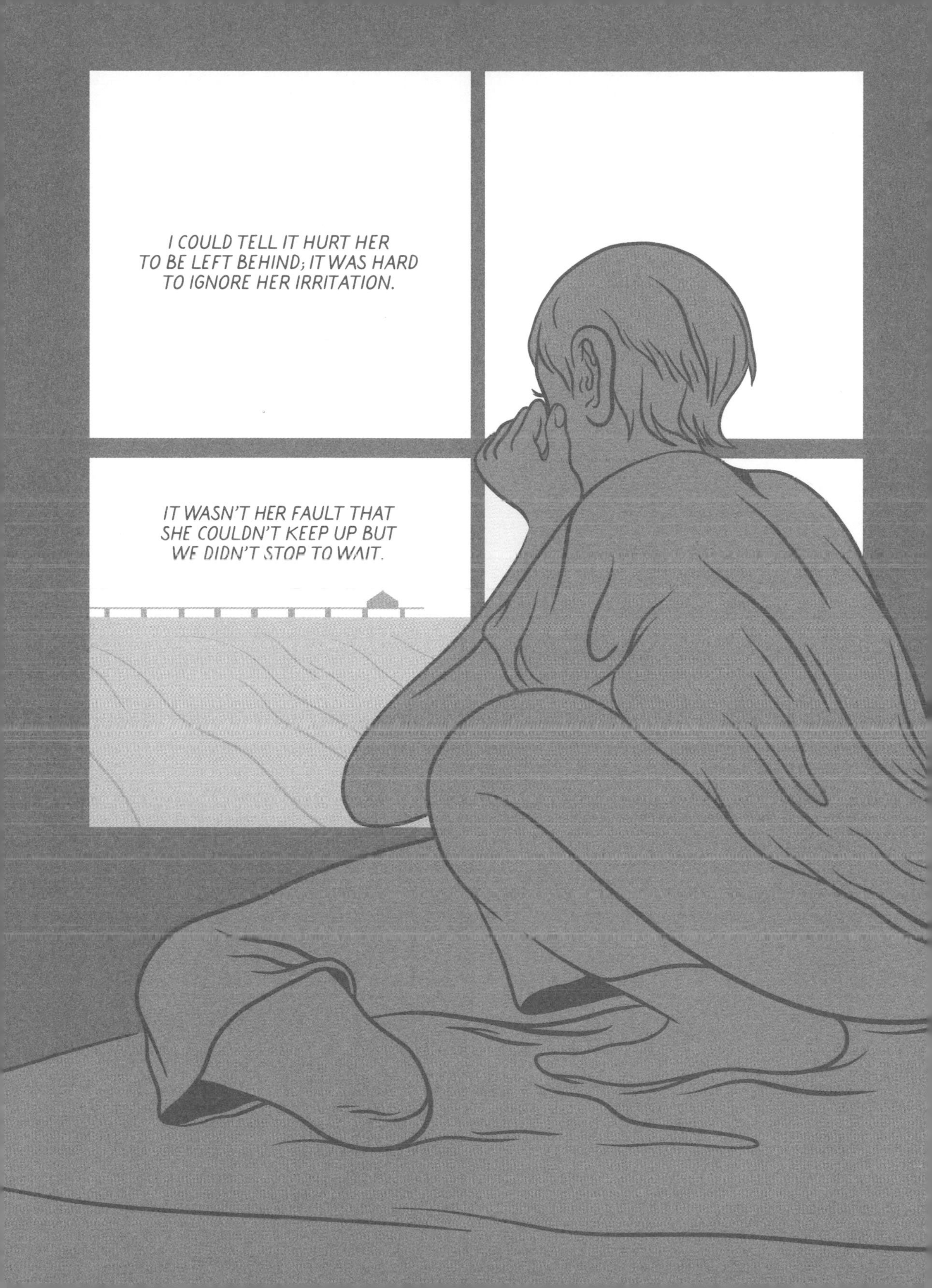
I COULD TELL IT HURT HER TO BE LEFT BEHIND; IT WAS HARD TO IGNORE HER IRRITATION.
IT WASN'T HER FAULT THAT SHE COULDN'T KEEP UP BUT WE DIDN'T STOP TO WAIT.

SURFING WITHOUT KRISTEN FELT WRONG BUT OUR GUILT COULDN'T KEEP US AWAY.

AFTER EACH SESSION, WE'D VISIT HER WHILE SHE RESTED IN BED,

AND TRY OUR HARDEST NOT TO RUB SEA SALT INTO HER WOUNDS.

EVEN THOUGH SHE DIDN'T HAVE THE ENERGY TO SURF, KRISTEN WOULD JOIN US WHEN SHE WAS FEELING WELL ENOUGH.

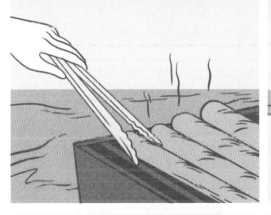

SHE'D MAKE HOTDOGS FOR US;

OUR AUDIENCE OF ONE.

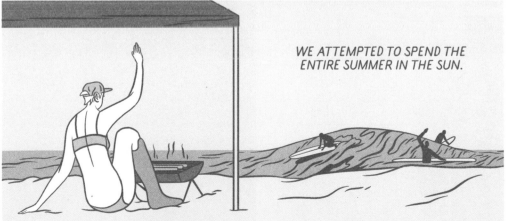

WE ATTEMPTED TO SPEND THE ENTIRE SUMMER IN THE SUN.

BUT WHEN SUMMER ENDED...

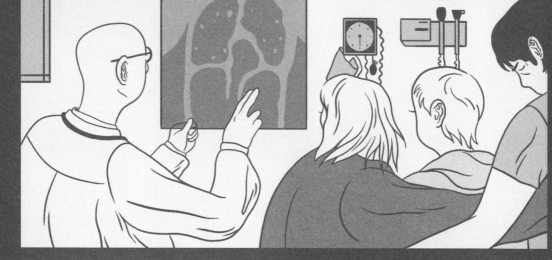

...THE GOOD TIMES DID TOO.

KRISTEN HAD HER SEVENTH LUNG SURGERY, THE THIRD ON THE RIGHT LUNG.

WHAT WAS SUPPOSED TO BE A FIVE-HOUR SURGERY TOOK TEN.

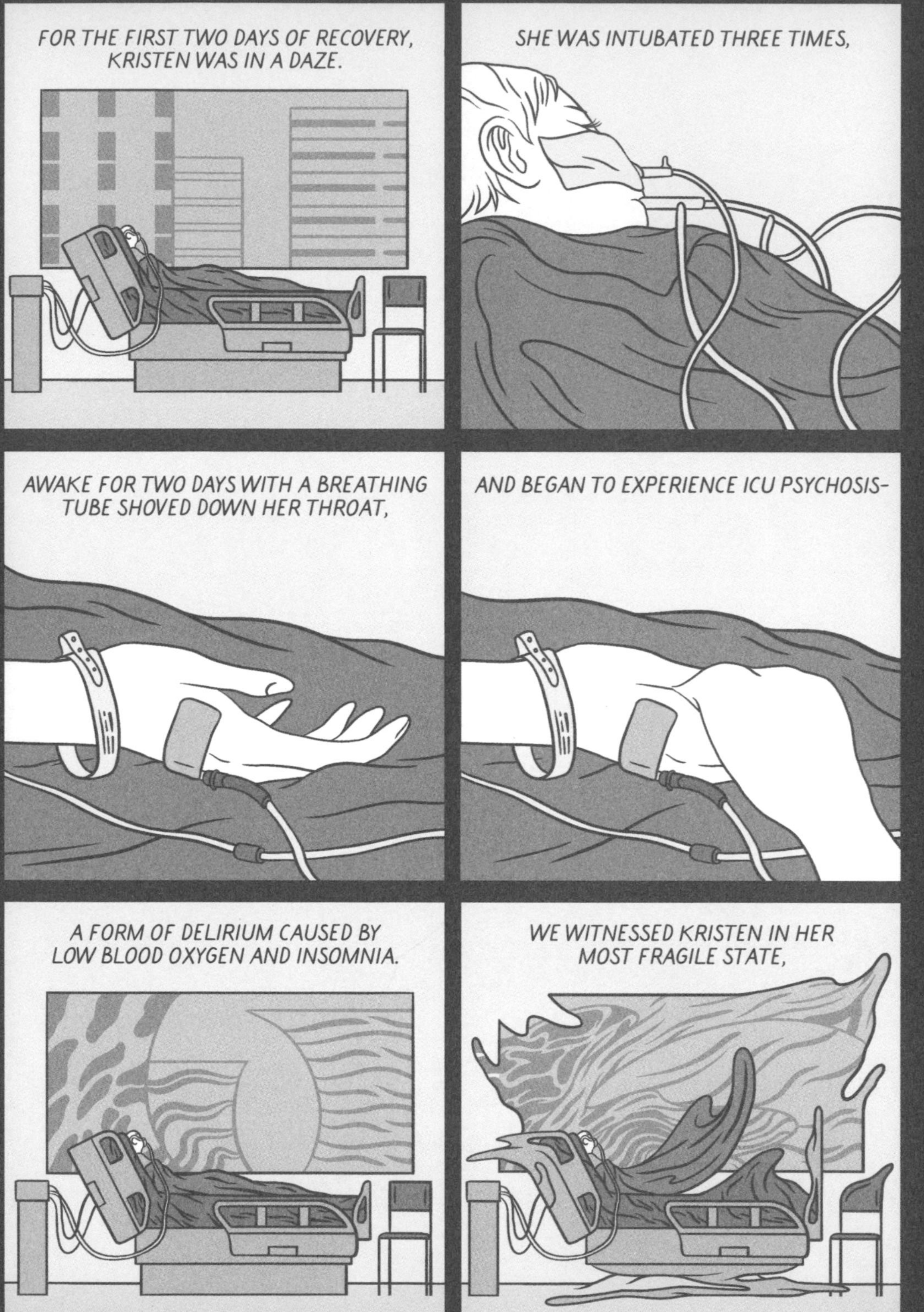
FOR THE FIRST TWO DAYS OF RECOVERY, KRISTEN WAS IN A DAZE.
SHE WAS INTUBATED THREE TIMES,
AWAKE FOR TWO DAYS WITH A BREATHING TUBE SHOVED DOWN HER THROAT,
AND BEGAN TO EXPERIENCE ICU PSYCHOSIS-
A FORM OF DELIRIUM CAUSED BY LOW BLOOD OXYGEN AND INSOMNIA.
WE WITNESSED KRISTEN IN HER MOST FRAGILE STATE,

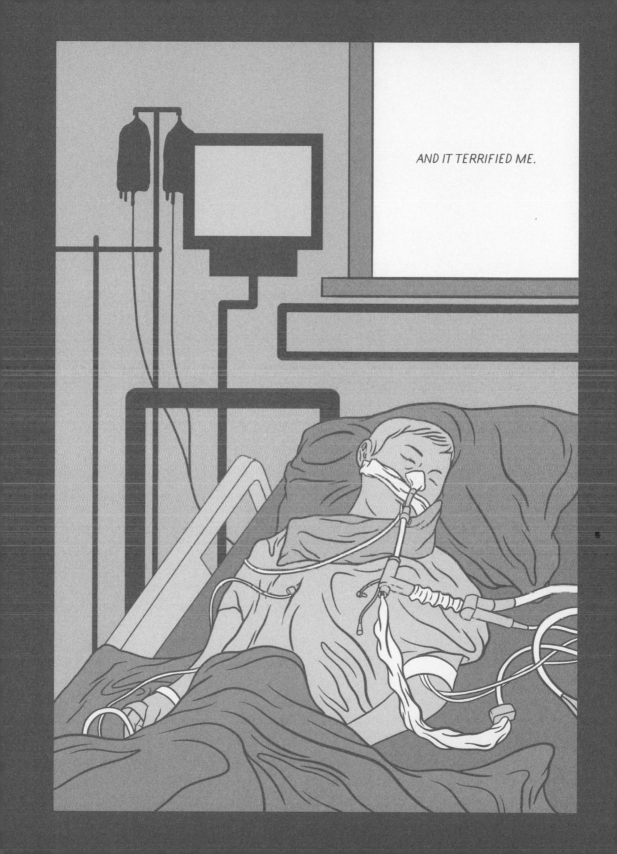

AND IT TERRIFIED ME.

KRISTEN ALWAYS BOUNCED BACK AFTER HER SURGERIES
BUT THIS TIME WAS DIFFERENT. EVERYTHING BECAME LIMITED.
HER ENERGY, HER BREATHING, HER APPETITE, HER SPEECH.

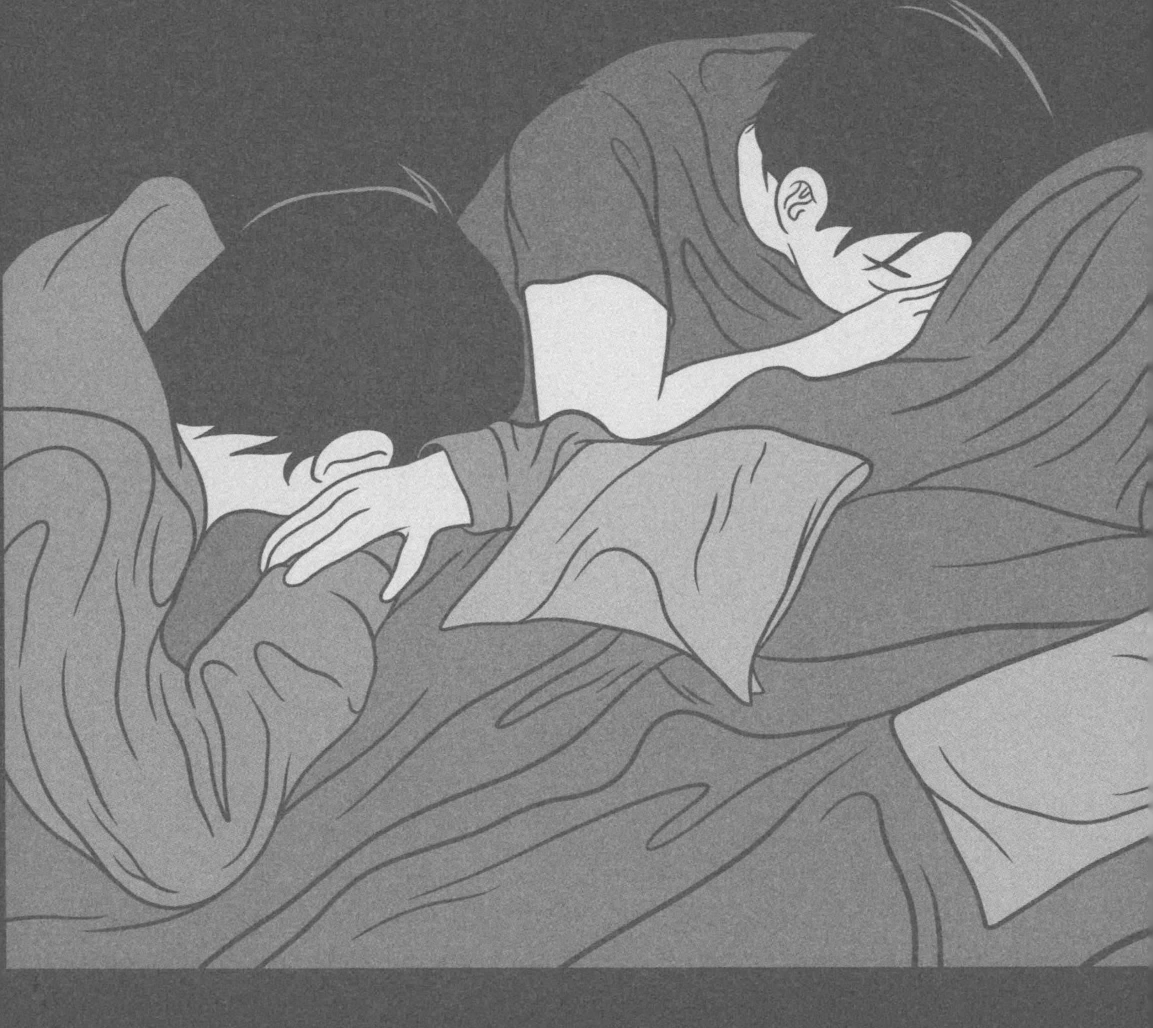

BUT SHE MADE IT WORK FOR AS LONG AS SHE COULD.

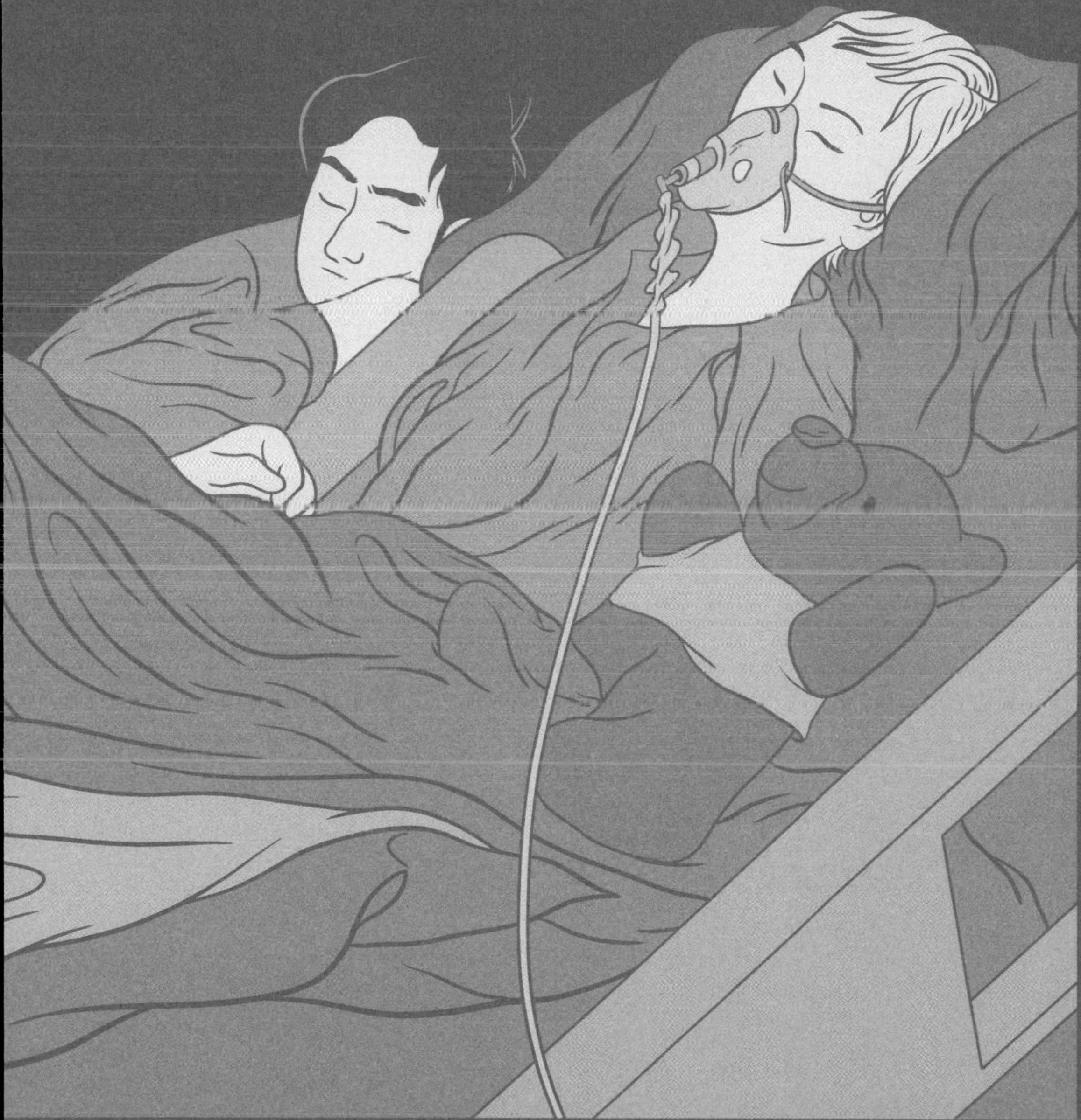

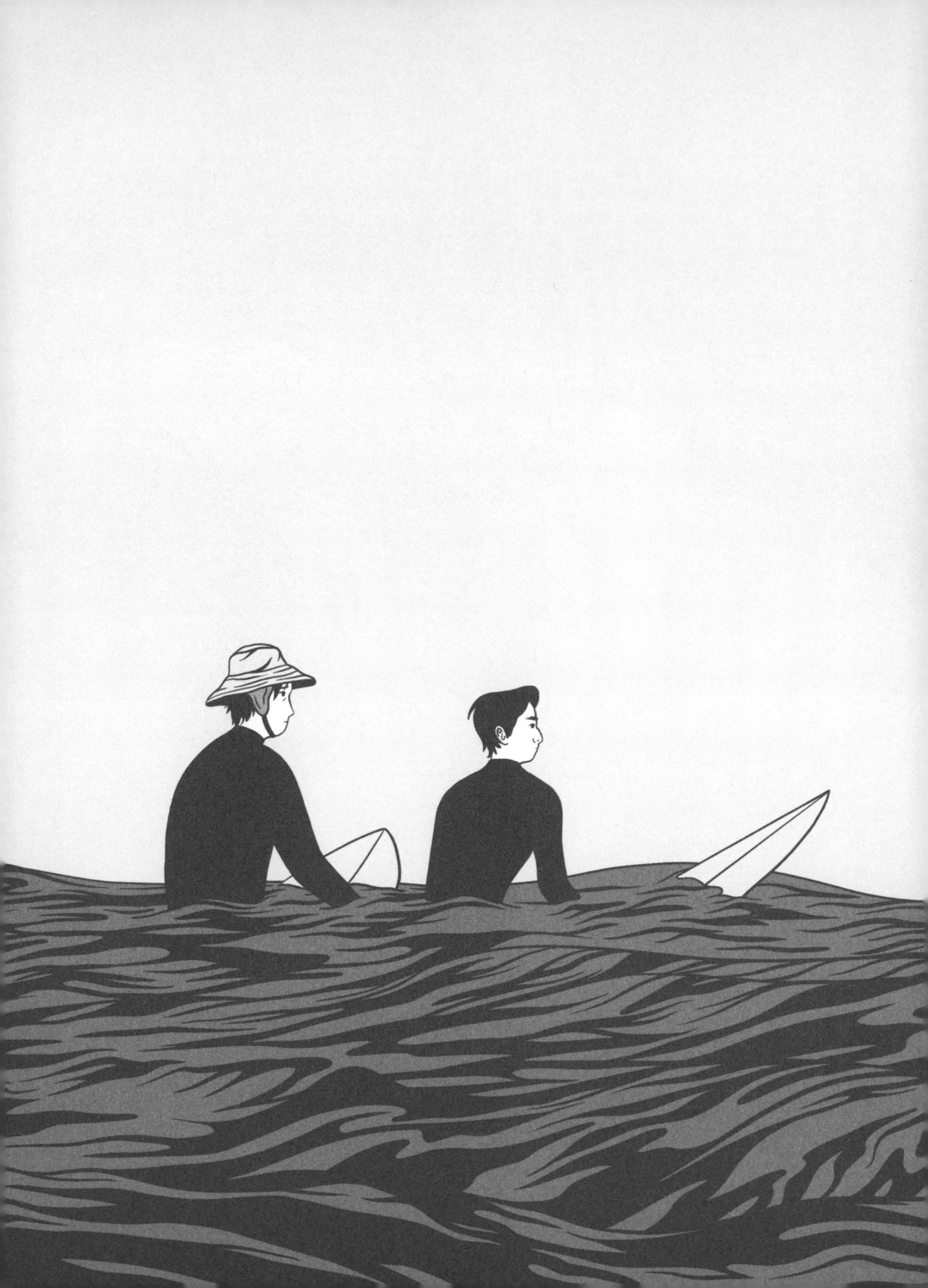

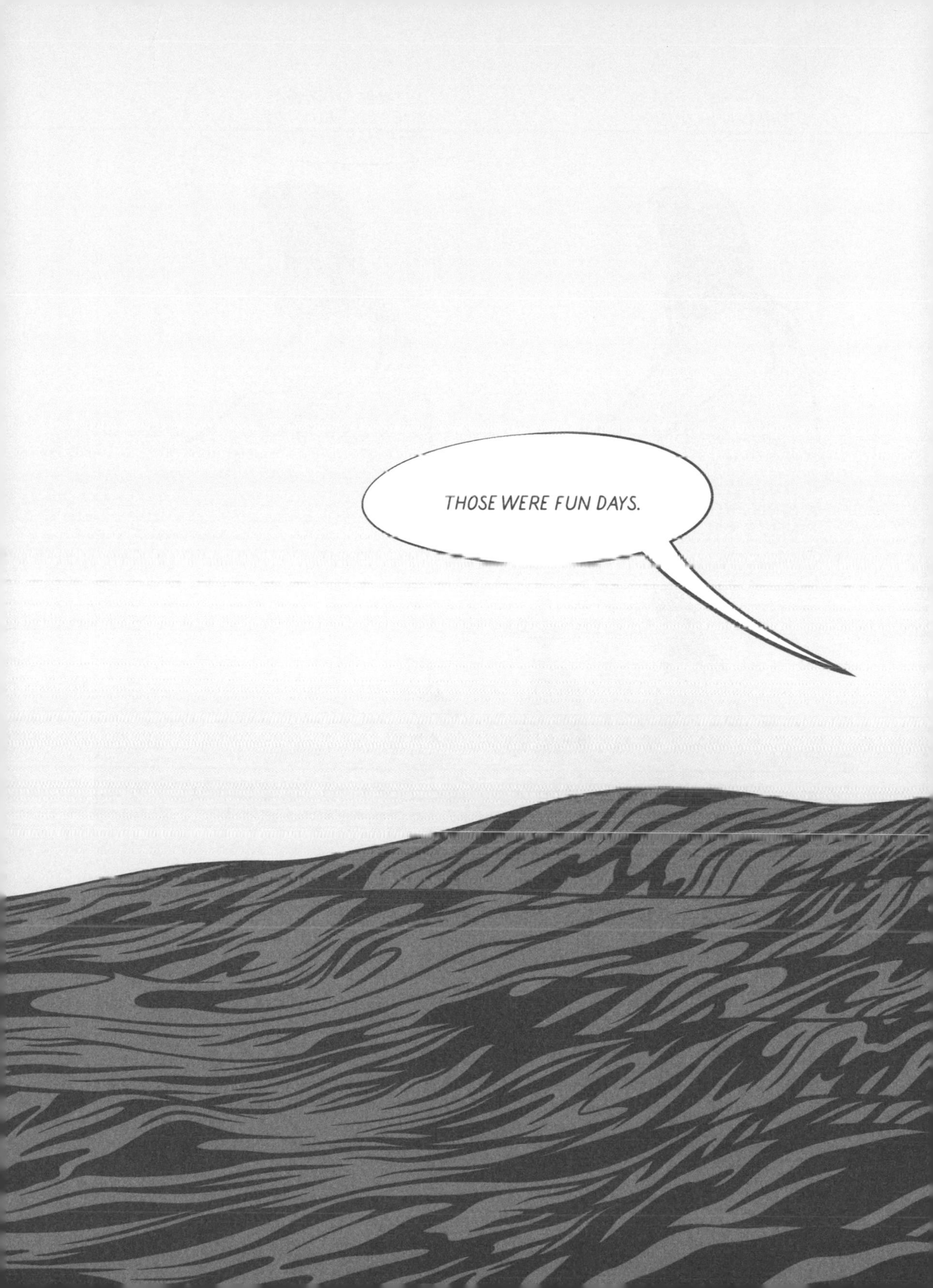
THOSE WERE FUN DAYS.

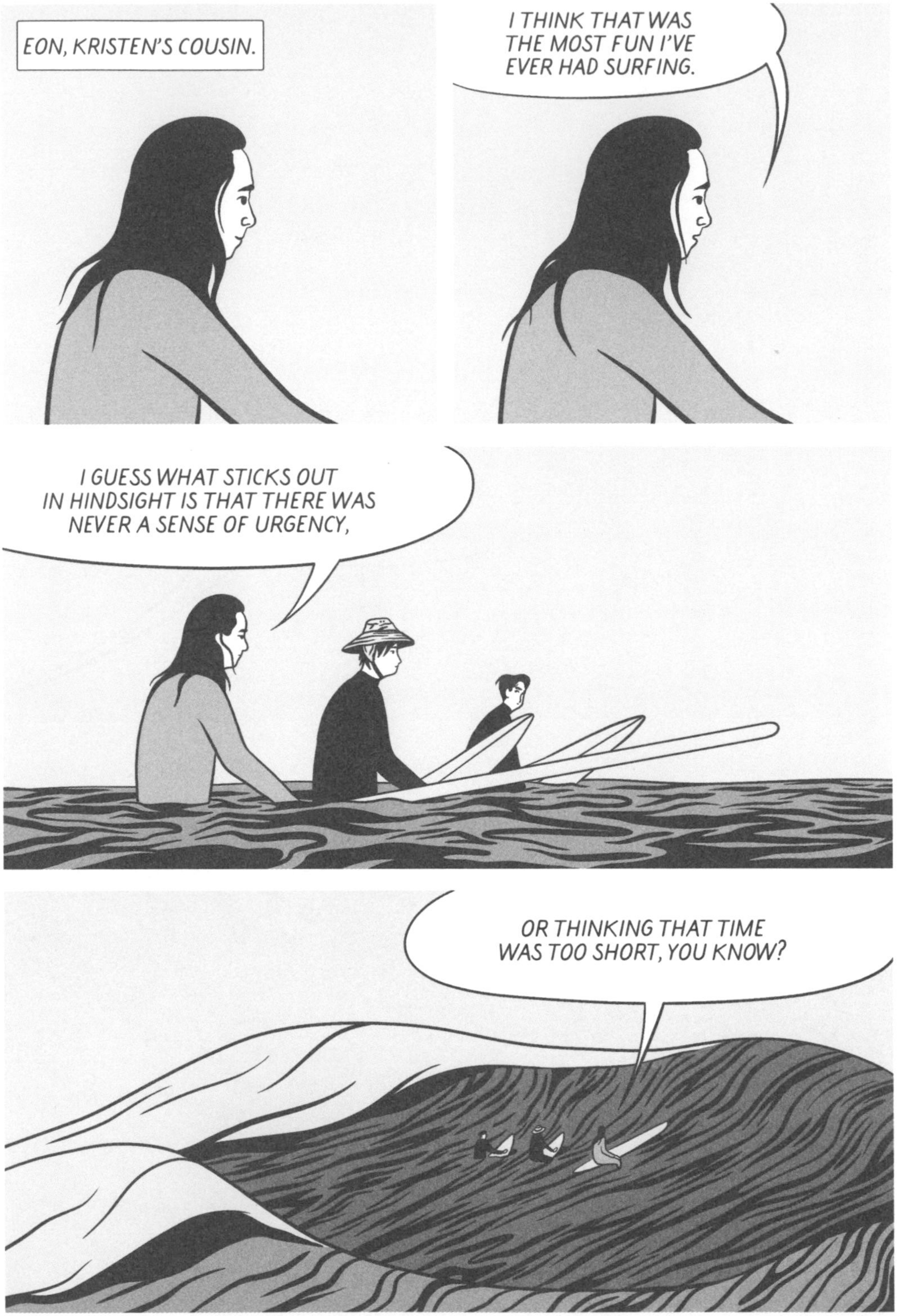
EON, KRISTEN'S COUSIN.
I THINK THAT WAS THE MOST FUN I'VE EVER HAD SURFING.
I GUESS WHAT STICKS OUT IN HINDSIGHT IS THAT THERE WAS NEVER A SENSE OF URGENCY,
OR THINKING THAT TIME WAS TOO SHORT, YOU KNOW?

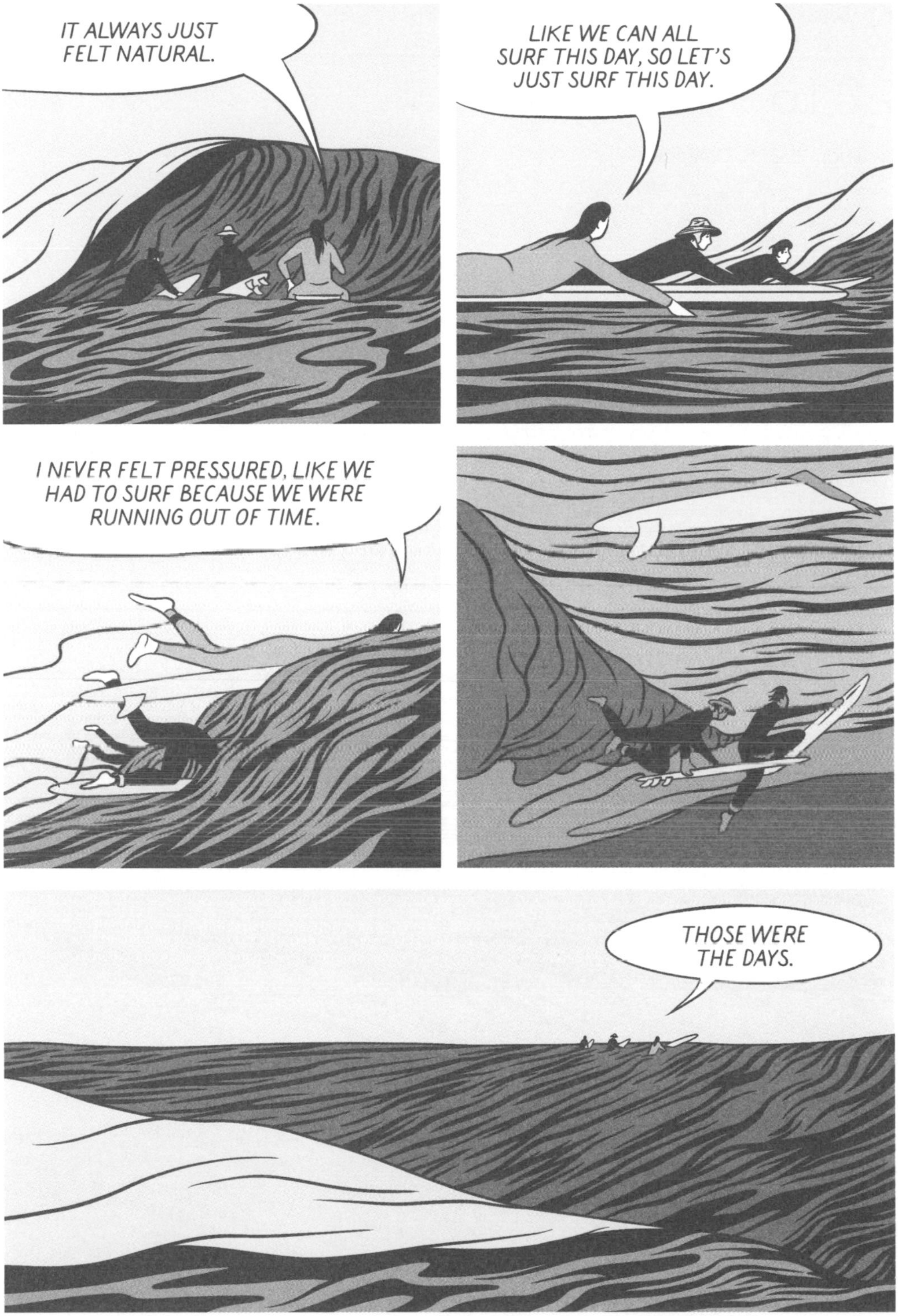
IT ALWAYS JUST FELT NATURAL.
LIKE WE CAN ALL SURF THIS DAY, SO LET'S JUST SURF THIS DAY.
I NEVER FELT PRESSURED, LIKE WE HAD TO SURF BECAUSE WE WERE RUNNING OUT OF TIME.
THOSE WERE THE DAYS.

Spring
2016

Newport Beach, California

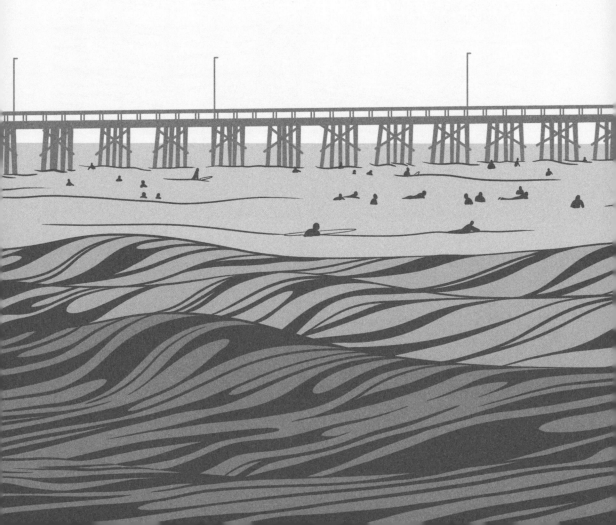

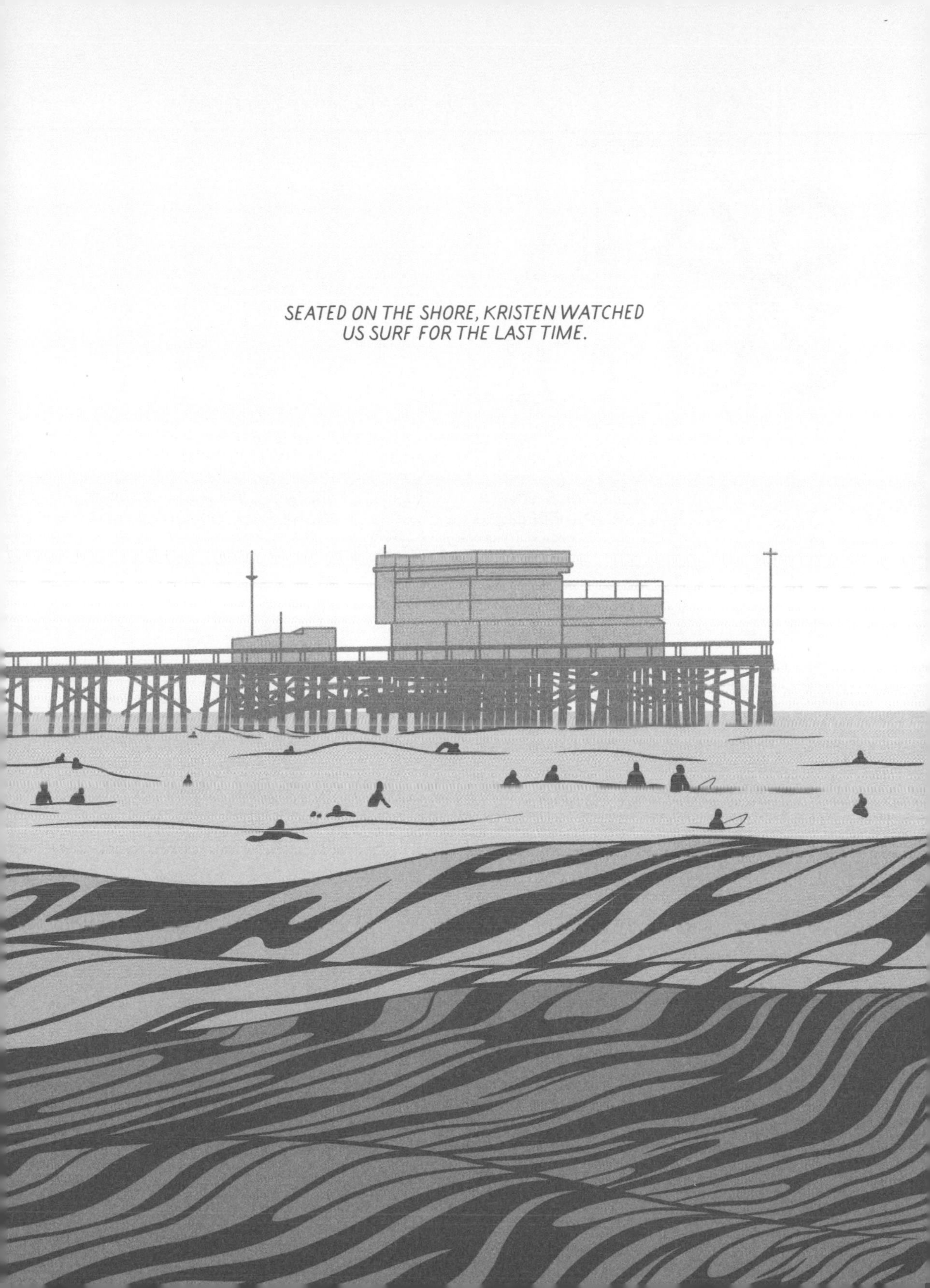
SEATED ON THE SHORE, KRISTEN WATCHED US SURF FOR THE LAST TIME.

SHE WATCHED FROM HER WHEELCHAIR,

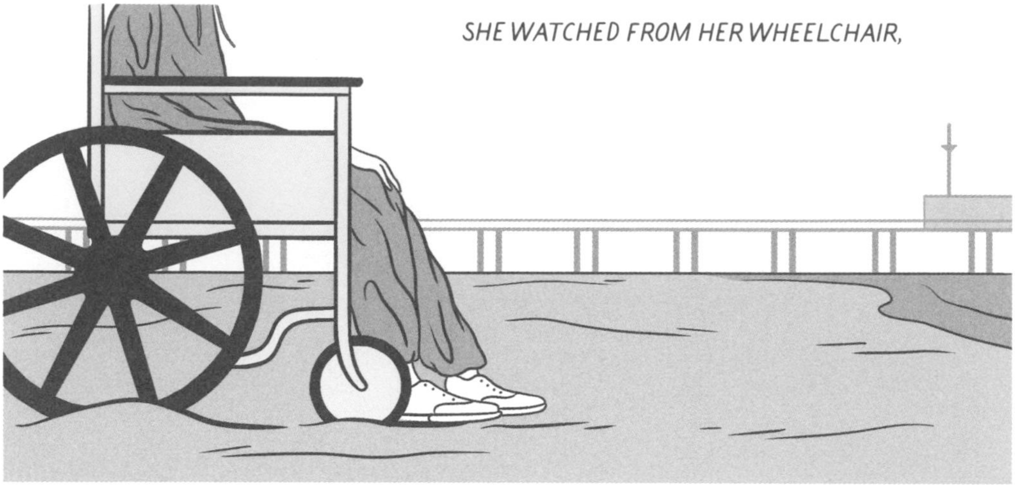

HER BREATHING NOW SHALLOW AND FORCED.

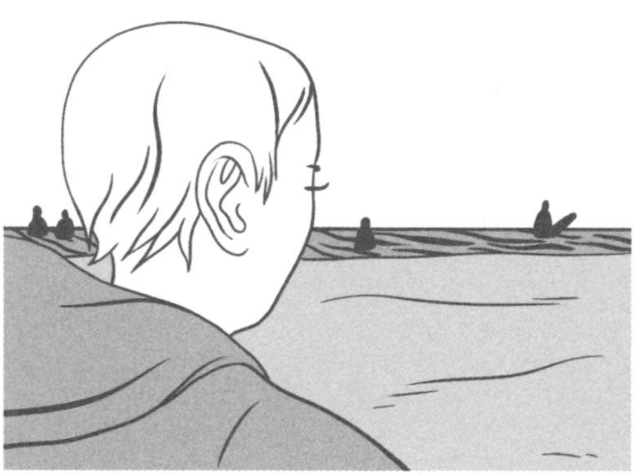

SHE WOULD INHALE SHARPLY AS SHE PULLED EACH BREATH.

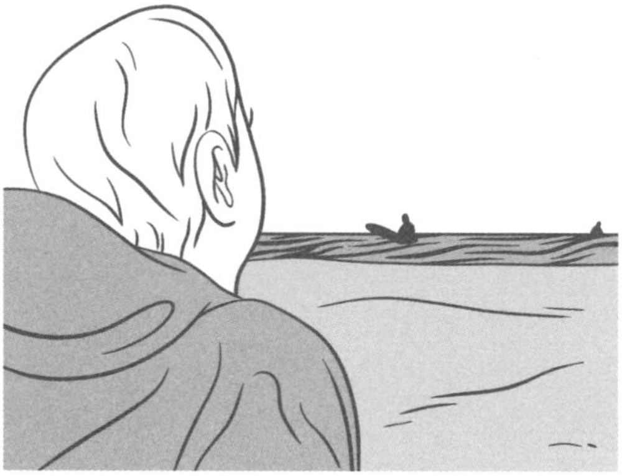

EVEN AS SHE SAT STILL, KRISTEN'S HEART WAS RACING, COMPENSATING FOR HER WEAKENING LUNGS.

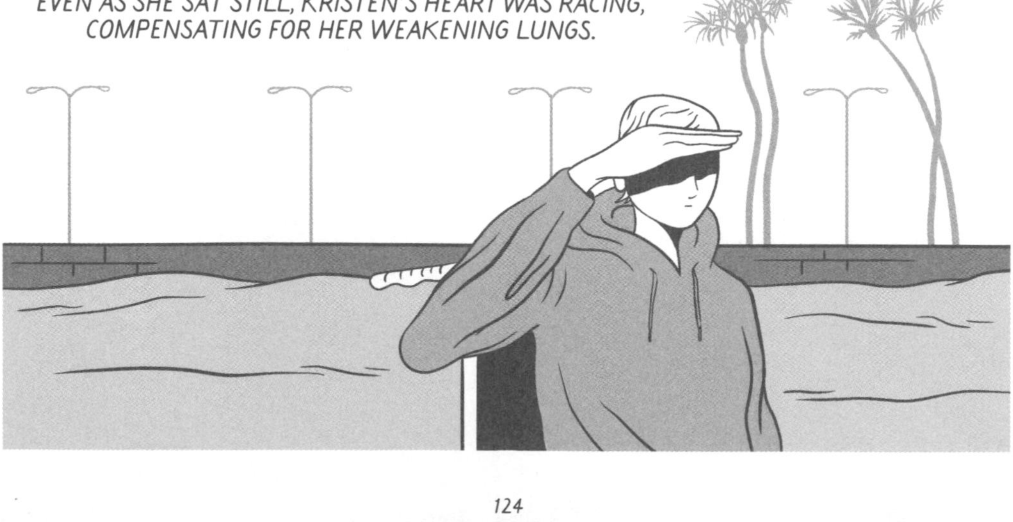

AFTER THE LUNG SURGERY, SHE WAS FORCED TO USE AN OXYGEN TANK.
SHE DESPISED IT AND INSISTED WE LEAVE IT BEHIND.

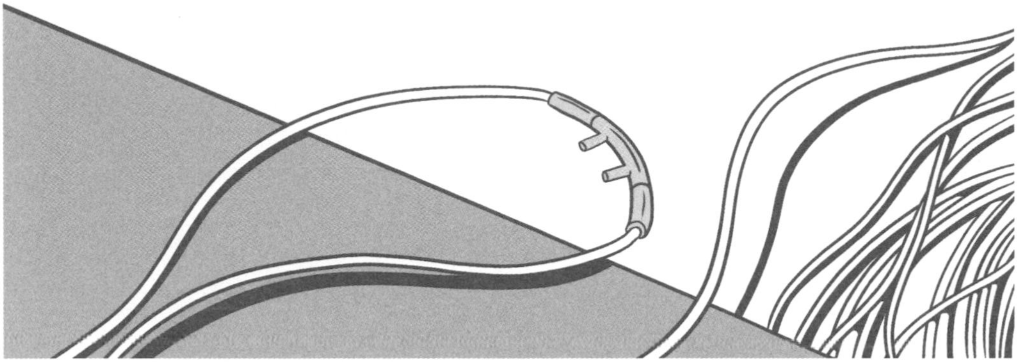

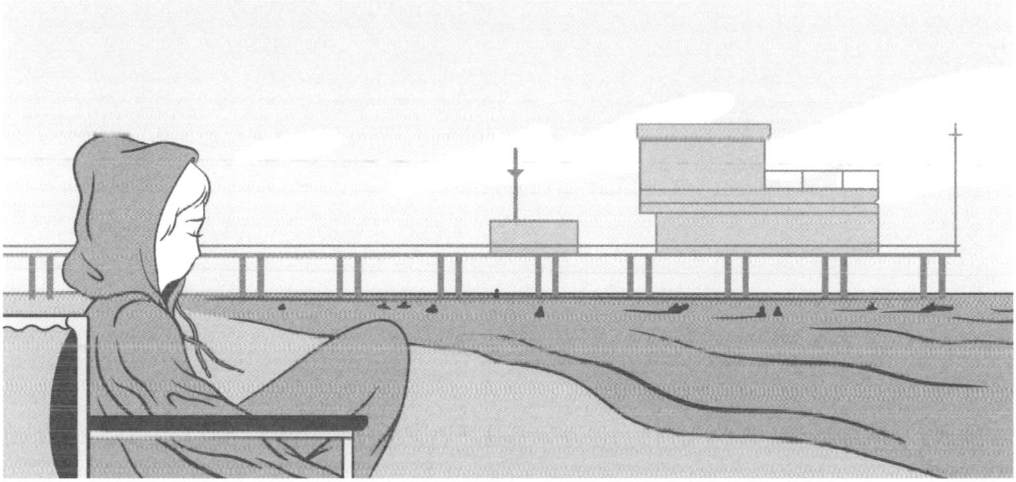

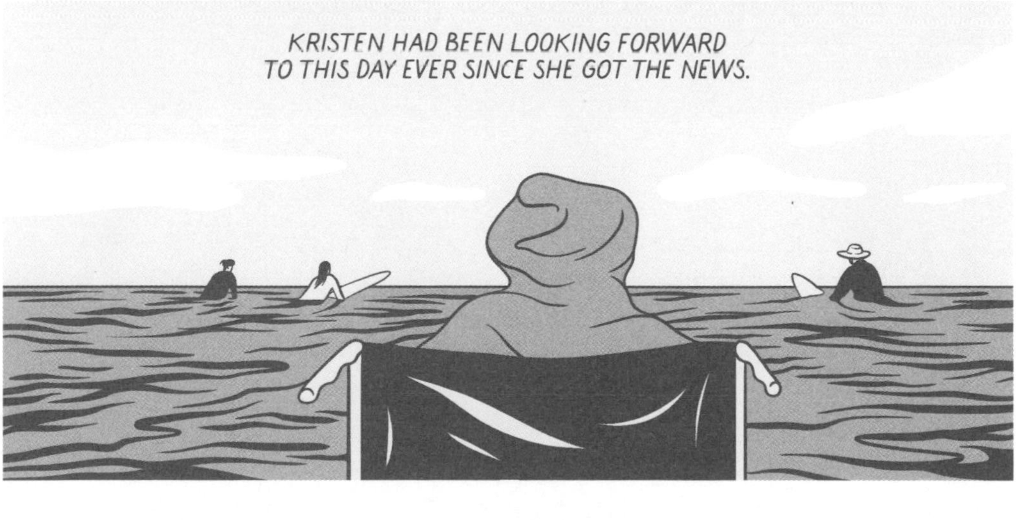
KRISTEN HAD BEEN LOOKING FORWARD TO THIS DAY EVER SINCE SHE GOT THE NEWS.

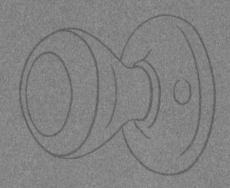

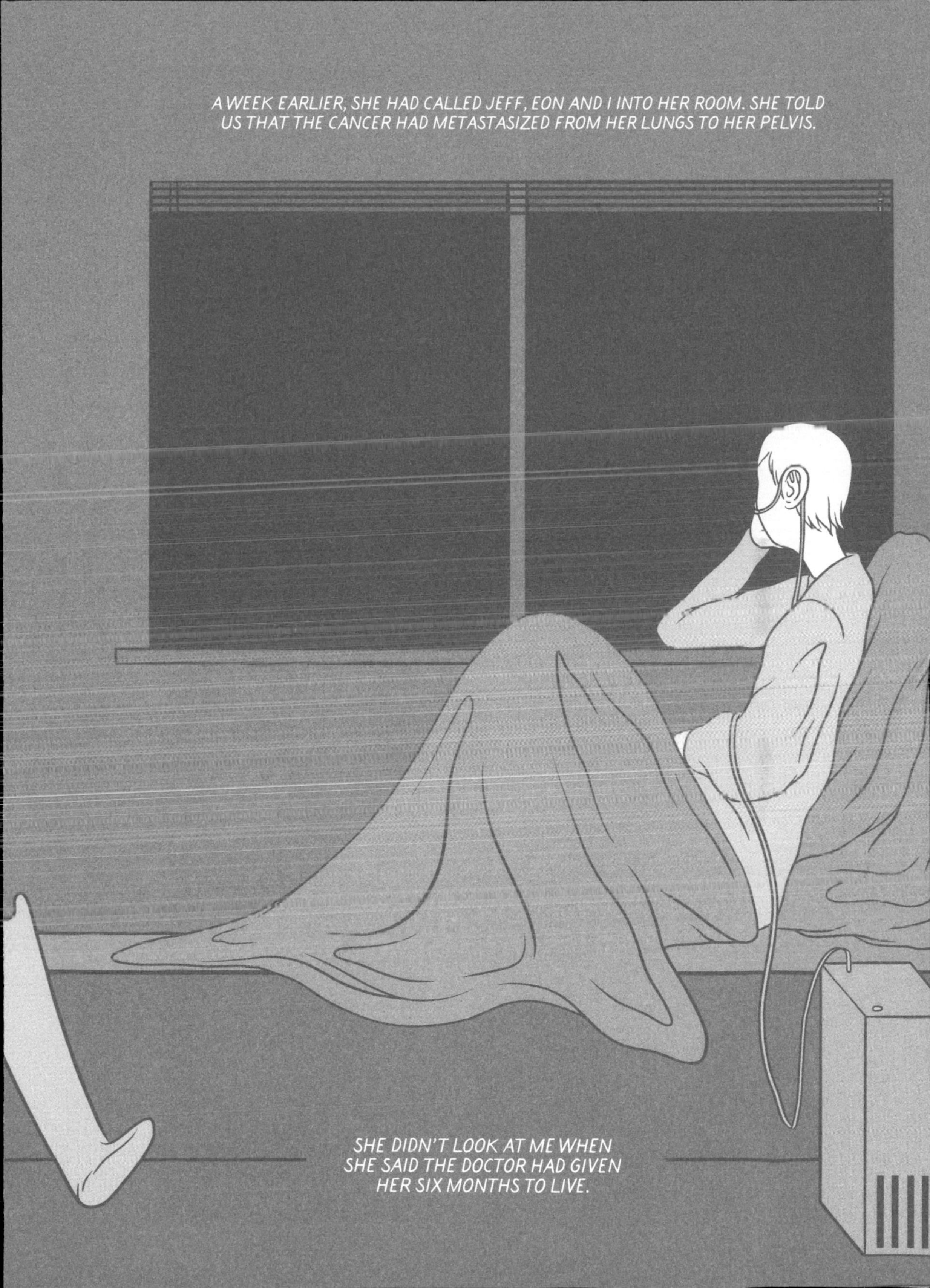
A WEEK EARLIER, SHE HAD CALLED JEFF, EON AND I INTO HER ROOM. SHE TOLD US THAT THE CANCER HAD METASTASIZED FROM HER LUNGS TO HER PELVIS.
SHE DIDN'T LOOK AT ME WHEN SHE SAID THE DOCTOR HAD GIVEN HER SIX MONTHS TO LIVE.

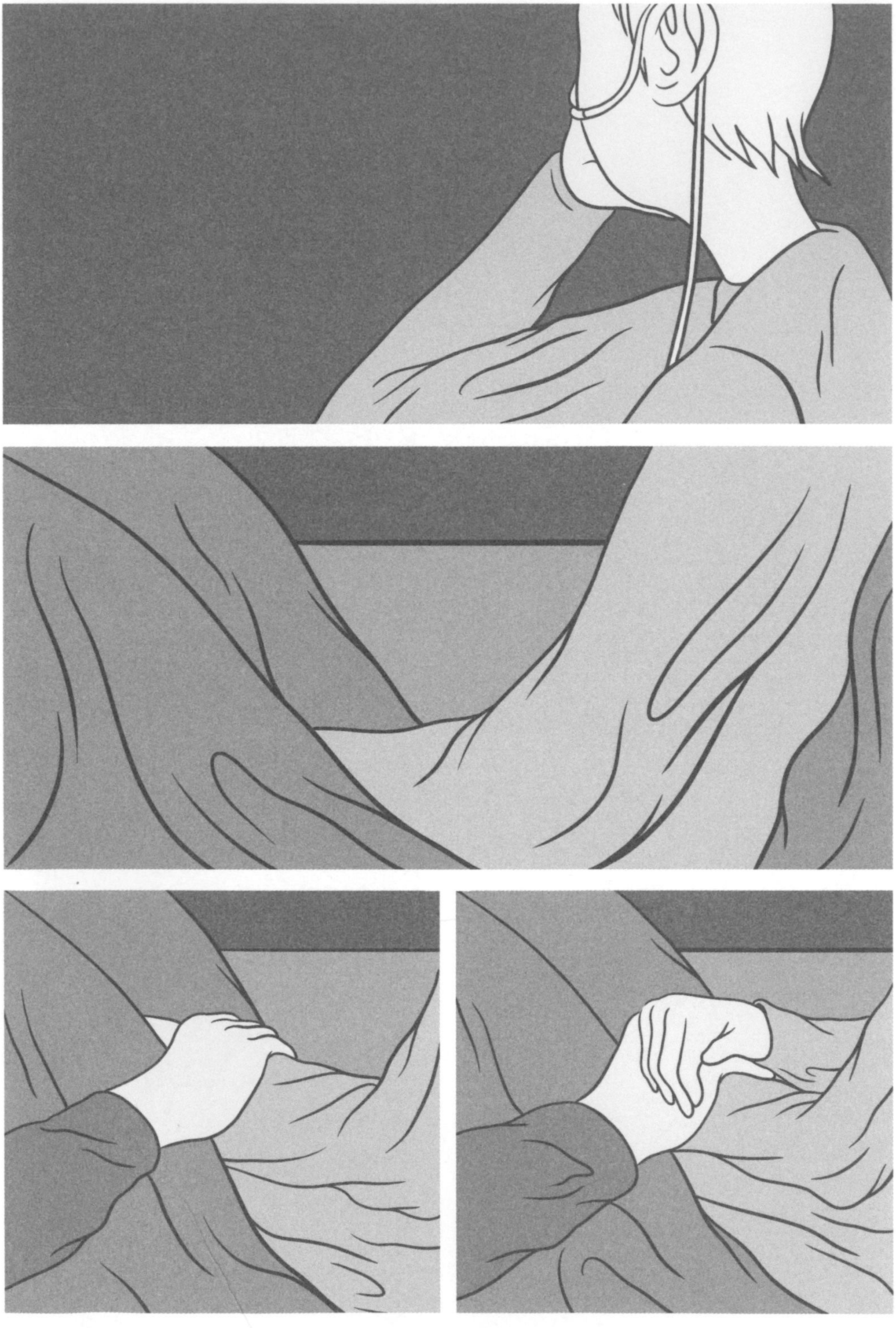

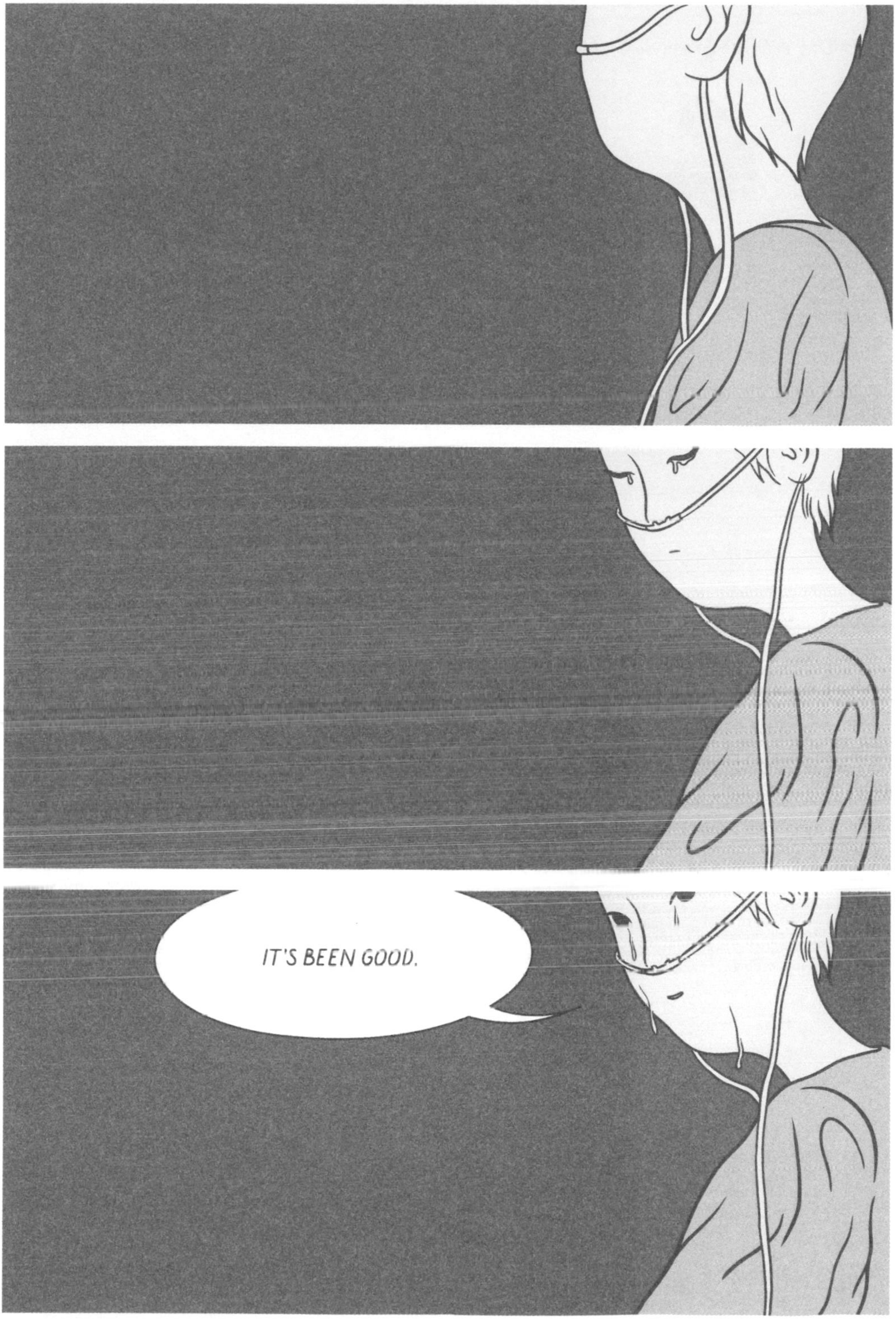
IT'S BEEN GOOD.

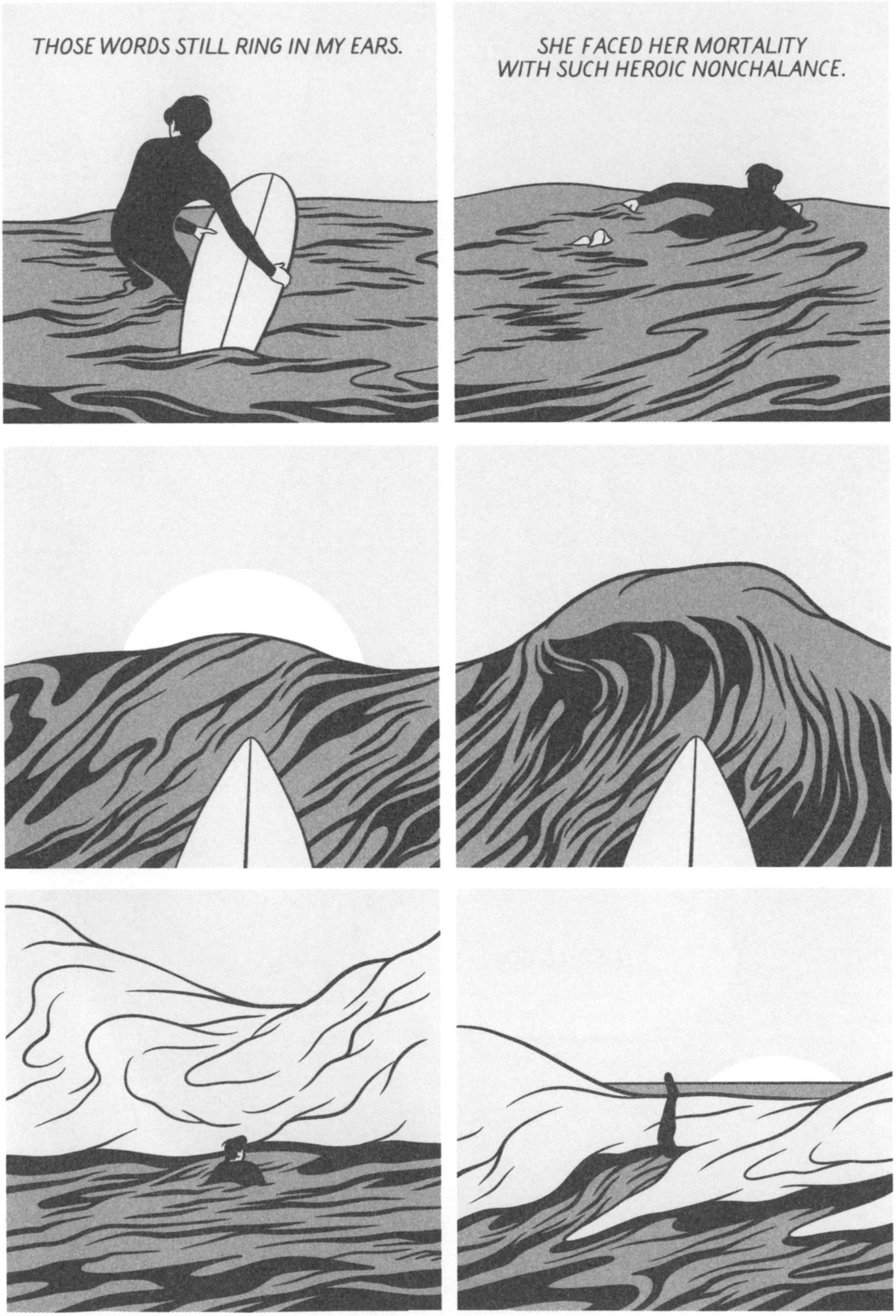
THOSE WORDS STILL RING IN MY EARS.
SHE FACED HER MORTALITY WITH SUCH HEROIC NONCHALANCE.

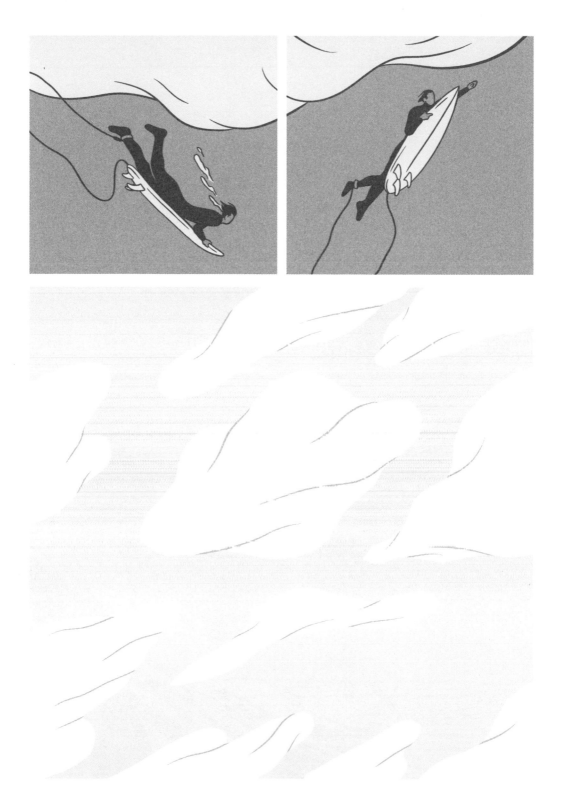

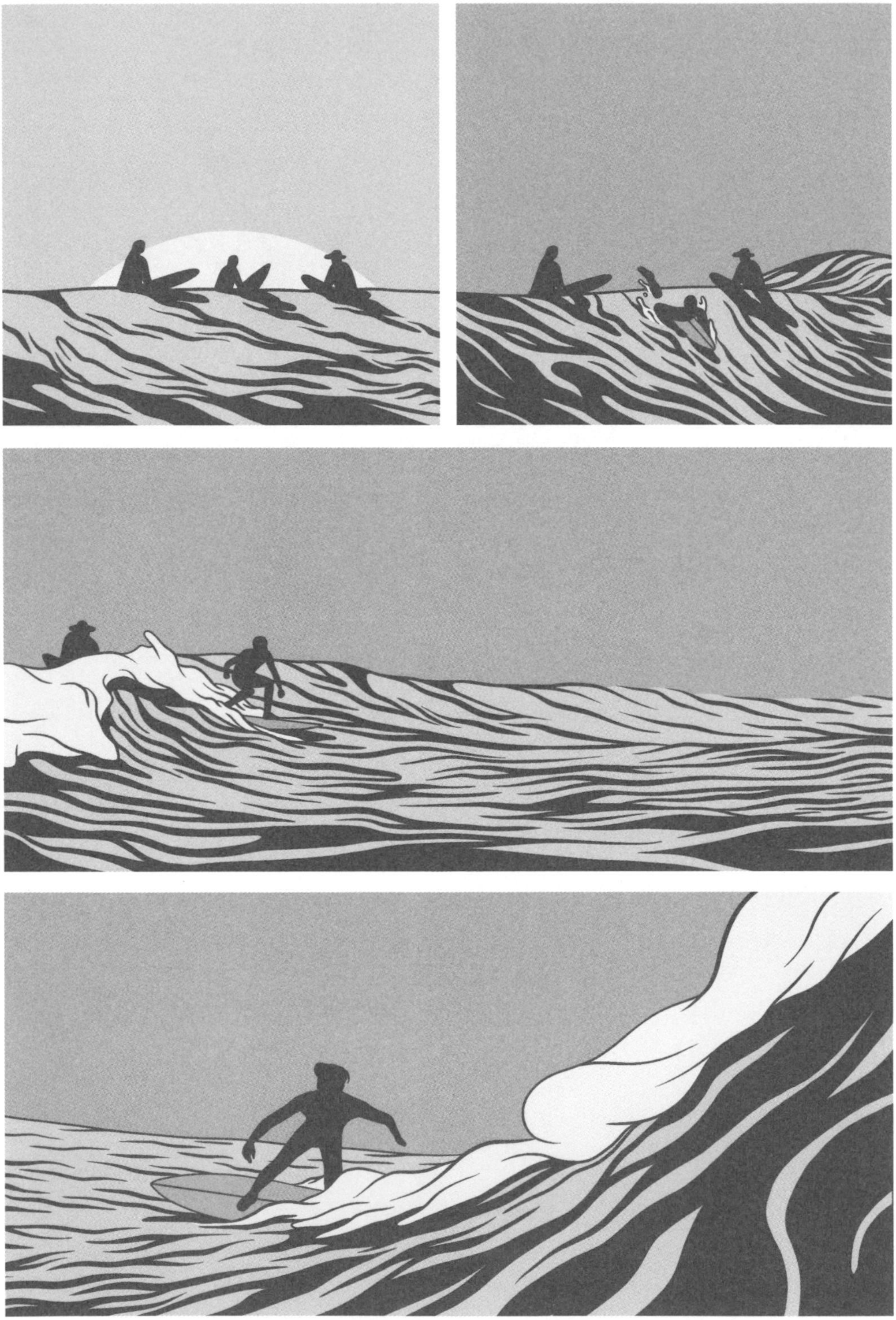

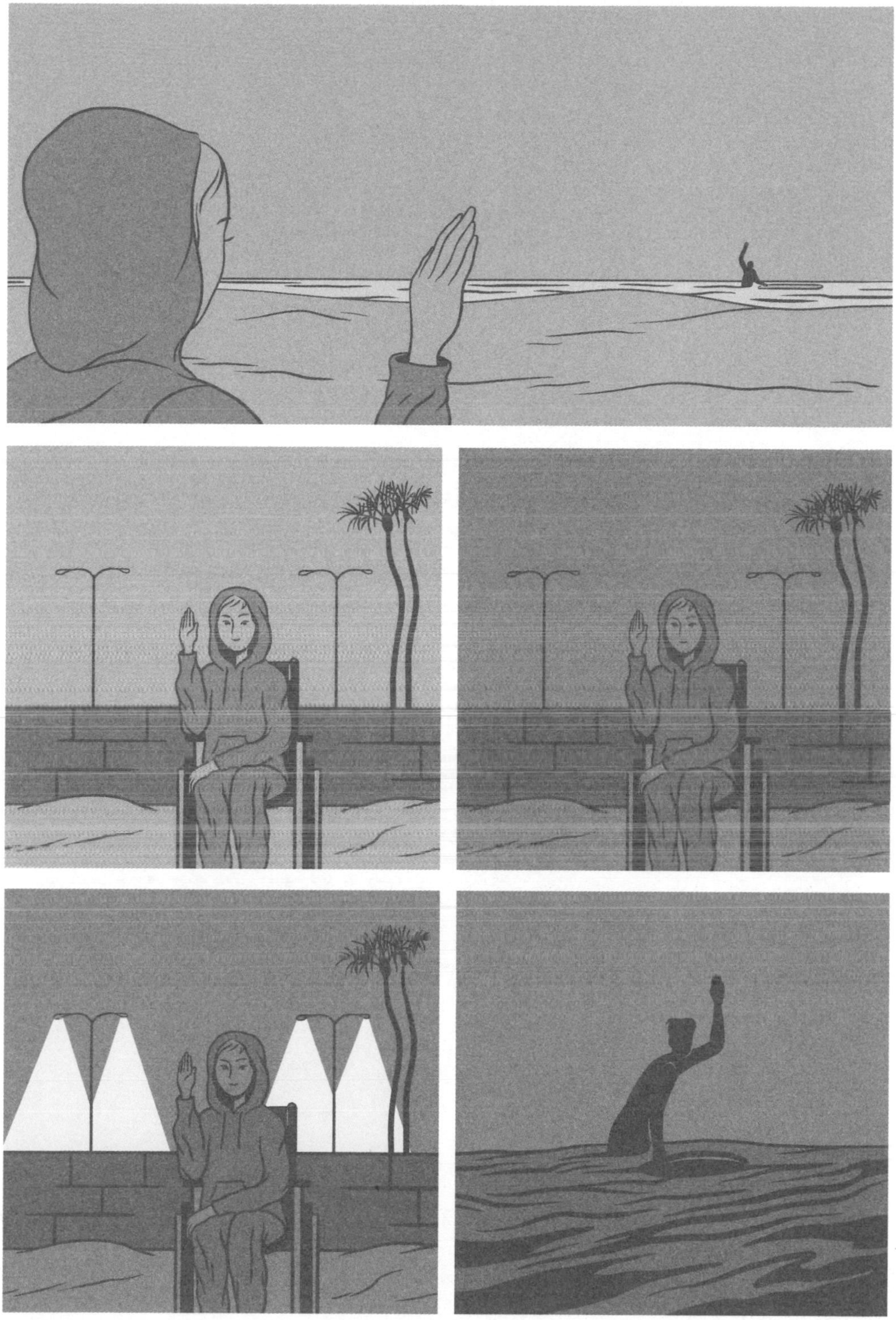

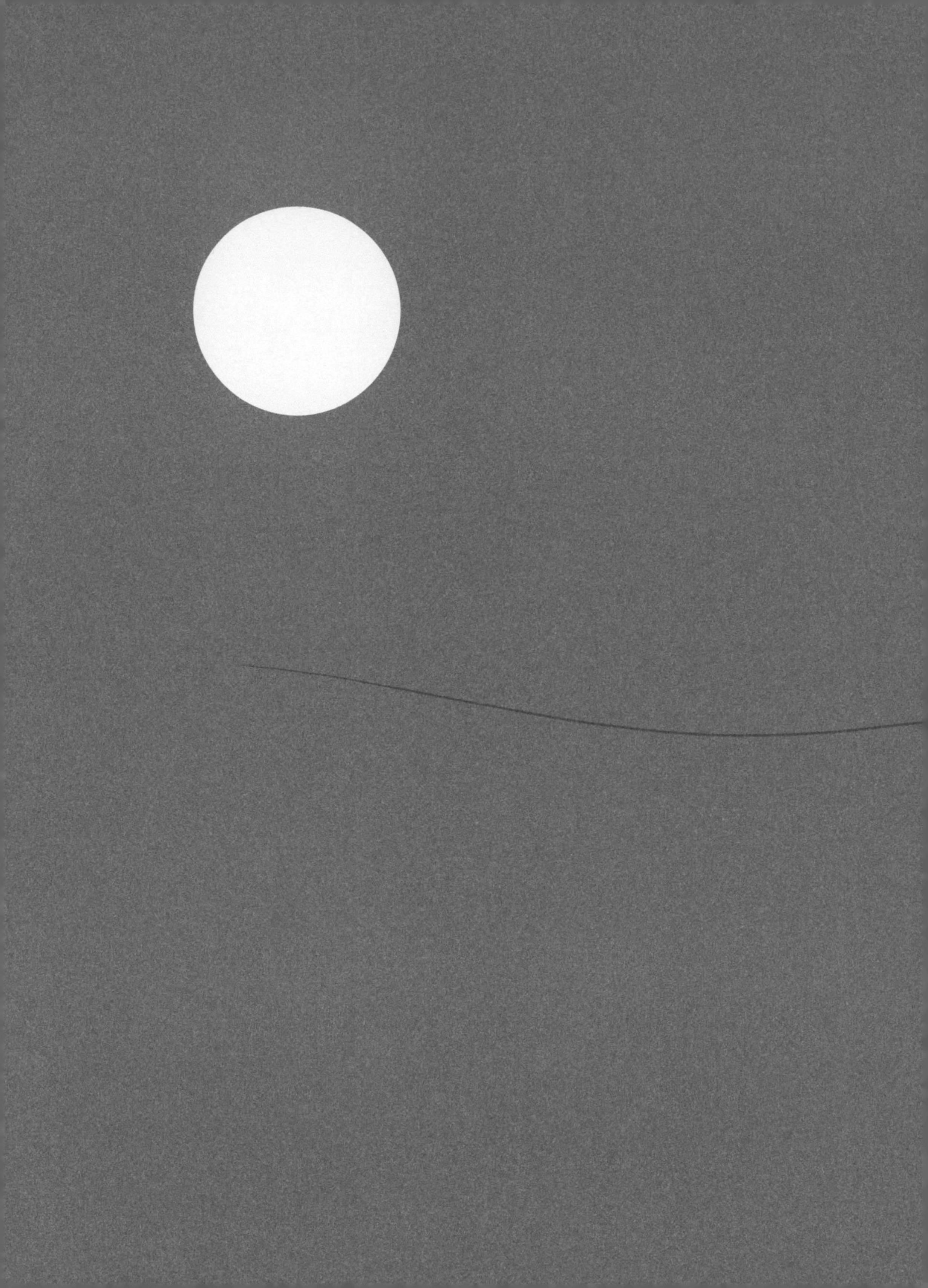

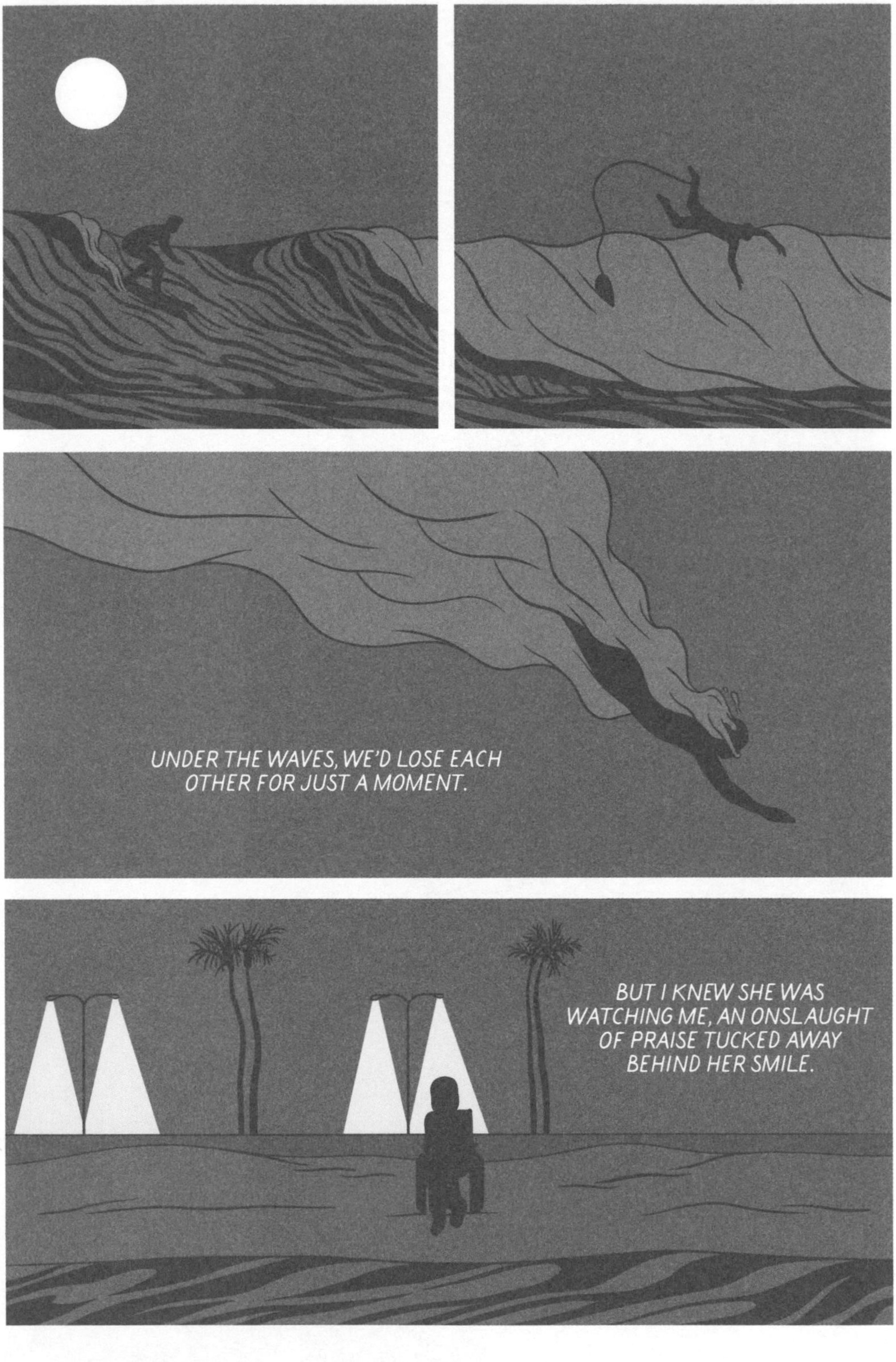
UNDER THE WAVES, WE'D LOSE EACH
OTHER FOR JUST A MOMENT.
BUT I KNEW SHE WAS
WATCHING ME, AN ONSLAUGHT
OF PRAISE TUCKED AWAY
BEHIND HER SMILE.

*MONTHS LATER, I WOULD DISCOVER KRISTEN'S JOURNAL.
IN ONE OF HER LAST PASSAGES SHE WROTE:*

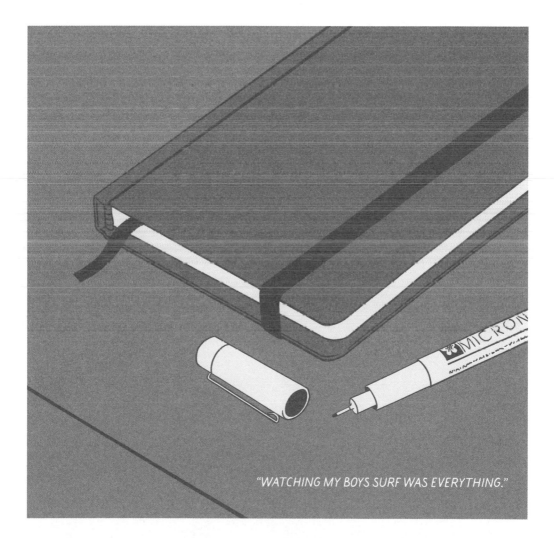

"WATCHING MY BOYS SURF WAS EVERYTHING."

VIII. MOVING PICTURES

Winter
2016

Pasadena, California

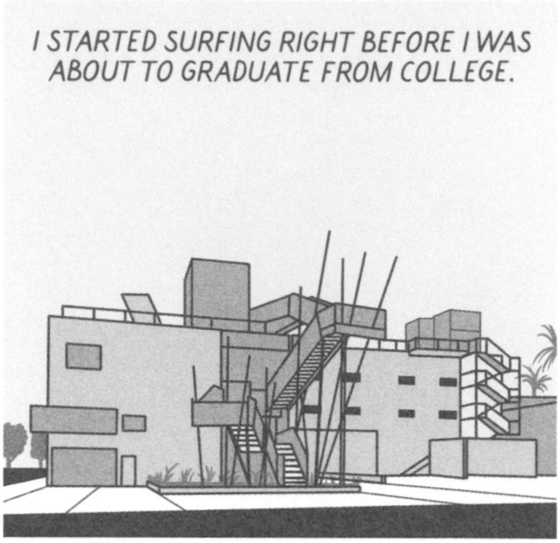
I STARTED SURFING RIGHT BEFORE I WAS ABOUT TO GRADUATE FROM COLLEGE.

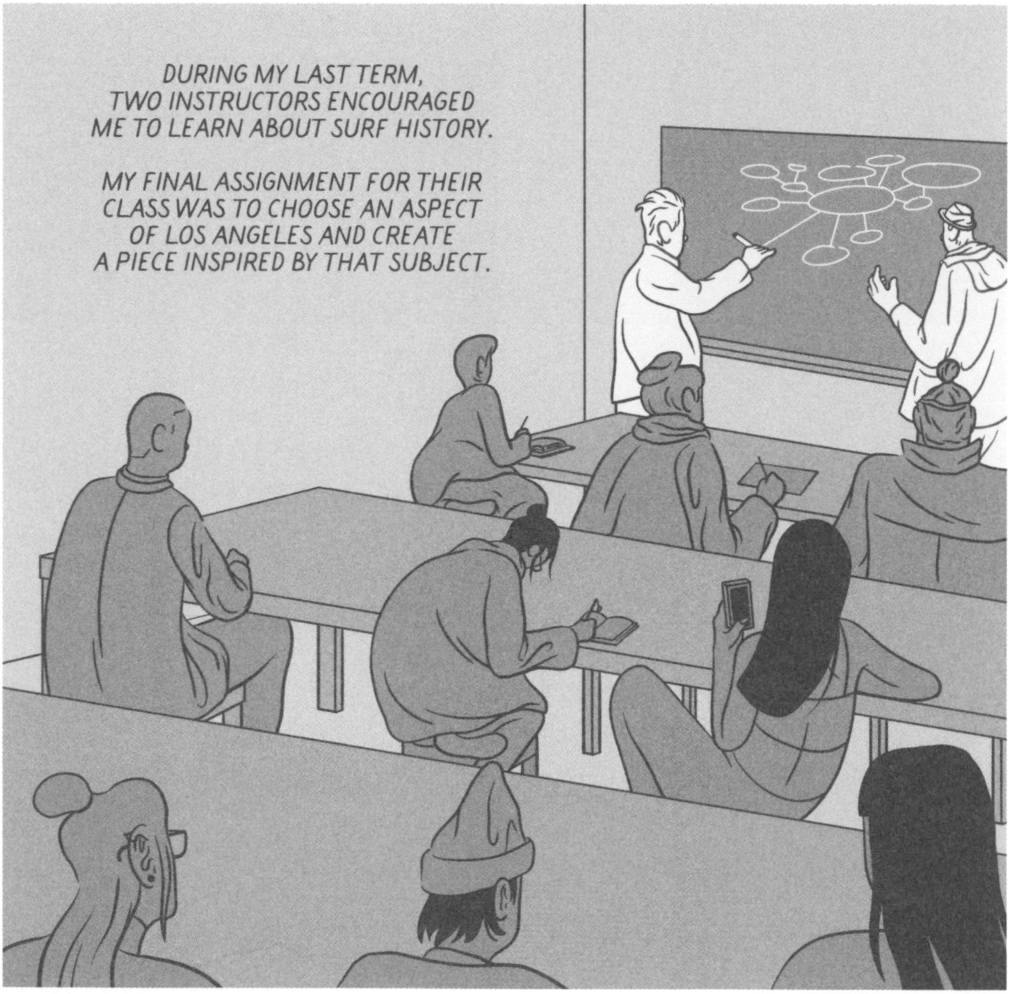
DURING MY LAST TERM, TWO INSTRUCTORS ENCOURAGED ME TO LEARN ABOUT SURF HISTORY.
MY FINAL ASSIGNMENT FOR THEIR CLASS WAS TO CHOOSE AN ASPECT OF LOS ANGELES AND CREATE A PIECE INSPIRED BY THAT SUBJECT.

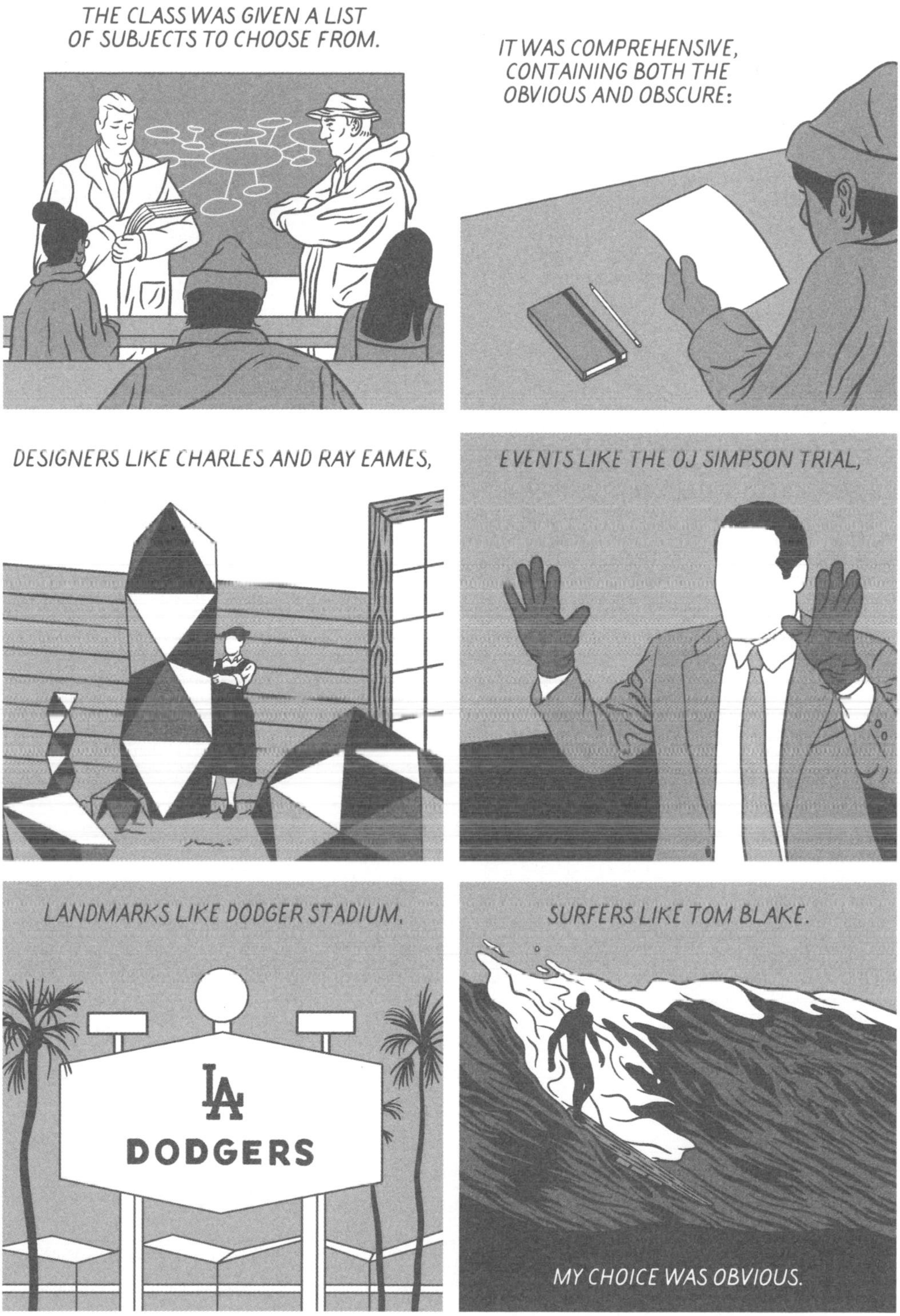
THE CLASS WAS GIVEN A LIST OF SUBJECTS TO CHOOSE FROM.
IT WAS COMPREHENSIVE, CONTAINING BOTH THE OBVIOUS AND OBSCURE:
DESIGNERS LIKE CHARLES AND RAY EAMES,
EVENTS LIKE THE OJ SIMPSON TRIAL,
LANDMARKS LIKE DODGER STADIUM,
LA
DODGERS
SURFERS LIKE TOM BLAKE.
MY CHOICE WAS OBVIOUS.

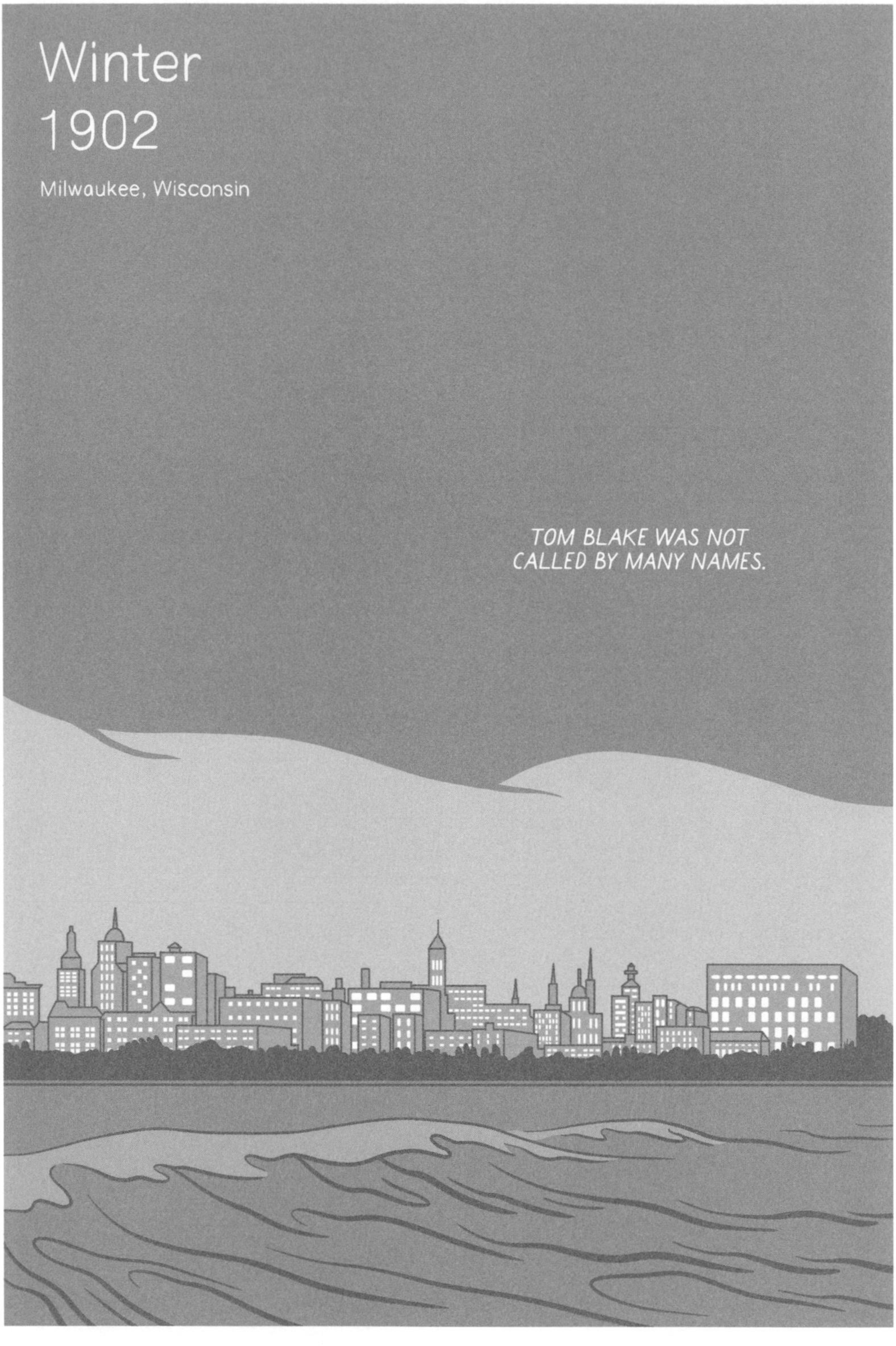
Winter
1902
Milwaukee, Wisconsin
TOM BLAKE WAS NOT CALLED BY MANY NAMES.

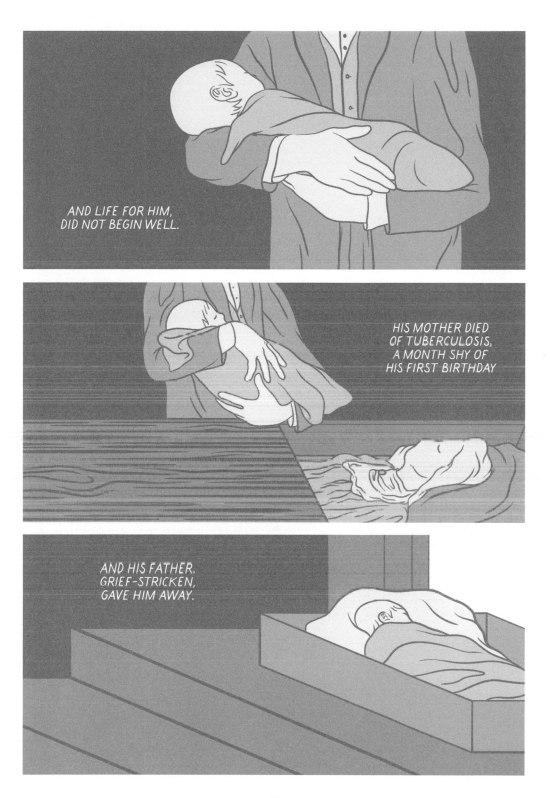

AND LIFE FOR HIM,
DID NOT BEGIN WELL.

HIS MOTHER DIED
OF TUBERCULOSIS,
A MONTH SHY OF
HIS FIRST BIRTHDAY

AND HIS FATHER,
GRIEF-STRICKEN,
GAVE HIM AWAY.

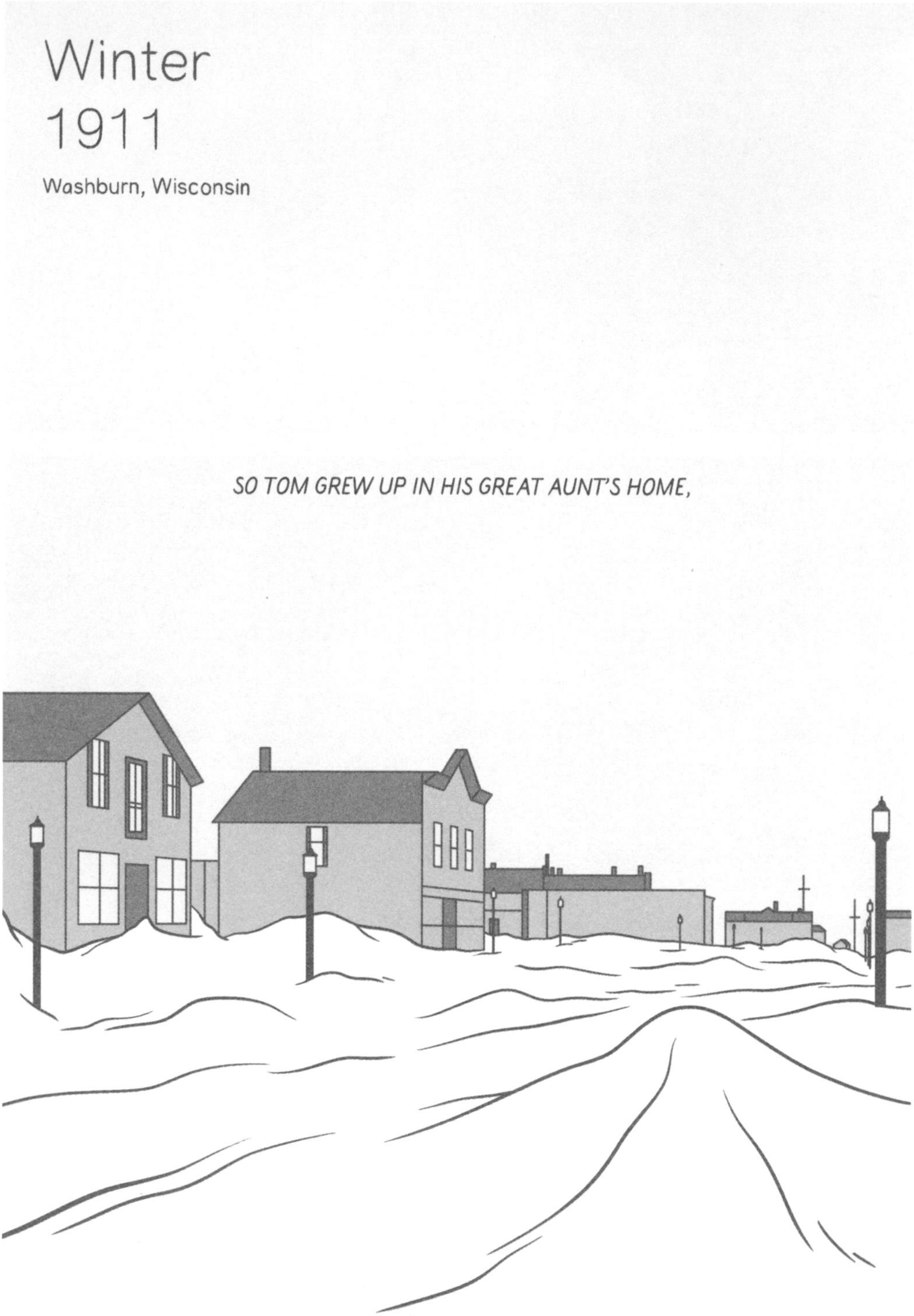
Winter
1911
Washburn, Wisconsin
SO TOM GREW UP IN HIS GREAT AUNT'S HOME,

AND ATTENDED ST. LOUIS CATHOLIC CHURCH AND RECTORY.

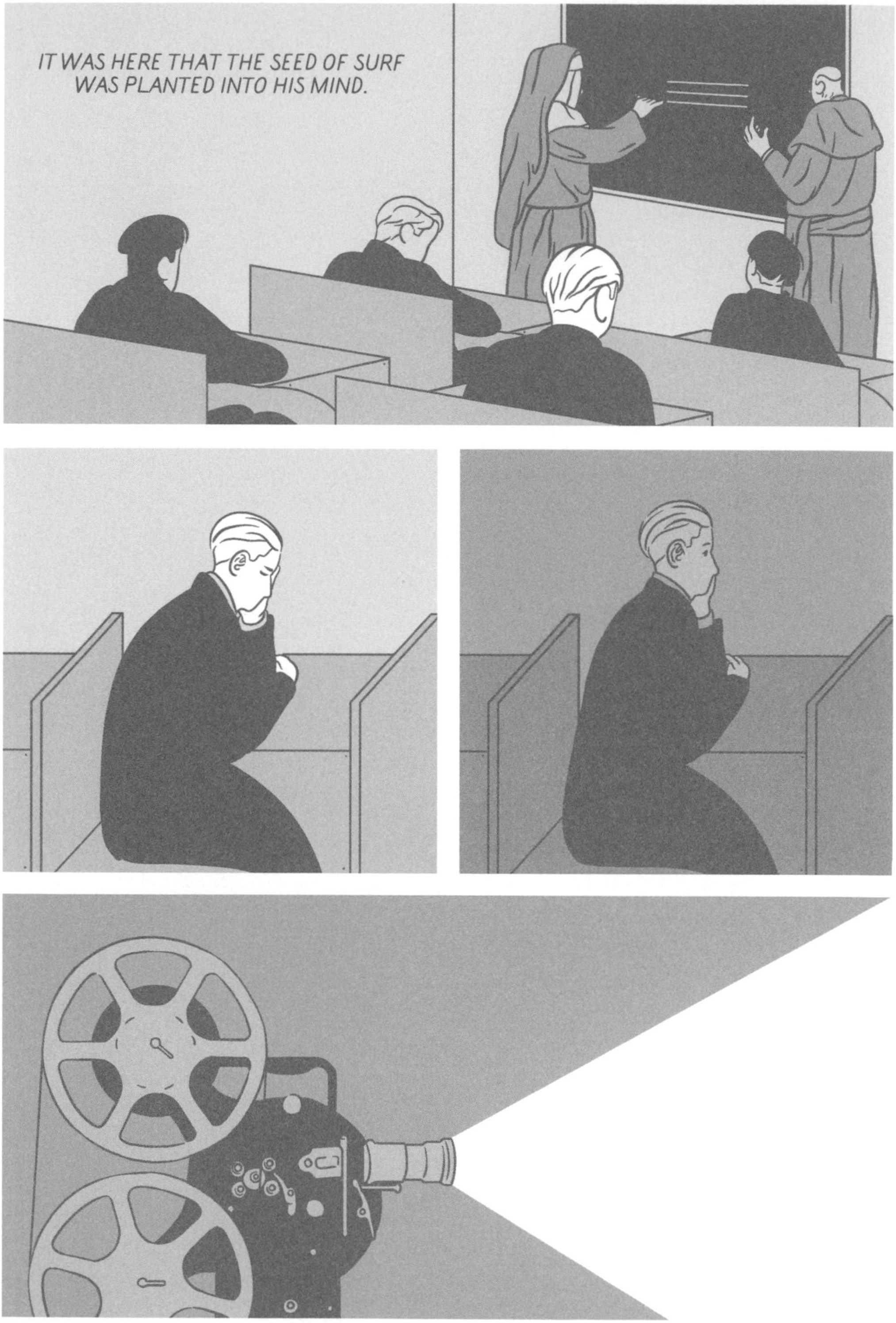
IT WAS HERE THAT THE SEED OF SURF
WAS PLANTED INTO HIS MIND.

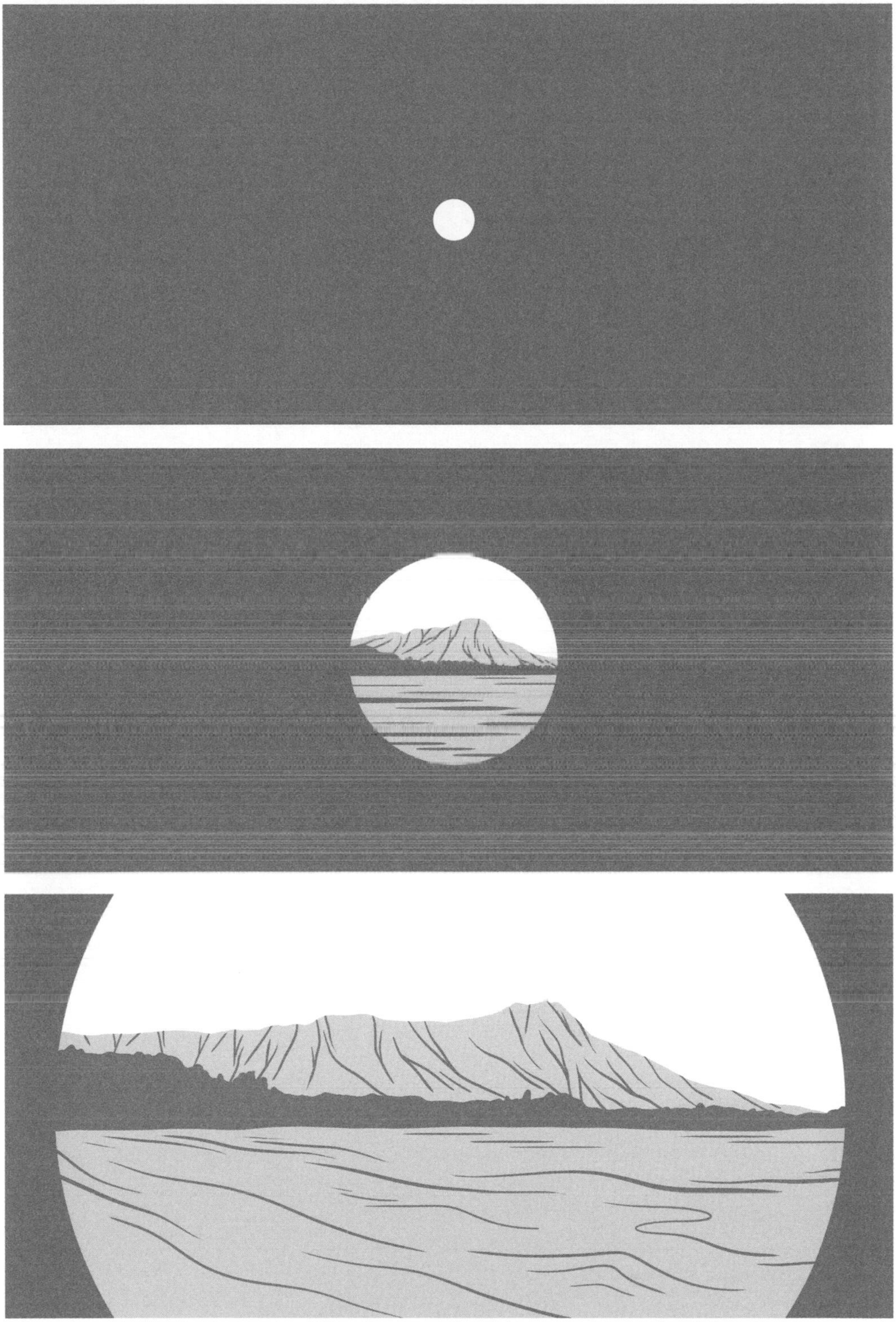

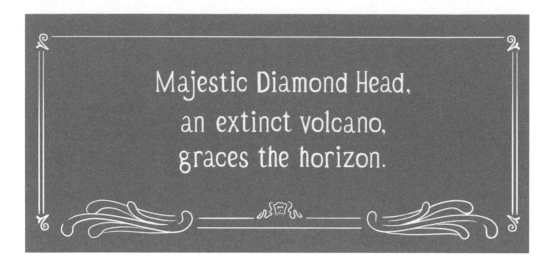

Majestic Diamond Head,
an extinct volcano,
graces the horizon.

All Hawaii
takes to the
waves.

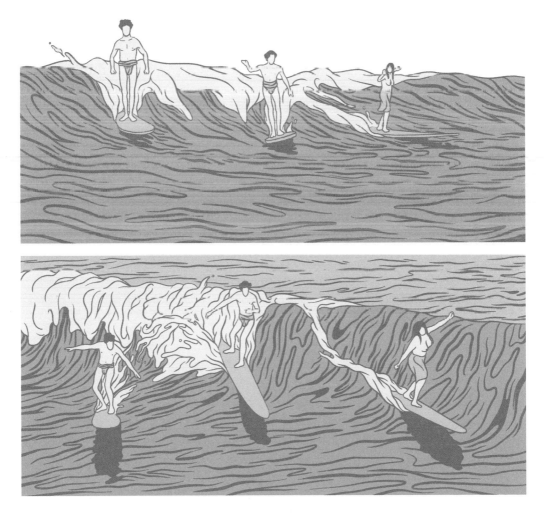

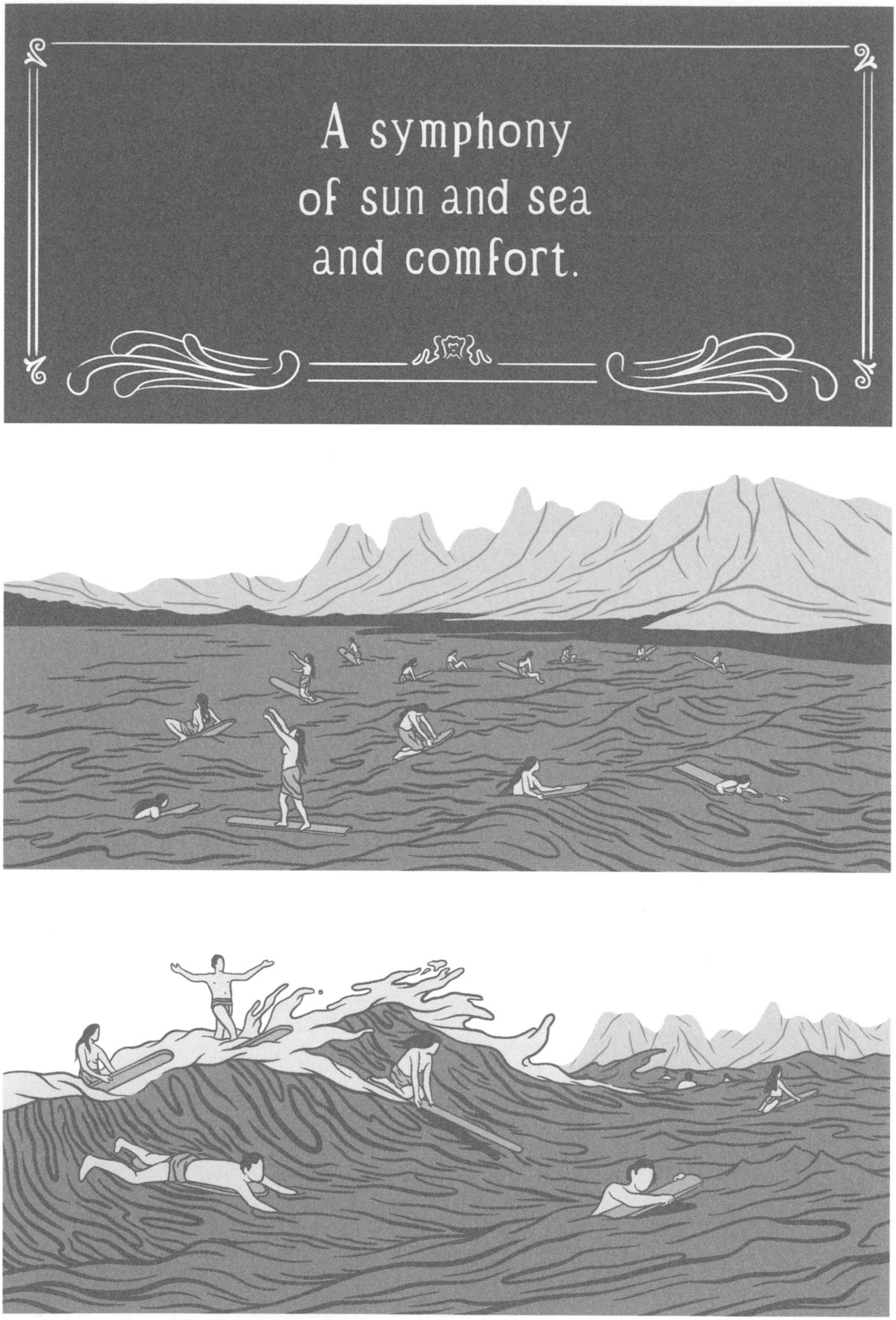
A symphony
of sun and sea
and comfort.

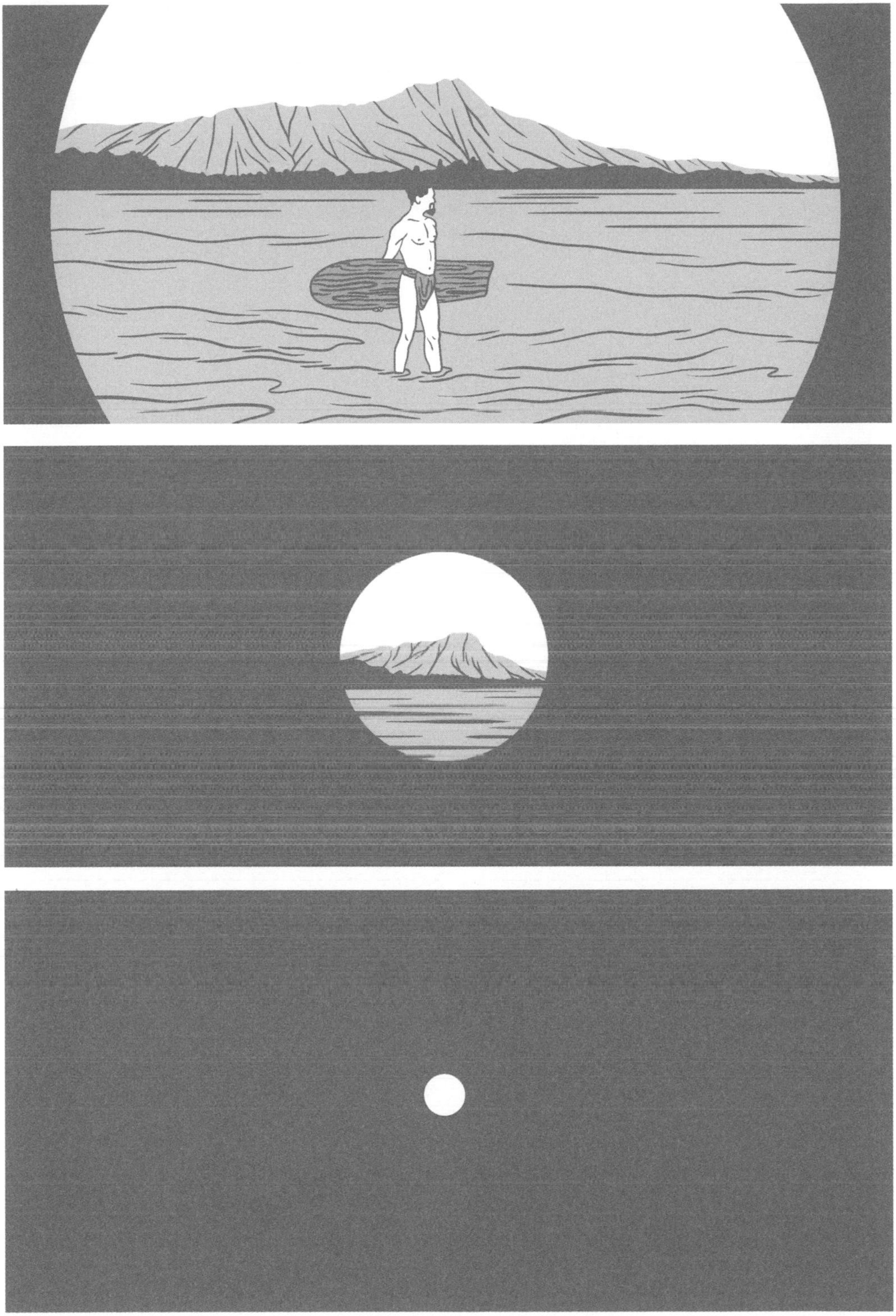

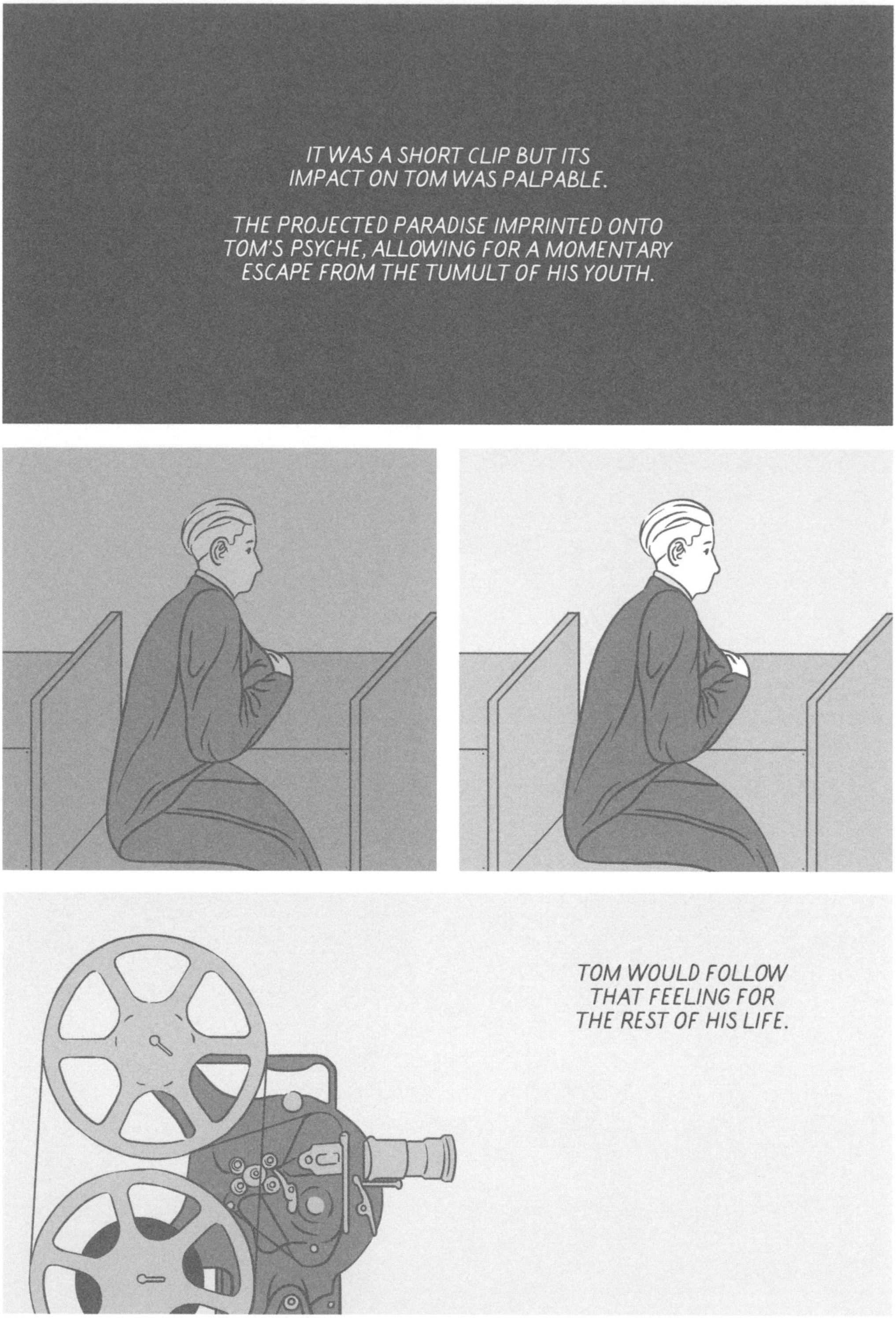
IT WAS A SHORT CLIP BUT ITS IMPACT ON TOM WAS PALPABLE.
THE PROJECTED PARADISE IMPRINTED ONTO TOM'S PSYCHE, ALLOWING FOR A MOMENTARY ESCAPE FROM THE TUMULT OF HIS YOUTH.
TOM WOULD FOLLOW THAT FEELING FOR THE REST OF HIS LIFE.

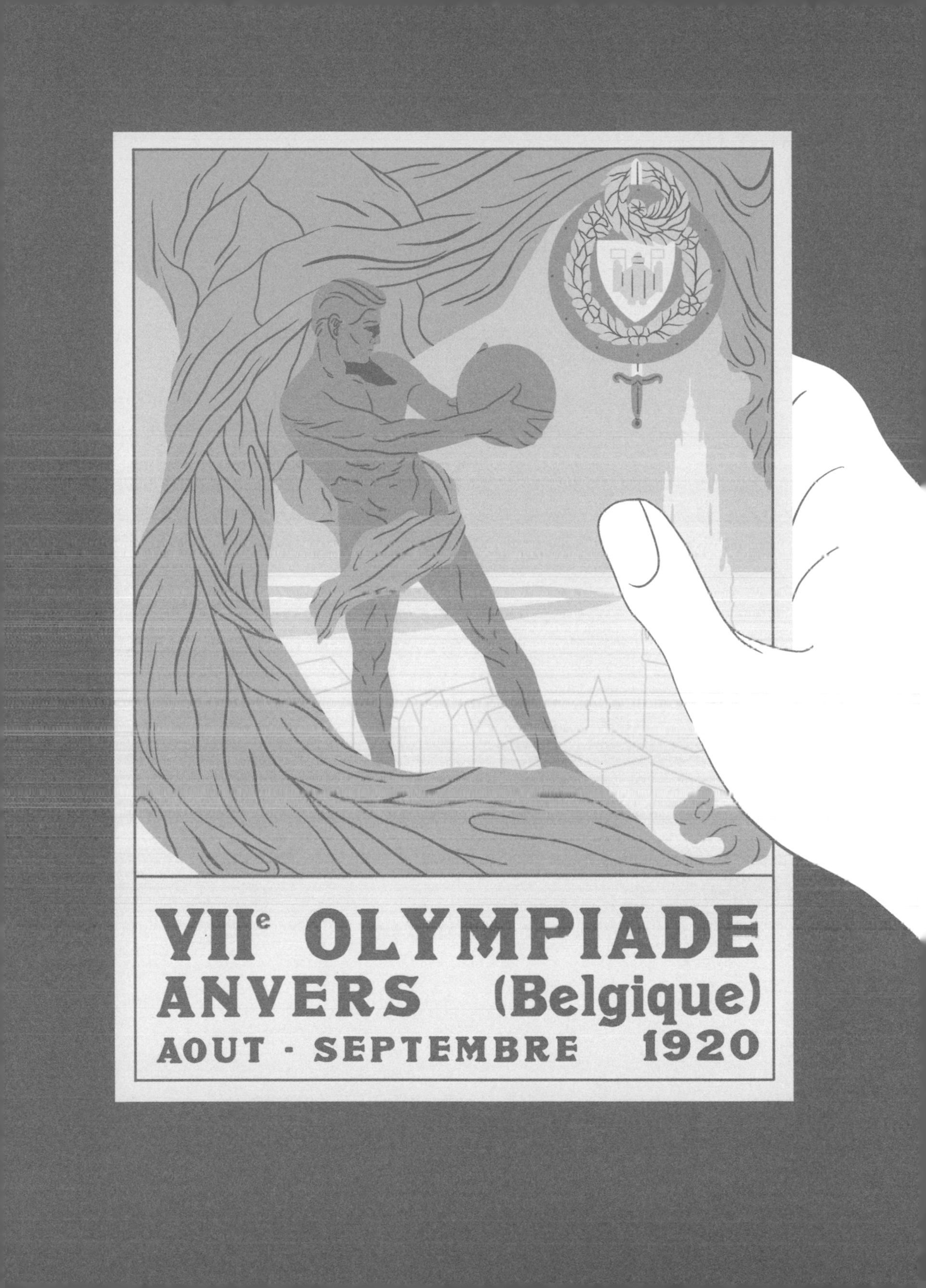
VIIe OLYMPIADE
ANVERS (Belgique)
AOUT - SEPTEMBRE 1920

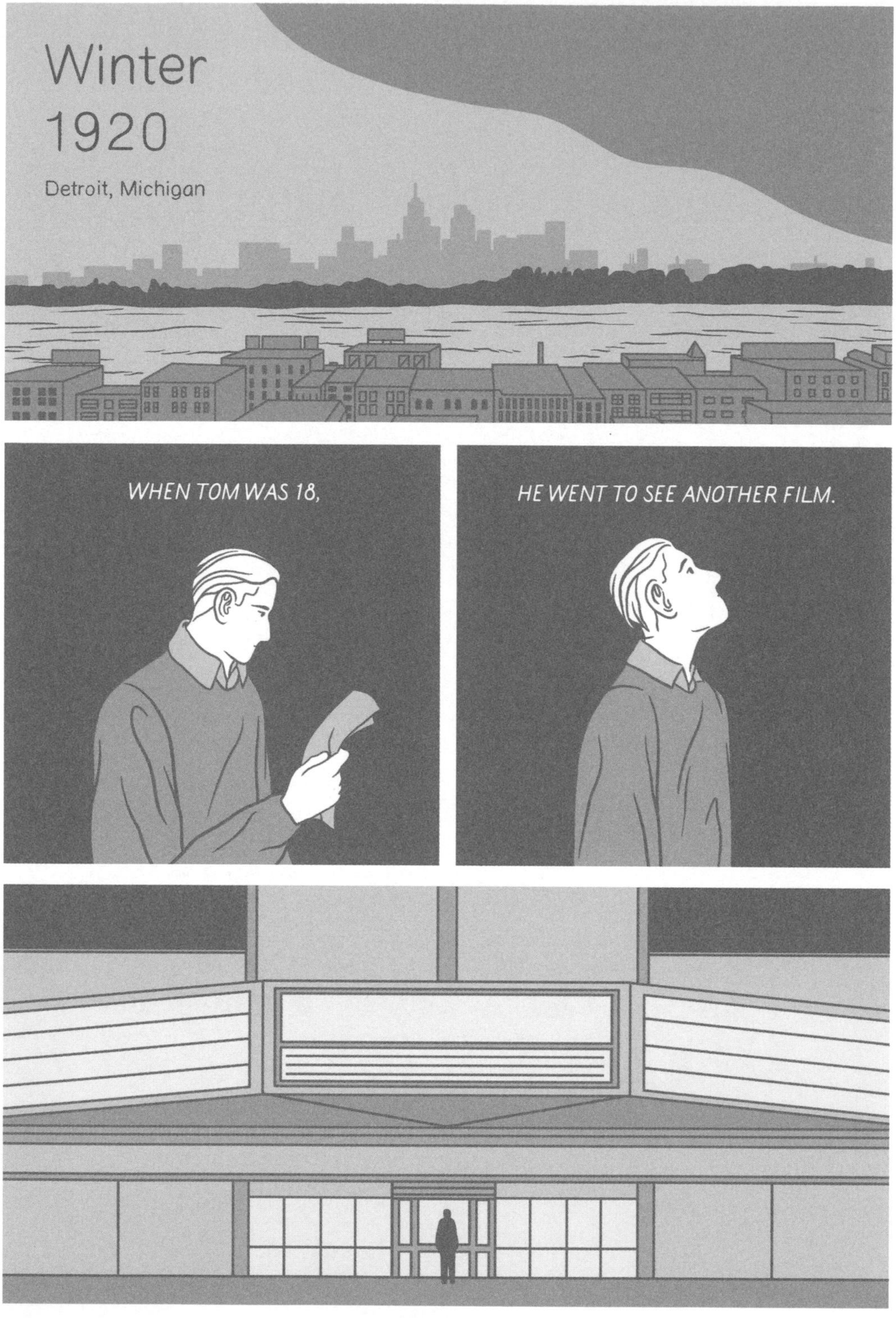
Winter
1920
Detroit, Michigan
WHEN TOM WAS 18,
HE WENT TO SEE ANOTHER FILM.

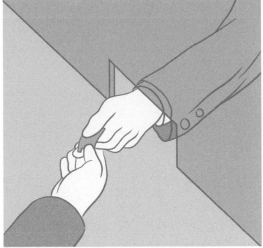
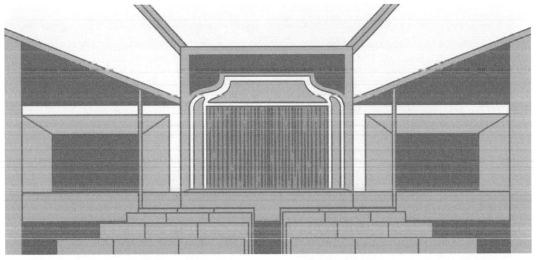
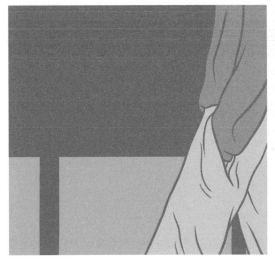

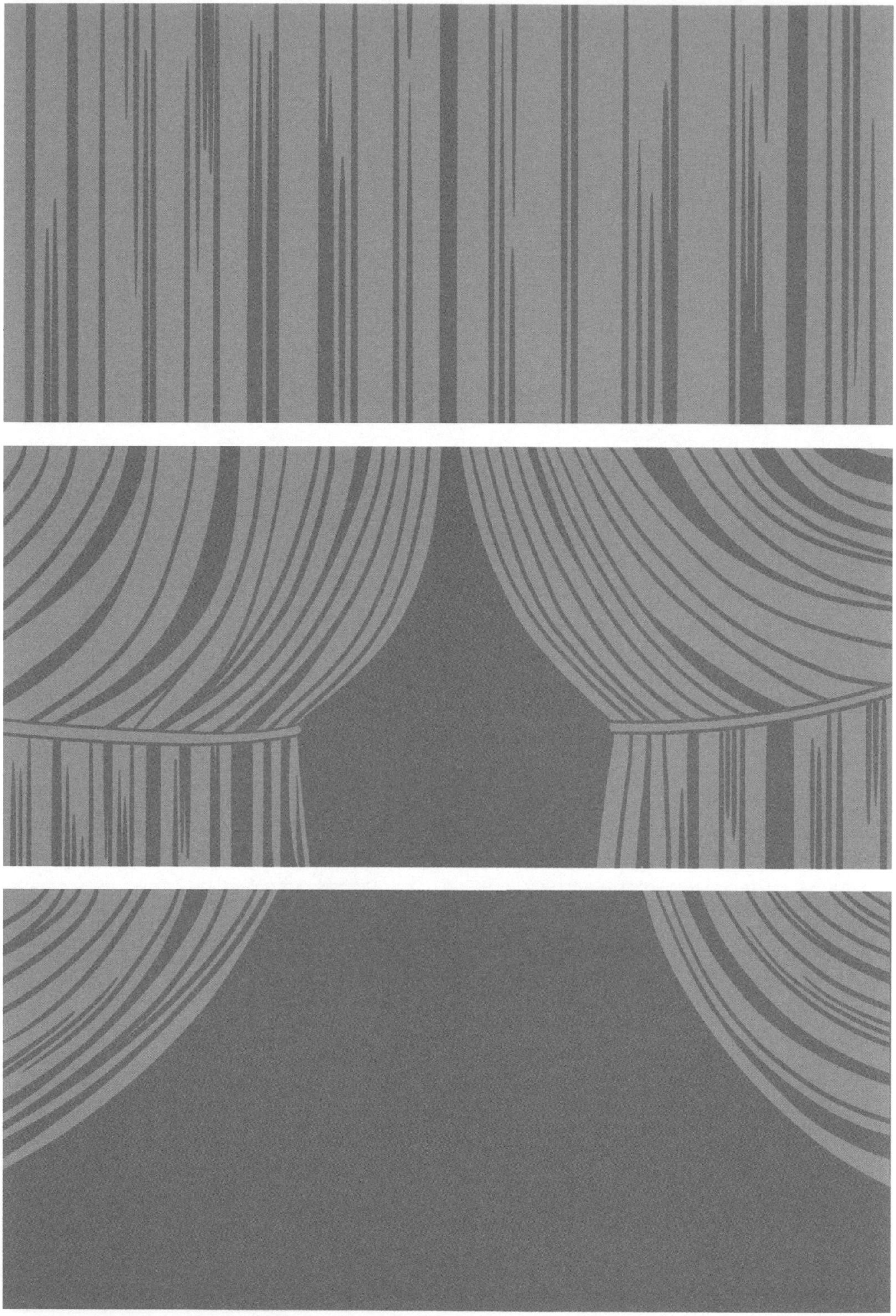

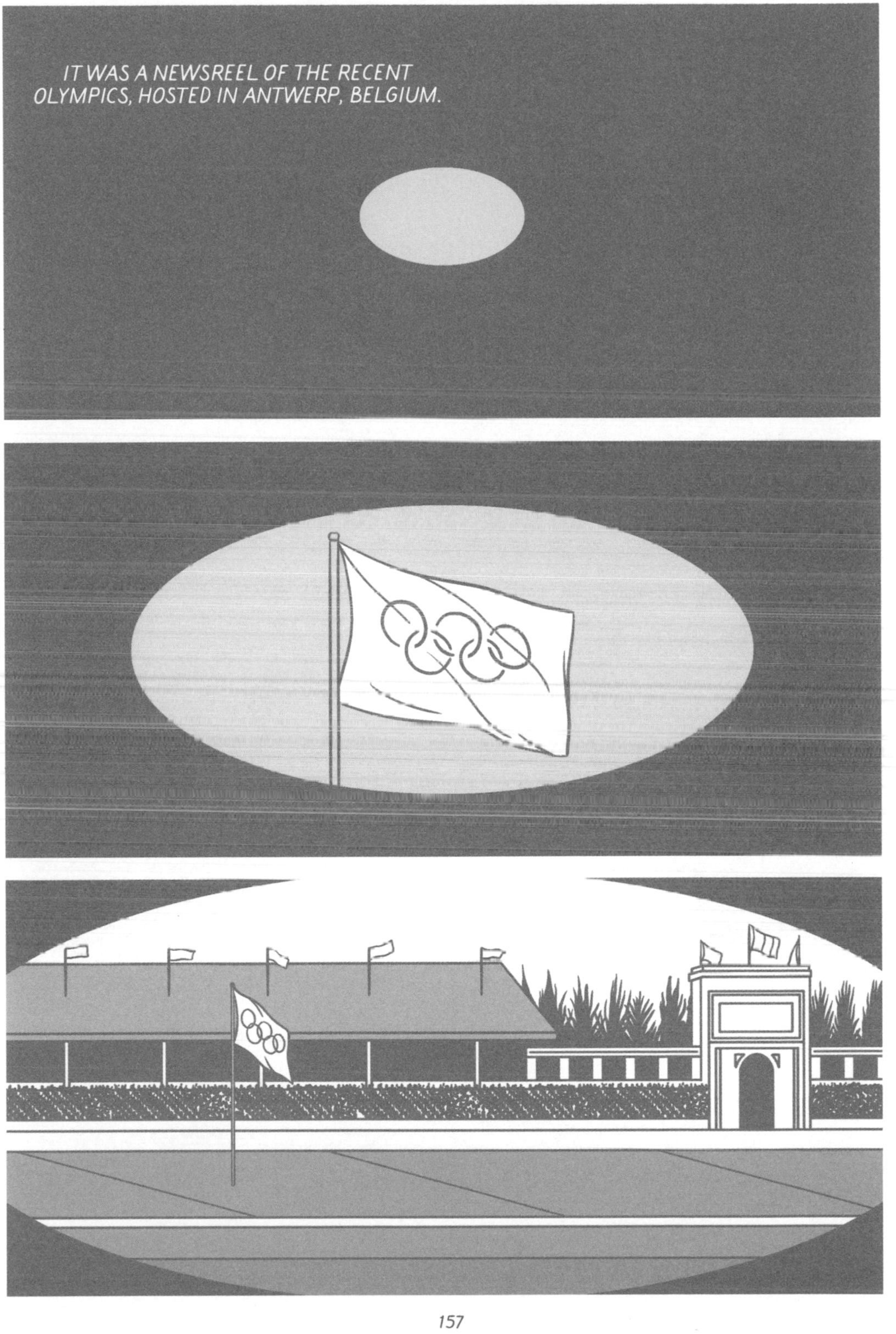
IT WAS A NEWSREEL OF THE RECENT OLYMPICS, HOSTED IN ANTWERP, BELGIUM.

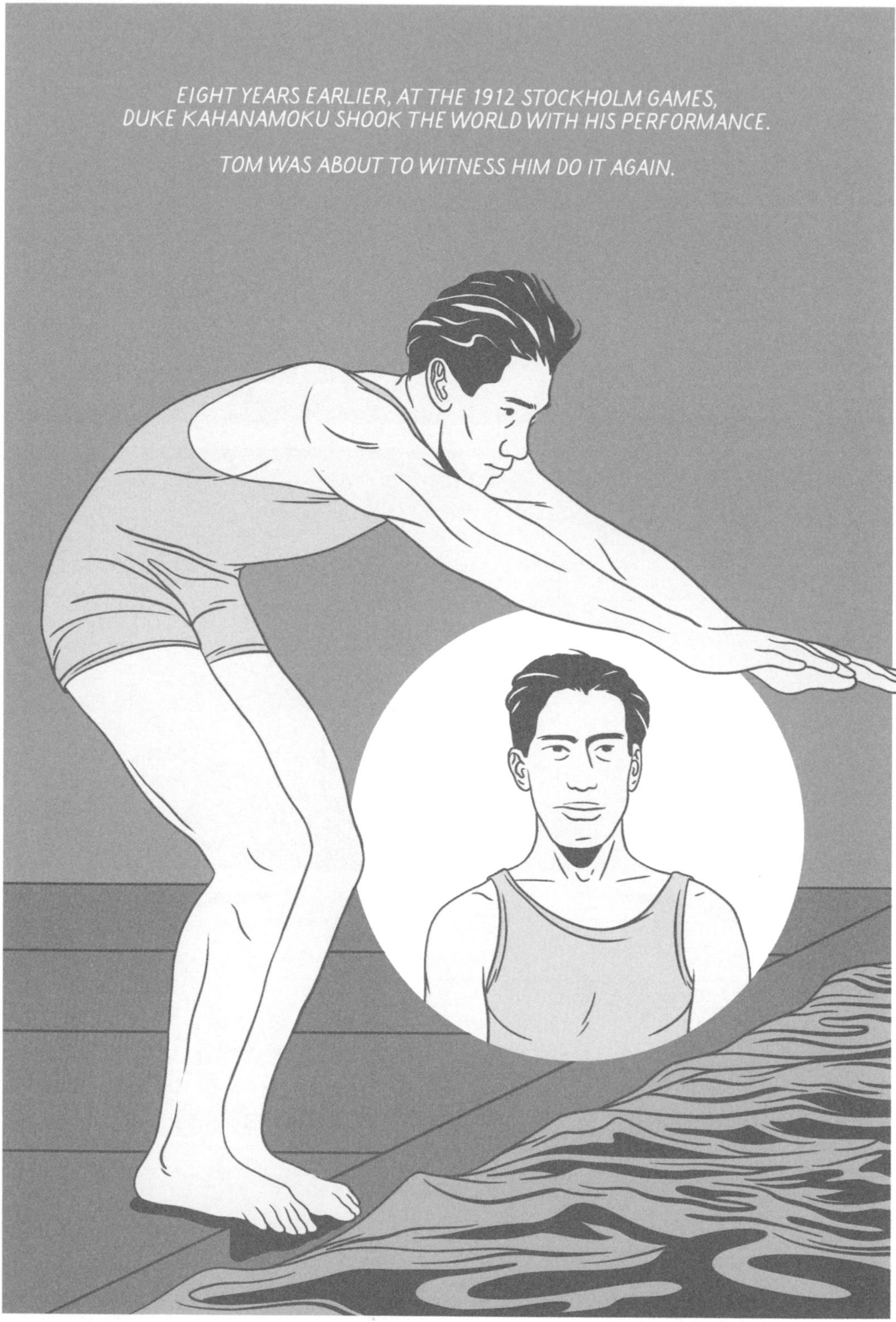
EIGHT YEARS EARLIER, AT THE 1912 STOCKHOLM GAMES, DUKE KAHANAMOKU SHOOK THE WORLD WITH HIS PERFORMANCE.
TOM WAS ABOUT TO WITNESS HIM DO IT AGAIN.

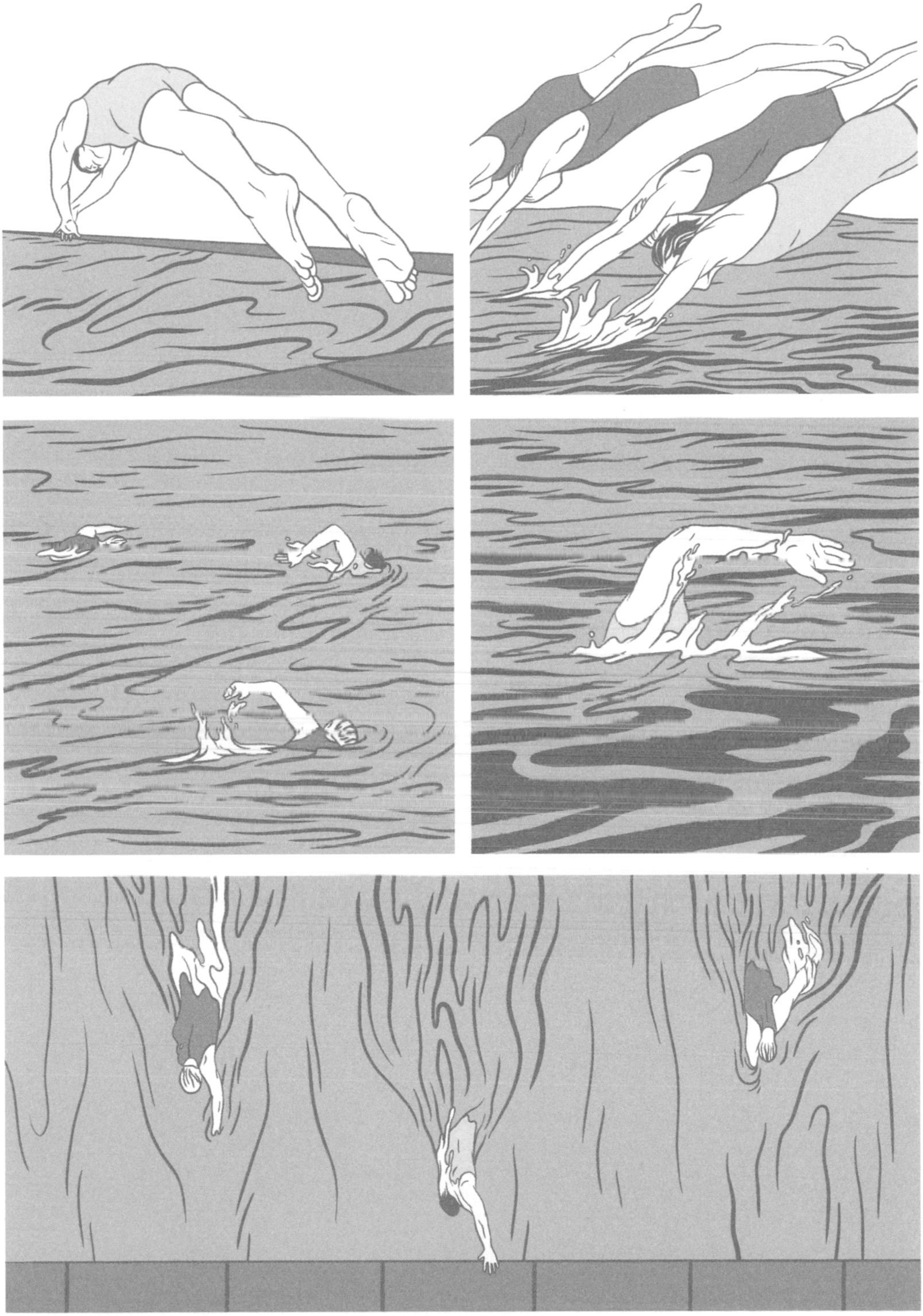

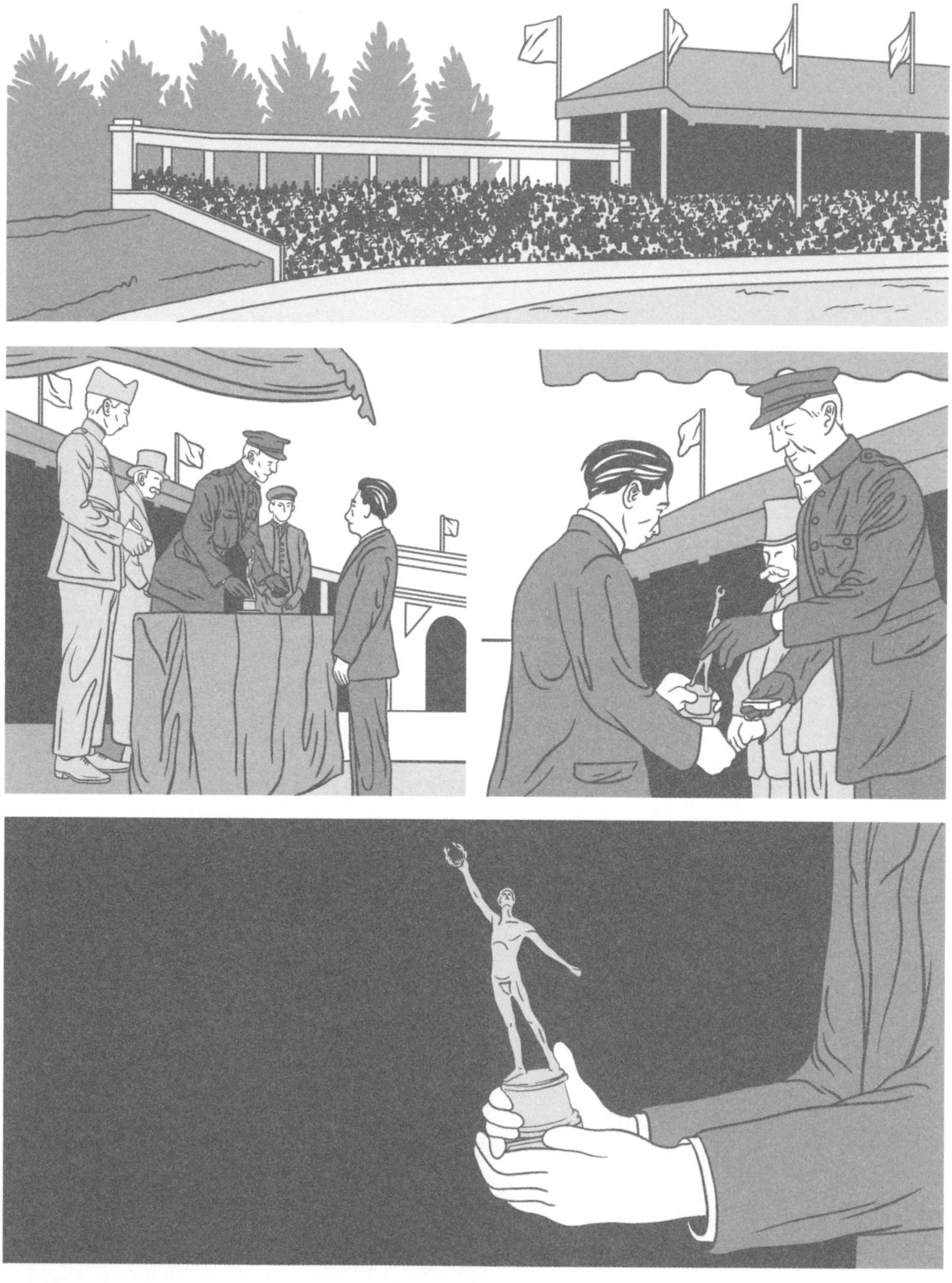

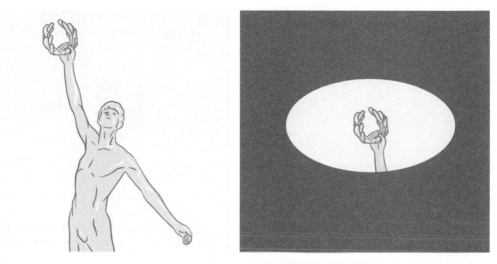

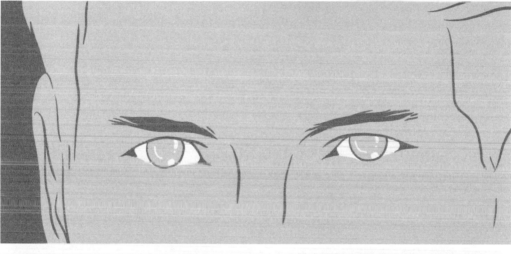

TOM WAS FLOORED.

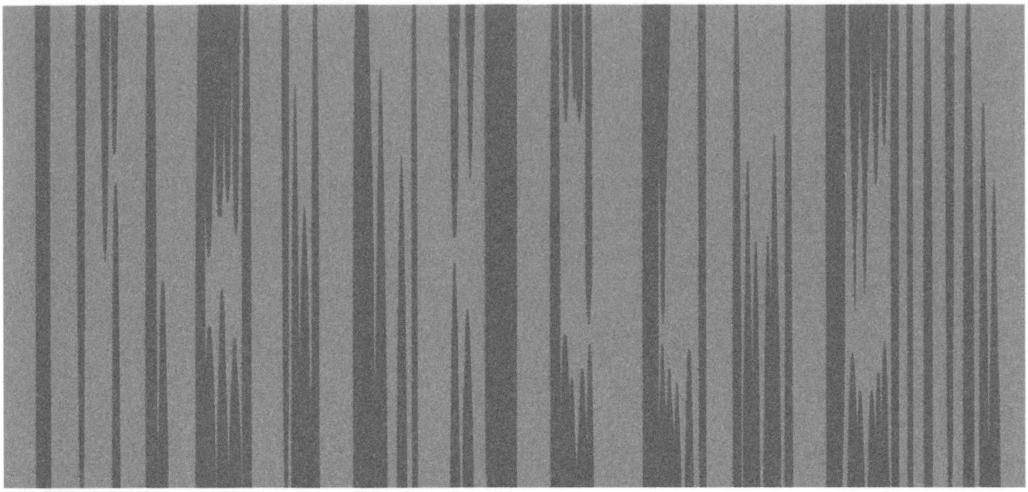

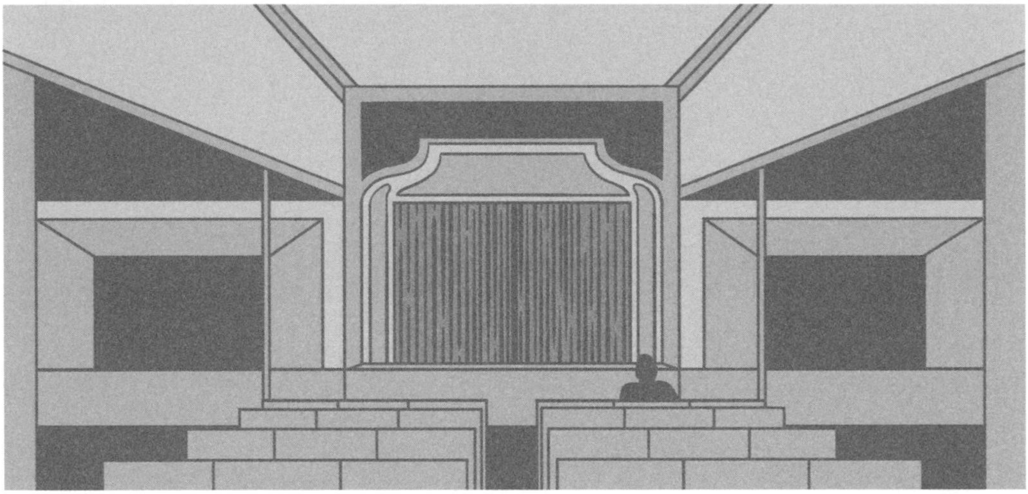

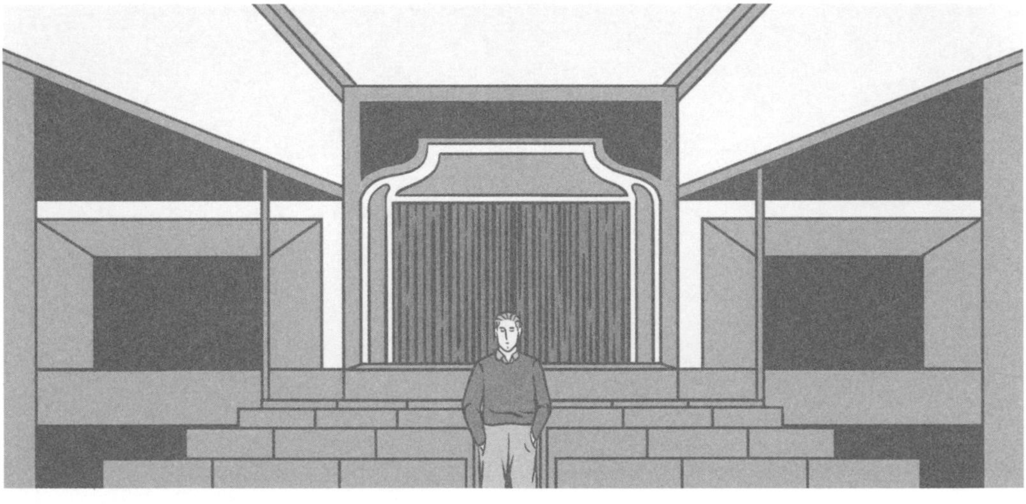

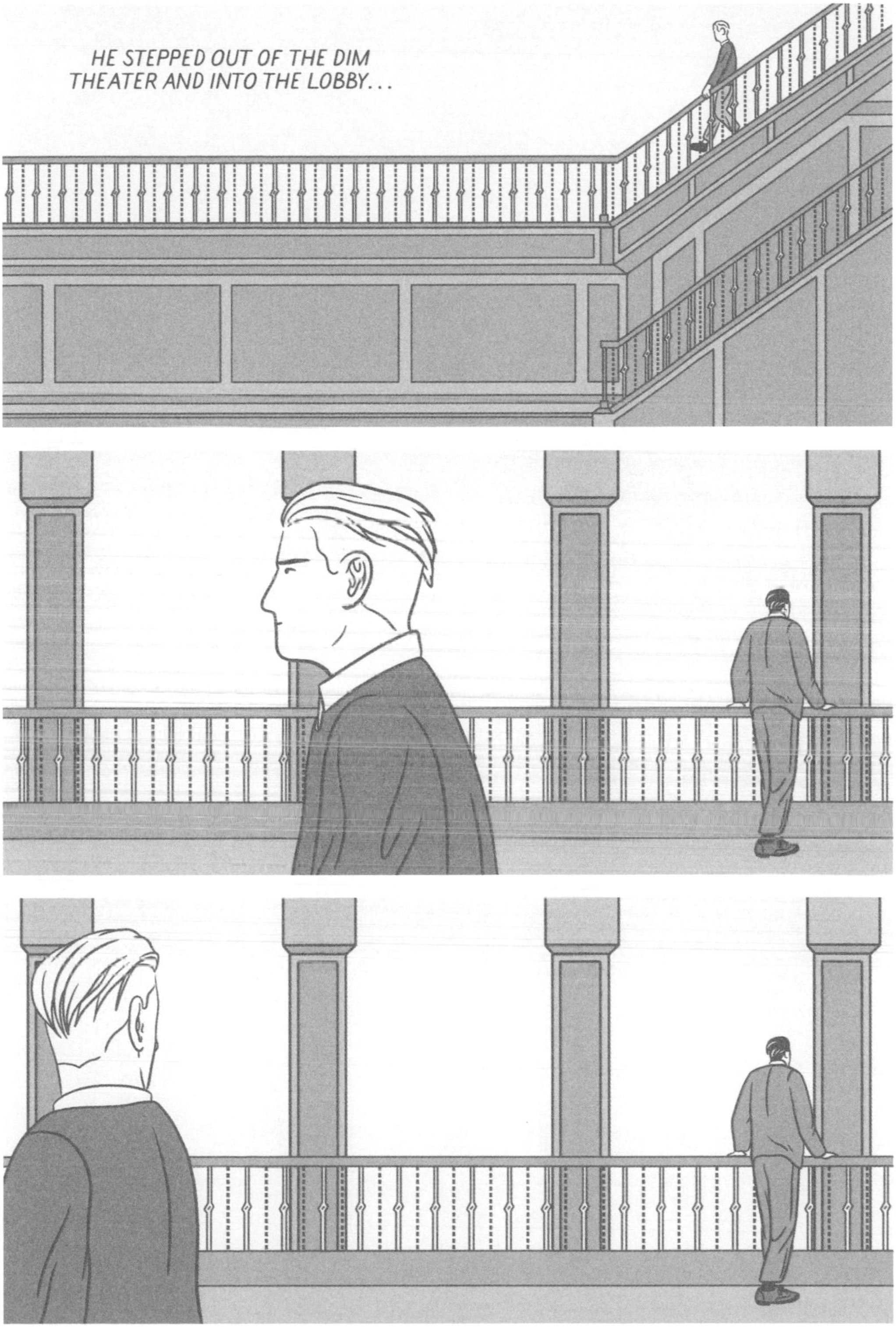
HE STEPPED OUT OF THE DIM THEATER AND INTO THE LOBBY...

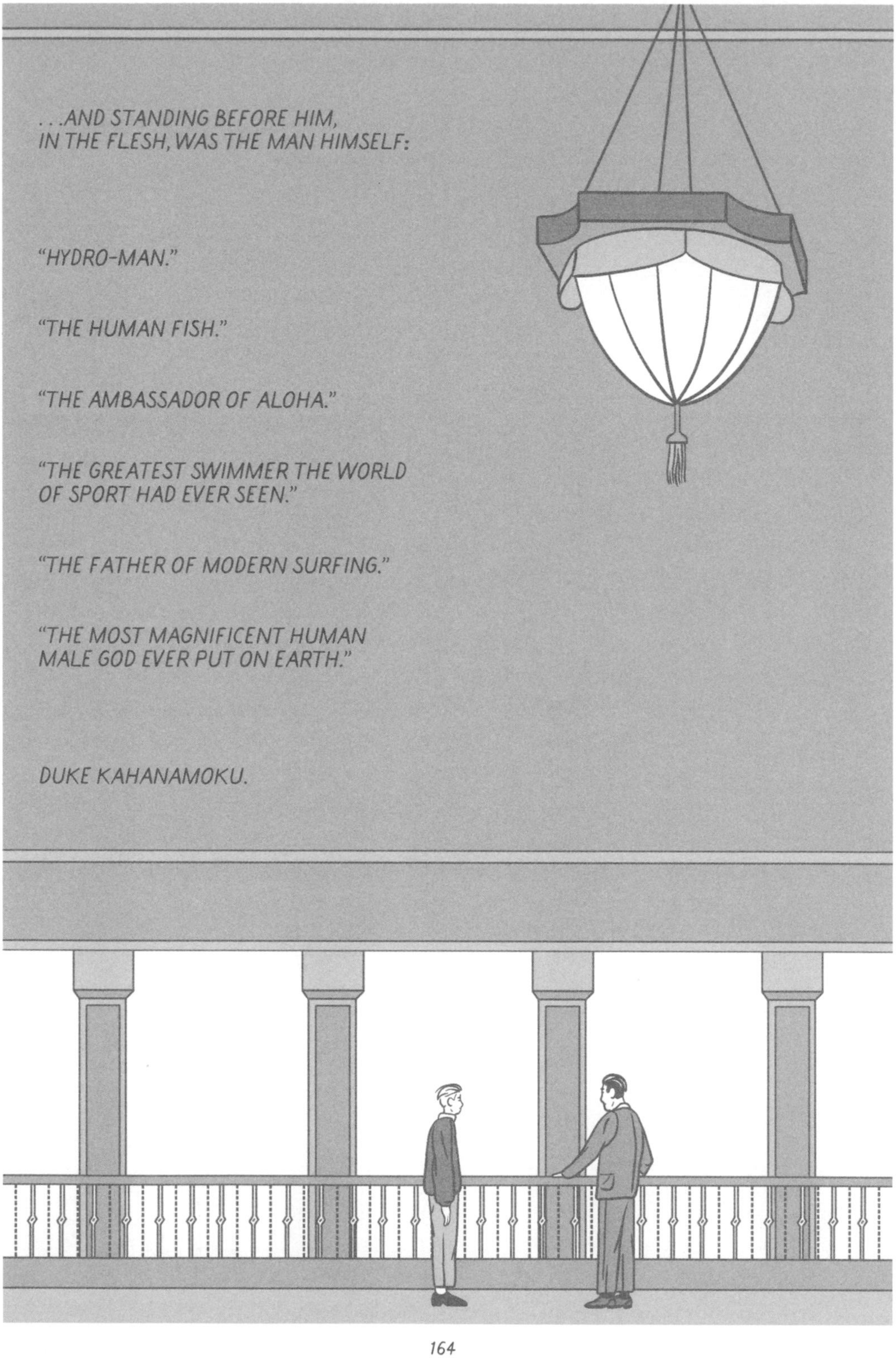
. . .AND STANDING BEFORE HIM,
IN THE FLESH, WAS THE MAN HIMSELF:
"HYDRO-MAN."
"THE HUMAN FISH."
"THE AMBASSADOR OF ALOHA."
"THE GREATEST SWIMMER THE WORLD
OF SPORT HAD EVER SEEN."
"THE FATHER OF MODERN SURFING."
"THE MOST MAGNIFICENT HUMAN
MALE GOD EVER PUT ON EARTH."
DUKE KAHANAMOKU.

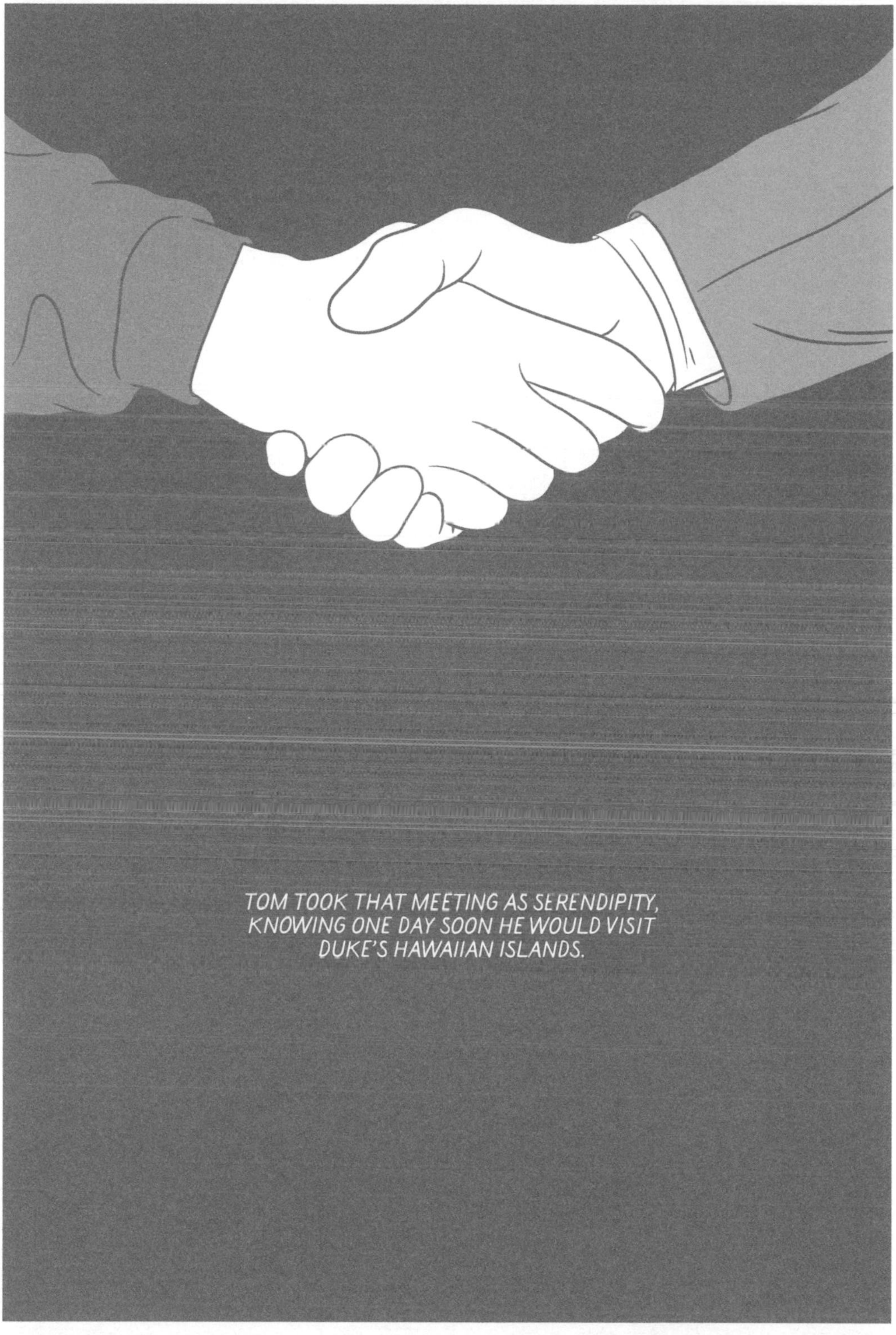
TOM TOOK THAT MEETING AS SERENDIPITY, KNOWING ONE DAY SOON HE WOULD VISIT DUKE'S HAWAIIAN ISLANDS.

IX. SCHOOL DANCE

Fall
2017

Cypress, California

I CAN'T REALLY RECALL EXACTLY HOW WE MET.

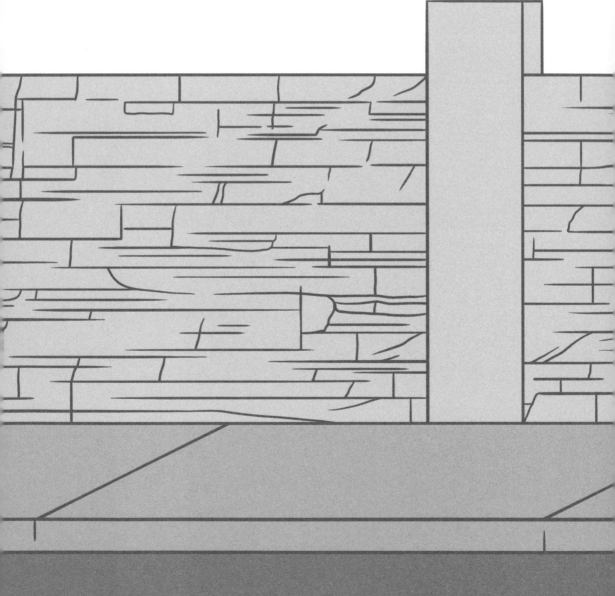

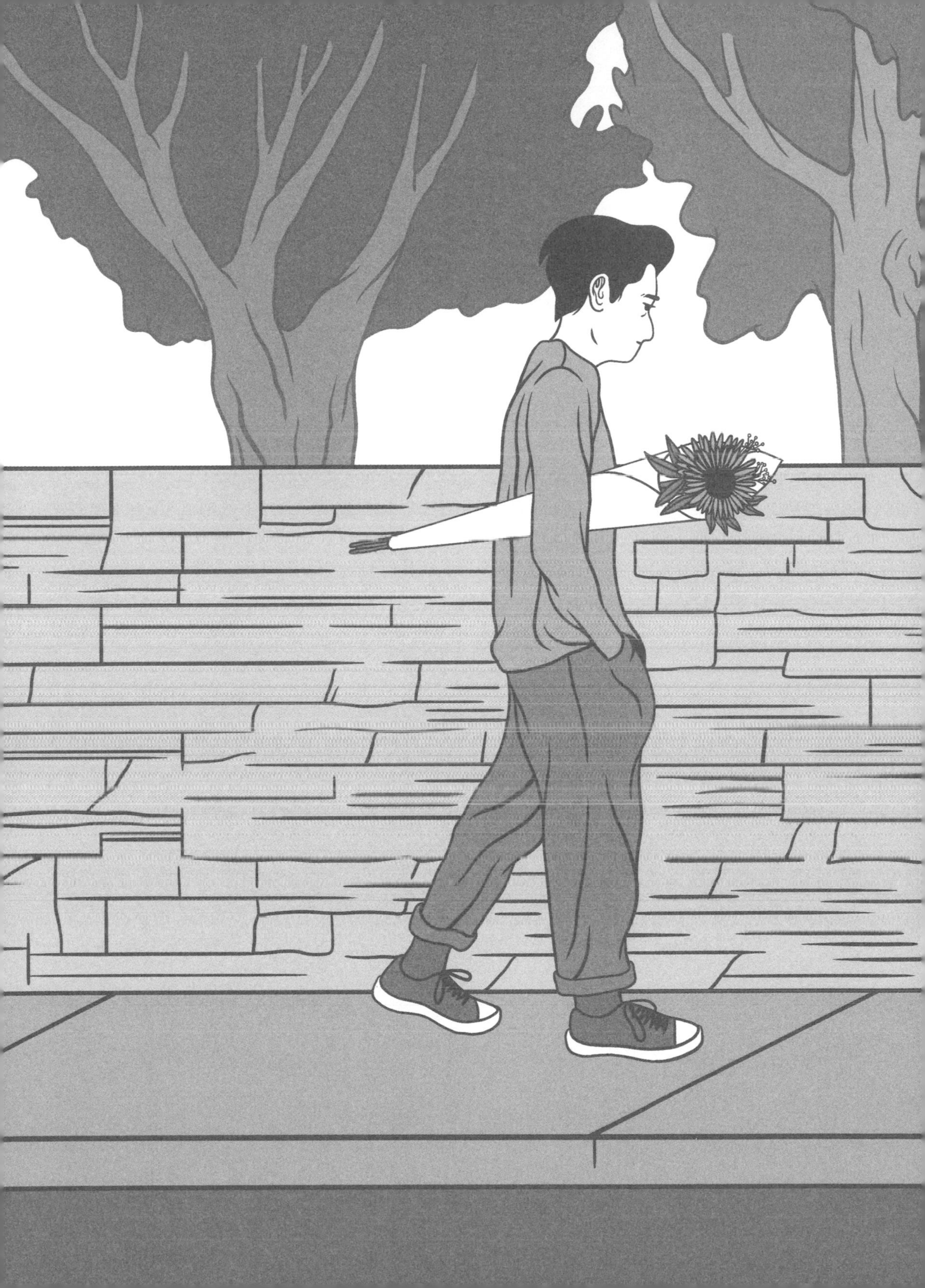

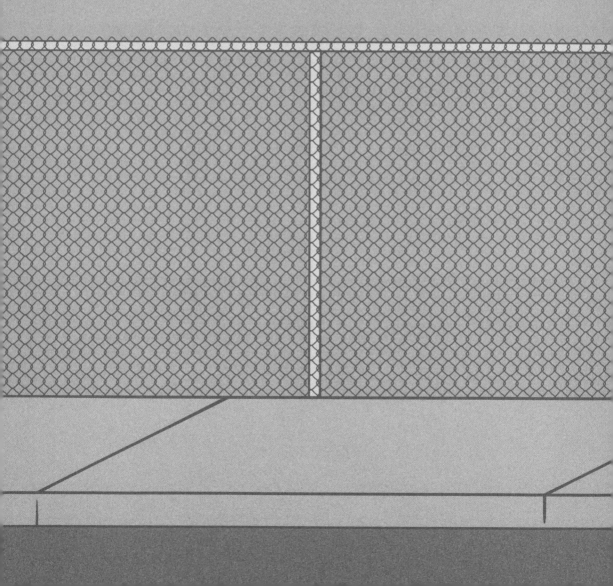

Fall
2005

Bellflower, California

BUT I CAN PIECE TOGETHER SMALL MOMENTS.

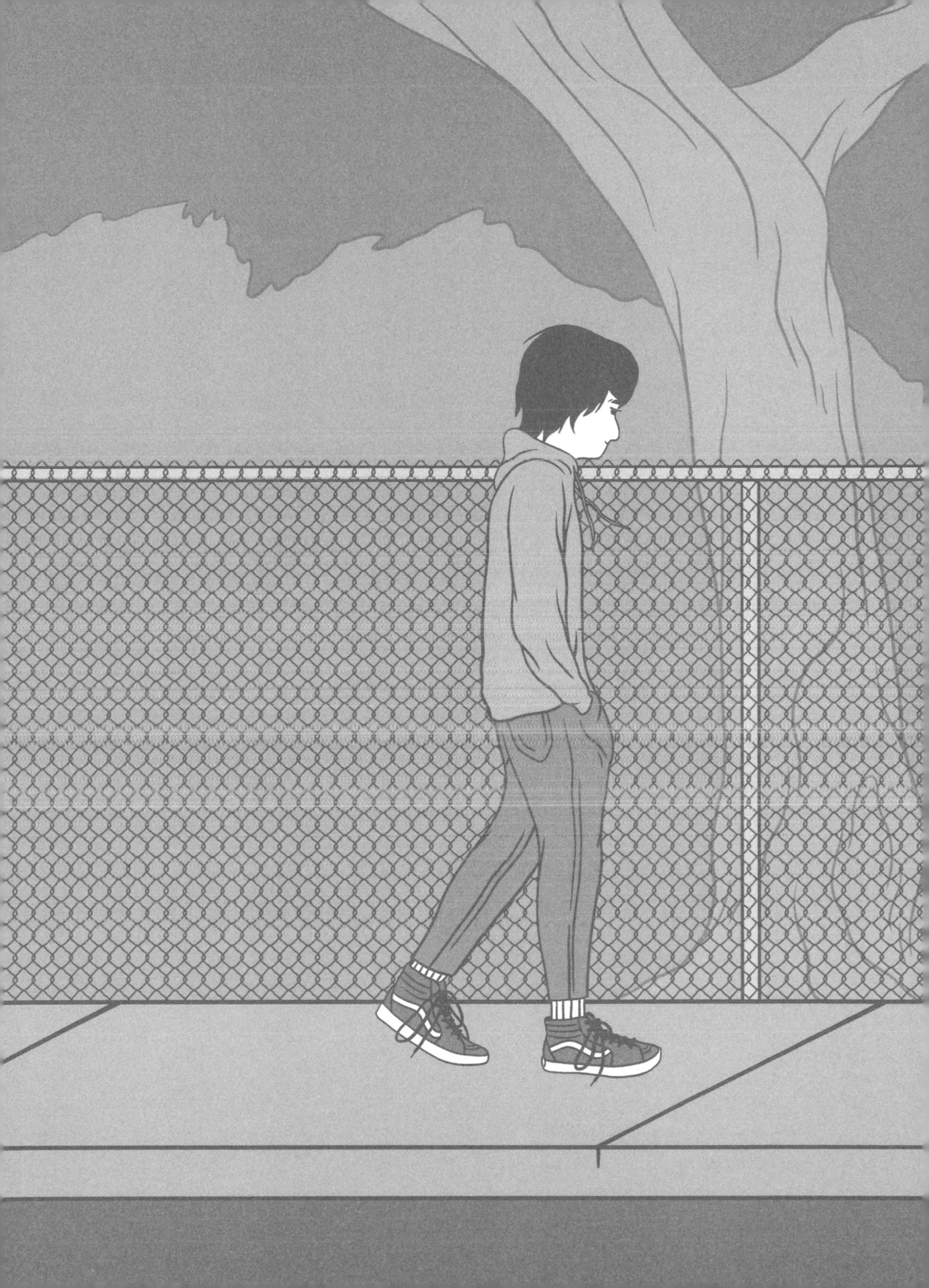

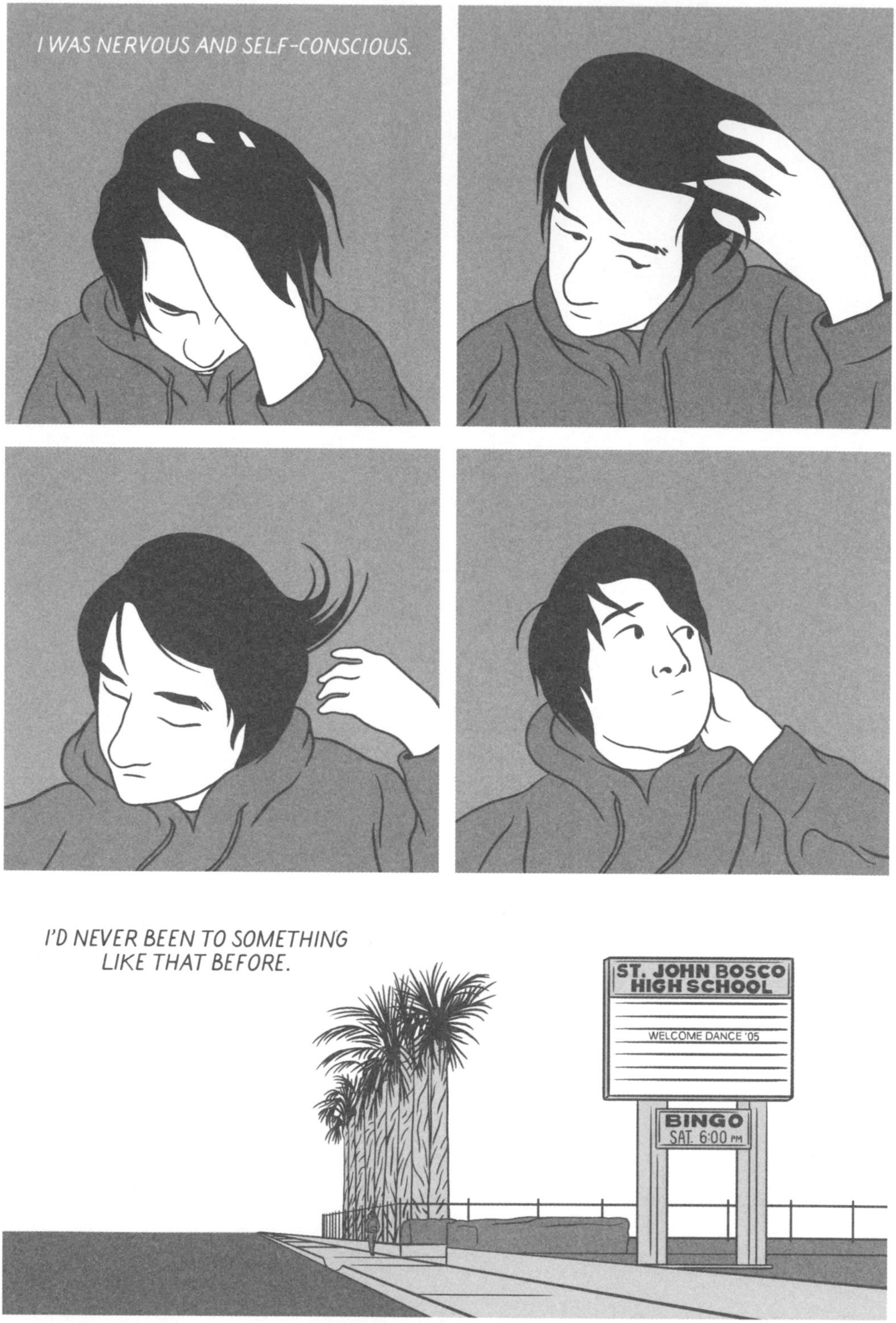
I WAS NERVOUS AND SELF-CONSCIOUS.
I'D NEVER BEEN TO SOMETHING LIKE THAT BEFORE.
ST. JOHN BOSCO HIGH SCHOOL
WELCOME DANCE '05
BINGO
SAT. 6:00 PM

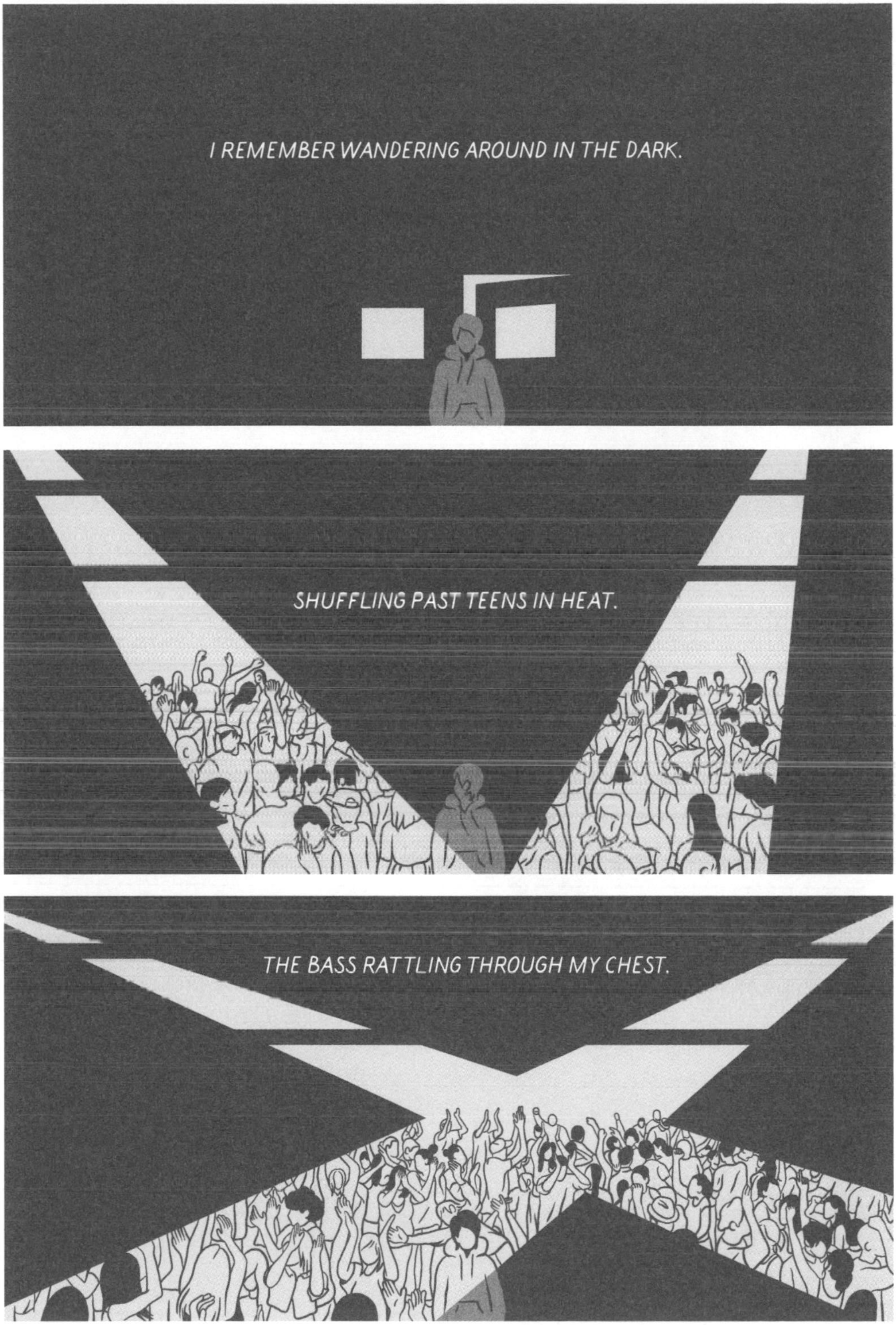
I REMEMBER WANDERING AROUND IN THE DARK.
SHUFFLING PAST TEENS IN HEAT.
THE BASS RATTLING THROUGH MY CHEST.

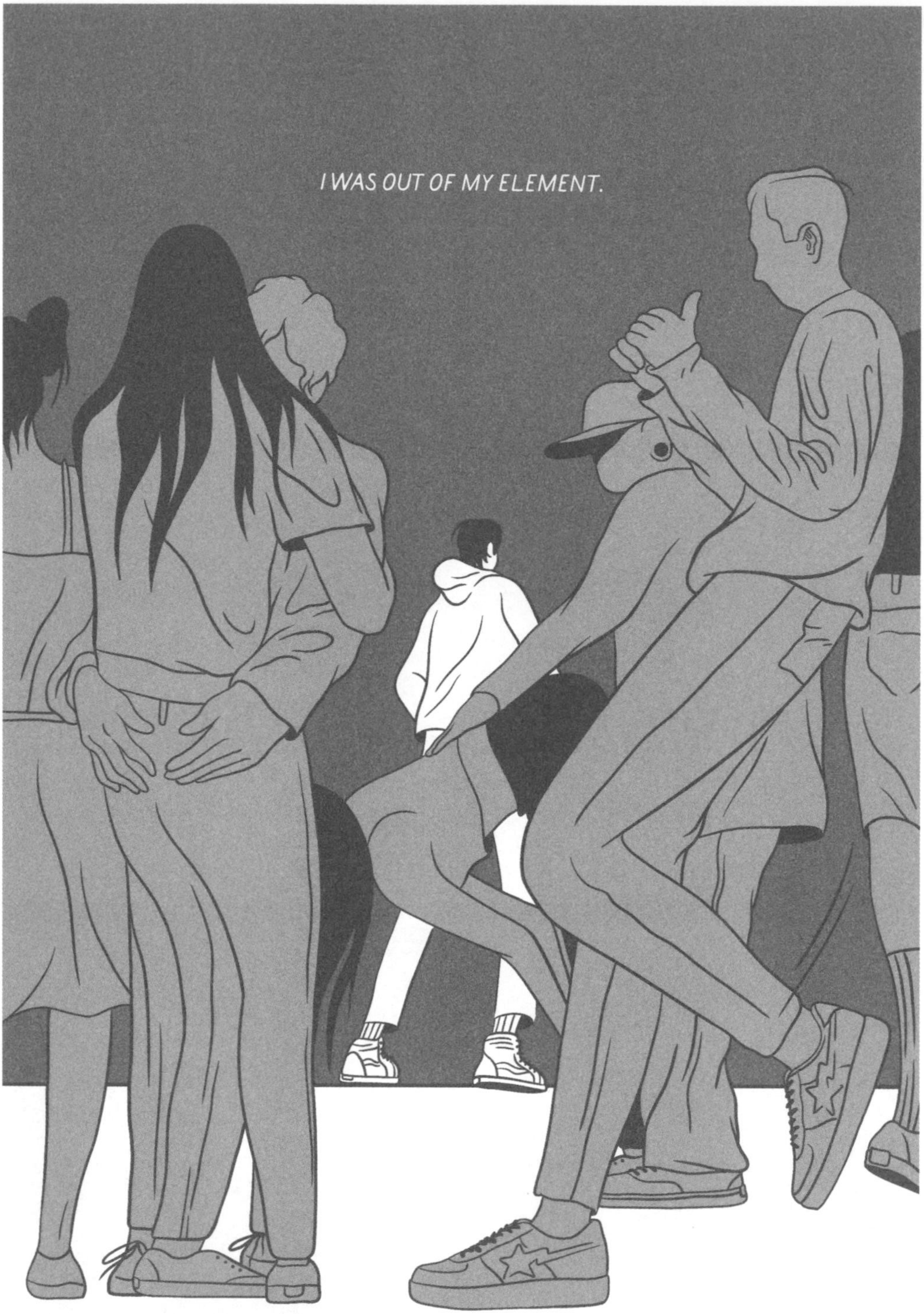
I WAS OUT OF MY ELEMENT.

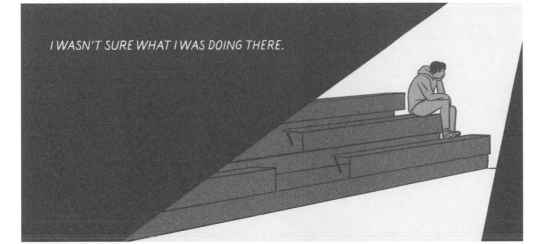

I WASN'T SURE WHAT I WAS DOING THERE.

I SPOTTED A GROUP OF PEOPLE THAT I KNEW.

THEY HUDDLED IN A CIRCLE AND MOVED IN TANDEM.

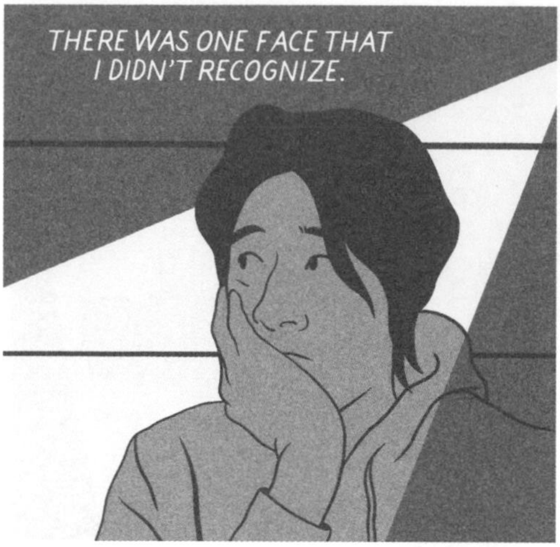
THERE WAS ONE FACE THAT
I DIDN'T RECOGNIZE.

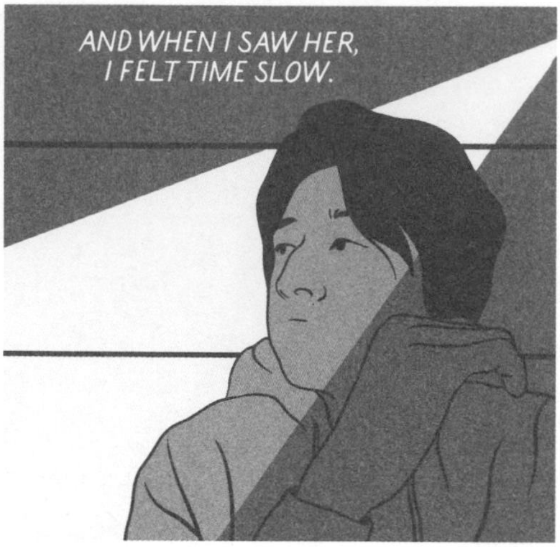
AND WHEN I SAW HER,
I FELT TIME SLOW.

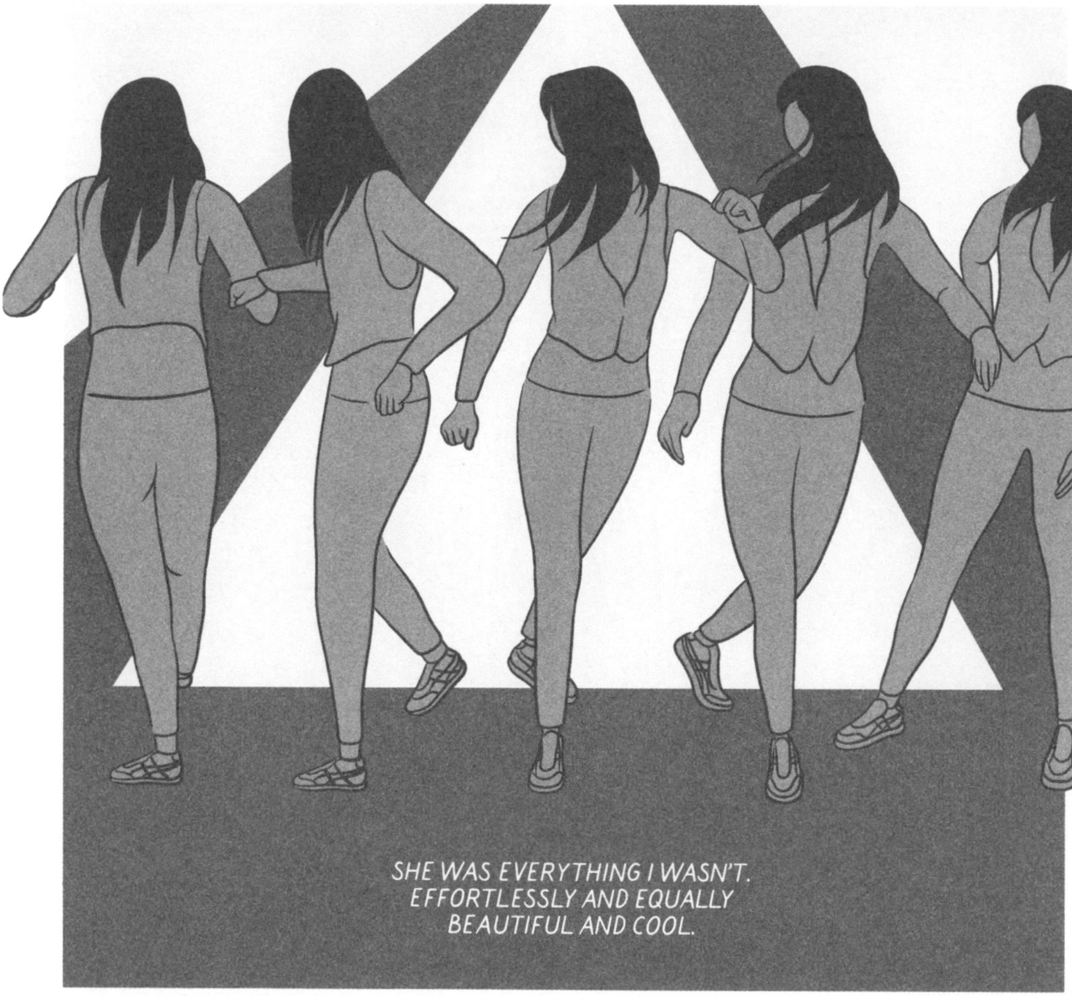
SHE WAS EVERYTHING I WASN'T.
EFFORTLESSLY AND EQUALLY
BEAUTIFUL AND COOL.

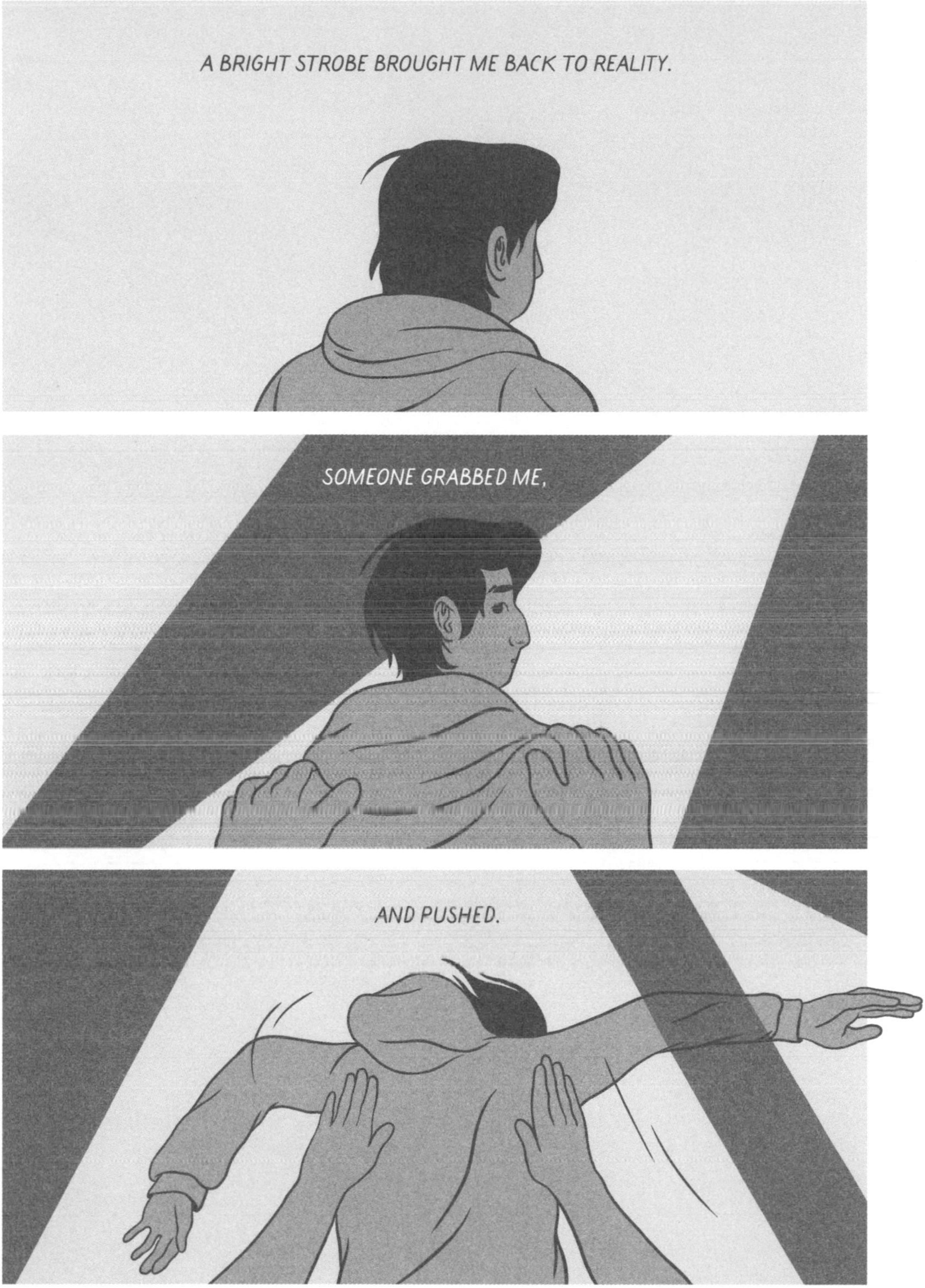
A BRIGHT STROBE BROUGHT ME BACK TO REALITY.
SOMEONE GRABBED ME,
AND PUSHED.

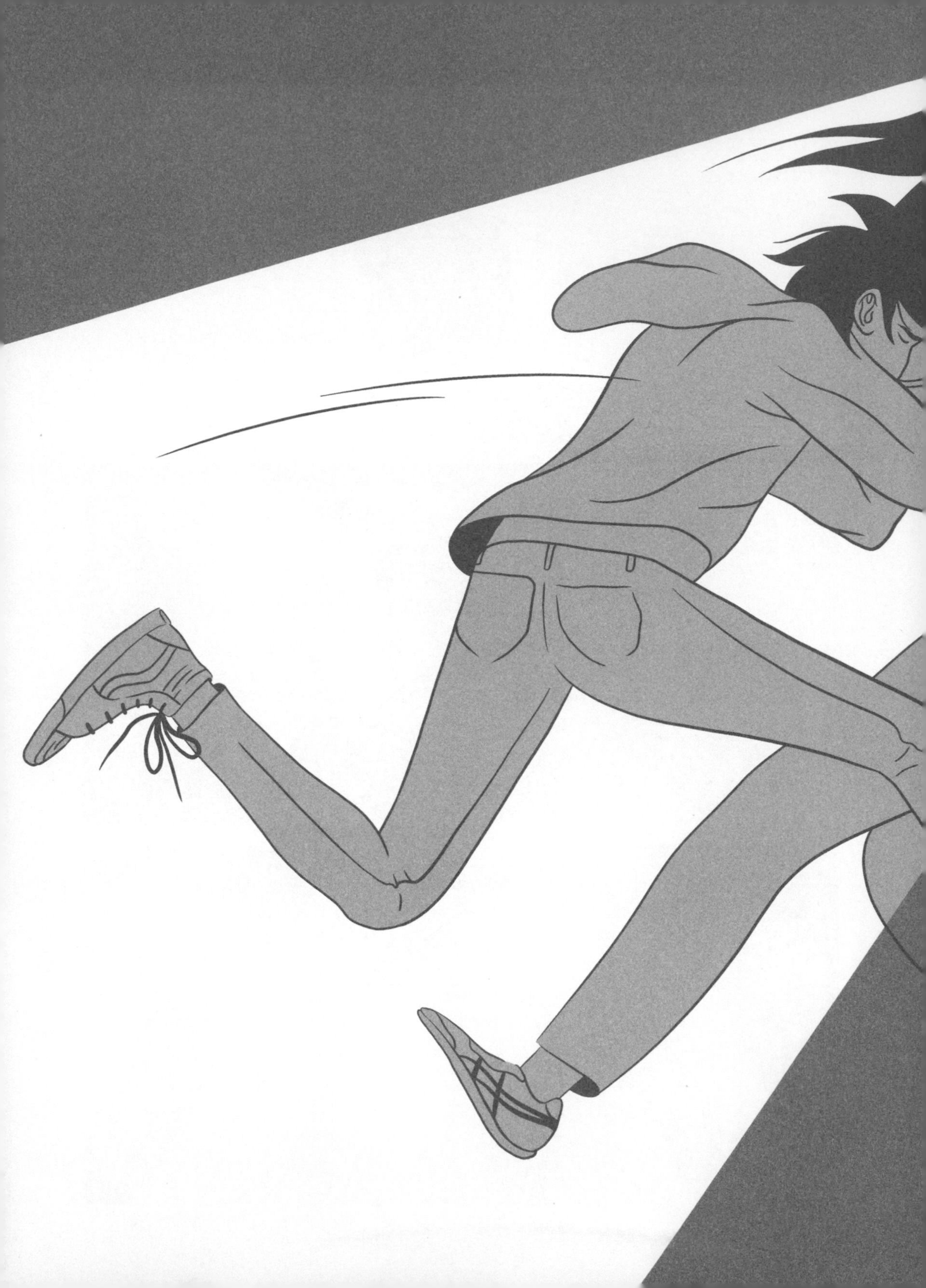

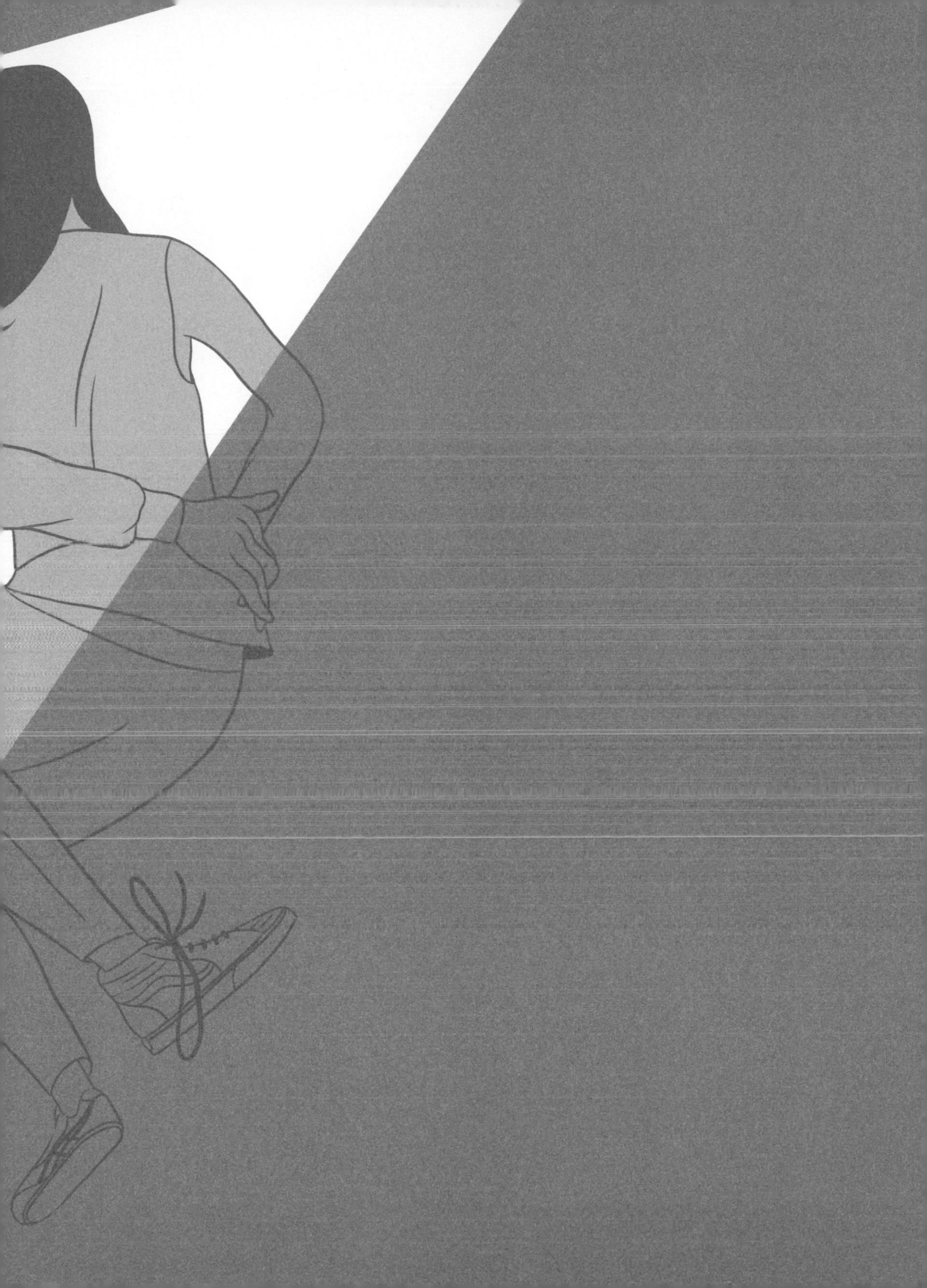

OUR COLLISION DIDN'T FAZE HER AT ALL.

THE CIRCLE ENSNARED US,

AND SHE JUST KEPT DANCING.

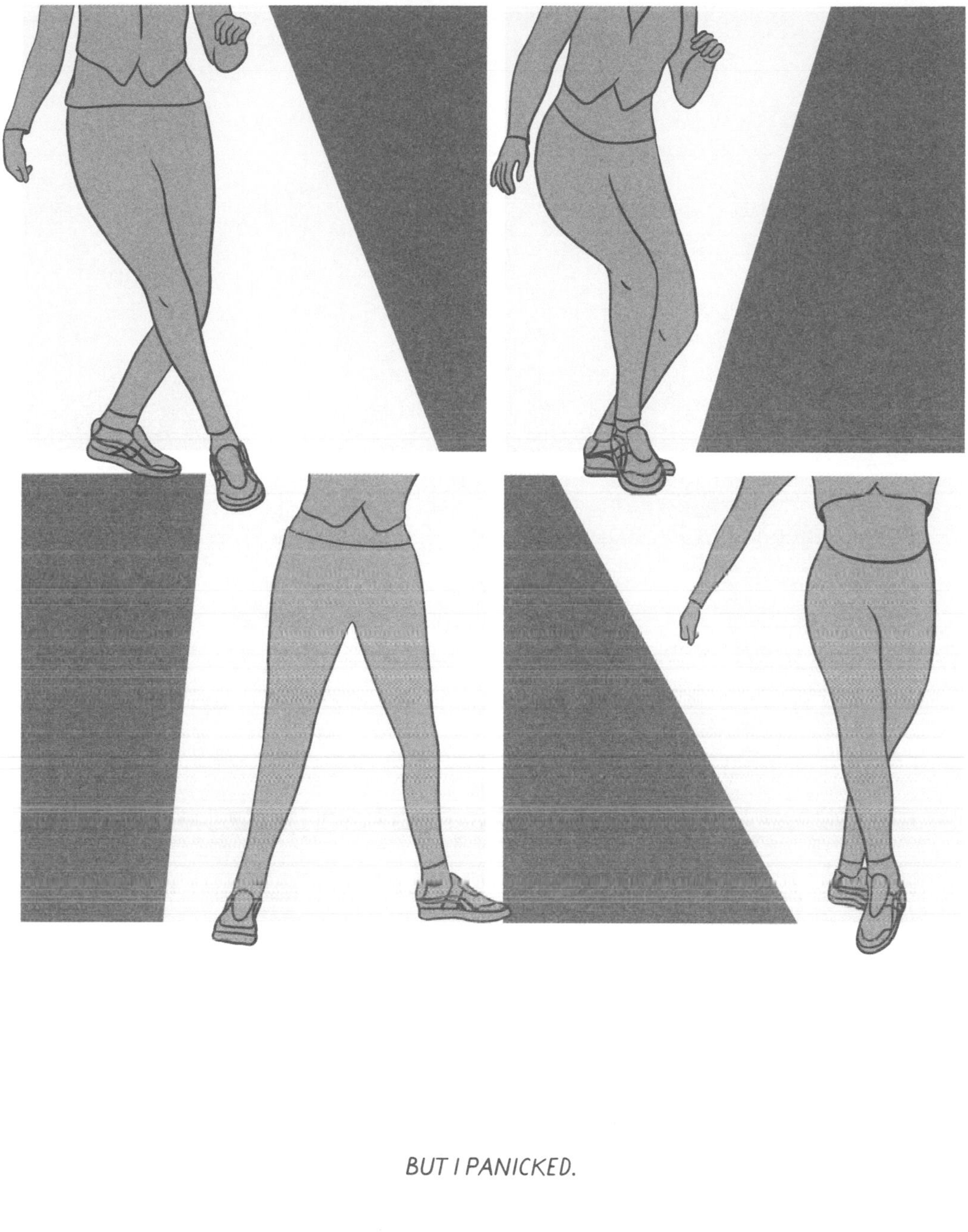

BUT I PANICKED.

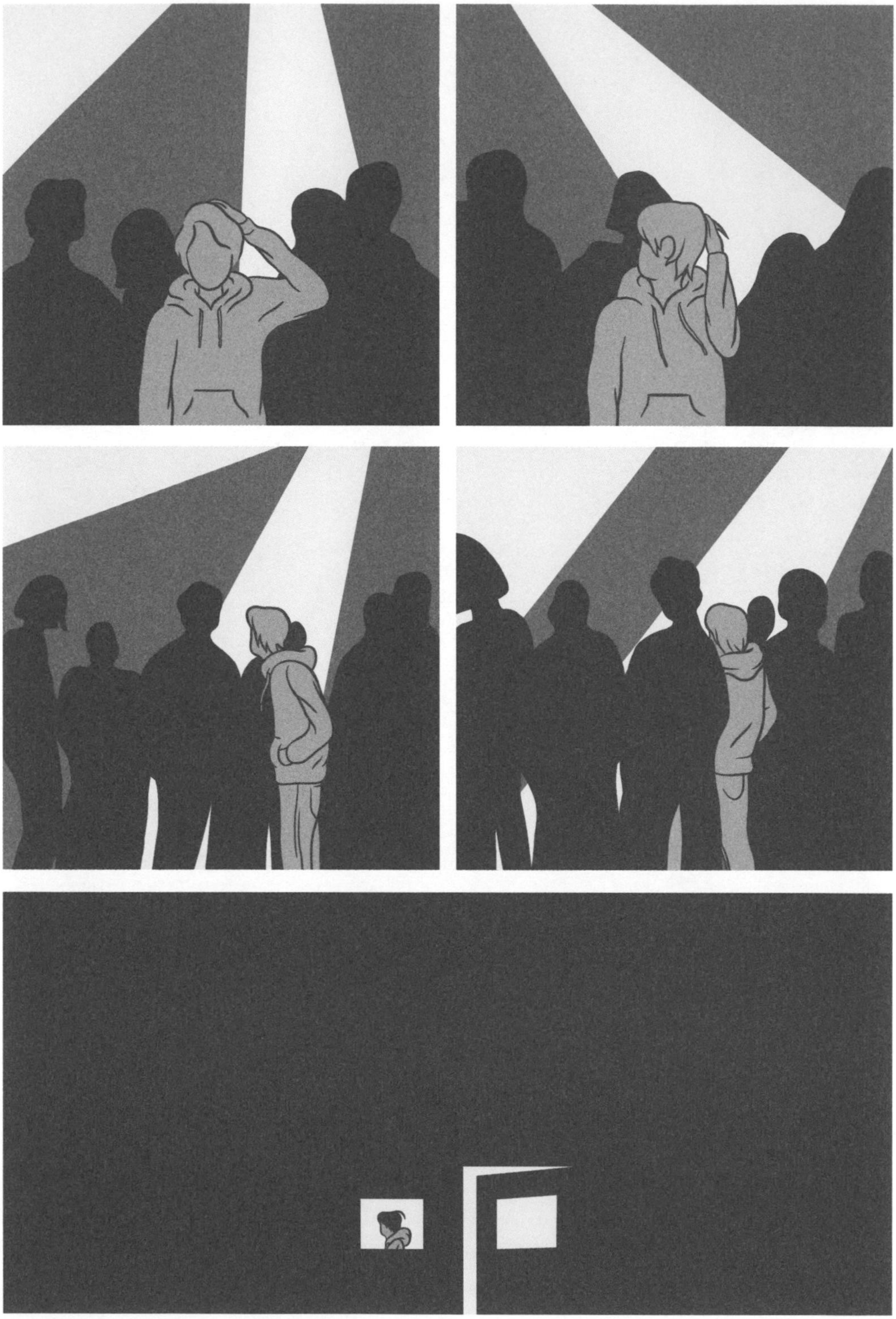

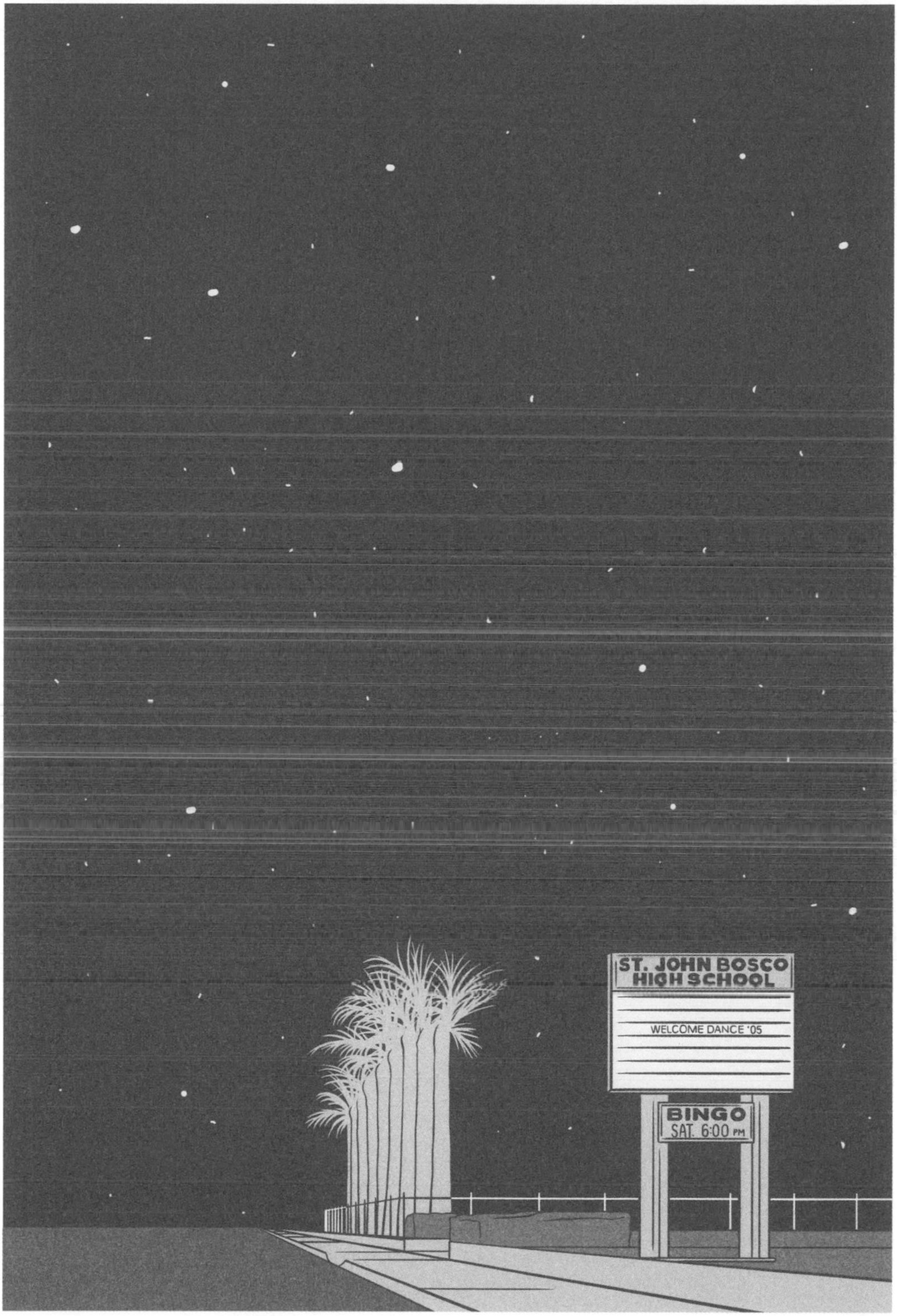
ST. JOHN BOSCO HIGH SCHOOL
WELCOME DANCE '05
BINGO SAT. 6:00 PM

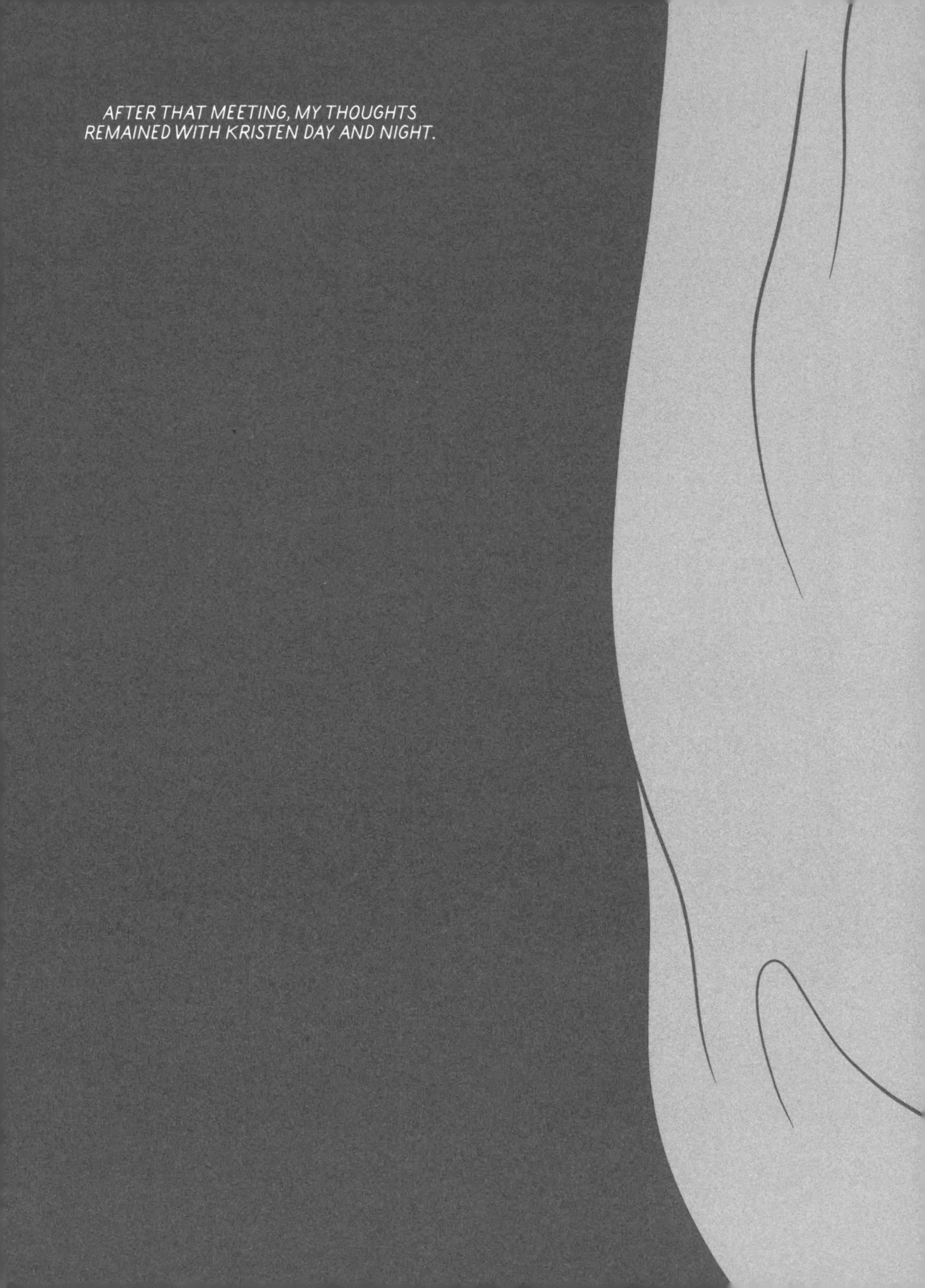
AFTER THAT MEETING, MY THOUGHTS
REMAINED WITH KRISTEN DAY AND NIGHT.

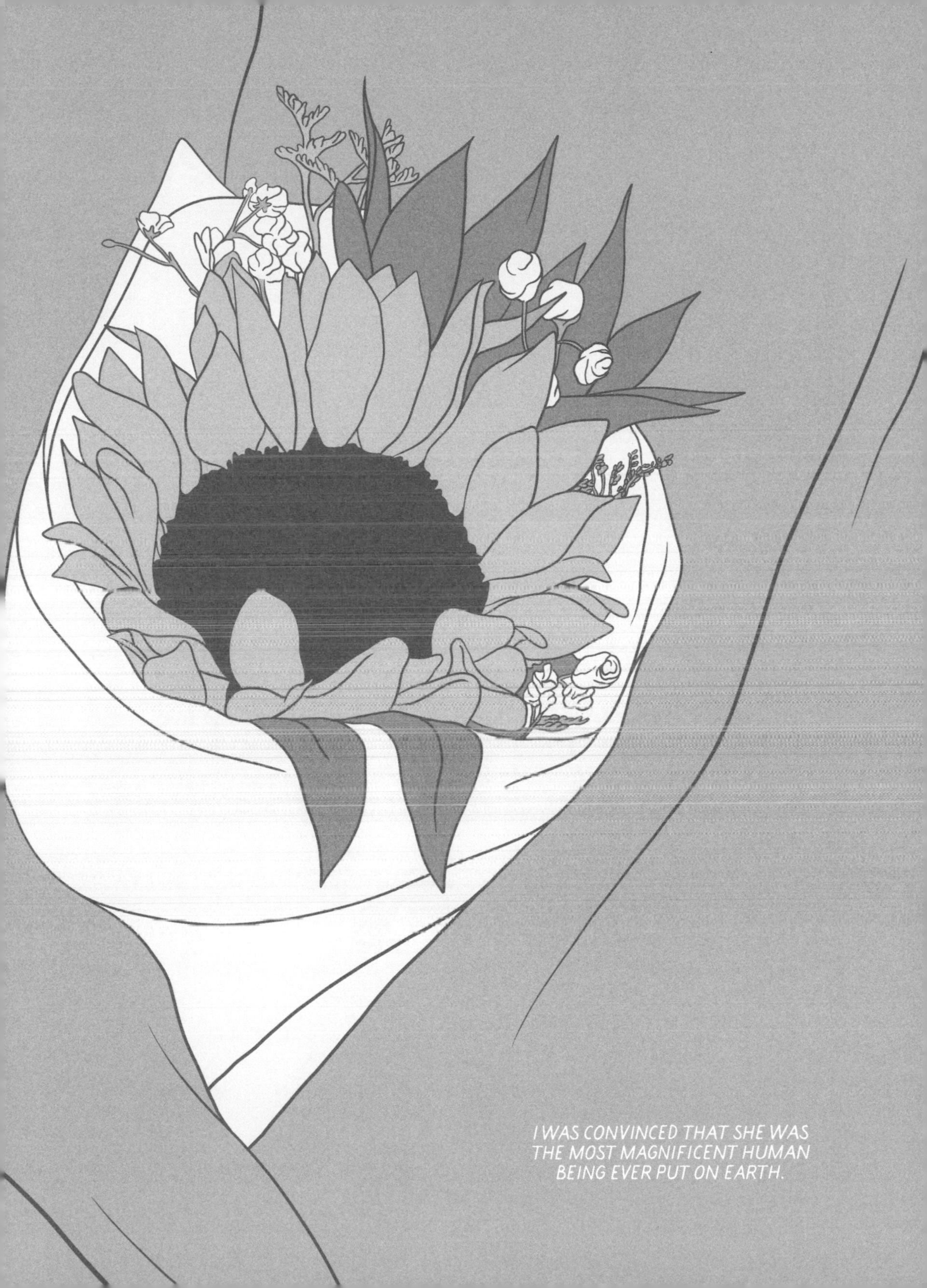
I WAS CONVINCED THAT SHE WAS
THE MOST MAGNIFICENT HUMAN
BEING EVER PUT ON EARTH.

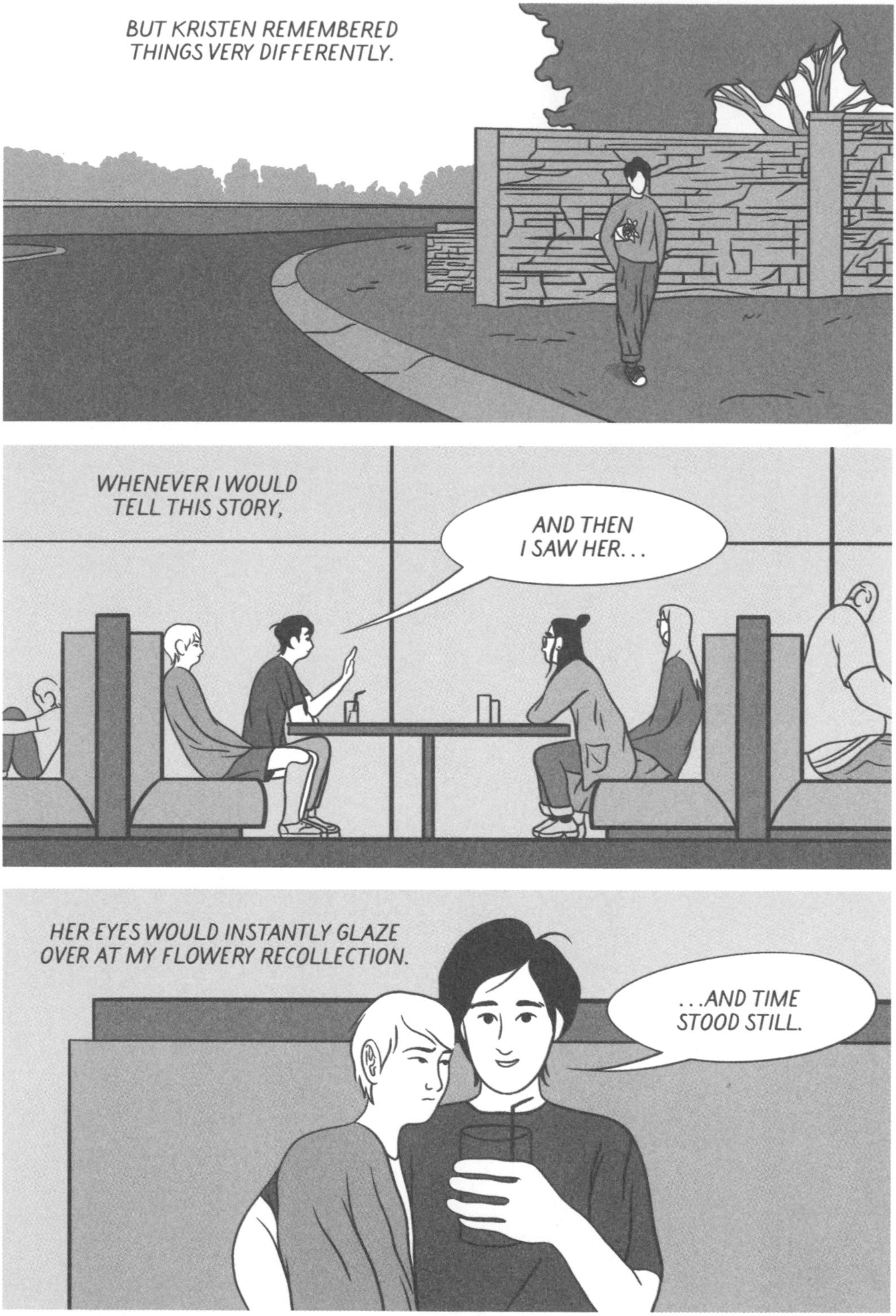
BUT KRISTEN REMEMBERED THINGS VERY DIFFERENTLY.
WHENEVER I WOULD TELL THIS STORY,
AND THEN I SAW HER...
HER EYES WOULD INSTANTLY GLAZE OVER AT MY FLOWERY RECOLLECTION.
...AND TIME STOOD STILL.

TO KRISTEN, THAT
WAS JUST ANOTHER NIGHT.

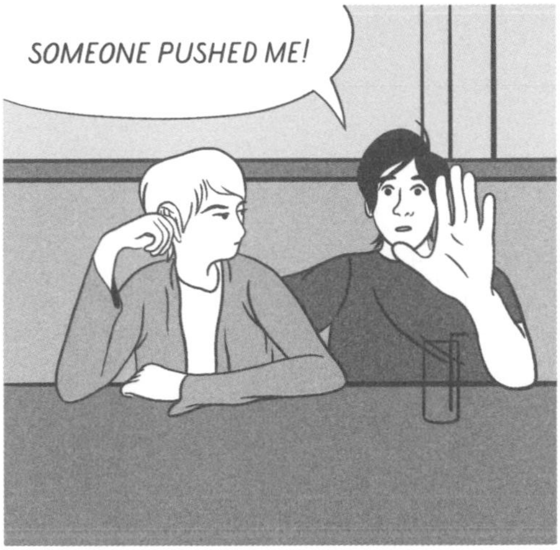
SOMEONE PUSHED ME!

OUR MAGICAL MEETING WAS
A FLEETING ANNOYANCE TO HER.

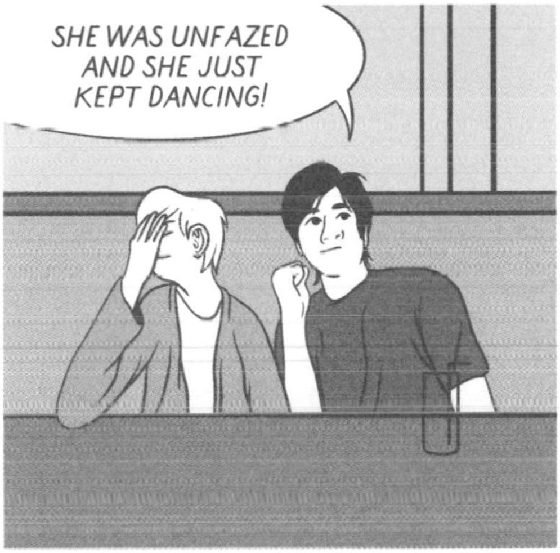
SHE WAS UNFAZED AND SHE JUST KEPT DANCING!

IF I TOLD THE STORY IN HER
COMPANY, SHE'D INCLUDE ALL
THE HUMILIATING DETAILS
THAT I FAILED TO MENTION.

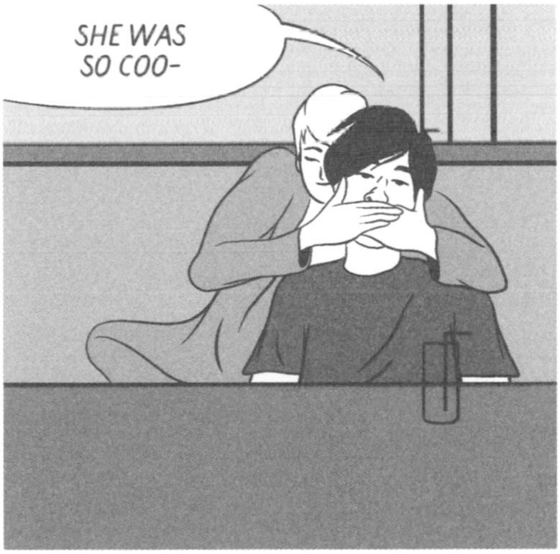
SHE WAS SO COO-

ALMOST IMMEDIATELY
AFTER THE DANCE,

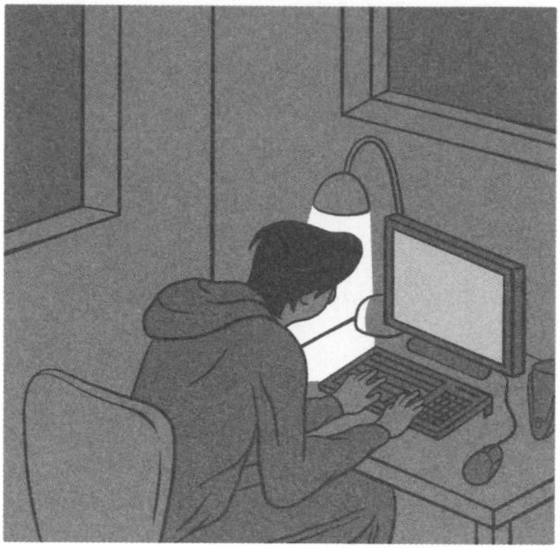

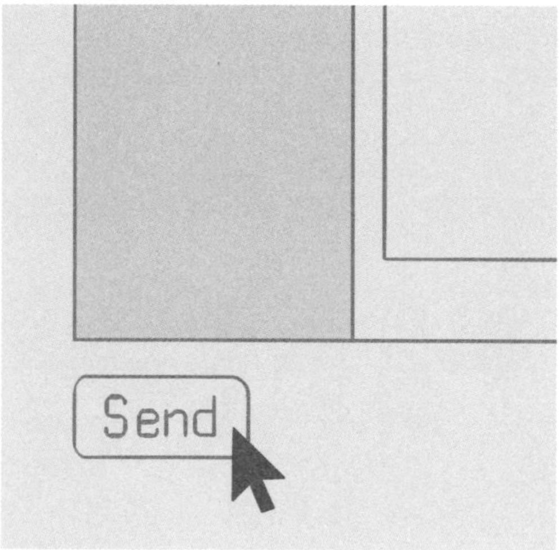
Send

AS KRISTEN WOULD
GLEEFULLY RECALL,

I SENT HER A MESSAGE.

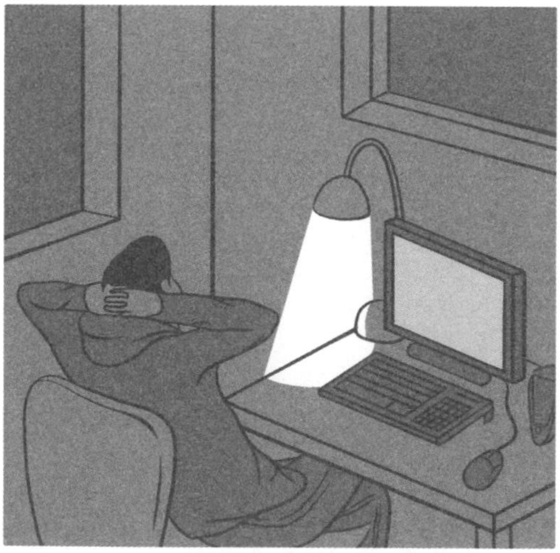

My Mail

☒ New Messages!

inbox

sent

I POURED MY HEART OUT.

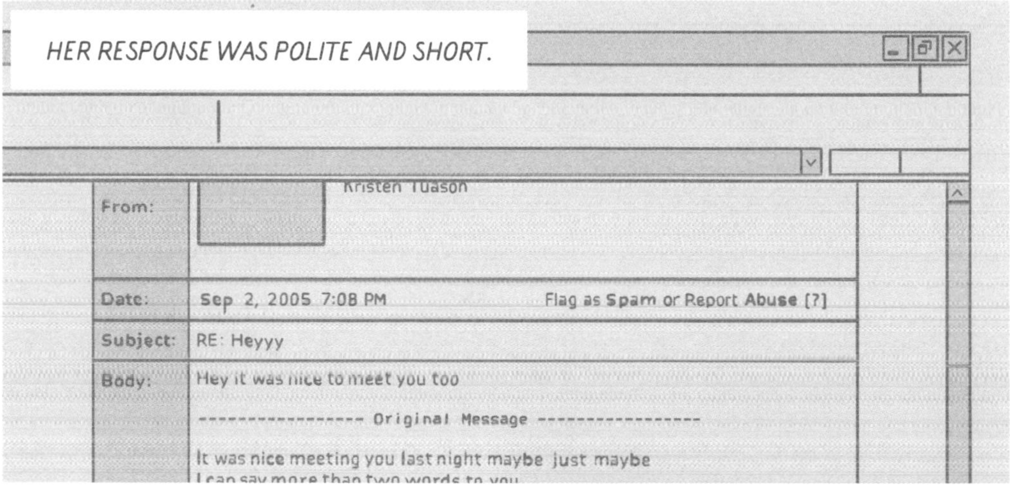

HER RESPONSE WAS POLITE AND SHORT.

From:	Kristen Tuason
Date:	Sep 2, 2005 7:08 PM Flag as Spam or Report Abuse [?]
Subject:	RE: Heyyy
Body:	Hey it was nice to meet you too

------------------ Original Message ------------------

It was nice meeting you last night maybe just maybe
I can say more than two words to you

*SHE DIDN'T THINK TWICE
ABOUT OUR INTERACTION.*

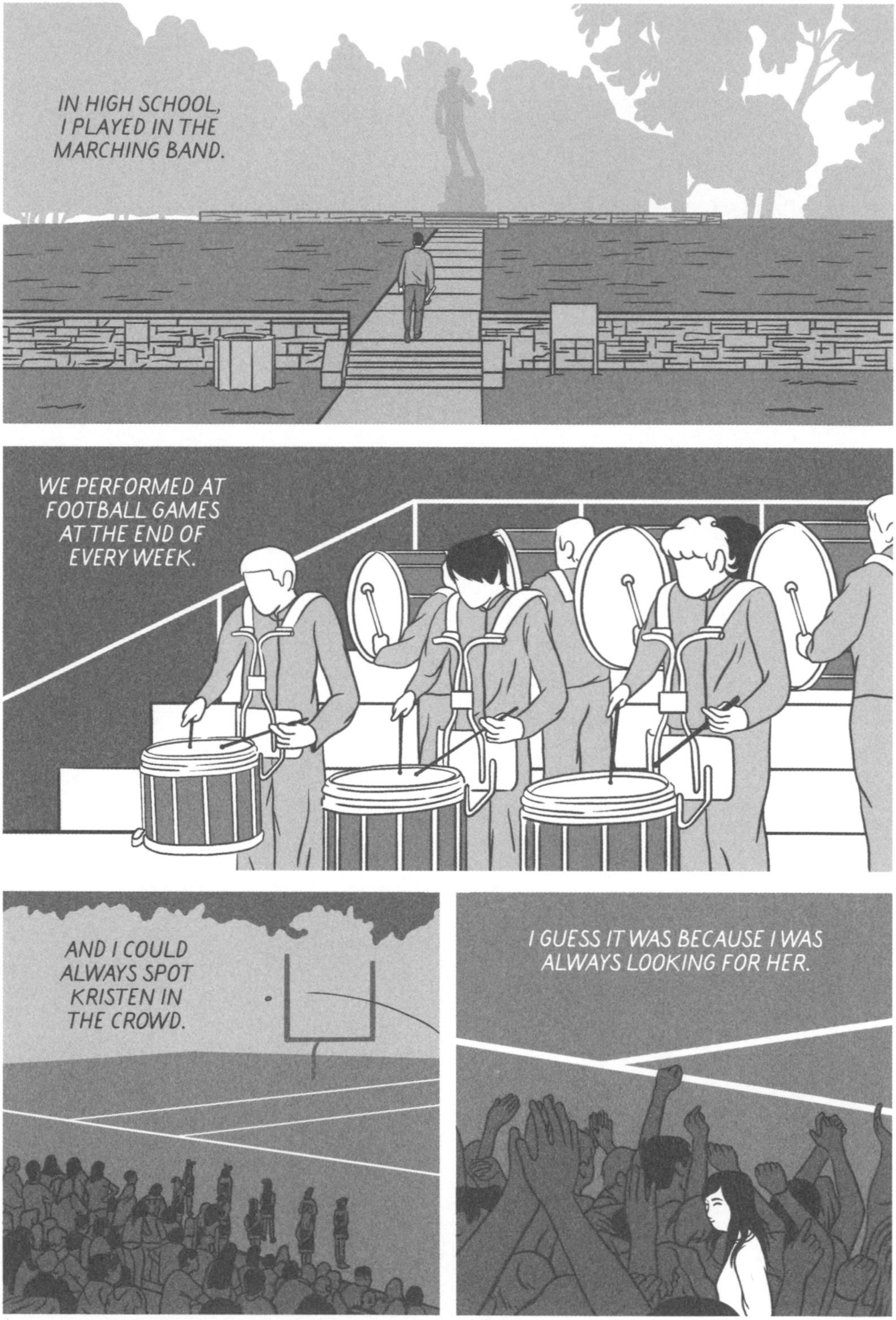
IN HIGH SCHOOL, I PLAYED IN THE MARCHING BAND.
WE PERFORMED AT FOOTBALL GAMES AT THE END OF EVERY WEEK.
AND I COULD ALWAYS SPOT KRISTEN IN THE CROWD.
I GUESS IT WAS BECAUSE I WAS ALWAYS LOOKING FOR HER.

YEARS LATER SHE'D TELL ME THAT MY CONSTANT VIGILANCE WAS IRRITATING.

SHE WAS UNINTERESTED AND RIGHTFULLY SO.

SHE HAD HER FRIENDS HIDE HER WHEN THEY SAW ME COMING.

I WAS SO EMBARRASSED.

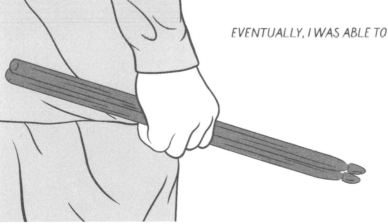

EVENTUALLY, I WAS ABLE TO TAKE THE HINT.

BUT I NEVER STOPPED LIKING HER.

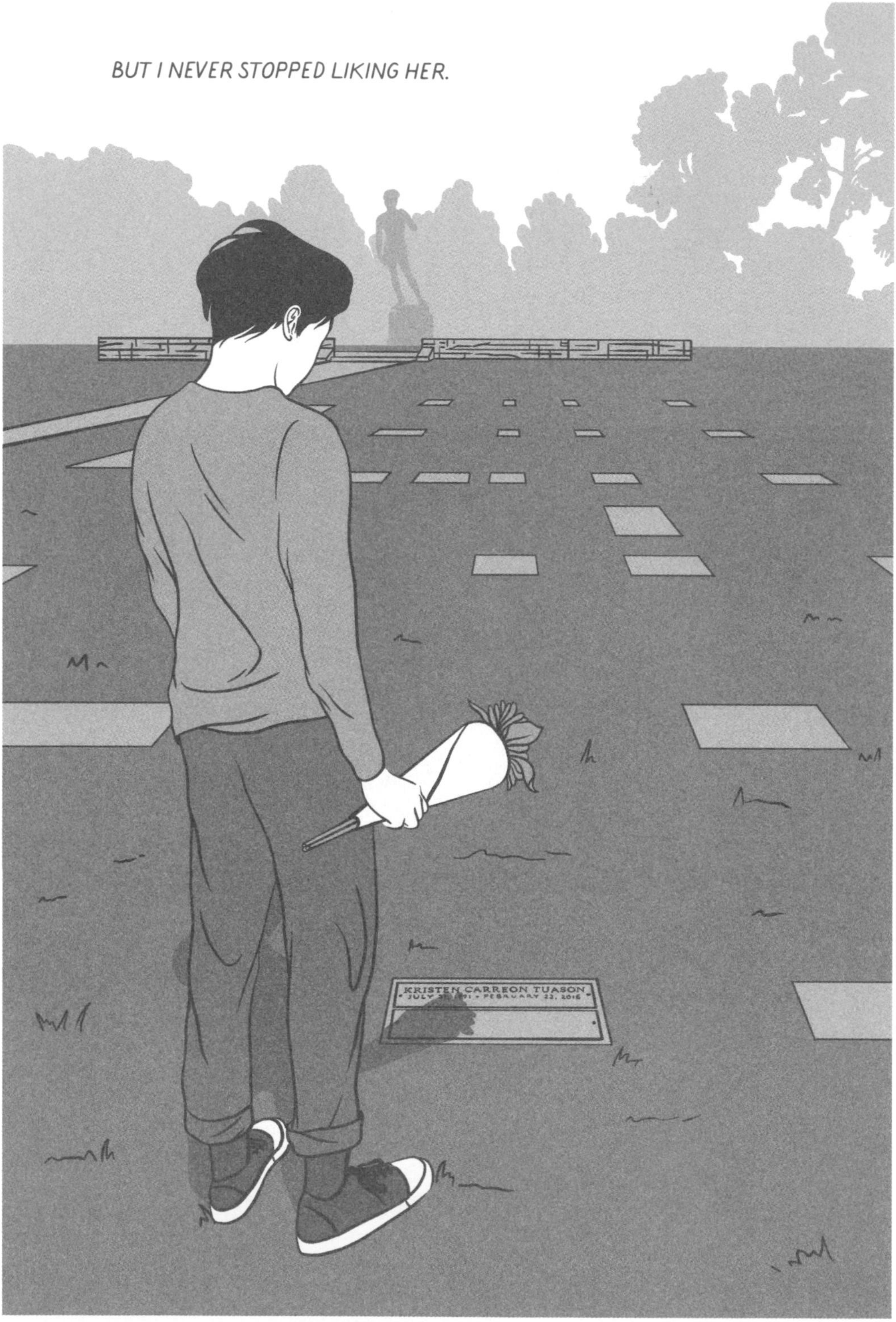
KRISTEN CARREON TUASON
FEBRUARY 22, 2016

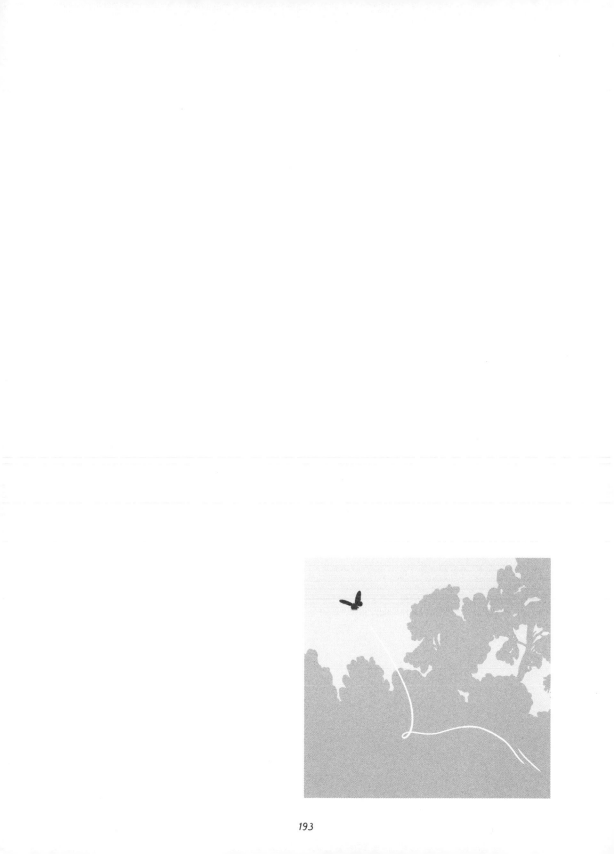

X. HUNGER

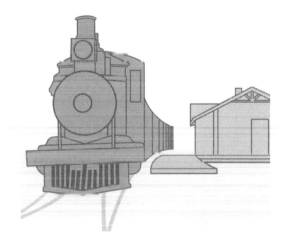

Fall
1920

Detroit, Michigan

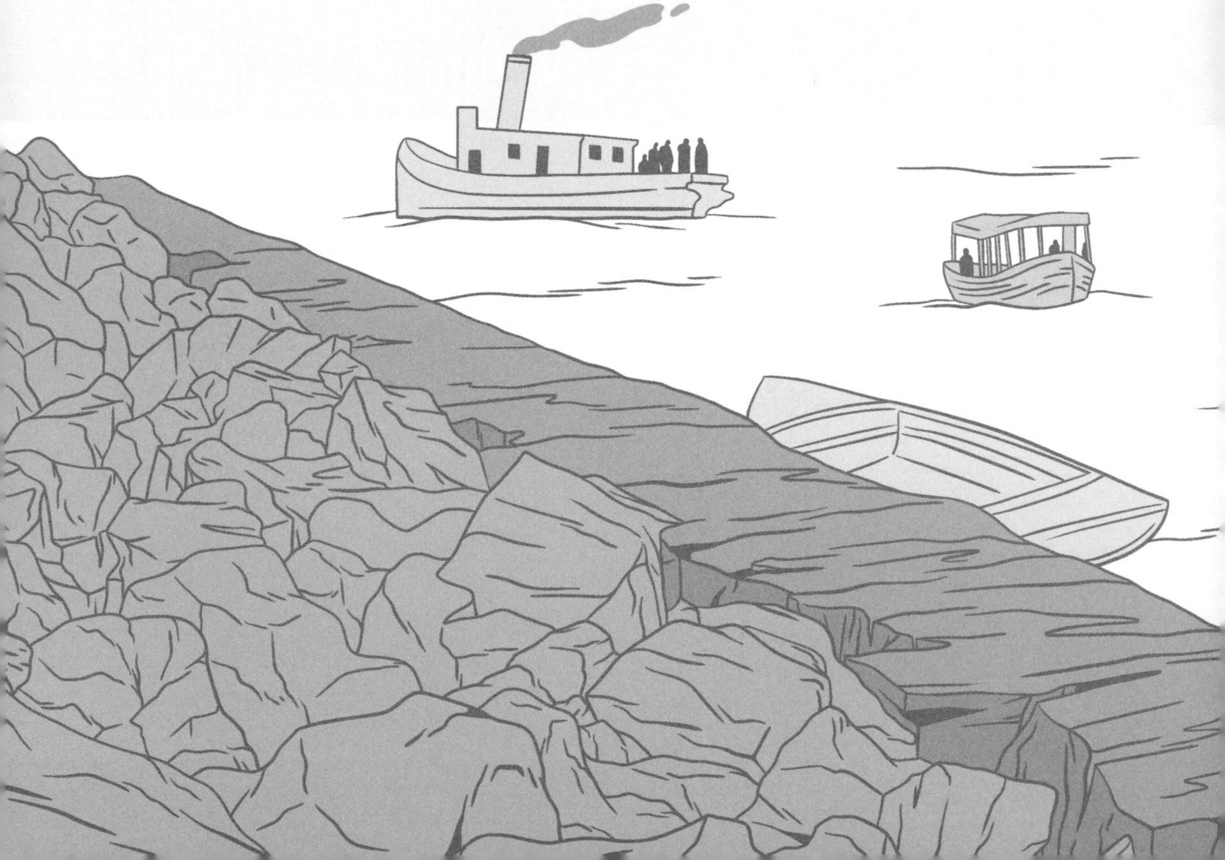

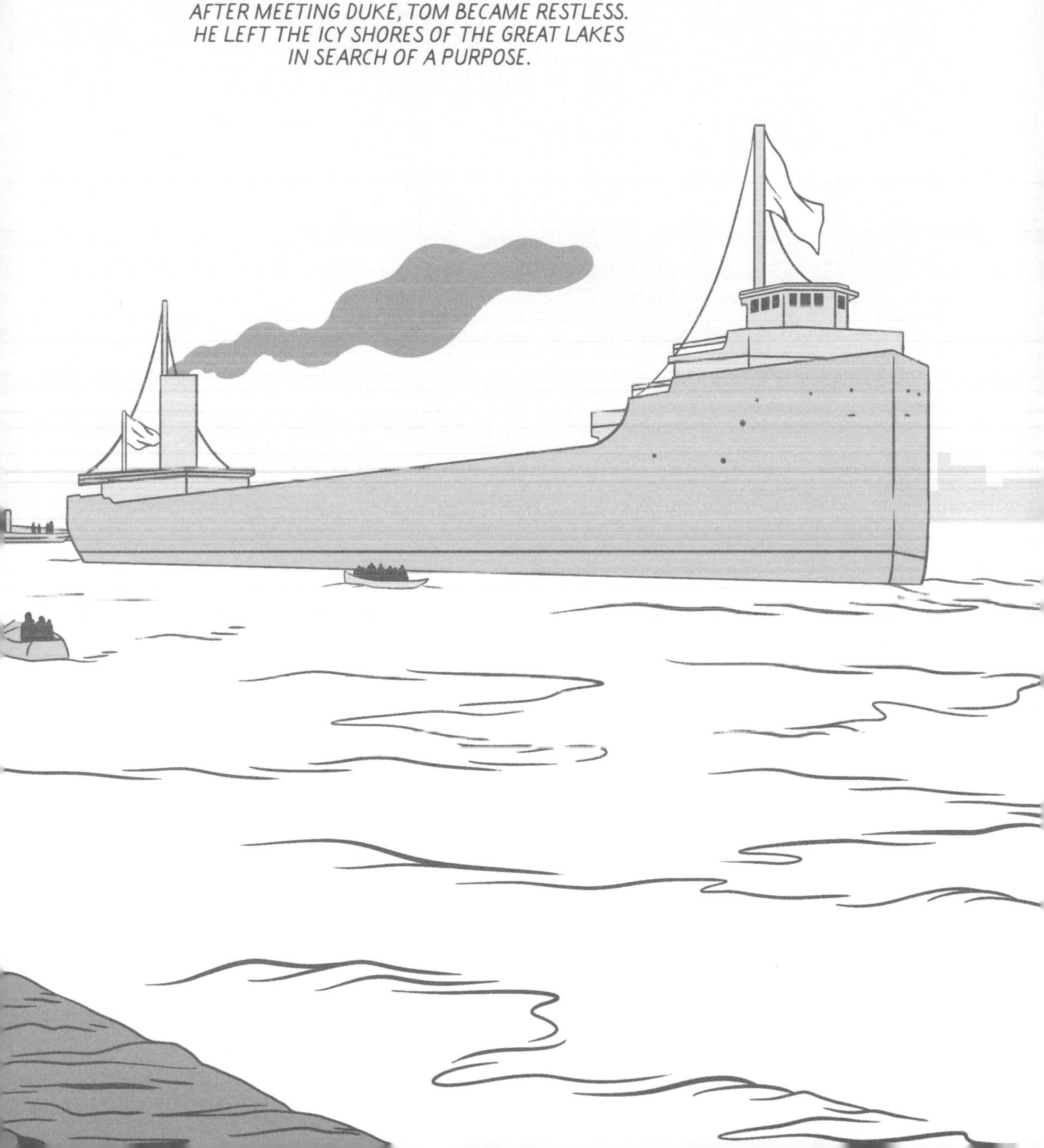
AFTER MEETING DUKE, TOM BECAME RESTLESS.
HE LEFT THE ICY SHORES OF THE GREAT LAKES
IN SEARCH OF A PURPOSE.

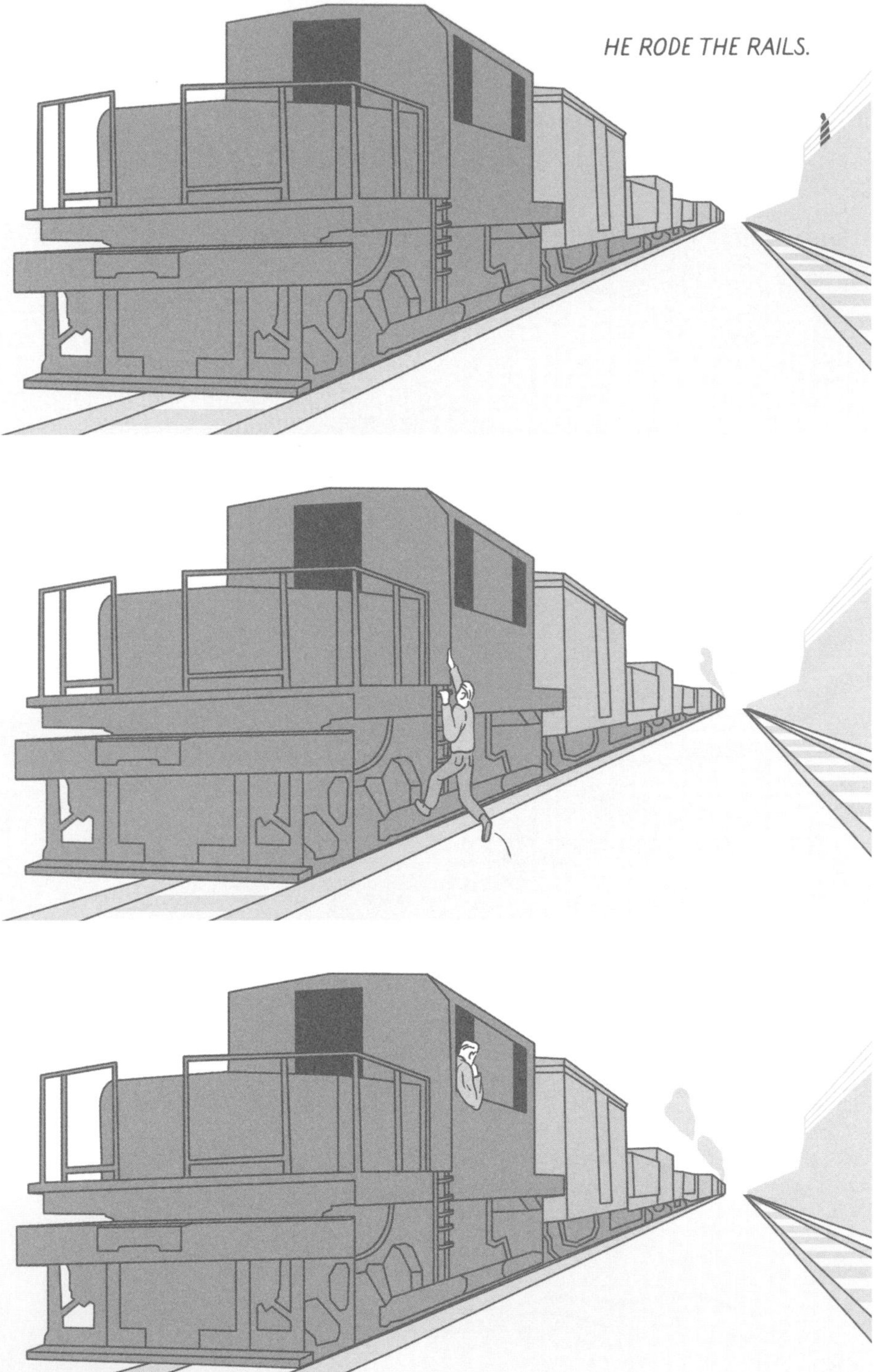
HE RODE THE RAILS.

FIRST STOP, NEW YORK.

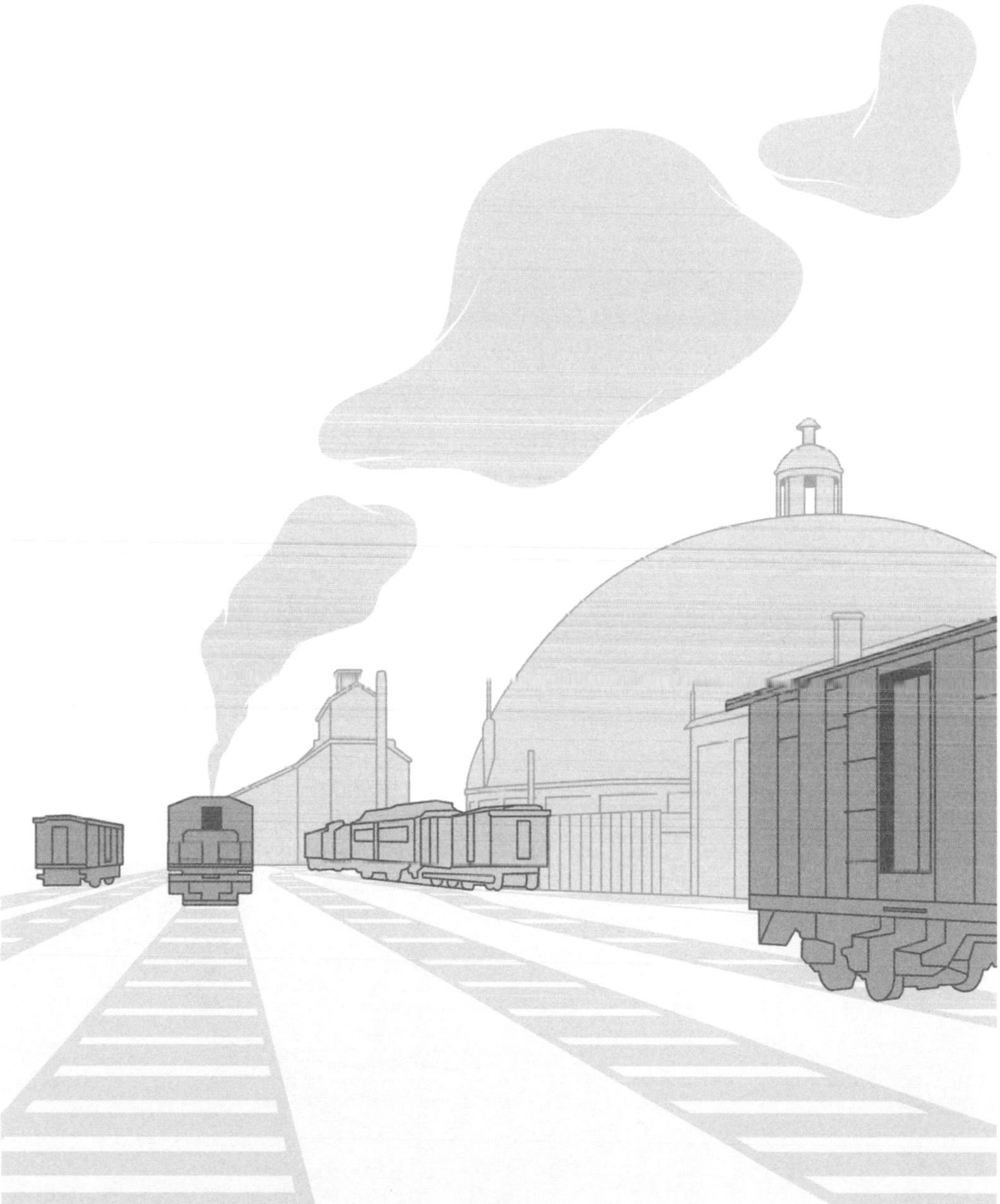

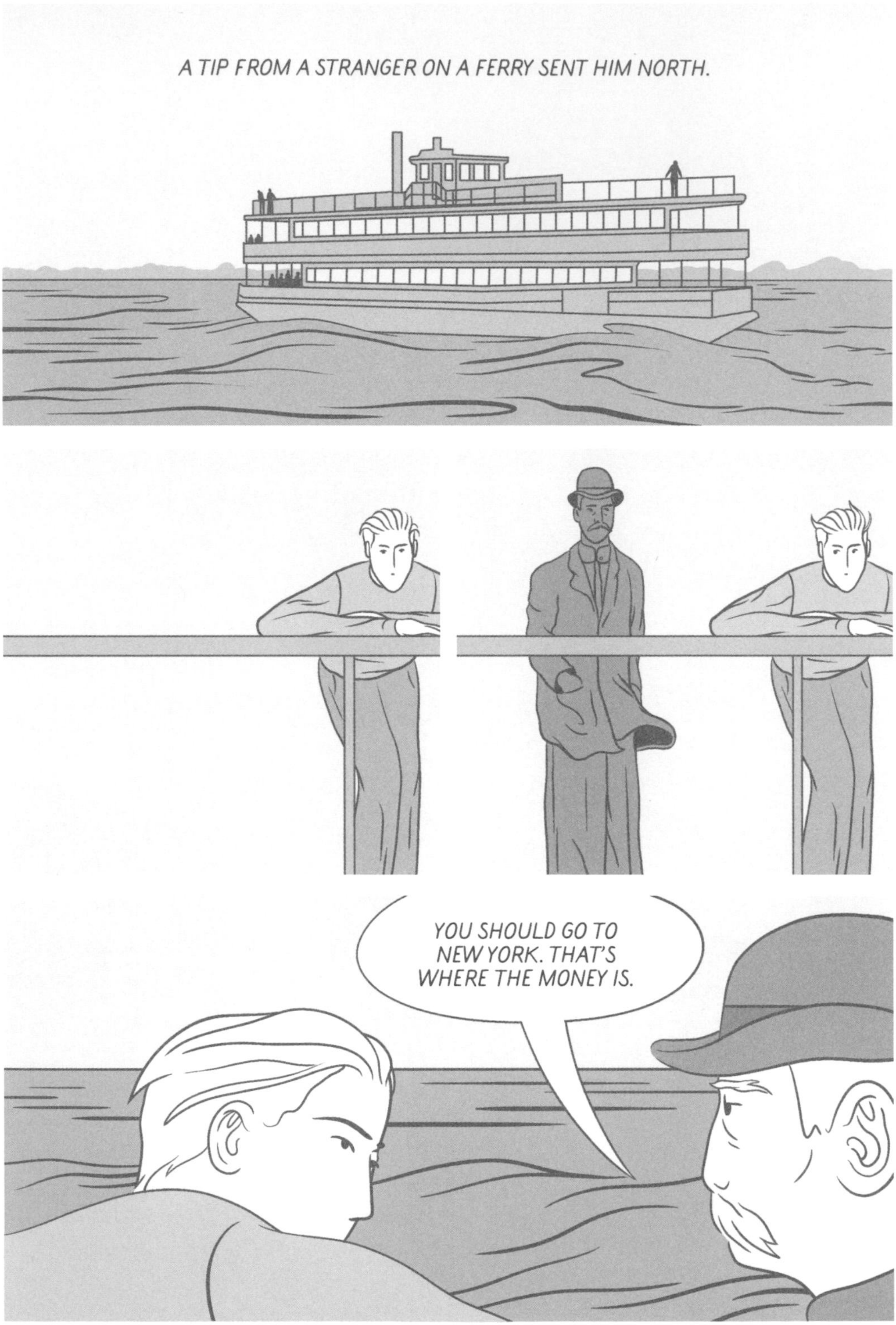
A TIP FROM A STRANGER ON A FERRY SENT HIM NORTH.
YOU SHOULD GO TO NEW YORK. THAT'S WHERE THE MONEY IS.

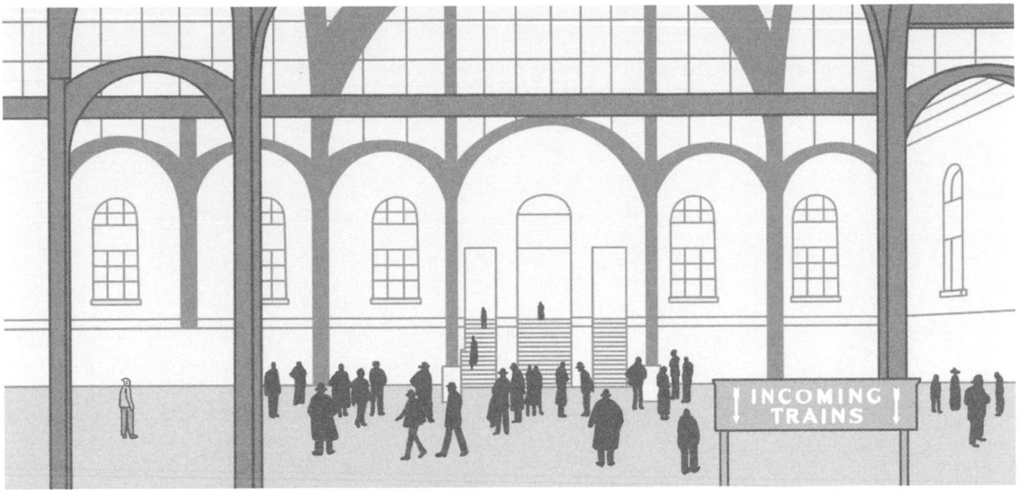
INCOMING TRAINS

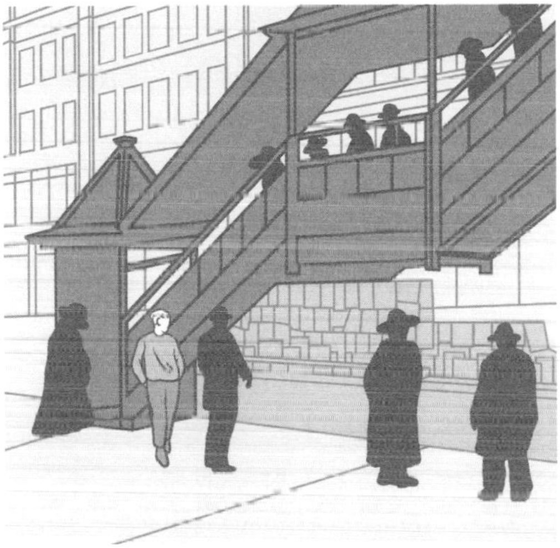

HE QUICKLY REALIZED IT WASN'T THE PLACE FOR HIM.

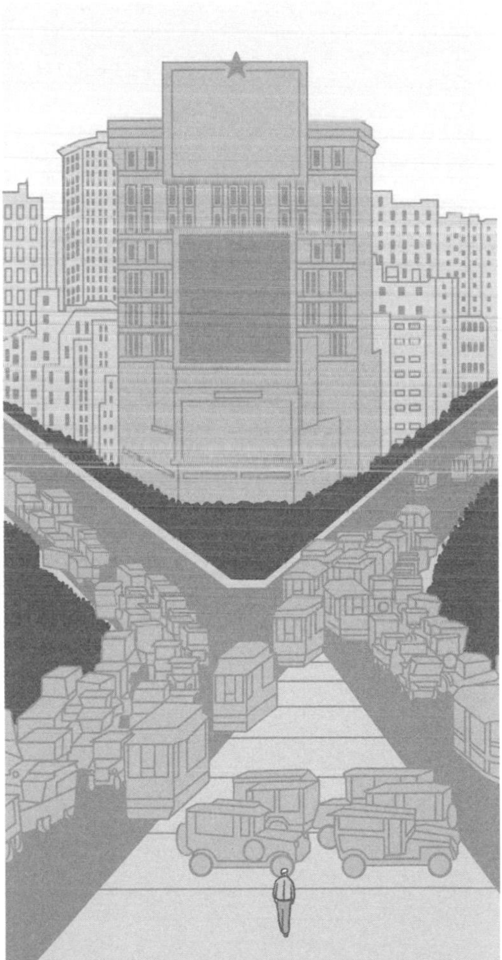

TOM WAS HUNGRY AND BROKE ON HIS WAY TO LONG ISLAND.

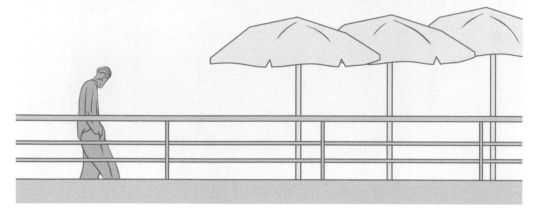

HE TOOK UP WORK AT A CARNIVAL WITH THE PROMISE OF A STEAK DINNER AS PAYMENT.

THEY LIED, SO HE LEFT.

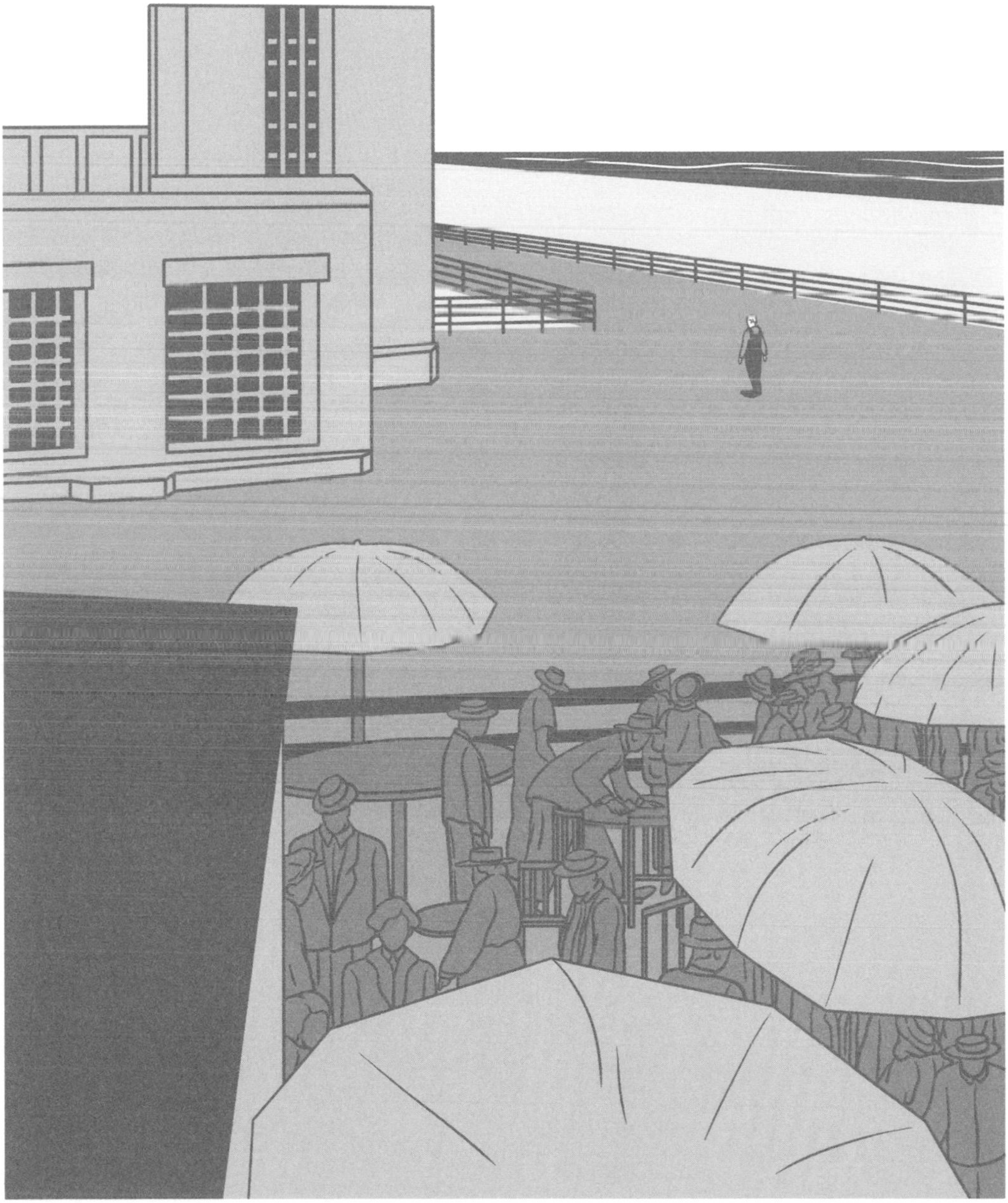

HIS NEXT STOP WAS CHICAGO,

WHERE HE LEARNED MAIL TRAINS THERE WENT STRAIGHT TO CALIFORNIA.

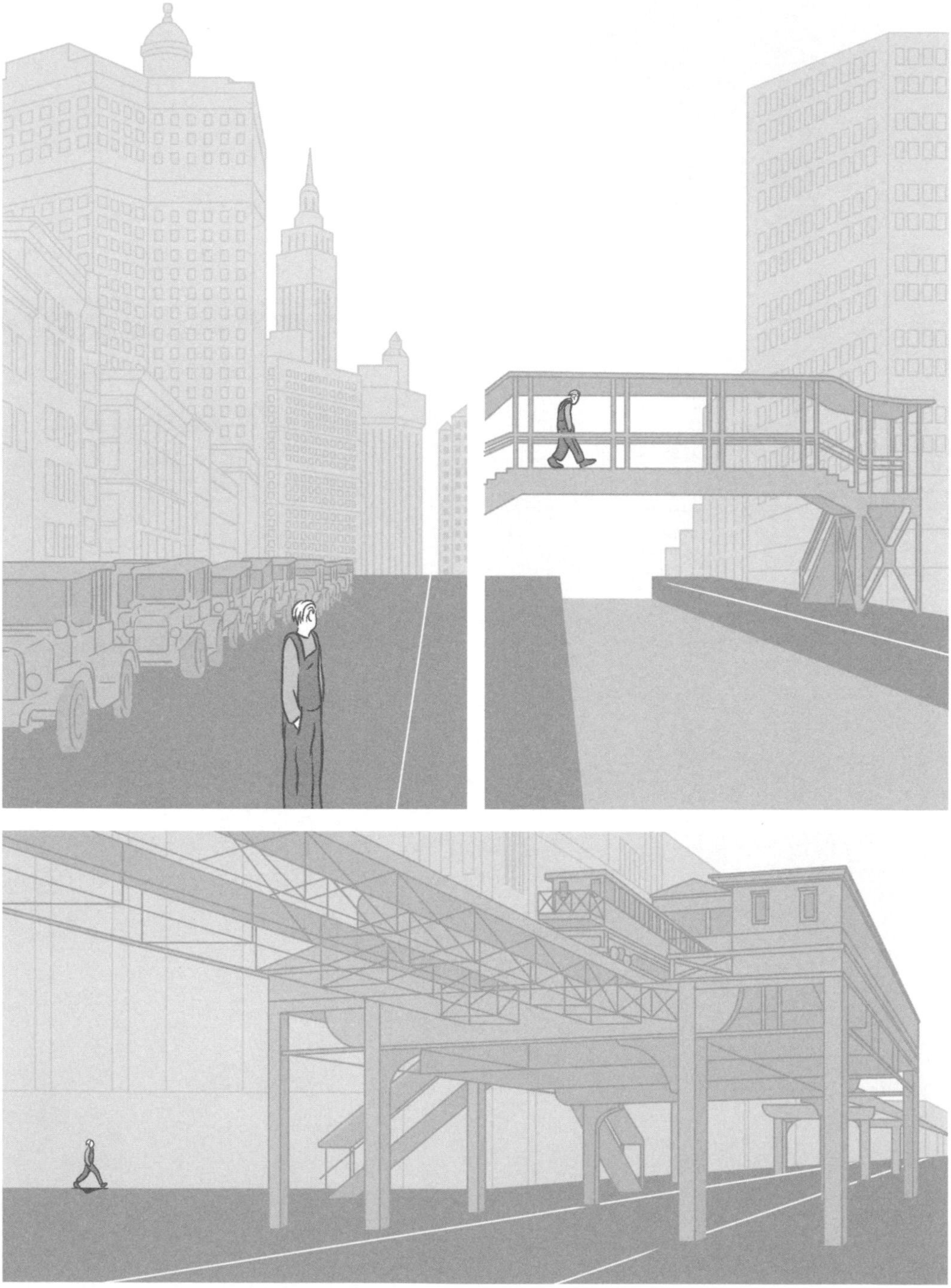

SO HE HEADED WEST.

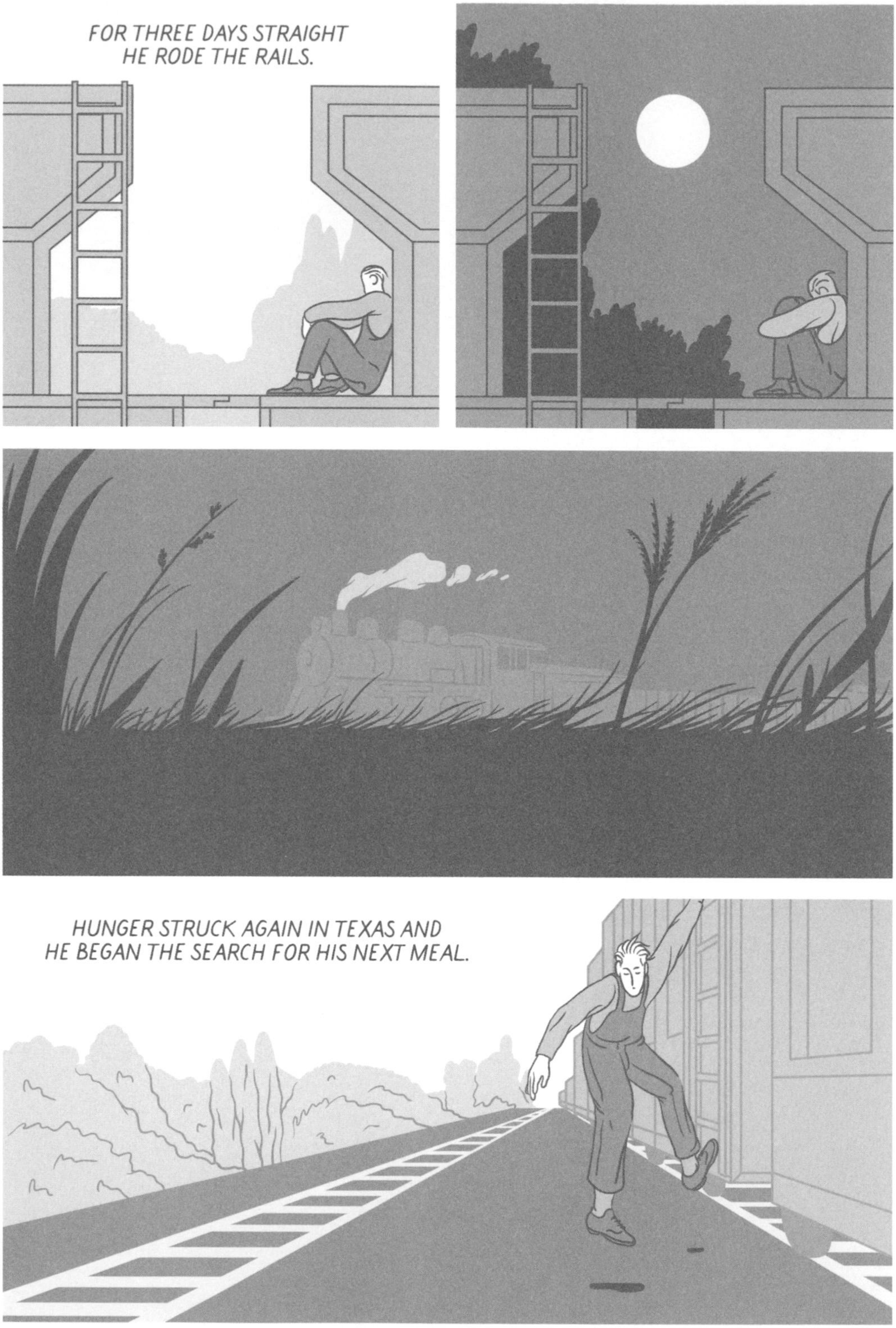
FOR THREE DAYS STRAIGHT HE RODE THE RAILS.
HUNGER STRUCK AGAIN IN TEXAS AND HE BEGAN THE SEARCH FOR HIS NEXT MEAL.

HE FOUND WORK ON A CATTLE RANCH.

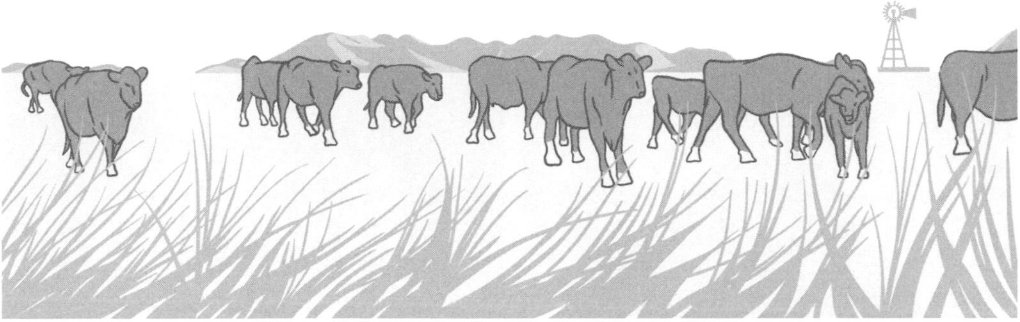

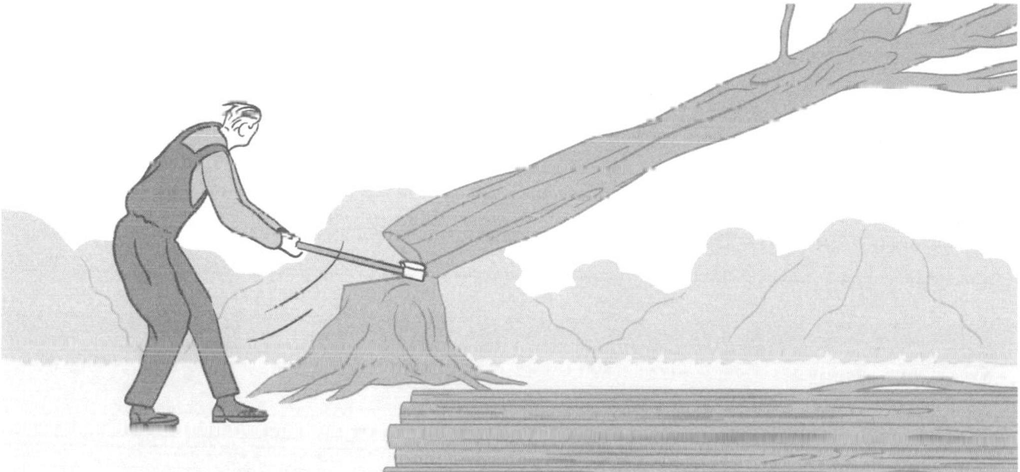

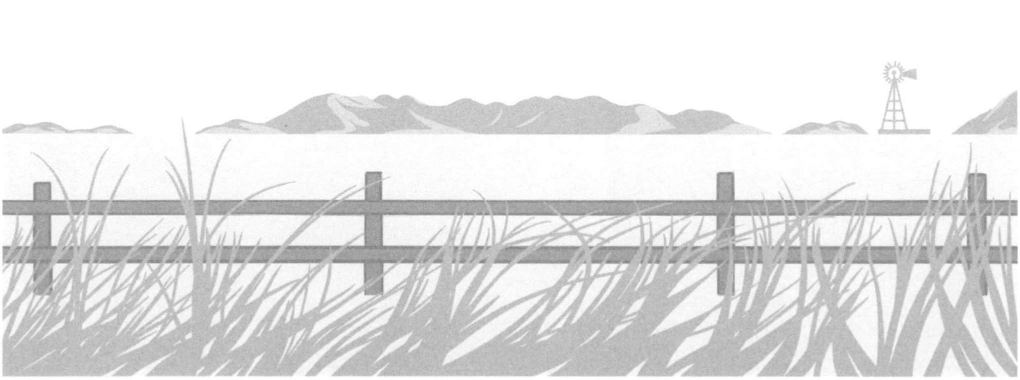

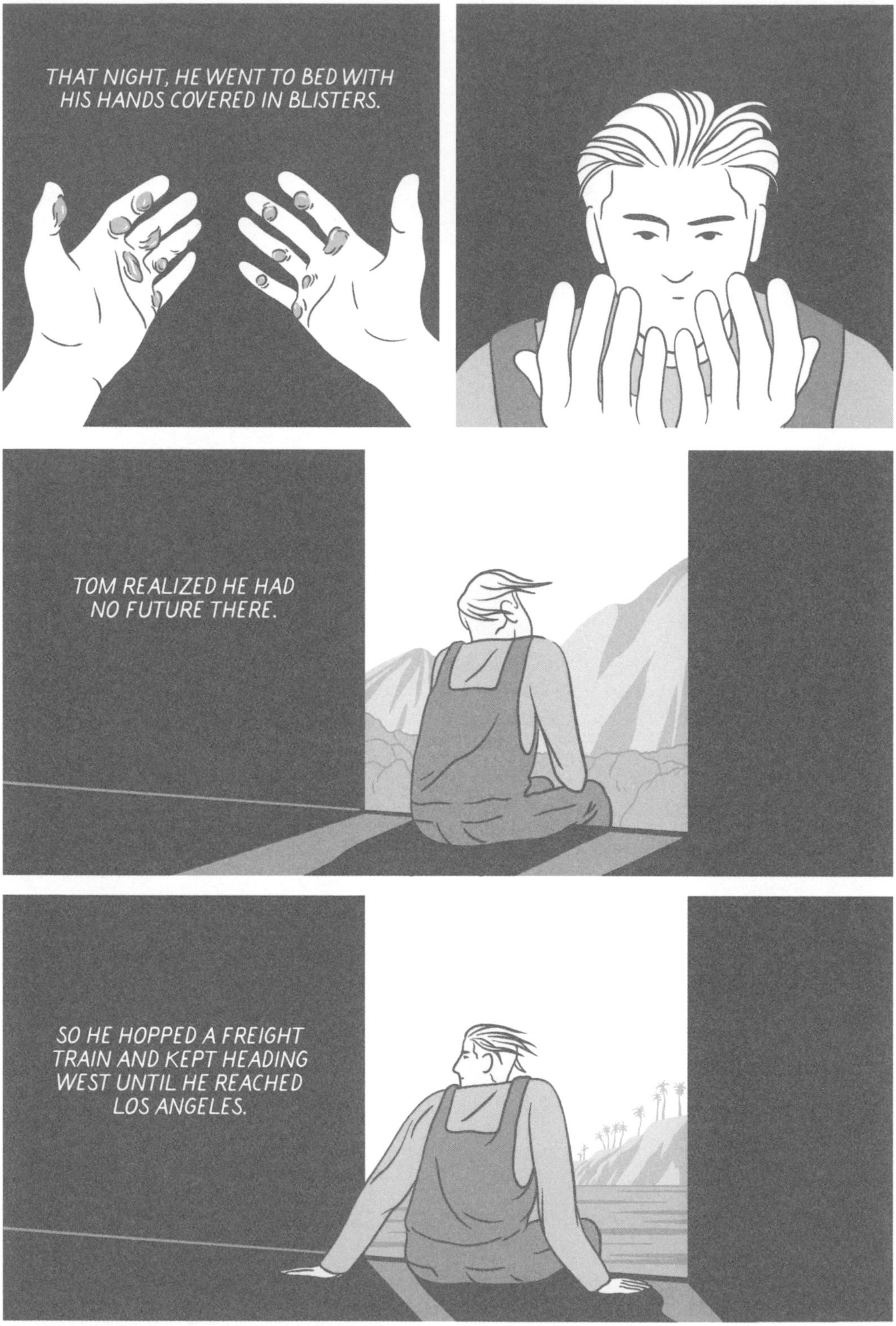
THAT NIGHT, HE WENT TO BED WITH HIS HANDS COVERED IN BLISTERS.
TOM REALIZED HE HAD NO FUTURE THERE.
SO HE HOPPED A FREIGHT TRAIN AND KEPT HEADING WEST UNTIL HE REACHED LOS ANGELES.

ARRIVING IN CALIFORNIA, HE TRIED HIS HAND AT ACTING.

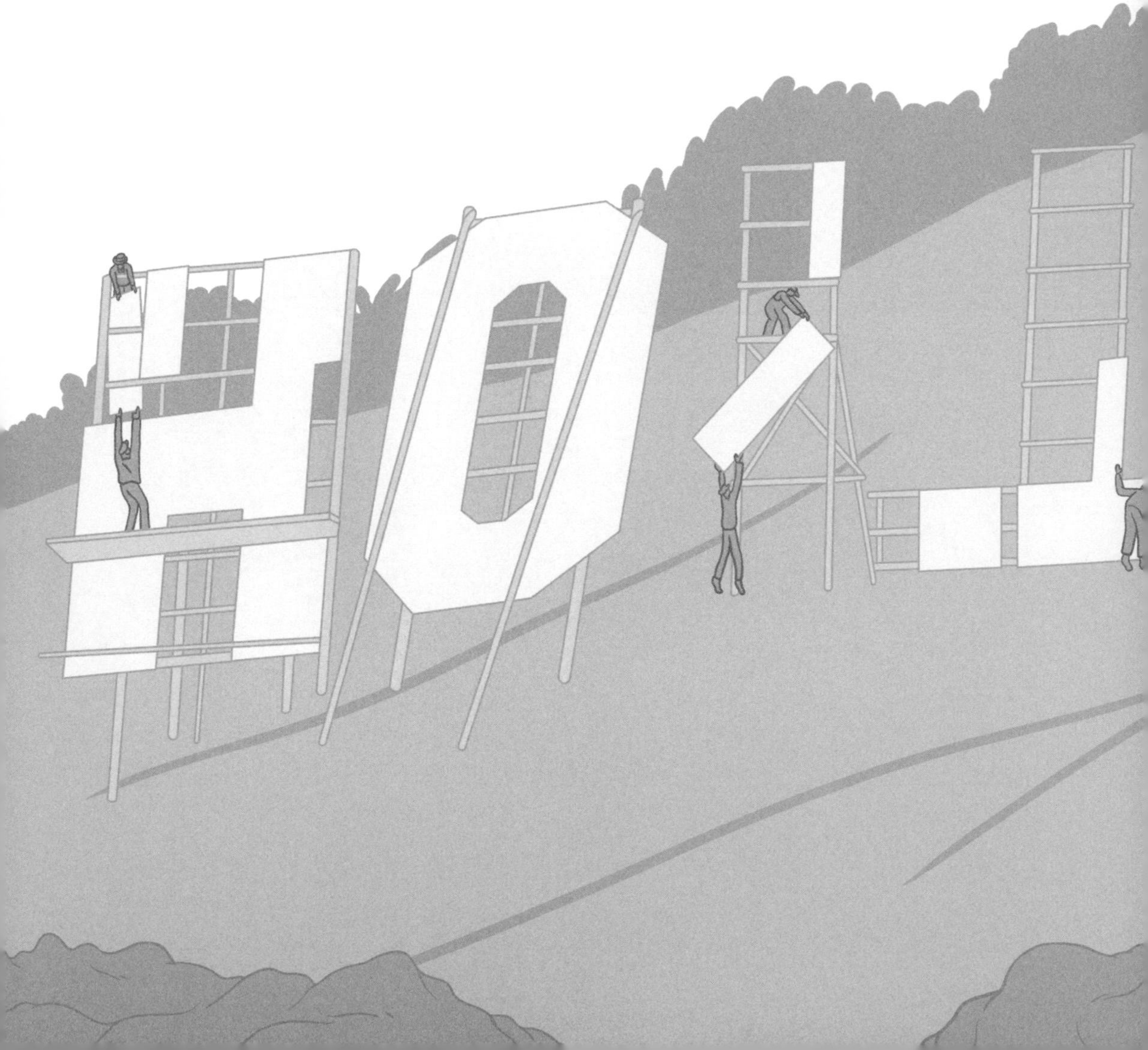

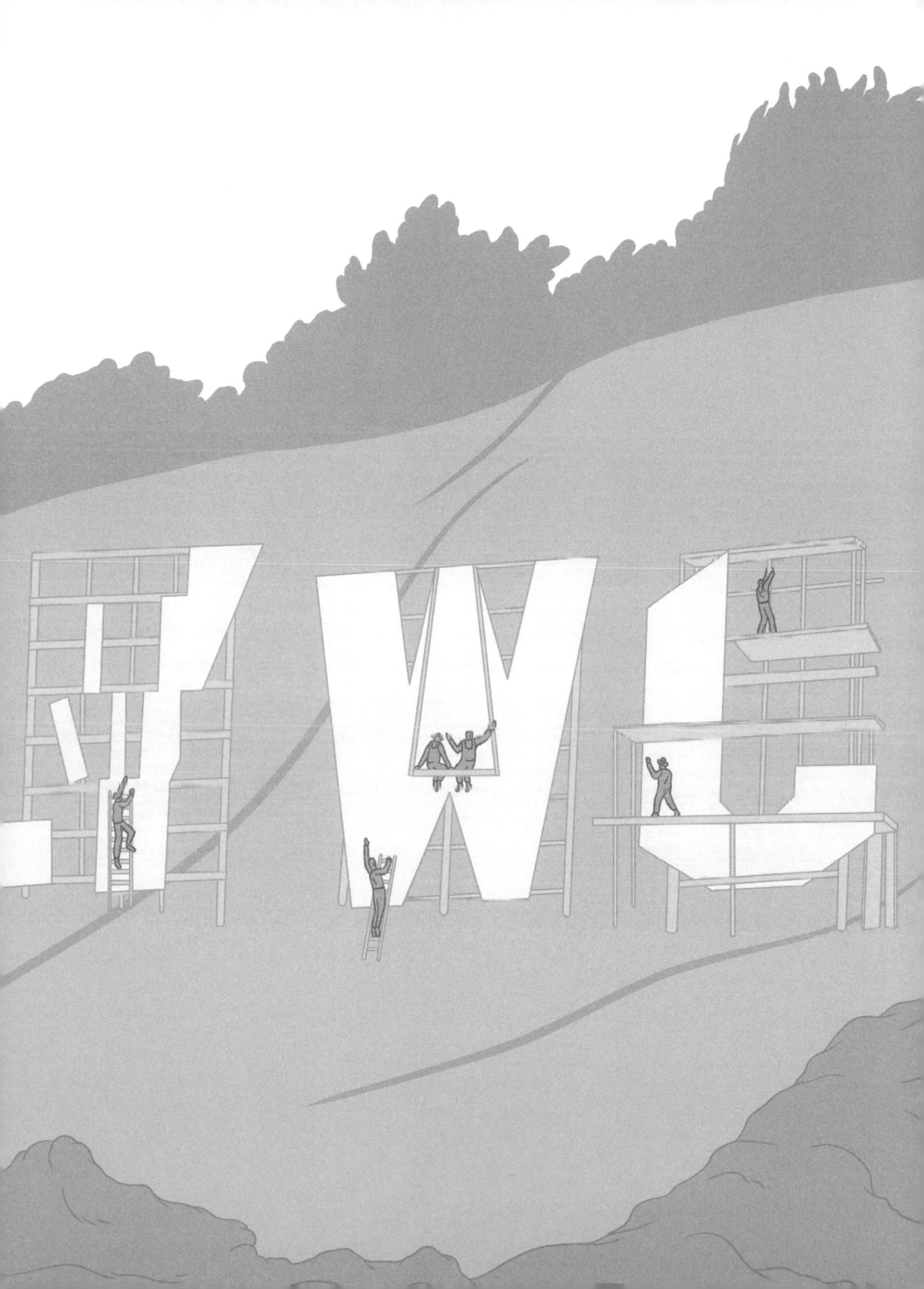

WHICH HE WAS SURPRISINGLY WELL CUT OUT FOR.

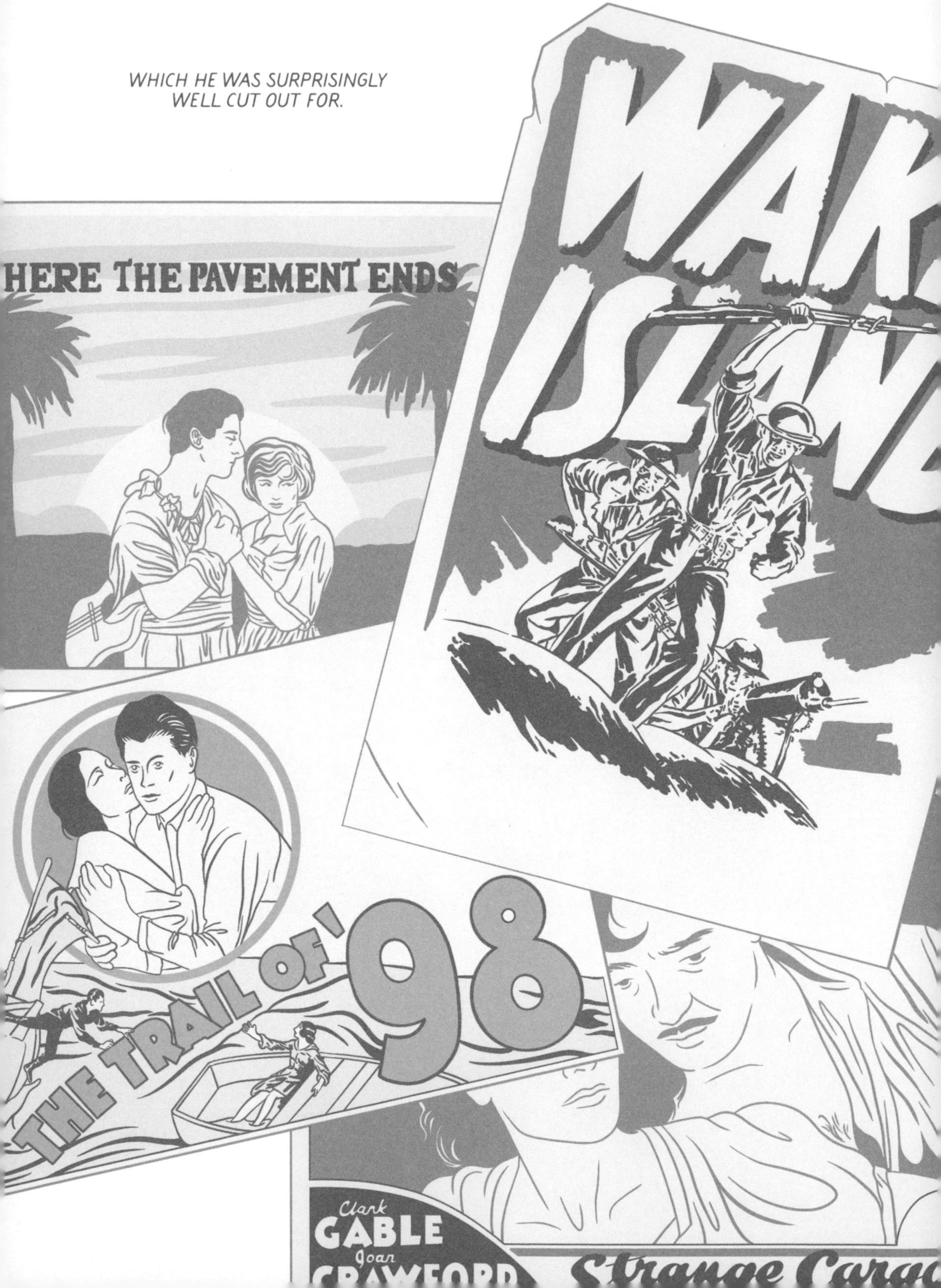
HERE THE PAVEMENT ENDS
THE TRAIL OF '98
Clark
GABLE
Joan

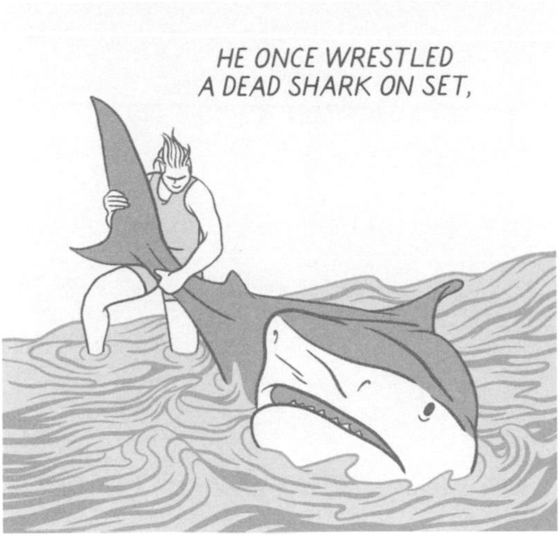
HE ONCE WRESTLED
A DEAD SHARK ON SET,

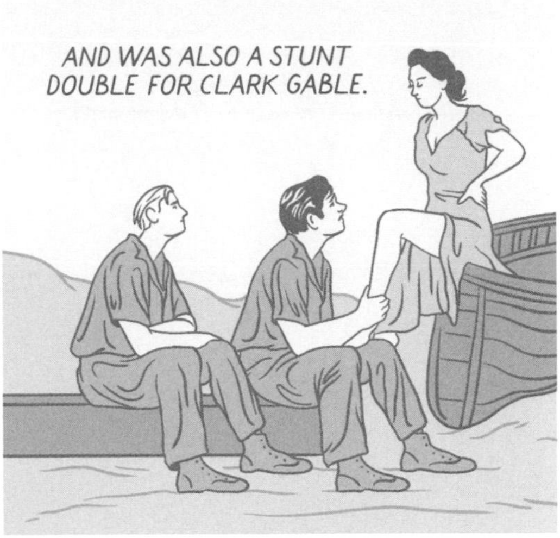
AND WAS ALSO A STUNT
DOUBLE FOR CLARK GABLE.

BUT THE FLASHING LIGHTS OF HOLLYWOOD SOON GREW DIM.
DURING THE FILMING OF "THE TRAIL OF '98", SEVERAL ACTORS DROWNED
DURING A SCENE DUE TO THE FILMMAKERS' NEGLIGENCE.

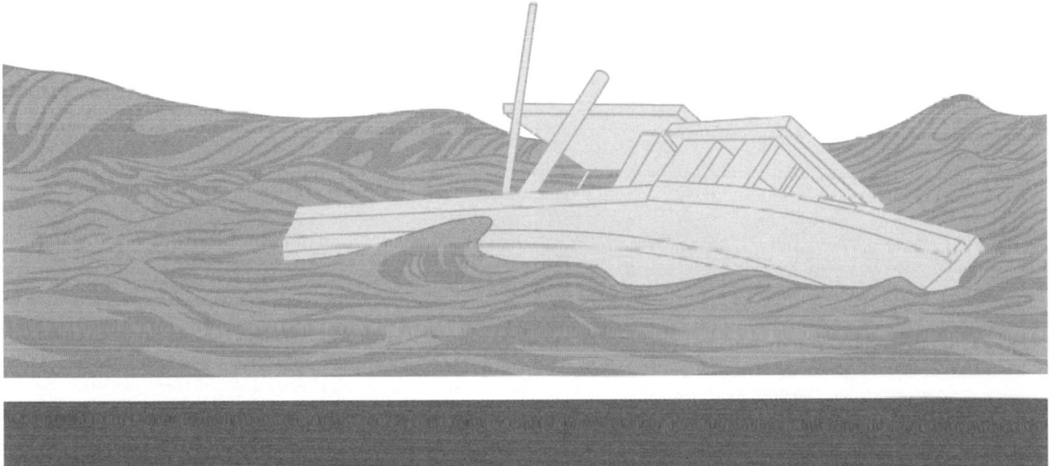

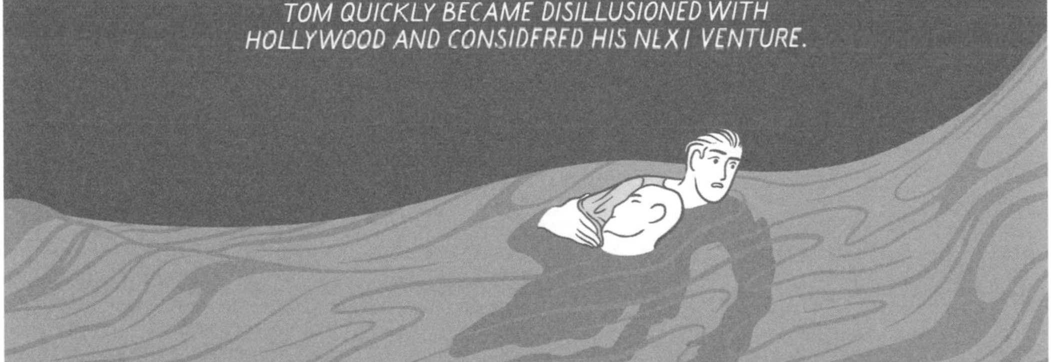
TOM QUICKLY BECAME DISILLUSIONED WITH
HOLLYWOOD AND CONSIDERED HIS NEXT VENTURE.

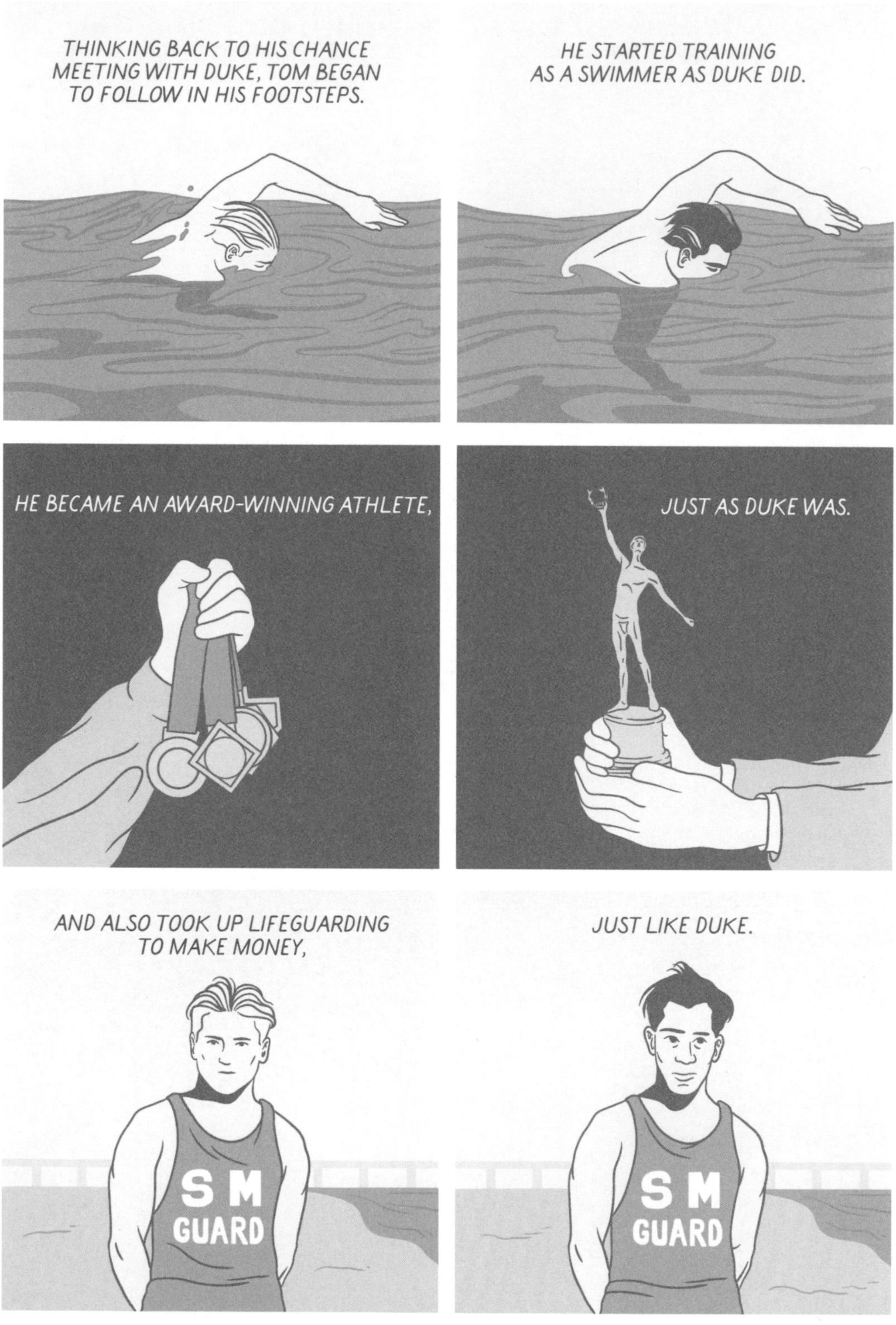
THINKING BACK TO HIS CHANCE MEETING WITH DUKE, TOM BEGAN TO FOLLOW IN HIS FOOTSTEPS.
HE STARTED TRAINING AS A SWIMMER AS DUKE DID.
HE BECAME AN AWARD-WINNING ATHLETE,
JUST AS DUKE WAS.
AND ALSO TOOK UP LIFEGUARDING TO MAKE MONEY,
S M GUARD
JUST LIKE DUKE.
S M GUARD

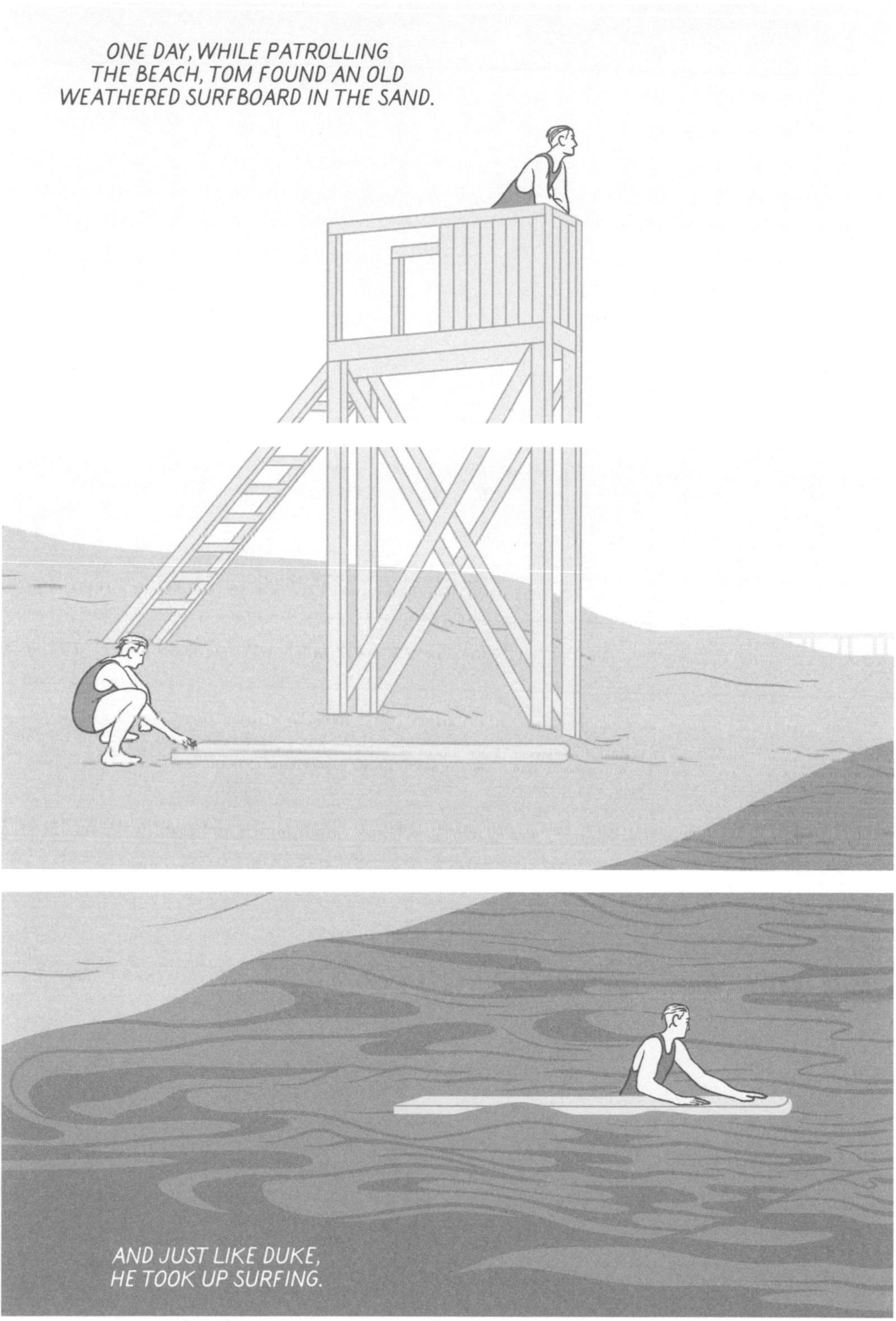
ONE DAY, WHILE PATROLLING THE BEACH, TOM FOUND AN OLD WEATHERED SURFBOARD IN THE SAND.
AND JUST LIKE DUKE, HE TOOK UP SURFING.

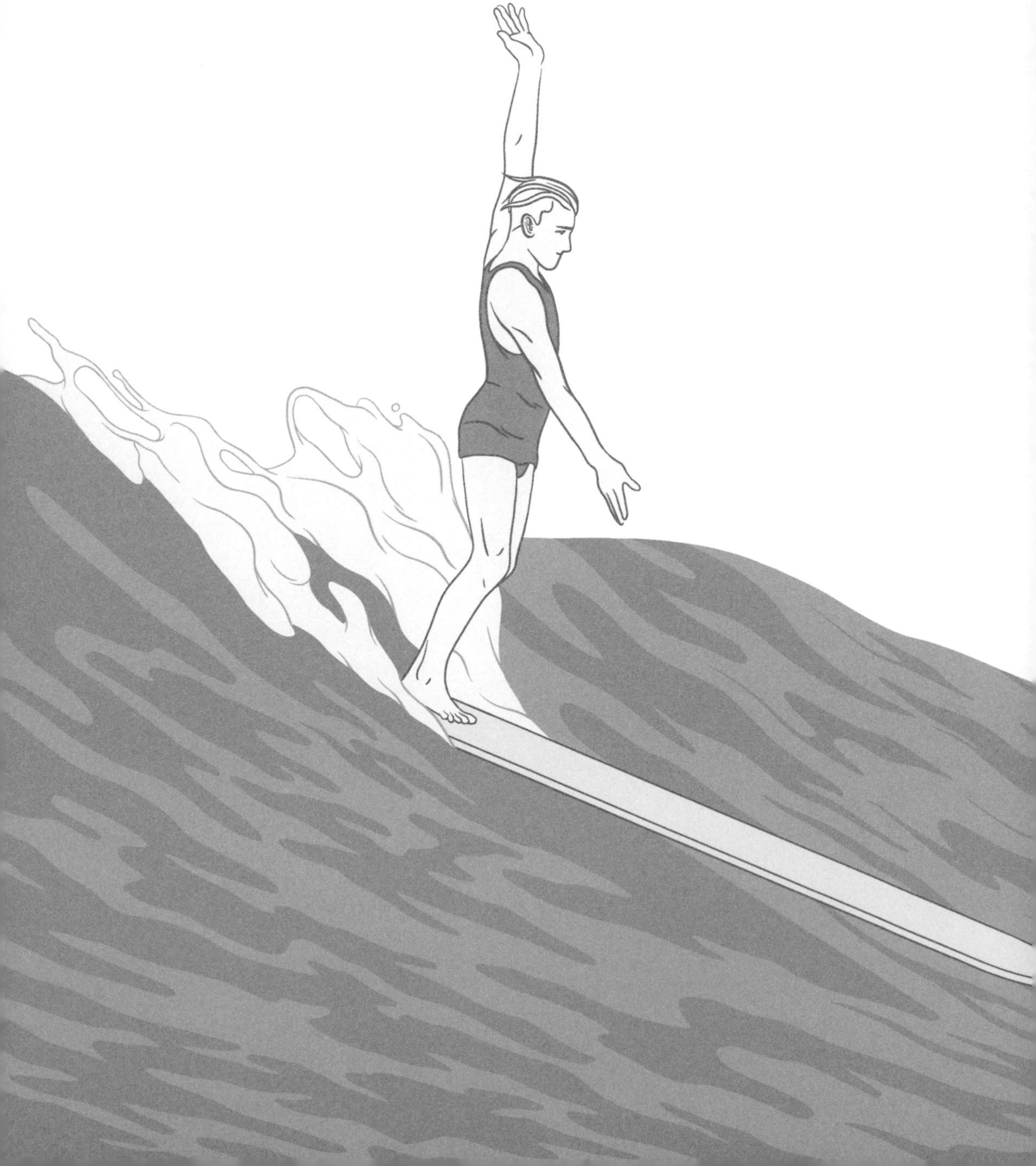

TOM CAUGHT HIS FIRST WAVE, AND HE WAS HOOKED.

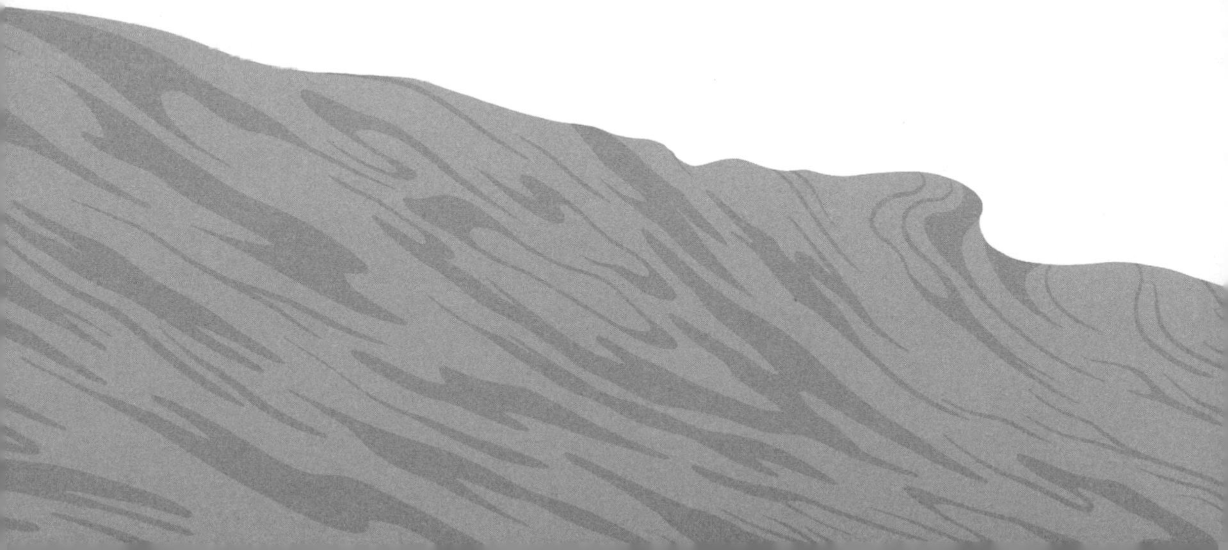

XI. FALLING

NOKIA

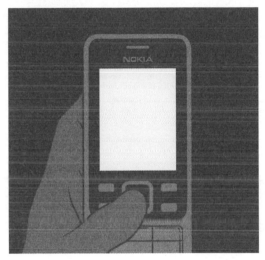

Summer 2007

Buena Park, California

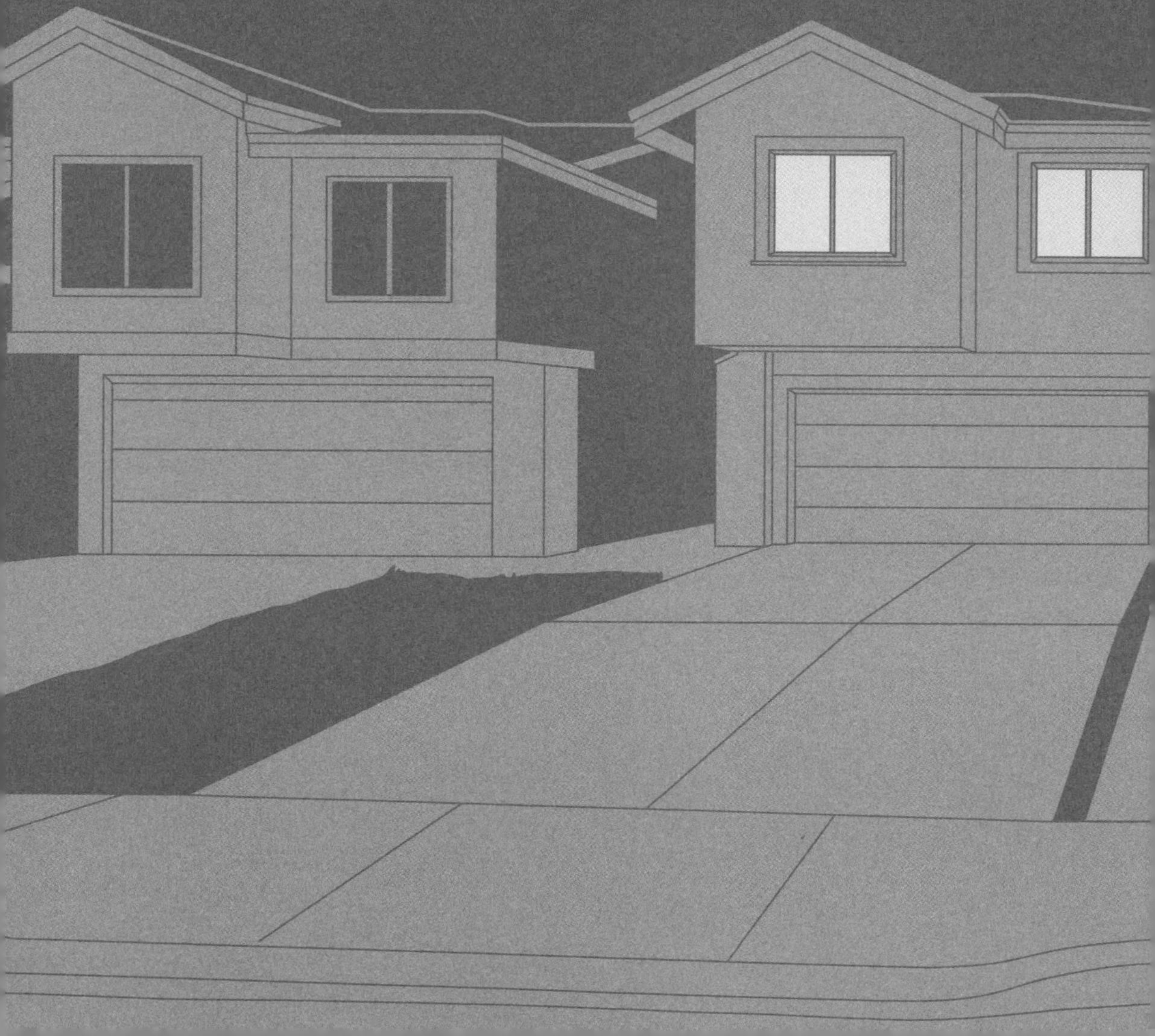

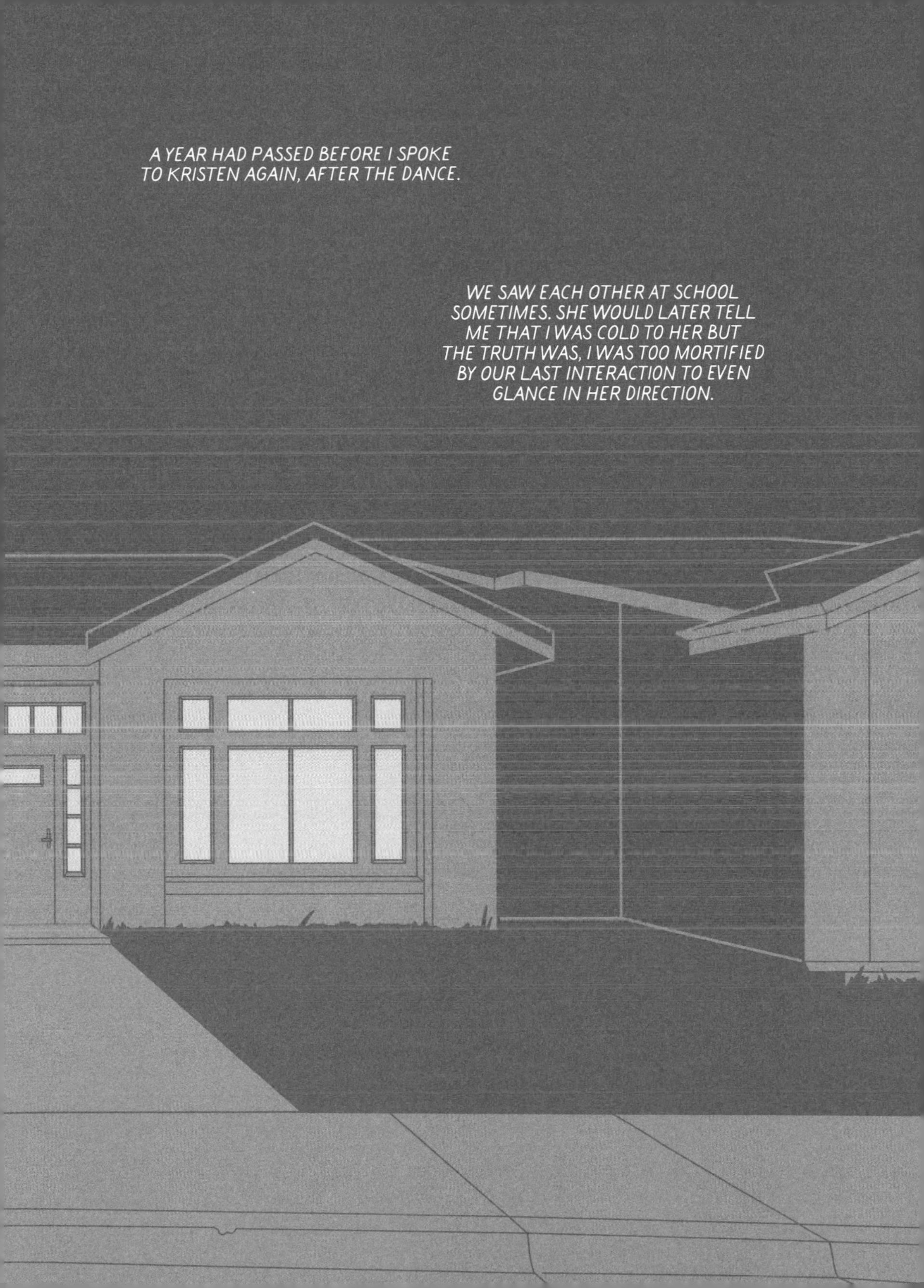
A YEAR HAD PASSED BEFORE I SPOKE TO KRISTEN AGAIN, AFTER THE DANCE.
WE SAW EACH OTHER AT SCHOOL SOMETIMES. SHE WOULD LATER TELL ME THAT I WAS COLD TO HER BUT THE TRUTH WAS, I WAS TOO MORTIFIED BY OUR LAST INTERACTION TO EVEN GLANCE IN HER DIRECTION.

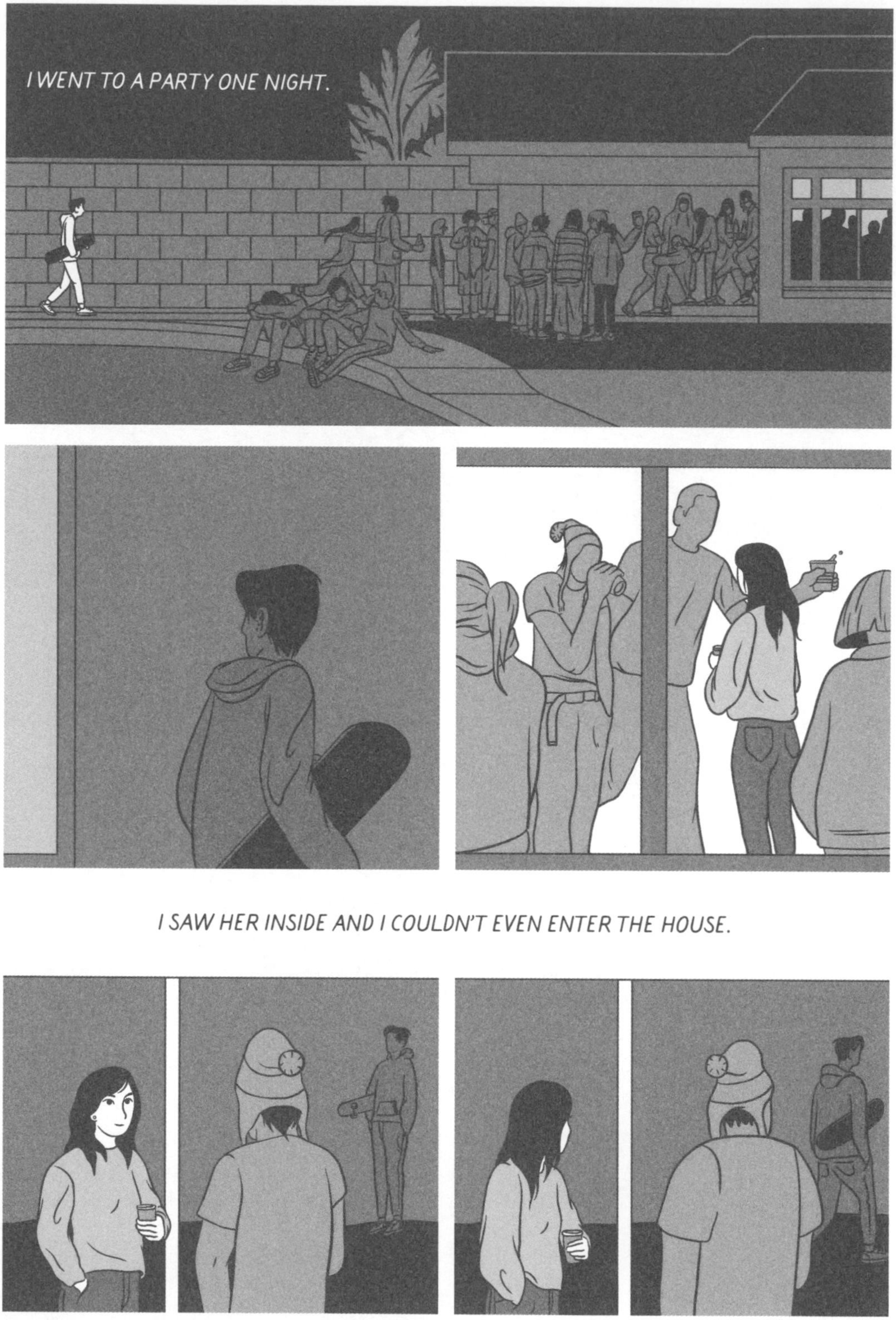
I WENT TO A PARTY ONE NIGHT.
I SAW HER INSIDE AND I COULDN'T EVEN ENTER THE HOUSE.

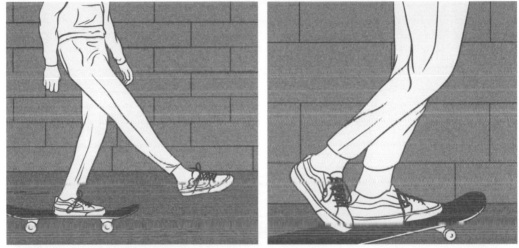

WHILE I WAS OUT FRONT, AN OLDER
GROUP OF KIDS WALKED UP TO THE PARTY.

ONE OF THEM APPROACHED ME,

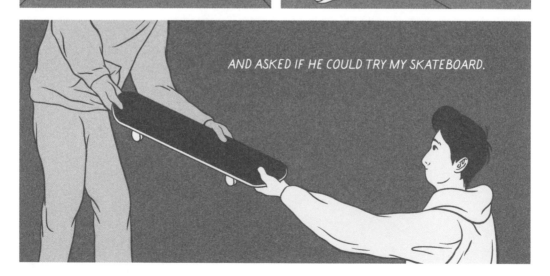

AND ASKED IF HE COULD TRY MY SKATEBOARD.

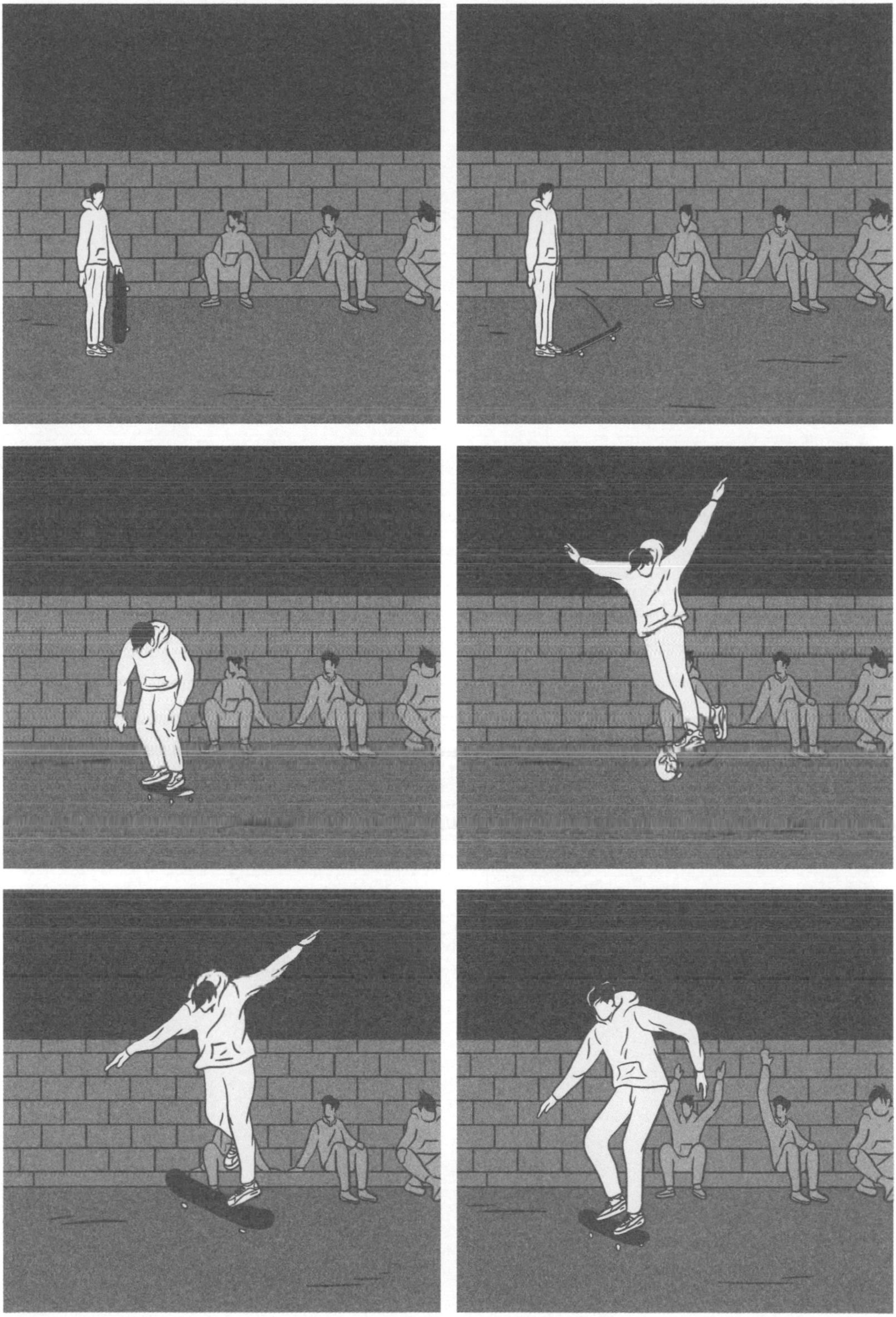

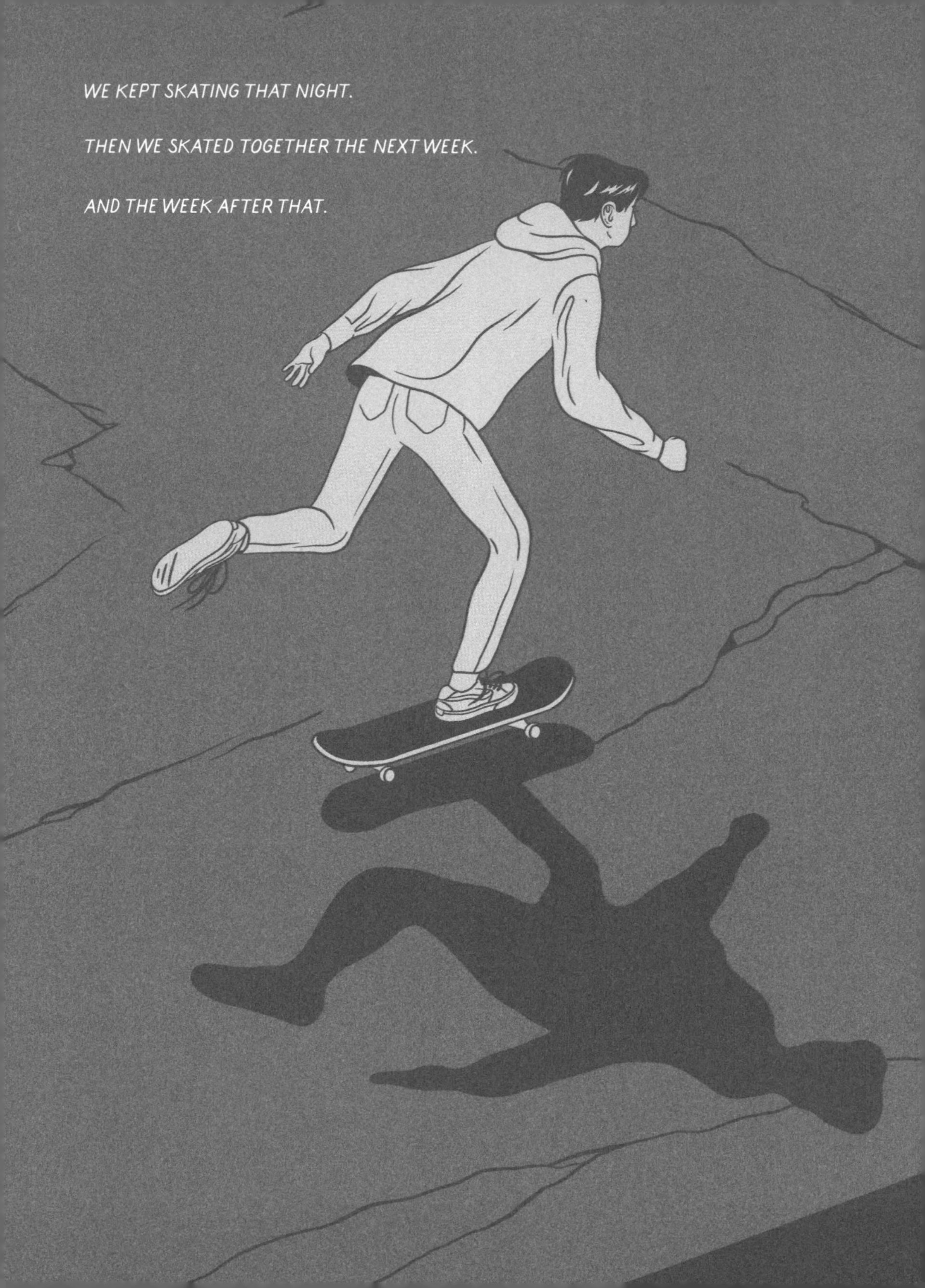
WE KEPT SKATING THAT NIGHT.
THEN WE SKATED TOGETHER THE NEXT WEEK.
AND THE WEEK AFTER THAT.

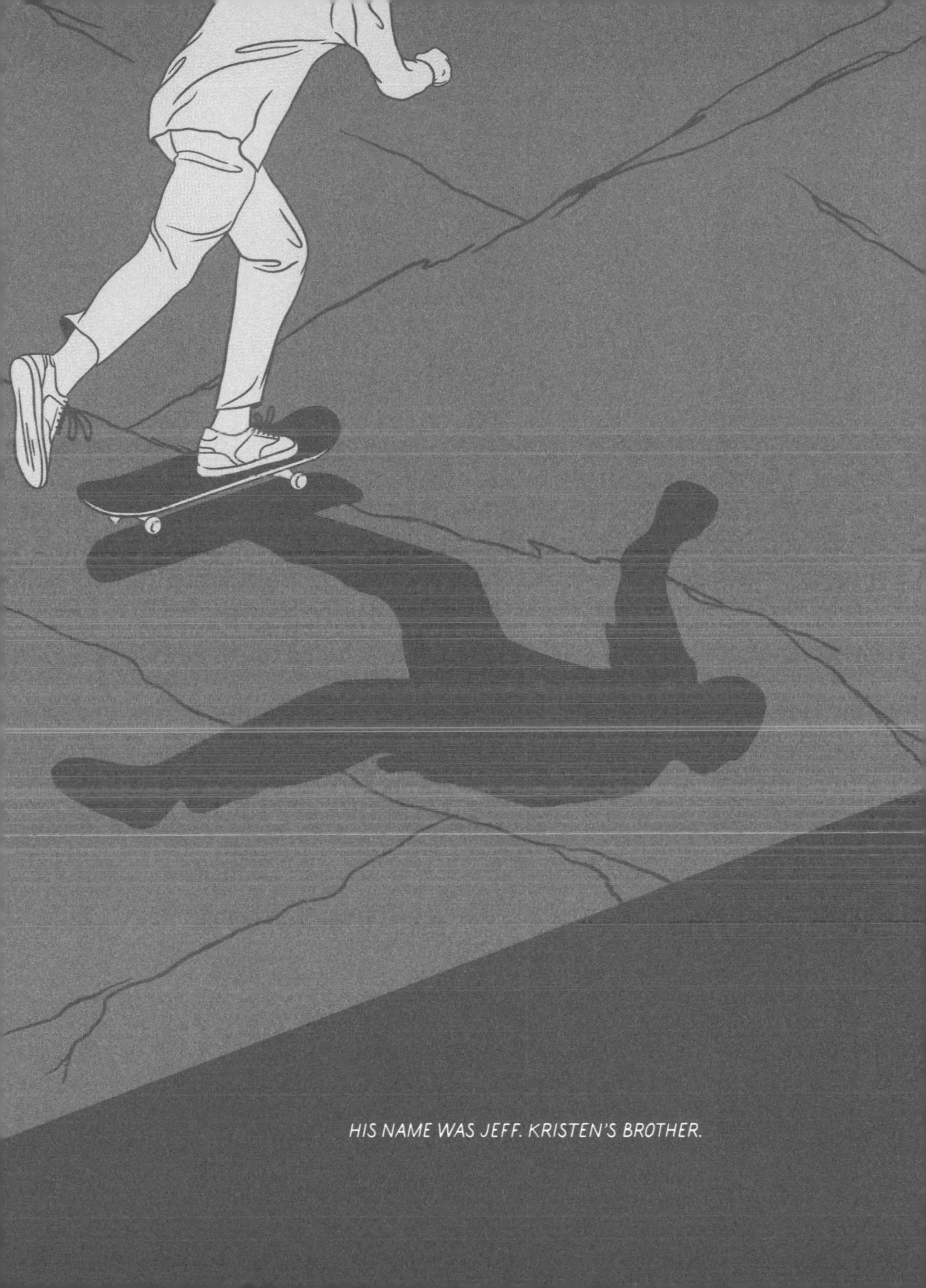
HIS NAME WAS JEFF. KRISTEN'S BROTHER.

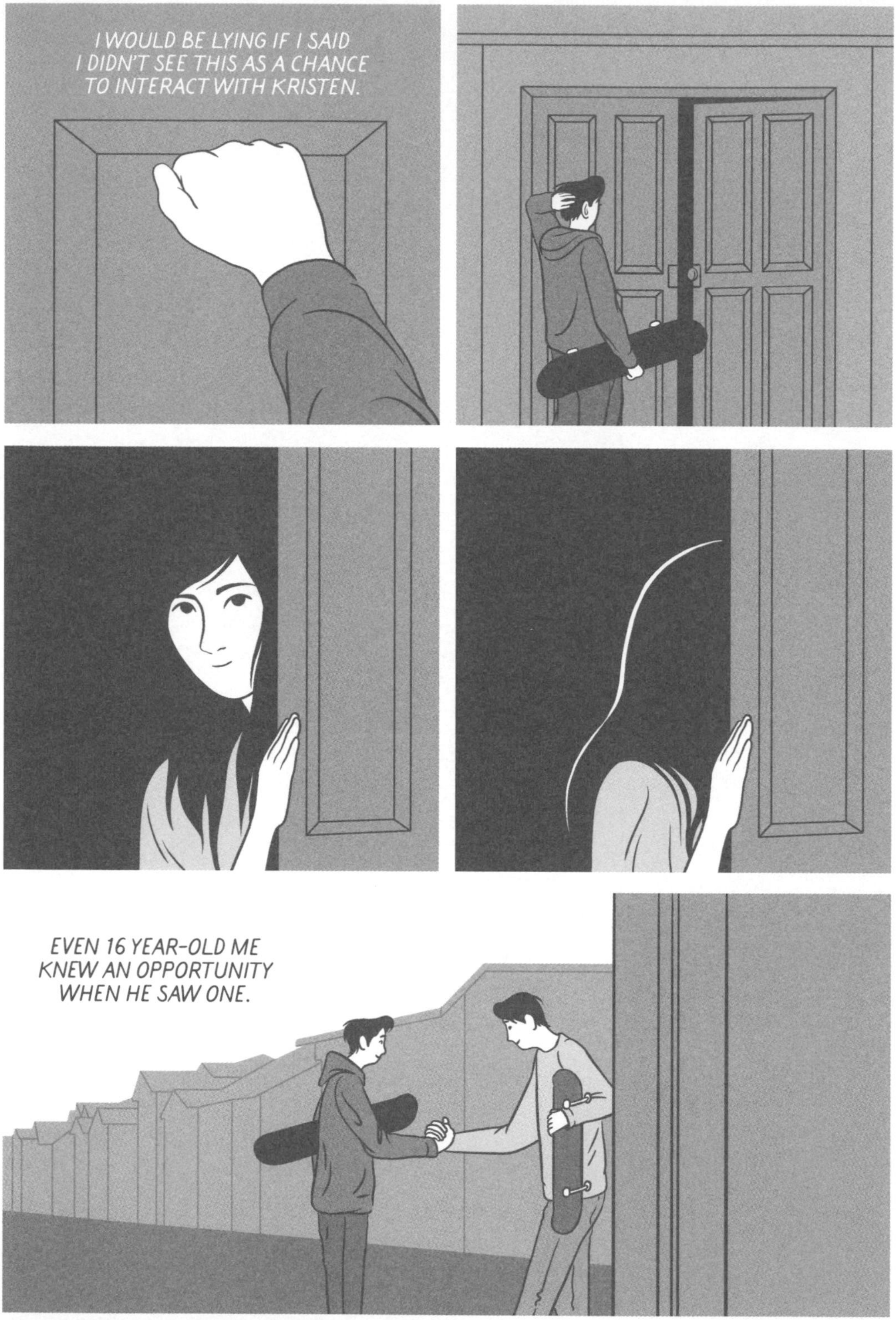
I WOULD BE LYING IF I SAID I DIDN'T SEE THIS AS A CHANCE TO INTERACT WITH KRISTEN.
EVEN 16 YEAR-OLD ME KNEW AN OPPORTUNITY WHEN HE SAW ONE.

EVENTUALLY, KRISTEN BECAME CURIOUS AS TO WHY
I WAS SPENDING SO MUCH TIME WITH HER BROTHER.

WE WOULD SKATE AND KRISTEN WOULD QUIETLY OBSERVE.

I THINK HAVING HER BROTHER'S APPROVAL MADE
KRISTEN START TO LOOK AT ME DIFFERENTLY.

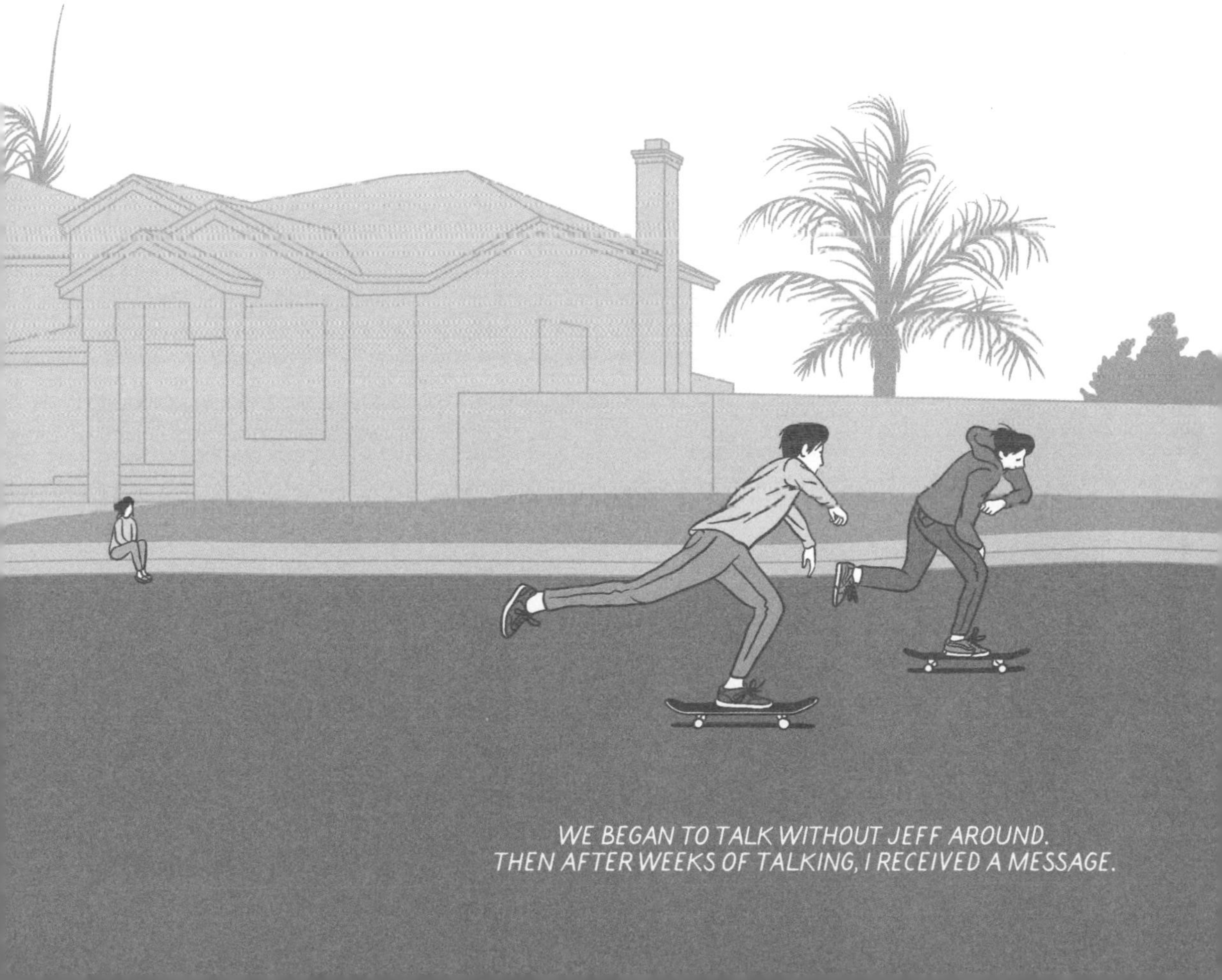
WE BEGAN TO TALK WITHOUT JEFF AROUND.
THEN AFTER WEEKS OF TALKING, I RECEIVED A MESSAGE.

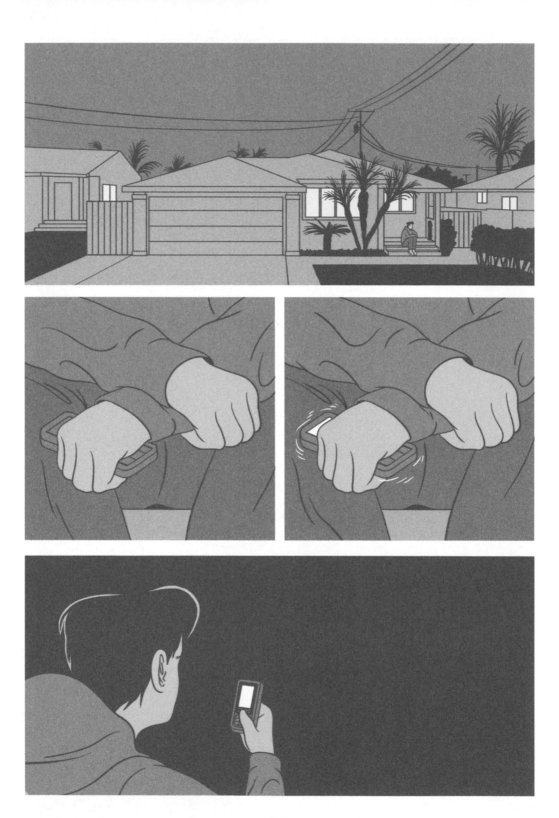

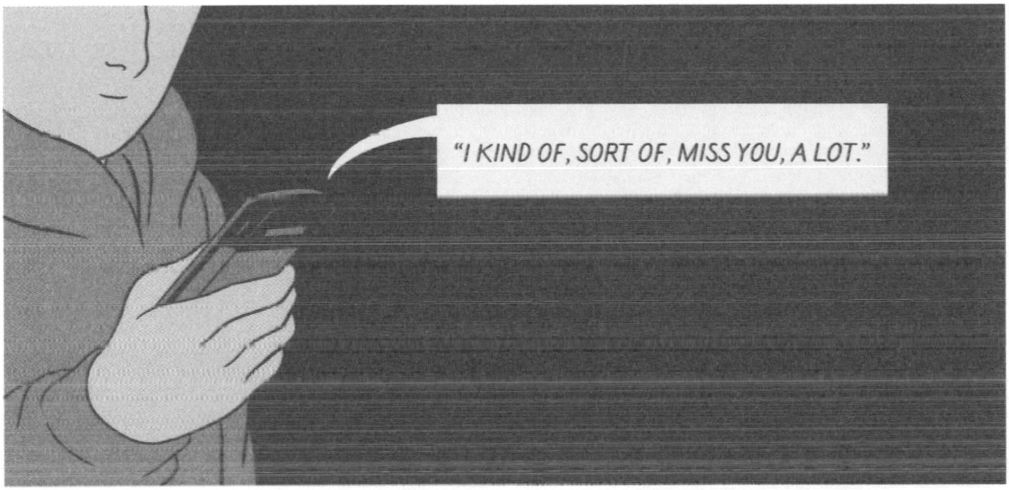
"I KIND OF, SORT OF, MISS YOU, A LOT."

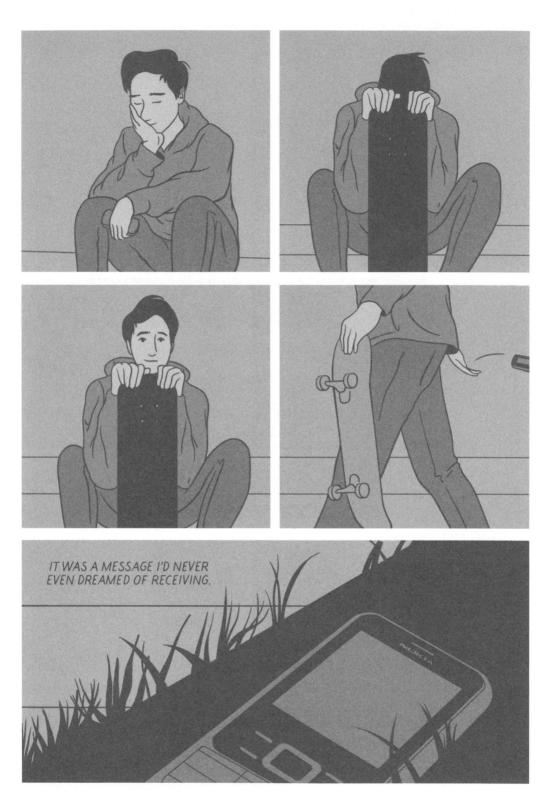

IT WAS A MESSAGE I'D NEVER
EVEN DREAMED OF RECEIVING.

232

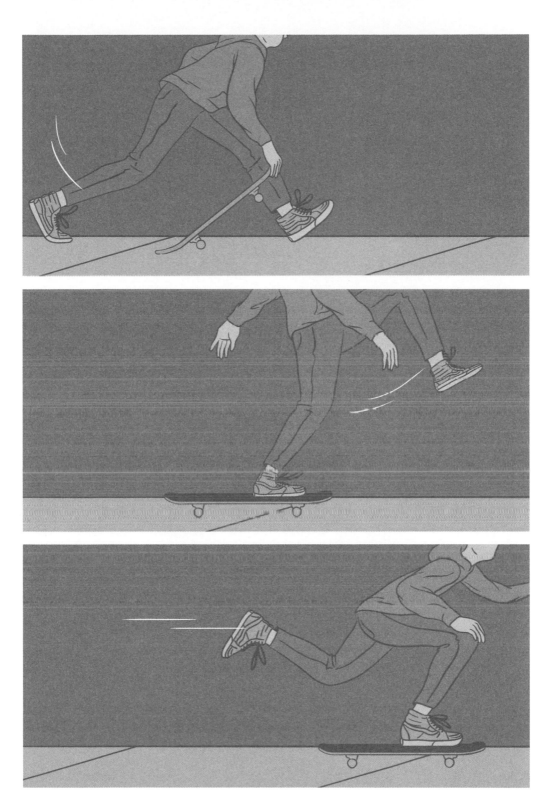

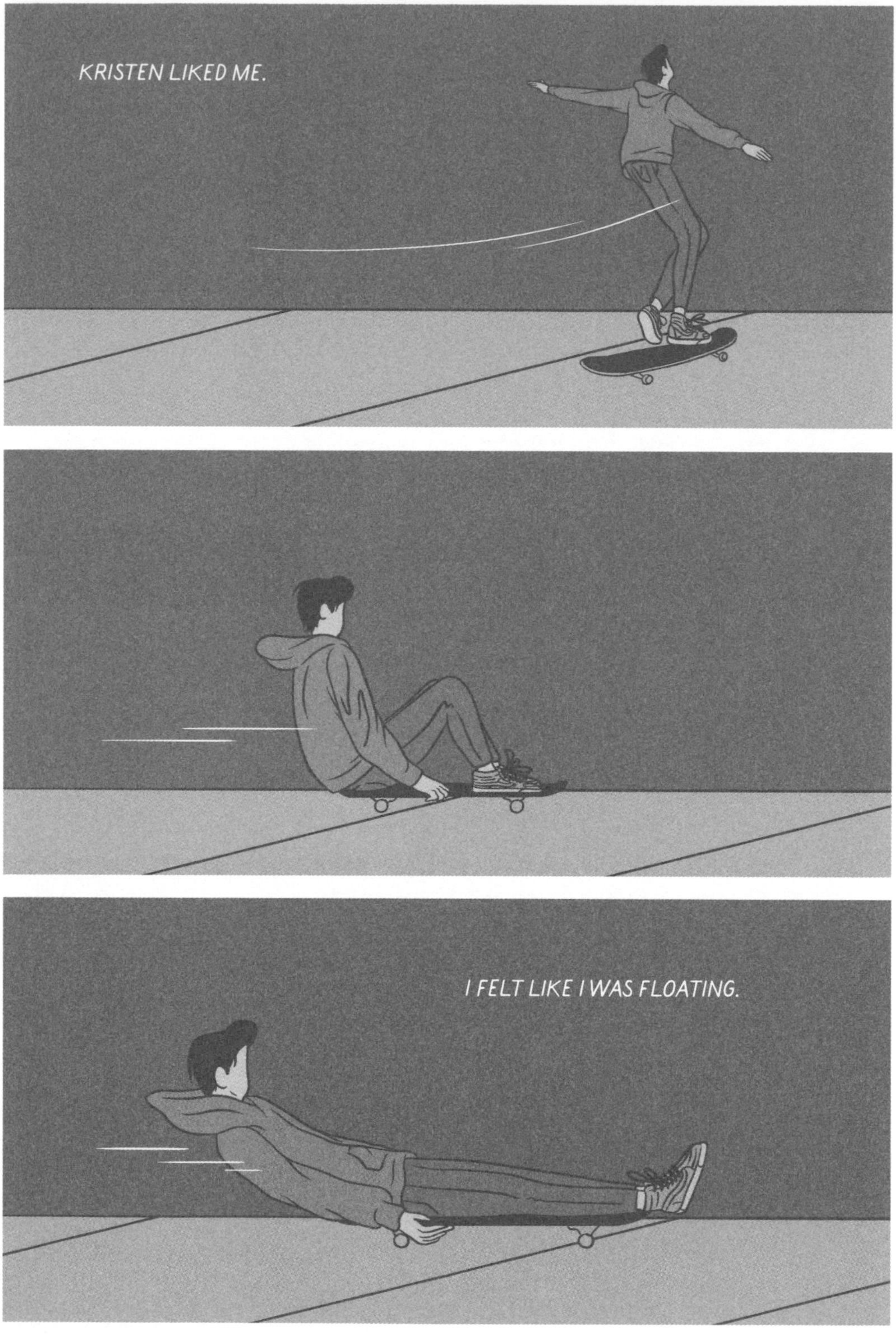
KRISTEN LIKED ME.
I FELT LIKE I WAS FLOATING.

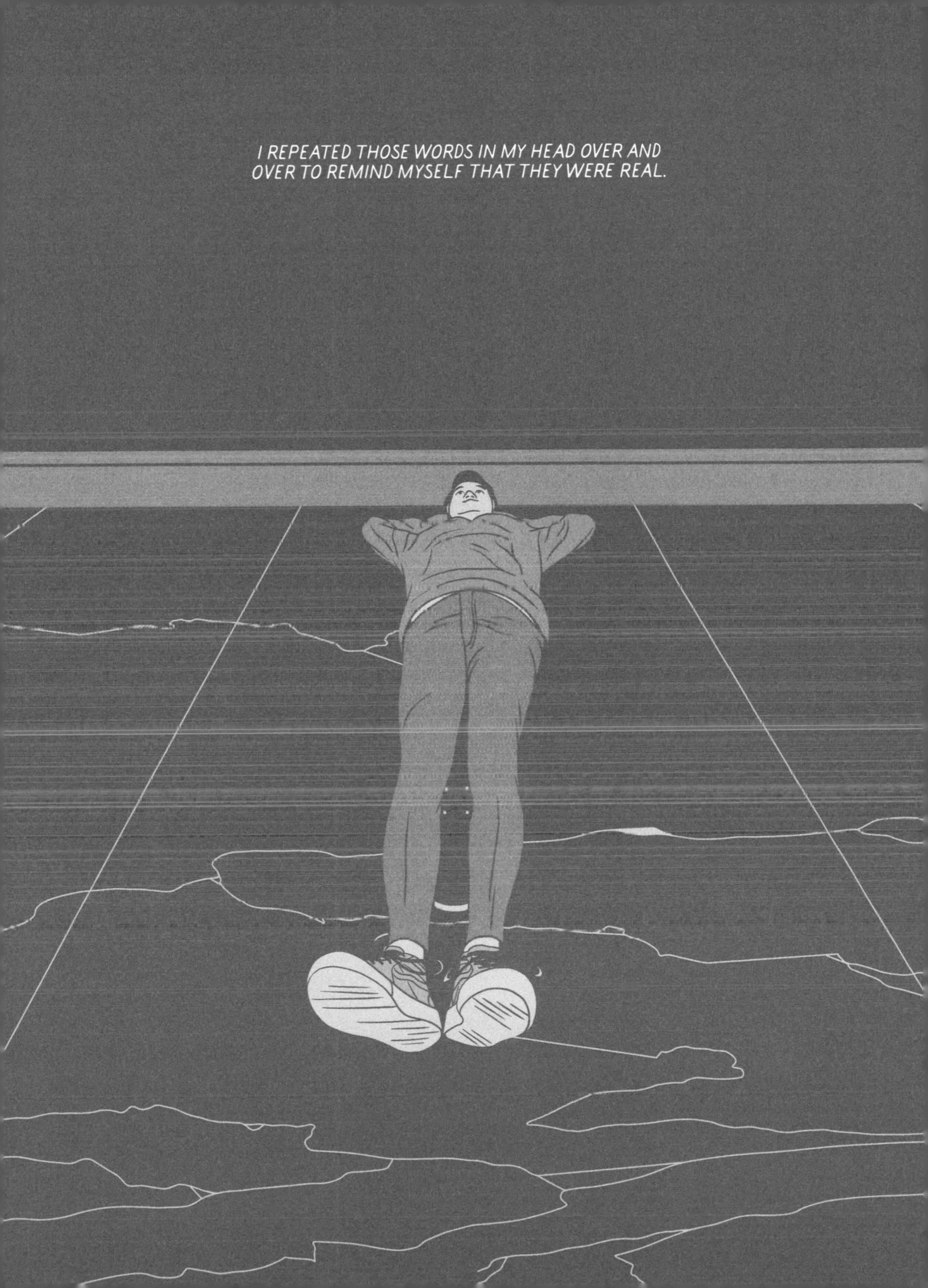
I REPEATED THOSE WORDS IN MY HEAD OVER AND OVER TO REMIND MYSELF THAT THEY WERE REAL.

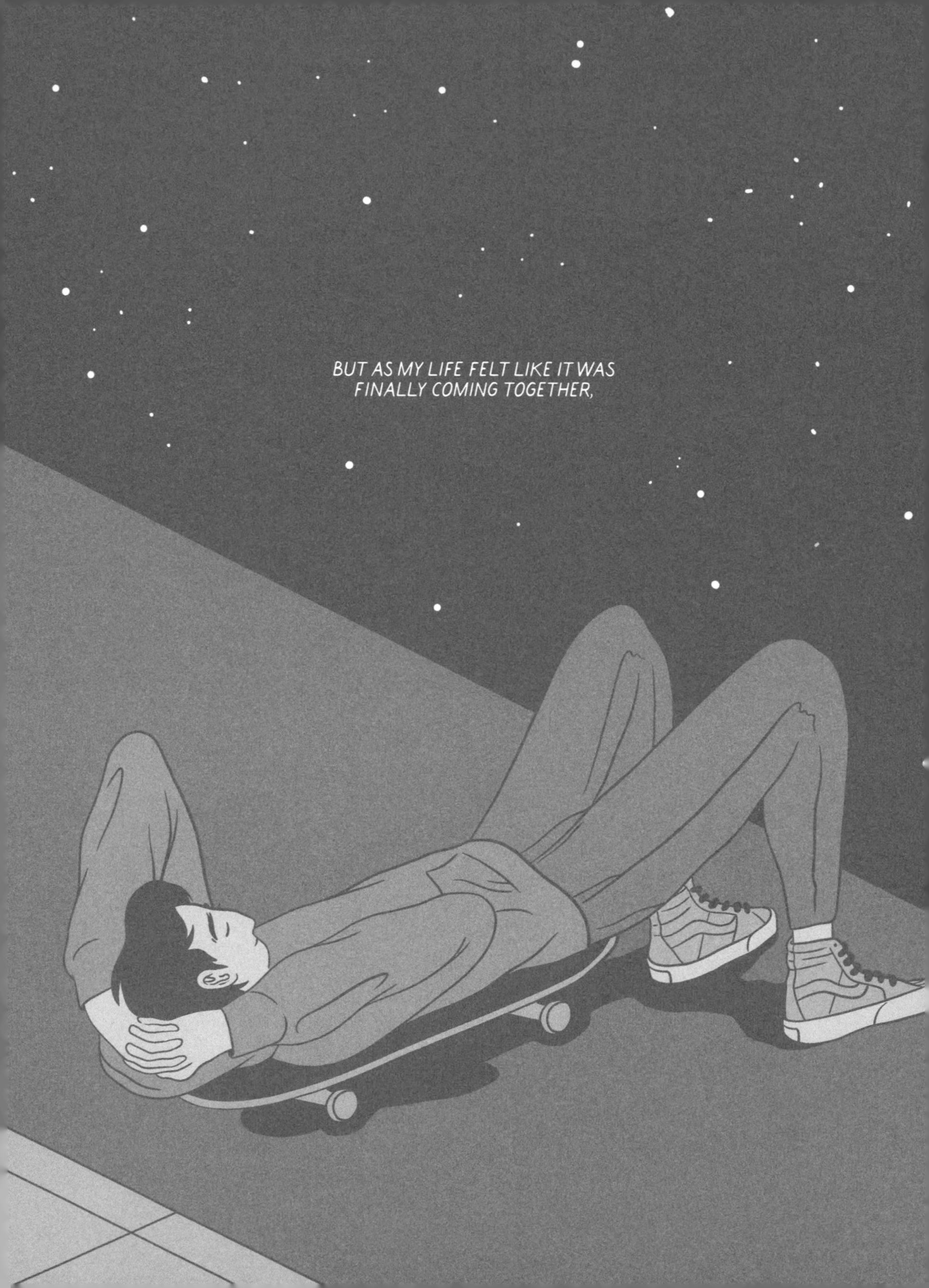
BUT AS MY LIFE FELT LIKE IT WAS FINALLY COMING TOGETHER,

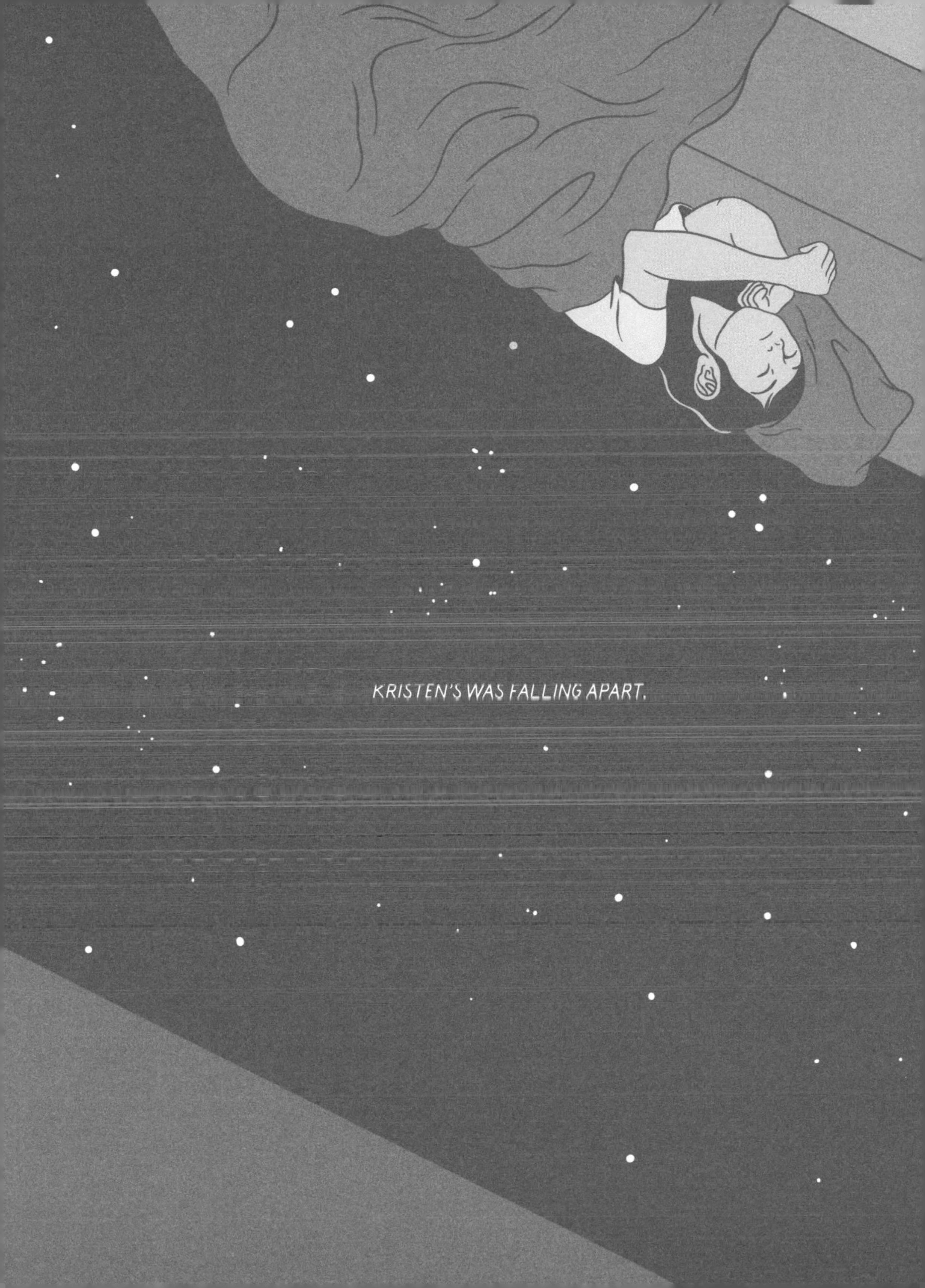
KRISTEN'S WAS FALLING APART.

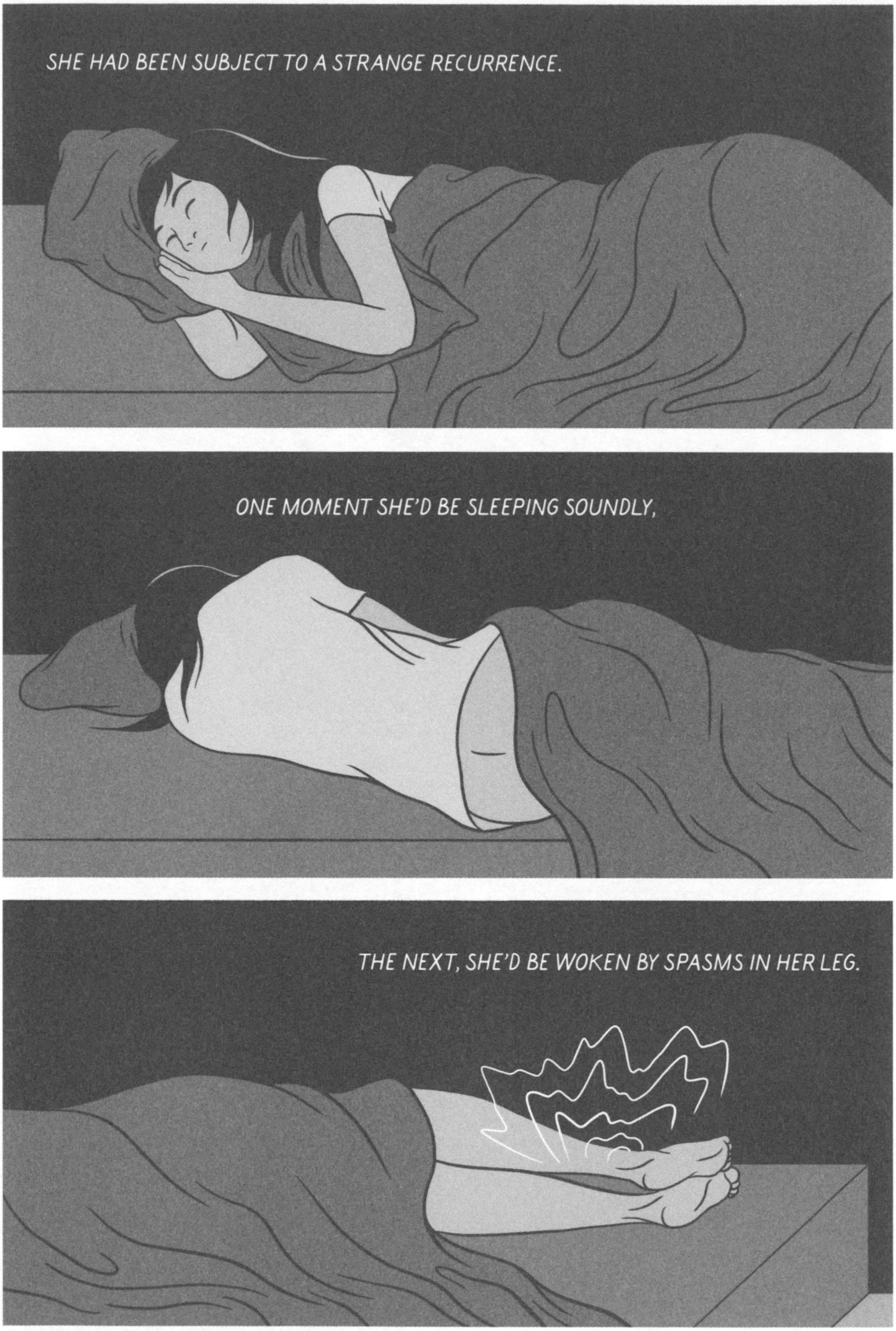
SHE HAD BEEN SUBJECT TO A STRANGE RECURRENCE.
ONE MOMENT SHE'D BE SLEEPING SOUNDLY,
THE NEXT, SHE'D BE WOKEN BY SPASMS IN HER LEG.

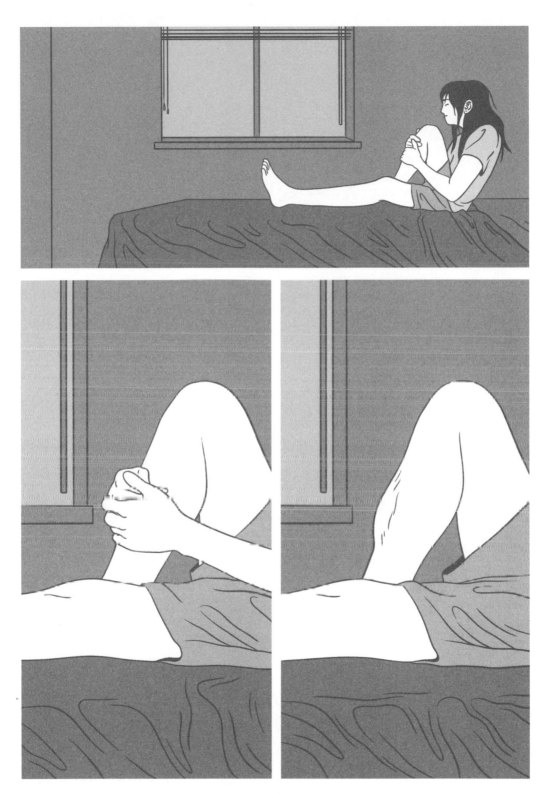

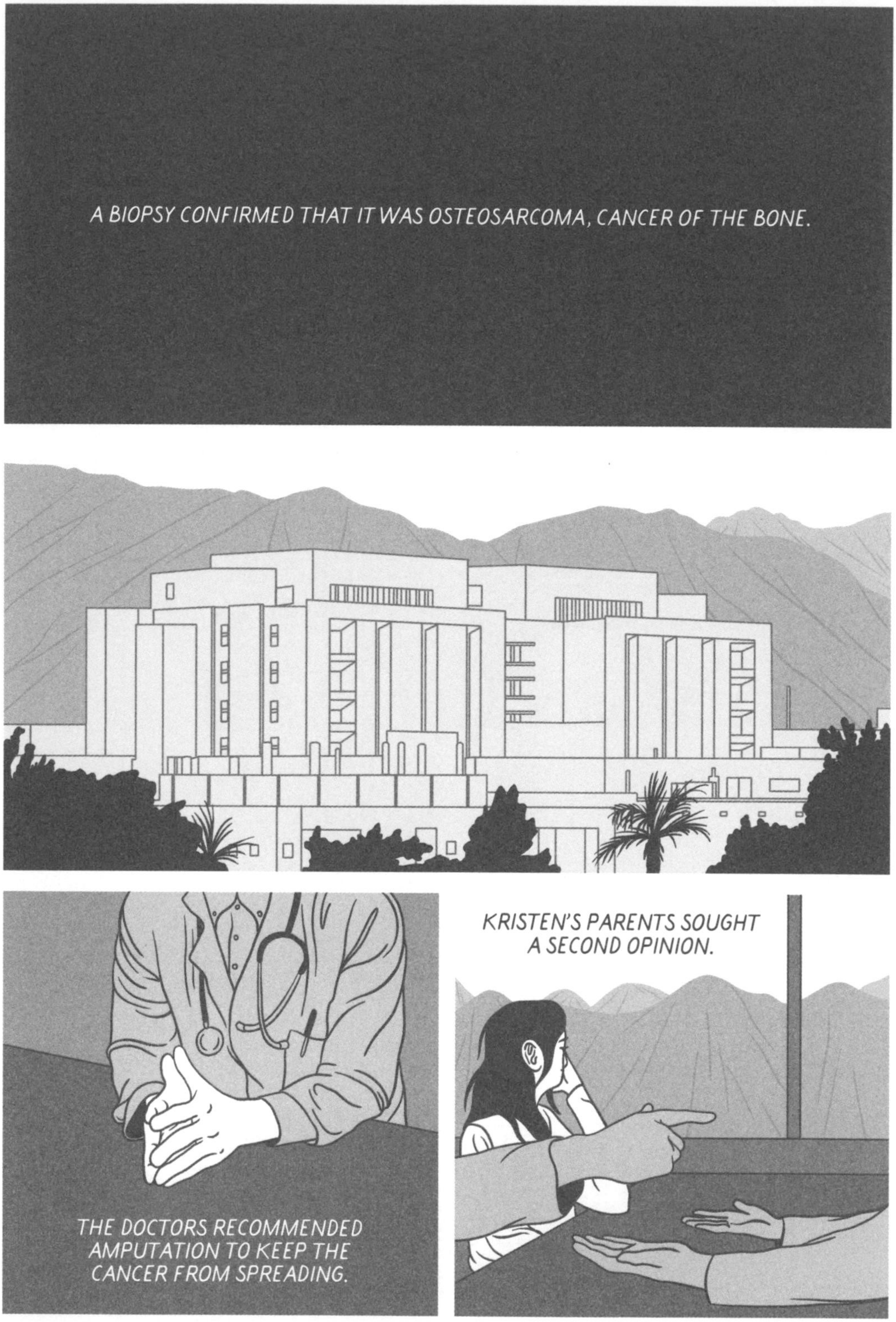
A BIOPSY CONFIRMED THAT IT WAS OSTEOSARCOMA, CANCER OF THE BONE.
THE DOCTORS RECOMMENDED AMPUTATION TO KEEP THE CANCER FROM SPREADING.
KRISTEN'S PARENTS SOUGHT A SECOND OPINION.

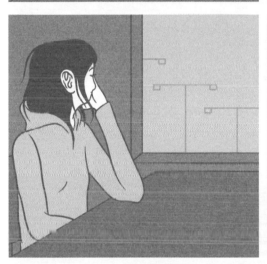

AFTER SITTING THROUGH MEETING AFTER MEETING, KRISTEN DECIDED THAT SHE WOULD RATHER LOSE HER LEG THAN HER LIFE.

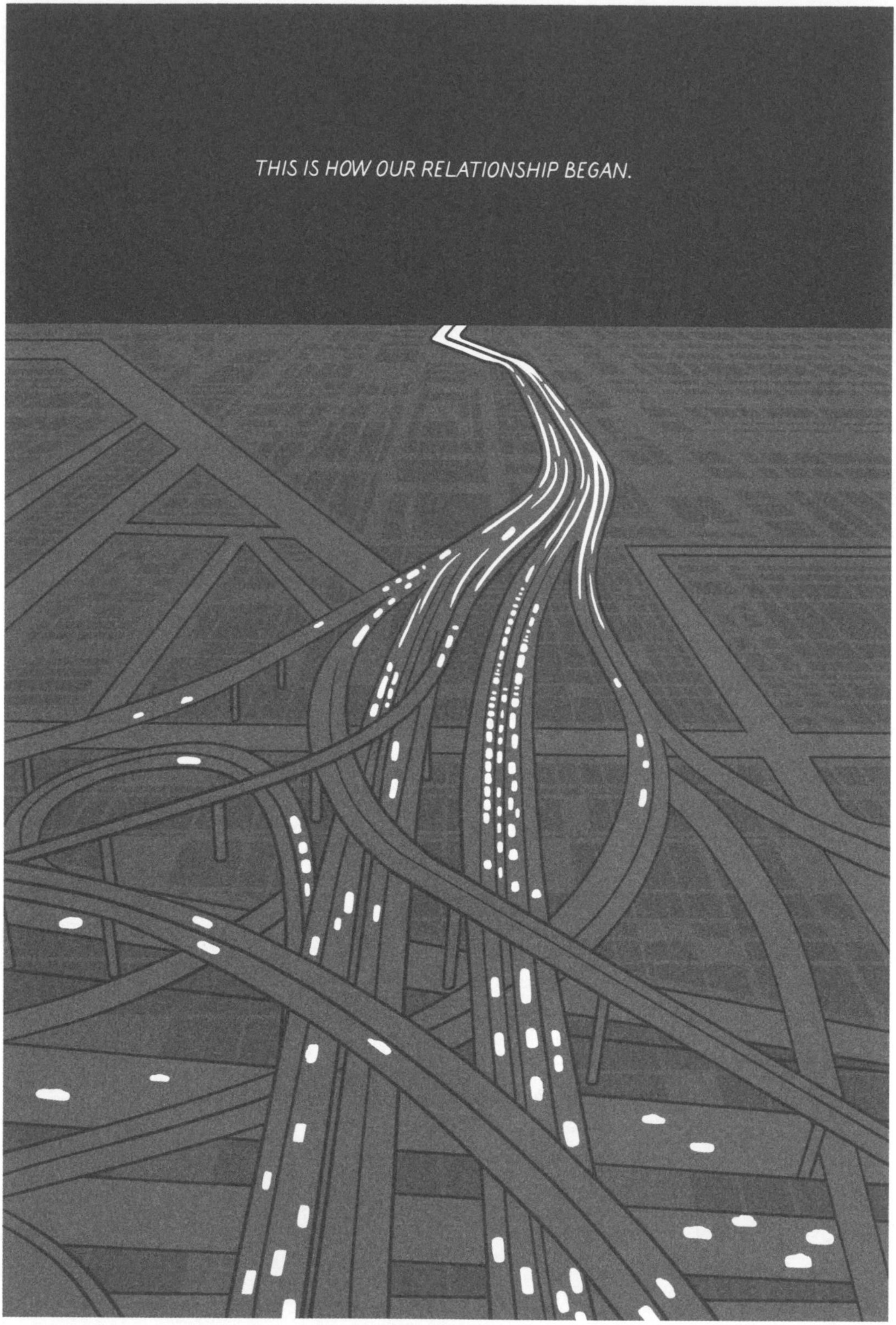
THIS IS HOW OUR RELATIONSHIP BEGAN.

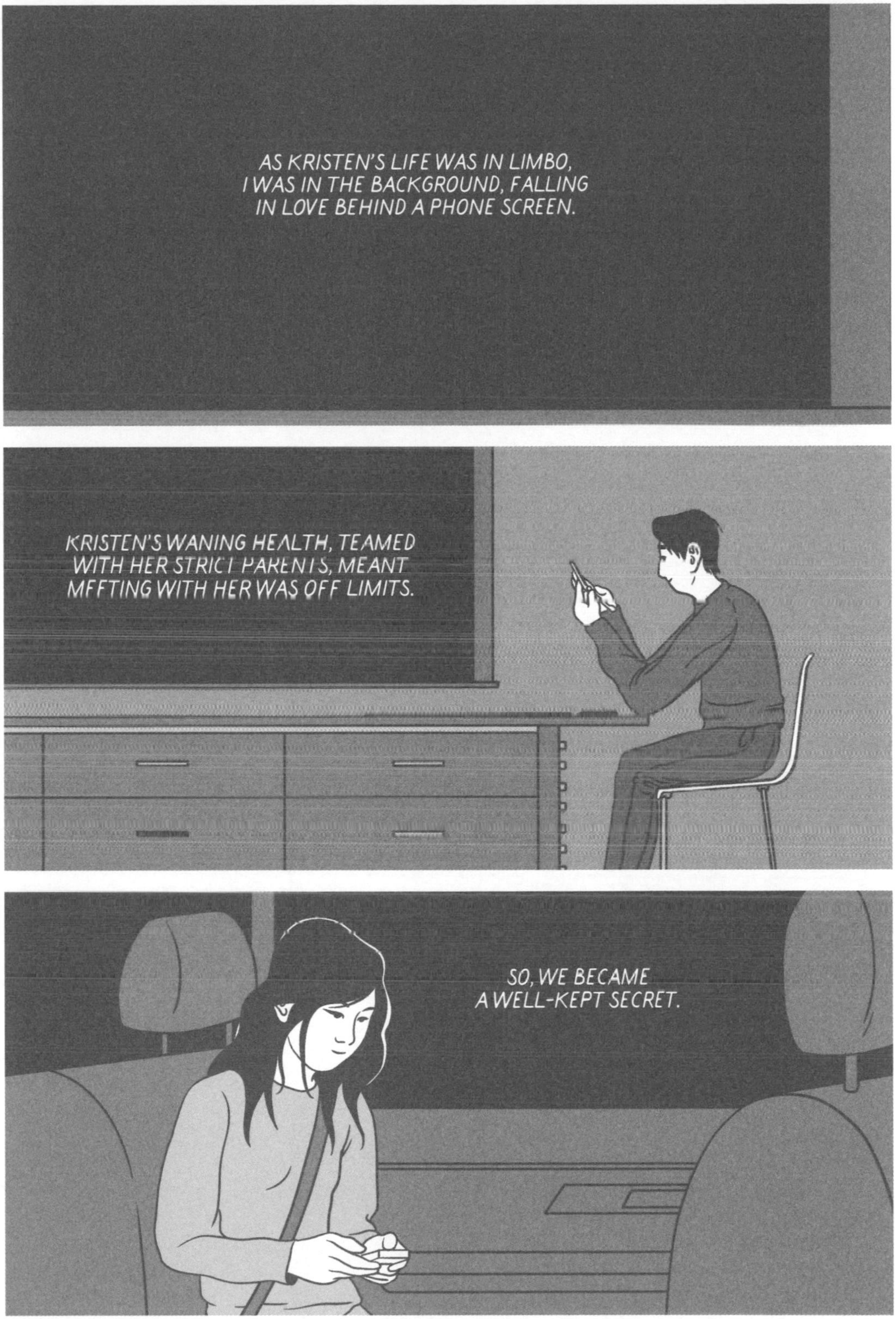
AS KRISTEN'S LIFE WAS IN LIMBO, I WAS IN THE BACKGROUND, FALLING IN LOVE BEHIND A PHONE SCREEN.
KRISTEN'S WANING HEALTH, TEAMED WITH HER STRICT PARENTS, MEANT MEETING WITH HER WAS OFF LIMITS.
SO, WE BECAME A WELL-KEPT SECRET.

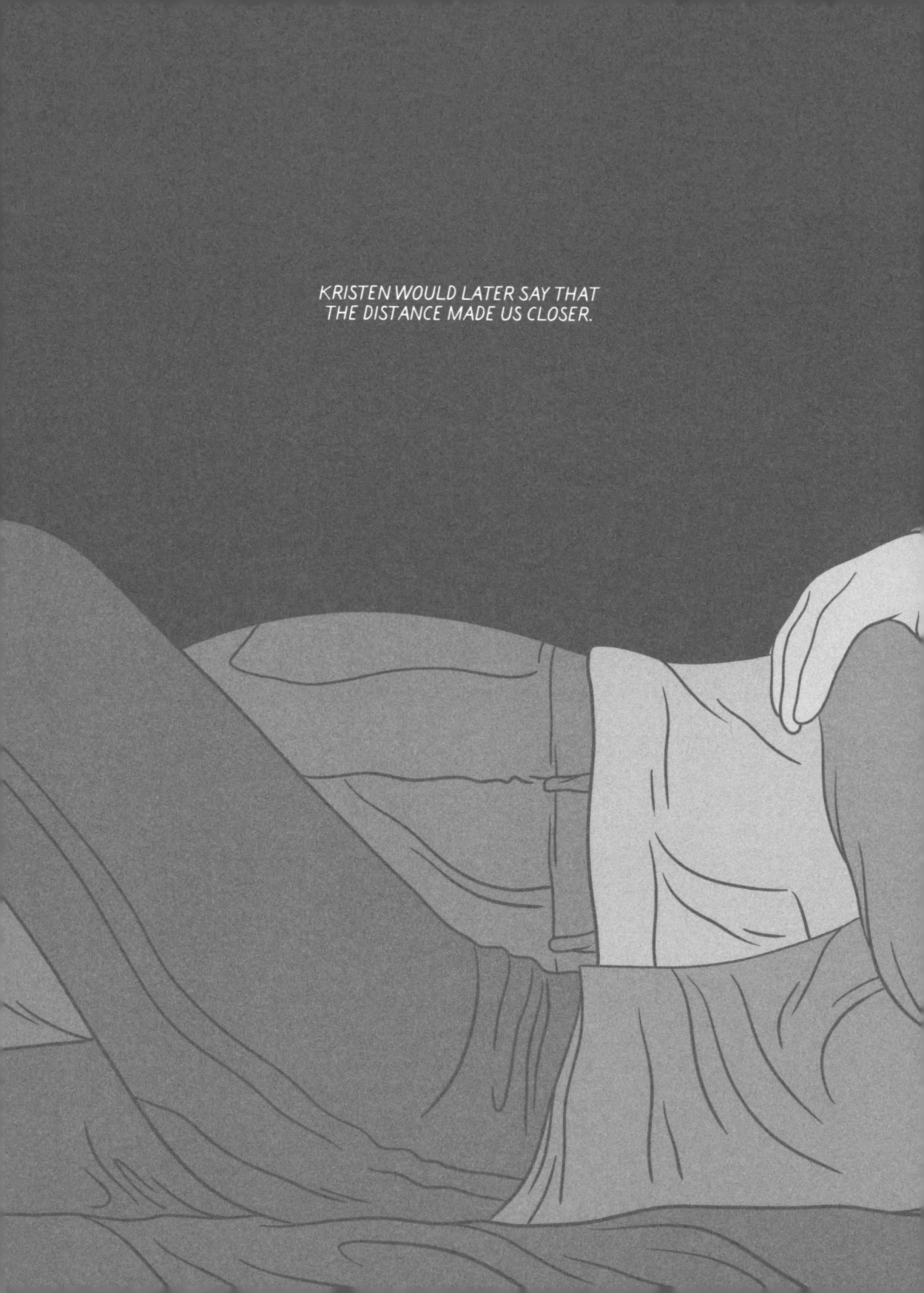
KRISTEN WOULD LATER SAY THAT THE DISTANCE MADE US CLOSER.

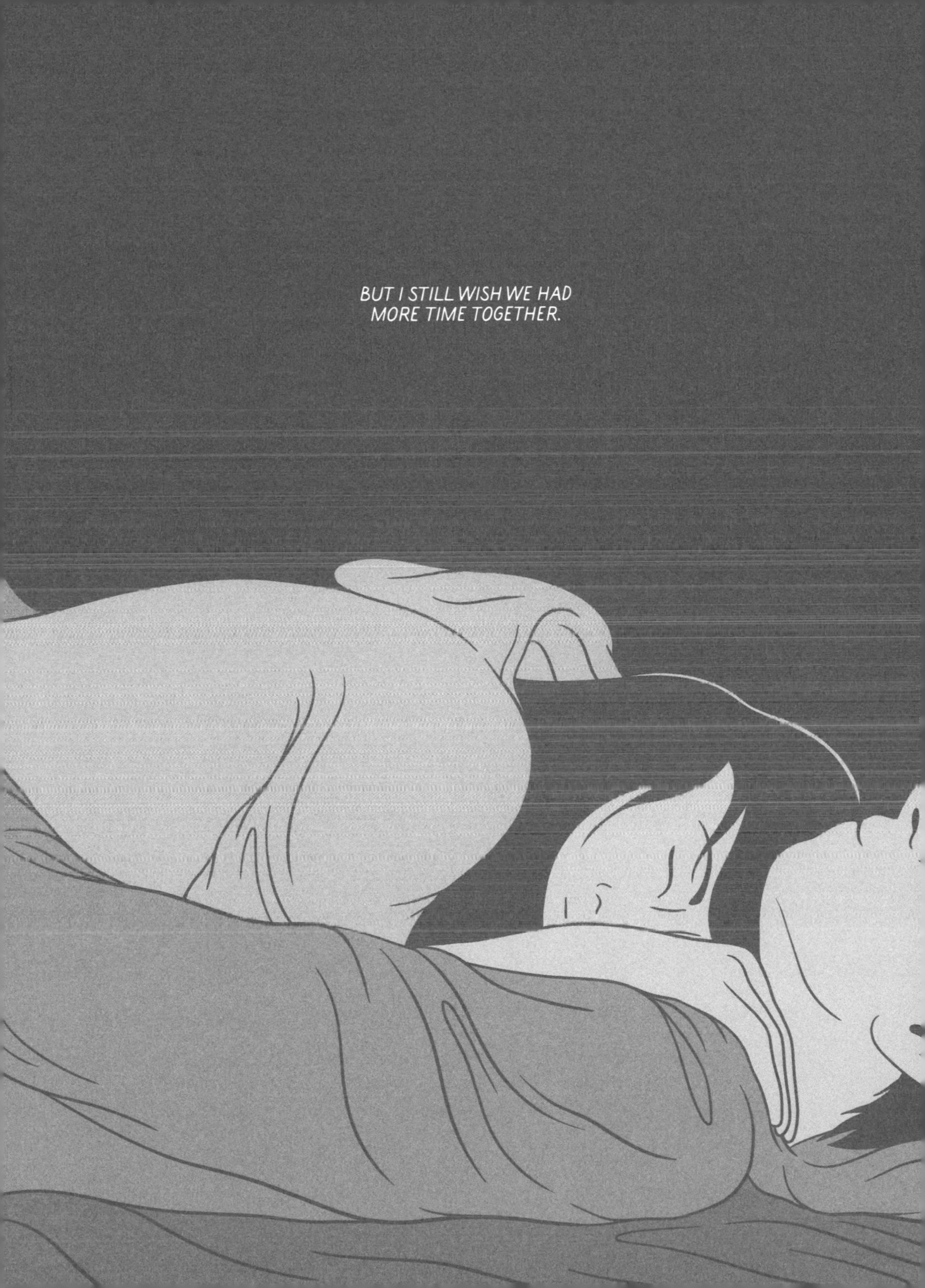
BUT I STILL WISH WE HAD MORE TIME TOGETHER.

WHEN KRISTEN HAD HER SURGERY,
I WAS WITH HER, THROUGH MY PHONE.

MESSAGING THINGS I THOUGHT
WOULD CHEER HER UP.

BUT STILL OBLIVIOUS TO HER
SUFFERING BECAUSE SHE NEVER
WANTED TO BURDEN ME WITH IT.

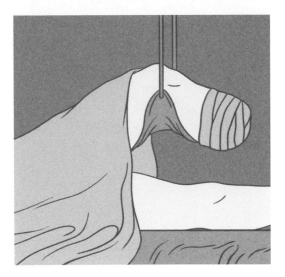

I WISHED I COULD TAKE HER PLACE.

I WANTED TO TAKE AWAY ALL OF HER PAIN.

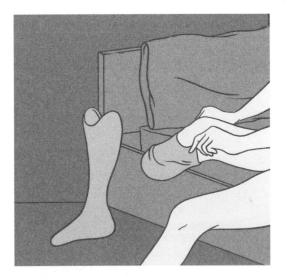

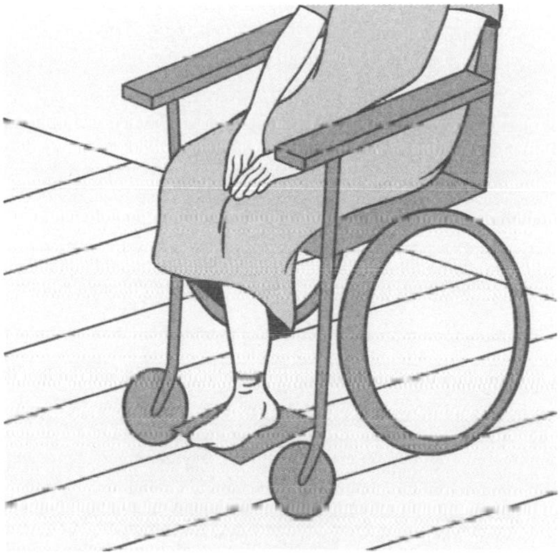

BUT SHE WOULDN'T LET ME.

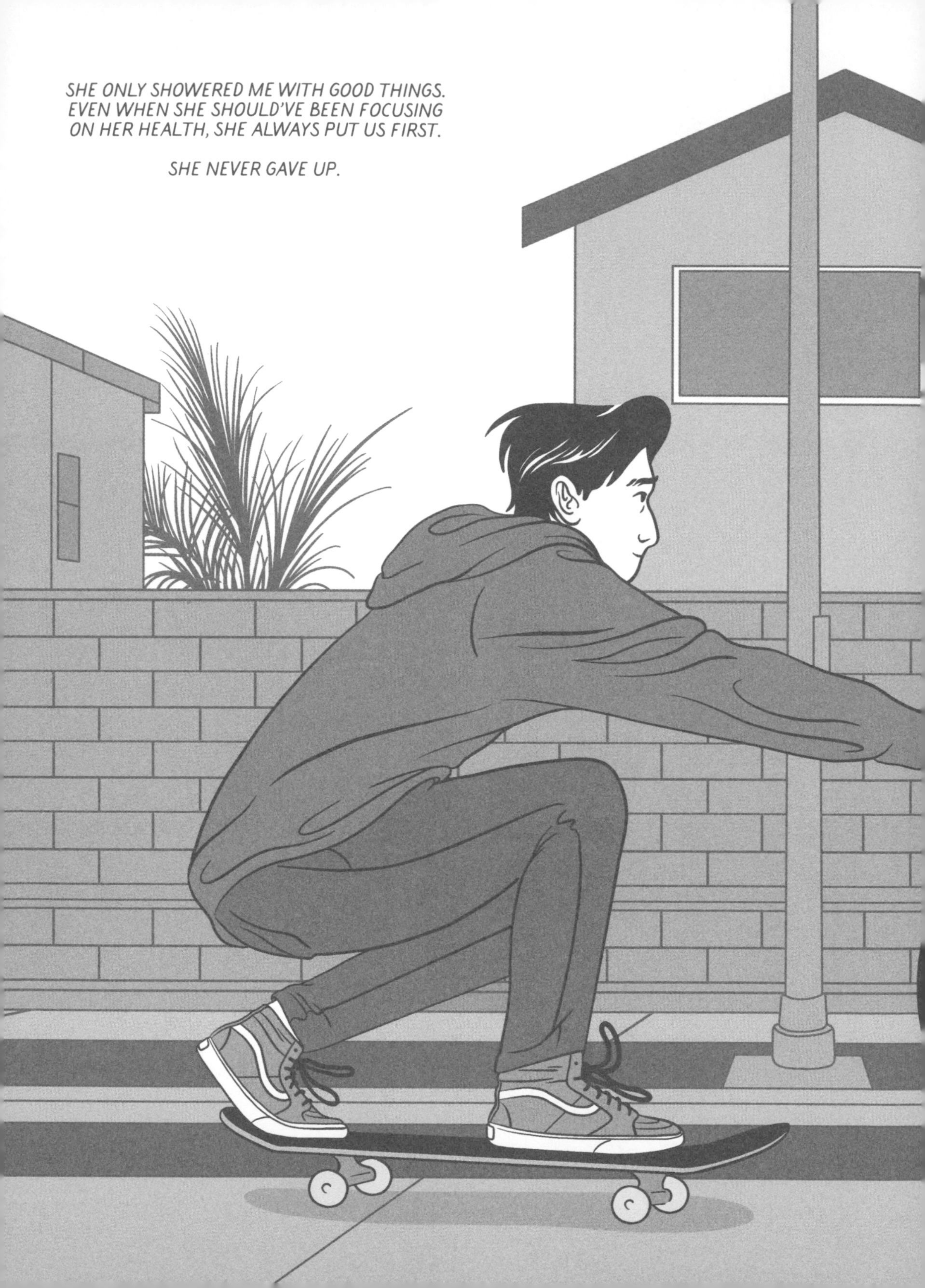
SHE ONLY SHOWERED ME WITH GOOD THINGS. EVEN WHEN SHE SHOULD'VE BEEN FOCUSING ON HER HEALTH, SHE ALWAYS PUT US FIRST.
SHE NEVER GAVE UP.

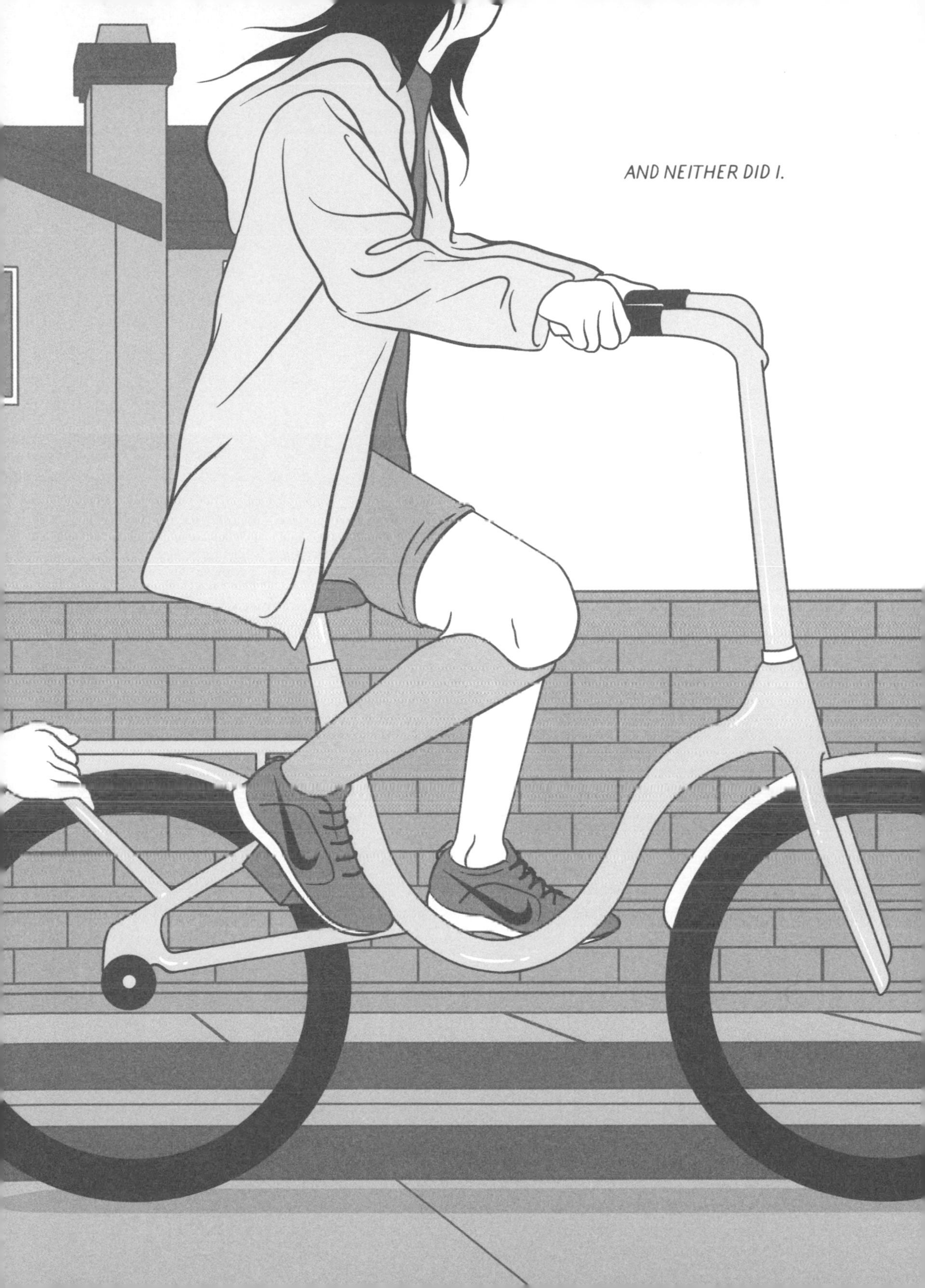
AND NEITHER DID I.

XII. INVENTION

Fig-3-
Fig-5-

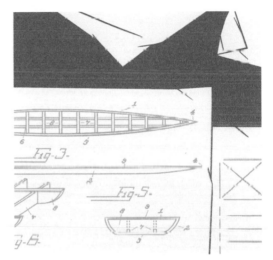

Fall
1926

Malibu, California

TOM TRAVELED ACROSS CALIFORNIA IN SEARCH OF UNCHARTED BEACHES AND UNTOUCHED WAVES.

HE BECAME ONE OF THE FIRST EVER TO SURF MALIBU.

HIS LUST FOR WAVES GREW, AS DID HIS CHILDHOOD DESIRE FOR ESCAPE.

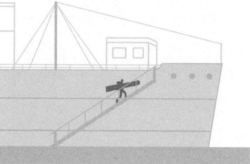

HE CAUGHT A STEAMSHIP TO HAWAII, THE LAND THAT FIRST ENCHANTED HIM.

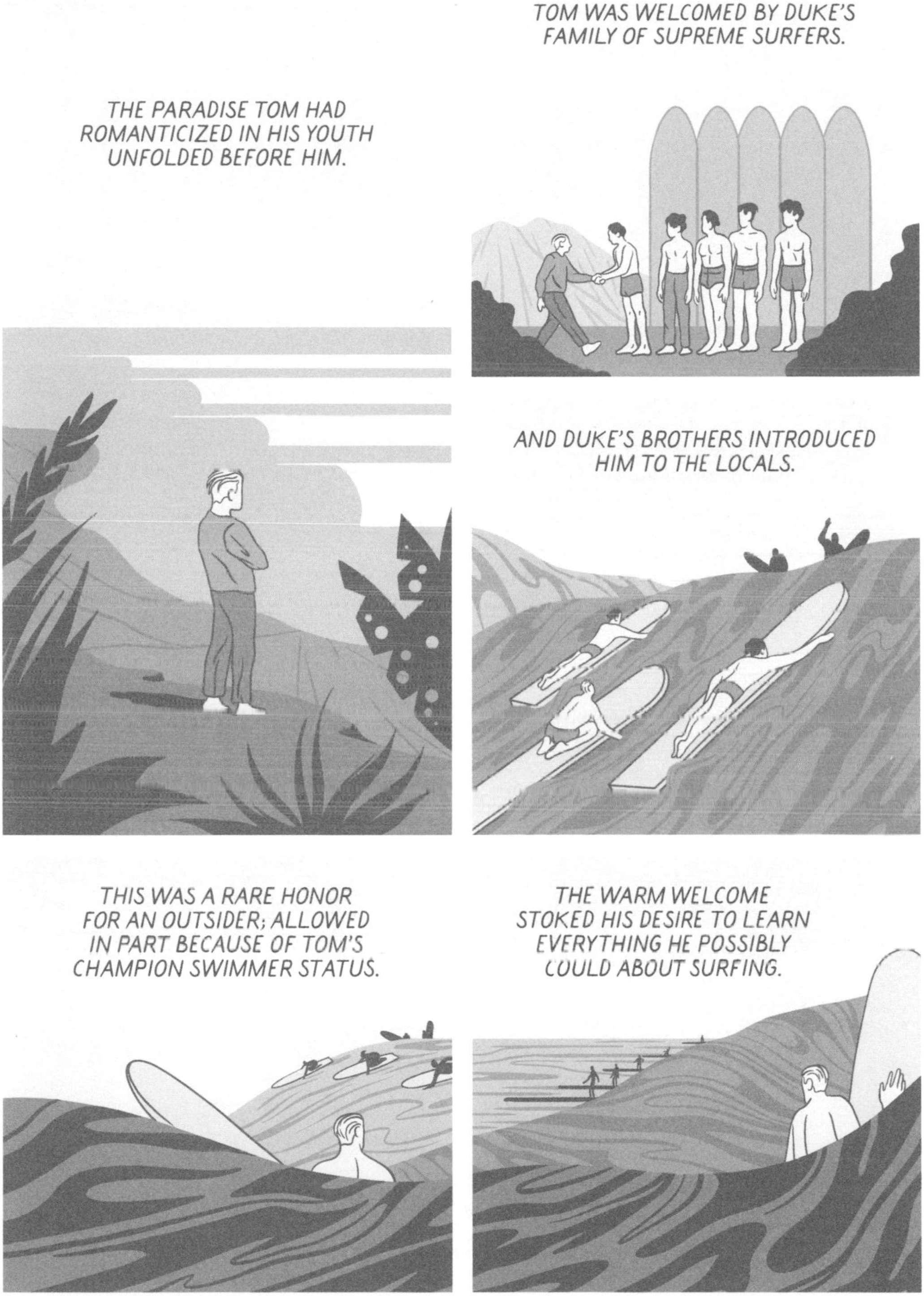
THE PARADISE TOM HAD ROMANTICIZED IN HIS YOUTH UNFOLDED BEFORE HIM.
TOM WAS WELCOMED BY DUKE'S FAMILY OF SUPREME SURFERS.
AND DUKE'S BROTHERS INTRODUCED HIM TO THE LOCALS.
THIS WAS A RARE HONOR FOR AN OUTSIDER; ALLOWED IN PART BECAUSE OF TOM'S CHAMPION SWIMMER STATUS.
THE WARM WELCOME STOKED HIS DESIRE TO LEARN EVERYTHING HE POSSIBLY COULD ABOUT SURFING.

DURING HIS STAY, TOM WAS INVITED TO VISIT HONOLULU'S BISHOP MUSEUM.

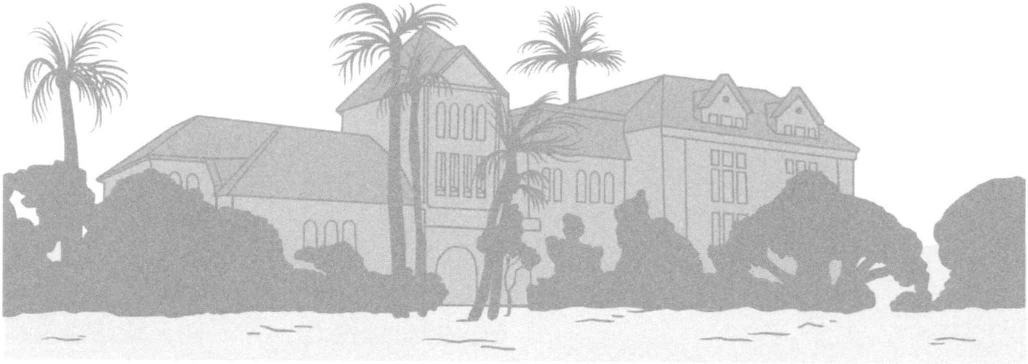

THERE, HE BEGAN TO STUDY THEIR COLLECTION OF ANCIENT SURFBOARDS. THESE WERE RIDDEN BY NATIVE SURFERS LONG BEFORE THE INFLUENCE OF A FOREIGN NATION TOOK OVER THE ISLANDS.

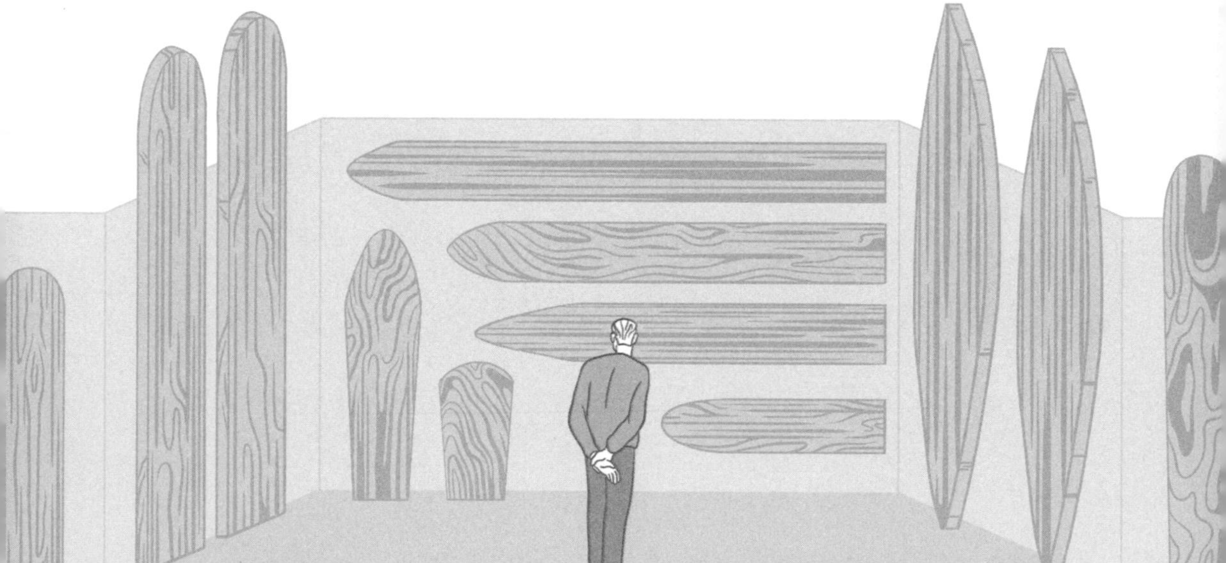

TOM SAW POTENTIAL IN THIS ANCIENT TECHNOLOGY, WHERE OTHERS JUST SAW ANTIQUES.

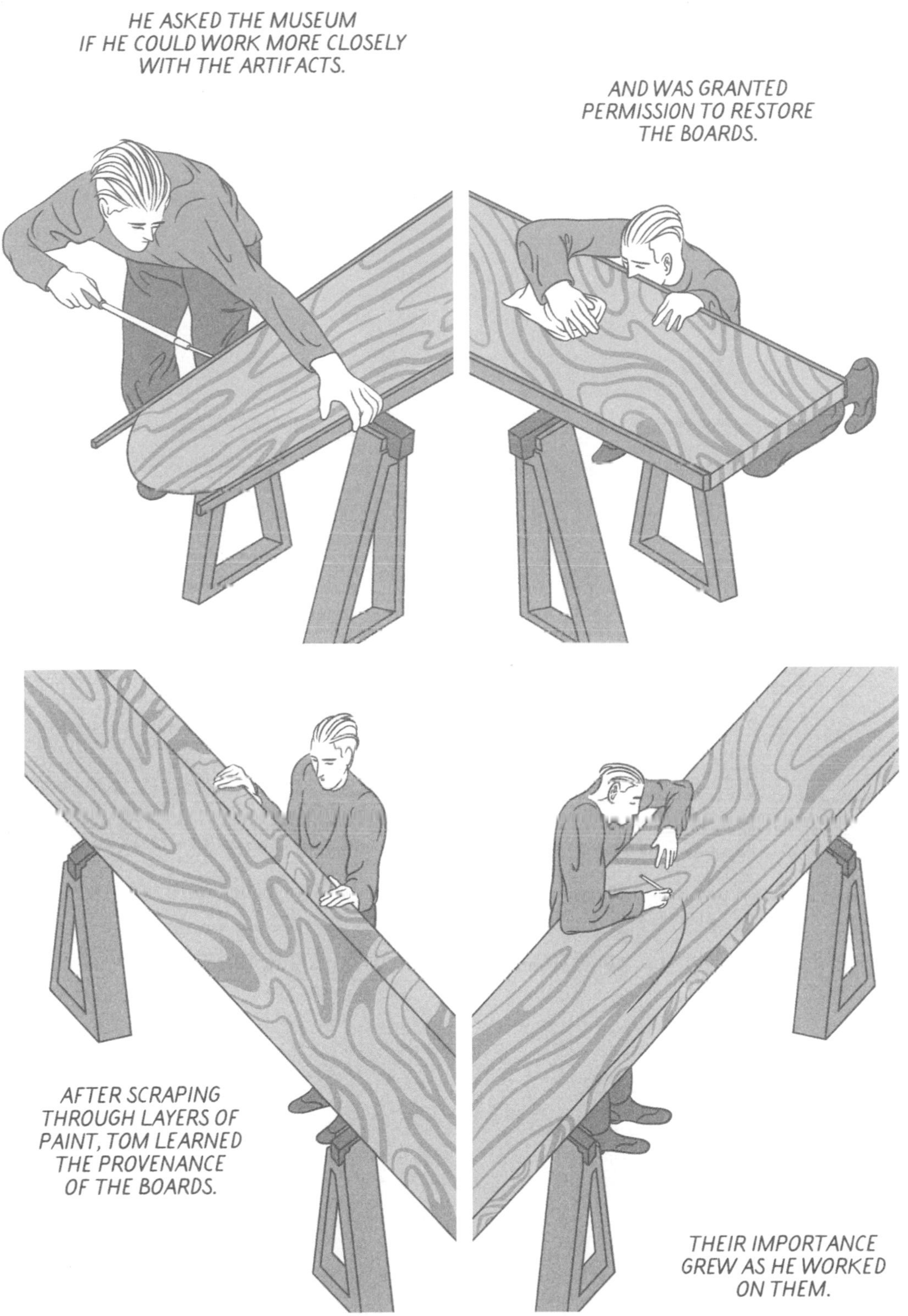
HE ASKED THE MUSEUM IF HE COULD WORK MORE CLOSELY WITH THE ARTIFACTS.
AND WAS GRANTED PERMISSION TO RESTORE THE BOARDS.
AFTER SCRAPING THROUGH LAYERS OF PAINT, TOM LEARNED THE PROVENANCE OF THE BOARDS.
THEIR IMPORTANCE GREW AS HE WORKED ON THEM.

THE SUBJECTS OF TOM'S RESTORATIONS WERE CALLED
OLO BOARDS. AT 16 FEET LONG, THEY WERE SURFBOARDS
TRADITIONALLY RESERVED FOR HAWAIIAN ROYALTY.
TOM SOUGHT TO DUPLICATE IT.

WHILE SHAPING THE OLO REPLICA, TOM DISCOVERED THAT IT WAS
TOO HEAVY TO BE CARRIED BY THE AVERAGE SURFER, SO HE DRILLED
HOLES INTO THE DECK TO TAKE SOME OF THE WEIGHT OUT.

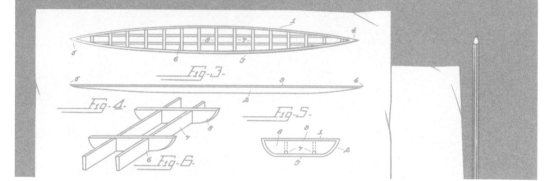

WHAT HE CREATED IN THE PROCESS WAS
A COMPLETELY NEW TYPE OF BOARD.

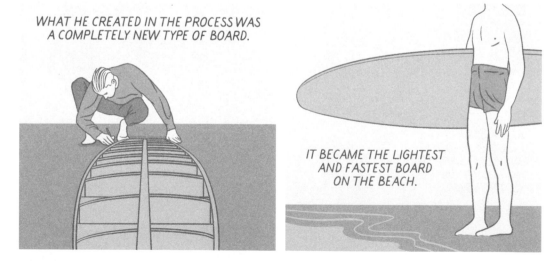

IT BECAME THE LIGHTEST
AND FASTEST BOARD
ON THE BEACH.

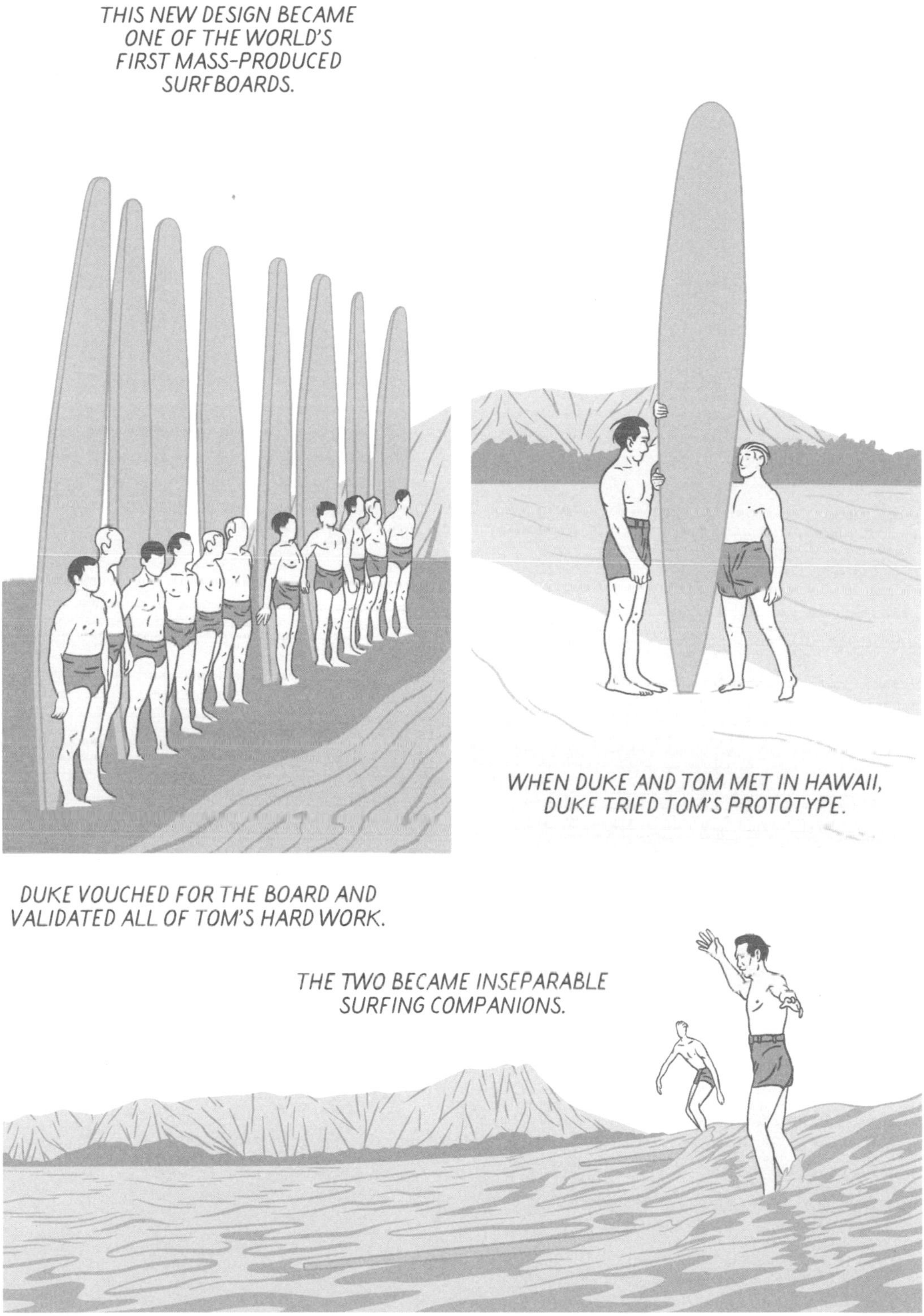
THIS NEW DESIGN BECAME ONE OF THE WORLD'S FIRST MASS-PRODUCED SURFBOARDS.
WHEN DUKE AND TOM MET IN HAWAII, DUKE TRIED TOM'S PROTOTYPE.
DUKE VOUCHED FOR THE BOARD AND VALIDATED ALL OF TOM'S HARD WORK.
THE TWO BECAME INSEPARABLE SURFING COMPANIONS.

TOM CAME TO HIS NEXT INVENTION
WHILE OBSERVING WASHED-UP JUNK.

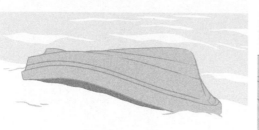

HE WAS THE FIRST TO ATTACH A FIN
TO A SURFBOARD, AS YOU WOULD A BOAT.

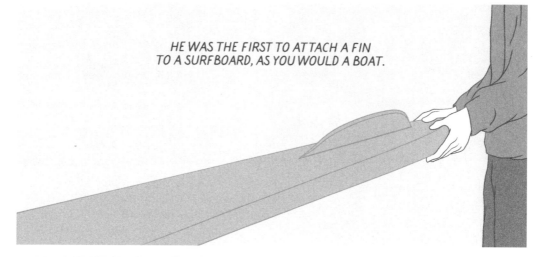

HE HAD NEVER EXPERIENCED SUCH CONTROL.

HIS CURIOSITY INFLUENCED ALL FUTURE ADVANCES ON SURFBOARDS.

TOM WROTE THE FIRST BOOK ABOUT SURFING. IT DISSECTED SURF HISTORY AND SHED LIGHT ON THE SPORT FOR ALL TO CONSUME; HIGHLIGHTING THE NICHE PASTIME FOR ITS BEAUTY AND CULTURAL SIGNIFICANCE.

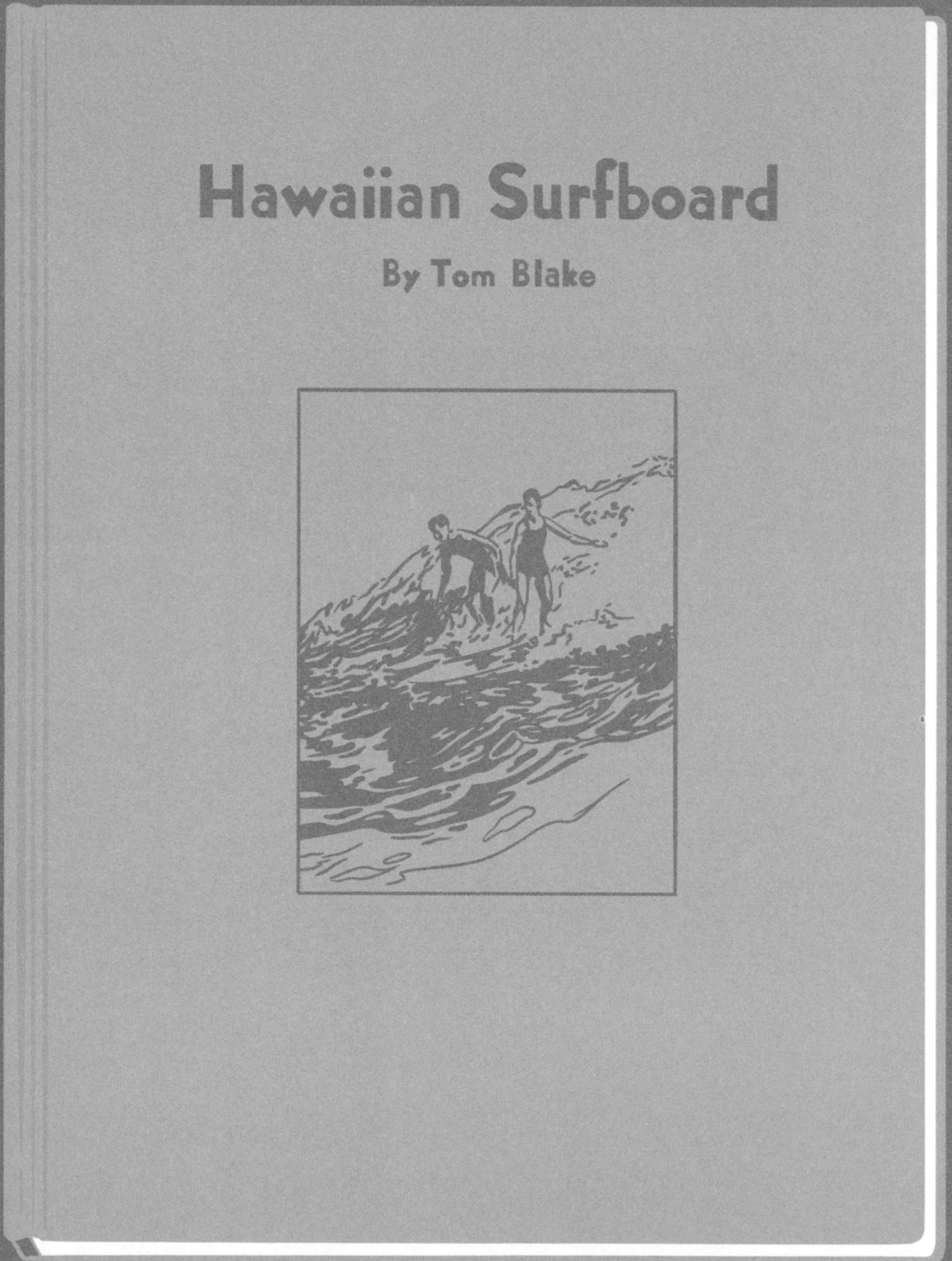
Hawaiian Surfboard
By Tom Blake

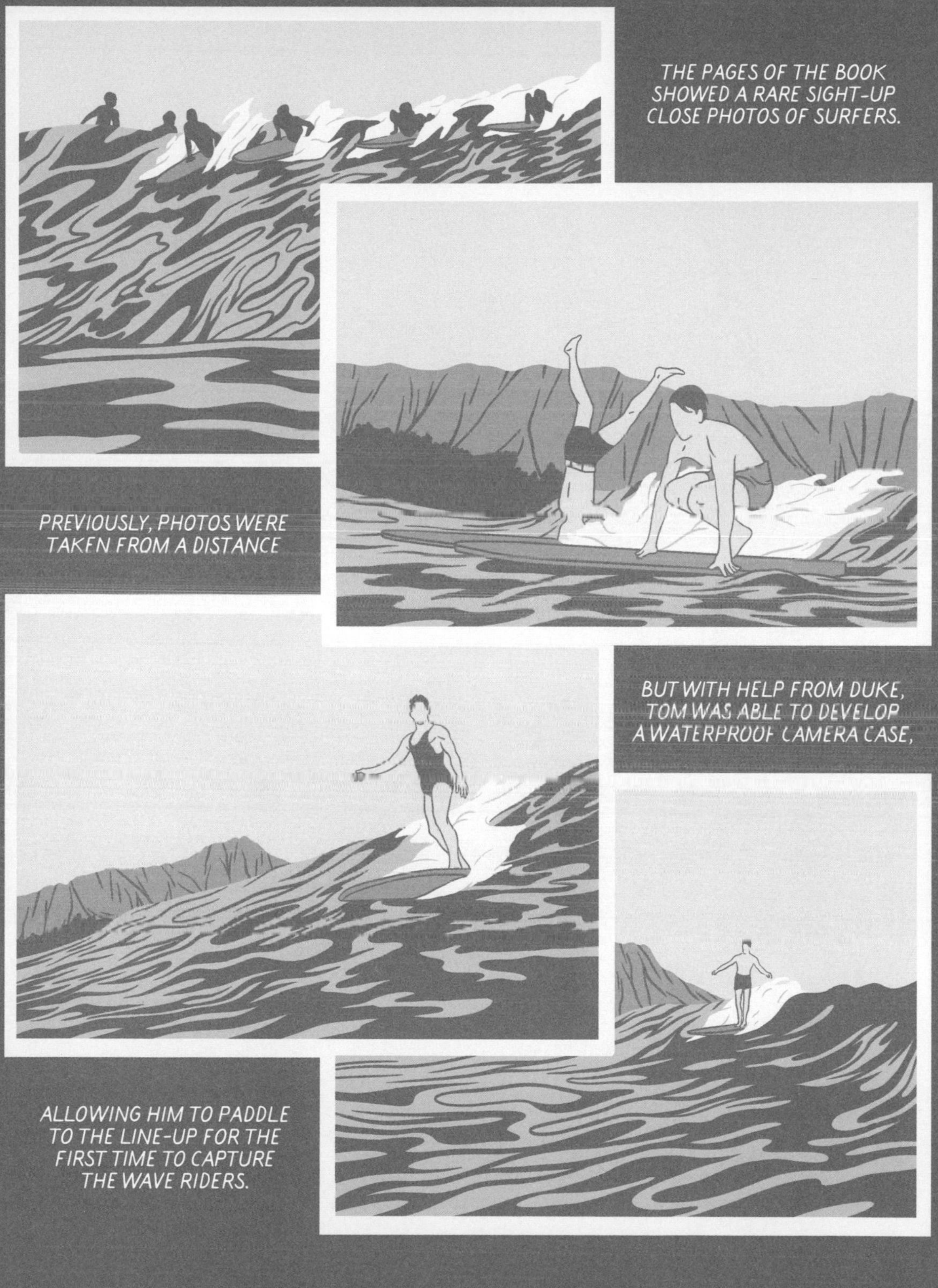
THE PAGES OF THE BOOK SHOWED A RARE SIGHT-UP CLOSE PHOTOS OF SURFERS.
PREVIOUSLY, PHOTOS WERE TAKEN FROM A DISTANCE
BUT WITH HELP FROM DUKE, TOM WAS ABLE TO DEVELOP A WATERPROOF CAMERA CASE,
ALLOWING HIM TO PADDLE TO THE LINE-UP FOR THE FIRST TIME TO CAPTURE THE WAVE RIDERS.

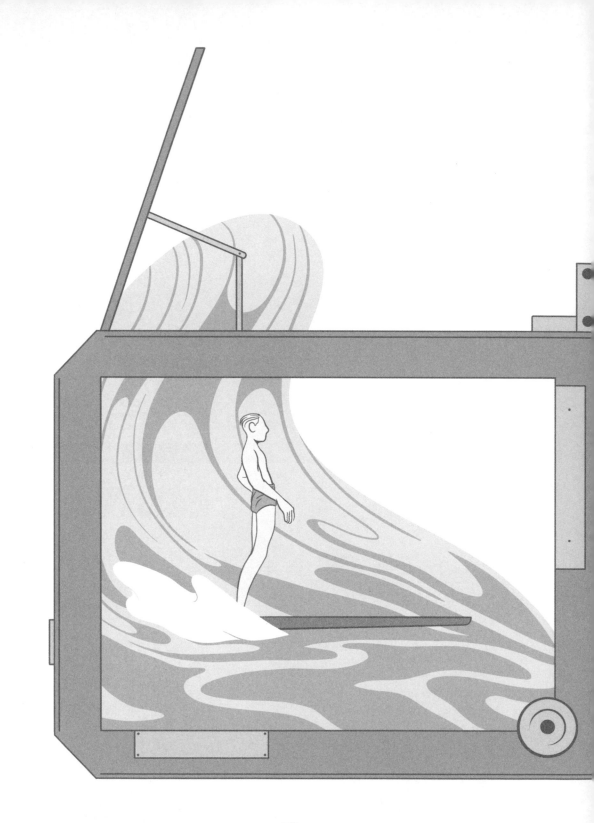

THROUGH HIS INVENTIONS, TOM DEMYSTIFIED
SURFING AND MADE IT ACCESSIBLE TO A BROADER
AUDIENCE, JUST LIKE DUKE HAD DONE.

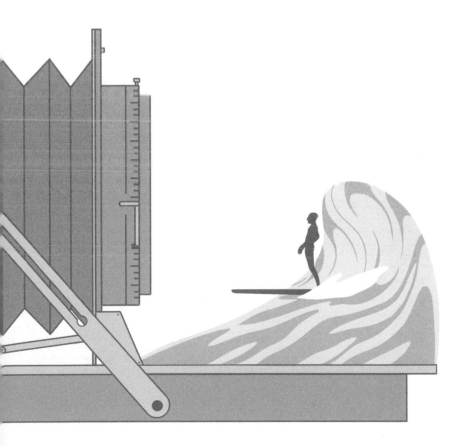

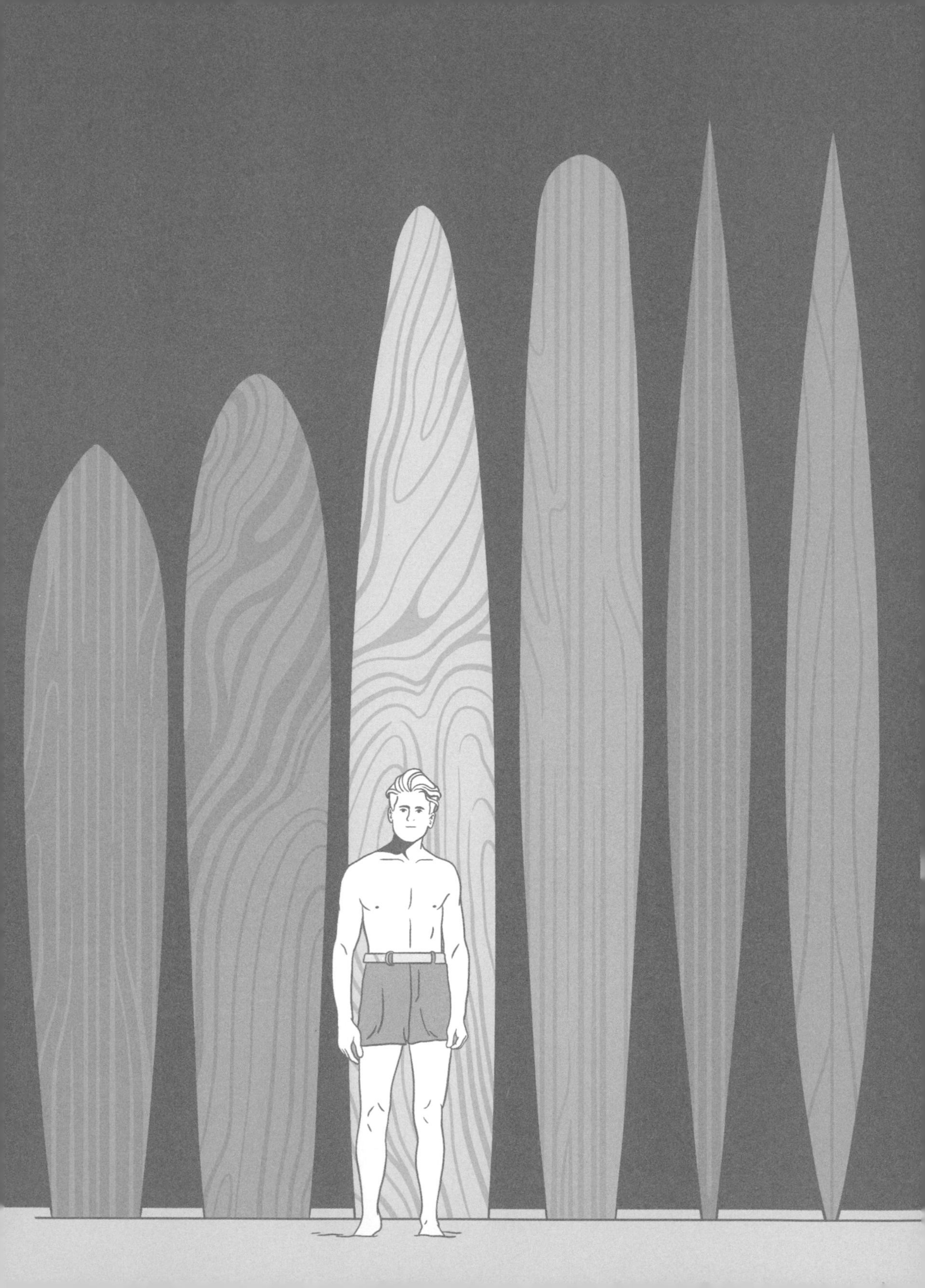

THE OCEAN HAD GIVEN TOM A PURPOSE AND DUKE HAD GIVEN HIM A VISION. WITH HIS TWO HANDS, TOM SHARED BOTH WITH THE WORLD.

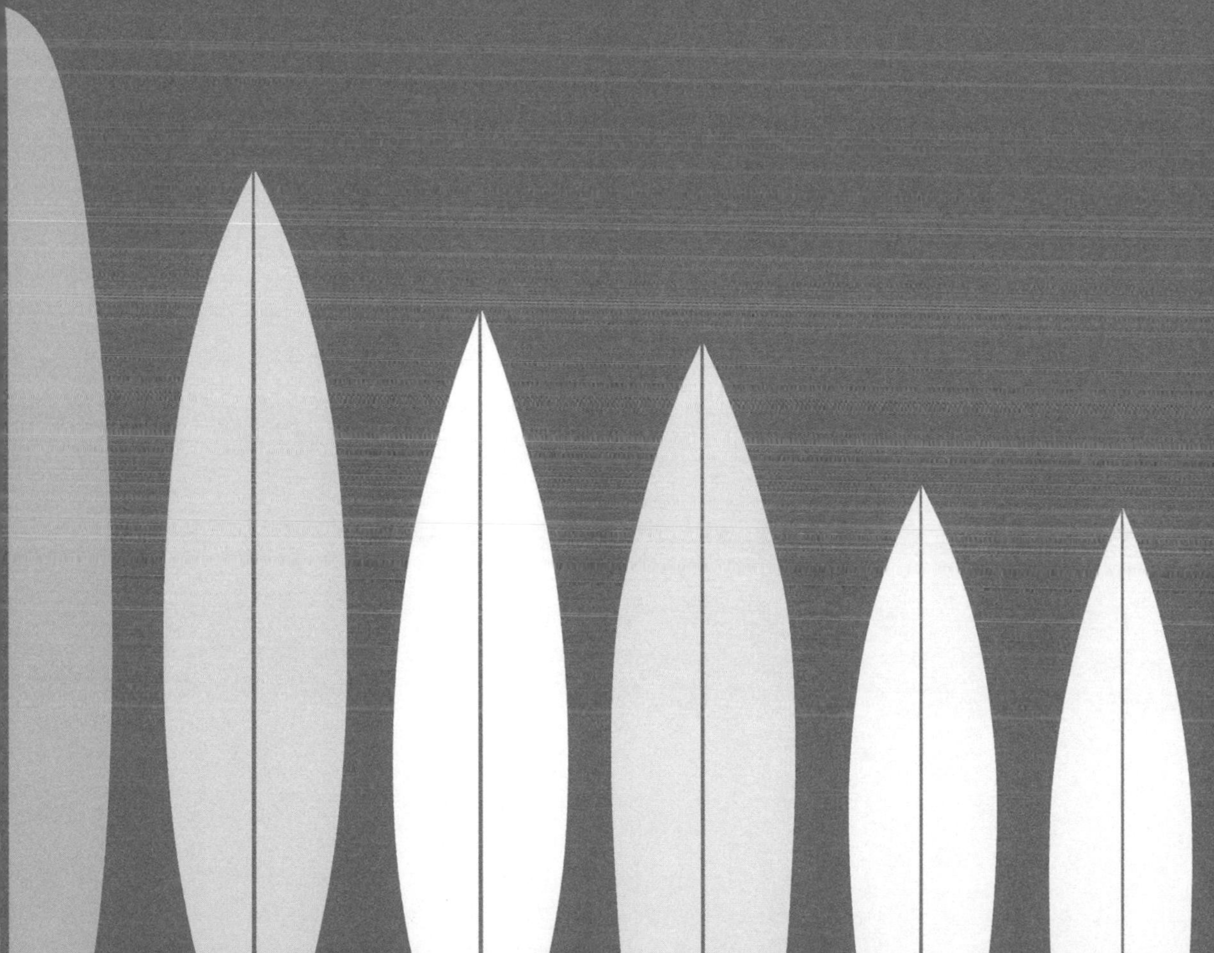

XIII. THE LIST

Winter 2016

Portland, Oregon

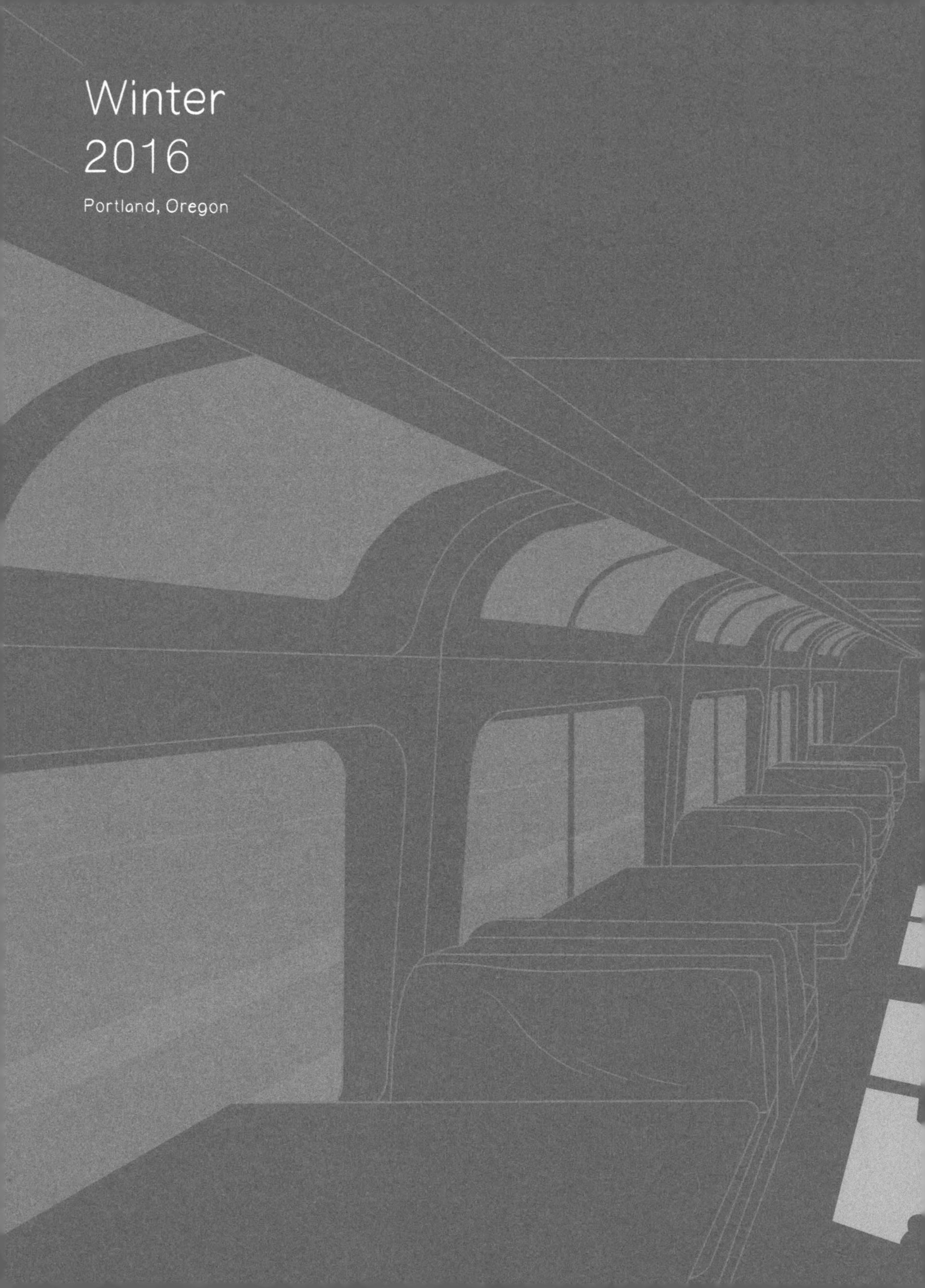

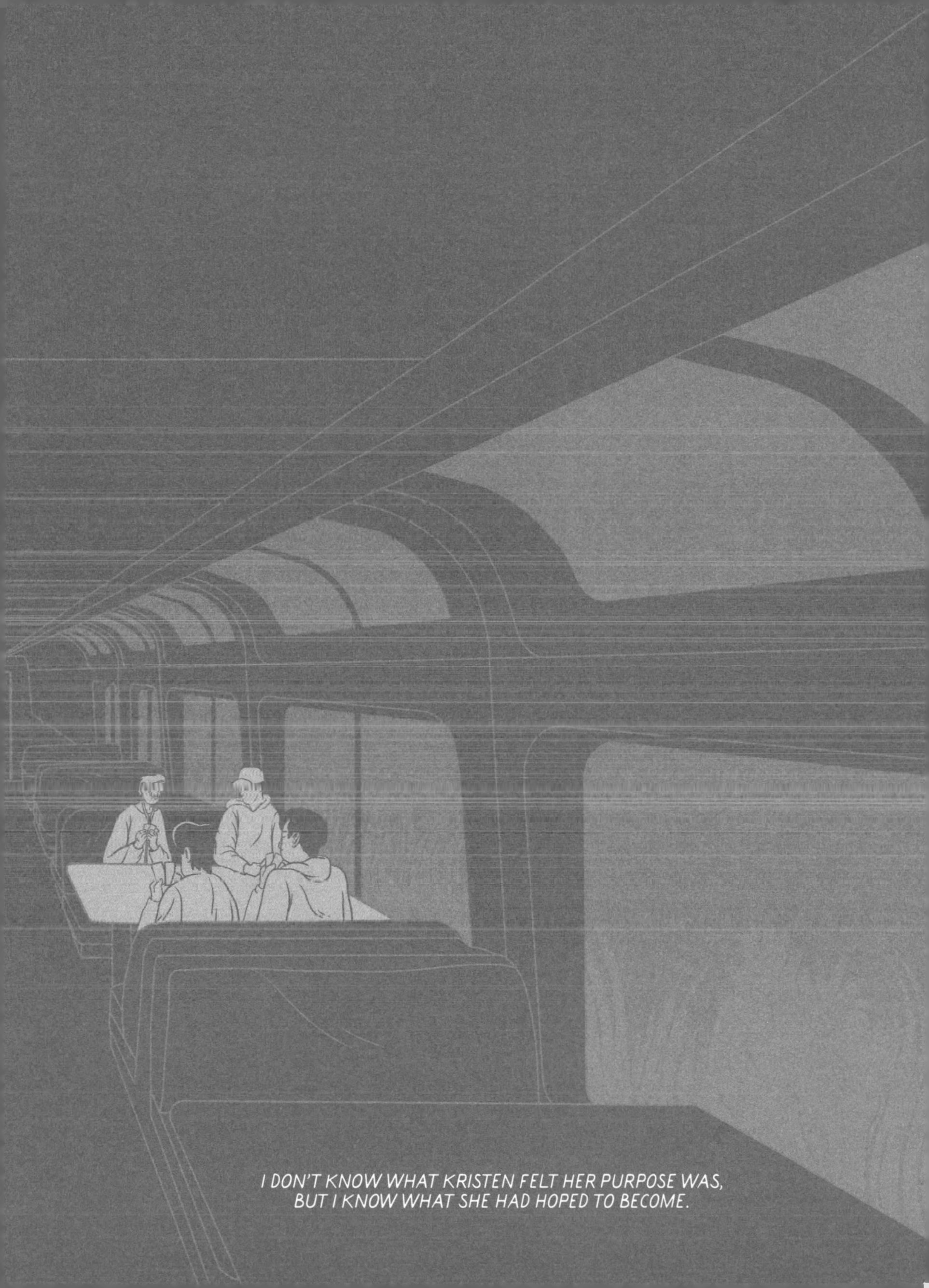
I DON'T KNOW WHAT KRISTEN FELT HER PURPOSE WAS,
BUT I KNOW WHAT SHE HAD HOPED TO BECOME.

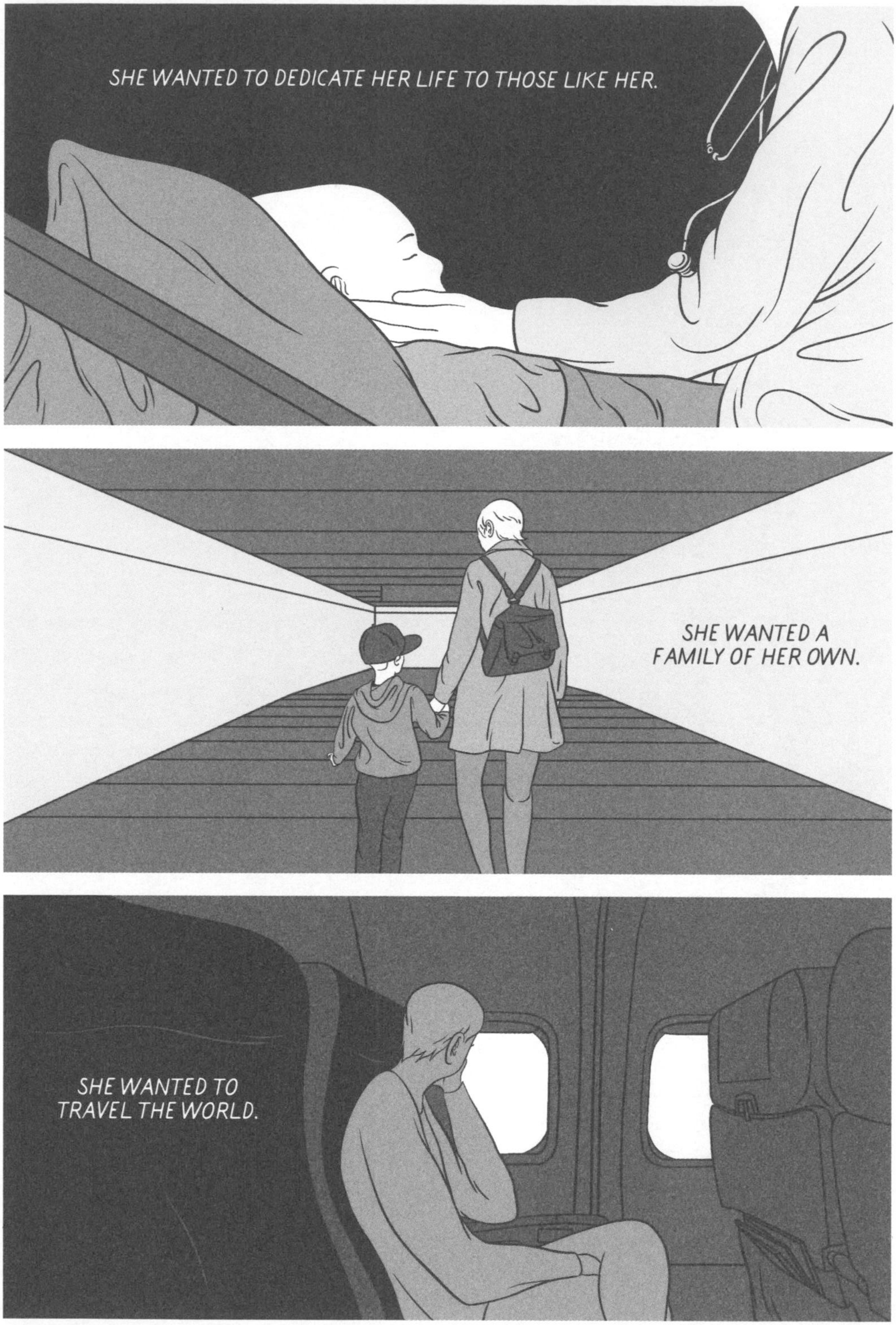
SHE WANTED TO DEDICATE HER LIFE TO THOSE LIKE HER.
SHE WANTED A FAMILY OF HER OWN.
SHE WANTED TO TRAVEL THE WORLD.

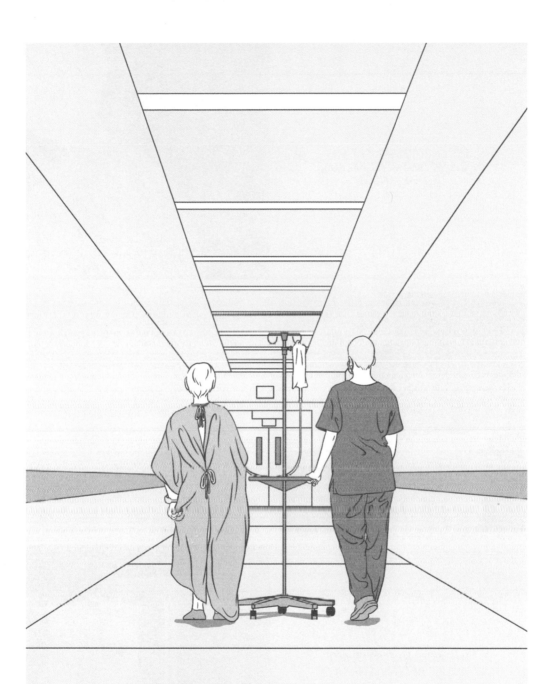

MORE THAN ANYTHING, SHE WANTED TO BE HEALTHY.

SHE ENDURED A LIFETIME
OF DISAPPOINTMENT BECAUSE
OF HER CANCER.

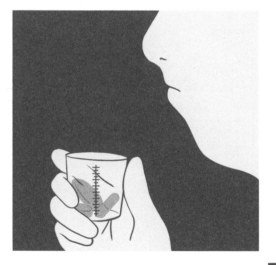

HER CONDITION TAUNTED HER.

SHE WOULD RECOVER BUT
IT WOULD RETURN, STRONGER.

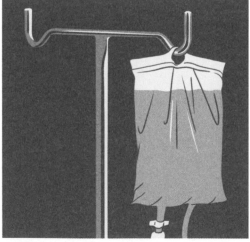

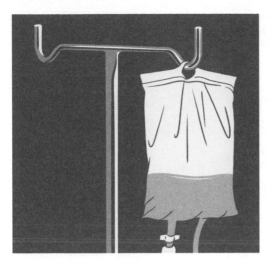

THE CRUEL CYCLE
OF REMISSION AND RELAPSE
SEEMED NEVER-ENDING.

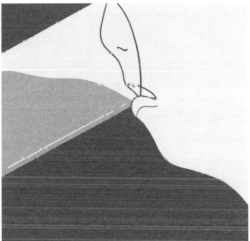

STILL, THROUGH ALL THE
CHEMOTHERAPY AND SURGERY,

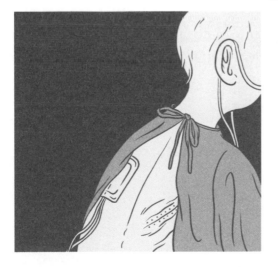

WE ALWAYS
REMAINED HOPEFUL.

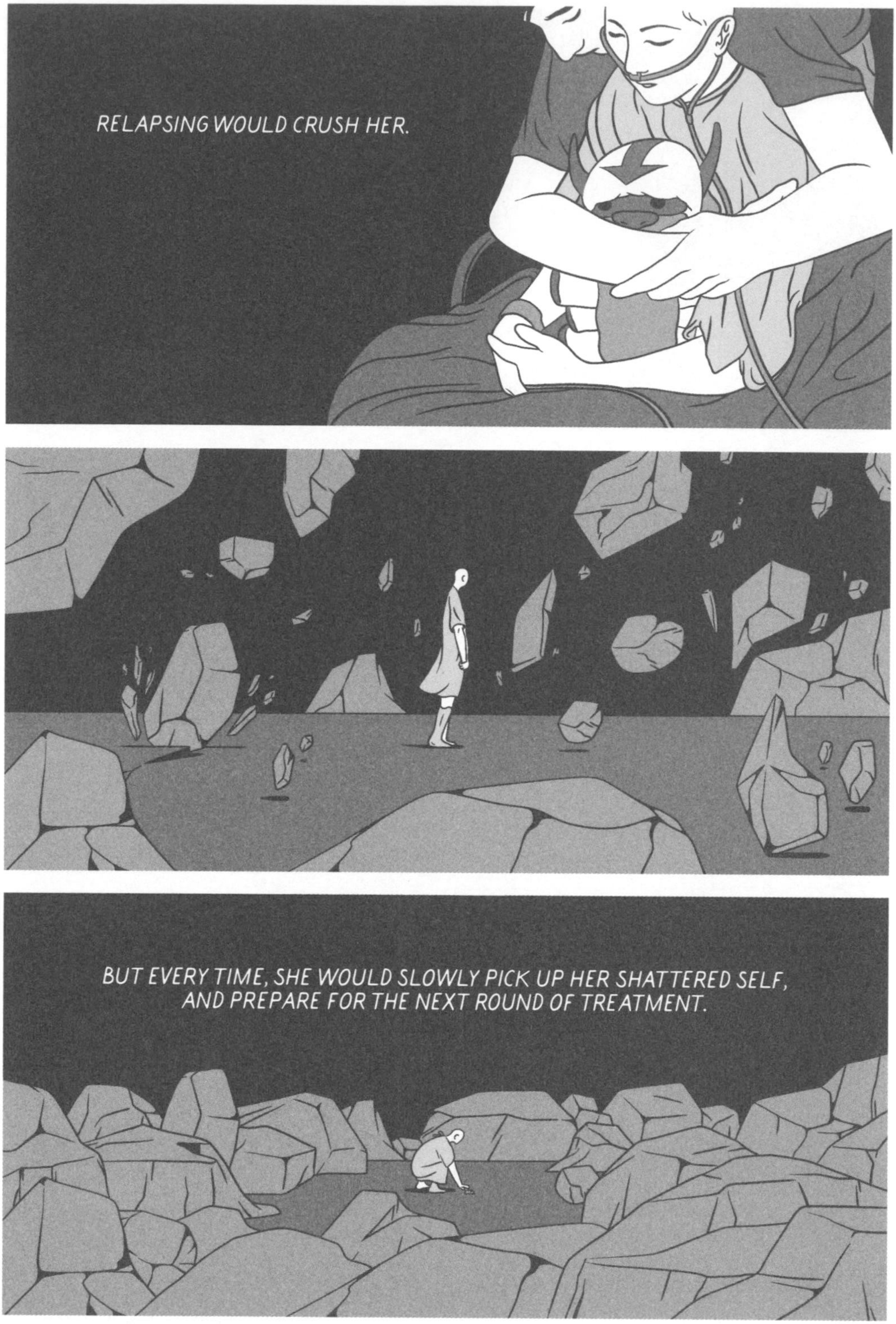
RELAPSING WOULD CRUSH HER.
BUT EVERY TIME, SHE WOULD SLOWLY PICK UP HER SHATTERED SELF, AND PREPARE FOR THE NEXT ROUND OF TREATMENT.

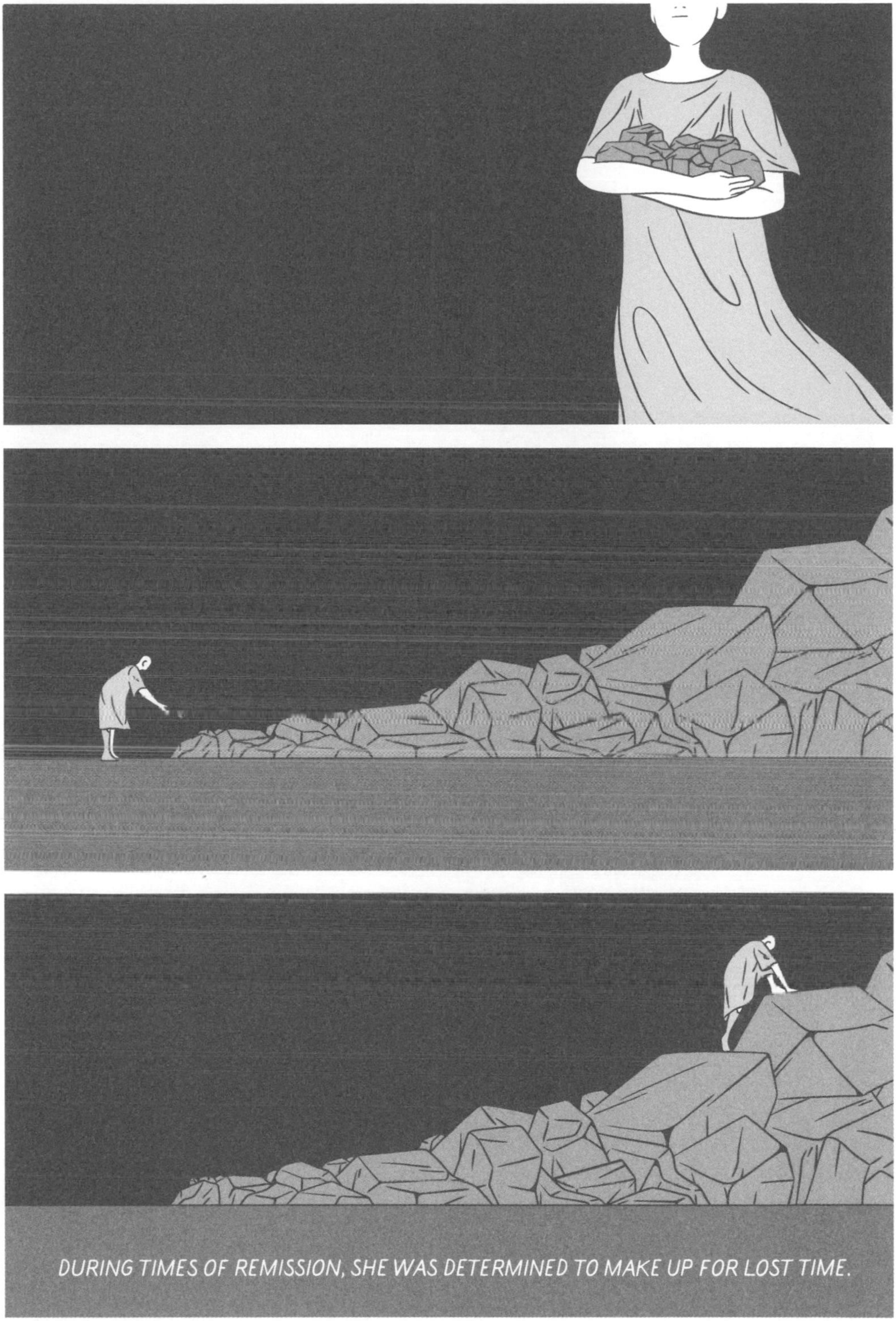
DURING TIMES OF REMISSION, SHE WAS DETERMINED TO MAKE UP FOR LOST TIME.

KRISTEN NEVER LET HERSELF BECOME DEFINED BY HER PHYSICAL LIMITATIONS.

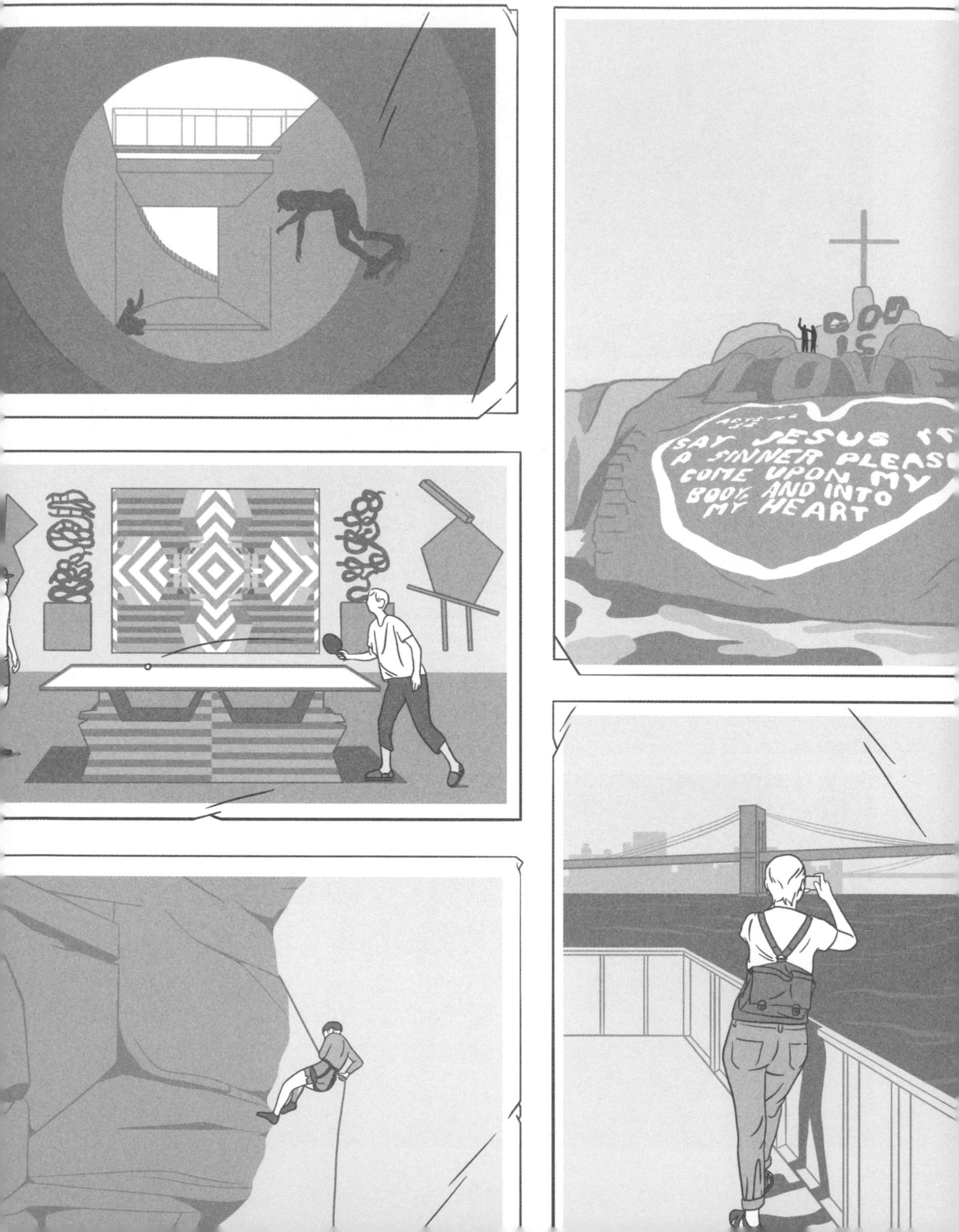
GOD IS LOVE
SAY JESUS I
A SINNER PLEAS
COME UPON MY
BODY, AND INTO
MY HEART

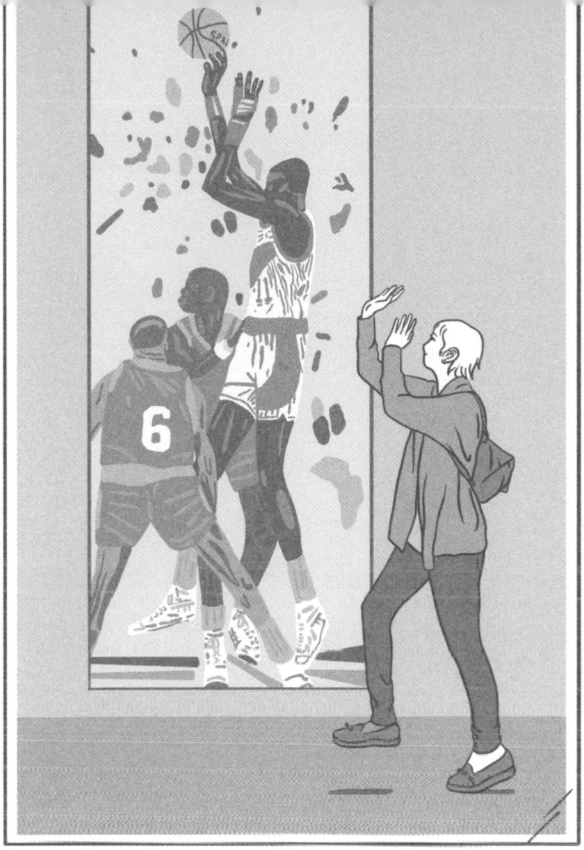

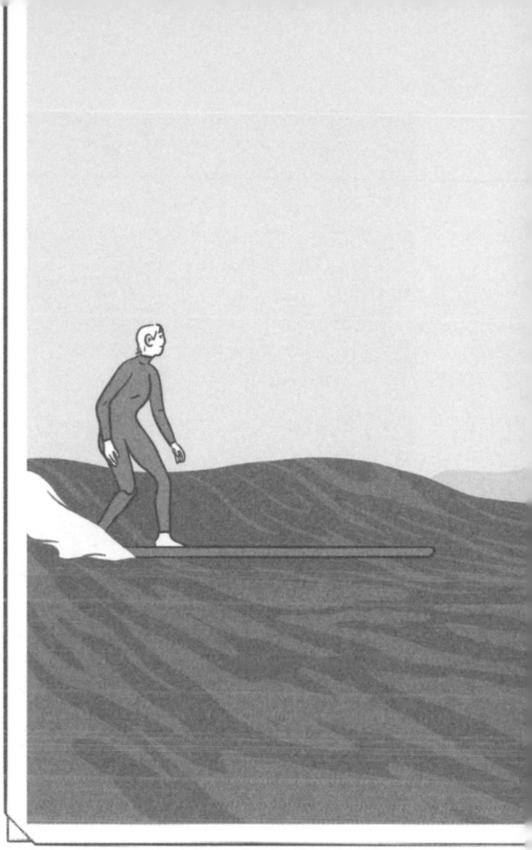

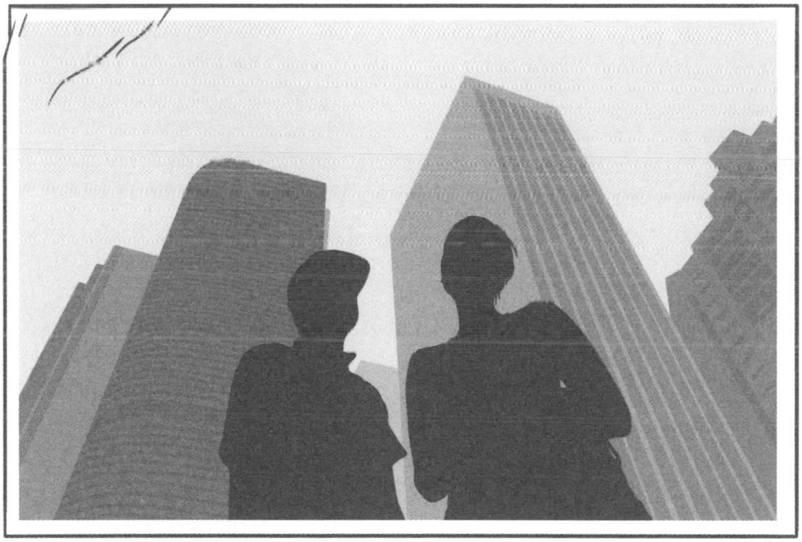

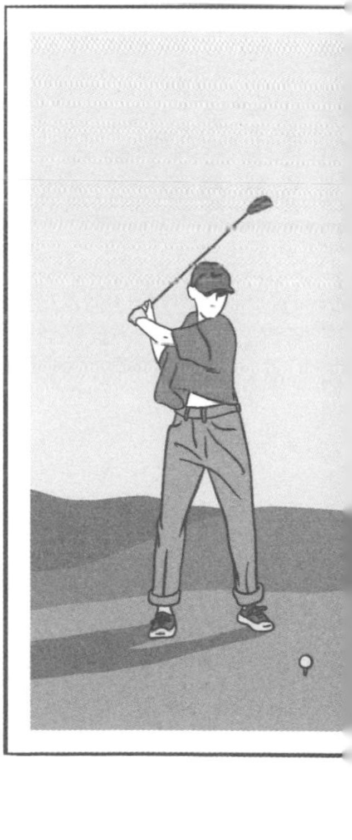

AND TOOK ADVANTAGE OF EVERY HEALTHY MOMENT.

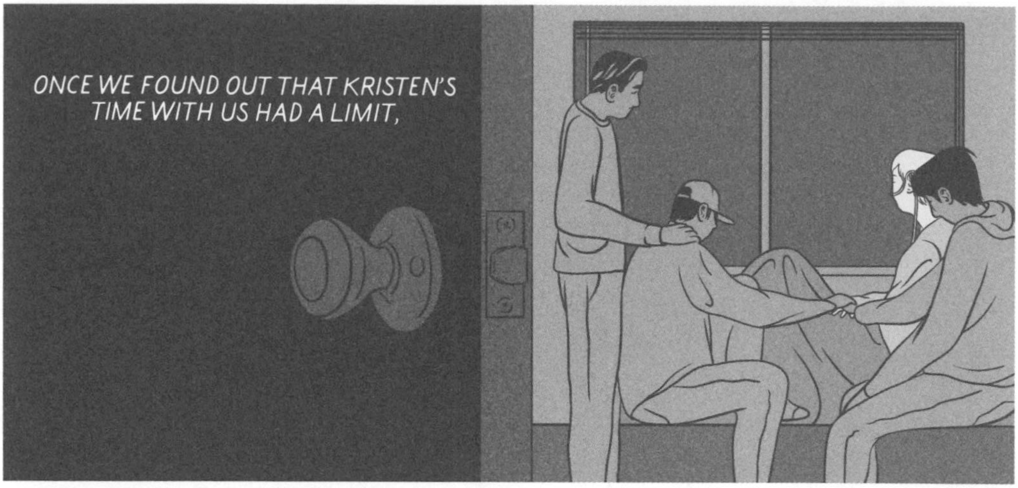
ONCE WE FOUND OUT THAT KRISTEN'S TIME WITH US HAD A LIMIT,

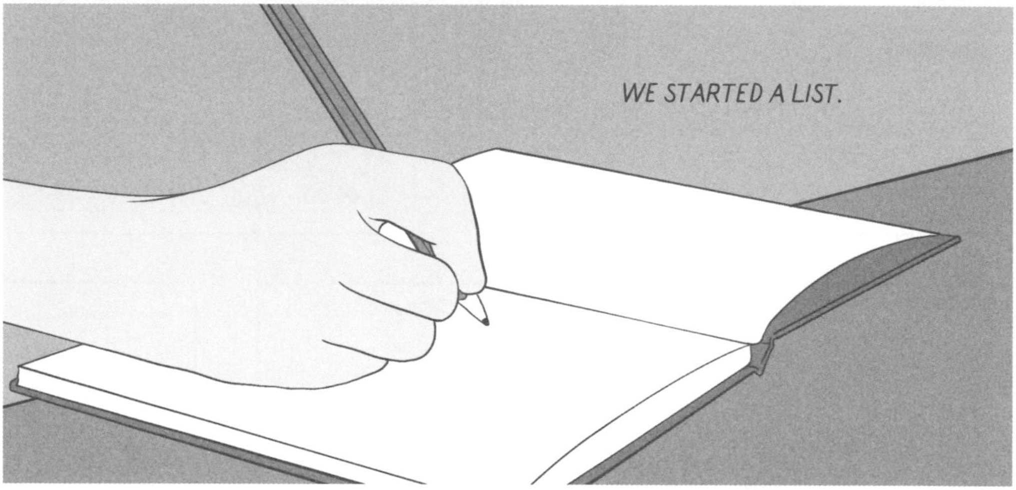
WE STARTED A LIST.

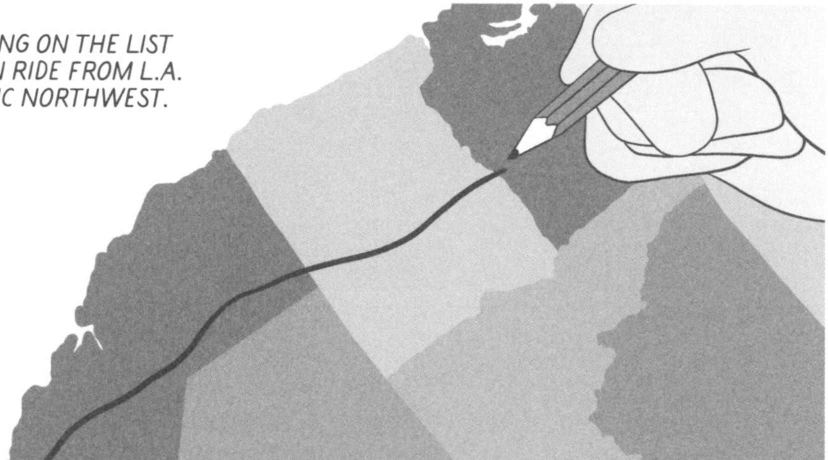
THE FIRST THING ON THE LIST WAS THE TRAIN RIDE FROM L.A. TO THE PACIFIC NORTHWEST.

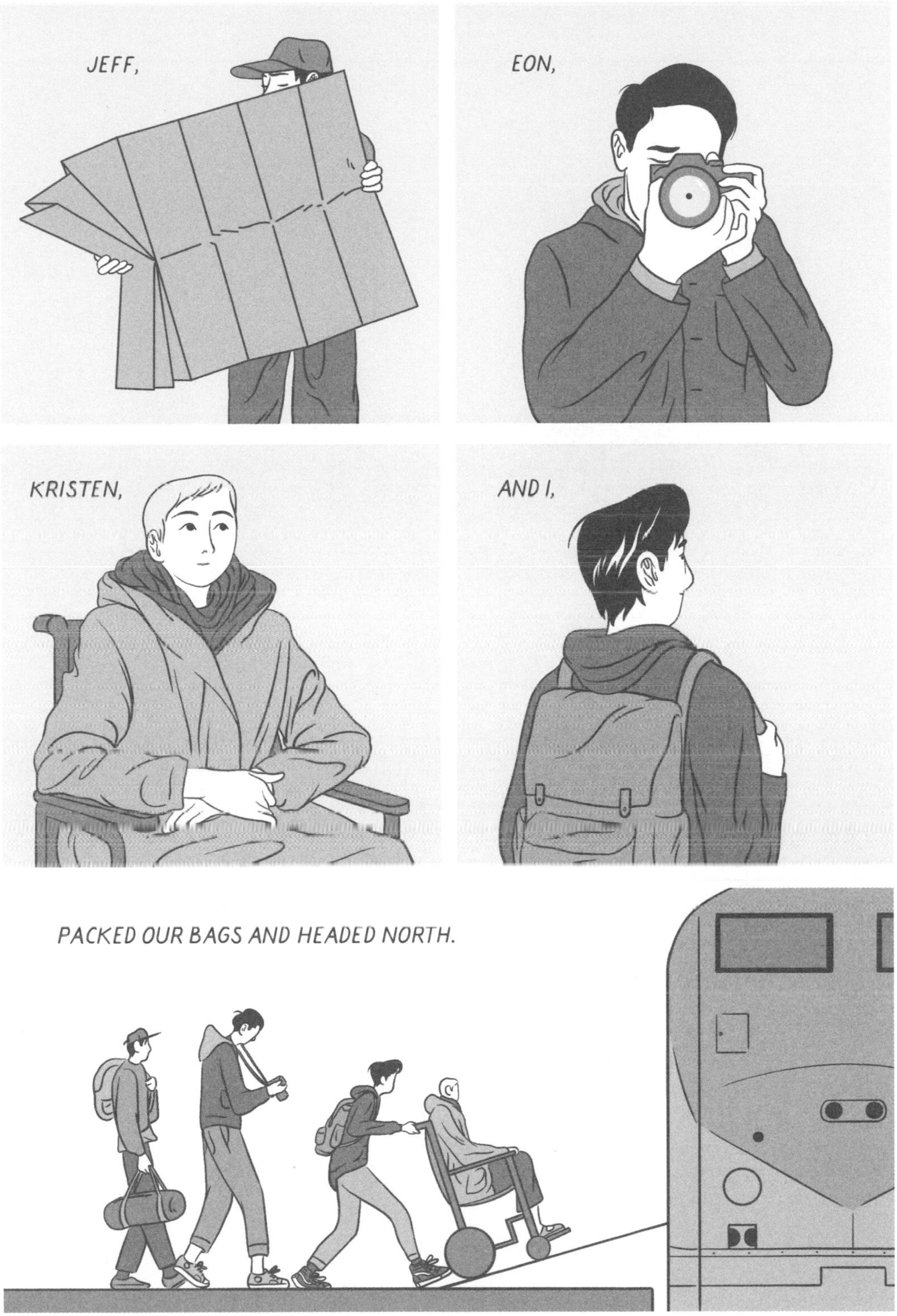
JEFF,
EON,
KRISTEN,
AND I,
PACKED OUR BAGS AND HEADED NORTH.

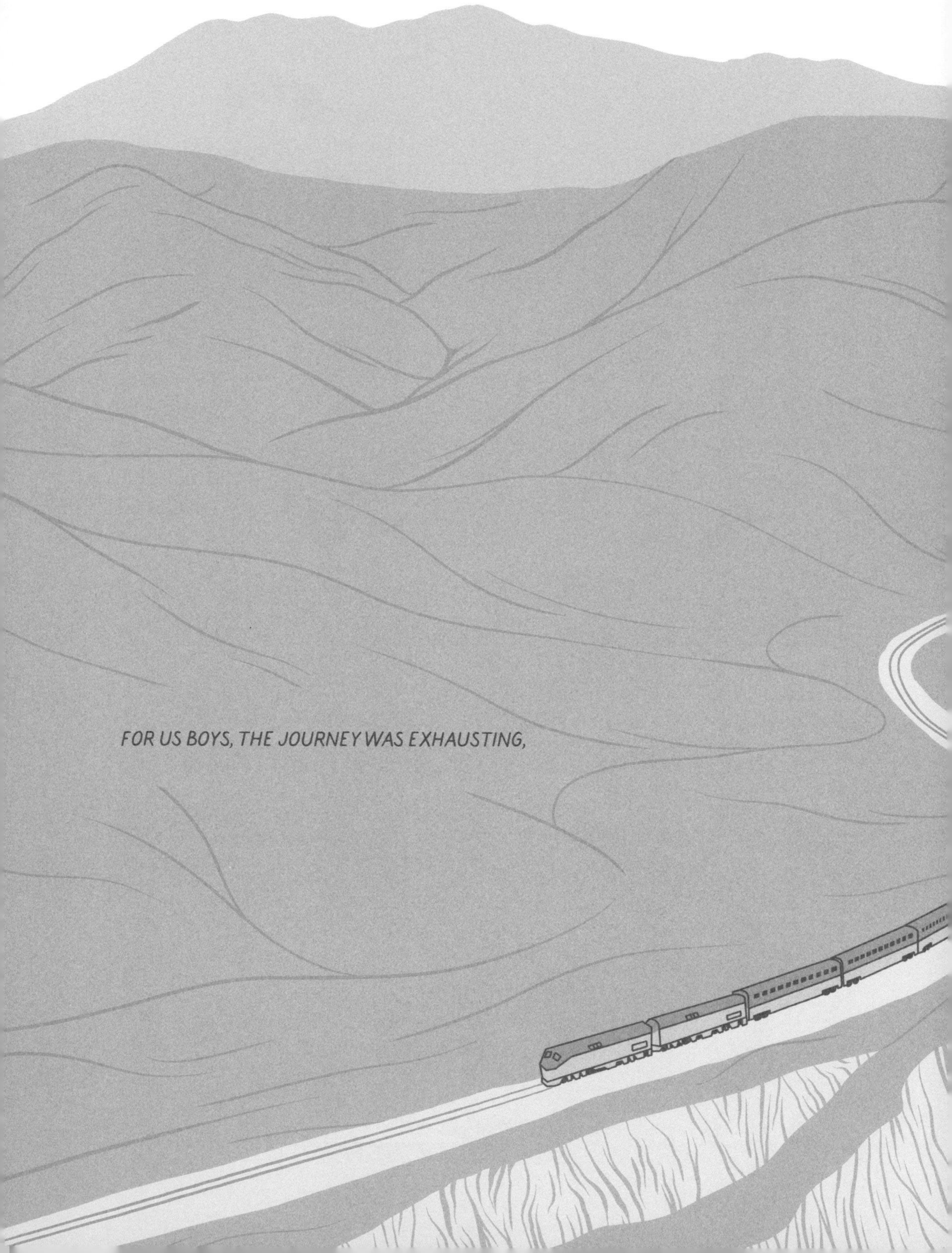
FOR US BOYS, THE JOURNEY WAS EXHAUSTING,

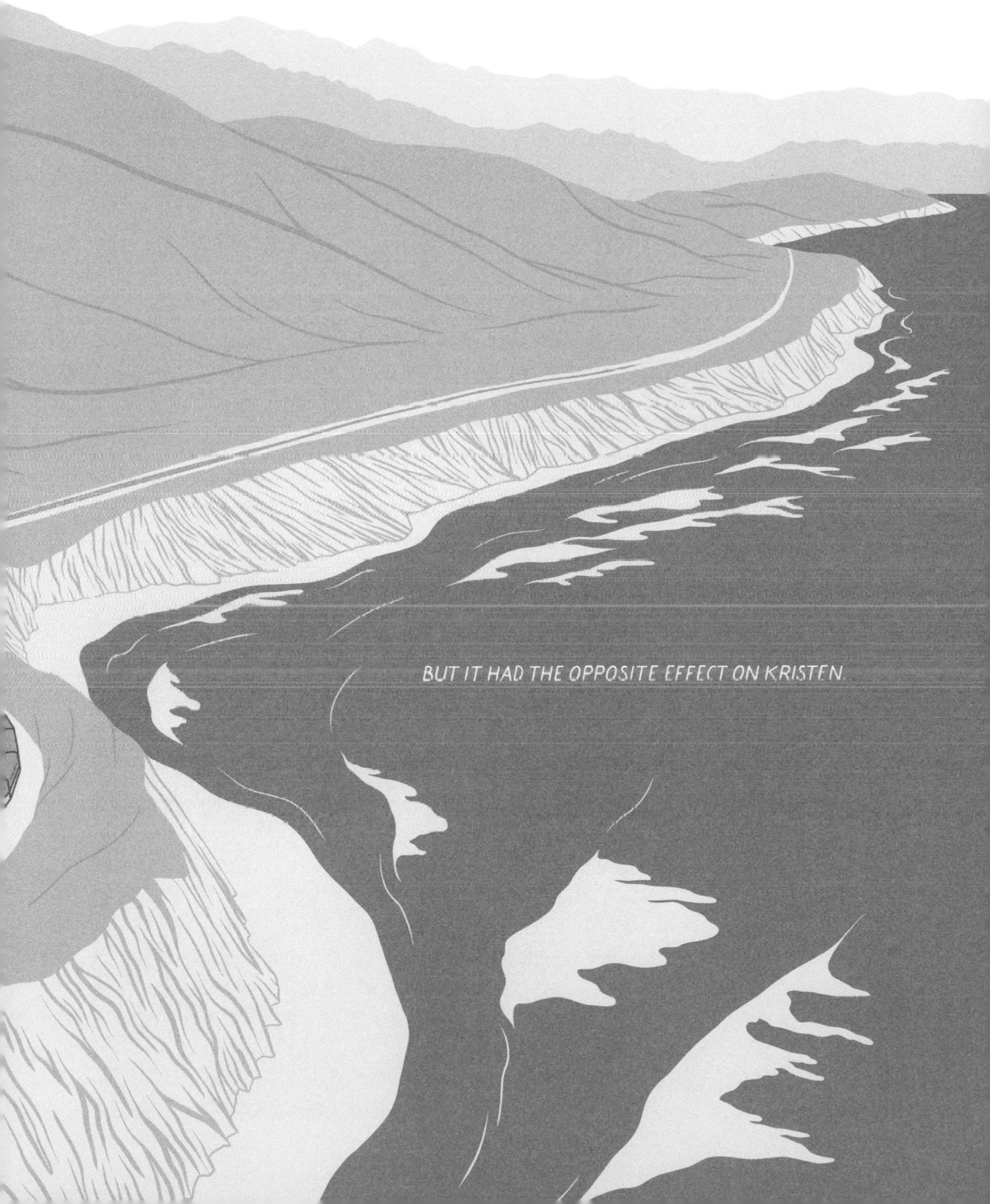
BUT IT HAD THE OPPOSITE EFFECT ON KRISTEN.

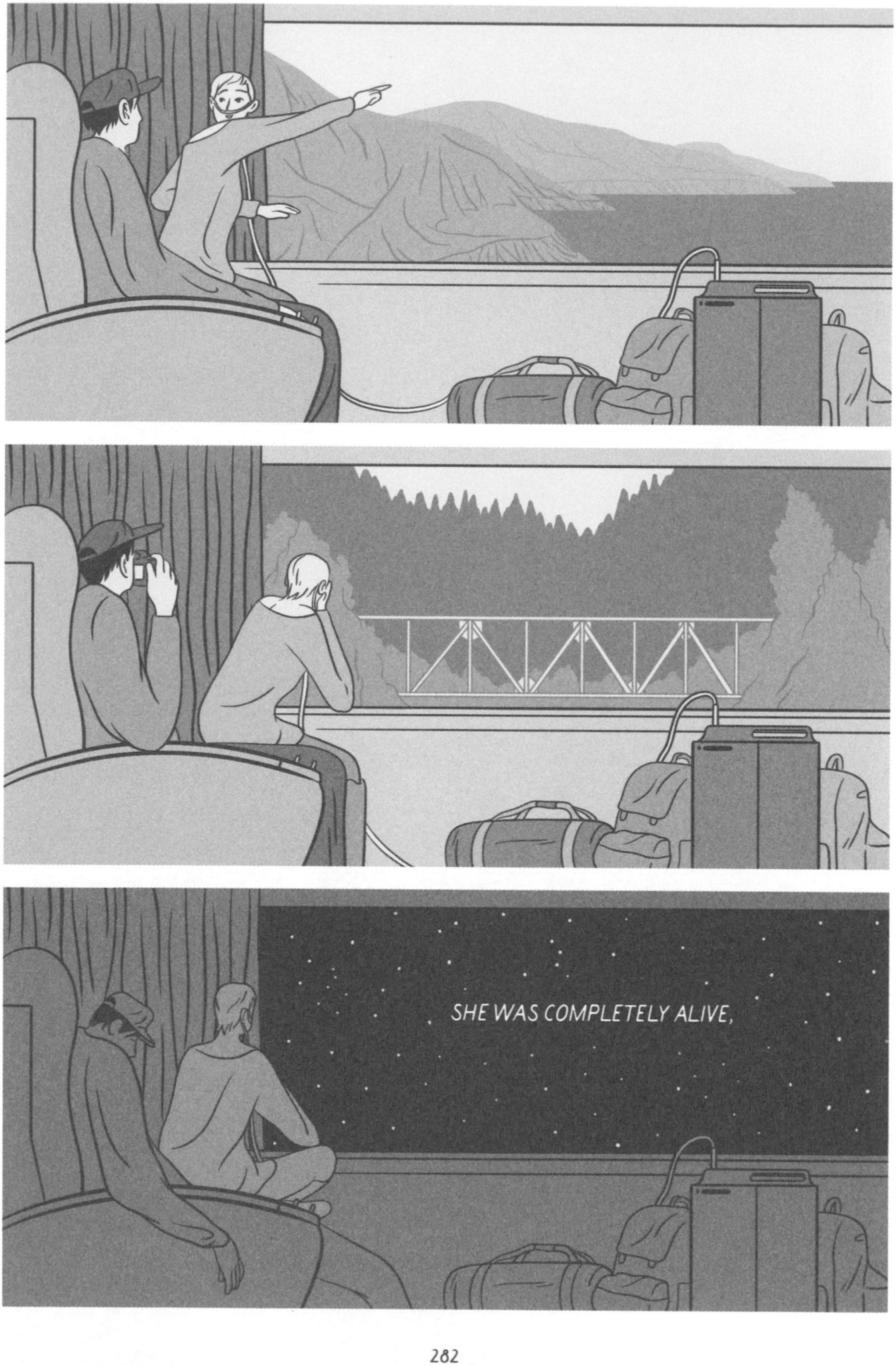
SHE WAS COMPLETELY ALIVE,

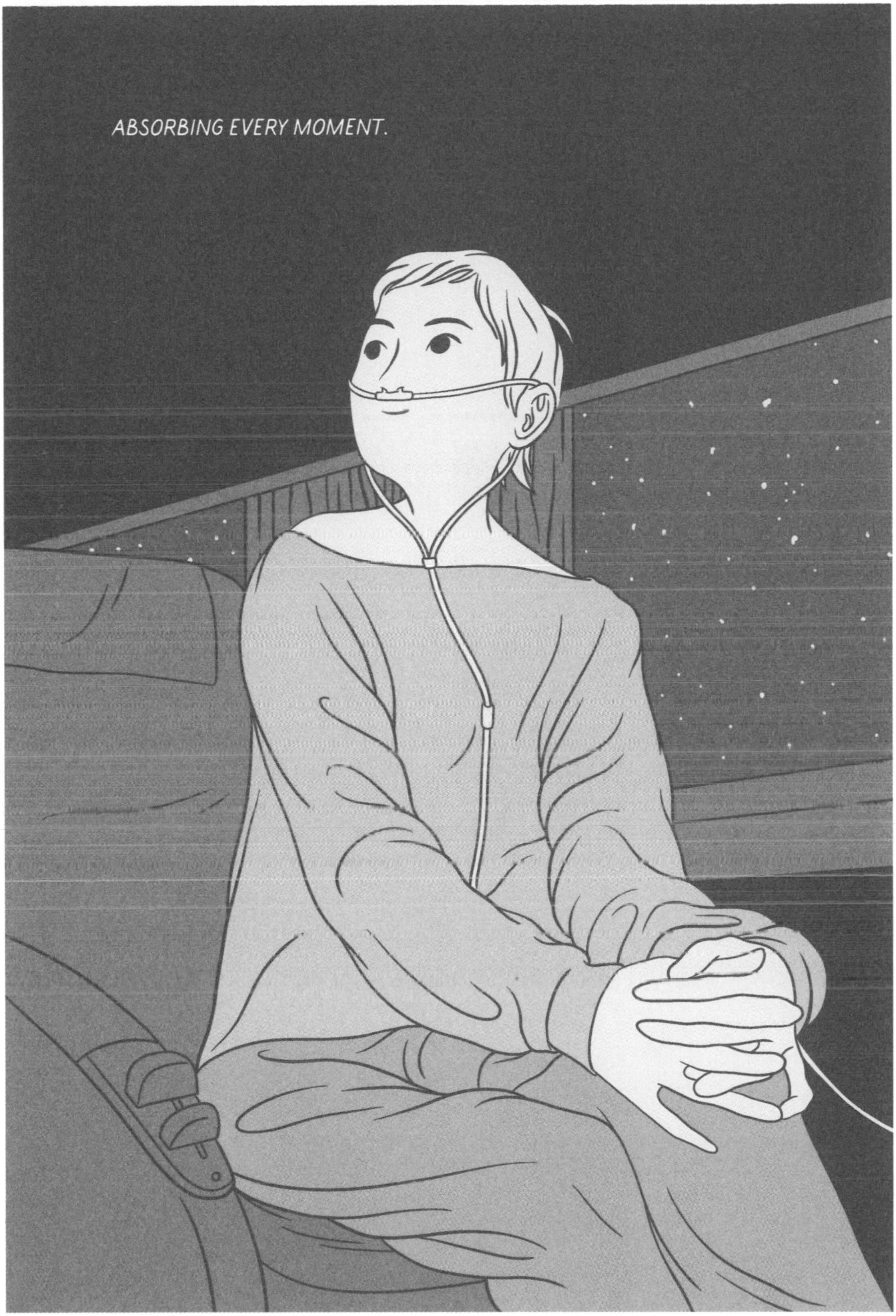
ABSORBING EVERY MOMENT.

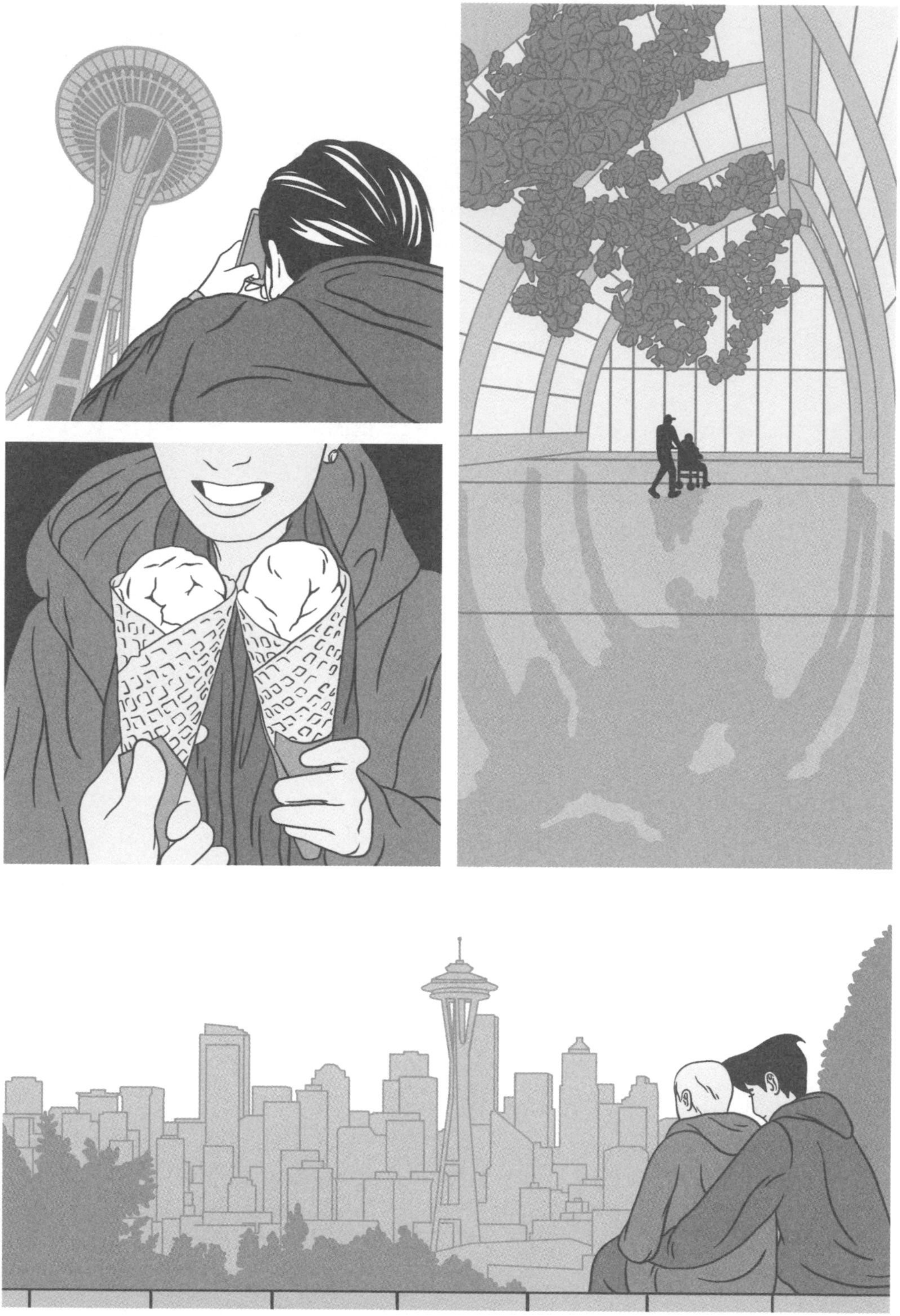

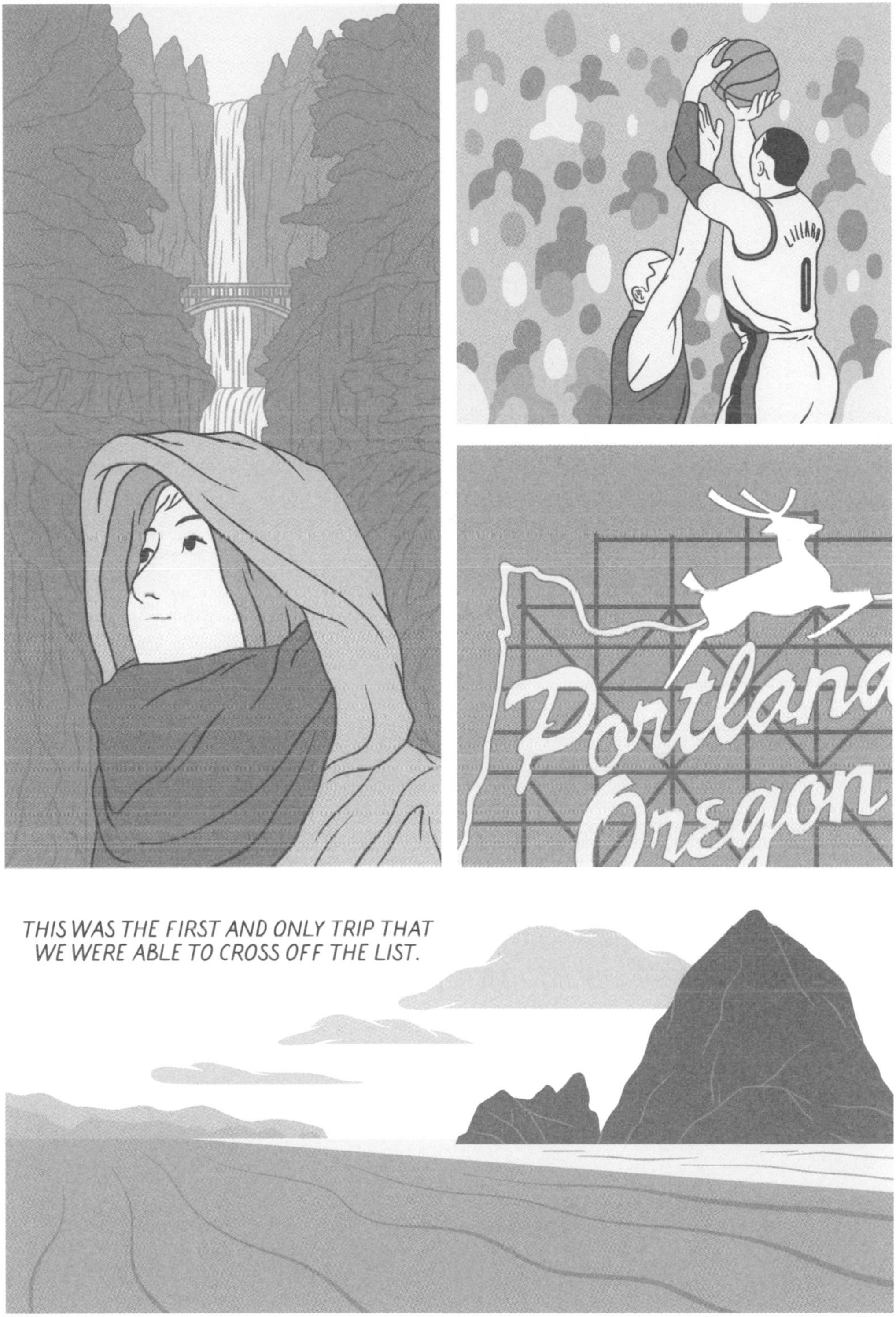
Oregon
THIS WAS THE FIRST AND ONLY TRIP THAT
WE WERE ABLE TO CROSS OFF THE LIST.

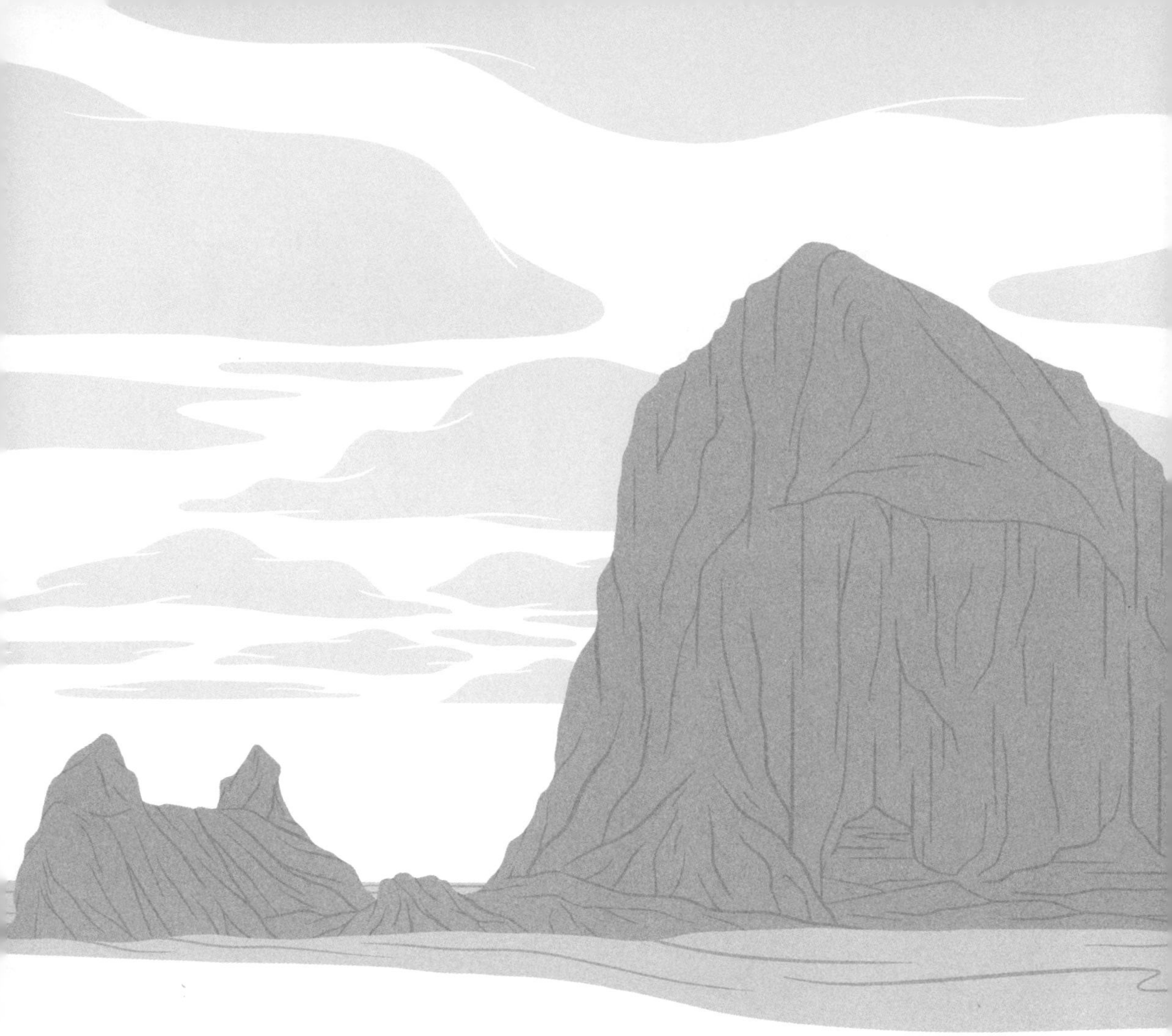

AFTER OUR TRIP, KRISTEN STARTED A ROUND OF CHEMO–A LAST-DITCH EFFORT BY HER DOCTORS.

AT FIRST, KRISTEN REFUSED, BUT FOR THE SAKE OF HER MOM, SHE TRIED ONE MORE TIME.

SHE WAS SO WEAK THAT THE INITIAL DOSE WIPED HER OUT. DAYS LATER SHE WAS HOSPITALIZED FOR A LUNG INFECTION. WITHIN A WEEK SHE QUICKLY BEGAN TO FADE.

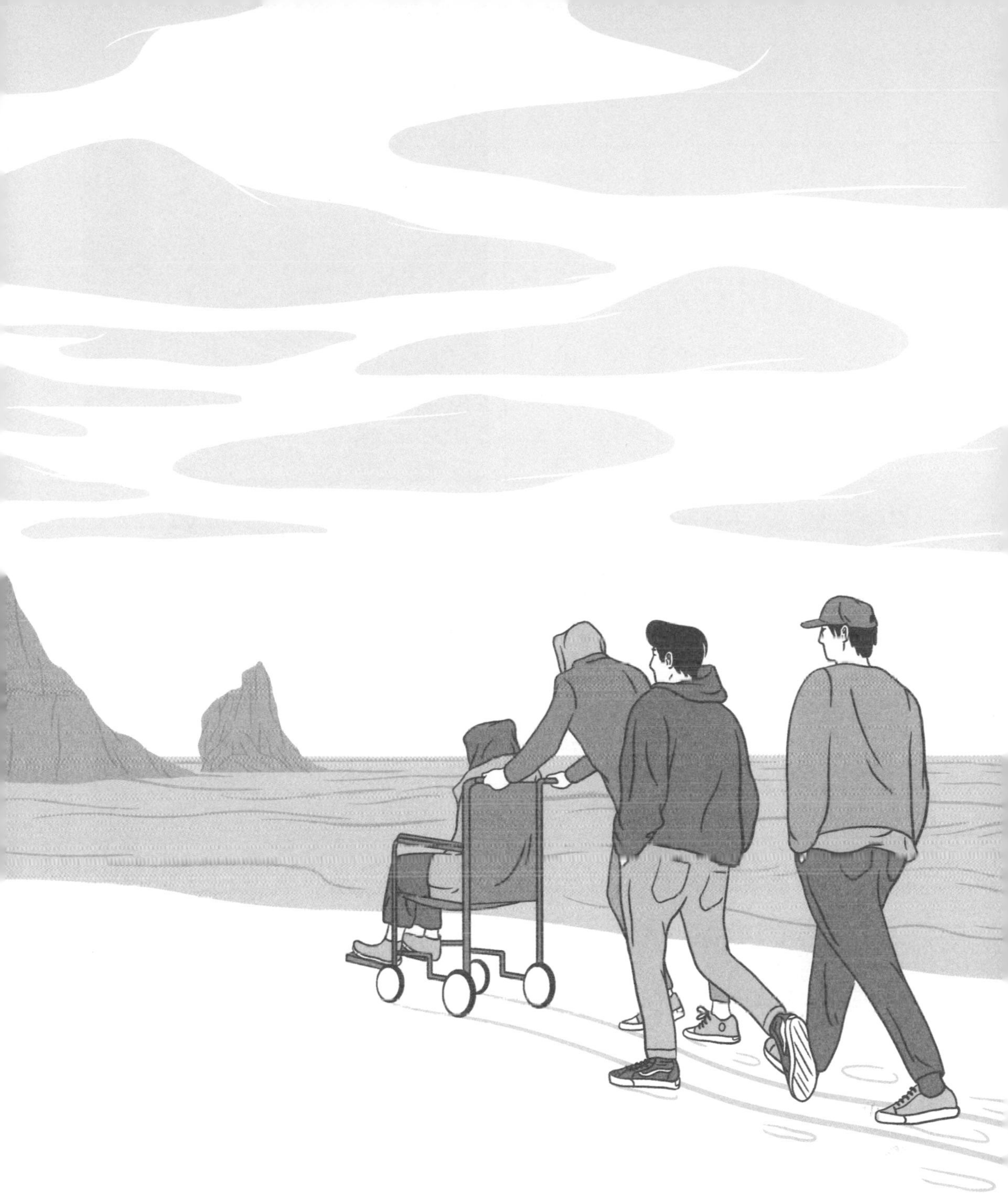

HER SIX-MONTH EXPECTANCY SEEMED LIKE
A LIFETIME COMPARED TO THIS NEW REALITY.

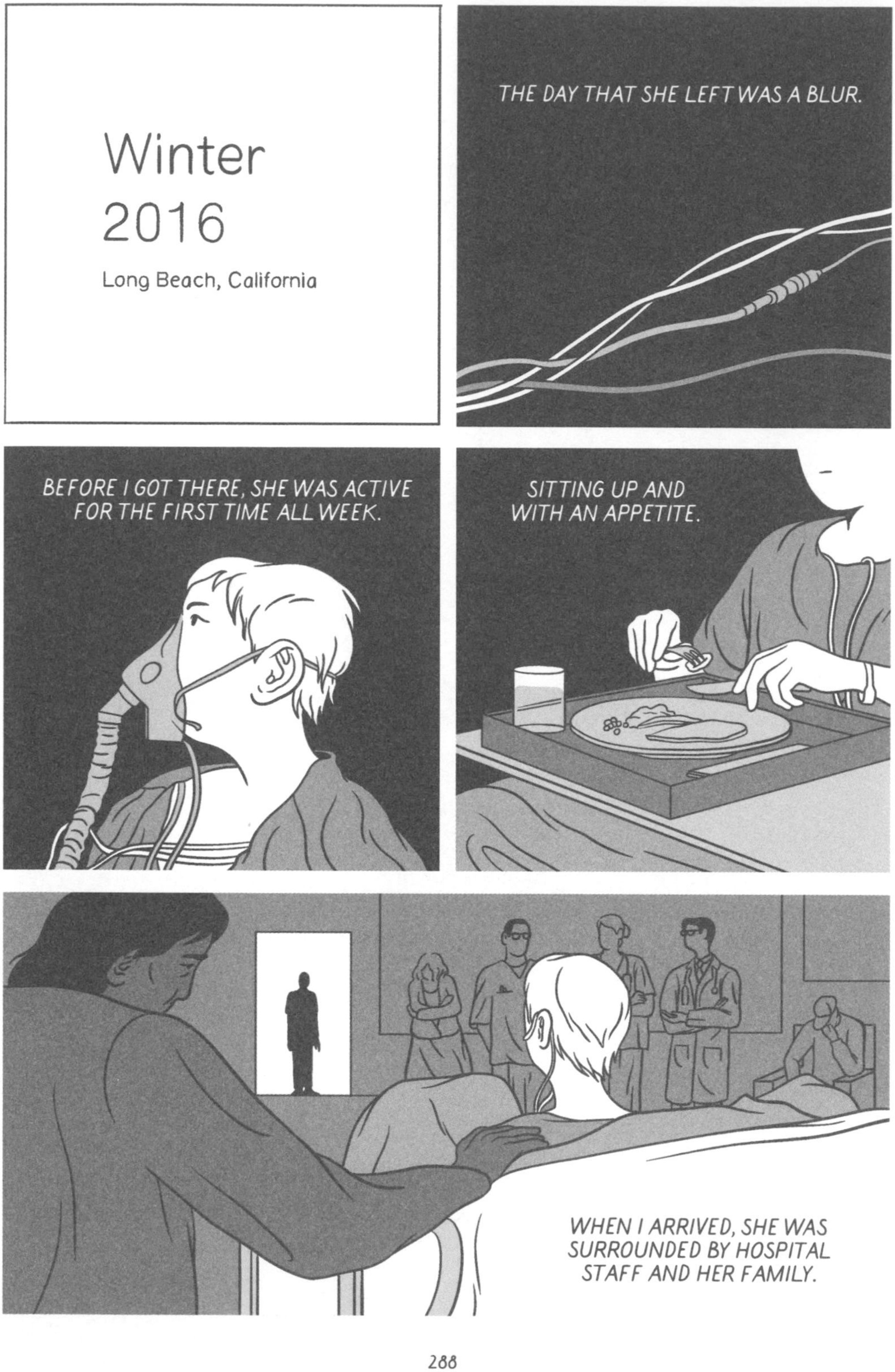
Winter
2016
Long Beach, California
THE DAY THAT SHE LEFT WAS A BLUR.
BEFORE I GOT THERE, SHE WAS ACTIVE FOR THE FIRST TIME ALL WEEK.
SITTING UP AND WITH AN APPETITE.
WHEN I ARRIVED, SHE WAS SURROUNDED BY HOSPITAL STAFF AND HER FAMILY.

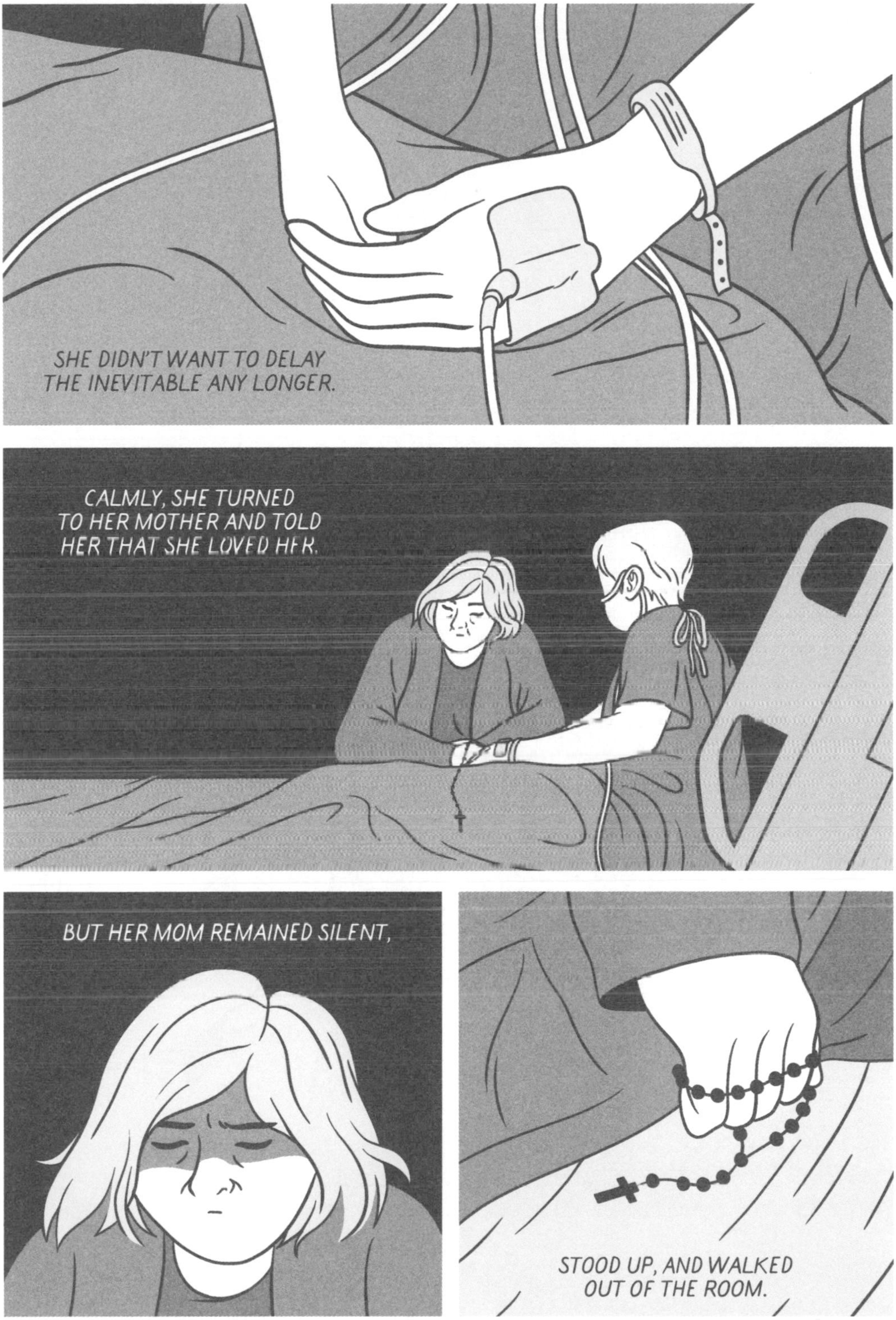
SHE DIDN'T WANT TO DELAY THE INEVITABLE ANY LONGER.
CALMLY, SHE TURNED TO HER MOTHER AND TOLD HER THAT SHE LOVED HER.
BUT HER MOM REMAINED SILENT,
STOOD UP, AND WALKED OUT OF THE ROOM.

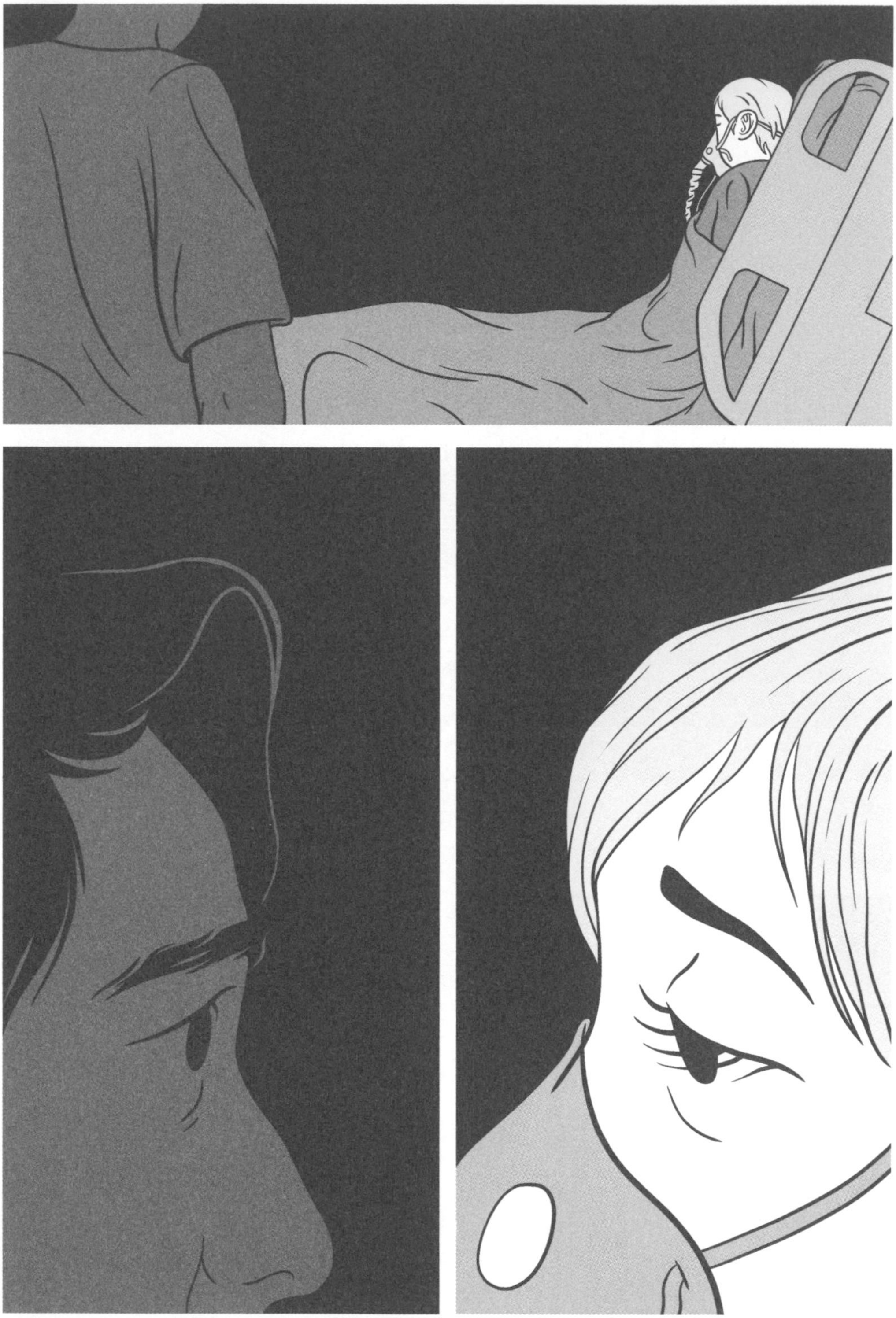

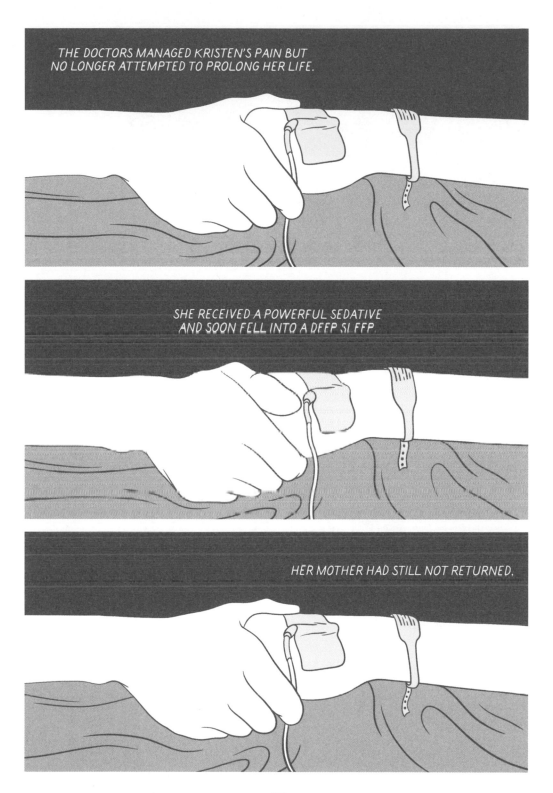

THE DOCTORS MANAGED KRISTEN'S PAIN BUT
NO LONGER ATTEMPTED TO PROLONG HER LIFE.

SHE RECEIVED A POWERFUL SEDATIVE
AND SOON FELL INTO A DEEP SLEEP.

HER MOTHER HAD STILL NOT RETURNED.

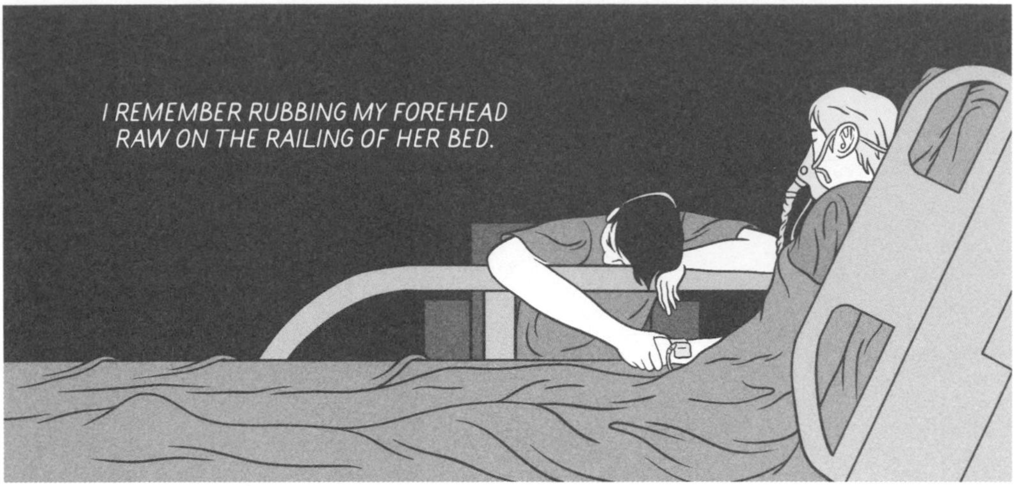
I REMEMBER RUBBING MY FOREHEAD RAW ON THE RAILING OF HER BED.

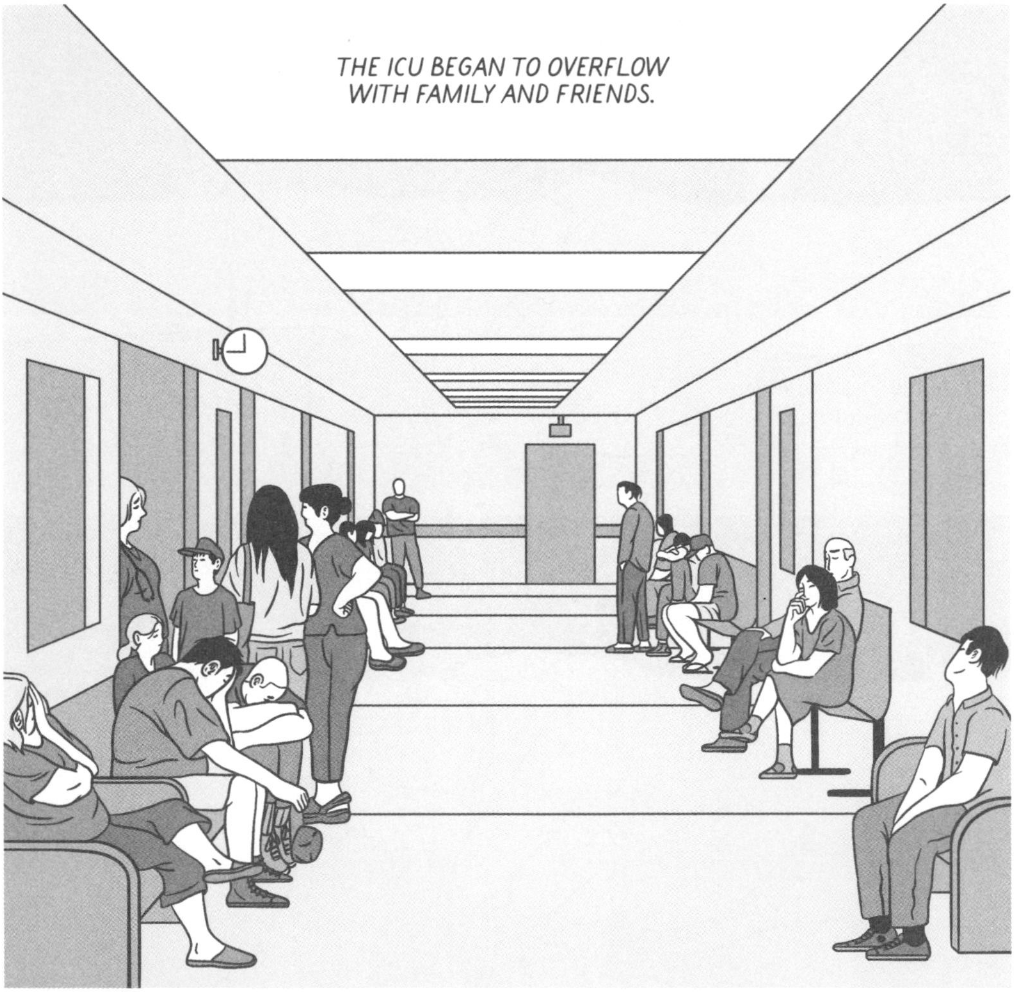
THE ICU BEGAN TO OVERFLOW WITH FAMILY AND FRIENDS.

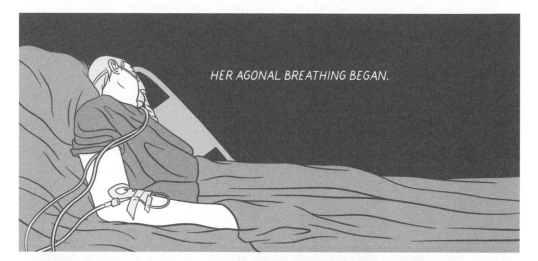

HER AGONAL BREATHING BEGAN.

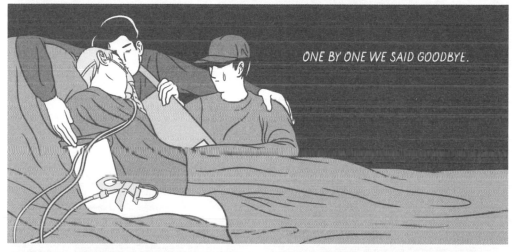

ONE BY ONE WE SAID GOODBYE.

WHEN IT WAS MY TURN.

I DIDN'T REALIZE HER FAMILY HAD CLEARED THE ROOM FOR US.

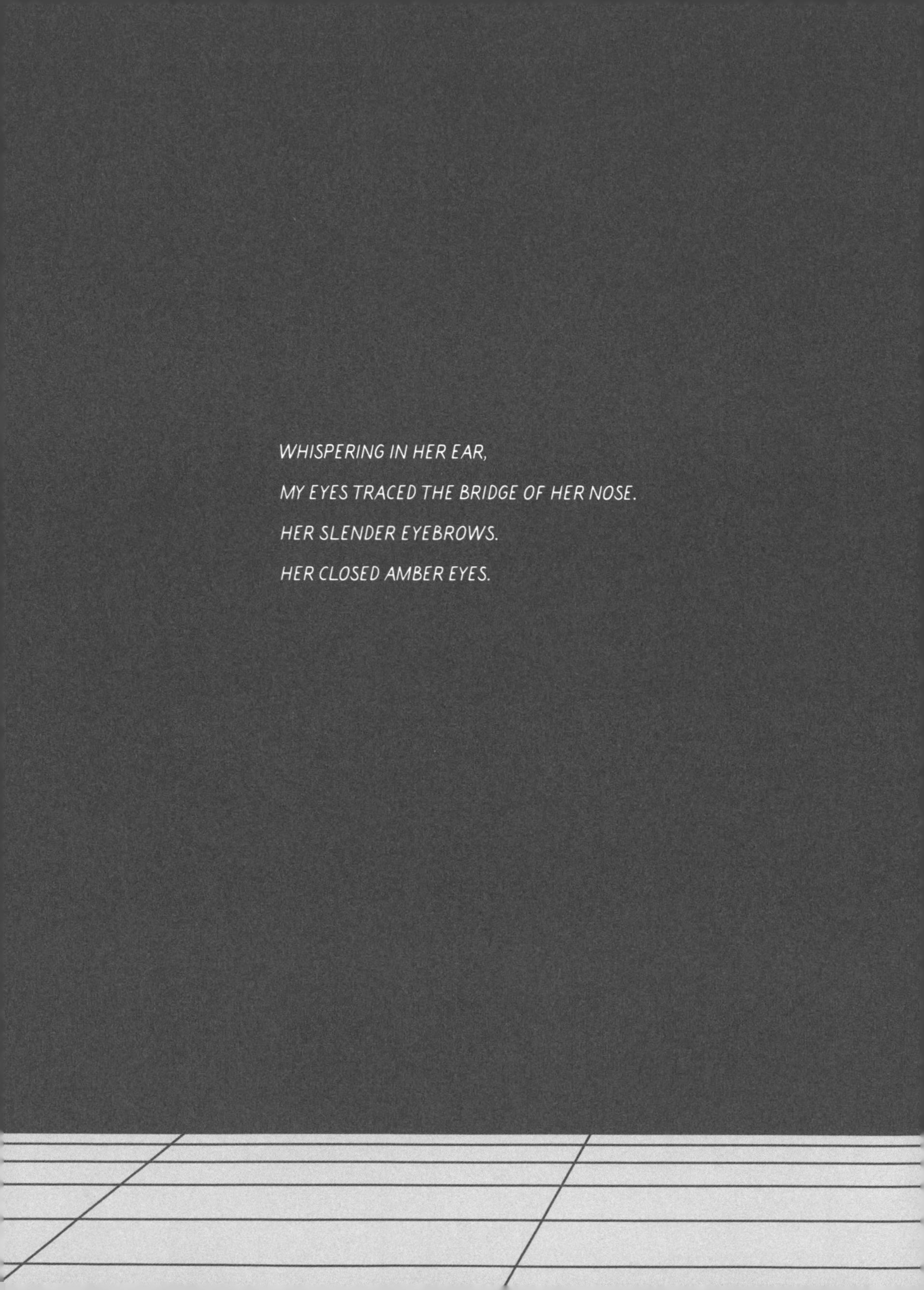
WHISPERING IN HER EAR,
MY EYES TRACED THE BRIDGE OF HER NOSE.
HER SLENDER EYEBROWS.
HER CLOSED AMBER EYES.

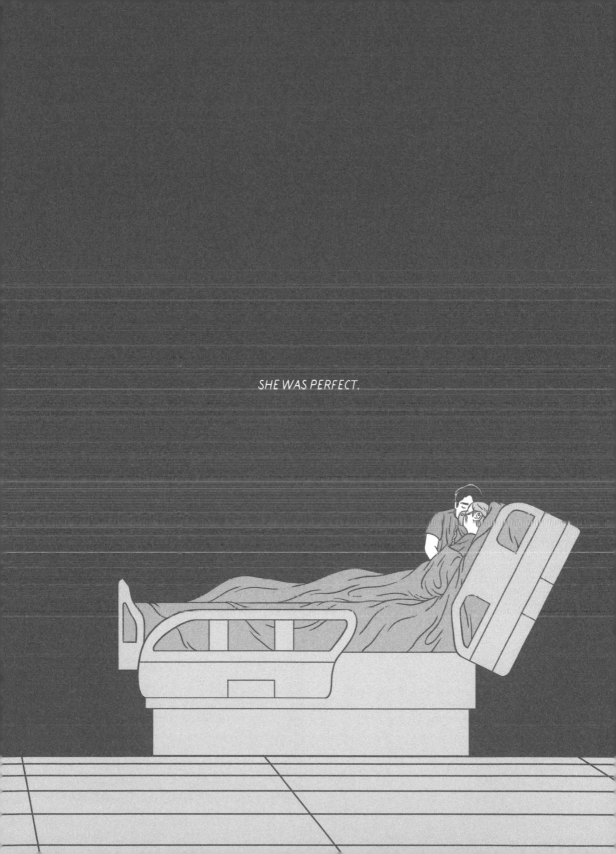

SHE WAS PERFECT.

SHORTLY BEFORE MIDNIGHT,
HER MOM CAME BACK.

SHE WENT STRAIGHT TO HER
CHILD AND TOLD HER HOW MUCH
SHE LOVED HER, HOW PROUD
OF HER SHE WAS, AND THAT
IS WAS OKAY TO LEAVE NOW.

UPON HEARING HER MOTHER SPEAK,
KRISTEN'S PULSE BEGAN TO DROP.

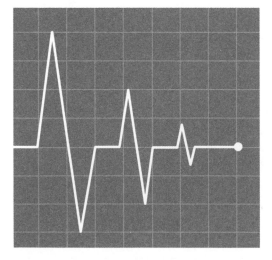

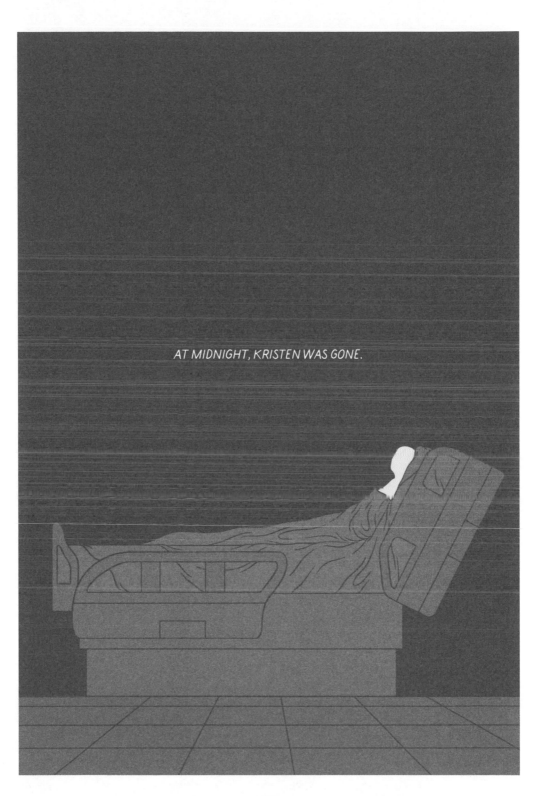

AT MIDNIGHT, KRISTEN WAS GONE.

A WAVE OF PEACE FILLED THE ROOM.

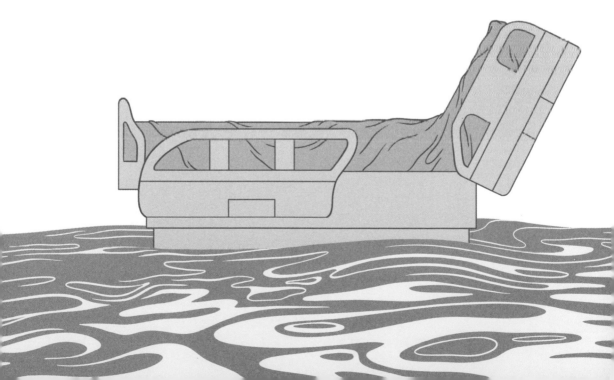

Fall
2017

Cypress, California

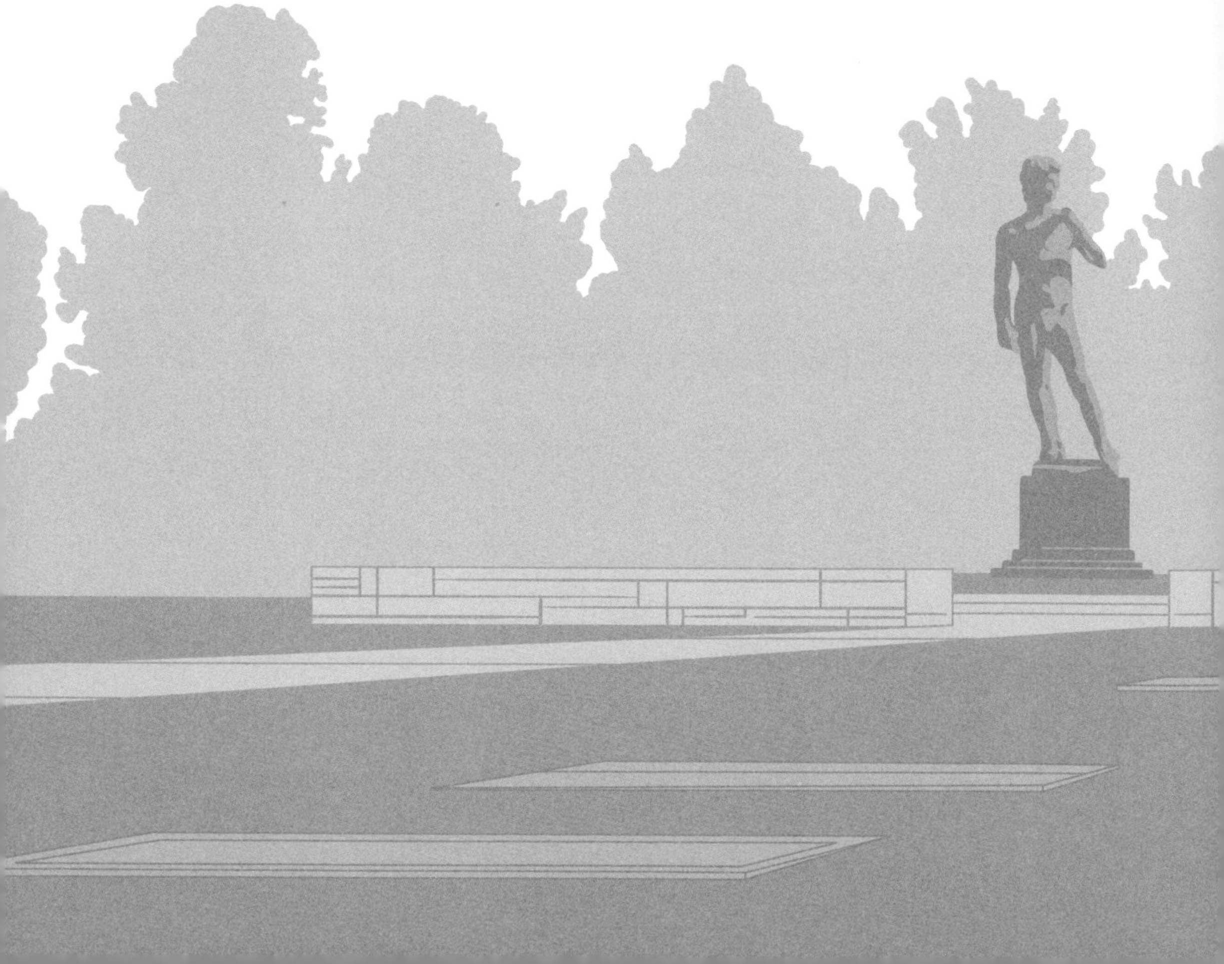

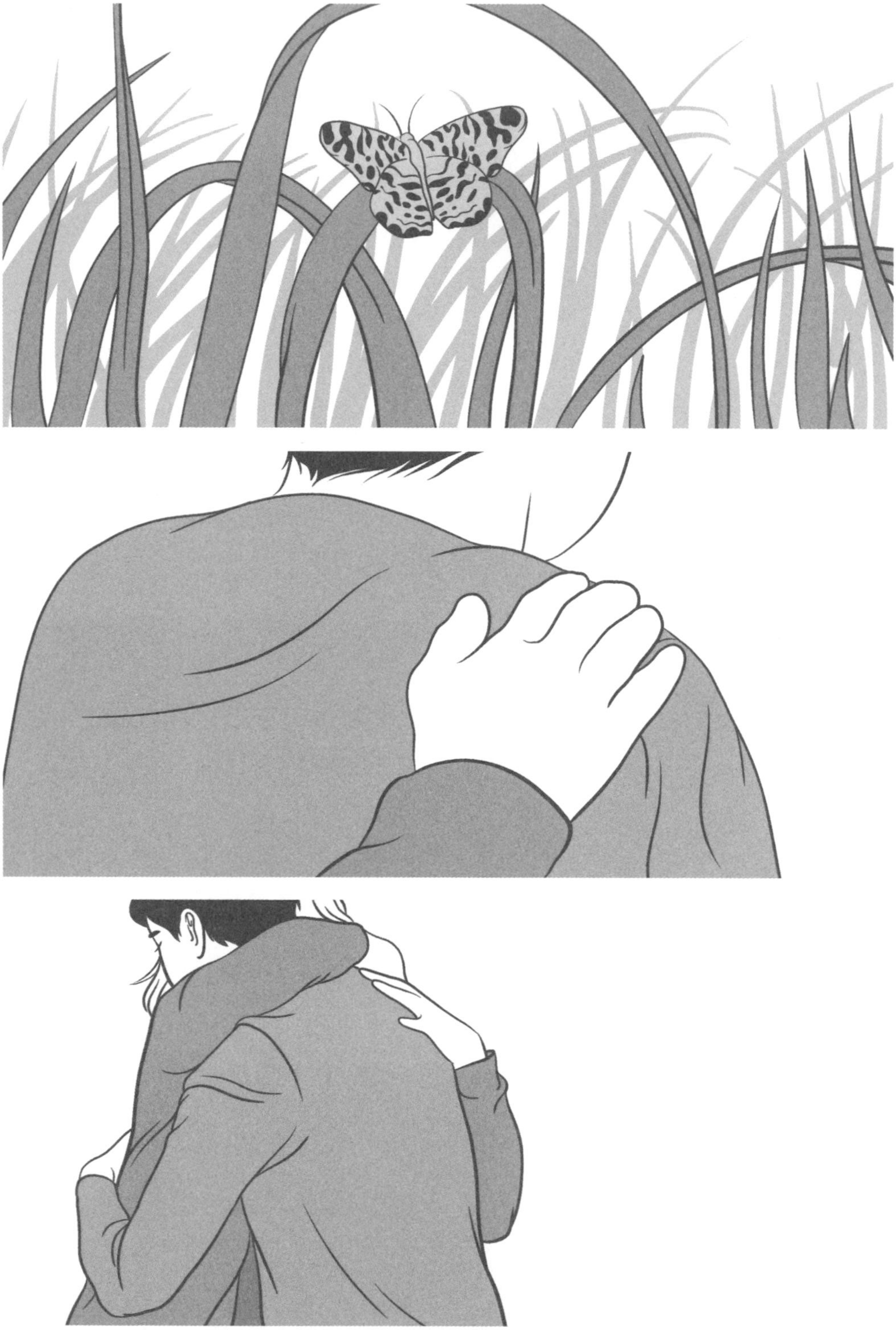

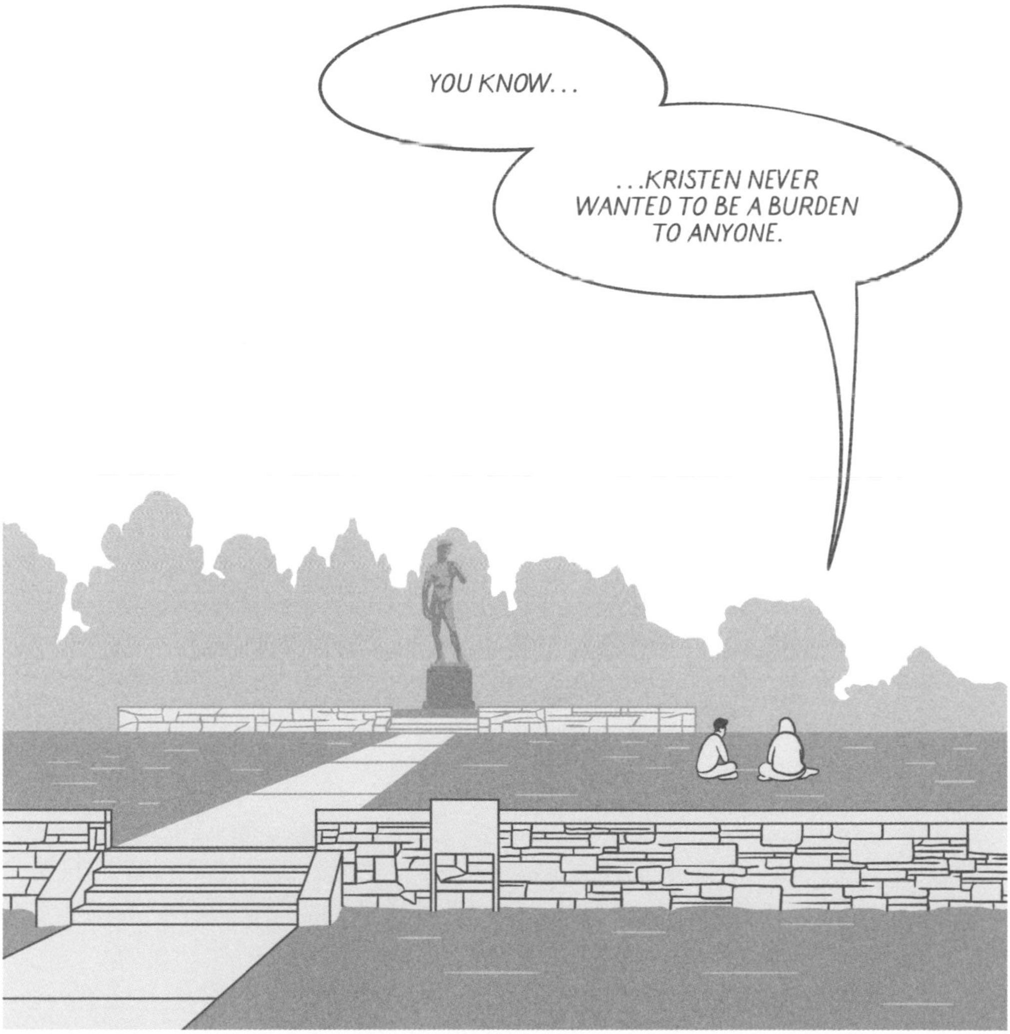
YOU KNOW...
...KRISTEN NEVER WANTED TO BE A BURDEN TO ANYONE.

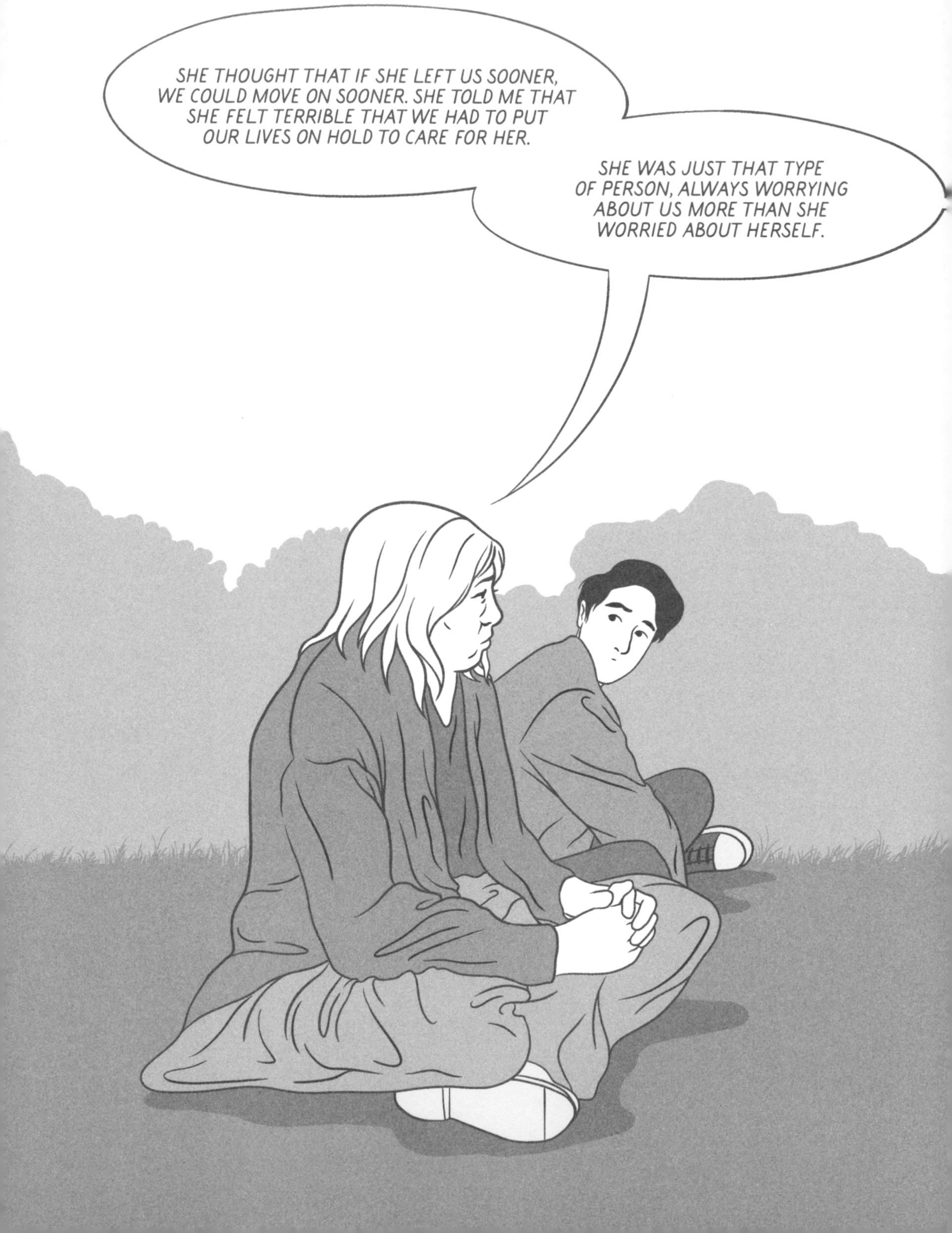
SHE THOUGHT THAT IF SHE LEFT US SOONER, WE COULD MOVE ON SOONER. SHE TOLD ME THAT SHE FELT TERRIBLE THAT WE HAD TO PUT OUR LIVES ON HOLD TO CARE FOR HER.
SHE WAS JUST THAT TYPE OF PERSON, ALWAYS WORRYING ABOUT US MORE THAN SHE WORRIED ABOUT HERSELF.

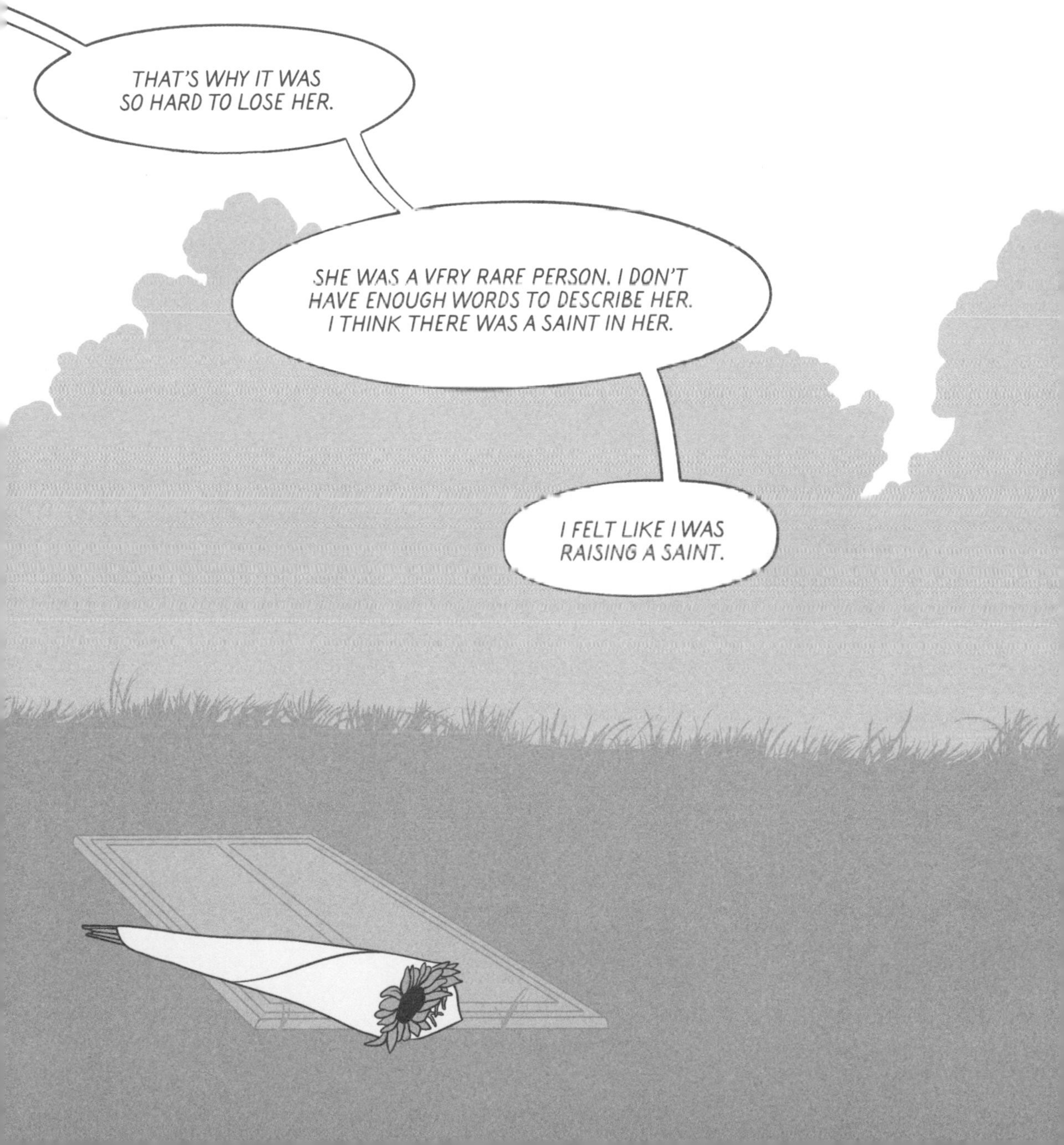
THAT'S WHY IT WAS SO HARD TO LOSE HER.
SHE WAS A VERY RARE PERSON. I DON'T HAVE ENOUGH WORDS TO DESCRIBE HER. I THINK THERE WAS A SAINT IN HER.
I FELT LIKE I WAS RAISING A SAINT.

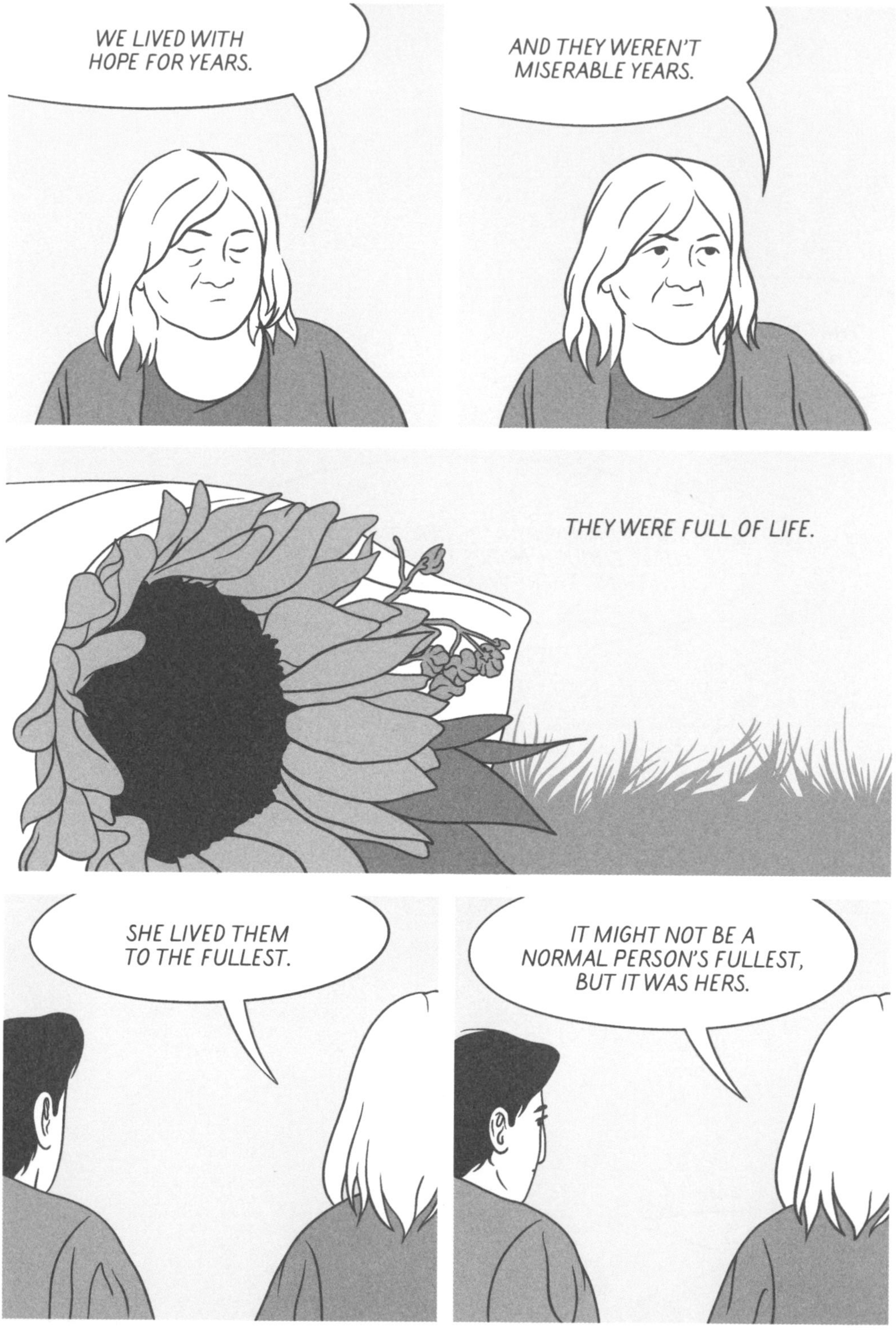
WE LIVED WITH HOPE FOR YEARS.
AND THEY WEREN'T MISERABLE YEARS.
THEY WERE FULL OF LIFE.
SHE LIVED THEM TO THE FULLEST.
IT MIGHT NOT BE A NORMAL PERSON'S FULLEST, BUT IT WAS HERS.

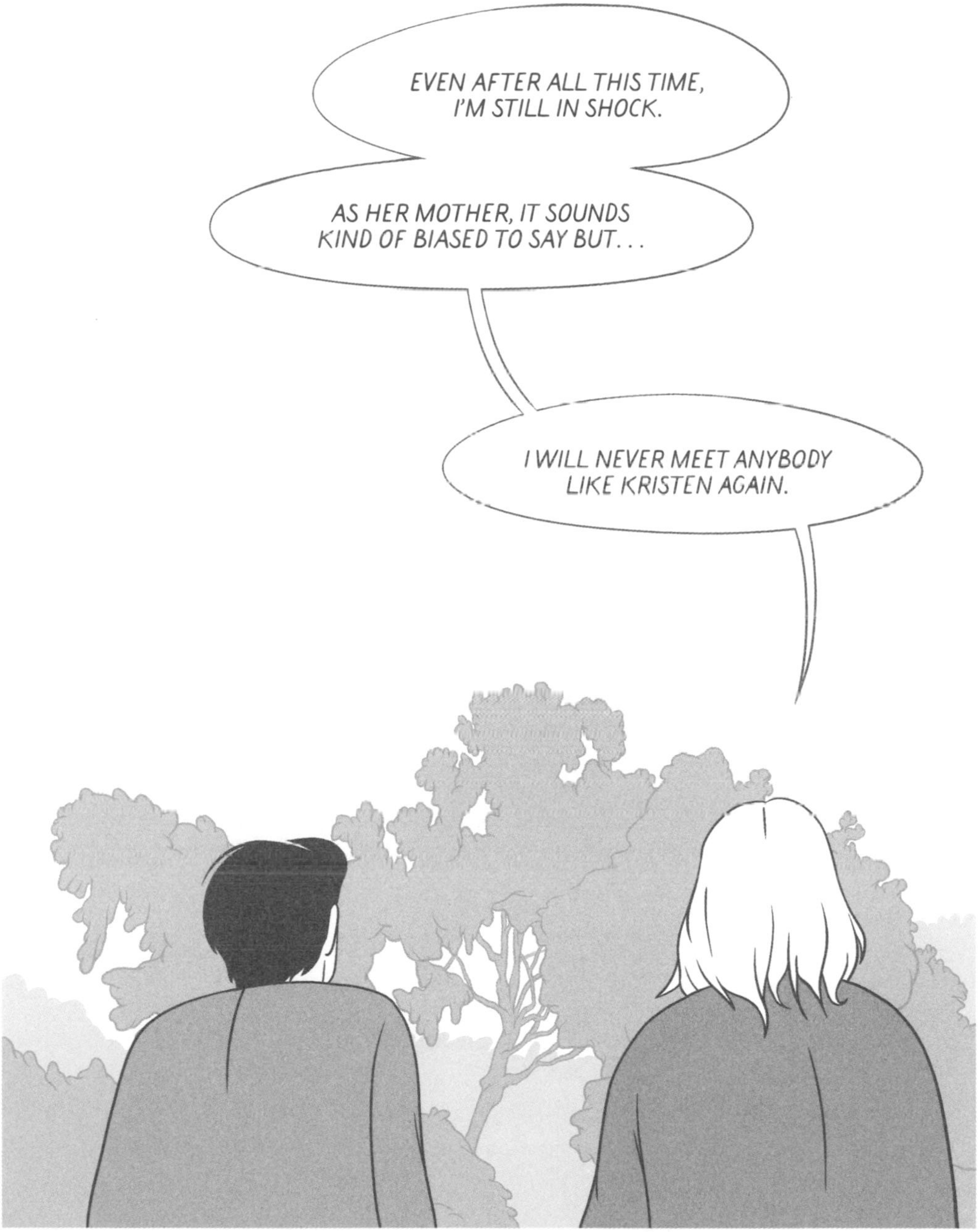
EVEN AFTER ALL THIS TIME, I'M STILL IN SHOCK.
AS HER MOTHER, IT SOUNDS KIND OF BIASED TO SAY BUT...
I WILL NEVER MEET ANYBODY LIKE KRISTEN AGAIN.

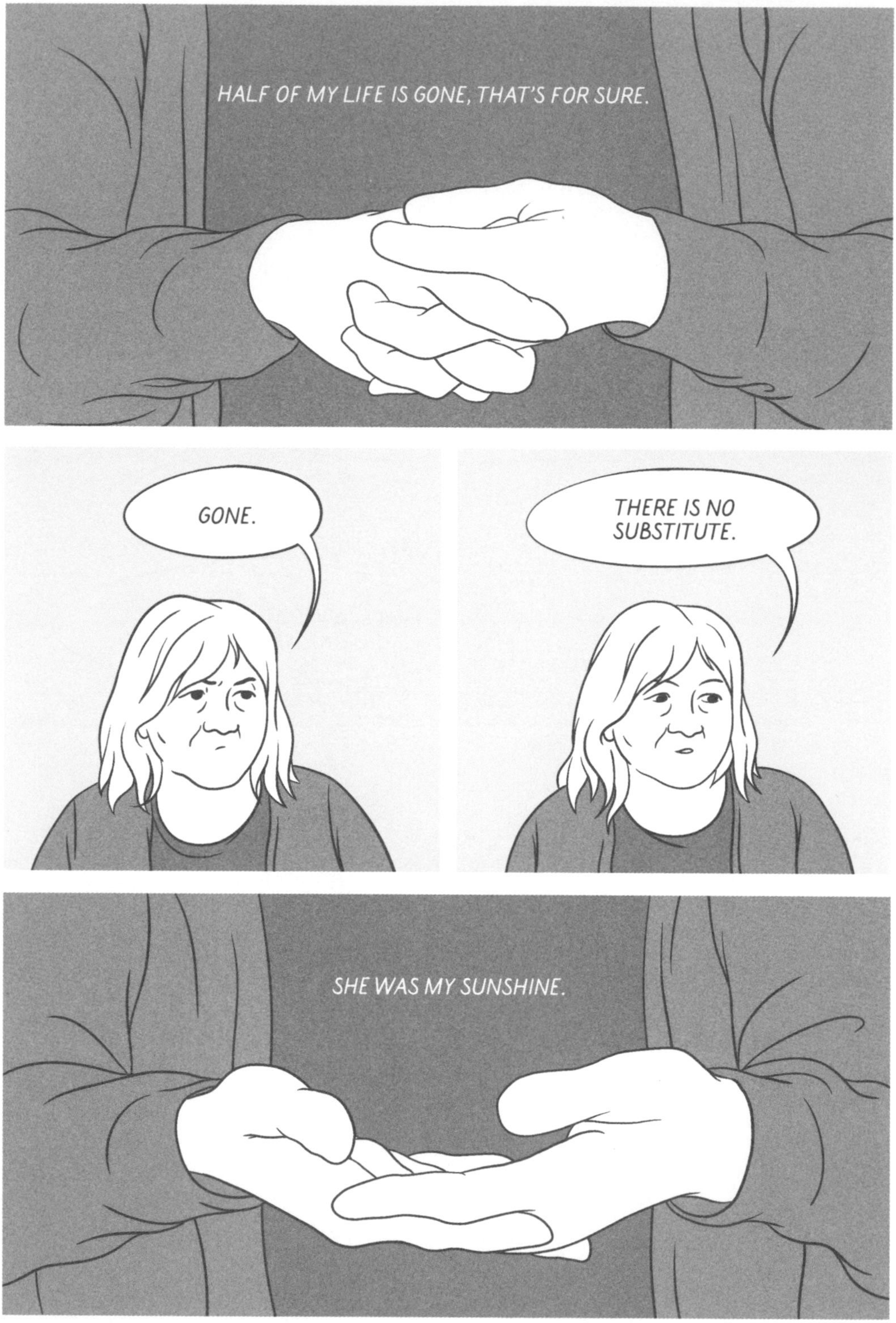
HALF OF MY LIFE IS GONE, THAT'S FOR SURE.
GONE.
THERE IS NO SUBSTITUTE.
SHE WAS MY SUNSHINE.

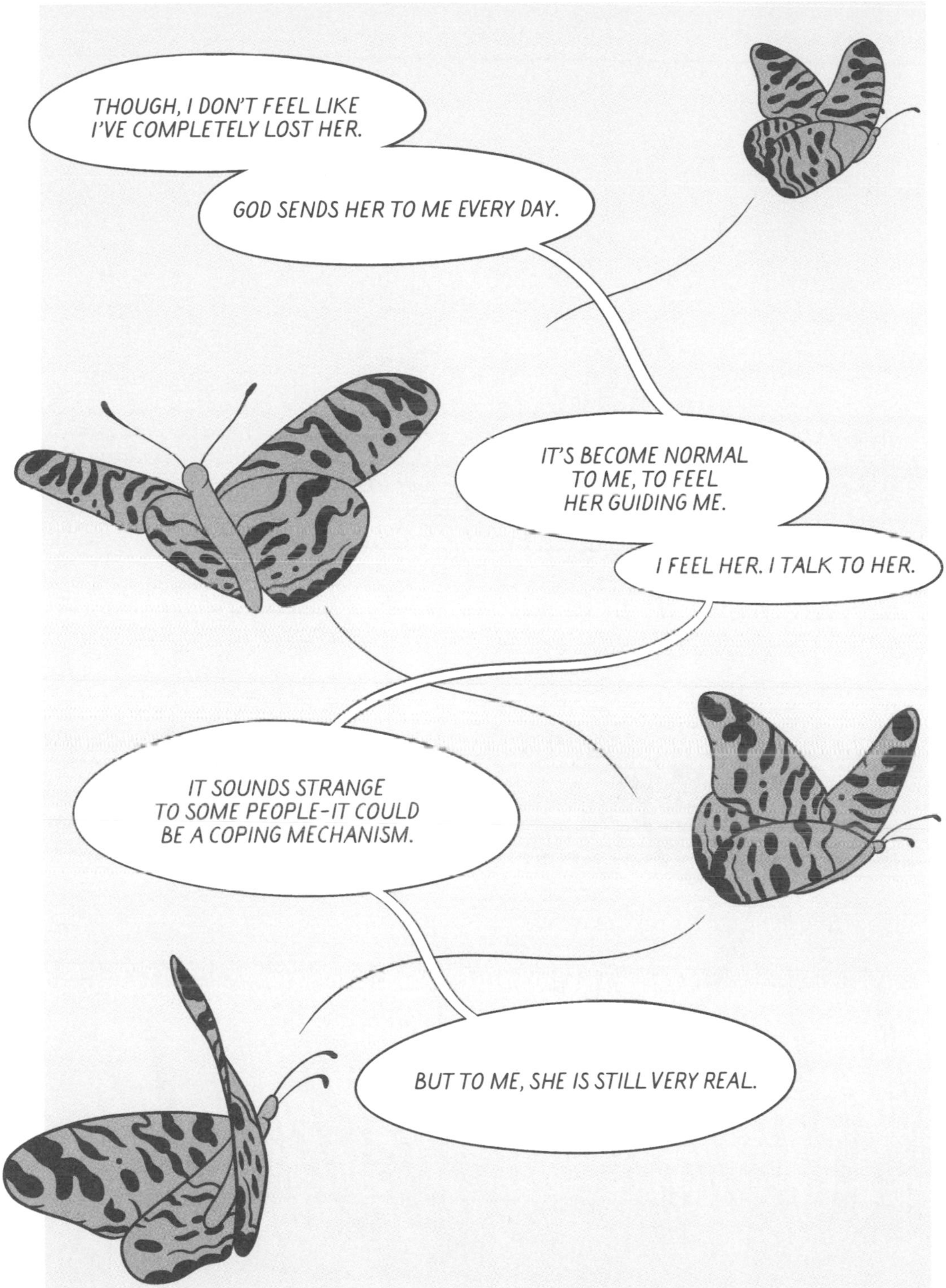
THOUGH, I DON'T FEEL LIKE I'VE COMPLETELY LOST HER.
GOD SENDS HER TO ME EVERY DAY.
IT'S BECOME NORMAL TO ME, TO FEEL HER GUIDING ME.
I FEEL HER. I TALK TO HER.
IT SOUNDS STRANGE TO SOME PEOPLE-IT COULD BE A COPING MECHANISM.
BUT TO ME, SHE IS STILL VERY REAL.

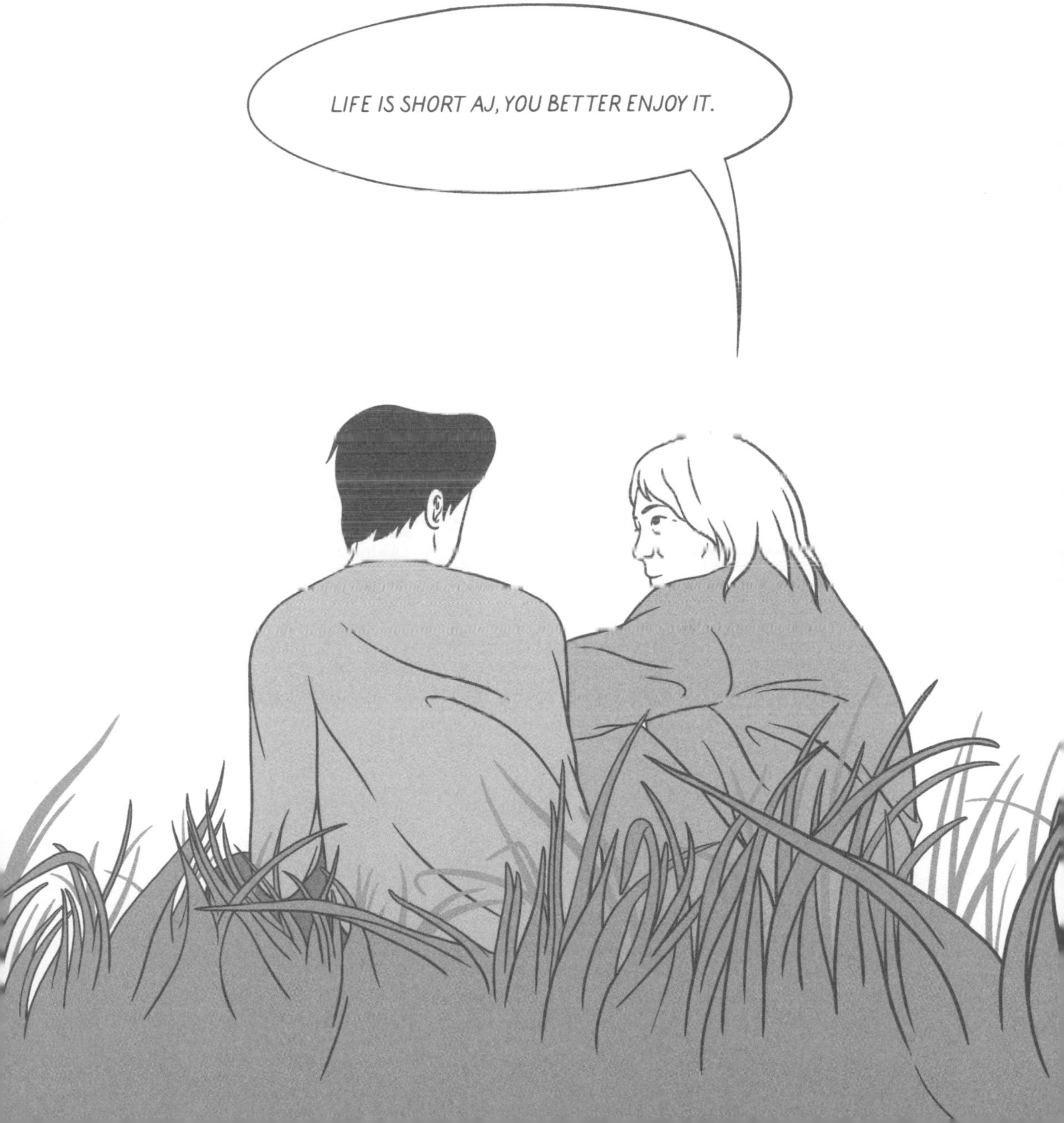
LIFE IS SHORT AJ, YOU BETTER ENJOY IT.

XIV. SOLITUDE

Spring 1950

Waikiki, Hawaii

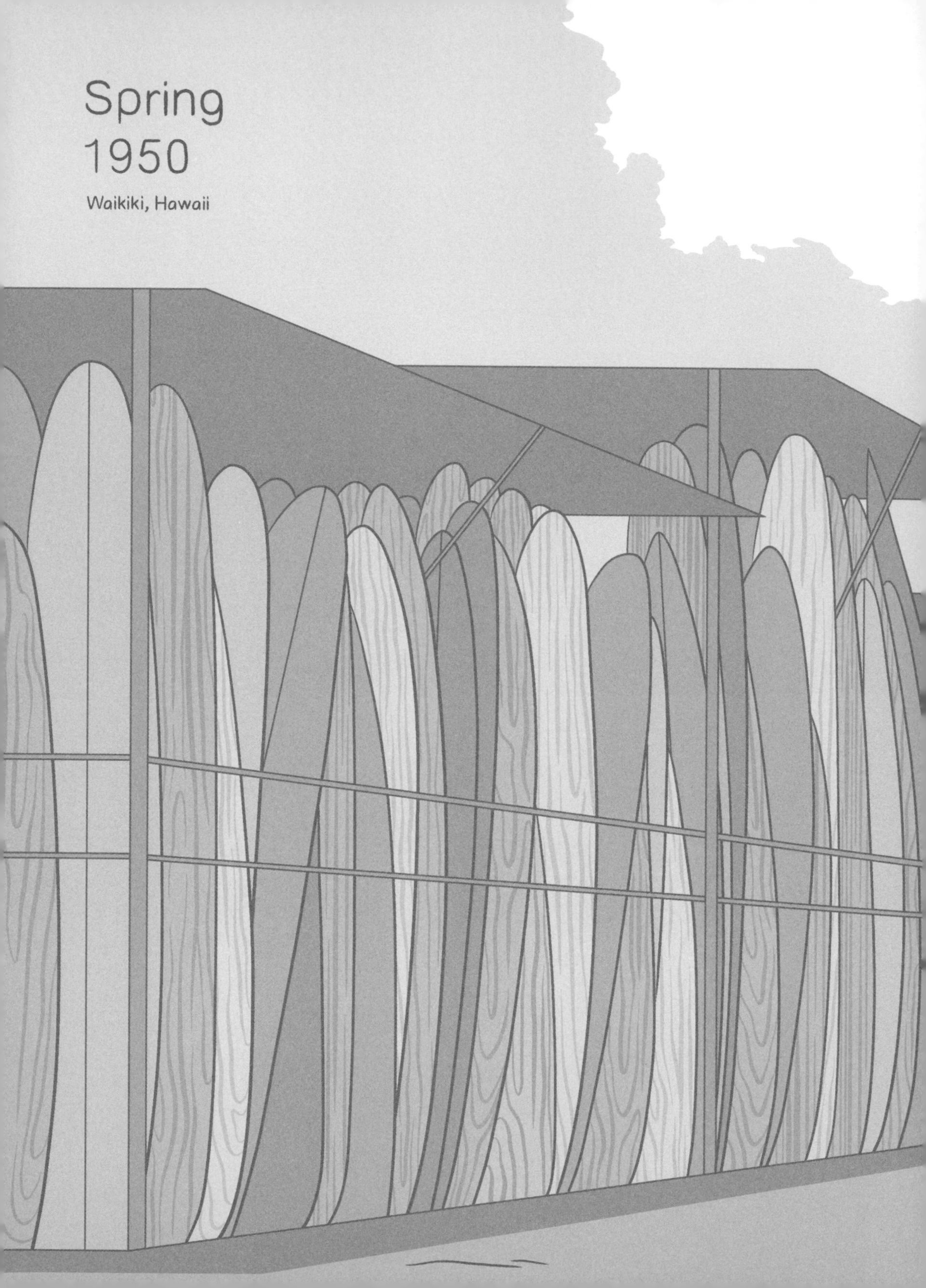

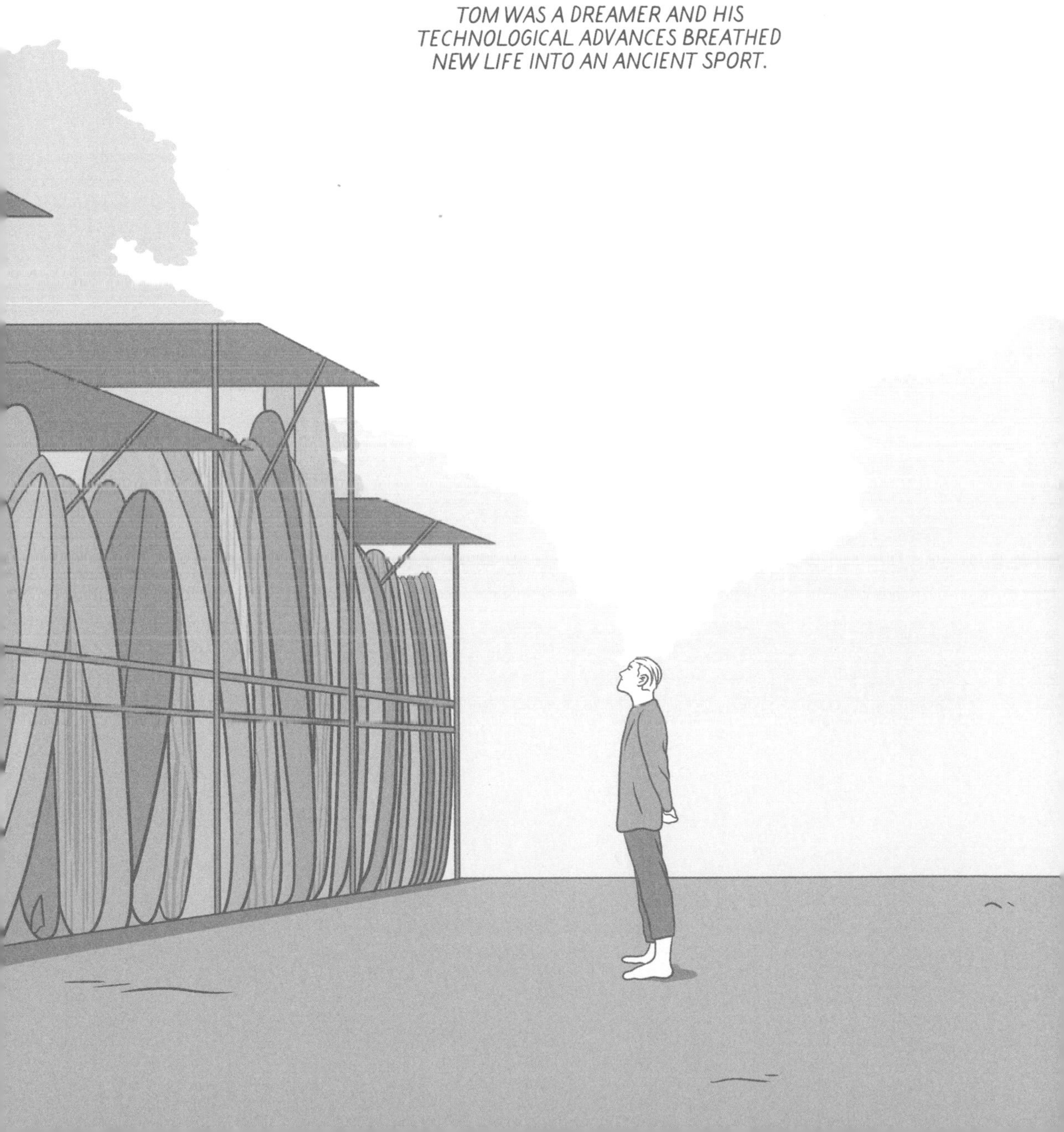
TOM WAS A DREAMER AND HIS TECHNOLOGICAL ADVANCES BREATHED NEW LIFE INTO AN ANCIENT SPORT.

BUT HIS CREATIONS WERE
NOT IMMUNE TO OPPOSITION.

TOM PERFECTED HIS PROTOTYPE
AND CALLED IT THE HOLLOW BOARD.

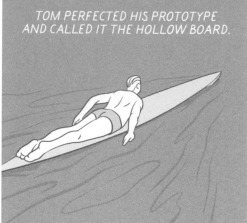

WHEN HE COMPETED
WITH HIS INVENTION...

...HE WOULD RIDE LONGER,
FARTHER, AND FASTER THAN
ALL OF THE OTHER SURFERS.

THIS DID NOT SIT WELL WITH PURISTS OF THE SPORT.

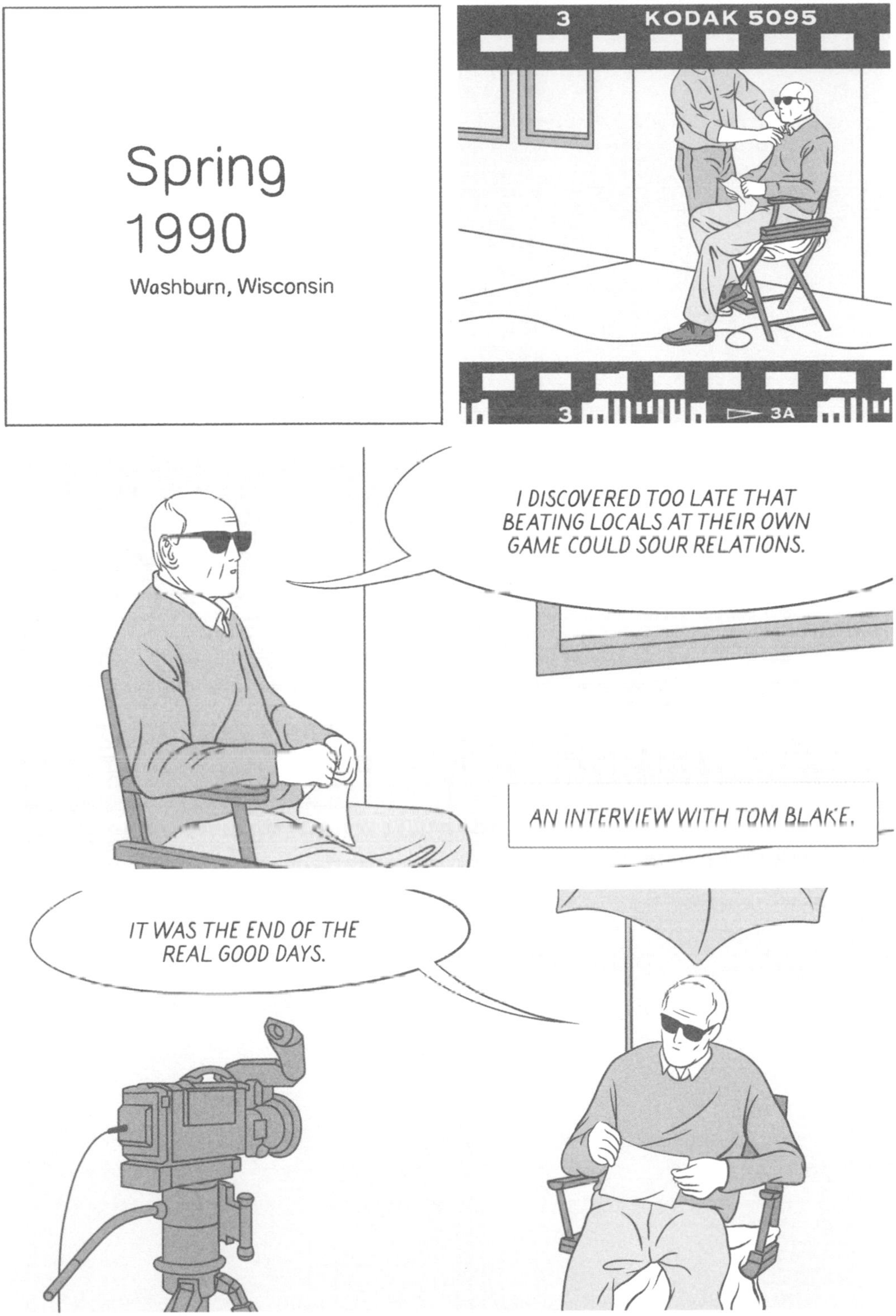
Spring
1990
Washburn, Wisconsin
3 KODAK 5095
3 3A
I DISCOVERED TOO LATE THAT BEATING LOCALS AT THEIR OWN GAME COULD SOUR RELATIONS.
AN INTERVIEW WITH TOM BLAKE.
IT WAS THE END OF THE REAL GOOD DAYS.

WHEN TOM'S SURFBOARD BECAME A HOUSEHOLD NAME,
BEGINNERS EVERYWHERE EMBRACED THE HOLLOW BOARD.

IT WAS QUICK AND PRACTICALLY WEIGHTLESS
COMPARED TO THE SOLID PLANKS THAT
SEASONED SURFERS RODE AT THE TIME.

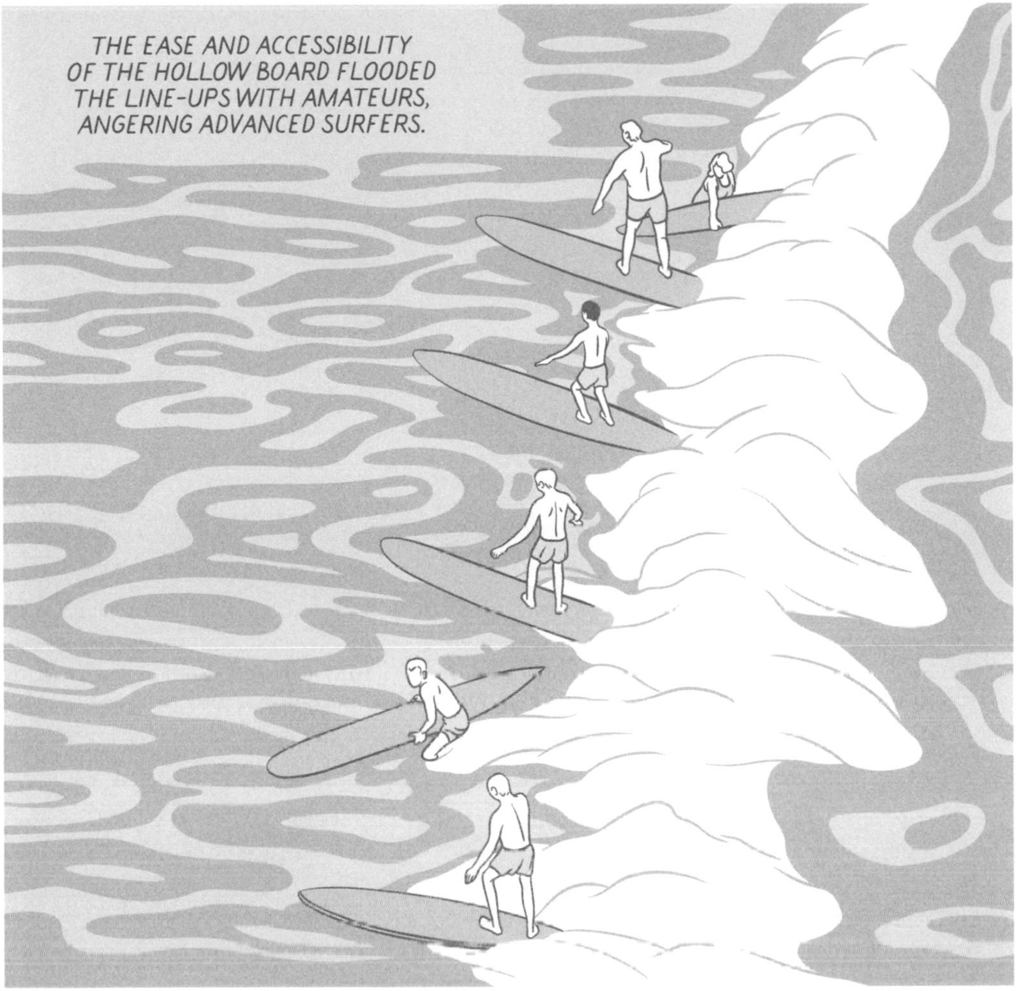
THE EASE AND ACCESSIBILITY OF THE HOLLOW BOARD FLOODED THE LINE-UPS WITH AMATEURS, ANGERING ADVANCED SURFERS.

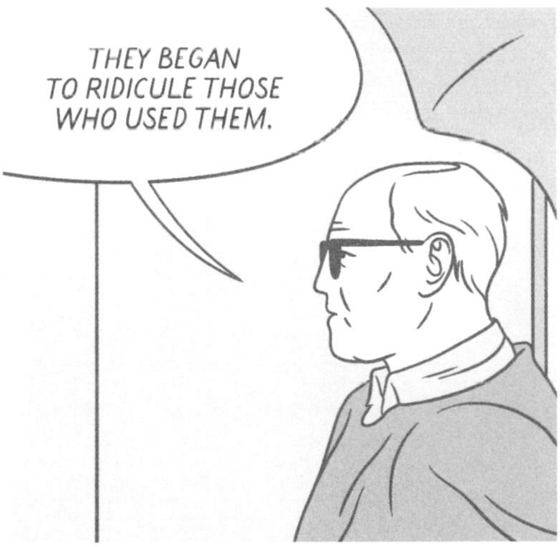
THEY BEGAN TO RIDICULE THOSE WHO USED THEM.

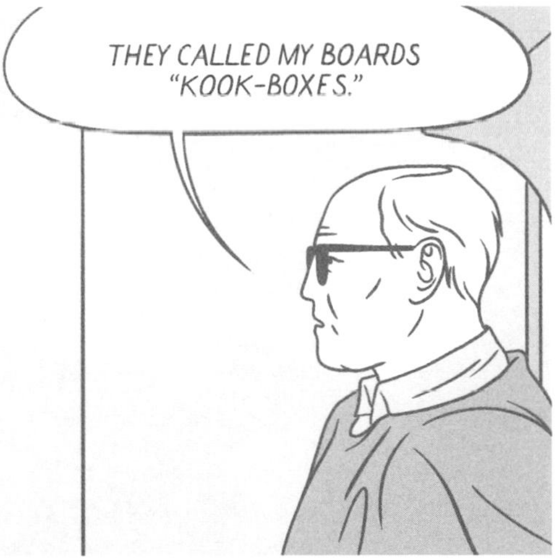
THEY CALLED MY BOARDS "KOOK-BOXES."

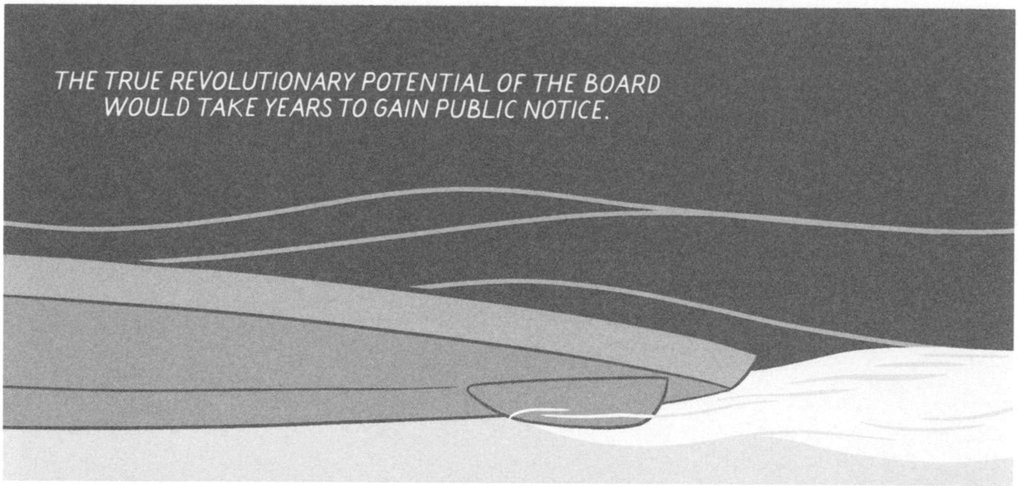
THE TRUE REVOLUTIONARY POTENTIAL OF THE BOARD WOULD TAKE YEARS TO GAIN PUBLIC NOTICE.

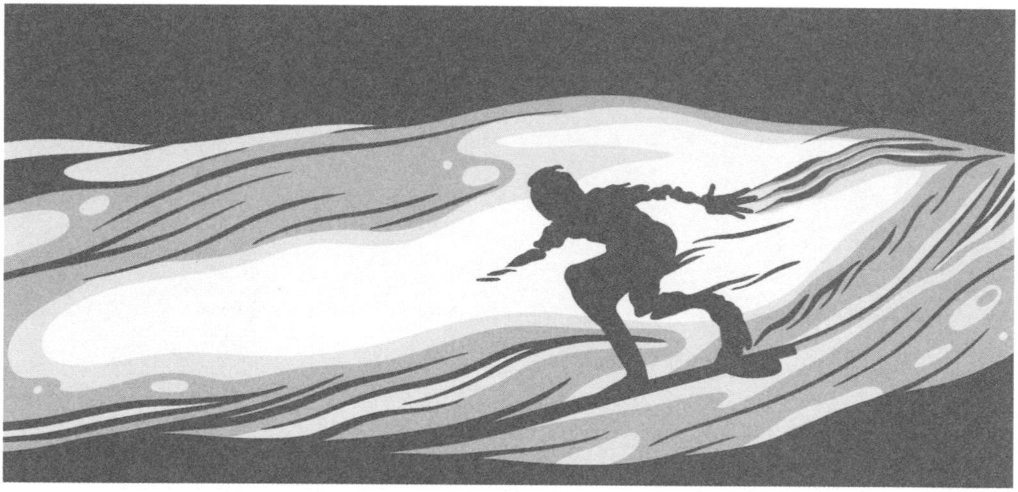

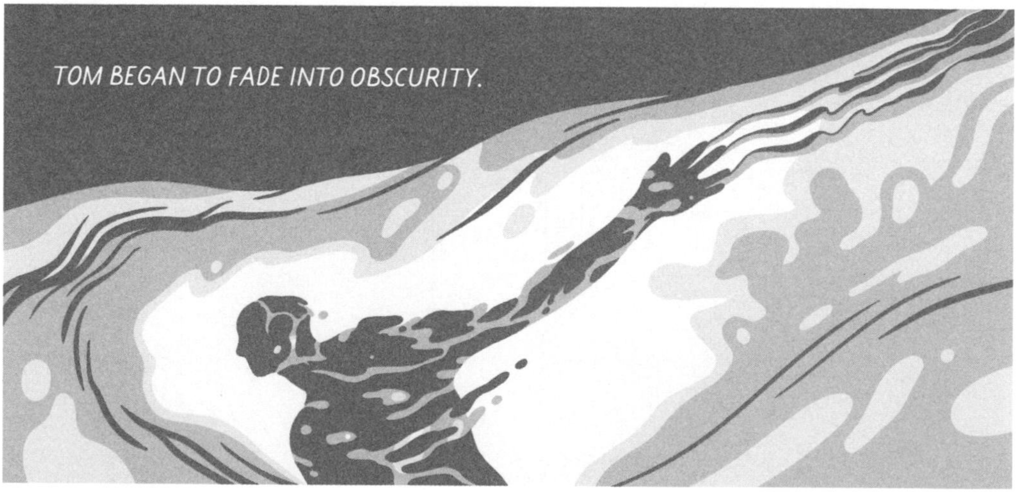
TOM BEGAN TO FADE INTO OBSCURITY.

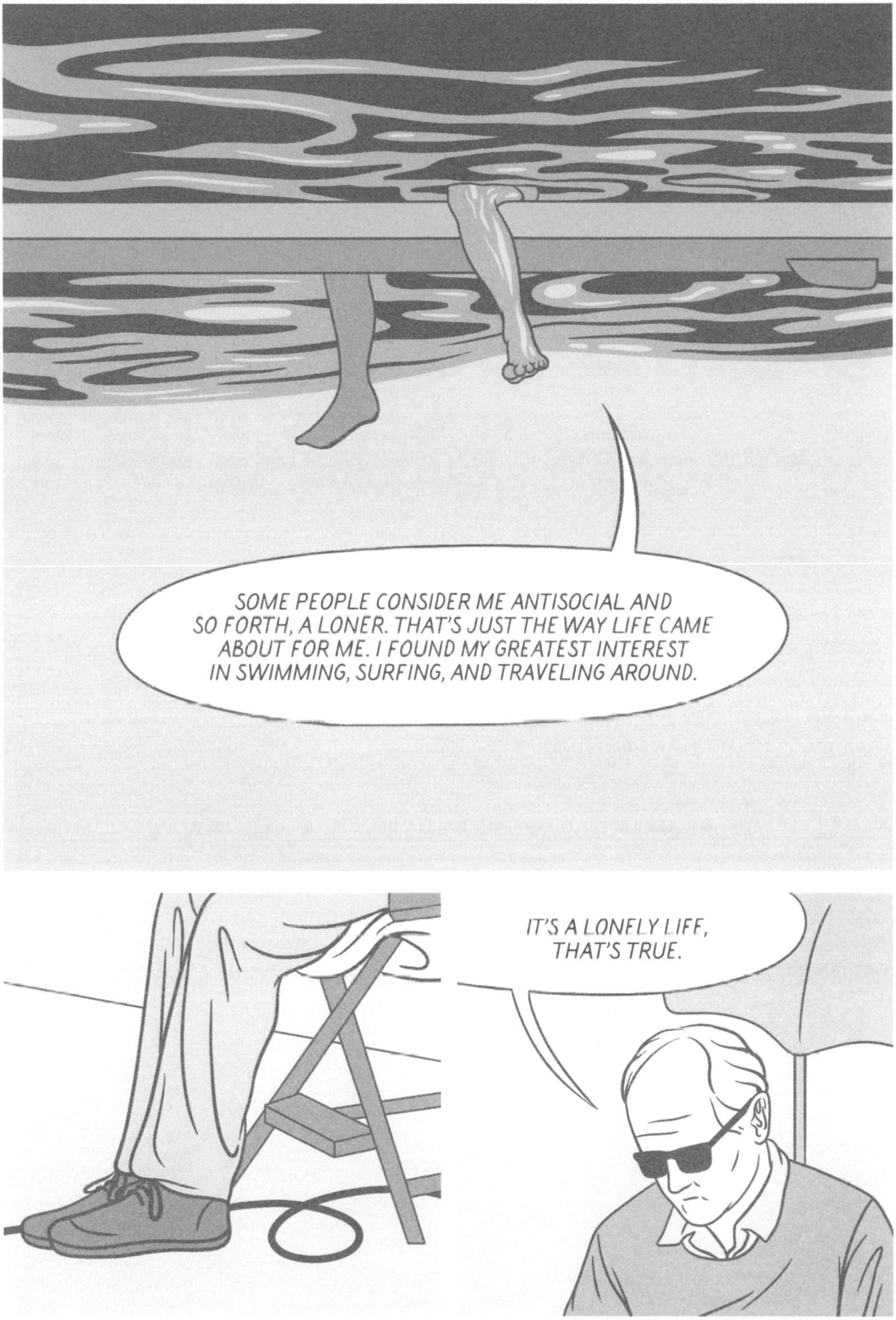
SOME PEOPLE CONSIDER ME ANTISOCIAL AND SO FORTH, A LONER. THAT'S JUST THE WAY LIFE CAME ABOUT FOR ME. I FOUND MY GREATEST INTEREST IN SWIMMING, SURFING, AND TRAVELING AROUND.
IT'S A LONELY LIFE, THAT'S TRUE.

DURING TOM'S LATER YEARS, WAIKIKI'S POPULATION EXPLODED.

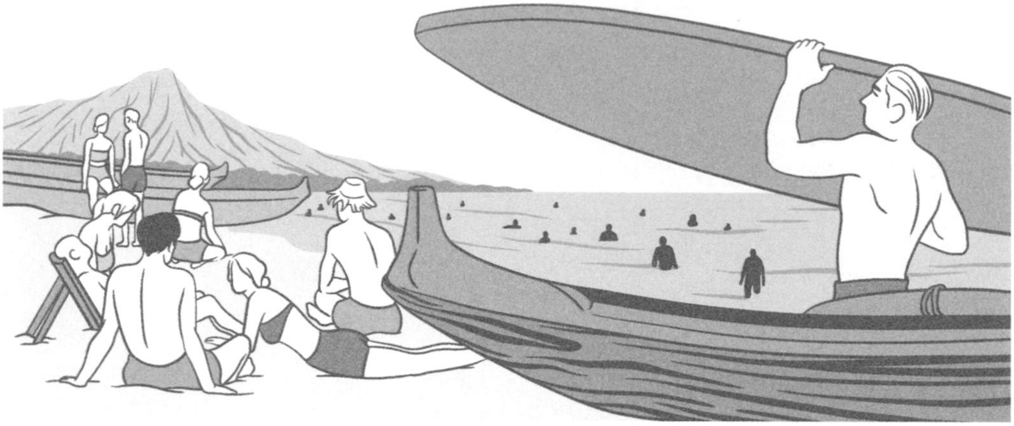

THE IRREVERENCE BROUGHT BY THE CROWDS WAS A JARRING COUNTER TO THE TRANQUIL SOLITUDE THAT THE ISLANDS HAD BROUGHT.

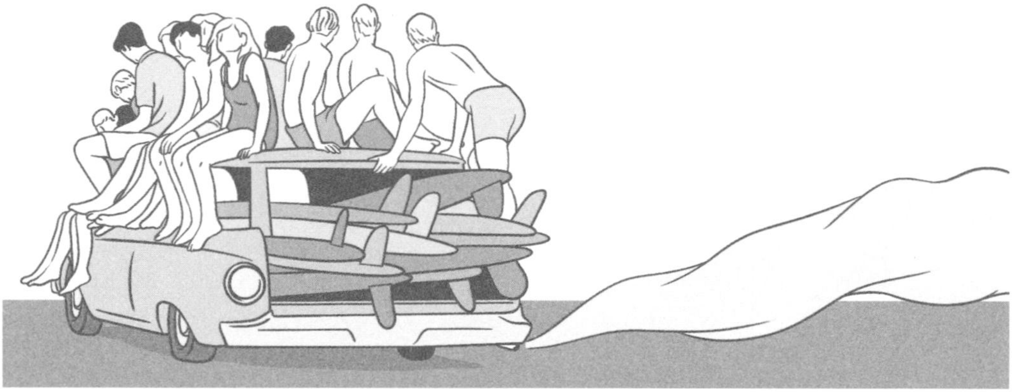

HE FELT LIKE HE COULD NO LONGER KEEP UP WITH THE OTHER SURFERS.

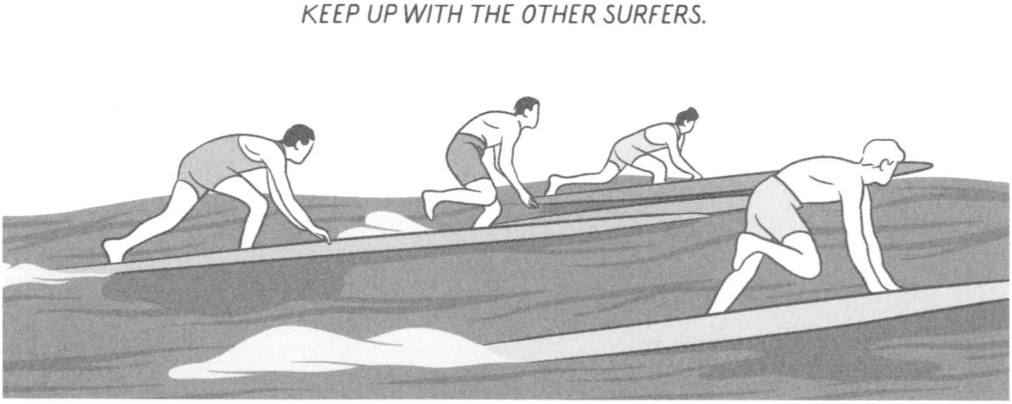

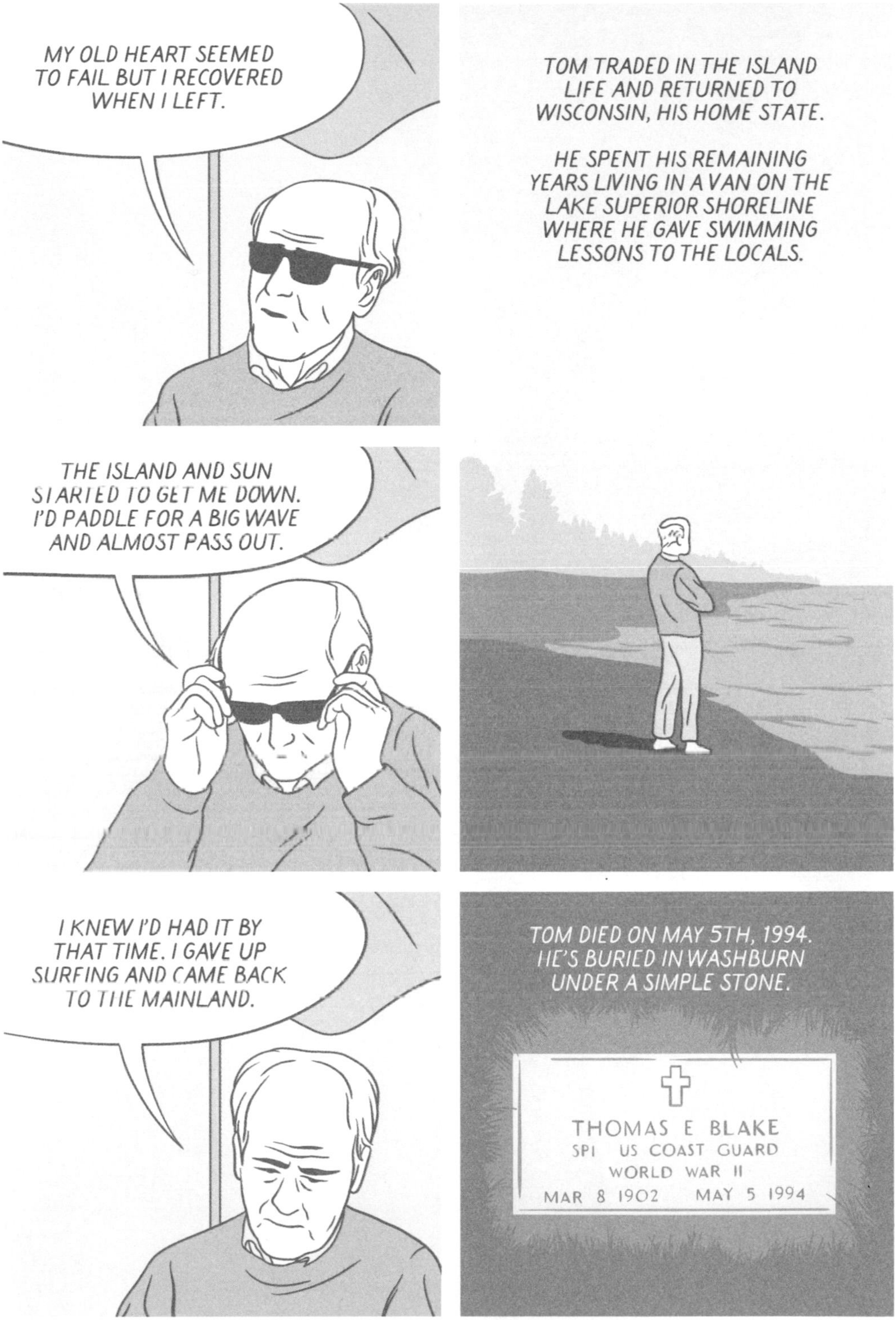
MY OLD HEART SEEMED TO FAIL BUT I RECOVERED WHEN I LEFT.
TOM TRADED IN THE ISLAND LIFE AND RETURNED TO WISCONSIN, HIS HOME STATE.
HE SPENT HIS REMAINING YEARS LIVING IN A VAN ON THE LAKE SUPERIOR SHORELINE WHERE HE GAVE SWIMMING LESSONS TO THE LOCALS.
THE ISLAND AND SUN STARTED TO GET ME DOWN. I'D PADDLE FOR A BIG WAVE AND ALMOST PASS OUT.
I KNEW I'D HAD IT BY THAT TIME. I GAVE UP SURFING AND CAME BACK TO THE MAINLAND.
TOM DIED ON MAY 5TH, 1994. HE'S BURIED IN WASHBURN UNDER A SIMPLE STONE.
THOMAS E BLAKE
SP1 US COAST GUARD
WORLD WAR II
MAR 8 1902 MAY 5 1994

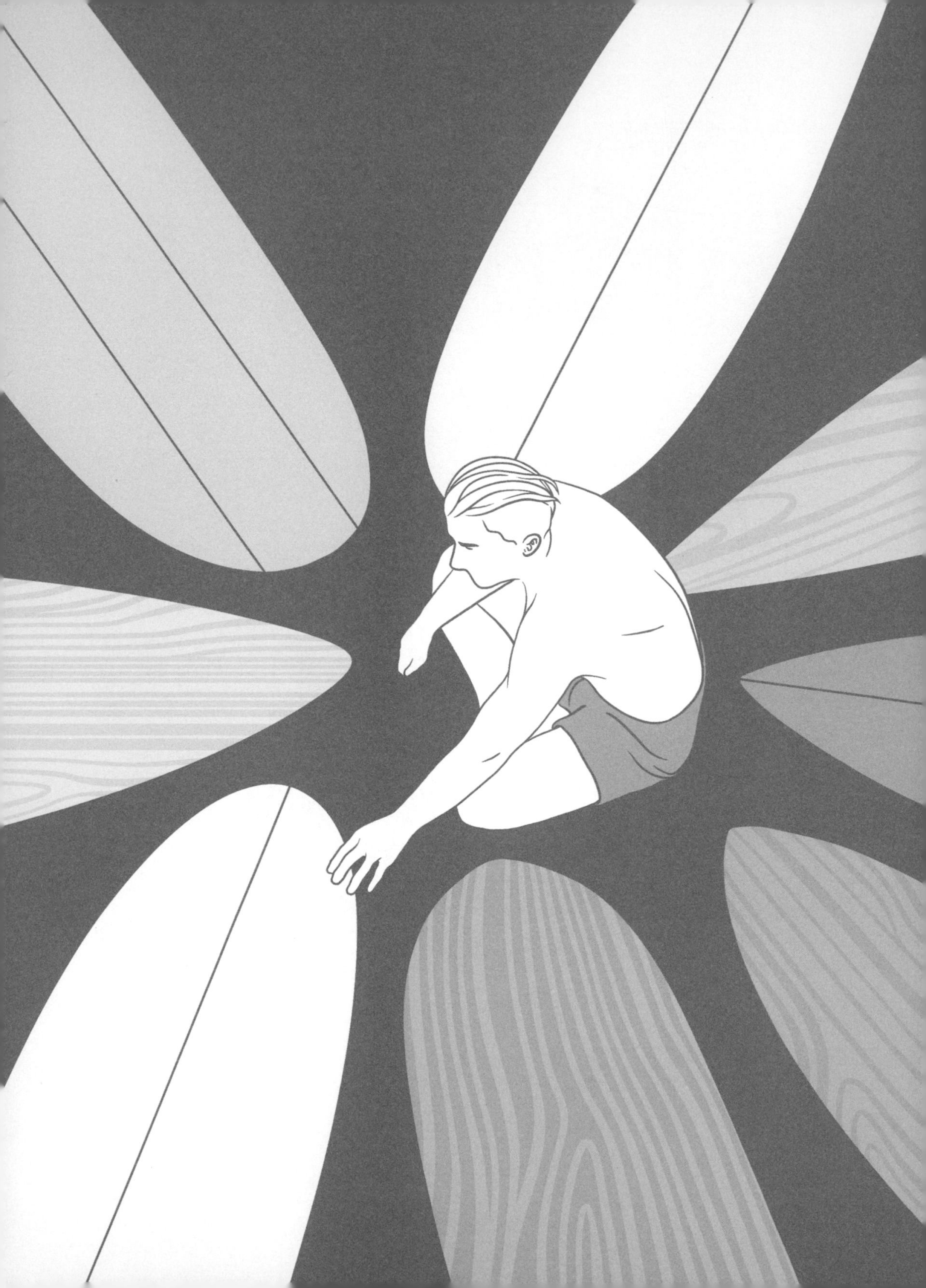

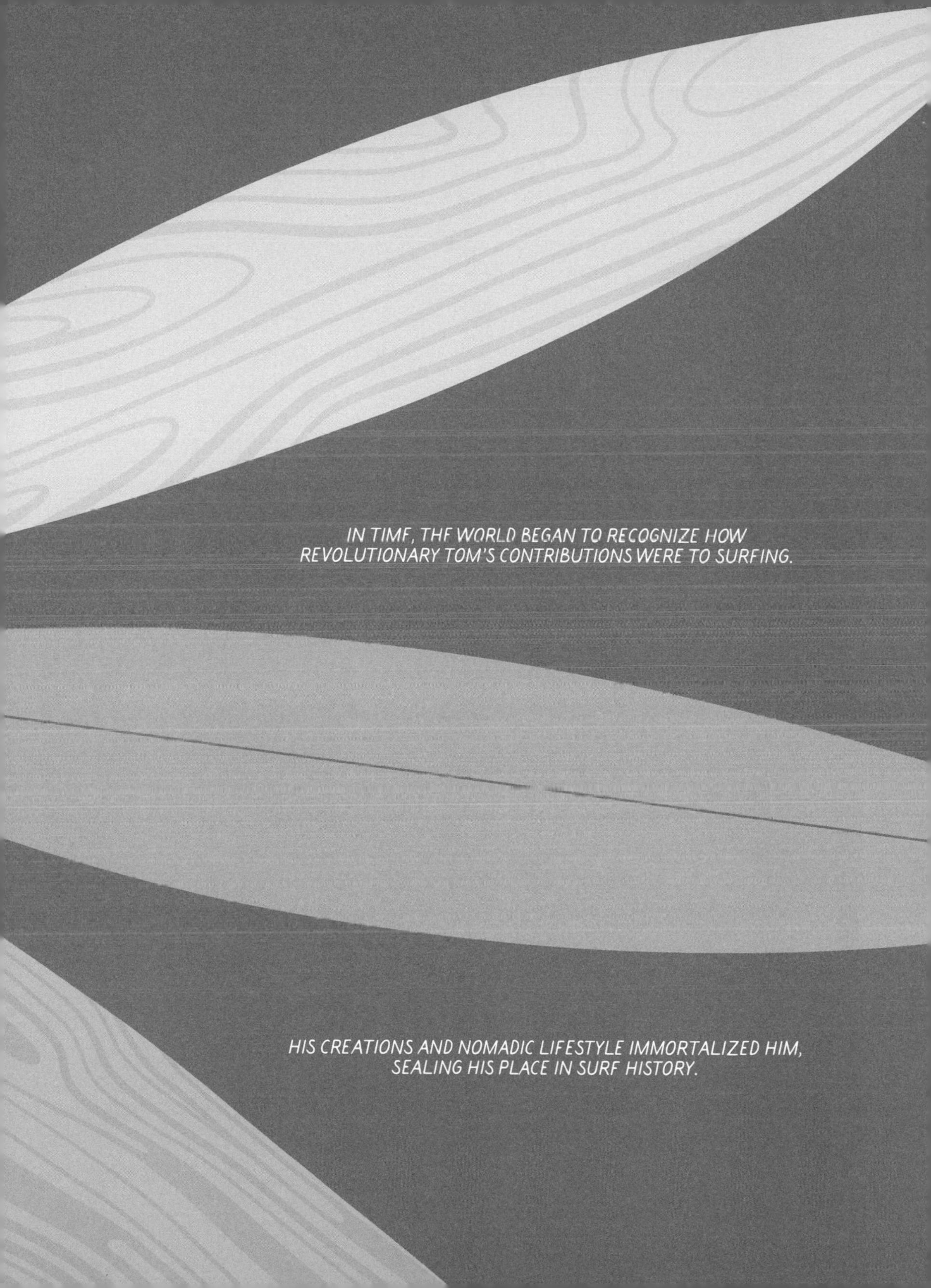
IN TIME, THE WORLD BEGAN TO RECOGNIZE HOW REVOLUTIONARY TOM'S CONTRIBUTIONS WERE TO SURFING.
HIS CREATIONS AND NOMADIC LIFESTYLE IMMORTALIZED HIM, SEALING HIS PLACE IN SURF HISTORY.

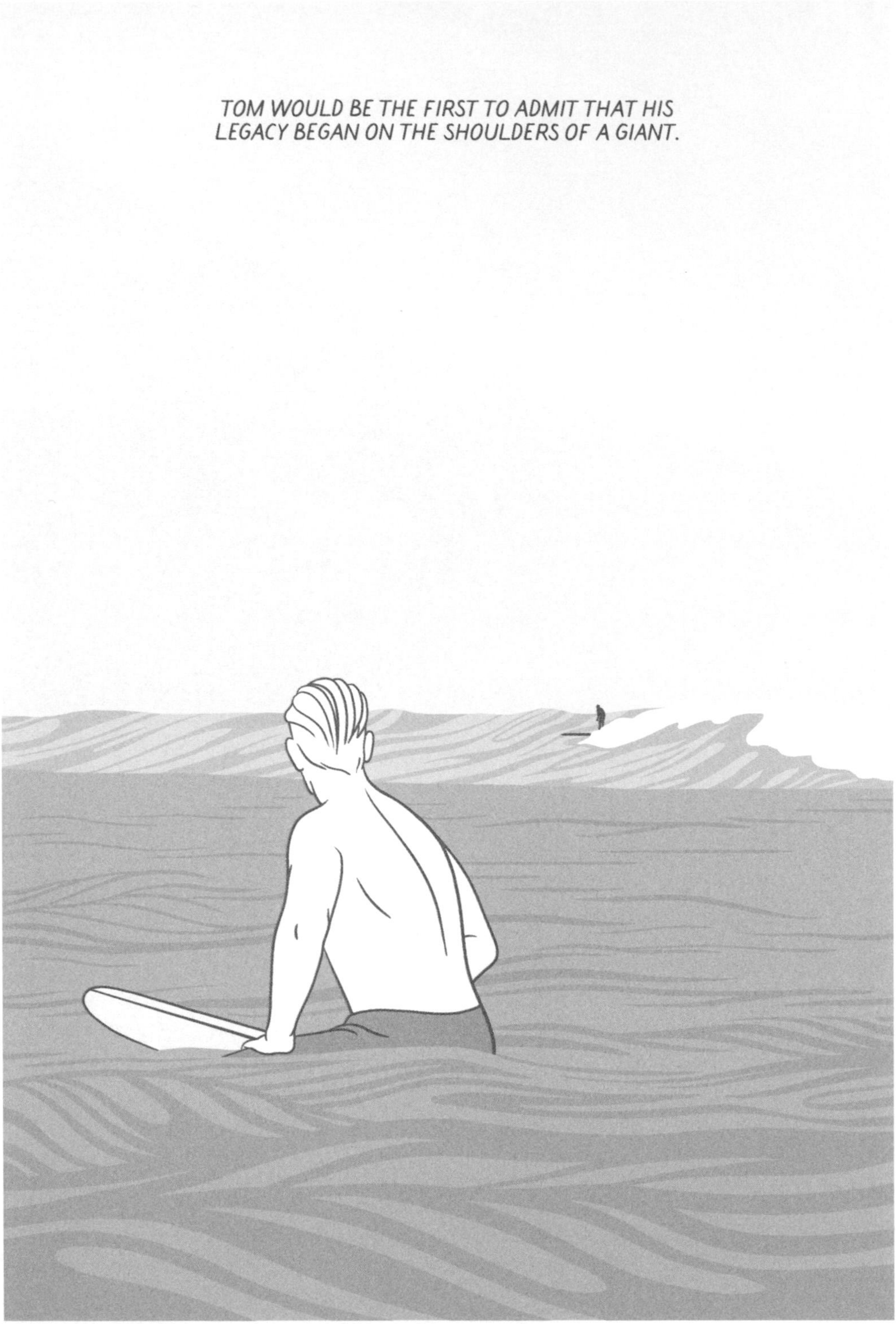
TOM WOULD BE THE FIRST TO ADMIT THAT HIS LEGACY BEGAN ON THE SHOULDERS OF A GIANT.

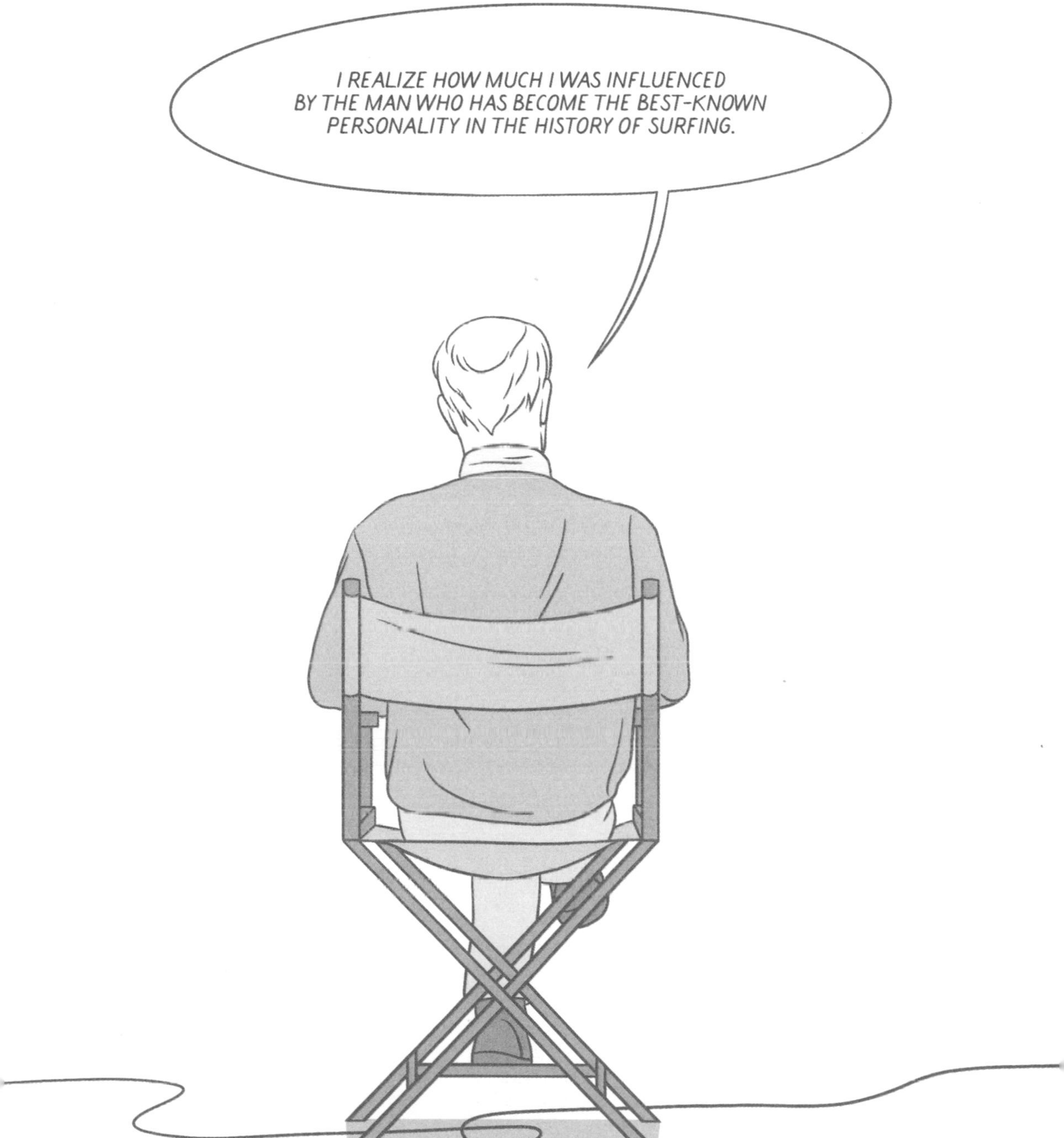
I REALIZE HOW MUCH I WAS INFLUENCED BY THE MAN WHO HAS BECOME THE BEST-KNOWN PERSONALITY IN THE HISTORY OF SURFING.

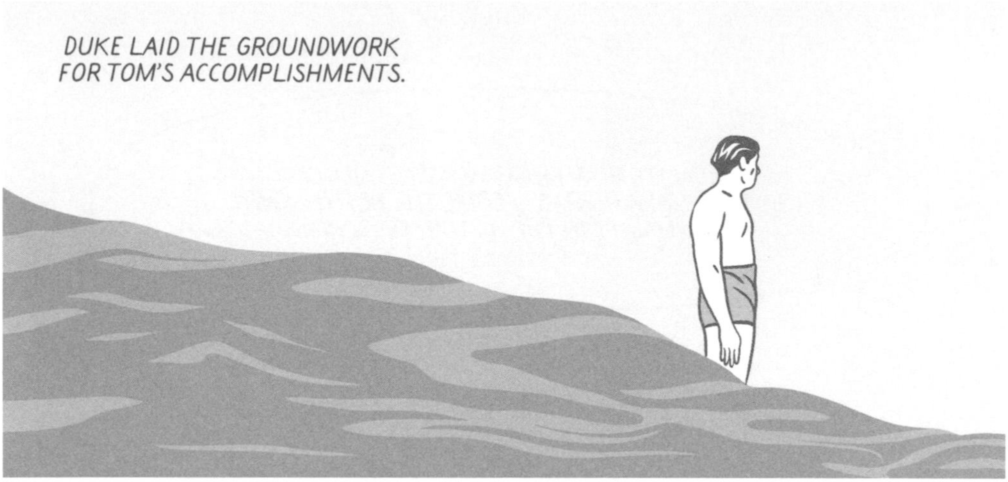
DUKE LAID THE GROUNDWORK FOR TOM'S ACCOMPLISHMENTS.

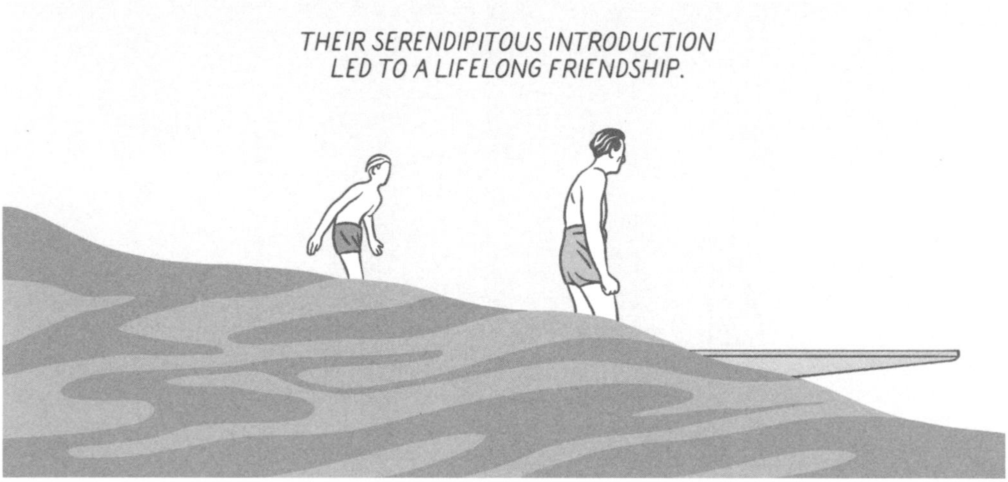
THEIR SERENDIPITOUS INTRODUCTION LED TO A LIFELONG FRIENDSHIP.

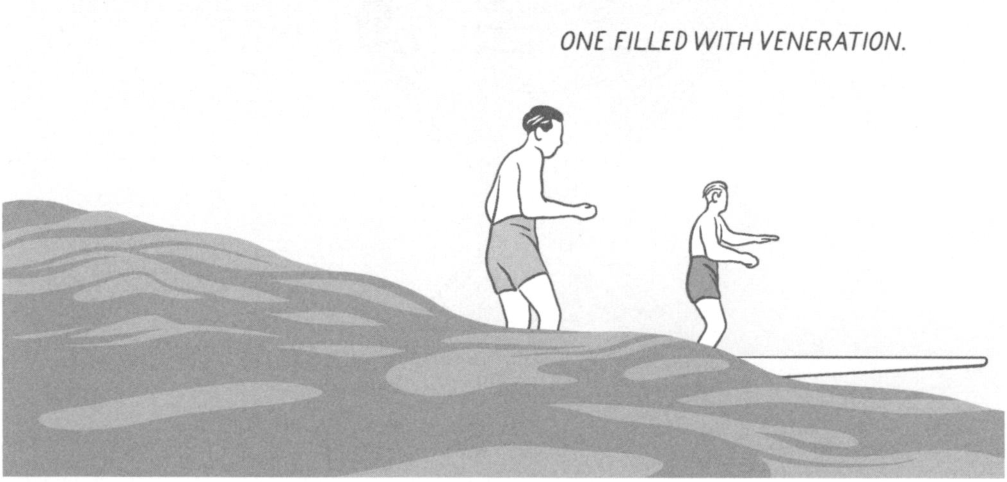
ONE FILLED WITH VENERATION.

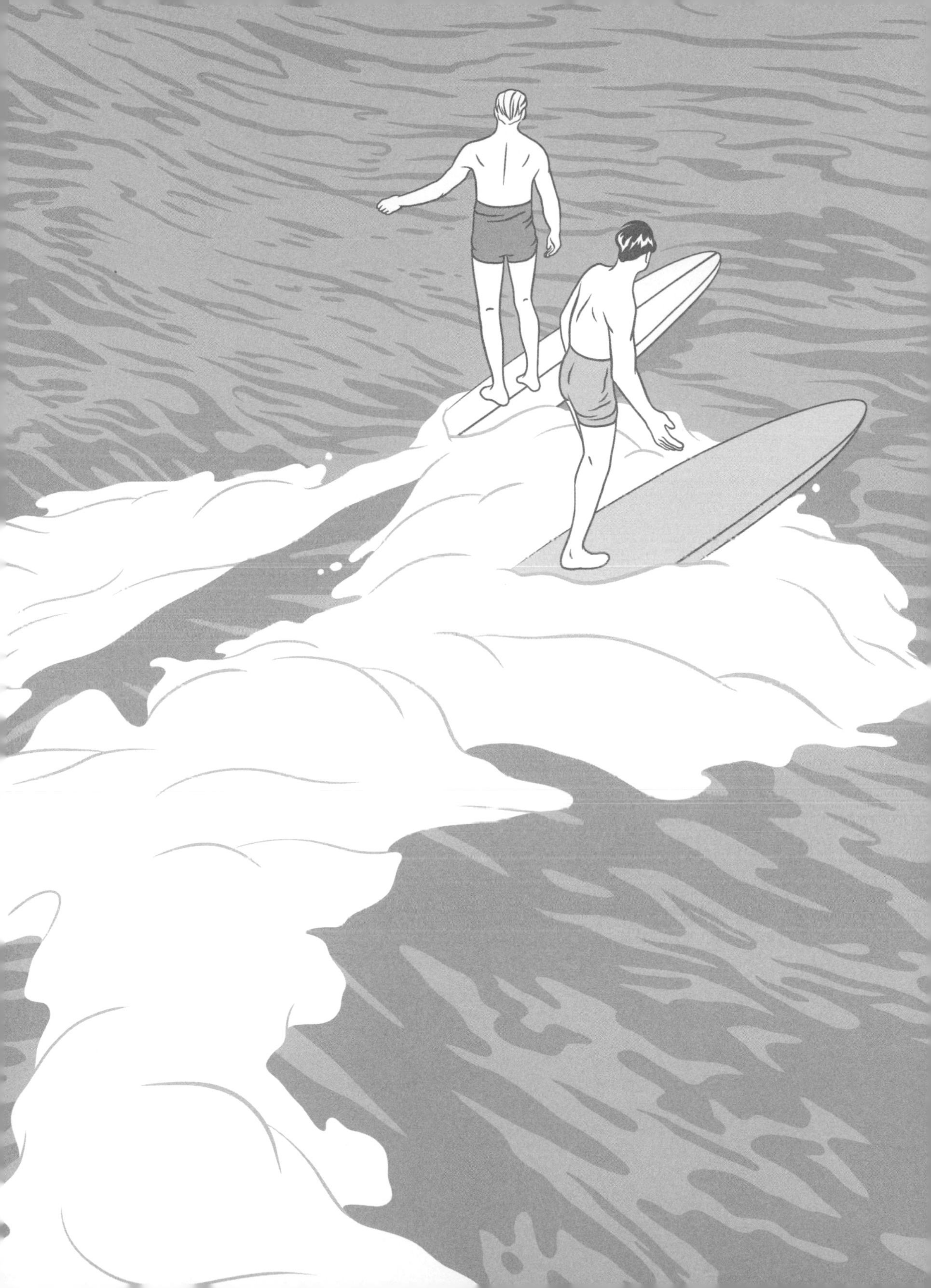

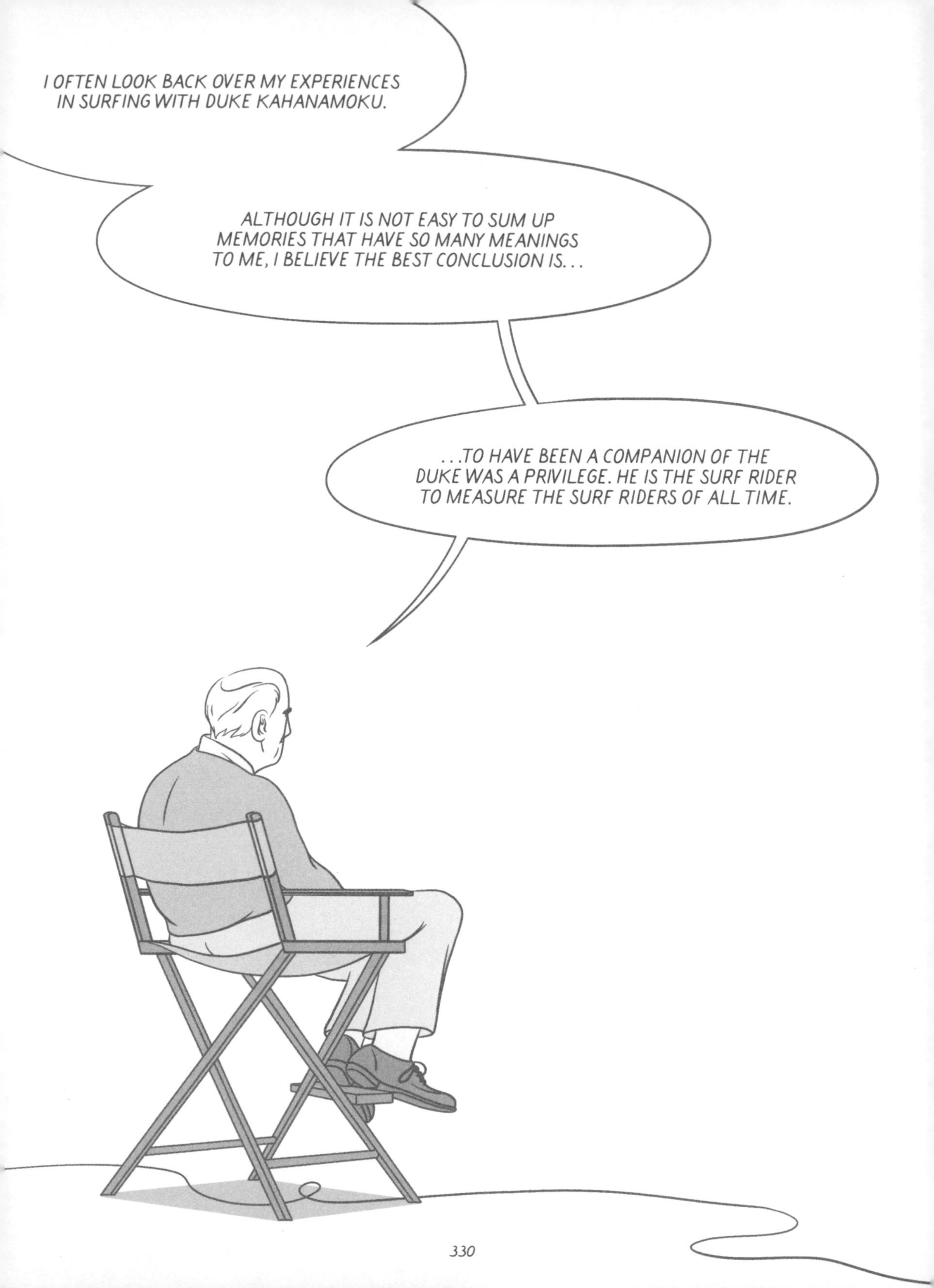
I OFTEN LOOK BACK OVER MY EXPERIENCES IN SURFING WITH DUKE KAHANAMOKU.
ALTHOUGH IT IS NOT EASY TO SUM UP MEMORIES THAT HAVE SO MANY MEANINGS TO ME, I BELIEVE THE BEST CONCLUSION IS. . .
. . .TO HAVE BEEN A COMPANION OF THE DUKE WAS A PRIVILEGE. HE IS THE SURF RIDER TO MEASURE THE SURF RIDERS OF ALL TIME.

TO THIS DAY, DUKE KAHANAMOKU IS ONE
OF THE MOST REVERED FIGURES IN SURFING.

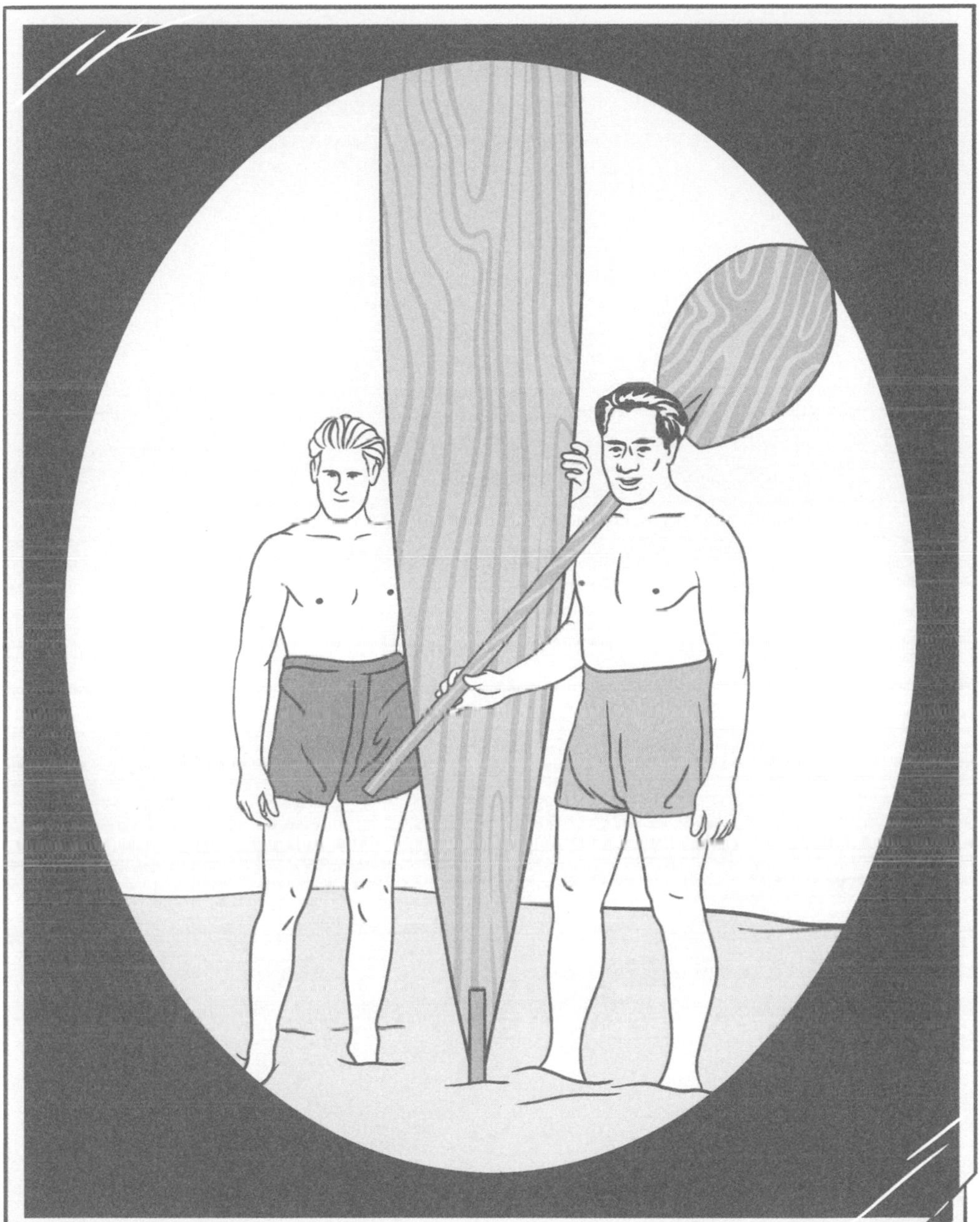

WHILE TOM BLAKE IS EQUALLY RESPECTED,
HE REMAINS AN ENIGMA, THOUGHT TO HAVE
BEEN A DAMAGED, ISOLATED INDIVIDUAL.

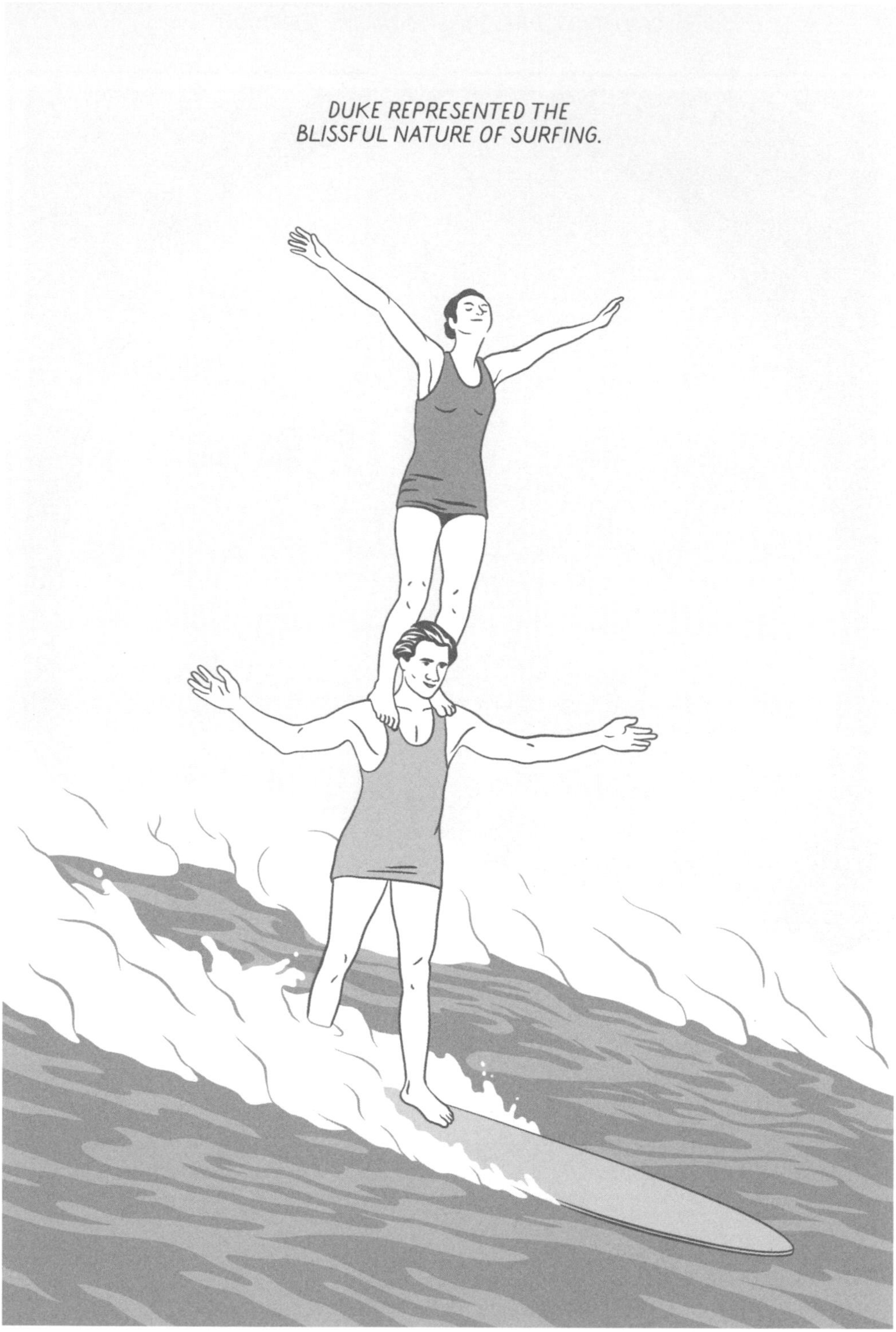
DUKE REPRESENTED THE
BLISSFUL NATURE OF SURFING.

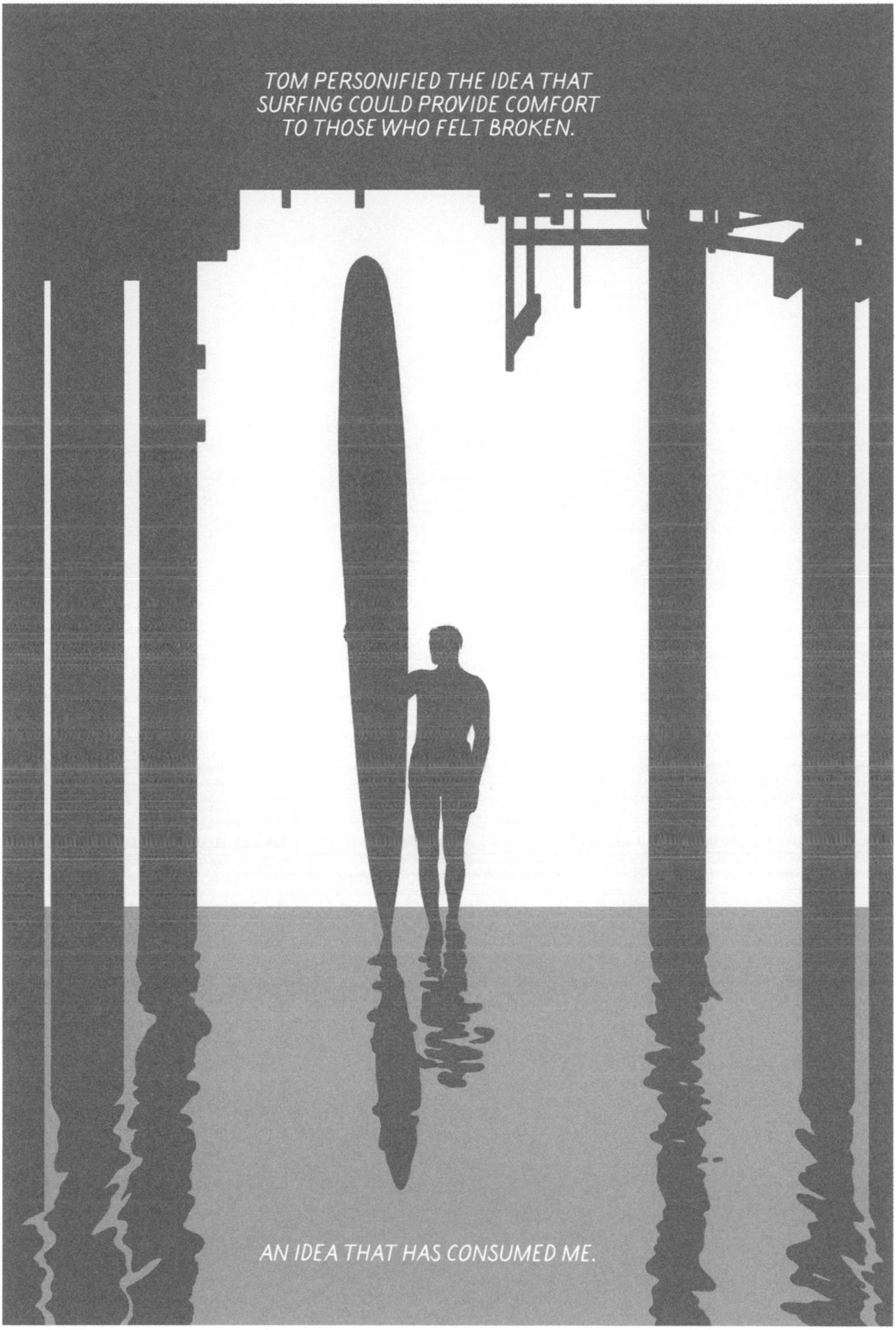
TOM PERSONIFIED THE IDEA THAT SURFING COULD PROVIDE COMFORT TO THOSE WHO FELT BROKEN.
AN IDEA THAT HAS CONSUMED ME.

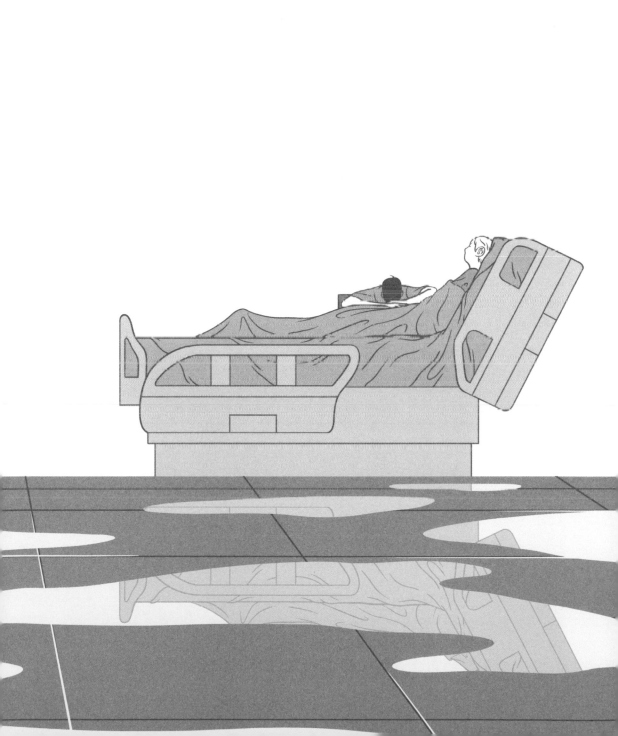

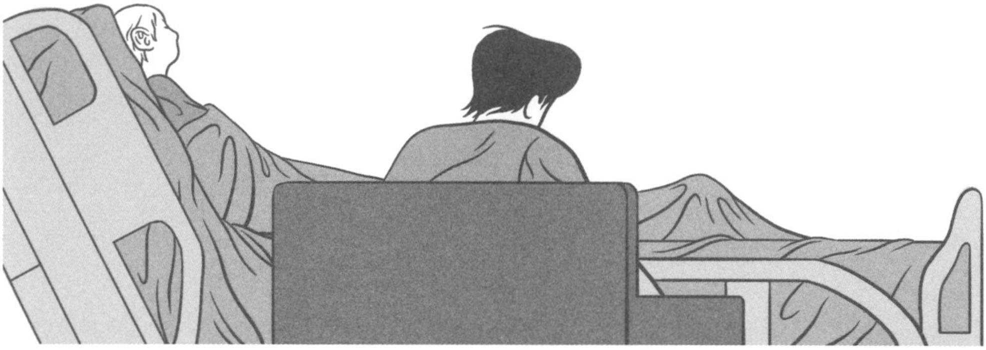

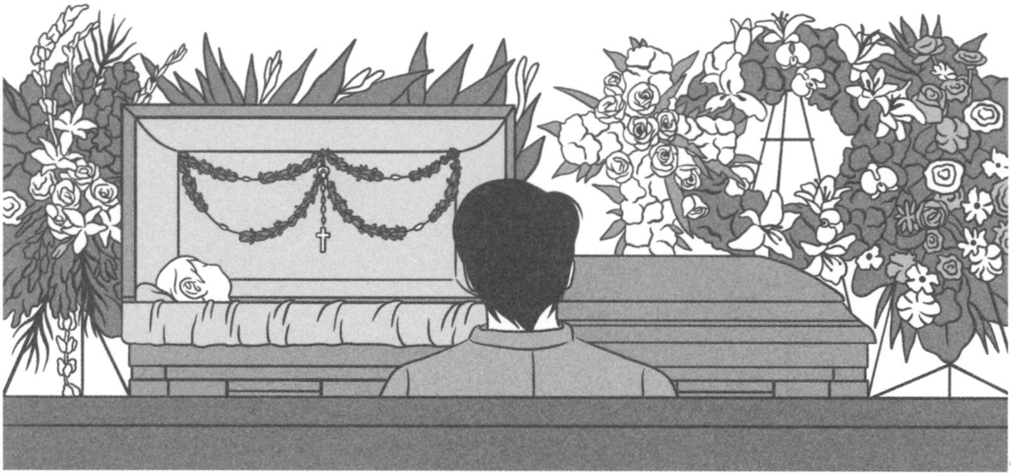

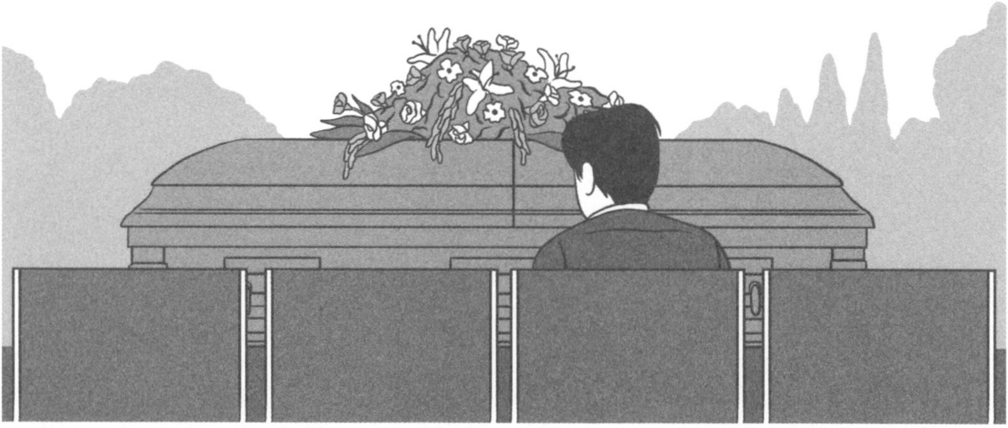

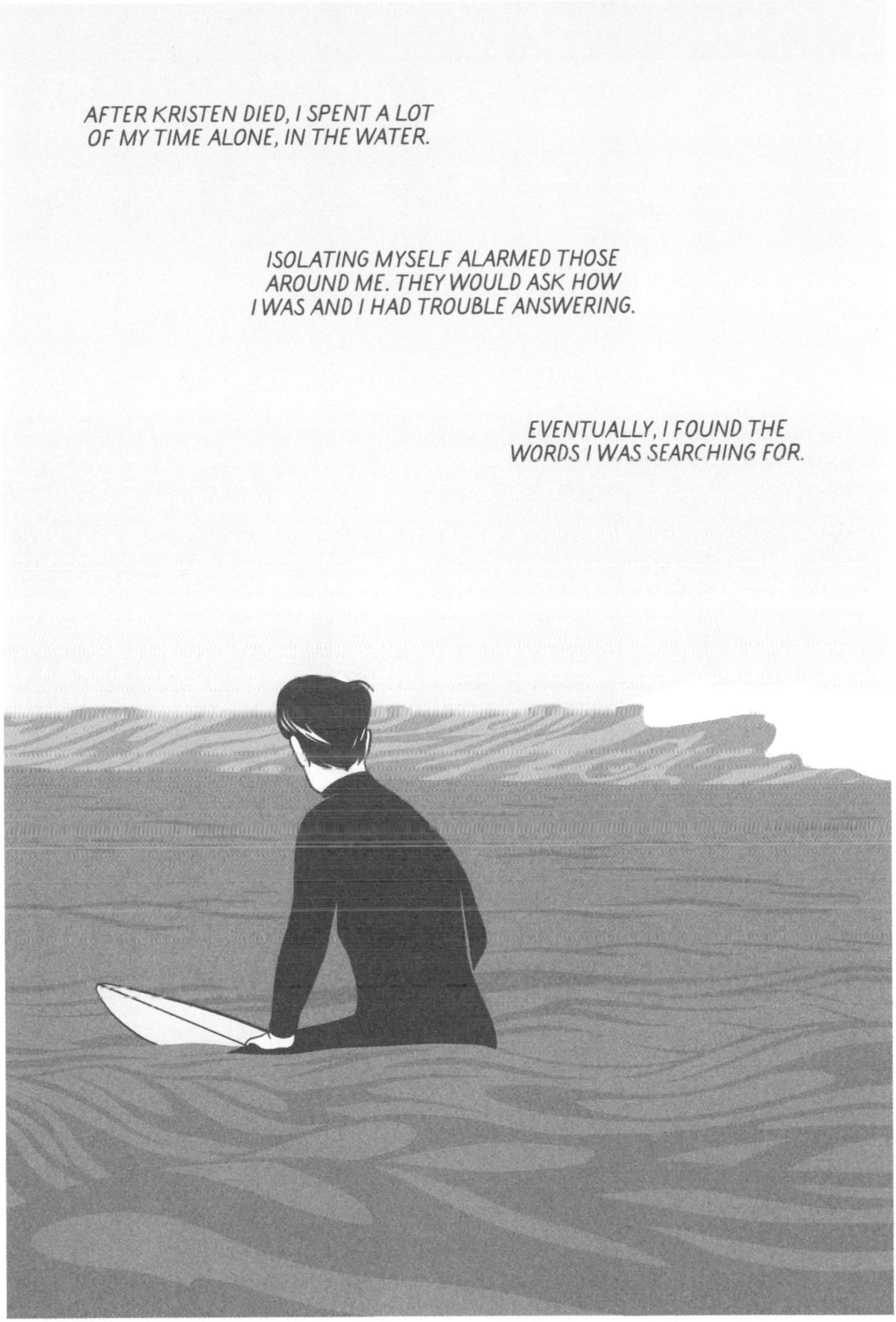
AFTER KRISTEN DIED, I SPENT A LOT OF MY TIME ALONE, IN THE WATER.
ISOLATING MYSELF ALARMED THOSE AROUND ME. THEY WOULD ASK HOW I WAS AND I HAD TROUBLE ANSWERING.
EVENTUALLY, I FOUND THE WORDS I WAS SEARCHING FOR.

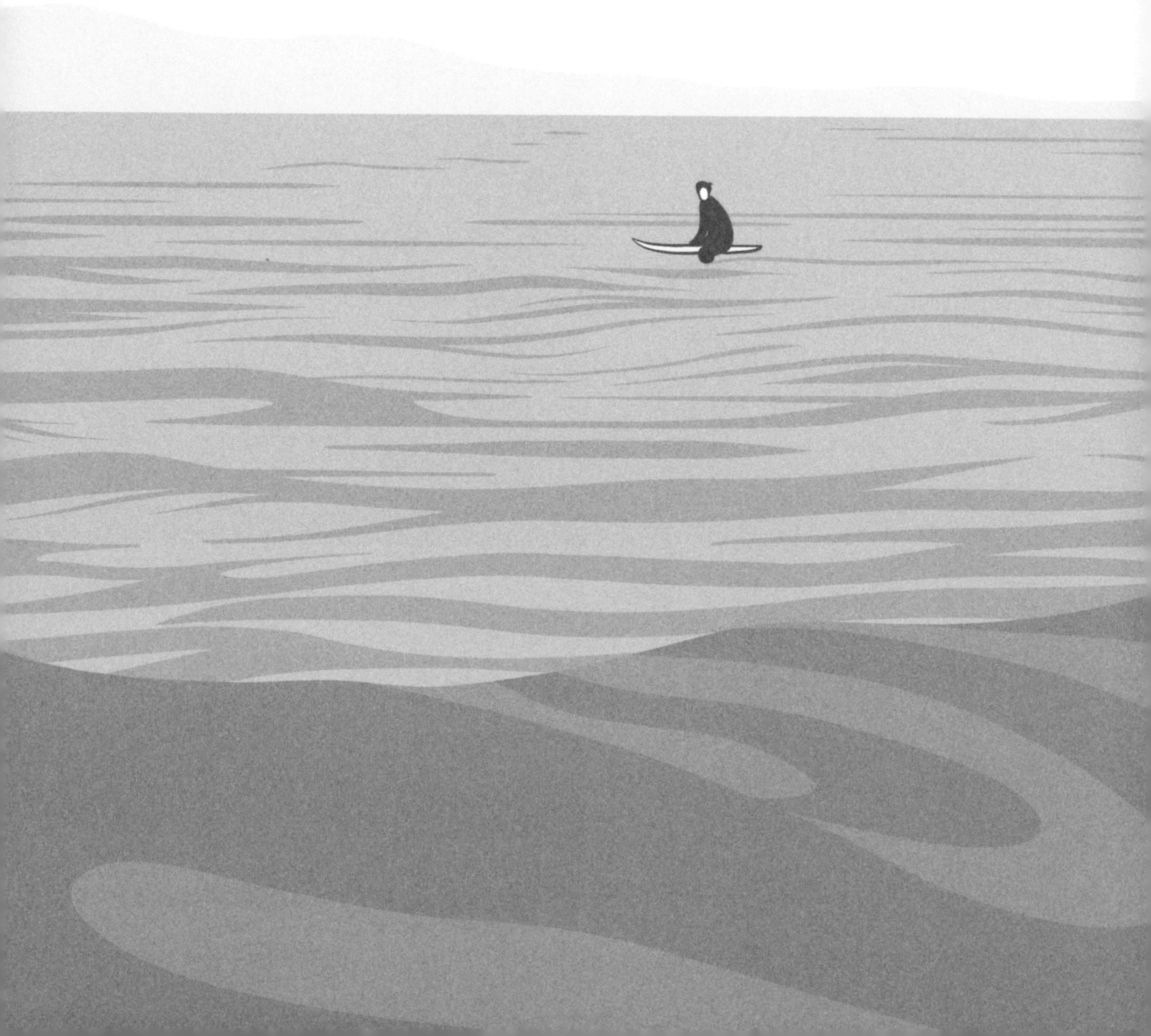

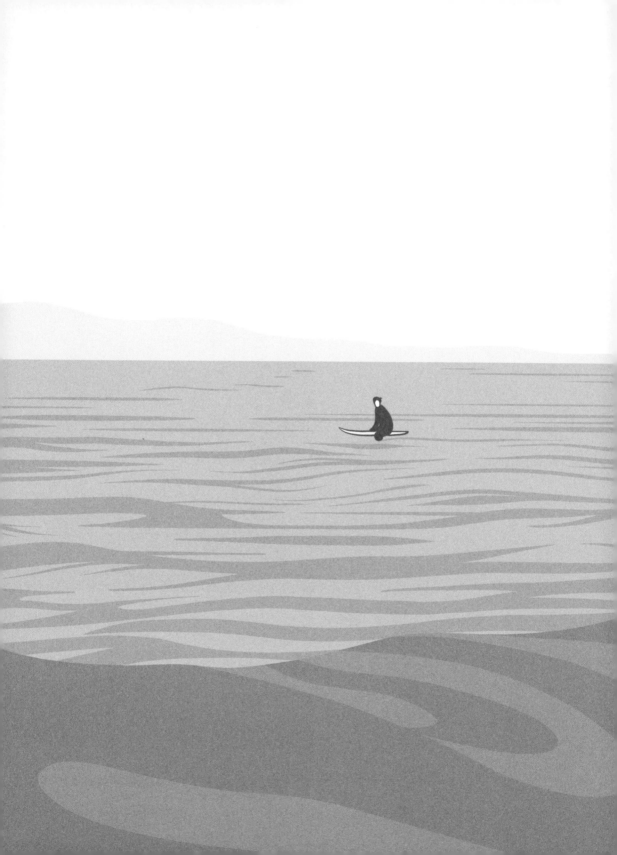

"IT COMES IN WAVES."

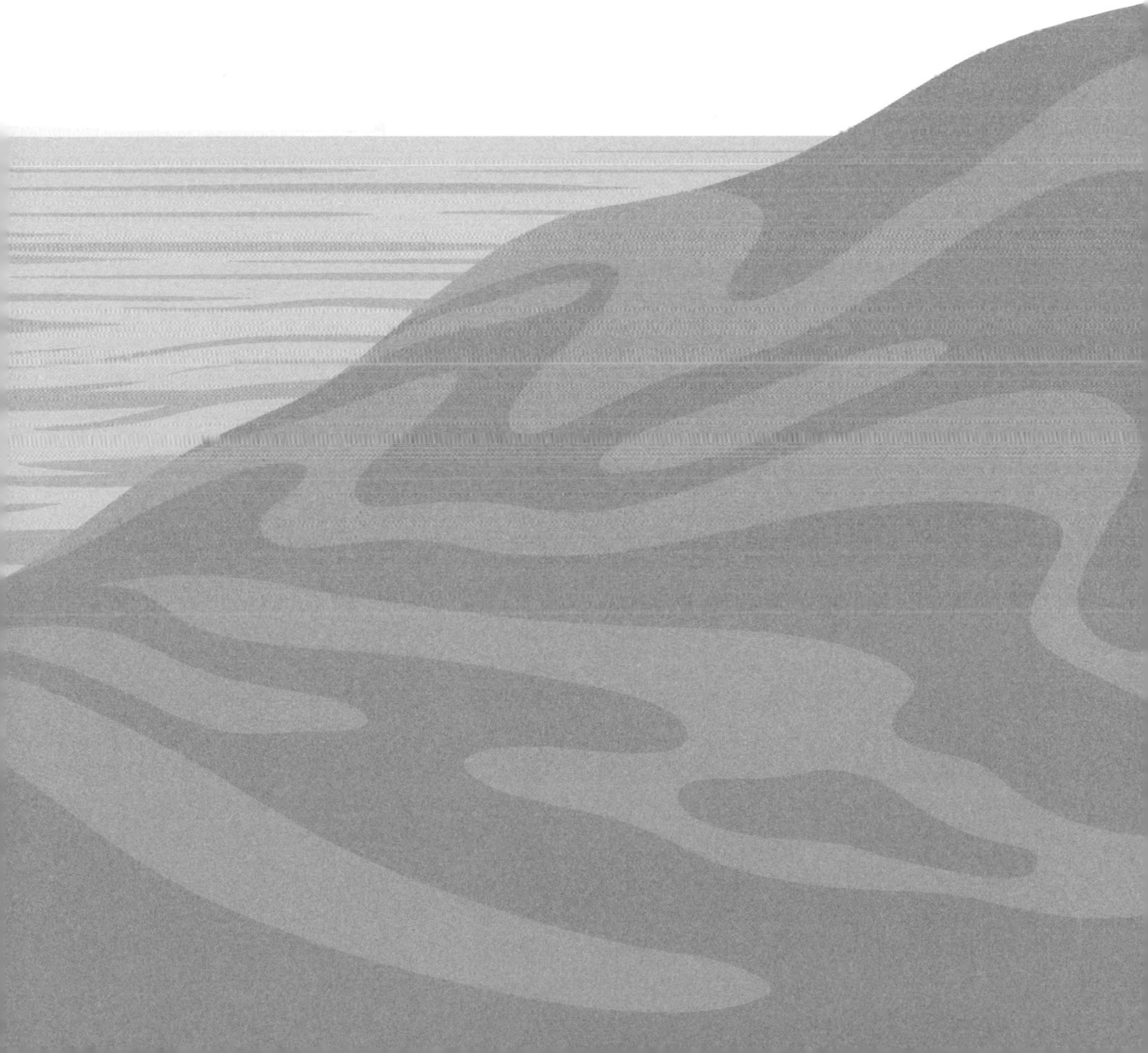

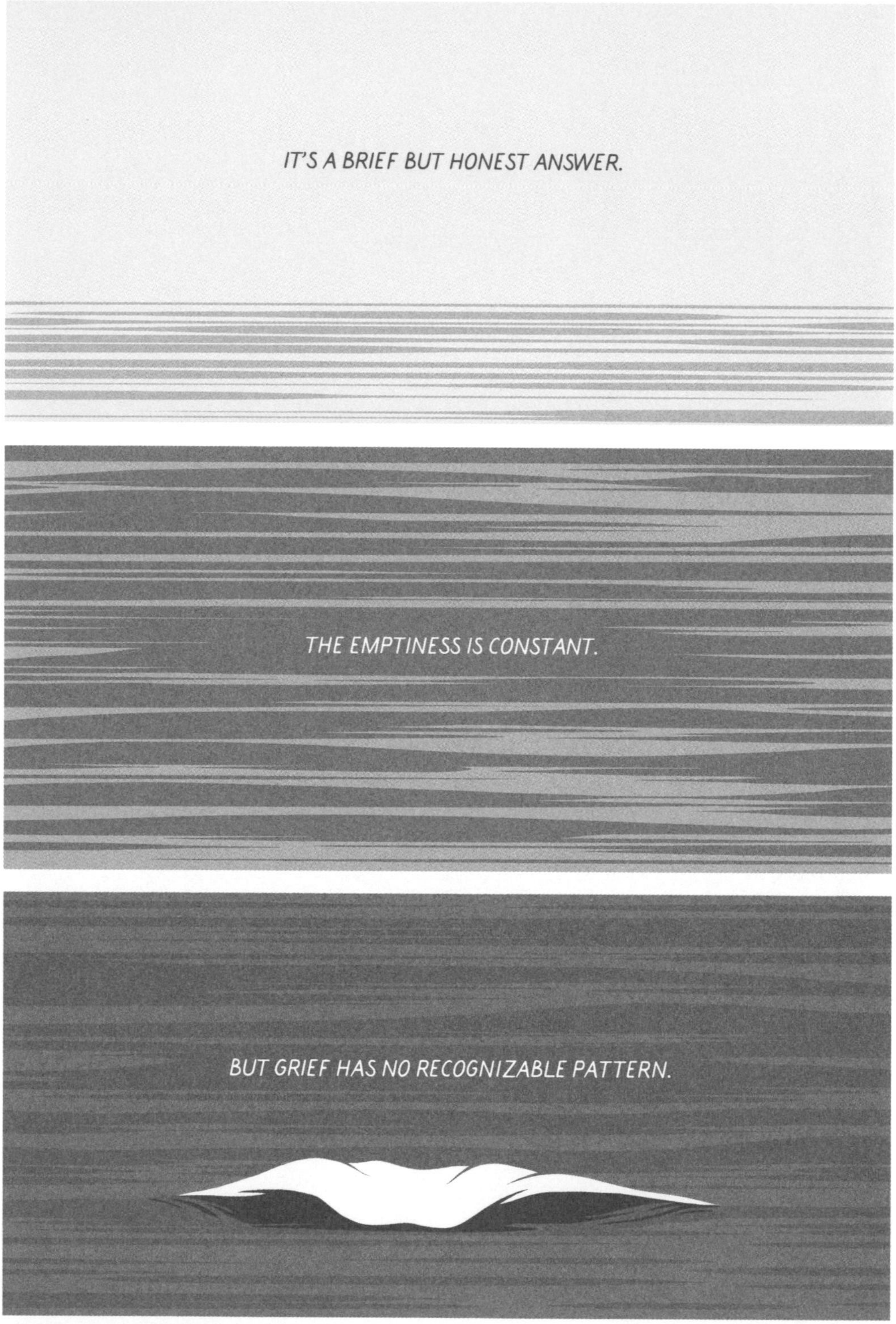
IT'S A BRIEF BUT HONEST ANSWER.
THE EMPTINESS IS CONSTANT.
BUT GRIEF HAS NO RECOGNIZABLE PATTERN.

IT JUST COMES AND GOES.

IT IS UNPREDICTABLE; BREWED BY A STORM IN THE DISTANCE, DEEP IN THE OCEAN, FAR FROM VIEW, CHURNING WATER ABOVE AND BELOW.

IT SURGES THROUGH CHANNELS, FORMING AND RUSHING WHILE CARRYING ITS MAGNITUDE FULL FORCE AS IT REACHES A BREAKING POINT.

IT GROWS UNTIL IT CANNOT SUSTAIN ITS SHAPE.
IT BECOMES UNSTABLE AND CRASHES.

EVENTUALLY, IT SETTLES INTO A CALM UNIFORM SURFACE.

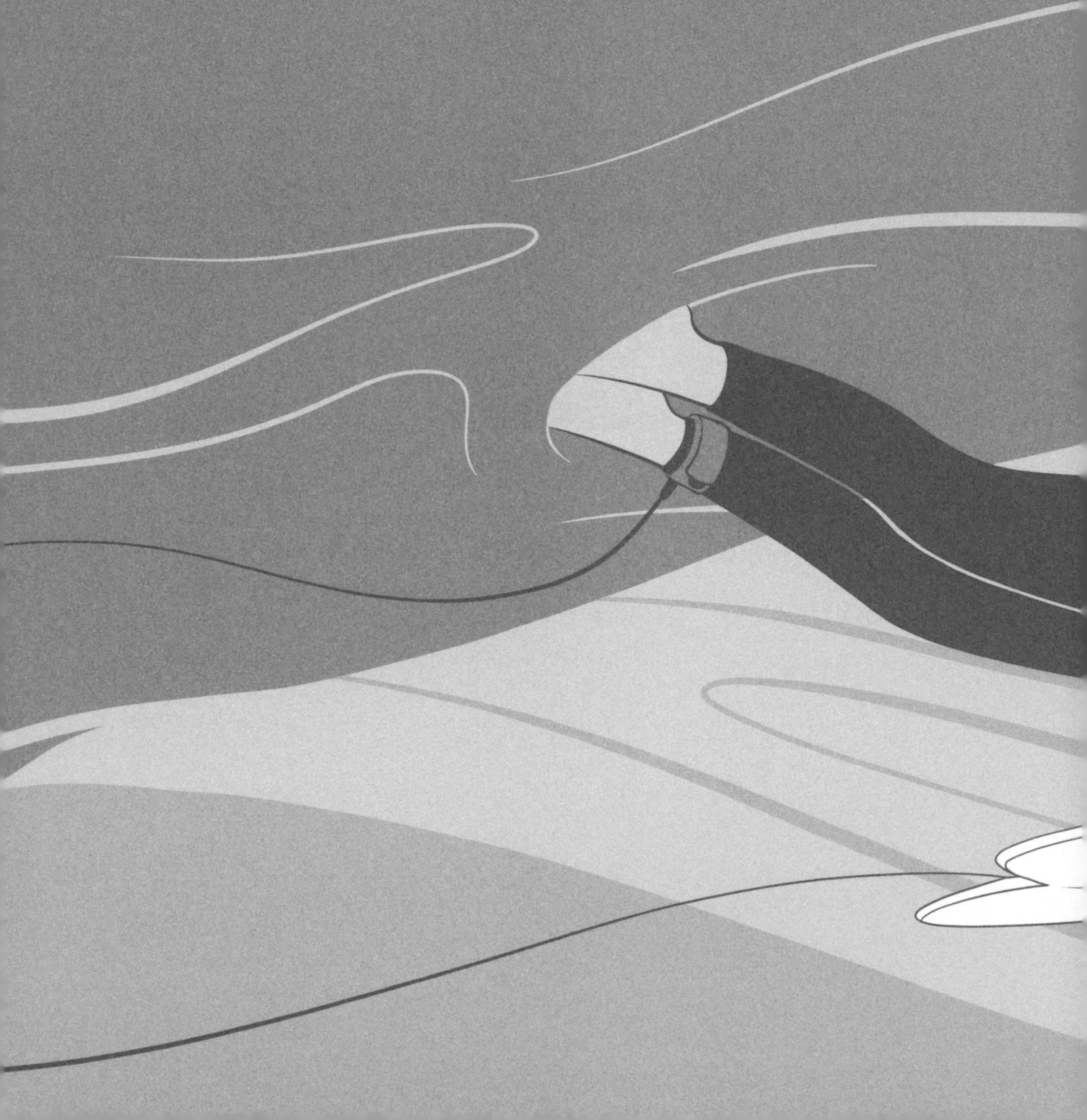

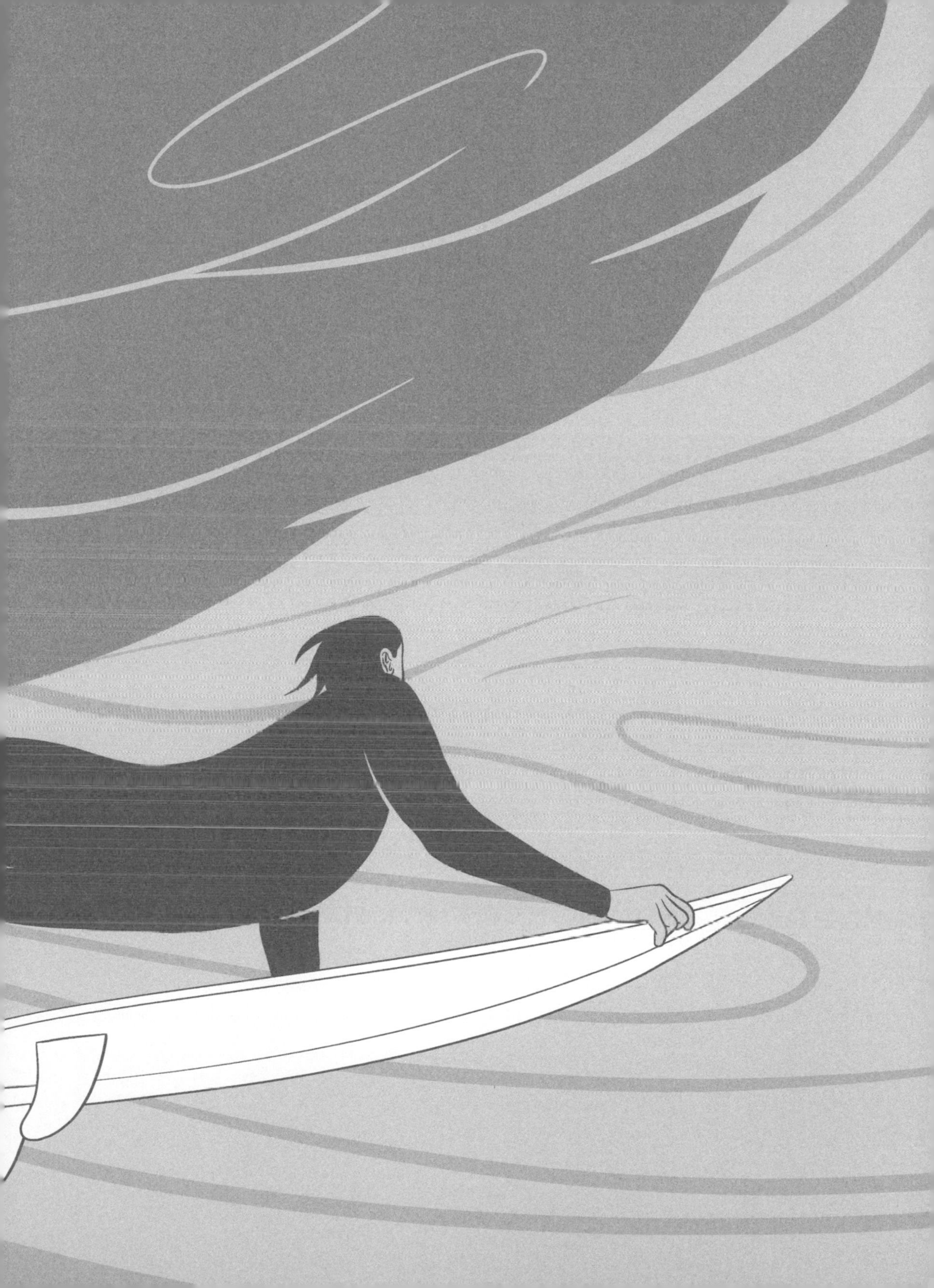

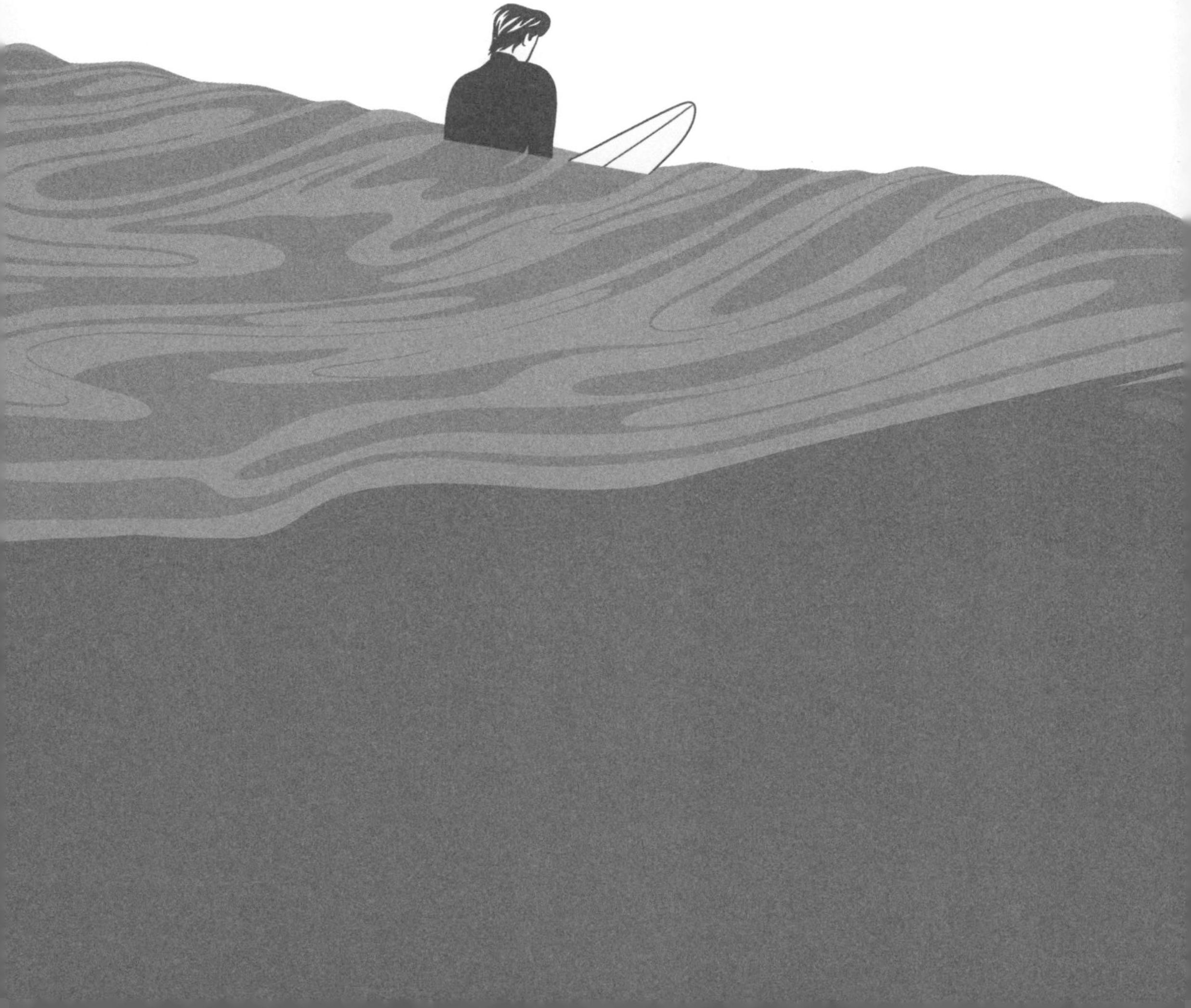

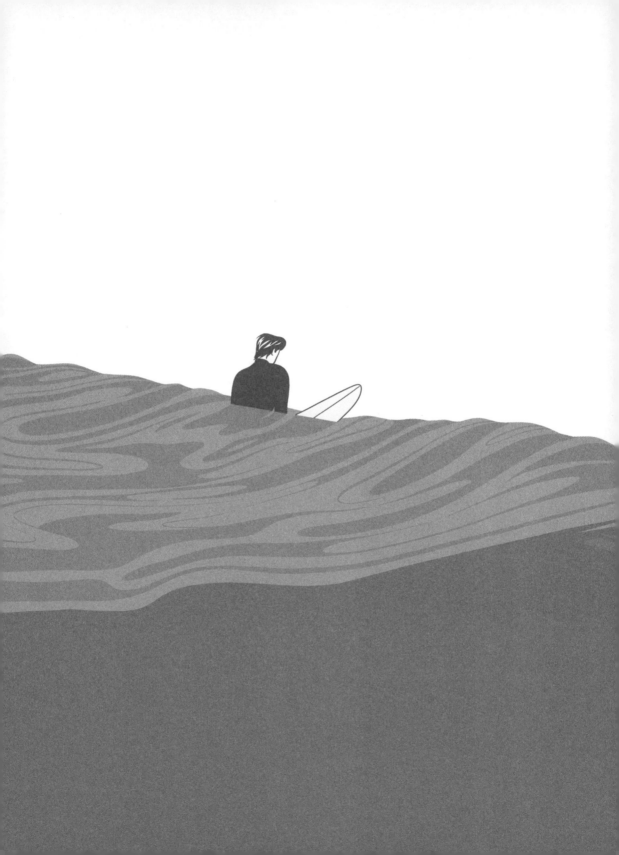

AND THEN THE WATER RETREATS, ONLY TO BEGIN AGAIN.

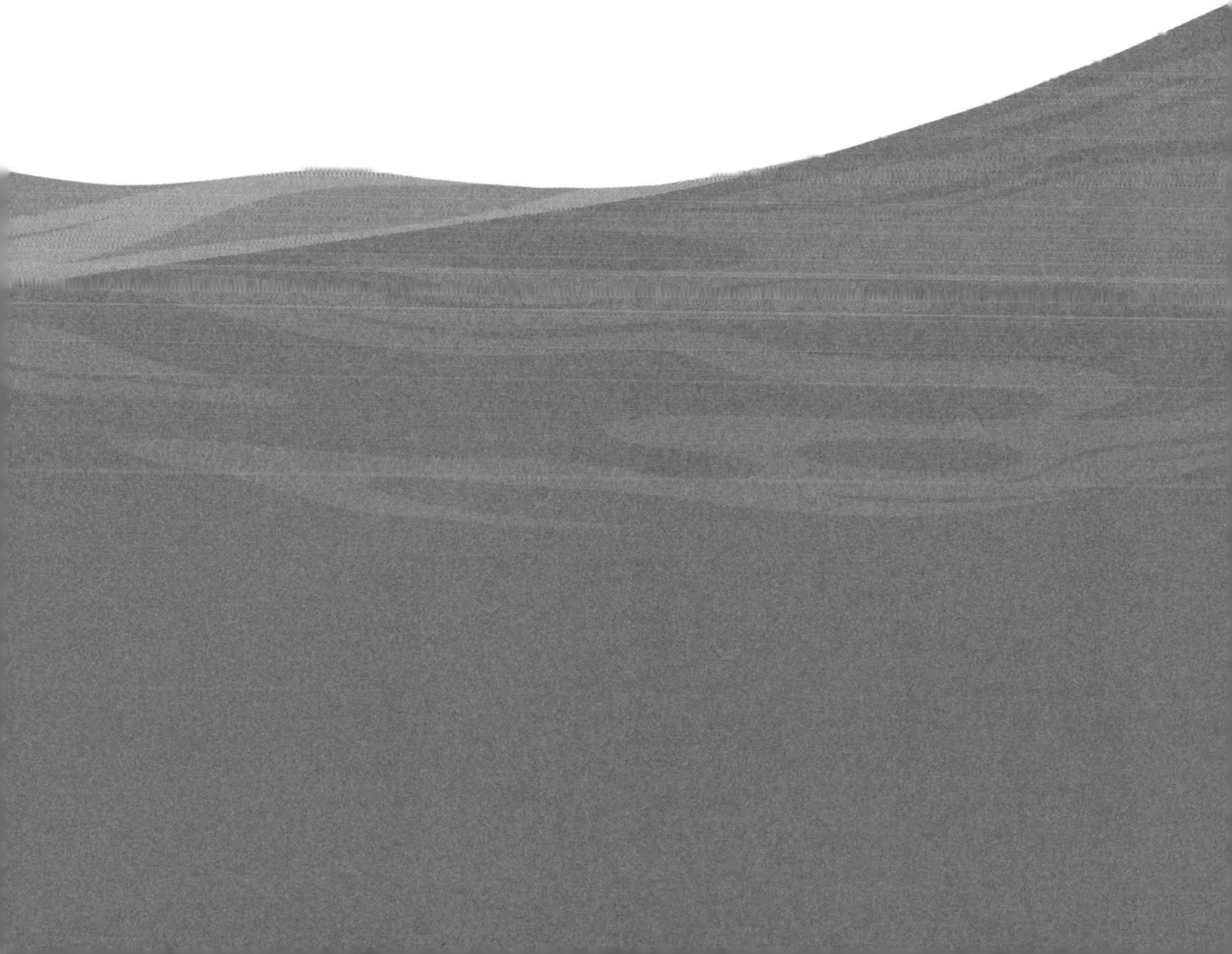

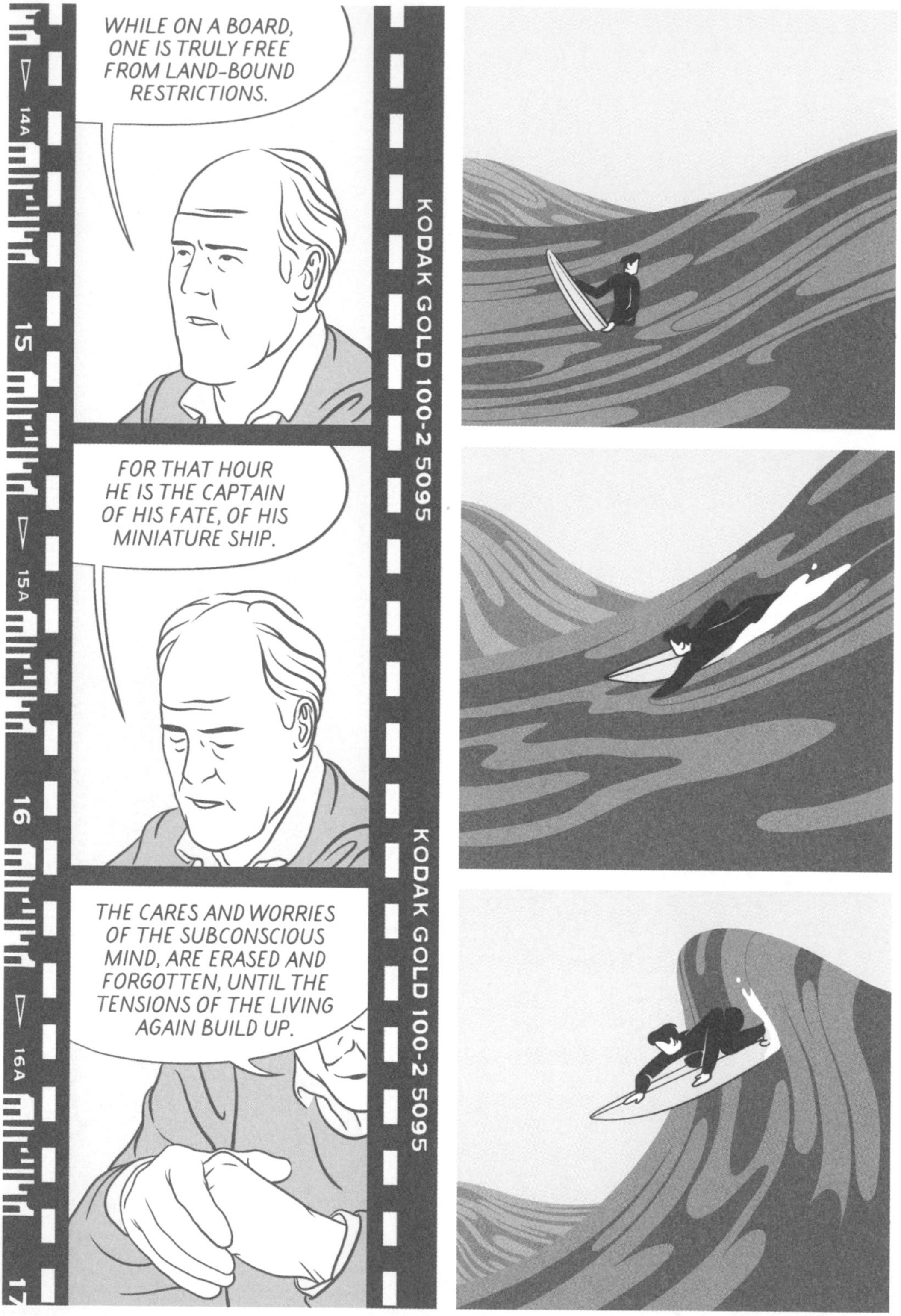
WHILE ON A BOARD, ONE IS TRULY FREE FROM LAND-BOUND RESTRICTIONS.
FOR THAT HOUR HE IS THE CAPTAIN OF HIS FATE, OF HIS MINIATURE SHIP.
THE CARES AND WORRIES OF THE SUBCONSCIOUS MIND, ARE ERASED AND FORGOTTEN, UNTIL THE TENSIONS OF THE LIVING AGAIN BUILD UP.
KODAK GOLD 100-2 5095
KODAK GOLD 100-2 5095
14A
15
15A
16
16A

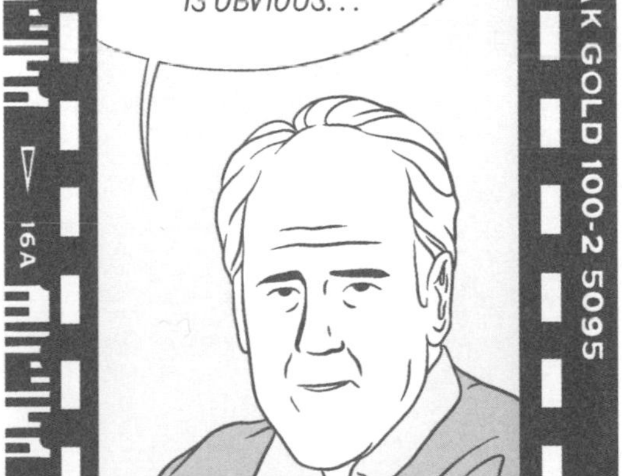
THE REMEDY AGAIN IS OBVIOUS. . .
KODAK GOLD 100-2 5095
16A

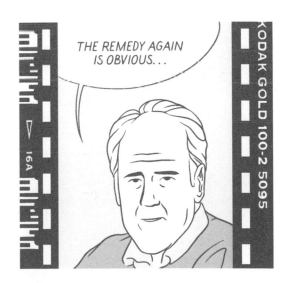

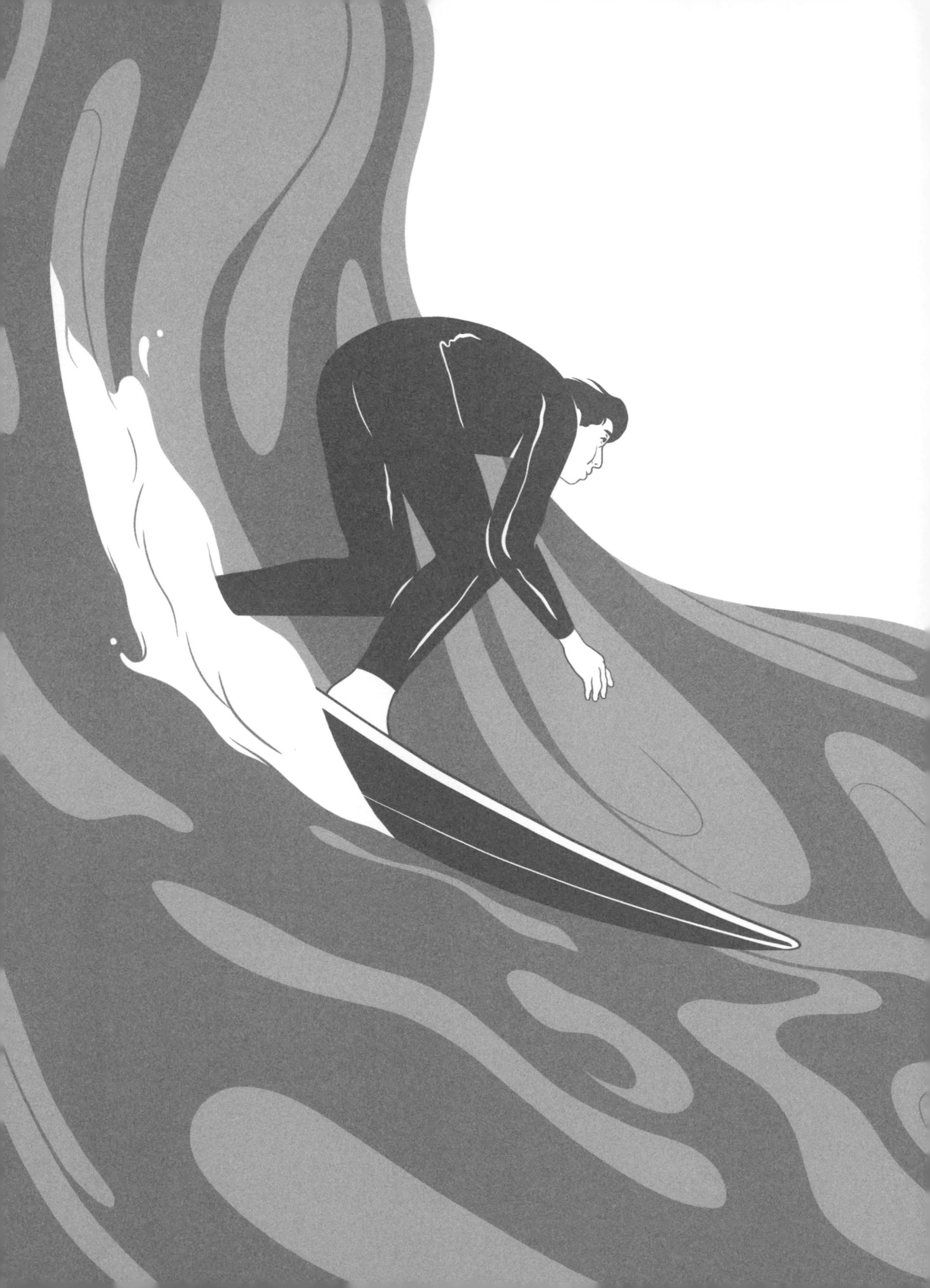

GO SURFING.

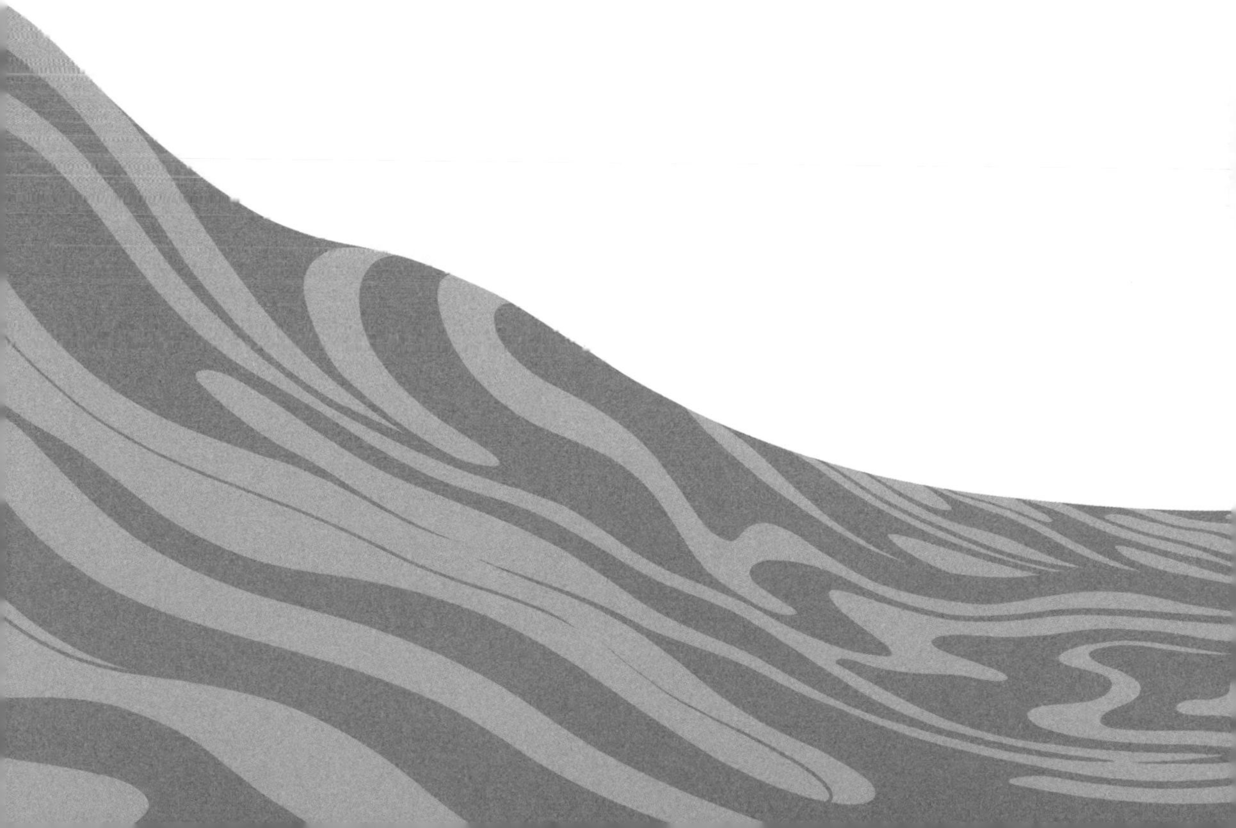

XV. BUSHWICK REQUEST

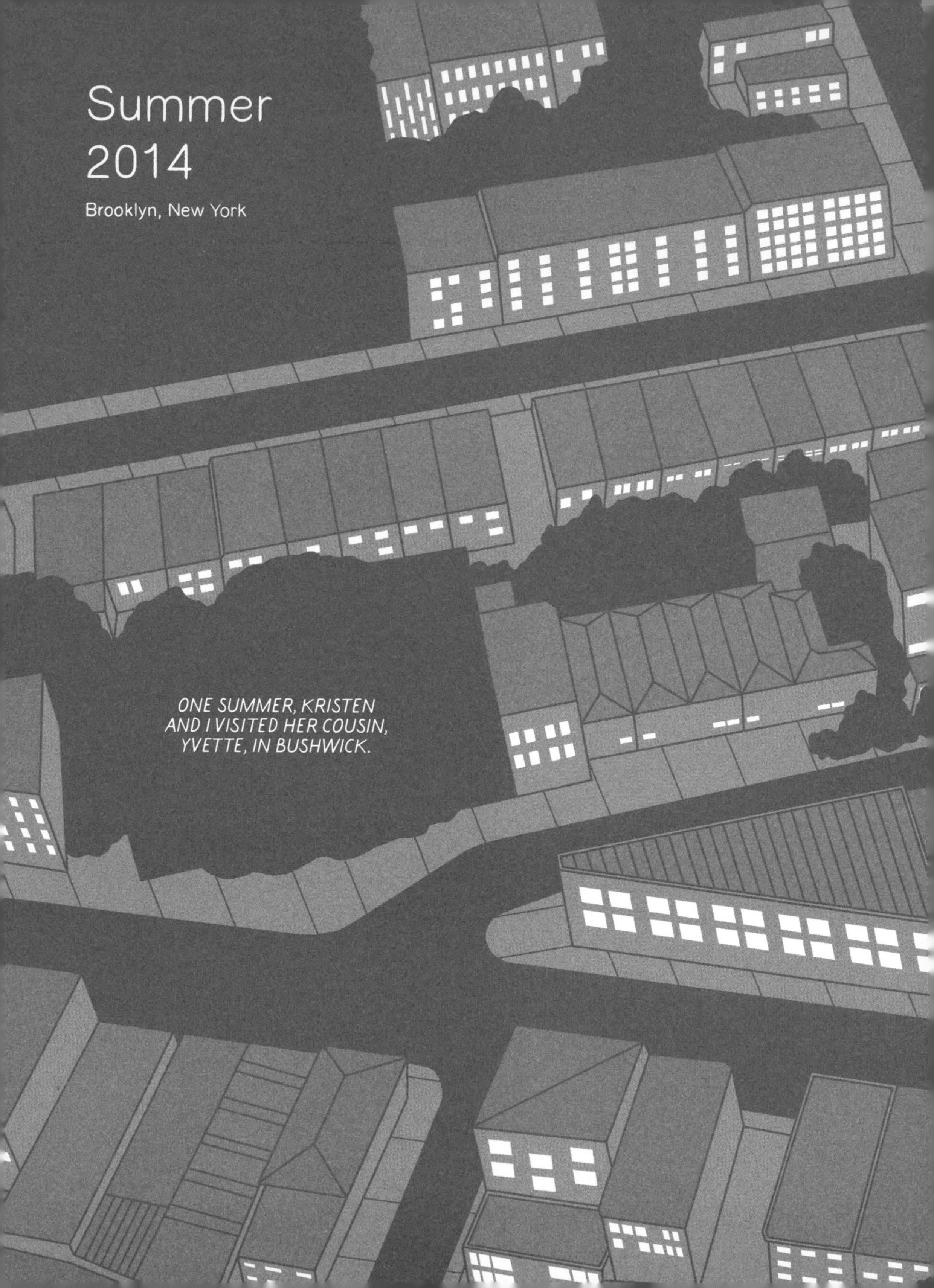
Summer
2014
Brooklyn, New York
ONE SUMMER, KRISTEN AND I VISITED HER COUSIN, YVETTE, IN BUSHWICK.

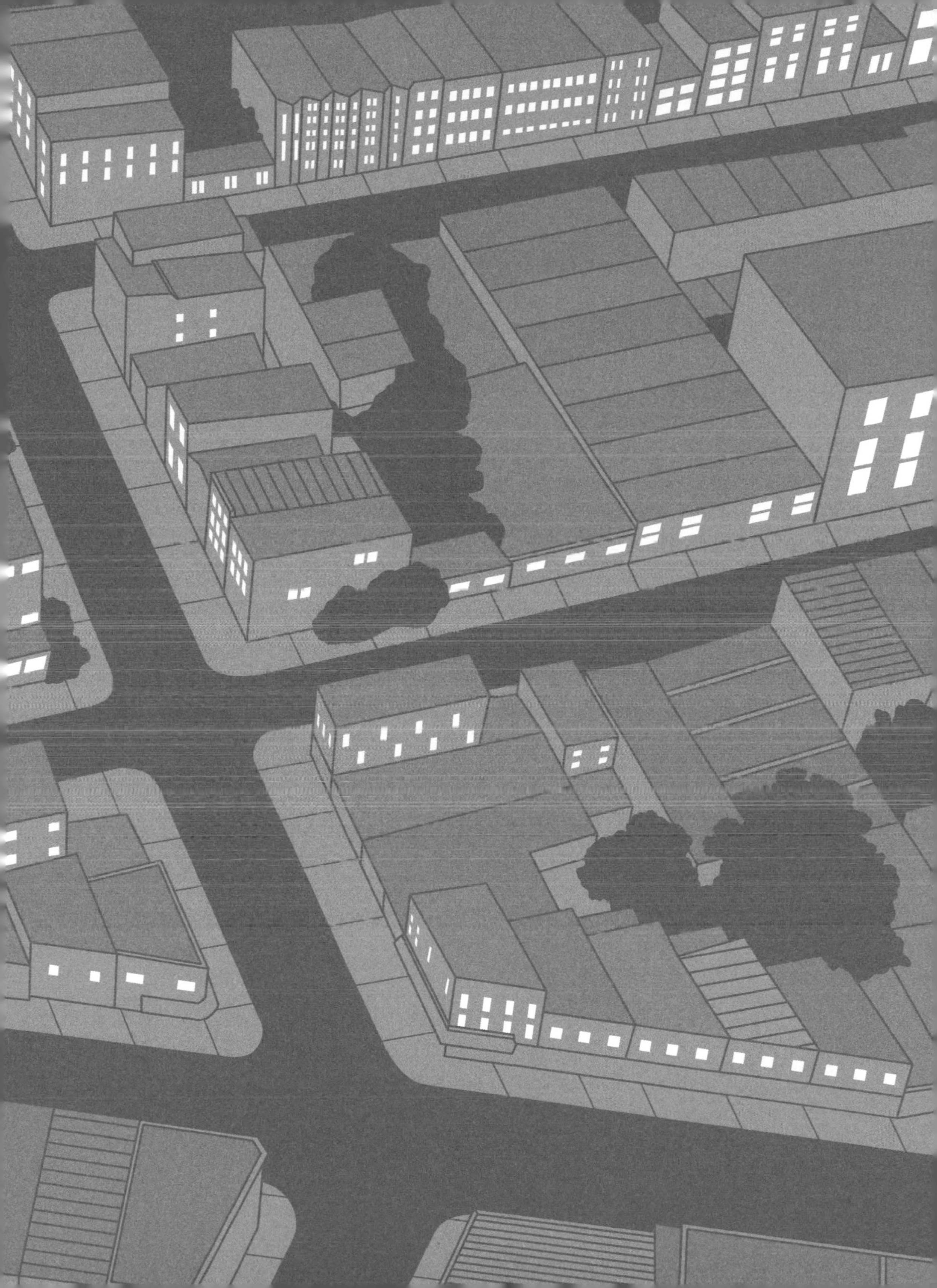

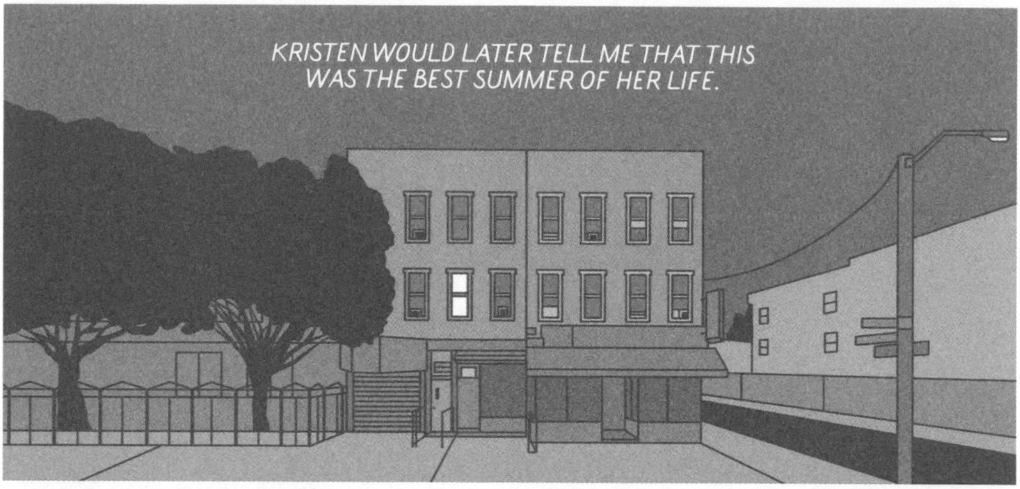
KRISTEN WOULD LATER TELL ME THAT THIS
WAS THE BEST SUMMER OF HER LIFE.

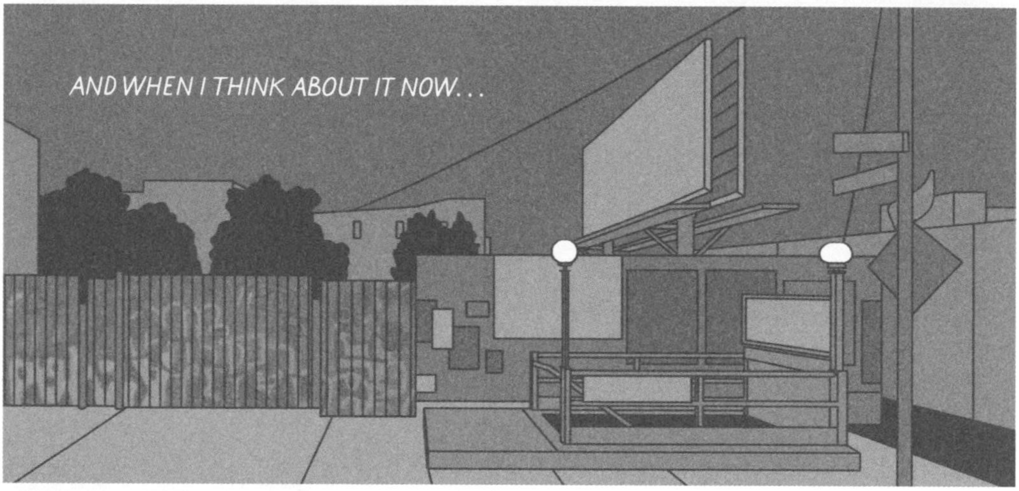
AND WHEN I THINK ABOUT IT NOW. . .

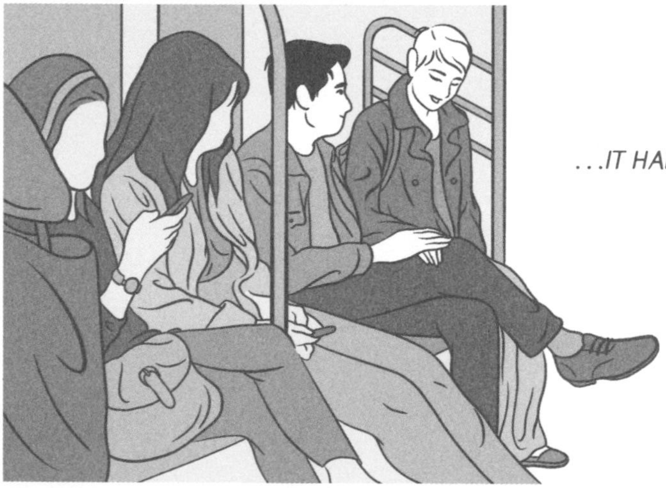

. . .IT HAD BEEN MY BEST TOO.

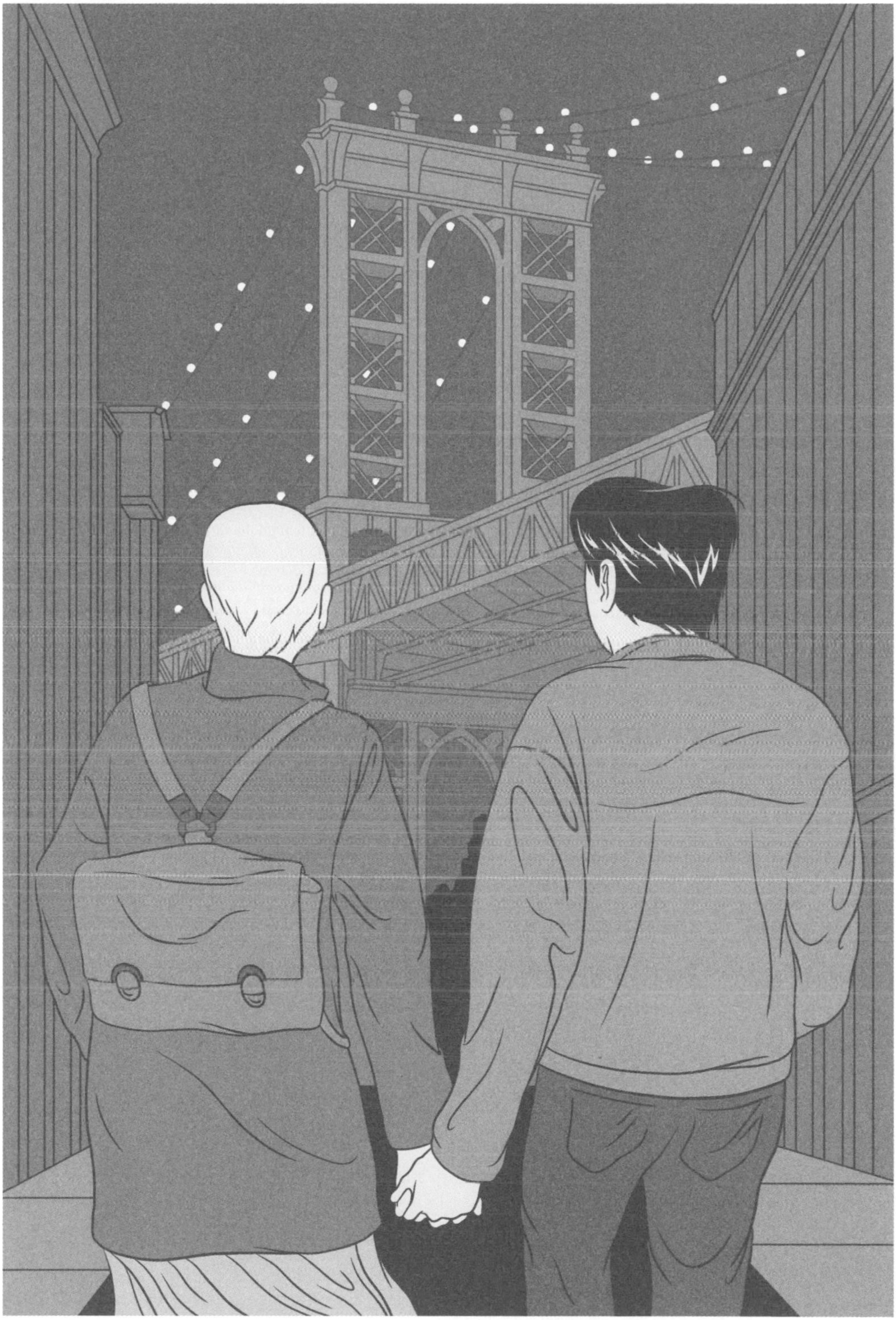

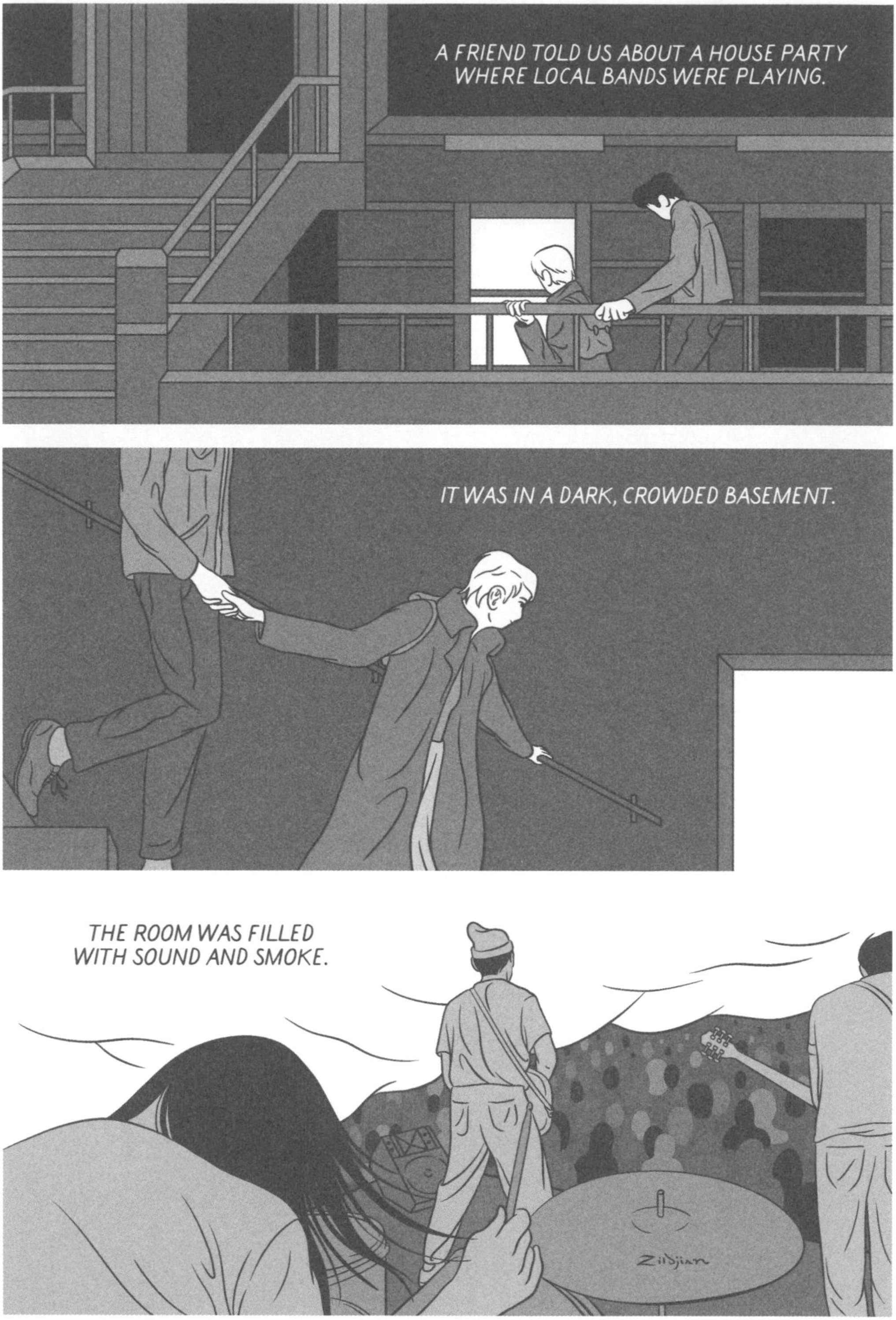
A FRIEND TOLD US ABOUT A HOUSE PARTY WHERE LOCAL BANDS WERE PLAYING.
IT WAS IN A DARK, CROWDED BASEMENT.
THE ROOM WAS FILLED WITH SOUND AND SMOKE.
Zildjian

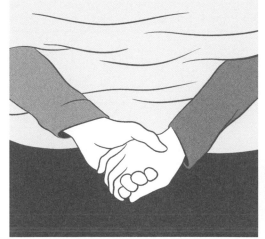

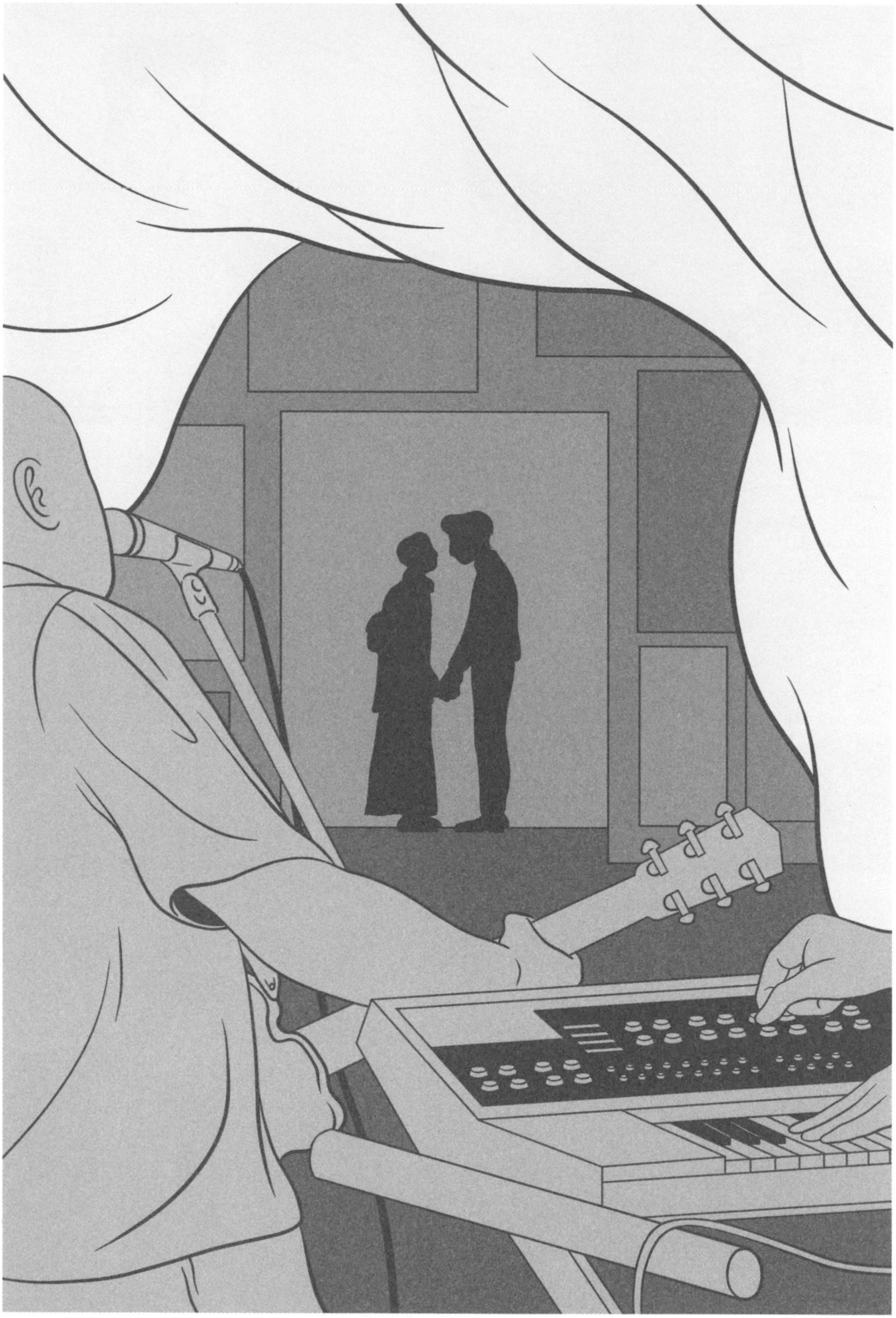

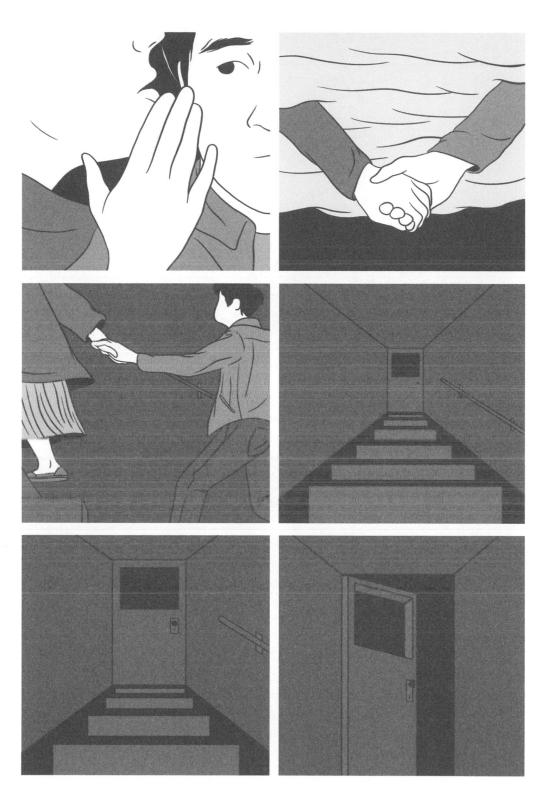

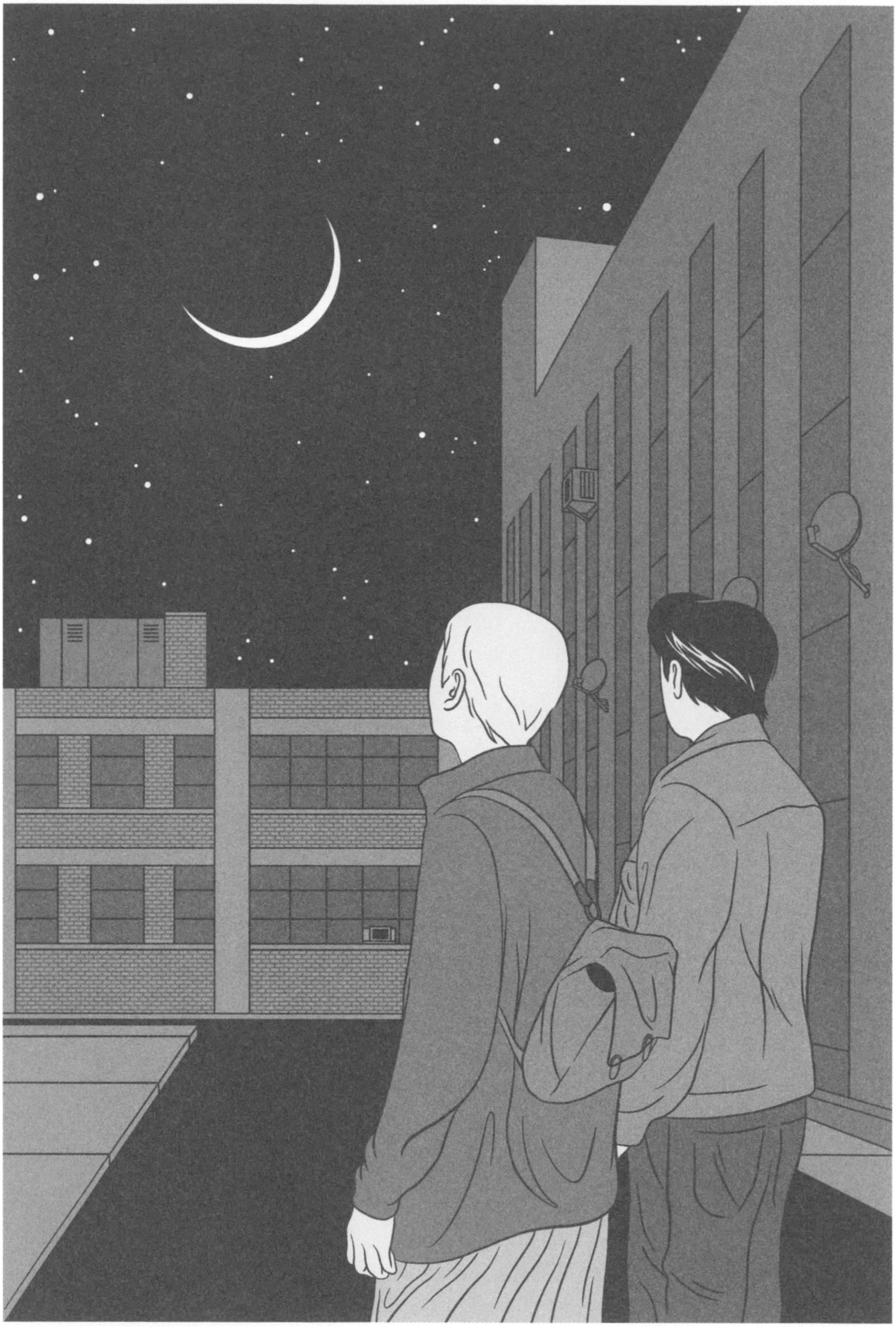

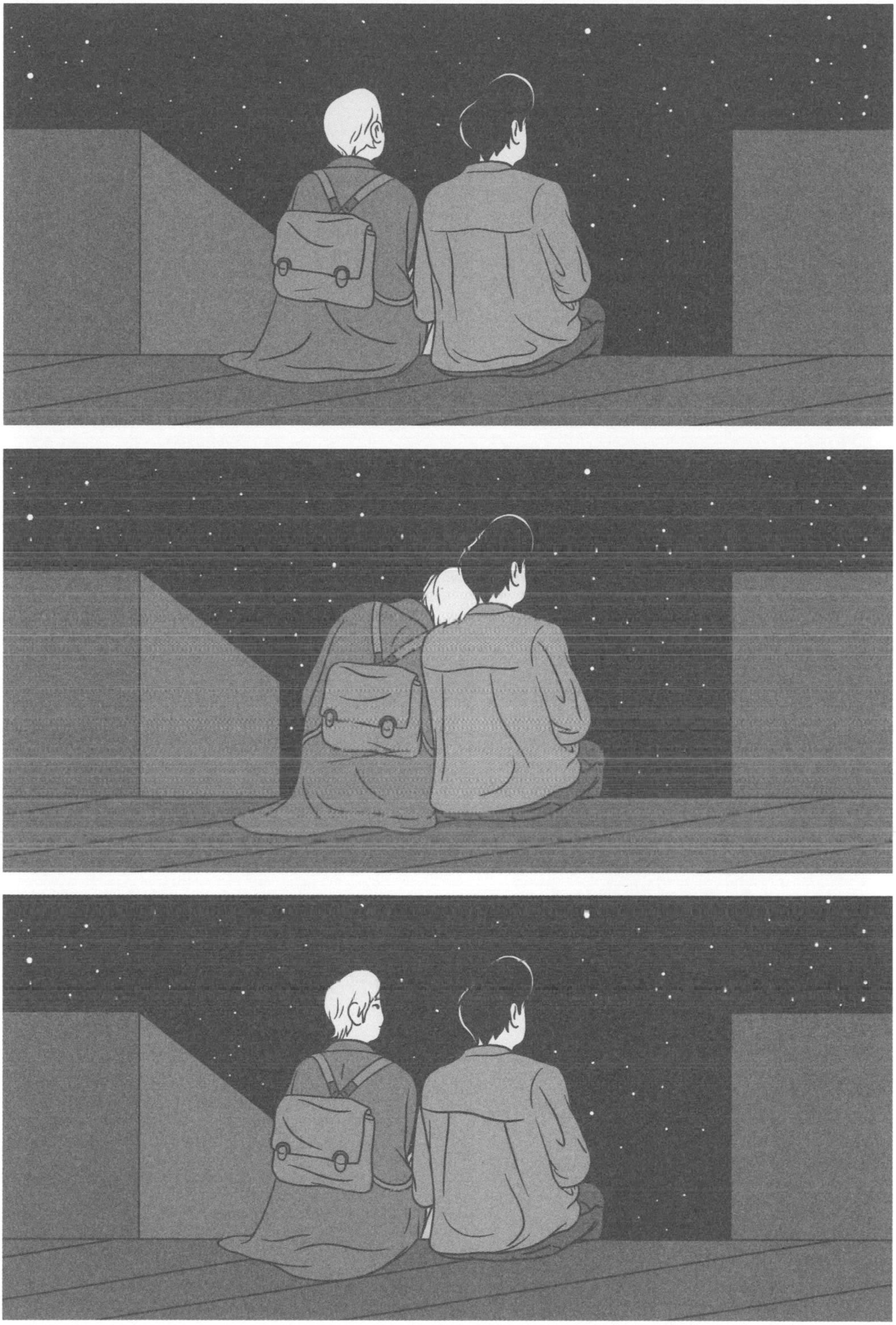

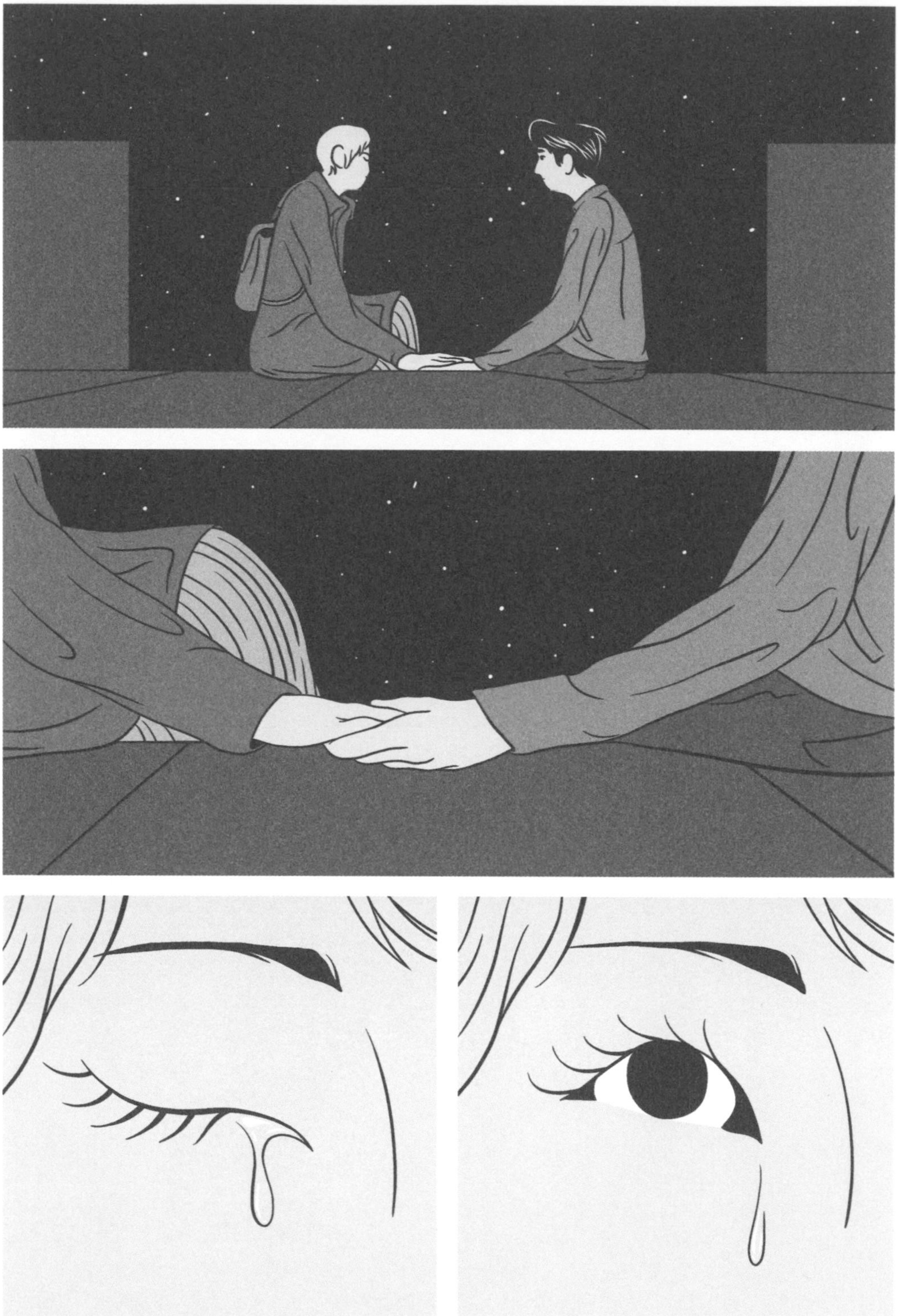

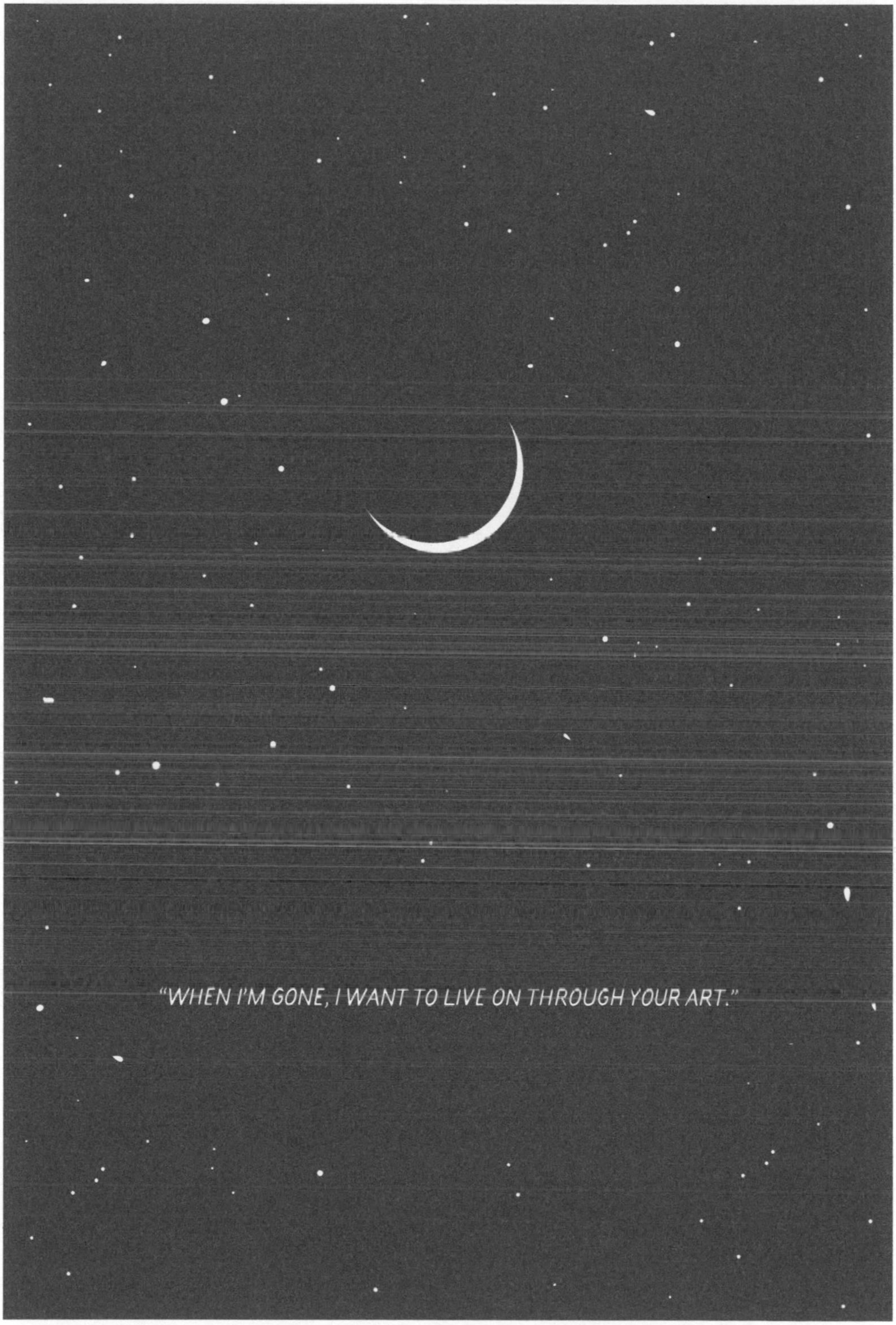
"WHEN I'M GONE, I WANT TO LIVE ON THROUGH YOUR ART."

"THAT'S ALL I WANT."

"PROMISE ME THAT YOU'LL TELL OUR STORY."

I PROMISED HER I WOULD.

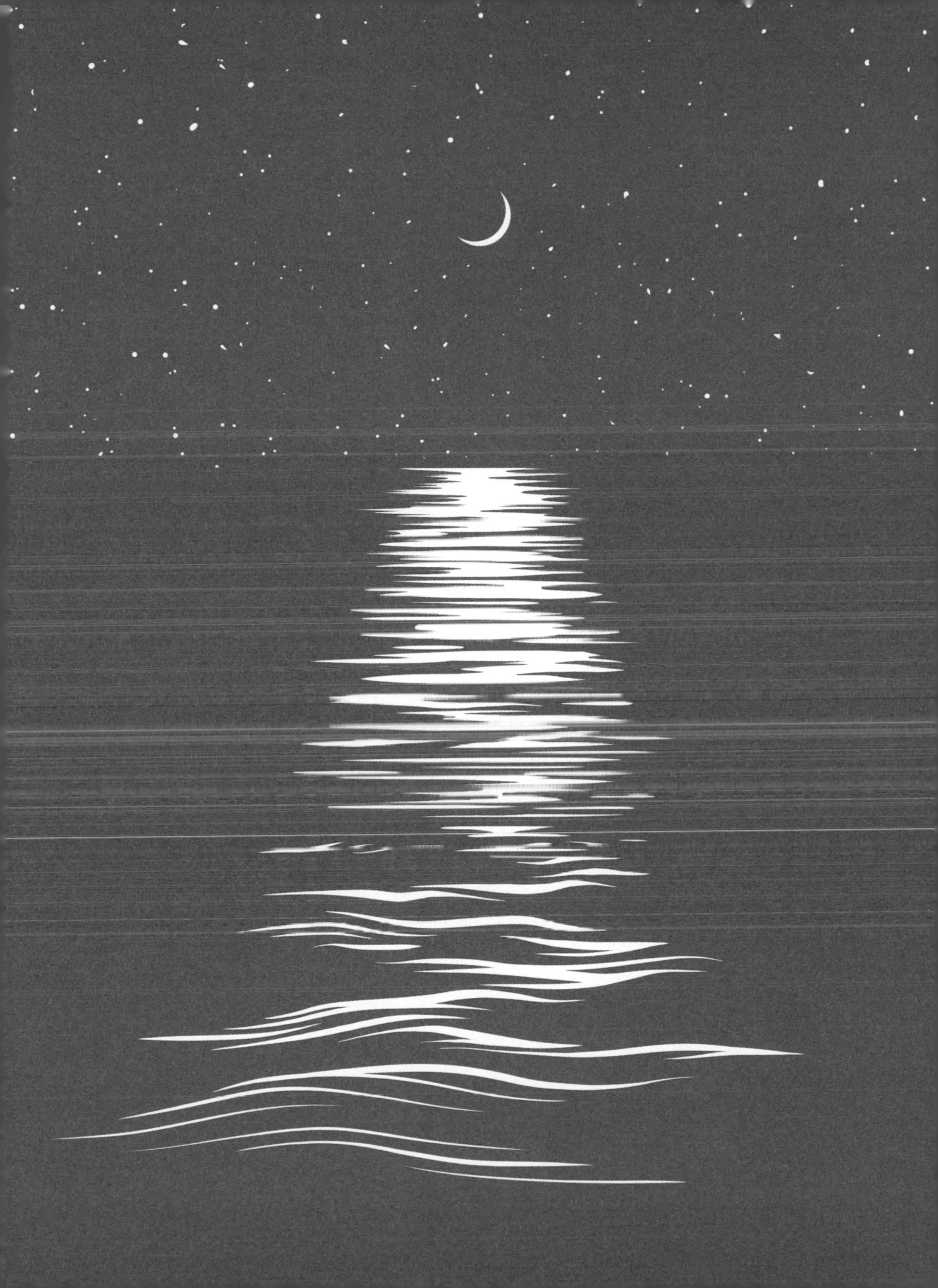

Acknowledgments

THANK YOU TO MY FAMILY, MY FRIENDS, AND EVERYONE WHO
BELIEVED IN ME. THANK YOU MOM, DAD, KUYA KEV, ATE, LOR, RINA,
SILVIA, AND NATE. THANK YOU TITA AIDA, JEFF, YVETTE, JULIAN, AUNTIE
LOY, AND UNCLE WILLY. THANK YOU EON AND LAUREN. THANK YOU
TO THE ENTIRE TUASON FAMILY. THANK YOU CLIVE, PAUL, AND ANN.
THANK YOU ARTCENTER. THANK YOU RANDY, SPENCER, AND MIKE.
THANK YOU SKECHERS. THANK YOU BRANDON. THANK YOU BOMS.
THANK YOU TO SAM AND EVERYONE AT NOBROW.
THANK YOU FOR YOUR LOVE, KRISTEN CARREON TUASON.

-AJ DUNGO

About the Author

AJ DUNGO IS AN ILLUSTRATOR LIVING IN LOS ANGELES. HE STUDIED
AT THE ARTCENTER COLLEGE OF DESIGN. WHEN HE ISN'T WORKING,
YOU CAN FIND HIM IN THE WATER OR SITTING IN A PARKING LOT,
EYEING A FRESHLY-PAINTED CURB.

Bibliography

BLAKE, TOM. HAWAIIAN SURFRIDERS. MOUNTAIN AND SEA, 1983.

"BLAKE, TOM." ENCYCLOPEDIA OF SURFING BY MATT WARSHAW, EOS.SURF/ENTRIES/BLAKE-TOM.

BRENNAN, JOSEPH L. DUKE: THE LIFE STORY OF HAWAI'I'S DUKE KAHANAMOKU. KU PA'A PUBLISHING, 1994.

FINNEY, BEN R., AND JAMES D. HOUSTON. SURFING: A HISTORY OF THE ANCIENT HAWAIIAN SPORT. POMEGRANATE ARTBOOKS, 1996.

HALL, SANDRA KIMBERLEY. DUKE: A GREAT HAWAIIAN. BESS PRESS, 2004.'.

HALL, SANDRA KIMBERLEY, AND GREG AMBROSE. MEMORIES OF DUKE: THE LEGEND COMES TO LIFE: DUKE PAOA KAHANAMOKU, 1890-1968. BESS PRESS, 1995.

HEIMANN, JIM. SURFING: 1778-2015. TASCHEN, 2016.

HONOLULU STAR-BULLETIN. "DUKE, WORLD-CHAMPION, WELCOMED HOME." OCTOBER 1, 1912.

"KAHANAMOKU, DUKE." ENCYCLOPEDIA OF SURFING BY MATT WARSHAW, EOS.SURF/ENTRIES/ KAHANAMOKU-DUKE.

LUERAS, LEONARD. SURFING; THE ULTIMATE PLEASURE. WORKMAN, 1984.

LYNCH, GARY, ET AL. TOM BLAKE: THE UNCOMMON JOURNEY OF A PIONEER WATERMAN. SPENCER CROUL AND CROUL PUBLICATIONS, 2013.

LYNCH, GARY. TOM BLAKE SURFING: 1922-1932. T. ADLER BOOKS, 1999.

MARGAN, FRANK, AND BEN R. FINNEY. A PICTORIAL HISTORY OF SURFING. HAMLYN, 1970.

PHILLIPS, JOHN, DIRECTOR. TOM BLAKE INTERVIEW, 1971. TOM BLAKE INTERVIEW, 1971, 8 JAN. 2019. VIMEO.COM/54489933.

"ON THE WAVES AT WAIKIKI." 1930.

SAUNDERS, JOSH T. "TOM BLAKE WAS A BADASS." SURFER MAGAZINE, SURFER MAGAZINE, 22 JULY 2013, WWW.SURFER.COM/BLOGS/REVIEWS/BOOKS/TOM-BLAKE-THE-UNCOMMON-JOURNEY-OF-A-PIONEER-WATERMAN/.

THE SALT LAKE TRIBUNE. "KANAKA SWIMMER HAS NO EQUAL IN THE WATER: THIS HAWAIIAN A HUMAN FISH." FEBRUARY 2, 1913.

WARSHAW, MATT. THE HISTORY OF SURFING. CHRONICLE BOOKS, 2010.

YOUNG, NAT. THE HISTORY OF SURFING. GIBBS SMITH, 1983.

10 CENTS FROM EVERY COPY OF THIS EDITION SOLD WORLDWIDE
WILL BE DONATED TO CANCER RESEARCH AND TREATMENT.

FIRST PUBLISHED IN 2019 BY NOBROW LTD.
27 WESTGATE STREET, LONDON E8 3RL.

2 4 6 8 10 9 7 5 3 1

PUBLISHED IN THE US BY NOBROW (US) INC.

PRINTED IN LATVIA ON FSC® C002795 CERTIFIED PAPER.

ISBN: 978-1-910620-63-2

WWW.NOBROW.NET

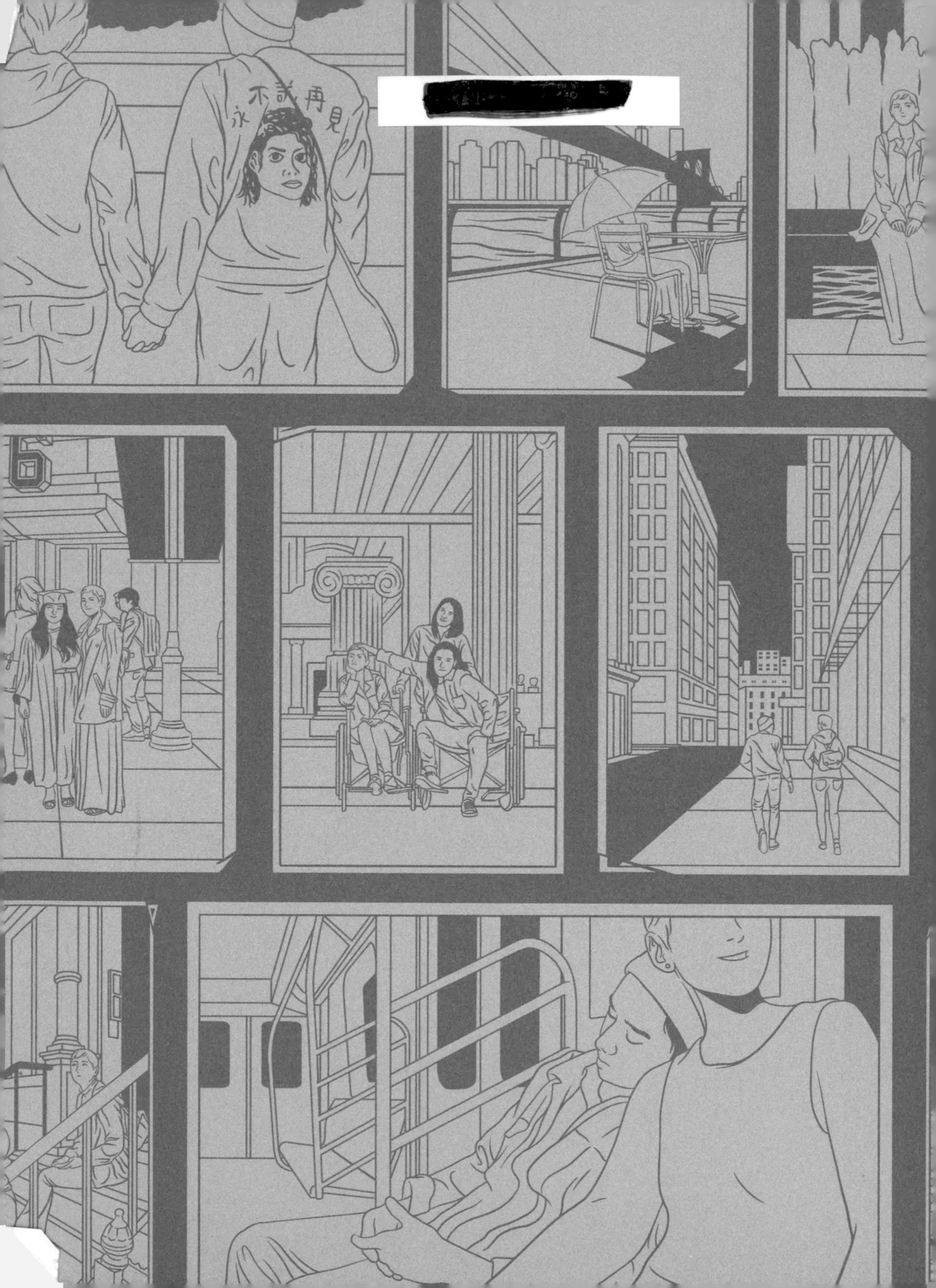
永不說再見
[redacted]